The Eton register; compiled for the Old Etonian Association

Eton College

With Compliments

from the O. E. A

The Hon. Sec. O.E.A. has much pleasure in calling the attention of Members to the careful compilation of this Part of the "Eton Register," and to the pains bestowed upon it by the Secretary, MR. W. CLAY, *and his assistants, as well as by* MESSRS. SPOTTISWOODE & CO., *the Printers. It is hardly possible that no mistakes will be detected, but the Hon. Sec. is convinced that every effort has been made to ensure absolute accuracy and completeness.*

Eton, November 1903.

THE ETON REGISTER

PART I.

1841–1850

THE

ETON REGISTER

PART I.

1841—1850

COMPILED FOR THE

OLD ETONIAN ASSOCIATION

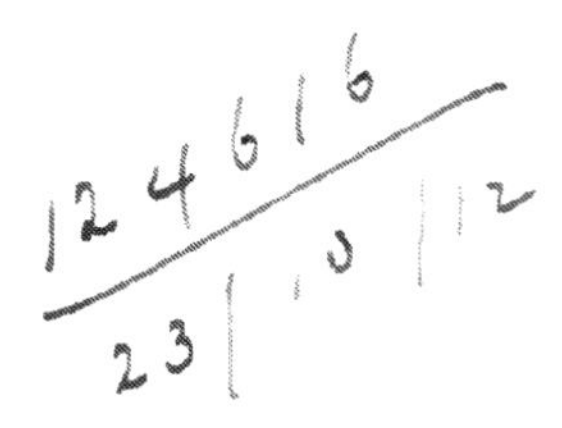

PRIVATELY PRINTED FOR THE MEMBERS
BY
SPOTTISWOODE & CO. LTD., ETON
1903

LIST OF

Provosts, Fellows, Masters, Assistant Masters, &c.

FROM 1840 TO 1850.

PROVOST.

Rev. Francis Hodgson, B.D., 1840^{2}–52^{3}.

VICE-PROVOST.

Rev. John Septimus Grover, M.A. . . . . . 1833–50^{3}

FELLOWS.

Rev. George Bethell, M.A. . . .	1818–50^{3}	Rev. George Rowney Green, M.A. .	1833–60^{1}
Rev. John Francis Plumptree, M.A. .	1822–64^{1}	Rev. George John Dupuis, M.A. .	1838–68^{2}
Rev. Thomas Carter, M.A. . . .	1829–56^{3}	Rev. John Wilder, M.A.	1840^{2}–84^{3}

STEWARDS OF THE COURTS.

John Greatheed Harris . . .	1833–50^{2}	Thomas Batcheldor	1850^{3}–66^{1}

HEAD MASTER.

Rev. Edward Craven Hawtrey, D.D. . . . . 1834–52^{3}

LOWER MASTERS.

Rev. Richard Okes, D.D. .	1838^{3}–50^{2}	Rev. Edward Coleridge, M.A.	1850^{3}–56^{3}

ASSISTANT MASTERS.

With Initials by which referred to in Lists.

Rev. Richard Okes, D.D. .	1821–38^{2}	R.O.
Rev. John Wilder . . .	1824–40	J.W.
Rev. Edward Coleridge, M.A.	1825–50^{2}	E.C.
Rev. Charles Luxmoore, M.A.	1829–53^{3}	C.L.
Rev. William Gifford Cookesley, M.A. . .	1830–54^{3}	W.G.C.

Name	Years	Initials
Rev. Edward Hayes Pickering, M.A.	1830-52[1]	E.H.P.
Charles Wilder	1831-38	C.W.
Rev. Harry Dupuis, B.D.	1835-52[1]	H.D.
Rev. Charles Old Goodford, M.A.	1835-52[3]	C.O.G.
Rev. William Laurence Eliot, M.A.	1836-62[1]	W.L.E.
Rev. Stephen Thomas Hawtrey, M.A., *Math.*	1836-72[2]	S.T.H.
Rev. Charles John Abraham, M.A.	1839-49[3]	C.J.A.
Rev. William Adolphus Carter, M.A.	1839-57[1]	W.A.C.
Rev. Francis Edward Durnford, M.A.	1839-64[1]	F.E.D.
Rev. Edward Balston, M.A.	1840[2]-60[1]	E.B.
Rev. John Eyre Yonge, M.A.	1840[3]-75[2]	J.E.Y.
Rev. John William Hawtrey, M.A.	1842-69[2]	J.W.H.
Rev. Charles Ross de Havilland, M.A., *Math.*	1843[1]-44[3]	C.R.deH.
Rev. George Frewer, M.A., *Math.*	1844[1]-73[3]	G.F.
Henry Mildred Birch, M.A.	1844[1]-49[1]	H.M.B.
Rev. William Cufaude Davie, B.A., *Math.*	1845[1]-46[2]	W.C.D.
William Johnson (aft. Cory), M.A.	1845[3]-72[1]	W.J.
Rev. Robert Arrowsmith, B.A., *Math.*	1846[3]-49[1]	R.A.
Rev. James Leigh Joynes, M.A.	1849[1]-77[3]	J.L.J.
Francis John Ottley, M.A., *Math.*	1849[2]-68[1]	F.J.O.
Rev. Wharton Booth Marriott, B.C.L.	1850[1]-60[2]	W.B.M.
Rev. Charles Wolley (aft. Wolley-Dod), M.A.	1850[1]-78[3]	C.Wo.
Charles Chepmell, B.A., *Math.*	1850[1]-50[3]	C.C.
Rev. Edward Hale, M.A., F.G.S., *Math.*	1850[1]-94[1]	E.H.
Rev. Russell Day, M.A.	1851[1]-74[2]	R.D.
Rev. Augustus Frederick Birch, M.A.	1852[2]-64[2]	A.F.B.
Rev. William Wayte, M.A.	1853[1]-75[3]	W.W.

EXTRA MASTERS.

Name	Subject	Years
Mr. Hexter	*Writing, Arith., and Maths.*	1823[2]-42[3]
W. Evans	*Drawing*	1823[2]-53[3]
H. Angelo	*Fencing*	1823[2]-64[3]
Mr. Venua	*Dancing*	1824[2]-64[3]
Mr. Tarver	*French*	1826[2]-51[1]
Mr. Schönerstedt	*German and Hebrew*	1836[2]-64[1]
Rev. Dr. Di Menna	*Italian*	1842[2]-42[3]
Signor Girolamo Picchioni	*Italian*	1843[1]-48[2]
H. Tarver	*Assist. French Master*	1843[2]-51[1]
Signor Sinibaldi	*Italian*	1848[3]-55[2]
Samuel Evans	*Assist. Drawing Master*	1849[2]-53[3]

Miss A. = Miss Angelo
Miss B. = Miss Bearblock
Mrs. de R. = Mrs. de Rosen
Mrs. D. = Mrs. Dodd
Mrs. Dr. = Mrs. Drury
Miss Edg. = Miss Edgar
Miss Edw. = Miss Edwards
W.E. = W. Evans
Miss G. = Miss Gulliver
Mrs. Hol. = Mrs. Holt
R.F.H. = R. F. Holt
Mrs. Hor. = Mrs. Horsford
Miss M. = Miss Middleton
Mrs. P. = Mrs. Parker
Mrs. Ri. = Mrs. Rishton
Mrs. Ro. = Mrs. Roberts (*née* Slingsby)
Misses S. = Misses Slingsby
T.H.S. = T. H. Stevens
Miss A. T. = Miss Ann Tyrrell
Mrs. Vall. = Mrs. Vallancey
Mrs. Vav. = Mrs. Vavasour
Mrs. Vo. = Mrs. Voysey
F.V. = Rev. F. Vidal
Miss W. = Miss Ward
Mrs. Y. = Mrs. Yonge

K.S. = King's Scholar.

NEWCASTLE SCHOLARS AND SELECT. 1840-1850.

1840.

Examiners.—Lord Lyttelton
W. E. Gladstone

A. Seymour
H. F. Hallam
W. Johnson, K.S.
F. J. Coleridge *ma.*
G. Smith
J. F. Mackarness, K.S.
A. Pott *ma.*
C. T. Buckland
R. N. Cust
W. J. Farrer
W. F. J. Kaye
H. S. Milman
J. M. Rice, K.S.
E. Thring, K.S.

1841.

Examiners.—Rev. W. E. Jelf
G. T. Pennington

W. Johnson, K.S.
G. Smith
F. J. Coleridge
A. Pott
M. J. Blacker, K.S.
C. T. Buckland
B. W. F. Drake, K.S.
R. W. Fiske, K.S.
H. James, K.S.
J. L. Joynes, K.S.
W. F. J. Kaye
J. M. Rice, K.S.
E. Thring, K.S.
J. A. Yonge, K.S.

1842.

Examiners.—E. S. Creasy
Rev. W. Adams

J. M. Rice, K.S.
J. L. Joynes, K.S.
C. B. Scott
J. Simpson

1843.

Examiners.—W. Selwyn
Rev. R. Durnford

J. L. Joynes, K.S.
J. Simpson
E. R. P. Bastard
B. W. F. Drake, K.S.
C. B. Scott

1844.

Examiners.—Sir F. H. Doyle
Rev. J. Chapman

B. W. F. Drake, K.S.
C. Wolley, K.S.
G. W. Hunt
Mr. R. C. Herbert *mi.*
E. McNiven
W. S. Pearce-Serocold
J. C. Wright, K.S.
M. E. M. Buller
J. J. Hornby
J. C. Patteson
O. A. Smith

1845.

Examiners.—G. C. Lewis
Rev. W. L. Sampson

R. Day, K.S.
J. Back
Mr. R. C. Herbert
J. J. Hornby
W. Wayte, K.S.
W. J. Beamont
E. McNiven
G. E. Ranken
H. J. Simonds, K.S.
M. E. Welby

1846.

Examiners.—Rev. J. F. Jackson
H. Cotton

W. Wayte, K.S.
W. J. Beamont
E. W. Blore
C. B. Borradaile, K.S.
W. S. Dugdale
T. F. Fremantle
C. C. James, K.S.
E. H. Rogers, K.S.
M. E. Welby
F. H. Whymper

1847.

Examiners.—Rev. R. Scott
Goldwin Smith

F. H. Whymper
H. Coleridge
E. W. Blore
C. Booth, K.S.
T. F. Fremantle
W. E. Welby
G. C. Brodrick
C. C. James, K.S.
J. N. Luxmoore
C. S. Parker
G. G. Tyler

1848.

Examiners.—Rev. R. L. Brown
Rev. J. F. Mackarness

H. Coleridge
T. F. Fremantle
G. C. Brodrick
C. C. James, K.S.
C. S. Parker
C. Booth, K.S.
C. B. Borradaile, K.S.
F. H. Curtis, K.S.
R. Duckworth
W. L. Lewis
W. E. Ridler, K.S.

1849.

Examiners.—Rev. J. G. Lonsdale
Rev. R. Shilleto

W. L. Lewis
W. H. Fremantle
R. G. W. Herbert
S. C. Bosanquet
H. Bradshaw, K.S.
H. Drake, K.S.
C. J. Evans, K.S.
H. J. Reynolds, K.S.
W. E. Ridler, K.S.
E. D. Stone, K.S.

1850.

Examiners.—Rev. W. E. Jelf
Rev. C. Badham

R. G. W. Herbert
H. J. Reynolds, K.S.
E. D. Stone, K.S.
S. C. Bosanquet
F. J. Coltman
H. Drake, K.S.
W. C. Green, K.S.
F. B. M. Montgomerie
C. T. Procter, K.S.
W. E. Ridler, K.S.

TOMLINE PRIZEMEN AND SELECT. 1840-1850.

1840.
- H. J. Hotham
- W. A. Houston
- W. F. J. Kaye

1841.
- W. F. J. Kaye
- E. R. P. Bastard

1842.
- C. B. Scott
- E. R. P. Bastard

1843.
- E. R. P. Bastard
- T. Lomax

1844.
- J. G. Scott
- T. Bendyshe

1845.
- E. W. Blore
- N. M. Ferrers

1846.
- N. M. Ferrers
- C. E. Coleridge

1847.
- E. W. Blore
- C. S. Parker
- A. Newdigate

1848.
- F. J. Coltman
- H. Barnard
- G. E. Martin

1849.
- S. C. Bosanquet
- J. V. Longbourne
- H. A. Martin

1850.
- A. B. Cotton
- H. A. Martin
- A. G. Giles-Puller

H.R.H. THE PRINCE CONSORT'S PRIZES. 1841-1850.

1841.

French and German: 1 J. Simpson
2 J. G. Dodson

1842.

French and German: 1 H. R. Lambton
2 J. G. Dodson
French and Italian: 1 J. G. Dodson
2 E. R. P. Bastard

1843.

French and German: 1 F. H. Whymper
2 M. W. J. Marsh

1844.

French and Italian: 1 W. J. Beamont
French and German: 2 J. E. Boileau *ma.*
French: 1 J. E. Boileau *ma.*
Italian: 1 W. J. Beamont

1845.

French: 1 M. C. Close
2 C. L. Peel
German: 1 W. S. Dugdale
2 C. S. Parker
Italian: 1 M. C. Close
2 F. G. M. Boileau

1846.

French: 1 G. H. C. Byng *ma.*
2 C. Foster
German: 1 C. S. Parker
2 C. H. Barton
Italian: 1 F. G. M. Boileau
2 H. Bradshaw, K.S.

1847.

French: 1 C. R. Wilson
2 { F. G. M. Boileau
F. B. C. Tarver, K.S. }
German: 1 G. H. C. Byng *ma.*
2 J. Stratton
Italian: 1 H. Coleridge
2 Marquis of Lothian

1848.

French: 1 Lord Grey de Wilton
2 P. H. W. Currie
Italian: 1 C. C. James, K.S.
2 Mr. W. J. B. W. Venables-Vernon
German: 1 L. Guy-Phillips
2 W. Egerton

1849.

French: 1 C. H. Marillier, K.S.
2 G. H. J. Chapman
German: 1 E. A. A. K. Cowell
2 Mr. W. N. Jocelyn
Italian: 1 E. A. A. K. Cowell
2 Mr. F. E. C. Byng

1850.

French: 1 E. A. A. K. Cowell
2 Mr. F. E. C. Byng
German: 1 F. W. Lambton *ma.*
2 S. H. Gem
Italian: 1 Mr. W. J. B. W. Venables-Vernon
2 W. J. Rous

LIST OF

Cricket Elevens, Boats' Crews, &c. &c.

FROM 1840 TO 1850.

EIGHTS.

1840.

Bow H. J. Farquharson
2 F. J. Richards
3 Hon. J. Yarde-Buller
4 J. Wolley
5 A. Chichester
6 W. Duckett
7 J. D. Rochfort
Stroke W. R. A. H. Arundell, *Capt.*
Cox. T. J. Bradshawe

Eton *v.* Old Etonians.
Won by Eton.

1841.

Bow. T. R. Smyth-Temple
2 E. Fellows
3 F. J. Richards
4 H. F. Radford
5 Hon. J. Yarde-Buller
6 F. Palmer
7 F. E. Tuke
Stroke W. R. A. H. Arundell, *Capt.*
Cox. T. Lyon

Eton *v.* a Cambridge VIII.
Won by Eton.

Eton *v.* Westminster.

1842.

Bow W. Chetwynd-Stapylton
2 W. U. Heygate
3 W. W. Codrington
4 F. M. Wilson
5 J. ffolliott
6 E. Fellows
7 F. E. Tuke
Stroke F. J. Richards, *Capt.*
Cox. R. T. Whitmore

Won by Westminster. Time, 38 mins. 35 secs.

1843.

Bow W. Chetwynd-Stapylton
2 H. A. F. Luttrell
3 Lord Henley
4 W. Babington
5 W. W. Codrington
6 F. M. Wilson
7 J. ffolliott
Stroke F. E. Tuke, *Capt.*
Cox. Lord B. T. M. Cecil

Won by Eton. Time, 24 mins.

1844.

Bow W. W. Codrington, *Capt.*
2 C. G. Sutton
3 H. A. F. Luttrell
4 G. H. Errington
5 W. Speke
6 T. Milles
7 E. Ethelston
Stroke G. R. Winter
Cox. Mr. D. G. Finch

No race this year.

1845.

Bow E. Ethelston
2 A. Tremayne
3 G. F. Luttrell
4 F. Talfourd
5 H. A. F. Luttrell, *Capt.*
6 H. S. Adlington
7 H. W. P. Richards
Stroke G. R. Winter
Cox. J. A. Shaw-Stewart

Won by Westminster. Time, 26 mins.

1846.

Bow W. J. Marshall
2 R. H. Barnes
3 A. R. Thompson
4 C. H. Miller
5 G. F. Luttrell, *Capt.*
6 C. M. Buller
7 W. L. G. Bagshawe
Stroke E. J. Bunny
Cox. W. T. Markham

Won by Westminster.

1847.

Bow A. W. Baillie
2 J. G. Holden
3 H. H. Tremayne
4 C. H. Miller, *Capt.*
5 A. R. F. M. De Rutzen
6 H. J. Miller
7 A. R. Thompson
Stroke W. L. G. Bagshawe
Cox. J. Greenwood

Won by Eton. Time, 25 mins. 50 secs.

1848.

Bow G. F. Slade
2 F. G. H. Smith
3 G. Irlam
4 A. W. Adair
5 H. H. Tremayne, *Capt.*
6 H. B. H. Blundell
7 J. Grant-Suttie
Stroke H. C. Herries
Cox. C. J. W. Miles

Rowed a race against a scratch crew from Boveney to Windsor. Won by Eton.

1849.

Bow T. B. H. Blundell
2 G. F. R. Jervis
3 W. R. Coleridge
4 B. W. M. Lysley
5 R. J. Buller
6 L. Cust
7 G. M. Robertson
Stroke H. B. H. Blundell, *Capt.*
Cox. J. Bateson

No race this year.

1850.

Bow T. H. Marshall
2 W. O. Meade-King
3 Mr. I. de V. E. Fiennes
4 P. H. Nind
5 J. W. Malcolm
6 R. Swann
7 F. A. Powys
Stroke G. M. Robertson
Cox. Mr. R. P. Nevill

Rowed two races.
1st, against a scratch crew from Cambridge; 'won by Eton.'
2nd, against an Oxford crew containing six University oars; 'won by Oxford.'

WINNERS OF SCHOOL PULLING.

1840.
C. H. Rhys
W. Chetwynd-Stapylton
E. L. Clutterbuck, *Cox.*

1841.
J. Yarde-Buller
W. Chetwynd-Stapylton
R. T. Whitmore, *Cox.*

1842.
W. U. Heygate
W. Chetwynd-Stapylton
Lord B. T. M. Cecil, *Cox.*

1843.
O. J. B. Rowley
H. F. S. Robinson
Smith *mi.*, *Cox.*

1844.
E. Ethelston
H. Williamson
F. Blomfield, *Cox.*

1845.
Evans
W. L. G. Bagshawe
F. G. Foster *mi.*, *Cox.*

1846.
C. J. Holden *ma.*
J. G. Holden *mi.*
Johnson, *Cox.*

1847.
W. L. G. Bagshawe
R. H. Barnes
E. W. Haywood *mi.*, *Cox.*

1848.
H. B. H. Blundell
G. F. Slade
Thompson, *Cox.*

1849.
F. Wykeham-Martin
G. M. Robertson
Mr. R. P. Nevill, *Cox.*

1850.
W. O. Meade-King
T. H. Marshall
Thompson, *Cox.*

WINNERS OF SCHOOL SCULLING.

1840.
G. E. Clayton-East

1841.
J. Spankie

1842.
P. J. W. Miles

1843.
W. Chetwynd-Stapylton

1844.
E. Ethelston

1845.
J. Greenwood

1846.
E. J. Bunny

1847.
W. L. G. Bagshawe

1848.
H. B. H. Blundell

1849.
F. A. Powys

1850.
G. Nevile

LIST OF ELEVENS AT LORD'S, WITH RESULTS.

1840.
J. R. L. E. Bayley, *Capt.*
W. B. Gwyn, K.S.
M. M. Ainslie
H. L. Bean
A. Robarts, K.S.
M. J. Blacker, K.S.
W. J. Farrer
R. W. Fiske, K.S.
J. W. Hay
R. J. C. R. Ker
W. S. Monck, K.S.
Eton *v.* Harrow.
Eton won by 31 runs.
Eton *v.* Winchester.
Winchester won by 43 runs.

1841.
J. R. L. E. Bayley, *Capt.*
H. L. Bean
W. S. Monck, K.S.
L. H. Bayley
T. G. Carter, K.S.
H. W. Fellows
H. Garth
W. Marcon, K.S.
C. Randolph
T. M. Townley
G. E. Yonge, K.S.
Eton *v.* Harrow.
Eton won by an innings and 175 runs.
Eton *v.* Winchester.
Winchester won by 109 runs.

1842.
M. M. Ainslie, *Capt.*
W. Marcon, K.S.
G. E. Yonge, K.S.
H. Garth
T. G. Carter, K.S.
L. H. Bayley
H. W. Fellows
T. M. Townley
C. Randolph
W. B. Marriott, K.S.
Hon. G. W. Milles
Eton *v.* Harrow.
Harrow won by 65 runs.
Eton *v.* Winchester.
Eton won by 7 wickets.

1843.
G. E. Yonge, K.S., *Capt.*
H. Garth
T. G. Carter, K.S.
L. H. Bayley
T. M. Townley
C. Randolph
E. McNiven
J. C. Patteson
R. Honywood
S. T. Clissold
S. T. Abbott
Eton *v.* Harrow.
Harrow won by 20 runs.
Eton *v.* Winchester.
Winchester won by 8 wickets.
J. B. Helm played instead of T. M. Townley.

1844.
L. H. Bayley, *Capt.*
J. C. Patteson
R. Honywood
S. T. Abbott
J. A. James, K.S.
E. McNiven
Hon. L. Neville
F. J. Coleridge, K.S.
C. E. Coleridge
J. W. Chitty
N. W. Streatfeild
Eton *v.* Harrow.
Eton won by an innings and 69 runs.
Eton *v.* Winchester.
Eton won by 27 runs.

1845.
E. McNiven, *Capt.*
J. A. James, K.S.
F. J. Coleridge, K.S.
C. E. Coleridge
J. W. Chitty
N. W. Streatfeild
F. S. P. Wolferstan
W. S. Deacon
A. F. Holland
J. J. Hornby
E. W. Blore
Eton *v.* Harrow.
Eton won by an innings and 174 runs.
Eton *v.* Winchester.
A tie.

1846.
F. J. Coleridge, K.S., *Capt.*
C. E. Coleridge
J. W. Chitty
N. W. Streatfeild
W. S. Deacon
E. W. Blore
D. S. Collings
J. Aitken
H. M. Aitken
F. H. Whymper
R. C. Antrobus
Eton *v.* Harrow.
Eton won by an innings and 135 runs.
Eton *v.* Winchester.
Eton won by an innings and 55 runs.

1847.
J. W. Chitty, *Capt.*
N. W. Streatfeild
W. S. Deacon
E. W. Blore
J. Aitken
H. M. Aitken
F. H. Whymper
R. C. Antrobus
A. Earle, K.S.
A. D. Coleridge, K.S.
W. E. Barnett
Eton *v.* Harrow.
Eton won by 9 wickets.
Eton *v.* Winchester.
Eton won by an innings and 78 runs.
A. R. Thompson played instead of A. D. Coleridge.

1848.
H. M. Aitken, *Capt.*
A. D. Coleridge, K.S.
W. E. Barnett
T. F. Fremantle
J. A. Bayley
A. Buckley
H. J. Cheales, K.S.
F. E. Stacey, K.S.
C. L. Norman
W. A. Norris, K.S.
T. E. Lloyd-Mostyn
Eton *v.* Harrow.
Harrow won by 41 runs.
Eton *v.* Winchester.
Eton won by 65 runs.

1849.
H. M. Aitken, *Capt.*
H. J. Cheales, K.S.
F. E. Stacey, K.S.
C. L. Norman
W. A. Norris, K.S.
C. Thackeray, K.S.
F. T. A. H. Bathurst
E. Cutler
G. H. Philips
W. P. Prest
F. J. Alderson
Eton *v.* Harrow.
Harrow won by 77 runs.
Eton *v.* Winchester.
Eton won by an innings and 27 runs.

1850.
C. L. Norman, *Capt.*
C. Thackeray, K.S.
F. T. A. H. Bathurst
W. P. Prest
F. J. Alderson
T. D. Tremlett, K.S.
T. O. Reay, K.S.
A. J. Coleridge, K.S.
H. Drake
L. Guy-Phillips
F. J. Coltman
Eton *v.* Harrow.
Eton won by 7 wickets.
Eton *v.* Winchester.
Eton won by 5 wickets.

KEEPERS OF THE FIELD AND LIST OF FIELD ELEVENS.

1847.

Keepers: { H. H. Tremayne / A. R. Thompson

F. M. Eden
A. R. F. M. De Rutzen
H. B. H. Blundell
T. F. Fremantle
J. Aitken
G. F. Slade
C. K. Crosse
W. E. Barnett
J. Grant-Suttie
Biddulph (12th man)

1848.

Keepers: { H. B. H. Blundell / J. Grant-Suttie

F. J. Coltman
R. J. M. Buller
G. L. Goodlake
A. D. Coleridge
Lord Pevensey
A. Congreve
R. P. Ethelston
H. Aitken
L. Guy-Phillips
W. H. Fremantle (12th man)

1849.

Keepers: { F. J. Coltman / R. P. Ethelston

L. Guy-Phillips
W. H. Fremantle
W. R. Coleridge
Hon. I. de V. E. Fiennes
R. M. King
E. W. Northey
E. F. Luttrell
C. L. Norman
G. F. R. Jervis
R. G. W. Herbert (12th man)

1850.

Keepers: { L. Guy-Phillips / E. W. Northey

Hon. R. P. Nevill
E. F. Luttrell
D. H. Mytton
Johnstone
F. W. Lambton
R. E. Welby
W. Watson
F. J. Alderson
J. Giles
P. H. Nind (12th man)

KEEPERS OF WALL AND LIST OF WALL ELEVENS.

1841.

COLLEGERS.

H. James, *Capt.*
J. Tarver
W. Marcon
J. L. Joynes
H. Phillott
H. S. Polehampton
T. Brocklebank
J. B. Helm
F. L. A. Goertz
H. Herbert

OPPIDANS.

J. Yarde-Buller, *Capt.*
J. Wolley
M. M. Ainslie
Hon. C. E. Pepys
F. M. Wilson
J. Craster
J. Spankie
F. J. Richards
T. Lomax

Oppidans won by 2 shies.

1842.

COLLEGERS.

J. Tarver, *Capt.*
W. Marcon
J. L. Joynes.
H. Phillott
T. Brocklebank
J. B. Helm
F. L. A. Goertz
J. A. James
F. A. James

OPPIDANS.

F. M. Wilson, *Capt.*
W. W. Codrington
W. Chetwynd-Stapylton
H. Garth
S. T. Clissold
R. Harkness
W. Babington
Lord Guernsey
Sir M. Shaw-Stewart
J. Courtenay
W. U. Heygate

Collegers won by 1 goal and 19 shies.

1843.

COLLEGERS.

J. L. Joynes, *Capt.*
T. Brocklebank
J. B. Helm
F. L. A. Goertz
J. A. James
F. A. James
C. Wolley
W. J. Smith
F. J. Coleridge
J. G. Hammond
B. W. F. Drake

OPPIDANS.

F. M. Wilson, *Capt.*
W. W. Codrington
R. Harkness
W. Babington
Sir M. Shaw-Stewart
A. B. Dickson
E. McNiven
J. H. Prinsep
H. W. P. Richards
F. Vansittart
J. F. Peel

Oppidans won by 8 shies.

1844.

COLLEGERS.

J. A. James, *Capt.*
F. A. James
C. Wolley
W. J. Smith
M. E. Stanborough
H. J. Simonds
A. Earle
A. F. Birch
H. S. Mackarness
W. Day
R. Day

OPPIDANS.

F. J. Holland, *Capt.*
A. B. Dickson
E. McNiven
H. W. P. Richards
H. A. F. Luttrell
E. Ethelston
H. V. B. Johnstone
H. A. Bosanquet
A. Tremayne
J. F. Peel
J. C. Patteson

Oppidans won by 10 shies to 2 shies.

1845.

COLLEGERS.

W. J. Smith, *Capt.*
F. J. Coleridge
H. J. Simonds
A. Earle
H. S. Mackarness
M. E. Stanborough
C. W. Moffat
W. A. Slade-Gully
C. Booth
F. E. Stacey
F. B. C. Tarver

OPPIDANS.

C. V. Spencer, *Capt.*
F. J. Holland
J. C. Patteson
F. H. Whymper
W. S. Deacon
C. T. McCausland
F. S. Pipe-Wolferstan
P. W. Jones-Bateman
H. V. B. Johnstone
A. R. Thompson
W. J. Marshall

Collegers won by 7 shies to 6 shies.

1846.

COLLEGERS.

W. J. Smith, *Capt.*
F. L. Yonge
H. S. Mackarness
M. E. Stanborough
C. W. Moffat
W. A. Slade-Gully
C. Booth
F. E. Stacey
F. B. C. Tarver
H. J. Cheales
R. J. Villers

OPPIDANS.

C. Foster
F. H. Whymper
W. S. Deacon
A. R. Thompson
W. J. Marshall
J. W. Chitty
C. H. Miller
A. R. F. M. De Rutzen
H. H. Tremayne
A. Buchanan
E. F. Luttrell

Draw.

1847.

COLLEGERS.

W. J. Smith, *Capt.*
H. J. Cheales
C. Booth
F. E. Stacey
F. B. C. Tarver
F. L. Yonge
W. A. Norris
W. M. Wollaston
A. D. Coleridge
C. C. James
A. J. Coleridge

OPPIDANS.

A. R. F. M. De Rutzen, *Capt.*
A. R. Thompson
H. H. Tremayne
J. Aitken
R. J. M. Buller
H. B. H. Blundell
G. F. Slade
J. Grant-Suttie
F. R. Thackeray
J. A. Atkinson
F. M. Eden

Collegers won by 6 shies.

1848.

COLLEGERS.

H. J. Cheales, *Capt.*
F. E. Stacey
F. L. Yonge
W. A. Norris
W. M. Wollaston
A. D. Coleridge
C. C. James
A. J. Coleridge
H. Drake
G. A. Caley
G. C. Green

OPPIDANS.

R. J. M. Buller, *Capt.*
H. B. H. Blundell
J. Grant-Suttie
Lord Pevensey
H. Aitken
E. F. Luttrell
L. Guy-Phillips
C. K. Crosse
E. Hoskins
T. H. C. Burder
D. F. B. Buckley

Collegers won by 14 shies to nil.

1849.

COLLEGERS.

F. E. Stacey, *Capt.*
W. M. Wollaston
A. J. Coleridge
H. Drake
N. L. Shuldham
J. O. Bent
W. Goodall
C. Thackeray
W. H. Whitting
H. Moody
O. C. Waterfield

OPPIDANS.

W. R. Coleridge
P. H. Nind
R. P. Ethelston
F. J. Coltman
L. Guy-Phillips
R. Meade-King
E. F. Luttrell
G. F. R. Jervis
Hon. I. de V. E. Fiennes
S. J. Blane
C. L. Norman

Collegers won by 1 shy

1850.

COLLEGERS.

W. M. Wollaston, *Capt.*
A. J. Coleridge
J. O. Bent
W. Goodall
C. Thackeray
W. H. Whitting
H. Moody
E. Carter
H. J. Reynolds
H. W. Younger
T. T. Tremlett

OPPIDANS.

P. H. Nind, *Capt.*
L. Guy-Phillips
E. F. Luttrell
D. H. Mytton
F. J. Alderson
T. B. H. Blundell
F. W. Lambton
R. E. Welby
C. H. Russell
W. Watson
R. L. Pemberton

Oppidans won by 3 shies to nil.

WINNERS OF SCHOOL STEEPLECHASE.

1846.
C. Foster

1847.
F. R. Thackeray

1848.
H. Holt

1849.
G. F. R. Jervis

1850.
W. C. Pearson

OFFICERS OF ETON SOCIETY.

1840.
President: C. J. Monk
Chairman: A. Pott
W. Johnson, K.S.

1841.
President: Hon. J. Yarde-Buller
Hon. R. Windsor-Clive
Chairman: H. G. Hulse

1842.
President: T. G. Carter, K.S.
Chairman: J. H. Turner
C. S. Hogg

1843.
President: J. L. Joynes, K.S.
Chairman: J. C. Patteson

1844.
President: C. Wolley, K.S.
F. J. Holland
Chairman: Hon. G. Herbert
F. J. Coleridge, K.S.

1845.
President: F. J. Coleridge, K.S.
J. W. Chitty
Chairman: J. W. Chitty
J. Greenwood

1846.
President: J. W. Chitty
Chairman: J. Greenwood

1847.
President: Hon. T. F. Fremantle
Chairman: A. D. Coleridge, K.S.
Auditor: J. Aitken, K.S.

1848.
President: A. D. Coleridge, K.S.
H. J. Cheales, K.S.
Chairman: W. H. Fremantle
Auditor: H. J. Cheales, K.S.
F. E. Stacey, K.S.

1849.
President: F. E. Stacey, K.S.
Chairman: W. H. Fremantle
J. P. Cobbold
Auditor: J. P. Cobbold
Hon. I. de V. E. Fiennes

1850.
President: P. H. Nind
H. Moody, K.S.
Chairman: R. E. Welby
Hon. F. E. Byng
Auditor: H. Moody, K.S.
A. J. Coleridge, K.S.

ELECTION, 1841.

The small superior figures after the years of entering and leaving denote the first, second, and third schooltimes.

SIXTH FORM.

Yonge *ma.* (K.S., J.E.Y.) — JAMES ARTHUR. 3rd son of Rev. C. Y., M.A., Assist. Master Eton Coll. 1803–29, Lower Master 1829; 1829^{3}–1841^{2}; Newc. Select 1841: King's Coll. Camb.; Fellow of King's, Camden Med. 1843; Barrister W. Circuit; Recorder of Barnstaple and Bideford; *m.* Hannah, *d.* of A. Rogers of Dublin; died Sept. 1864.

Blacker (K.S.) — REV. MAXWELL JULIUS. 2nd son of Lieut.-Col. V. B., C.B., of the Madras Army; 1832^{2}–1841^{3}; Eton XI. 1840; Newc. Select 1841; Merton Coll. Oxf. 3rd Class Lit. Hum.; died 1888.

Monck (K.S.) — REV. WILLIAM STANLEY. Son of J. B. M. of Coley Park, Reading; 1832^{1}–1841^{2}; Eton XI. 1840–1; Univ. Coll. Oxf. B.A.; Curate at St. Peter's, Leeds; died of typhus fever, July 11, 1847.

Baverstock (K.S.) — REV. JOHN. 1832^{2}–1841^{2}; St. John's Coll. Camb. M.A.; Assist. Master Uppingham School; died 1868.

James *ma.* (K.S., E.C.) — REV. EDWARD STANLEY. Son of Rev. Canon E. J., Canon of Winchester and Vicar of Alton, Winchester; 1834^{2}–1841^{1}; Merton Coll. Oxf. M.A.; gained an open Postmastership; Vicar of Letcombe Regis, Wantage, 1853–68; *m.* 1st, Sarah Rennell, *d.* of Rev. James Jolliffe; 2nd, Frances Catherine, *d.* of William Abbott; died July 24, 1868.

Johnson (K.S., W.G.C.) — WILLIAM (aft. Cory). Son of C. W. J. of Great Torrington, Devon; 1832^{3}–1841^{2}; Newc. Select 1839–40, Sch. 1841; King's Coll. Camb. M.A., Chancellor's English Med., Camden Med., Craven Univ. Sch. 1844; Assist. Master at Eton, 1845–72; author of 'Ionica,' etc.; *m.* Rosa Caroline, *d.* of Rev. G. de C. Guille, Rector of Little Torrington, Devon; died June 11, 1892.

Browning *ma.* (K.S., C.Wi., & C.J.A.) — REV. WILLIAM THOMAS. Son of W. S. B.; 1832^{2}–1842^{2}; Exeter Coll. Oxf. M.A.; Clergyman and Schoolmaster: *m.* Margaret, *d.* of Rev. G. R. Green, Fellow of Eton, 1833; died 1882.

Brine *ma.* (K.S.) — ANDREW GRAM. 4th son of Capt. J. B. of Claremont, Sidmouth, Devon; 1831^{3}–1841^{2}; Capt. 32nd Foot; served in the East Indies, severely wounded at the siege of Mooltan, 1849; died unm. June 23, 1873.

James (Misses S., aft. K.S., C.Wi., & W.G.C.) — REV. HERBERT. Son of W. R. J.; 1831^{3}–1842^{2}; Newc. Select 1841; Capt. Coll. Wall 1841, won Coll. Pulling twice; King's Coll. Camb. M.A., Crosse Sch. 1847; Rector of Livermere and Rural Dean; *m.* Mary Emily, *d.* of Adm. Horton. *Livermere Rectory, Bury St. Edmund's.*

Evans (K.S., W.G.C.) — WILLIAM VERNON. Son of W. E., Drawing Master at Eton; 1829 [illegible] 1841 [illegible]; went out with Bishop Selwyn to New Zealand, and died at Wellington, New Zealand 1842.

Smyth-Pigott *max.* (E.H.P.) — HENRY THOMAS COWARD. 2nd son of J. H. S.-P. of Brockley Hall, West Town, Bristol; 1835^{3}–1841^{2}; was in Scots Greys: *m.* Elizabeth, *d.* of James Mells Nairne of Dunsinnan, Balbeggie, Perth; died 1858.

Fiske (K.S., H.D.) — REV. ROBERT WHITE. 1835^{2}–1841^{3}; Eton XI. 1840; Newc. Select 1841; Trin. Coll. Camb. 2nd Cl. Class. Trip.; Vicar of North Leigh, Oxfs.

Tarver *ma.* (K.S., W.G.C.) — REV. JOSEPH. Son of J. C. T. of Eton; 1832^{3}–1845^{3}; Coll. Wall 1841–2, Keeper 1842; Worc. Coll. Oxf. M.A.; *m.* 1st, *d.* of J. H. Talbot; 2nd, *d.* of M. Knapp. *Filgrave Rectory, Newport Pagnell.*

Arundell (C.L.) — WILLIAM REINFRED ARUNDELL HARRIS-. Eld. son of W. A. H.-A. of St. Mary's, Lifton, Devon; 1834^{2}–1841^{3}; Eton VIII. 1839–41. Capt. of the Boats, 1840–1.

Hulse (R.O.) — HENRY GORE. 5th son of Sir C. H., 4th Bt., of Breamore House, Salisbury; 1835^{3}–1842^{2}; Merton Coll. Oxf.; died at Messina, June 1, 1851.

Polehampton *ma.* (K.S.) — REV. EDWARD THOMAS WILLIAM. 1832^{2}–1841^{3}; Pembroke Coll. Oxf. M.A., Fellow of Pembroke Coll.; Rector of Hartfield, Tunbridge Wells; died Dec. 8, 1890.

Rice (K.S., C.L.) — REV. JOHN MORLAND. Son of E. R. R. of Dane Court, Dover; 1836^{1}–1842^{2}; Newc. Select 1840 and 1841, Sch. 1842; Magd. Coll. Oxf.: Fellow of Magd. B.D.; formerly Rector of Bramber, Sussex; *m.* Caroline Penelope, *d.* of Edward York of Wighill Park, York; died Aug. 1897.

Smyth-Pigott *ma.* (E.H.P.) — EDWARD FREDERICK. 3rd son of J. H. S.-P. of Brockley Hall, West Town, Bristol; 1836^{1}–1842^{2}; Ball. Coll. Oxf.; Sub-Editor of 'Daily News'; Late Examiner of Stage Plays; died 1897.

Mr. Neville *ma.* (E.H.P.) — HON. CHARLES CORNWALLIS (5th Lord Braybrooke). 2nd son of Richard, 3rd Lord B.; 1836^{1}–1841^{3}; Magd. Coll. Camb. M.A.; J.P. and D.L. for Essex, late Vice-Lieut. of Essex; Hereditary Visitor of Magd. Coll. Camb.; *m.* Hon. Florence Priscilla Alicia Maude, *d.* of Cornwallis, 3rd Visct. Hawarden; died June 7, 1902.

Dodd — GEORGE WILLIAM. Son of Mrs. D., a Dame at Eton; 1831^{3}–1841^{3}; Queen's Coll. Oxf.

Bayley *ma.* (R.F.H., R.O. & C.L.) — REV. JOHN ROBERT LAURIE EMILIUS (Rev. Sir E. Laurie, Bt.), assumed surname of Laurie 1887. Son of Sir J. E. G. B., 2nd Bt., of Maxwelton, Moniaive, Thornhill; 1835^{3}–1841^{3}; Eton XI 1838–41, Capt. 1840 and 1841; Trin. Coll. Camb. B.D.; Vicar of Woburn, 1853–6; Rector of St. George's, Bloomsbury, 1856–87; Vicar of St. John's, Paddington, 1867–88; [illegible] *d.* of Edward R. Rice, [illegible] Dover. 14 *Hyde* [illegible] W.

B

Hallam (E.C.)
HENRY FITZMAURICE. Son of the Historian; 1836^{3}–1841^{3}; Newc. Med. 1840; Trin. Coll. Camb.; 9th in Class. Trip.; Chanc. Med. 1846; died at Siena, 1850.

Kaye (E.H.P.)
VEN. ARCHDN. WILLIAM FREDERICK JOHN. Son of Rt. Rev. J. K., Bp. of Lincoln; 1836^{3}–1841^{3}; Newc. Select 1840–1; Tomline Prizeman 1840–1; Ball. Coll. Oxf. M.A., 3rd Cl. Class., 2nd Math. 1844; Rector of Riseholme since 1846; Archdeacon and Canon of Lincoln since 1863; *m.* Mary, *d.* of Rt. Rev. John Jackson, Bp. of Lincoln and London. *Lincoln.*

Smith *ma.* (E.C.)
GOLDWIN. Son of R. P. S., M.D., of Mortimer, Berks; 1836^{3}–1841^{3}; Newc. Select 1840, Med. 1841; Magd. and Univ. Coll. Oxf.; Hon. D.C.L., Hertford Sch. 1842; Lat. V. and Ireland, 1845; 1st Cl. 1845; Chanc. Prize for Latin V. 1845; Latin Essay 1846; Regius Prof. of Mod. Hist. 1858–66 and Fellow of Univ. Coll. 1846; English Essay 1847; Barr. Lincoln's Inn; Prominent Champion of the North during American Civil War 1864; went to U.S. 1868; Hon. Prof. of English and Constitutional Hist. in Cornell Univ. U.S.A.; went to Canada 1871; Literary; *m.* Harriet, widow of Henry Boulton and *d.* of Thomas Dixon. *The Grange, Toronto, Canada.*

Buckland (Mrs. Hor., E.C.)
CHARLES THOMAS. Son of Rev. J. B. of Laleham, Staines; 1836^{1}–1841^{3}; Newc. Select 1840–1; Haileybury E. I. Coll. 1842–4; Bengal Civil Service 1844–81; Member of the Bengal Board of Revenue, and Bengal Legislative Council; *m.* Mary Ann Letitia, *d.* of Sir Henry Ricketts, K.C.S.I., of the Bengal Civil Service; died March 1894.

Ainslie (C.O.G.)
MONTAGUE MORDAUNT. 1836^{3}–1842^{2}; Eton XI. 1839–42, Capt. 1842; Opp. Wall 1841; Oxf. XI. 1843–5; Barrister; formerly in the Office of the Examiner of Recognizances, House of Commons.

Luxmoore *ma.* (Misses S., J.W.)
CHARLES (aft. Luxmoore-Brooke). Of Witherdon, Broadwood Widger, Lifton, N. Devon, and aft. of Ashbrook Hall, Cheshire; son of Rev. C. T. C. L., Vicar of Guilsfield, Welshpool; 1836^{1}–1842^{2}; Capt. 37th Regt. and A.D.C. to Governor of Ceylon; served in Indian Mutiny 1857–8, mentioned in despatches (med.); *m.* Mary Rosalie, *d.* of Rev. Charles Thomas Carpenter of Launceston; died Jan. 9, 1890.

FIFTH FORM—UPPER DIVISION.

Carter (K.S., E.H.P.)
THOMAS GARDEN. 1836^{3}–1843^{3}; Eton XI. 1841–3; Pres. Eton Soc. 1842; Trin. Coll. Camb. M.A.; formerly Vicar of Linton, Kent.

Browning *mi.* (K.S.)
ARTHUR HENRY. Son of W. S. B.; 1834^{3}–1843^{3}; Lincoln Coll. Oxf.; City Merchant; *m.* Ellen, *d.* of J. Booth; died at Genoa 1880.

Simonds *ma.* (K.S., C.W. & C.O.G.)
HENRY ADOLPHUS. Son of W. M. S.; 1834^{3}–1843^{3}; Brewer; *m.* Emily, *d.* of — Boulger. *Audley's Wood, Basingstoke.*

Marriott (Mrs. P., aft. K.S., H.D.)
REV. WHARTON BOOTH, B.D., F.S.A. Son of G. W. M., B.C.L., of the Inner Temple; 1836^{3}–1843^{3}; Eton XI. 1842; Sch. of Trin. Coll. Oxf., B.A.; 2nd Cl., Lit. Hum., and Fellow of Exeter Coll. 1846; Assist. Master at Eton 1850^{1}–60^{3}; Editor of 'Adelphi' of Terence; *m.* Julia, *d.* of William Soltau; died Dec. 16, 1871.

Marcon (aft. K.S.)
REV. WALTER. Son of J. M., J.P., of Swaffham, Norfolk; 1834^{3}–1842^{3}; Eton XI. [illegible] 1841 2; [illegible] 1844; Rector of [illegible] *d.* of Rev. Henry [illegible]

Yonge *mi.* (K.S., J.E.Y.)
GEORGE EDWARD. 4th son of Rev. C. Y., M.A., Assist. Master at Eton 1803–29, Lower Master 1829; 1832^{1}–1843^{3}; Eton XI. 1841–3, Capt. 1843; Keeper of Upper Club 1842–3; Trin. Coll. Oxf.; Oxf. XI. 1844–8; Treas. of Hants County; *m.* Lucy, *d.* of Gideon Acland. *Stoke Lodge, Bishopstoke, Eastleigh, R.S.O., Hants.*

King (K.S., E.H.P.)
REV. RICHARD HENRY. 1835^{3}–1843^{3}; Merton Coll. Oxf. M.A.; formerly Rector of Little Glenham, Wickham Market, Suffolk; died 1886.

Joynes *ma.* (Mrs. P., aft. K.S., J.W. & E.C.)
REV. JAMES LEIGH. Son of Rev. — J., Rector of Gravesend; 1836^{3}–1844^{1}; Newc. Select 1841, Med. 1842, Sch. 1843; Coll. Wall 1841–3, Keeper 1843; Pres. Eton Soc. 1843; Sch. of King's Coll. Camb. M.A.; Camden Med. 1843; Fellow of King's; Assist. Master at Eton 1849–77; Lower Master 1877–87. 171 *Montpelier Road, Brighton.*

Phillott (K.S., C.Wi.)
REV. HERBERT. Son of Rev. P., Rector of Stanton-Prior, near Bath; 1835^{3}–1843^{3}; Coll. Wall 1841–2; Ch. Ch. Oxf.; dead.

Mr. Campbell (E.C.)
HON. WILLIAM FREDERICK (2nd Lord Stratheden and Campbell). Eld. son of Sir John, 1st Lord Campbell (Lord Chanc. 1859) and Baroness Stratheden; 1836^{1}–1841^{3}; Hon. Col. 7th Vol. Bn. K.R.R.C.; D.L. for co. Roxburgh; M.P. for Cambridge 1847–52, and for Harwich 1859–60; died unm. Jan. 21, 1893.

Clive (W.E., E.C.)
HON. ROBERT WINDSOR-. Eld. son of Hon. R. H. C., M.P. of Oakly Park, Salop, and the Baroness Windsor; 1836^{3}–1842^{3}; Pres. Eton Soc. 1841; St. John's Coll. Camb. M.A.; M.P. for Ludlow 1852–4, and S. Salop 1854–9; *m.* Lady Mary Selina Louisa Bridgeman, *d.* of 2nd Earl of Bradford; died August 4, 1859.

Mr. Curzon *ma.* (E.O.)
HON. HENRY DUGDALE. 4th son of Richard William Penn, 1st Earl Howe; 1836^{1}–1841^{3}; Ch. Ch. Oxf.; J.P. and D.L. for Hants; formerly Capt. Leicestershire Yeo. Cav.; *m.* Eleanor Young, *d.* of Major-Gen. Thomas R. Swinburne. *East Dean, Romsey.*

Mitchell (H.D.)
JAMES WILLIAM. 1836^{3}–1841^{3}.

Brocklebank (K.S.)
T. . 1844.

Bean (E.H.P.)
HENRY LUCAS. 1836^{1}–1841^{3}; Eton XI. 1839–41; Cornet N. Somerset Yeo.

Stephens (C.L., aft. K.S., C.L.)
R. . 1844.

Hutton (K.S.)
R. R. . 1844.

Goertz (K.S.)
F. L. A. . 1844.

Helm (K.S.)
J. B. . 1844.

Hamilton
PEREGRINE CHARLES BAILLIE. Eld. son of H. of Rambleton Law, Berwickshire; 1835^{3}–1841^{3}; late Capt. Rifle Brigd.; dead.

Brine *mi.* (K.S., R.O.)
C. C. . 1844.

Herbert (R.O., aft. K.S., R.O.)
REV. HENRY. Son of W. H. of Huntingdon; 1833^{3}–1842^{3}; Coll. Wall 1841; Worc. Coll. Oxf.; Rector of Hemingford Abbots since 1866. *Hemingford Abbots Rectory, St. Ives, Hunts.*

Polehampton *mi* (K.S.)
REV. HENRY STEDMAN. 1832^{3}–1842^{3}; Coll. Wall 1841; Pembroke Coll. Oxf.; Oxf. VIII. 1846; formerly Chaplain to the Residency at Lucknow; died in Hospital at Lucknow 1858.

Drake (K.S., C.O.G.) — B. W. F. . 1844.

Spankie *ma.* (H.D.) — JOHN. Eld. son of S. S.; 1837^{3}–1842^{2}; won School Sculling 1841; Opp. Wall 1841; Merton Coll. Oxf.; 2nd Cl. Class. 1846; Barrister, Lincoln's Inn; died Jan. 23, 1902.

Mount (E.C.) — WILLIAM GEORGE. Son of W. M. of Wasing Place, Reading; 1837^{1}–1842^{1}; Ball. Coll. Oxf. M.A.; called to the Bar, Inner Temple, 1849; M.P. for Newbury Div. of Berks 1885–1901; J.P. for Hants; Chmn. of C.C. and Chmn. of Qr. Sessions for Berks 1887, High Sheriff 1877; *m.* Marianne Emily, *d.* of Robert Clutterbuck of Watford House, Herts. *Wasing Place, near Reading.*

Spankie *mi.* (H.D.) — ROBERT. 2nd son of S. S.; 1837^{3}–1841^{3}; E. I. Coll. Haileybury; Bengal Civil Service, Magistrate and Coll. at Saharunpore; *m. d.* of Dr. Blakely, Dean of Down.

Hole (Mrs. P., E.C.) — REV. ROBERT. Son of Rev. G. H. of Chumleigh, Devon; 1837^{3}–1841^{2}; Univ. Coll. Oxf. B.A.; J.P. for Devon; Rector of North Tawton; *m.* Kate, *d.* of Robert Fulford of N. Tawton. *The Rectory, North Tawton, R.S.O., N. Devon.*

Wolley *ma.* (J. W.) — JOHN. Eld. son of Rev. J. W., Vicar of Beeston, Nottingham; 1836^{3}–1842^{1}; Eton VIII. 1840; Opp. Wall 1841; Trin. Coll. Camb. M.A.; a distinguished Naturalist, especially in British Birds' Eggs; died unm. 1859.

Ferard (Miss W., C.J.A.) — CHARLES COTTON. Of Winkfield Manor, Ascot; son of D. F. of Winkfield Manor; 1836^{3}–1841^{2}; Trin. Coll. Camb. M.A.; J.P. for Berks; Barrister; *m.* Emily Jane, *d.* of The Very Rev. Thomas Dale, Dean of Rochester; died 1886.

Sumner (E.C.) — RT. REV. GEORGE HENRY (LORD BISHOP OF GUILDFORD). Son of Rt. Rev. C. R. S., Bp. of Winchester; 1837^{1}–1842^{3}; Ball. Coll. Oxf. M.A. D.D.; Bishop Suffragan of Guildford 1888–96, late Rector of Old Alresford, Hants; Rural Dean, Archdn. and Canon of Winchester; Prolocutor of Lower Ho. of Convocation of Cant.; *m.* Mary Elizabeth, *d.* of Thomas Heywood of Hope End. *The Close, Winchester.*

Molesworth (H.D.) — WALTER HELE. 4th son of the Rev. W. M. of St. Breoke, Cornwall; 1837^{3}–1841^{3}; *m.* Frances Mary, *d.* of Adm. Henry Duncas Twysden, R.N.; died Jan. 11, 1885.

Master (H.D.) — REV. GEORGE STREYNSHAM. Eld. son of Ven. R. M. M., Archdn. of Manchester; 1837^{2}–1841^{3}; B.N.C. Oxf. M.A.; formerly Vicar of Twickenham, and late Rector of West Dean, Wilts; *m.* Harriet Susannah Ann, *d.* of Rev. Thomas Hunt, Rector of West Felton, Salop. *Bourton Grange, Co. Somerset.*

Welby *ma.* (E.C.) — WILLIAM EARLE. 3rd son of Rev. J. E. W., Rector of Harston, Grantham; 1837^{3}–1841^{5}; Oriel Coll. Oxf.; J.P. cos. Derby, Lincoln, and Northants; *m.* Adeline, *d.* of William Fane, Bengal C.S. *Barilton House, Stamford.*

Hoskins (K.S., C.O.G.) — C. T. . 1844.

Waring — WALTER THOMAS. Son of B. W., M.D., of St. Pauls Cray, Kent; 1833^{3}–1841^{3}; formerly Capt. Kent Artillery Militia; died Oct. 21, 1895.

Wright (K.S., E.C.) — J. C. . 1844.

Bastard (E.C.) — EDMUND RODNEY POLLEXFEN. Of Kitley, Devon; eld. son of E. P. B. of Kitley; 1838^{1}–1843^{2}; Newc. Select 1843; Tomline Select 1841–42, Prizeman 1843; Ball. Coll. Oxf. M.A., Double First, 1846; *m.* Florence Mary, *d.* of Simon Scrope of Danby Hall, Yorks; died June 12, 1856.

Carlyon (W.L.E.) — EDWARD AUGUSTUS. 2nd son of E. C. of Tregrehan, Par Station, Cornwall; 1838^{2}–1841^{2}; Trin. Coll. Camb. M.A.; Barrister; J.P. for Devon; died unm. Dec. 5, 1874.

Hughes (C.O.G.) — WILLIAM EDWARD. 2nd son of M. H. of Sherdley Hall, St. Helens, Lancaster; 1837^{2}–1841^{3}; Trin. Coll. Camb.; died unm. in Brussels, Dec. 17, 1885.

Butt *ma.* (R.O.) — WILLIAM PACKER COLSTON. Son of T. P. B. of Arle Court, Cheltenham; 1838^{3}–1841^{2}; Trin. Coll. Oxf. B.A.; member of Committee of O.U.B.C. 1842–3; died 1848.

Franks (E.C.) — CHARLES WILLIAM. Only son of the London banker; 1838^{3}–1843^{1}; Ch. Ch. Oxf.; Colonial Treasurer, British Columbia.

Monk (E.C.) — CHARLES JAMES. Of Bedwell Park, Hatfield, and 5 Buckingham Gate, S.W.; son of Rt. Rev. J. H. M., Bishop of Gloucester and Bristol; 1838^{1}–1843^{2}; Pres. Eton Soc. 1840; Trin. Coll. Camb. M.A.; Epigrams, 1845; Brown's Med. 1845; Members' Prizeman 1846–7; called to the Bar, Lincoln's Inn, 1850; Chanc. of Bristol 1855–84, and Glouc. 1859–84; Pres. of the Associated Chamb. of Comm. of the United Kingdom 1881–4; M.P. for Glouc. 1859, 1865–85 and 1895–1900; J.P. and D.L. for co. Glouc.; Director of the Suez Canal; *m.* Julia, *d.* of P. S. Balli, Consul-Gen. of Greece; died Nov. 10, 1900.

Jenkins — JOHN HEYWARD. Son of Rev. J. J., of Kerry, Newtown; of Cross Wood, Welshpool; 1837^{3}–1841^{3}; Oriel Coll. Oxf.; formerly Capt. Montgoms. Rifles; *m.* Eliza, *d.* of John Jones; dead.

Houstoun (J.W.) — WILLIAM ADAM. 4th son of Gen. Sir R. H., K.C.B., of Clerkington, Haddington, N.B.; 1838^{3}–1841^{2}; Trin. Coll. Camb., Fellow Commoner; Capt. Madras Cav.; died unm. in India, Aug. 11, 1846.

Wodehouse (E.H.P.) — SIR JOHN, Bt. (3rd Lord Wodehouse, and 1st Earl of Kimberley, K.G., P.C., D.C.L.). Son of Hon. H. W., 2nd son of 2nd Lord Wodehouse; 1838^{3}–1843^{1}; Ch. Ch. Oxf., B.A., 1st Cl. Class. 1847; Hon. D.C.L. 1894; Under Sec. Foreign Office, 1852–6, 1859–61, and 1894–5; Envoy-Extraordinary to Russia, 1856–8; on special mission to Copenhagen, 1863; Under Sec. for India, 1864; Lord-Lieut. of Ireland, 1864–6; Lord Privy Seal, 1868–70; Sec. for Colonies 1870–4 and 1880–2; Chanc. of Duchy of Lanc. 1882; Sec. for India, 1882–6 and 1892–4; Lord Pres. of the Council, 1892–4; Sec. for For. Aff. 1894–5; Leader of Lib. Party Ho. of Lords, 1897; Pres. of Univ. Coll. London; J.P. and D.L. for Norfolk; *m.* Lady Florence Fitzgibbon, C.I., eld. *d.* of 3rd and last Earl of Clare; died April 8, 1902.

Wolley *mi.* (K.S., J.W. & E.H.P.) — C. (aft. Wolley-Dod). . 1844.

Peel *ma.* (E.C.) — ROBERT KENNEDY. Eld. son of Lieut.-Gen. J. P., P.C., D.C.L., M.P.; 1837^{3}–1843^{2}; Wall XI.; Ball. Coll. Oxf.; called to the Bar; died at Ardennes, April 17, 1863.

Mr. Milles (H.D.) — HON. GEORGE WATSON (1st Earl Sondes, D.L.). Eld. son of G. J. M., 4th Lord Sondes; 1838^{1}–1842^{3}; Eton XI. 1842; R.M. Coll. Sandhurst; Capt. R. Horse Gds.; M.P. for East Kent 1868–74; *m.* Charlotte, eld. *d.* of Sir Henry Stracey, 5th Bt.; died Sept. 10, 1894.

Hotham *ma.* (E.C.) — REV. FREDERICK HARRY. 2nd son of Vice-Adm. Sir H. H., K.C.B., of Silverlands, Chertsey; 1837^{3}–1841^{3}; Ch. Ch. [illegible] Rushbury, Salop, and [illegible] Annie, 4th *d.* of Robert [illegible] Park, Chertsey; died April 11, 1887.

Heygate (Mrs. Ev., R.O.) — WILLIAM UNWIN. Of Roecliffe Hall, Loughborough; 2nd son of Sir W. H., 1st Bt. (Lord Mayor of London, 1822), of Roecliffe Hall; 1837^{2}–1843^{3}; Eton VIII. 1842; Opp. Wall 1842; won Pulling and Double Sculling 1842; Merton Coll. Oxf. M.A.; Oxf. VIII. 1846; called to the Bar at Lincoln's Inn 1850; M.P. for Leicester 1861–5, Stamford 1868, S. Leicestershire 1870–80; J.P. and D.L. for Herts and Leicesters; has a medal from R. Humane Soc.; Banker; Railway Direc. and Alderman C.C.; *m.* Constance Mary, *d.* of Sir George H. Beaumont, 8th Bt., of Coleorton Hall, Ashby-de-la-Zouch; died March 2, 1902.

Foster (W.E., E.C.) — EDMUND BENSON. Only son of E. F. of Clewer Manor, Windsor; 1837^{1}–1843^{2}; Ball. Coll. Oxf. B.A.; J.P. and D.L. for Berks; Berks C.C. 1894–1902; *m.* Edith Eleanor, 2nd *d.* of Sir Thomas Fraser Grove, 1st Bt., of Ferne House, Salisbury. *Clewer Manor, Windsor.*

Greene *ma.* (H.D.) — REV. THOMAS HUNTLEY. 2nd son of T. G. of Slyne and Whittington; 1837^{2}–1841^{3}; Ball. Coll. Oxf.; formerly Rector of Marsh Gibbon, Bicester; Archdn. of Capetown; *m.* Helen, *d.* of Gen. Hon. Sir Patrick Stuart, G.C.M.G.; died Oct. 10, 1887.

Newdigate (W.E., E.C.) — REV. CHARLES JOHN. 2nd son of F. N. of Kirk and West Hallam; 1838^{2}–1841^{2}; Ch. Ch. Oxf. M.A.; Rector of West Hallam, Derby; died unm. 1876.

Stapylton (Mrs. Ev., C.J.A.) — REV. WILLIAM CHETWYND-. 3rd son of Major H. R. C.-S. of Wighill; 1838^{3}–1843^{3}; Eton VIII. 1842–3; Opp. Wall 1842; winner of Pair Oars 1840–2, and of Sculling and Double Sculling 1843; Merton Coll. Oxf. Fellow; Oxf. VIII. 1844–6; Rector of Hallaton, and Hon. Canon of Rochester; *m.* 1st, Elizabeth Biscoe, *d.* of Rev. Robert Tritton, Rector of Morden; 2nd, Mary Elizabeth, *d.* of Frederick Johnson. *Hallaton Rectory, Uppingham.*

Crawley *ma.* (R.O.) — JOHN SAMBROOK. Of Stockwood, Luton; eld. son of S. C. of Stockwood; 1837^{3}–1843^{3}; Trin. Coll. Camb.; J.P. for Beds, High Sheriff 1858; *m.* Sarah Bridget, *d.* of Frederick Octavius Wells, of the Bengal Civil Service; died Sept. 22, 1895.

Mr. Herbert *ma.* (E.C.) — HON. G. . 1844.

Miles (R.O.) — SIR PHILIP JOHN WILLIAM, 2nd Bt. Eld. son of Sir W. M., 1st Bt., of Leigh Court, Bristol; 1837^{3}–1843^{3}; won School Sculling 1842, Double Sculling 1842–3; Camb.; M.P. for East Somersets 1878–85; *m.* Frances Elizabeth, *d.* of Sir David Roche, Bt.; died June 5, 1888.

Sartoris *ma.* (R.O.) — CHARLES. Of Wilcote, Charlbury, Oxford; son of U. S. of Sceaux Park, near Paris; 1838^{2}–1842^{3}; Exeter Coll. Oxf. M.A.; J.P., co. Oxf., High Sheriff 1872; *m.* Mary Hermione, *d.* of James Henry Callander, of Craigforth House, Stirling; died 1884.

Clark (R.O.) — ERVING FREDERICK. Eld. son of E. C. of Efford Manor, Plymouth; 1838^{2}–1841^{3}; Trin. Coll. Camb.; died 1850.

Hanmer (Mrs. Hor.) — WILLIAM, J.P. Of Bodnod Hall, Denbighshire; eld. son of W. H., Barrister, of Bodnod; 1837^{1}–1841^{3}; formerly Major 87th Fusiliers; died May 26, 1894.

Lord Pomfret (H.D.) — 1837^{3}–1841^{3}; Ch. Ch. Oxf.; dead.

Vansittart (C.L.) — I. 1841.

Pryor (C.L.) — THOMAS. Of the Elms, Baldock, Herts; 4th son of V. P. of Baldock; 1837^{1}–1841^{3}; J.P. for Herts; Lord of the Manor of Baldock; a Brewer; *m.* Mary Matilda Willoughby, *d.* of Augustus Foster, of Warmwell Hall, co. Dorset; dead.

Day (K.S., R.O.) — W. . 1844.

James *ma.* (K.S., C.Wi. & C.J.A.) — J. A. . 1844.

Chilton (Miss W., E.H.P.) — REV. GEORGE ROBERT COMYN. Son of G. C.; 1837^{3}–1843^{3}; Ch. Ch. Oxf. M.A.; Curate of Redenhall 1853, Curate of Puttenham 1856; Vicar of Wanborough, Surrey, 1861–95; *m.* Frances Sophia, *d.* of Rev. Clement Strong. *Littleton, Guildford.*

Hammond *ma.* (K.S.) — J. G. . 1844.

Batchelor *ma.* (K.S.) — F. T. . 1844.

Drury (K.S., C.L.) — ARTHUR. 1837^{1}–1842^{3}; formerly in the Indian Army.

Seymour (C.L.) — ALFRED. Of Knoyle House, Salisbury; 2nd son of H. S. of Trent Manor House, Somerset; 1837^{1}–1842^{2}; Newc. Sch. 1840; Ch. Ch. Oxf.; M.P. for Totnes 1863–9, and Salisbury 1869–74; J.P. and D.L.; *m.* Isabella, *d.* of Sir Baldwin Leighton, Bt., and widow of Beriah Botfield, M.P., of Norton Hall; died 1888.

Scott *ma.* (C.O.G.) — REV. CHARLES BRODRICK, D.D. Son of J. S. S., Q.C., of 3 Merrion Sq., Dublin, and The Cottage, Delgany, Greystones; 1837^{2}–1843^{3}; Tomline Prizeman 1842; Newc. Select 1842–3; Trin. Coll. Camb. D.D., Fellow and Tutor of Trin.; Senior Classic, Chanc. Med. and 22nd Wrangler; Pitt Univ. Sch.; Le Bas and Member's Prizes; Headmaster of Westminster 1855–83, and Preb. of St. Paul's; *m.* Susan, *d.* of Prof. John Smyth of Norwich; died at Bournemouth, 1894.

McNiven *ma.* (Miss W., E.C.) — H. . 1844.

Dodson (E.C.) — JOHN GEORGE (1st Lord Monk Bretton), P.C., M.A. Of Conyboro, Lewes; son of Rt. Hon. Sir J. D., Knt., LL.D., Advocate of the Admiralty; 1837^{2}–1842^{3}; Prince Consort's Prize 1841–2; Fellow of Eton Coll. 1876–80; Ch. Ch. Oxf.; 1st Cl. Class. 1847; called to the Bar, Lincoln's Inn, 1853; M.P. for Sussex 1857–74, for Chester 1874–80, and for Scarborough 1880–4; Deputy Speaker of the House of Commons 1865–72; Financial Sec. to the Treasury 1873–4; Pres. of the Local Gov. Board 1880–2; Chanc. of the Duchy of Lancaster 1882–4; Chmn. of East Sussex Co. Council 1889–92; J.P. and D.L. for Sussex; *m.* Caroline Florence, *d.* of William John Campion of Danny, Hurstpierpoint, Hassocks, Sussex; died May 25, 1897.

Northmore (W.G.C.) — JOHN. 2nd son of Rev. T. W. N. of Cleve, Devon; 1838^{2}–1842^{1}; B.N.C. Oxf.; H.M. Civil Service, Ceylon; J.P. for Devon; *m.* 1st, Jemima Hayter, *d.* of Rev. William Hawes, Rector of Chagford, Devon; 2nd, Harriet Olympia Morshead, *d.* of Northmore Herle Pierce Lawrence of Launceston; 3rd, Sarah Selina Persse, *d.* of Stephen W. Cranglie and widow of Rev. R. H. Donovan. *The Rosery, Ashburton, Devon.*

Buller (E.C.) — SIR MORTON EDWARD MANNINGHAM-, 2nd Bt. Eld. son of Sir E. M.-B., 1st Bt., of Dilhorn; 1838^{3}-1844^{1}; Newc. Select 1844; Ball. Coll. Oxf. B.A.; J.P. and D.L. for co. Stafford; Hon. Col. 3rd Bn. N. Staffs Regt.; *m.* Mary, *d.* of William Davenport of Maer Hall, co. Stafford. *Dilhorn Hall, Cheadle.*

Bidgood (C.O.G.) — CHARLES HARRY. Son of H. F. B. of Rockbeare Court, Devon; 1838^{2}-1841^{3}; Trin. Coll. Camb.; died unm. June 1884.

Mr. Herbert *mi.* (Mrs. Vall., & W.E., E.B.) — HON. R. C. . 1841.

Back *ma.* (R.F.H., J.W.) — REV. HENRY. 1838^{3}-1842^{2}; Sch. of Trin. Coll. Camb.; 1st Cl. Class. 1847; formerly Vicar of Banbury.

Cra'ster (H.D.) — JOHN. Of Cra'ster Tower; eld. son of T. Wood-Cra'ster of Cra'ster Tower, Lesbury, Northumberland; 1838^{3}-1843^{3}; Opp. Wall 1841; St. John's Coll. Oxf. B.A.; J.P. and D.L. for Northumberland, High Sheriff 1879; formerly Capt. Northumb. L.I. Militia; *m.* Charlotte Pulleine, *d.* of William Roddam of Roddam Hall, Alnwick; died March 13, 1895.

Lord Henley — ANTHONY HENLEY (3rd Lord). Son of Robert, 2nd Lord H.; 1835^{3}-1843^{2}; Eton VIII. 1843; Ch. Ch. Oxf.; D.L., J.P. and C.C. Northants, High Sheriff 1854; M.P. for Northampton 1859-74; *m.* 1st, Julia Augusta, *d.* of the Very Rev. John Peel, D.D., Dean of Worcester; 2nd, Clara Campbell Lucy, *d.* of Joseph H. S. Jekyll; died Nov. 27, 1898.

Hotham *mi.* (E.C.) — BEAUMONT WILLIAMS. 3rd son of Vice-Adm. Sir H. H., K.C.B., of Silverlands, Chertsey; 1838^{3}-1842^{1}; late Capt. Gren. Gds.; H.M. Consul at Calais 1859-82; *m.* Charlotte Amelia, youngest *d.* of Adm. George F. Rich. 4 *Eaton Gardens, Hove, Brighton.*

Keene (Mrs. Y., H.D.) — CHARLES RUCK-. Son of Rev. C. E. R.-K. of Swyncombe House, Henley-on-Thames; 1838^{3}-1842^{3}; *m.* Emily, *d.* of J. Sweeting of Devon; died Feb. 14, 1886.

Cracroft (R.O.) — REV. ROBERT WENTWORTH. 3rd son of Col. R. C. of Hackthorn Hall, Lincoln; 1838^{3}-1841^{3}; Ball. Coll. Oxf. B.A.; Rector of Harrington and Brinkhill; *m.* Hon. Elizabeth Catherine Lane Fox, *d.* of Sackville Walter Lane Fox of Bramham Park, Yorks. *Harrington Rectory, Spilsby, Lincs.*

Lucy (J.W.) — WILLIAM FULKE. Eld. son of G. L. of Charlecote Park, Warwick; 1838^{3}-1841^{3}; Camb.; died unm. July 1, 1848.

Palmer (C.Wl.) — GEORGE JOHN. 3rd son of Sir J. H. P., 7th Bt., of Carlton Park, Rockingham; 1837^{3}-1841^{3}; a Barrister of Inner Temple.

Naper (Misses S., J.W.) — JAMES LENOX. Eld. son of J. L. W. N. of Loughcrew; 1838^{3}-1843^{3}; Ch. Ch. Oxf.; J.P. and D.L. for co. Meath, High Sheriff 1853; late Major, Meath Militia; *m.* Hon. Katherine Frances Rowley, *d.* of Clotworthy, 3rd Lord Langford. *Loughcrew, Oldcastle, R.S.O., co. Meath.*

Yarde-Buller (E.C.) — HON. JOHN. Eld. son of 1st Lord Churston; 1837^{3}-1841^{3}; Eton VIII. 1840-1; won School Pulling 1841; Capt. Opp. Wall 1841; Pres. Eton Soc. 1841; St. Mary Hall, Oxf. M.A.; Col. S. Devon Militia; *m.* Charlotte, *d.* of Edward Sacheverell Chandos-Pole of Radbourne Hall, Derby; died May 6, 1867.

Vaughan (Mrs. Rl., W.G.C.) — REV. JAMES STUART. Of Slapton, near Dartmouth; 1838 -1841 ; Ball. Coll. Oxf. B.A.; formerly C[illegible] of Street Chapel, Black[illegible]ton Devons.

Bill (C.O.G.) — AUGUSTUS HORSFALL. 3rd son of C. H. B. of Storthes Hall, Yorks; 1838^{1}-1842^{2}; Ch. Ch. Oxf.; died 1874.

Mr. Pierrepont (H.D.) — HON. SYDNEY WILLIAM HERBERT (3rd Earl Manvers). 2nd son of Charles Herbert P., 2nd Earl Manvers, of Thoresby Park, Nottingham; 1837^{3}-1841^{3}; Ch. Ch. Oxf. B.A.; J.P. and D.L. for Notts; M.P. for S. Nottingham 1852-60; Hon. Col. S. Notts Yeo. Cav.; *m.* Georgine Jane Elizabeth Fanny, 2nd *d.* of Augustin Louis Joseph Casimir Gustave de Franquetot (Duc de Coigny) of France; died Jan. 16, 1900.

Richards *ma.* (E.H.P.) — REV. FREDERICK JONATHAN. 2nd son of W. P. R. of Park Crescent, W.; 1837^{2}-1842^{3}; Eton VIII. 1840-2; Capt. of Boats 1842; Opp. Wall 1841; Merton Coll. Oxf. and Durham, M.A.; Cox. of Oxf. VIII. 1845; Vicar of Boxley, near Maidstone, 43 years; *m.* Dora Georgina Harrington, *d.* of George Moses Benson of Lutwyche Hall, Salop; died 1896.

Lyon (W.L.E.) — THOMAS. Eld. son of T. L. of Appleton Hall, near Warrington; 1837^{3}-1841^{3}; Cox. Eton VIII. 1841; formerly 17th Lancers; aft. settled in Sweden; *m.* Helena, *d.* of Baron Posse, of Aispånga, Sweden; died Nov 28, 1885.

Temple (E.H.P.) — THOMAS RAMSHAY SMYTH-. Only son of F. J. H. S.-T. of Ellerslie, Sussex; 1836^{1}-1841^{3}; Eton VIII. 1841; Trin. Coll. Camb. M.A.; Barrister, Lincoln's Inn; *m.* 1st, Catherine Victorie, *d.* of M. Larmane; 2nd, Henrietta, *d.* of Joseph Chitty; 3rd, Georgina Adelaide, *d.* of William Golden Lumley, Q.C. 10 *Sussex Square, Hyde Park, W.*

Marquis of Drogheda (W.G.C.) — HENRY FRANCIS SEYMOUR MOORE (8th Earl and 3rd and last Marquis of Drogheda), K.P., P.C. Son of Lord H. S. M., 2nd son of 1st Marq. of D.; 1836^{3}-1842^{3}; Trin. Coll. Dublin; Lord-Lieut. and custos rotulorum co. Kildare; Vice-Adm. of Leinster; Hon. Col. 3rd Bn. Royal Dublin Fusiliers; Lieut.-Col.-Comm. Kildare Rifles, and Ranger of the Curragh; J.P. and D.L. Queen's Co.; *m.* Hon. Mary Caroline Stuart Wortley, *d.* of John, 2nd Lord Wharncliffe; died suddenly June 29, 1892.

Sir V. Cornewall (H.D.) — SIR VELTERS, 4th Bt. Eld. son of Sir G. C., 3rd Bt., of Moccas Court, Hereford; 1837^{3}-1841^{3}; Master of Herts Hounds, and Capt. Herts Militia; died unm. Oct. 14, 1868.

MIDDLE DIVISION.

Campbell (J.W.) — SIR ARCHIBALD ISLAY, 3rd Bt. Of Garscube, Glasgow; son of J. C. and grandson of Sir A. C., 2nd Bt.; 1838^{1}-1842^{2}; Ch. Ch. Oxf., 2nd Cl. 1847; M.P. 1851-7; *m.* Agnes, *d.* of Richard, 2nd Marquis of Westminster; died Sept. 11, 1866.

Simpson (E.H.P.) — REV. JOSEPH. 1839^{1}-1843^{2}; Newc. Select 1842, Med. 1843; Prince Consort's French and German Prize, 1841; Sch. of Trin. Coll. Camb.; 3rd in Class. Trip. and Wrangler; Fellow of Jesus Coll.; aft. a Priest in the Roman Catholic Church.

Marston (Miss Edw., C.J.A.) — REV. CHARLES DALLAS. 1839^{1}-1841^{3}; Caius Coll. Camb. M.A.; formerly Rector of St. Mary's, Bryanston Sq., S.W.

McNiven *mi.* (Miss W., E.C.) — E. 1844.

Mr. Neville *[illegible]* ([illegible]) — [illegible] 1844.

Gilbert (C.O.G.)
ROBERT WINTLE (aft. Wintle). Son of Rev. A. T. G., Bishop of Chichester; 1838^{3}-1841^{2}; St. John's Coll. Oxf., 2nd Class Lit. Hum.; Canc. of the Diocese of Chichester; Barrister; *m.* Emma, *d.* of Ven. Henry Cotton, Archdn. of Cashel; died Aug. 1892.

Hogg (R.O.)
CHARLES SWINTON. 2nd son of Sir J. W. H., 1st Bt., P.C.; 1837^{3}-1843^{2}; Ch. Ch. Oxf.; Administrator-Gen. of Calcutta; Barrister; *m.* Harriet Anne, *d.* of Sir Walter G. Stirling, Bt.; died in Calcutta, March 16, 1870.

Birch (Mrs. Ri., aft. K.S., C.J.A.)
A. F. . 1844.

Garth (Mrs. Hor., E.H.P.)
REV. HENRY. Son of G. of Farnham; 1839^{3}-1843^{3}; Eton XI. 1841-3; Opp. Wall 1842; Keeper of Upper Club 1842-3; was an Army Chaplain at Aldershot; aft. Curate of Trinity, Vauxhall Br. Road; died 1859.

Bendyshe (Miss Edw., aft. K.S., H.D.)
T. . 1844.

Patteson *ma.* (E.C.)
J. C. (Bp. of Polynesia). 1844.

Macleod (C.L.)
GEORGE FORBES. 1839^{2}-1841^{3}.

Vance *ma.* (Mrs. P., W.L.E.)
E. B. . 1844.

Tuke (E.H.P.)
REV. FRANCIS EDWARD. 1838^{3}-1843^{3}; Eton VIII. 1841-3; Capt. of the Boats 1843; B.N.C. Oxf. M.A.; Stroke Oxf. VIII. 1844-5; formerly Incumbent of Wye, Kent; died April 1898.

Stuart (E.H.P.)
PAUL AMADEUS FRANCIS COUTTS. Only son of Lord Dudley Coutts Stuart, M.P.; 1838^{3}-1841^{2}; formerly Capt. 68th Regt.; died unm. Aug. 1889.

Gates (C.L.)
RICHARD SMYTHE. Son of G. of Bramley, near Guildford; 1838^{3}-1843^{3}.

Newman (C.L.)
F. . 1844.

Rogers *ma.* (W.E., E.C.)

Dashwood (W.L.E.)
THOMAS ALEXANDER. Son of T. J. D.; 1838^{3}-1843^{3}; Ch. Ch. Oxf. M.A.; J.P. for Herts; *m.* Charlotte Eliza, *d.* of Rev. C. W. Knyvett. *Everton House, Shanklin.*

Murdoch (E.H.P.)
GEORGE FRANCIS. 3rd son of J. G. M. of Frognal, Hampstead; 1837^{3}-1843^{3}; St. John's Coll. Camb. B.A.; Camb. VIII. 1846, Cox 1847; died unm. June 1850.

Spankie *min.* (Mrs. Y., H.D.)
JAMES SHIELS. 3rd son of S. S.; 1838^{3}-1842^{3}; formerly Bengal Civil Service.

Wilmot-Horton (E.H.P.)
REV. SIR GEORGE LEWIS, 5th Bt. 4th son of the Rt. Hon. Sir R. J. W.-H., 3rd Bt.; 1838^{3}-1841^{2}; Trin. Coll. Camb. M.A.; Rector of Garboldisham, Norfolk; J.P. co. Stafford; *m.* Frances Augusta, *d.* of Henry Pitches Boyce; died Oct. 24, 1887.

Parker *ma.* (Misses S., J.W.)
JOHN SKIPWITH. 1838^{3}-1842^{2}; Ch. Ch. Oxf.

Hibbert (E.H.P.)
[illegible]

Mr. Pepys (Mrs. Vall., E.C.)
HON. CHARLES EDWARD (2nd Earl of Cottenham). Eld. son of C. C. P., 1st Earl of C.; 1838^{3}-1842^{2}; Opp. Wall 1841; Trin. Coll. Camb.; Clerk of the Crown of Chancery; died unm. Feb. 18, 1863.

Crawley *mi.* (R.O.)
HENRY SAMBROOK. 2nd son of S. C. of Stockwood, Luton; 1837^{3}-1842^{2}; formerly in the Life Gds.; dead.

Tremayne *ma.* (H.D.)
JOHN. Of Heligan, St. Austell, Cornwall; eld. son of J. H. T. of Heligan; 1838^{3}-1842^{3}; Ch. Ch. Oxf. B.A.; J.P. and D.L. for Cornwall, High Sheriff 1859; J.P. for Devon; M.P. for E. Cornwall 1874-84, S. Devon 1884-5; *m.* Hon. Mary Charlotte Martha Vivian, *d.* of 2nd Lord Vivian; died at Biarritz, April 7, 1901.

Lambton (C.L.)
HENRY RALPH. Of Redfield, Winslow, Bucks; eld. son of W. H. L. of Biddick Hall, Durham; 1838^{3}-1843^{3}; Prince Consort's French and German Prize 1842; Univ. Coll. Oxf.; Banker; *m.* Elizabeth M. C., *d.* of William Bernard Harcourt of St. Leonard's Hill, Windsor; died Jan. 24, 1896.

Stuart *ma.* (H.D. & C.O.G.)
WILLIAM. Eld. son of W. S. of Aldenham Abbey, Watford; 1838^{3}-1843^{3}; St. John's Coll. Camb.; called to the Bar, Inner Temple, 1851; J.P. for Herts; J.P. and D.L. for Beds, High Sheriff 1875; J.P. for Hunts; Lieut.-Col. Beds Militia; M.P. for Bedford 1854-7 and 1859-68; Chmn. of Qr. Sessions for Beds; *m.* Katherine, *d.* of John Armitage Nicholson of Balrath, co. Meath; died Dec. 21, 1893.

Whitmore (C.O.G.)
ROBERT THOMAS. Of Sundridge, Kent; 1839^{1}-1843^{1}; Cox. Eton VIII. 1842; Merton Coll. Oxf.; died suddenly of apoplexy 1863.

Harvey (H.D.)
SIR ROBERT BATESON, 1st Bt. Son of R. H. of Langley Park, Slough; 1838^{2}-1841^{3}; Ch. Ch. Oxf.; J.P. and D.L. for Bucks; M.P. for Bucks over 18 years; Major Bucks Hussars and Capt. Bucks Volunteers; *m.* 1st, Diana Jane, *d.* of Archdn. Stephen Creyke, Rector of Bolton Percy; 2nd, Magdalen Breadalbane, widow of Alexander Anderson, and *d.* of Sir John Pringle, 5th Bt.; died March 23, 1887.

Woodbridge *ma.* (W.G.C.)
FREDERICK. 1838^{3}-1842^{2}; formerly a Brewer in London and living at Surbiton, Surrey.

Style (Miss W., C.J.A.)
SIR WILLIAM HENRY MARSHAM, 9th Bt. Of Glenmore, Stranorlar, co. Donegal; son of Capt. W. S., R.N., of Bicester House, Oxf., and cousin of Sir T. C. S., 8th Bt.; 1838^{3}-1842^{1}; Merton Coll. Oxf. M.A.; J.P. and D.L. for cos. Donegal and Monmouth; High Sheriff co. Donegal 1856; *m.* 1st, Hon. Rosamond Marion, *d.* of Charles, 1st Lord Tredegar; 2nd, Ellen Catharine, *d.* of Edward Taylor Massy of Cottesmore, co. Pembroke, widow of Henry Hyde Nugent, Banker. 1 *Trinity Villas, Folkestone.*

Turton (C.O.G.)
REV. HENRY MEYSEY. 1838^{1}-1842^{3}; Trin. Coll. Oxf. B.A.; Missionary in Nelson, New Zealand, formerly Vicar of Great Milton, Oxford, and Chaplain at Boulogne; died 1881.

Townley *ma.* (C.O.G.)
CHARLES WATSON. Of Fulbourne, Camb.; 2nd son of R. G. T. of Fulbourne; 1837^{3}-1842^{3}; Lord-Lieut. of co. Camb., and J.P. for Norfolk; *m.* Georgiana, *d.* of M. D. Dalison of Hamptons, Kent; died Oct. 17, 1893.

Currie (C.O.G.)
JAMES PATTISON. Eld. son of J. C., M.P., of Essendon, Herts; 1838^{3}-1841^{1}; Director of Bank of England since 1855, Governor 1885-7; one of H.M.'s Lieuts. for City of London; *m.* 1st, Anna Dora, *d.* of Rev. J. G. Brett of Ranelagh, Chelsea; 2nd, Euphemia Anna, *d.* of James Blyth of Woolhampton, Berks. *Sandown House, Esher.*

Harkness *ma.* (C.O.G.) — REV. WILLIAM. Of Garryfine and Temple Athea, co. Limerick; eld. son of Rev. R. H. of Garryfine and Temple Athea, Vicar of East Brent, Somerset; 1837[3]-1842[2]; St. John's Coll. Camb. M.A.; Camb. VIII. 1845; Vicar of Winscombe, Somersets; *m.* Sarah Anne, *d.* of John Peebles, M.D., of Dublin; died at Ventnor, Isle of Wight, 1863.

James *mi.* (K.S., C.Wi. & C.J.A.) — F. A. . 1844.

Parker (H.D.) — LIEUT.-COL. WILLIAM. Of Hanthorpe House, Bourne, co Lincoln; eld. son of W. P. of Hanthorpe: 1837[3]-1843[2]; Exeter Coll. Oxf. B.A.; J.P. and D.L. for co. Lincoln; Hon. Lieut.-Col. (ret.) R. S. Lincoln Militia; *m.* Augusta Millet Harriot, *d.* of Lieut.-Col. C. W. Short, Coldstream Gds.

Vernon-Smith *ma.* (C.Wi. & J.E.Y.) — HON. FITZPATRICK HENRY (aft. Vernon) (2nd Lord Lyveden). Eld. son of Robert, 1st Lord L., of Farming Woods, Northants; 1838[3]-1841[3]; in the Diplomatic Service, 1846-50; J.P. and D.L. for Northants; *m.* 1st, Lady Albreda Elizabeth, *d.* of Charles William, 5th Earl Fitzwilliam, K.G.; 2nd, Julia Katie, *d.* of Albert Emary of Hastings; died Feb. 25, 1900.

Vernon-Smith *mi.* (C.Wi. & J.E.Y.) — HON. GOWRAN CHARLES (aft. Vernon). 2nd son of Robert, 1st Lord Lyveden, of Farming Woods, Northants; 1838[3]-1843[3]; Trin. Coll. Camb.; Barrister and Recorder of Lincoln; *m.* Caroline, *d.* of John Nicholas Fazakerly, M.P. for Peterboro'; died Jan. 15, 1872.

Leigh (R.O.) — THOMAS. Son of L. of Luton Hoo, Beds; 1838[1]-1841[1]; a Partner in Allsopp's Brewery at Burton-on-Trent.

Douglas *ma.* (E.H.P.) — REV. WILLIAM WILLOUGHBY. Of Salwarpe, Droitwich; eld. son of Rev. H. D., Canon of Durham and Rector of Salwarpe; 1838[2]-1841[3]; St. John's Coll. Camb. M.A.; J.P. for co. Worcester, Hon. Canon of Worc.; Proctor in Convocation; *m.* Frances Jane, *d.* of William Wybergh How of Nearwell, Shrewsbury; died Feb. 19, 1898.

Battiscombe (C.L.) — MAJOR ROBERT CHARLES. Of Vere's Wootton, Dorset; eld. son of Rev. R. B. of Hactons, Upminster, Romford; 1838[3]-1841[2]; Royal Bombay Artillery; served in the Crimea in the Turkish Contingent; *m.* Mary Elizabeth Anne, *d.* of Patrick James Fahy of Hornchurch, Essex; died 1899.

Pearce *ma.* (C.O.G.) — WALTER SEROCOLD (aft. Pearce-Serocold). Of Cherry Hinton, Camb.; eld. son of Rev. E. S. P.-S. of Cherry Hinton; 1838[3]-1844[1]; Newc. Select 1844; Capt. 66th Regt.; *m.* Amelie, *d.* of Hon. Judge Duval of Quebec; died Aug. 14, 1880.

Hunt (C.J.A.) — G. W. . 1844.

Day (Mrs. Ro., aft. K.S., W.L.E.) — R. . 1844.

Mr. Hanbury *ma.* (H.D.) — HON. W. B. BATEMAN- (Lord Bateman). . 1844.

Plumer (Mrs. Ri., E.C.) — HALL. Of Malpas Lodge, Torquay; son of T. H. P. of Canons Park, Middlesex; 1839[2]-1841[3]; Registrar's Office, Court of Chancery; *m.* Louisa, *d.* of Henry Turnley; died 1888.

Hervey (W.G.C.) — FEL[illegible] 1846; 13th L[illegible] Dr[illegible]; [illegible] in Ireland; [illegible]

Blanchard (W.G.C.) — REV. HENRY DACRE. Son of Rev. J. B. of Middleton Rectory, near Beverley; 1839[2]-1843[2]; Trin. Coll. Camb. M.A.; Rector of Middleton-on-the-Wolds; *m.* 1st, Catharine Anne, *d.* of the Rev. W. P. Manclarke; 2nd, Grace, *d.* of Rev. Canon Houghton. *The Rectory, Middleton-on-the-Wolds, Driffield.*

Wilson *ma.* (Mrs. Vall, E.C.) — LIEUT.-COL. FULLER MAITLAND. Of Stowlangtoft Hall, Bury St. Edmunds; eld. son of H. W. of Stowlangtoft; 1838[3]-1843[3]; Eton VIII. 1842-3; Opp. Wall 1841-3, Keeper 1842-3; Ch. Ch. Oxf. M.A.; Oxf. VIII. 1844-5; J.P.; Lieut.-Col. W. Suffolk Militia; M.P. for W. Suffolk 1875, High Sheriff 1873; *m.* Agnes Caroline, *d.* of Rt. Hon. Sir Richard Torin Kindersley, Vice-Chanc.; died 1875.

Curzon (H.D.) — GEORGE NATHANIEL. Eld. son of Hon. and Rev. A. C. of Weston Underwood, Derby, and grandson of 2nd Lord Scarsdale; March 1839[1]-1843[3]; Ch. Ch. Oxf.; died unm. in St. George's Hospital from a fall from his horse in Hyde Park, June 17, 1855.

Mackarness (R.F.H., aft. K.S., R.O.) — H. S. . 1844.

Douglas (W.E., E.C.) — STAIR. 1839[2]-1843[3]; Oriel Coll. Oxf.; died about 1861.

Deacon *ma.* (Mrs. Hor., E.H.P.) — JOHN. Of Mabledon, Tonbridge; eld. son of J. D. of Mabledon; 1839[2]-1844[1]; Oriel Coll. Oxf. M.A.; formerly a Banker in London; *m.* Lucy Katherine, *d.* of Francis Pym of the Hasells, Beds; died 1901.

Hornby (R.O.) — J. J. . 1844.

Honywood (Mrs. P., C.O.G.) — R. . 1844.

Bennett (W.A.C.) — WILLIAM. 1839[2]-1844[1].

Clissold *ma.* (Mrs. D., W.L.E.) — STEPHEN THOMAS. Son of Rev. S. C., Rector of Wrentham, Suffolk; 1839[1]-1843[3]; Eton XI. 1843; Opp. Wall 1842; Trin. Coll. Camb. M.A.; Camb. XI. 1844 and 1846; Barrister and Stipendiary Magistrate at Ballarat, Australia; *m.* Ada Byron, *d.* of Charles Sievwright; dead.

West (Miss A., E.C.) — R. T. . 1844.

Higginson (C.J.A.) — GEN. SIR G. W. A., K.C.B. 1844.

Duckworth (Mrs. Hor., J. W. & C.O.G.) — GEORGE. Eld. son of W. D. formerly of Beechwood, New Forest, aft. of Orchardleigh Park, Frome; 1838[3]-1844[1]; Trin. Coll. Camb.; Capt. 5th Dragoon Gds.; died of cholera on board the 'Bombay' transport in Varna Bay on his way to the Crimea, Aug. 24, 1854.

Bowyer-Smijth (W.L.E.) — REV. ALFRED JOHN EDWARD. 2nd son of Rev. Sir E. B.-S., 10th Bt., of Hill Hall, Theydon Mount, Epping; 1837[3]-1842[2]; Univ. Coll. Oxf. M.A.; Rector of Attleborough, Norfolk; *m.* Mary Constantia, *d.* of Maj.-Gen. Sir John Rolt, K.C.B.; died Jan. 19, 1887.

Mr. Astley (E.H.P.) — REV. HON. DELAVAL LOFTUS (18th Lord Hastings). 2nd son of Sir Jacob A., Bt. (16th Lord Hastings), of Melton Constable, Norfolk; 1839[2]-1843[1]; Trin. Coll. Camb. M.A.; Vicar of East Barsham, [illegible] Hon. Frances [illegible] *d.* of 1st Visct. [illegible] 1872.

Stanley (C.J.A.) — E. J. . 1844

Palmer (C.L.) — COL. FREDERICK. 3rd son of Rev. H. P. of Carlton Curlieu, Leicester; 1839^{3}-1841^{3}; Eton VIII. 1841; Trin. Coll. Dublin; J.P. and D.L. for co. Leicester, High Sheriff 1865; J.P. for co. Rutland; formerly Capt. 27th Regt.; Hon. Col. Leicestershire Y.C (ret.); *m.* Mary, *d.* of William Henry Harrison of Conyngham Hall, Yorks, and sister of Col. W. H. Harrison-Broadley of Welton House, Brough. *Withcote Hall, Oakham.*

Thomas (Mrs. Y., R.O.) — RHYS GORING-. Of Plâs Llannon, Llanelly; eld. son of R. G.-T. of Gelly Wernu; 1838^{3}-1842^{2}; Ch. Ch. Oxf. M.A.; Barrister; J.P. and D.L., co. Carmarthen; *m.* Emily, *d.* of Richard Janion Nevill of Llangennech Park, co. Carmarthen; died Sept. 19, 1887.

Streatfeild *ma.* (R.F.H., C.O.G.) — LIEUT.-COL. HENRY DORRIEN. Of Chiddingstone, Edenbridge, Kent; eld. son of H. S. of Chiddingstone; 1839^{2}-1842^{3}; J.P. and D.L. for Kent, High Sheriff 1882; formerly Capt. 1st Life Gds., and late Lieut.-Col. West Kent Yeo.; *m.* Marion Henrietta, *d.* of Oswald Smith of Blendon Hall, Kent; died March 27, 1889.

Coleridge (W.E., aft. K.S., E.C.) — F. J. . 1844.

Peel *ma.* (C.J.A.) — ARTHUR LENNOX. 2nd son of L. P. of Brighton; 1839^{1}-1843^{1}; Col. comm. 52nd Oxfs L.I.; died unm. Jan. 14, 1875.

Sartoris *mi.* (R.O.) — A. U. . 1844.

Mr. Duncombe (W.A.C.) — HON. ALBERT. Eld. son of William, 2nd Lord Feversham; 1839^{3}-1844^{1}; died Sept. 14, 1846.

Speke (Mrs. Her., C.O.G.) — W. . 1844.

Brooke (C.L.) — JOHN WILLIAM. Of Sibton Park, Yoxford; son of J. B. of Armitage Bridge, Huddersfield; 1839^{1}-1842^{3}; Univ. Coll. Oxf. M.A.; Barrister; J.P. and D.L. for Suffolk, High Sheriff 1864; *m.* Jemima Charlotte, *d.* of James Brittlan of Buenos Ayres; died May 5, 1881.

Coleridge (E.C.) — C. E. . 1844.

Forster (C.O.G.) — JOHN GRANVILLE. 1838^{1}-1841^{3}; formerly 6th Dragoon Gds.

Rouse-Boughton (W.G.C.) — A. J. (aft. Rouse-Boughton-Knight). 1844.

Bayley *mi.* (R.F.H., R.O. & C.L.) — SIR L. H., Kt. . 1844.

Reid (W.L.E.) — FRANCIS NEVILLE. Son of N. R., Banker and Brewer at Windsor; 1839^{3}-1841^{3}; settled in Italy, near Naples.

Greathead (E.H.P.) — WILLIAM SAMUEL. Son of S. G. of Landford Lodge, Salisbury; 1838^{2}-1841^{3}; formerly Capt. Hants Militia; aft. 41st Regt.; *m.* Amelia, *d.* of Hugh Baillie; died Jan. 27, 1878.

Gulliver — HENRY WILLIAM. 1836^{2}-1841^{3}; formerly [illegible] Engineers.

Gully (C.O.G., aft. K[illegible]) — [illegible] . 1844.

Sir M. Shaw-Stewart (J.W. & R.O.) — SIR M. R., Bt. 1844.

Chandos-Pole *ma.* (R.O.) — E. S. . 1844.

Lee-Warner *ma.* (J.W., F.E.D.) — WILLIAM HENRY. Of Tyberton Court, co. Hereford; 8th son of Rev. D. H. L.-W. of Walsingham Abbey, Norfolk; 1838^{3}-1842^{1}; was in the 19th Regt.; died 1896.

Jodrell (W.G.C.) — REV. SIR EDWARD REPPS, 3rd Bt. 2nd son of Sir R. P. J., 2nd Bt., M.A., of Sall Park, Norfolk; 1836^{1}-1842^{2}; Queen's Coll. Oxf. M.A.; *m.* Lucinda Emma Maria, *d.* of Robert T. Garden of River Lyons, King's Co.; died Nov. 12, 1882.

Clayton-East (E.H.P.) — CHARLES WILLIAM. 3rd son of Sir E. G. C.-E., 1st Bt.; 1838^{2}-1841^{3}; formerly Lieut. 15th Regt.; *m.* 1st, Lillie Campbell, *d.* of Campbell Maclachlan; 2nd, Eliza Spooner, *d.* of Thomas Spooner Palmer of Bayview, co. Sligo; died Aug. 21, 1866.

Peel *mi.* (E.C.) — EDMUND YATES. 2nd son of the Rt. Hon. Gen. J. P., P.C., D.C.L., of Marble Hill, Twickenham; 1838^{3}-1843^{2}; R. M. Coll. Sandhurst; Lieut.-Col. 85th Regt.; served in the Eastern Campaign 1854-5, medal with two clasps, Turkish medal; Consul at Oran; aft. Resident Magistrate in Ireland; *m.* Maria Frances Knighton, *d.* of Richard Chadwick; died April 21, 1900.

Curtis (J.W.) — HORACE GOAD. 7th son of Sir W. C., 2nd Bt., of Callands Grove, Middlesex; 1838^{3}-1841^{3}; died unm. Feb. 4, 1878.

LOWER DIVISION.

Smith *ma.* (Mrs. Ri., J.W.) — OSWALD AUGUSTUS. Of Hammerwood Lodge, East Grinstead; eld. son of O. S. of Blendon Hall, Kent; 1840^{1}-1844^{1}; Newc. Select 1844; Trin. Coll. Camb. M.A.; D.L. for City of London; *m.* Rose Sophia, *d.* of Arthur Vansittart of Shottesbrooke, Berks, and Foots Cray, Kent; died Aug. 21, 1902.

De Horsey (W.E., E.C.) — WILLIAM HENRY BEAUMONT. 1840^{2}-1842^{3}; formerly Lt.-Col. Gren. Gds.

Plumptre (R.O.) — R. W. . 1844.

Simonds *mi.* (K.S., W.L.E.) — H. J. . 1844.

Wilson (Home, W.L.E.) — AYLMER ST. AUBYN. 1839^{1}-1841^{3}.

Back *mi.* (R.F.H., J.W.) — J. . 1844.

Rogers *mi.* (W.E., aft. K.S., W.A.C.) — E. H. . 1844.

Dent (Miss Edw., H.D.) — J. D. . 1844.

Mr. Campbell (R.O.) — HON. AND REV. ARCHIBALD GEORGE. Of Marchfield House, Bracknell; 2nd son of John Frederick, 1st Earl Cawdor; 1840^{2}-1842^{3}; Ball. Coll. Oxf. M.A.; Rector of Knipton, Grantham, 1853-83; *m.* Charlotte Henrietta, *d.* of Hon. and Very Rev. Henry Edward John Howard, Dean of Lichfield; died May 2, 1902.

Finch-Hatton (W.A.C.)
EDWARD HATTON. Eld. son of Hon. and Rev. D. H. F.-H., Rector of Great Weldon, Kettering; 1840^{1}–1842^{2}; Ch. Ch. Oxf. M.A.; Capt. Northants Militia; died April 6, 1887.

Mr. Hanbury *mi.* (H.D.)
HON. C. S. (aft. Bateman-Hanbury-Kincaid-Lennox). 1844.

Hayne (W.E., W.A.C.)
REV. PREB. RICHARD JAMES. Son of Rev. R. H., D.D., of Bradfield, Manningtree; 1839^{1}–1842^{3}; Exeter Coll. Oxf. M.A.; Vicar of Buckland Monachorum and Preb. of Exeter. *Buckland Vicarage, Yelverton, S. Devon.*

Luttrell (Mrs. Y., and Mrs. D., C.J.A.)
H. A. F. 1844.

Ffolliott (Misses S., J.W.)
JOHN. Of Hollybrook House, Boyle; son of J. Ff. of Hollybrook; 1839^{3}–1843^{3}; Eton VIII. 1842-3; Univ. Coll. Oxf. B.A.; J.P. and D.L. co. Sligo, High Sheriff Sligo 1851 and Leitrim 1882; Hon. Col. Sligo Militia; *m.* Grace Charlotte, *d.* of Col. Frederick Philips of Rhual, co. Flint; died Dec. 29, 1894.

Ernst (C.O.G.)
HENRY. Of Westcombe House, Evercreech, Bath; son of T. H. E. of Westcombe; 1839^{3}–1842^{3}; J.P. and D.L. for Somerset; High Sheriff 1893; Capt. and Hon. Major 3rd Somerset R.V., formerly Capt. 88th Regt.; *m.* Anne, *d.* of William Waring of Caerleon, Newport, Mon.; died Feb. 11, 1896.

Packe (Mrs. Hor., H.D.)
C. 1844.

Fanshawe (Miss B., W.A.C.)
JOHN GASPARD. Of Parsloes, Chadwell Heath, Essex; eld. son of Rev. T. L. F. of Parsloes and Vicar of Dagenham, Essex; 1839^{3}–1841^{2}; formerly Clerk in the Board of Trade; *m.* Barbara Frederica Beaujolois, *d.* of Hon. William James Coventry of Earle's Croome Court, co. Worcester. *The Cedars, St. Johns, Bedford.*

Welby *mi.* (Mrs. P., E.C.)
M. E. 1844.

Nanton (W.L.E.)
AUGUSTUS. 1840^{1}–1842^{2}; Univ. Coll. Oxf.; formerly a Barrister at Toronto, Canada.

Stone (Mrs. P., C.J.A.)
A. 1844.

Tremayne *mi.* (H.D.)
A. 1844.

Hames (C.L.)
REV. HAYTER GEORGE (aft. Hayter-Hames). Of Chagford, Newton Abbot; son of Rev. W. H. of Chagford; 1840^{3}–1842^{2}; Ch. Ch. Oxf. M.A.; Rector of Chagford; J.P. for Devon; *m.* Constance Harriet, 2nd *d.* of Sir Charles Henry Colvile, Kt., of Lullington, Burton-on-Trent; died Feb. 9, 1886.

Heald (E.H.P.)
GEORGE TRAFFORD. 1840^{2}–1844^{1}; formerly in Life Gds.; *m.* Lola Montes; died some years ago.

Reynolds (Miss A., C.J.A.)
H. R. 1844.

Randolph (Mrs. Hor., J.W., & E.H.P., J.W., & E.H.P.)
REV. CYRIL. Son of G. R.; 1839^{3}–1843^{3}; Eton XI. 1841-3; Ch. Ch. Oxf. M.A.; Oxf. X. 1844-5; Rector of Chartham; *m.* *d.* [illegible] Hervey. *Chartham Rectory, Canterbury.*

Brown (Miss A., J.W.)
ARTHUR HENRY CLERKE. Of Kingston Blount, Tetsworth; son of J. B. of Kingston Blount; 1840^{2}–1843^{2}; Ch. Ch. Oxf.; J.P. and D.L. for co. Oxf., High Sheriff 1877; *m.* Sophia, *d.* of Col. John William Fane of Wormsley, Stokenchurch, Wallingford; died 1889.

Hibbert (E.H.P.)
EDWARD GEORGE. Of Feltwell Lodge, Brandon, Norfolk; son of W. T. H. of Hare Hill, Alderley, Cheshire; 1839^{3}–1843^{3}; Lieut.-Col. Gren. Gds.; died July 18, 1901.

Ottley (Miss B., E.C.)
REV. FRANCIS JOHN. 1839^{1}–1842^{3}; Oriel Coll. Oxf. M.A., 1st Class Math. 1848, Sen. Math. Sch.; Math. Master at Eton 1849-68.

Parsons (Mrs. P., C.J.A.)
REV. JOHN TOURNAY. 1839^{3}–1841^{3}; Ball. Coll. Oxf. B.A.; Vicar of Much Dewchurch, Hereford; dead.

Marson (Mrs. Ro., E.H.P.)
FREDERICK BOYD. Son of T. F. M. of Highfield Park; 1839^{3}–1843^{1}; Trin. Coll. Camb. M.A.; Barrister; *m.* Mary Caroline, *d.* of Thomas Stead Carter of Moor Place, Much Hadham, Herts. *Highfield Park, Heckfield, Winchfield.*

Lord Dunkellin (C.J.A.)
HON. ULICK CANNING. Eld. son of Sir Ulick John, 14th Earl and 1st Marquis of Clanricarde; 1840^{3}–1843^{3}; M.P. for co. Galway; Lieut.-Col. Coldstream Gds.; Knt. of the Order of the Medjidie; died Aug. 16, 1867.

Woodcock (W.E., E.C.)
REV. ELBOROUGH. 1839^{3}–1841^{3}; took Orders, but has no preferment; formerly of Upper Seymour Street, London.

Bowles (E.H.P., C.J.A.)
EDWARD. Son of Col. B. of North Aston, Oxford; 1839^{3}–1842^{2}; Ch. Ch. Oxf.; Major 60th Rifles; A.D.C. to the Governor-General of India; served in the Indian Mutiny (medal); served in the China War of 1860 (medal and two clasps); ret. 1871; *m.* Jane Elizabeth, *d.* of Rev. Henry Hutton, Presidency Chaplain, Bengal; died Dec. 22, 1897.

Earle *ma.* (Miss W., aft. K.S., J.W. & F.E.D.)
A. 1847.

Smith (Mrs. P., H.D.)
RICHARD JAMES. 1840^{1}–1842^{3}.

Rouse (C.O.G.)
REV. WILLIAM GASKELL. 1838^{3}–1843^{3}; Ch. Ch. Oxf. M.A.; formerly Curate of Blunham, Sandy.

Sir W. Fraser (C.J.A.)
SIR W. A., Bt. 1844.

Smijth-Windham (W.E., E.C.)
W. G. (aft. Windham). 1844.

Foster (Mrs. Ro., J.W., & W.L.E.)
SIR WILLIAM, Bt. Eld. son of Sir W. F., 1st Bt., of Norwich; 1839^{1}–1842^{3}; J.P. and D.L. for Norfolk; Capt. 11th Hussars, 1843-57; Crimean medal; *m.* 1st, Georgina, 2nd *d.* of Richard Armit of Monkstown, co. Dublin; 2nd, Harriet, 4th *d.* of Capt. Thomas George Wills, R.N. *The Grove, Hardingham, Attleborough, Norfolk.*

Courtenay (Mrs. Y., R.O.)
JOHN. 2nd son of G. C. of Swerford Park, Enstone, Oxford; 1838^{3}–1842^{3}; Opp. Wall 1842; died at Trin. Coll. Oxf. 1844.

Mr. Eliot *ma.* (C.J.A.)
HON. EDWARD JOHN CORNWALLIS (Lord Eliot). Eld. son of Edward, 3rd Earl of St. Germans, of Port Eliot, St. Germans, Cornwall; 1839^{3}–1843^{3}; Ch. Ch. Oxf.; Capt. 1st Life Gds.; died unm. Nov. 26, 1864.

Crawley [illegible]
[illegible], 3rd son of S. C. [illegible] Gds.; 1839^{1}–1843^{3} [illegible]

Hyde (F.E.D.) — FRANCIS COLVILLE. Of Ashdown House, East Grinstead; son of J. H. of Syndale, Faversham, Kent; 1839^{3}–1842^{2}; Trin. Coll. Camb.; *m.* C. A., *d.* of Gen. Sir Ralph Darling; died March 1892.

Lord Belgrave (W.A.C.) — HUGH LUPUS GROSVENOR (1st Duke of Westminster). 2nd son of Richard, 2nd Marquis of Westminster; 1839^{3}–1843^{1}; Ball. Coll. Oxf.; K.G., P.C., Lord-Lieut. of London and Chester; M.P. for Chester 1847–69; Master of the Horse 1880–5; Hon. Col. Earl of Chester's Yeo. Cav. and Queen's Westminster Rifles; Supernumerary A.D.C. to the Queen for H.M.'s Vol. Forces; *m.* 1st, Lady Constance Gertrude Leveson-Gower, 4th *d.* of George Granville, 2nd Duke of Sutherland; 2nd, Hon. Catharine Caroline Cavendish, *d.* of William George, 2nd Lord Chesham; died Dec. 22, 1899.

Ryde (Mrs. Hor., W.G.C.) — HENRY JOHN. 1838^{3}–1842^{2}.

Ward (C.J.A.) — COL. MICHAEL FOSTER. Eld. son of T. R. W. of Ogbourne St. Andrew, Marlborough; 1839^{3}–1842^{1}; late 90th Lt. Infantry; J.P. co. Wilts; *m.* Helen Christina, *d.* of Robert Clerk-Rattray of Craighall-Rattray, co. Perth. *Bannerdown House, Batheaston, Bath, and Upton Park, Slough.*

Vance *mi.* (Mrs. P., aft. K.S., W.L.E.) — SIR H. P., Kt. . 1844.

Saltmarshe (W.L.E.) — PHILIP. Eld. son of P. S. of Saltmarshe; 1839^{1}–1843^{2}; J.P. and D.L. for co. York; formerly Lieut. 8th Hussars; Lieut.-Col. E. Yorks R.V.; *m.* 1st, Blanche, *d.* of Robert Denison of Waplington Manor, co. York; 2nd, Harriet, *d.* of Capt. George Hotham, R.E. *Saltmarshe, Howden.*

Campbell (E.H.P.) — WALTER BARRINGTON ODYNELL. Only son of J. G. C. of Ardpatrick, Tarbert, co. Argyll; 1838^{3}–1842^{2}; died 1851.

Barnard (C.O.G.) — EDWARD THOMAS. Son of Rev. H. W. B., Canon of Wells; 1837^{2}–1841^{3}; Lieut. 21st Fusiliers 1846–50; *m.* Ellen, *d.* of Major Thomas Clerk; died at Strathearne, Melbourne, March 23, 1901.

Townley *mi.* (C.O.G.) — THOMAS MANNERS. 3rd son of R. G. T. of Fulbourne, Camb.; 1838^{1}–1843^{2}; Eton XI. 1841–3; Camb. XI. 1847–8; was in the 10th Hussars; died April 1895.

Stephenson (W.L.E.) — REV. CHARLES. 1838^{1}–1843^{2}; Pemb. Coll. Camb. M.A.; formerly of Mitcham, Surrey; dead.

Lane (Mrs. Ri., J.W.) — MAJOR-GEN. CHARLES POWLETT. Eld. son of C. L. of Badgemore, co. Oxford; 1838^{3}–1841^{2}; J.P. and D.L. for Dorset; late Lieut.-Col. 21st Hussars; *m.* 1st, Caroline, *d.* of G. Lucy of Charlecote, Warwick; 2nd, Bertha D'Albiac, *d.* of John Du Boulay of Donhead Hall, Wilts. *Glanden, Wimborne.*

Stanhope (Miss Edw., H.D.) — EDWYN FRANCIS BRYDGES SCUDAMORE-. 4th son of Sir E. F. S.-S., 2nd Bt., of Holme Lacy, Hereford; 1838^{3}–1841^{3}; Capt. 39th Regt.; died unm. at Hong-Kong, Sept. 13, 1855.

Lautour (Misses S., C.O.G.) — ALBERT (aft. De Lautour). Son of L. of Hexton, Herts; 1838^{3}–1841^{2}; Capt. Rifle Bgde.; died 1861.

Porter (Mrs. Hor., C.O.G.) — REV. GEORGE. 1838^{3}–1842^{2}; Exeter Coll. Oxf.; Rector of Rackenford, Morchard Bishop, N. Devon; dead.

Radford (W.G.C.) — REV. HENRY FREER. Son of H. R.; [illegible] 1842; Eton VIII. 1841; Trin. Coll. Camb. B.A.; Rector of Broughton Astley, [illegible]; [illegible].

Graham (W.L.E., aft. K.S., W.L.E.) — FREDERICK VALPY. 1837^{2}–1844^{1}; Solicitor, at Kingsclere, Newbury.

Cholmeley (C.O.G., aft. K.S., C.O.G.) — J. . 1844.

Lord Anson (C.J.A.) — THOMAS GEORGE (2nd Earl of Lichfield). Eld. son of Thomas William, 1st Earl of L.; 1839^{1}–1841^{2}; M.P. for Lichfield 1847–54; Lord-Lieut. of Staffs 1863–71; *m.* Lady Harriet Georgiana Louisa Hamilton, *d.* of James, 1st Duke of Abercorn; died Jan. 7, 1892.

Pott *ma.* (W.A.C.) — ROBERT. Of Bentham Hill, Tunbridge Wells; son of W. P. of Bromley, Kent; 1838^{2}–1842^{2}; Distiller; *m.* Anna, *d.* of Donald Maclean, of Stanley House, co. Gloucester; died 1894.

Scott *mi.* (C.O.G.) — J. G. . 1844.

Dugdale (E.C.) — W. S. . 1844.

Lord Darnley (W.G.C.) — JOHN STUART BLIGH (6th Earl of Darnley), D.L., C.A. Eld. son of Edward, 5th Earl of Darnley; 1839^{3}–1843^{3}; Ch. Ch. Oxf. B.A.; Lieut.-Col. West Kent Yeo. Cav. 1863–74; *m.* Lady Harriet Mary Pelham, *d.* of Henry Thomas, 3rd Earl of Chichester; died Dec. 14, 1896.

Fitzwygram (F.E.D.) — REV. JOHN FITZROY. 4th son of Sir R. F., 2nd Bt., of Leigh Park, Havant; 1840^{3}–1843^{3}; Trin. Coll. Camb. M.A.; Vicar of New Hampton, Middlesex; *m.* Alice, *d.* of Sir Henry George Ward, G.C.M.G.; died Aug. 13, 1881.

Blackett (R.F.H., C.J.A.) — MONTAGU. Of Greenhills, co. Tipperary; 3rd son of C. B., of Wylam, Northumberland; 1839^{2}–1841^{2}; Ch. Ch. Oxf.; *m.* Emma Mary, 2nd *d.* of Very Rev. Gilbert Elliot, Dean of Bristol; died May 28, 1866.

Johnson (J.W.) — C. P. 1844.

Arbuthnot (R.F.H., F.E.D.) — WILLIAM REIRSON. Of Madras; 4th son of G. A. of Elderslie, Surrey; 1840^{3}–1844^{1}; Merchant; *m.* Mary Helen, *d.* of Philip Anstruther.

Franks (W.E., F.E.D.) — SIR AUGUSTUS WOLLASTON, K.C.B. Son of Capt. F. F., R.N.; 1839^{3}–1844^{1}; Trin. Coll. Camb.; Sec. of the Exhib. of Mediæval Art 1850; Assist. in Dept. of Antiquaries of the British Museum 1851; Director of the Soc. of Antiq.; Pres. of the Soc. of Antiq.; died May 21, 1897.

Curtis (R.F.H., aft. K.S., C.L.) — F. H. . 1847.

Wright (R.F.H., E.C.) — C. I. 1844.

Adlington (W.E., C.J.A.) — H. S. 1844.

Pellew (Mrs. Ro., E.C.) — H. E. . 1844.

Tarver *mi.* (Home, K.S., W.G.C. & C.J.A.) — F. B. C. . 1847.

Watson (R.F.H., C.L.) — JOHN WILLIAM. Son of Baron Watson; 1839^{3}–1843^{2}; Trin. Coll. Camb. B.A.; J.P. for Northumberland; *m.* Margaret G., *d.* of Patrick Forsse FitzPatrick. *Adderston Hall, Belford.*

Mr. Fitzwilliam (Miss M., J.W.) — HON. CHARLES WILLIAM WENTWORTH-, F.R.G.S. Of Alwalton, Peterborough; 4th son of Charles William, 5th Earl Fitzwilliam; 1839^{2}–1842^{2}; Trin. Coll. Camb.; M.P. for Malton 1852–85; J.P. and D.L. for Hunts; *m.* Anne, 4th *d.* of Hon. and Rev. Thomas Lawrence Dundas; died Dec. 20, 1894.

Peel *ma.* (F.E.D.) — AUGUSTUS ROBERT LAWRENCE. Eld. son of Very Rev. J. P., Dean of Worcester; 1839^{2}–1843^{2}; Ch. Ch. Oxf.; died June 2, 1870.

O'Brien *ma.* (H.D.) — DONAT JOHN HOSTE. Of Butler's Green, Herts; son of Adm. D. H. O'B., R.N., of Yew House, Hoddesdon, Herts; 1840^{2}–1843^{3}; St. John's Coll. Camb. B.A.; Barrister; J.P. for Herts; *m.* Martha Sheppard, *d.* of Rev. R. Morice; died April 16, 1881.

Crichton-Stuart (E.H.P.) — HERBERT. 2nd son of Lord Patrick James Herbert C.-S. of Bute; 1840^{2}–1843^{3}; Trin. Coll. Camb. M.A.; Foreign Office; *m.* Fanny Adelaide, 3rd *d.* of John Labouchere of Broomhall, Surrey; died Dec. 30, 1891.

Murray (F.E.D.) — ROBERT HAY. 3rd son of Right Rev. G. M., Bishop of Rochester; 1840^{2}–1842^{2}; Ch. Ch. Oxf.; called to the Bar at Lincoln's Inn 1853; J.P. and D.L. for Surrey, High Sheriff 1869, and J.P. for Bucks; *m.* Elizabeth, *d.* of Samuel Gregson. *Spinfield, Great Marlow.*

Heywood *ma.* (Miss A., C.J.A.) — OLIVER. 2nd son of Sir B. H., F.R.S., 1st Bt., of Claremont, Manchester; 1839^{3}–1842^{3}; J.P. and D.L. for Lancashire, High Sheriff 1888; Banker; *m.* Eleanor, *d.* of Richard Watson Barton, of Springwood, Lancaster; died March 17, 1892.

Foster (Mrs. Hor., W.A.C.) — AUGUSTUS BILLET. Eld. son of A. F. of Warmwell House, Dorchester, Dorset; 1839^{3}–1843^{1}; Exeter Coll. Oxf.; J.P. for Dorset; Col. Dorset Yeo.; *m.* Mildred, *d.* of Richard Fort; died 1892.

Venables (W.A.C.) — A. R. P. . 1844.

Walsh (Mrs. Hor., H.D.) — ARTHUR (Lord Ormathwaite). Eld. son of Sir J. B. W., Bt., 1st Lord Ormathwaite; 1840^{2}–1843^{2}; Trin. Coll. Camb.; Capt. 1st Life Gds., ret. 1855; M.P. for Leominster 1865–8, Radnorshire 1868–80; Lord-Lieut. of the co. of Radnor 1875–95; Chmn. Radnorshire County Council; J.P. Berks and Hereford; Hon. Col. 3rd Bn. South Wales Borderers since 1876; *m.* Lady Katherine Emily Mary Somerset, *d.* of Henry, 7th Duke of Beaufort. *Strettington House, Chichester.*

Fyfe (W.L.E.) — DOUGLAS MUNRO. 1839^{2}–1841^{2}; formerly Capt. in the Army and Adjutant of the Berks Rifle Vol.

Mr. Curzon *mi.* (E.C.) — MAJOR HON. WILLIAM HENRY. 5th son of Richard William Penn, 1st Earl Howe; 1839^{3}–1843^{2}; Merton Coll. Oxf. M.A.; formerly Major 17th Lancers; *m.* 1st, Beatrice Louisa Margaret, 2nd *d.* of Alexander Page; 2nd, Emily, *d.* of Frederick Cowper of Carlton Hall, Penrith. 17 *Eccleston Square, S.W.*

Joynes *mi.* (Mrs. P., aft. K.S., E.C.) — W. . 1847.

Vyse *ma.* (Mrs. Vall., & W.E., E.C.) — LIEUT.-GENERAL EDWARD HOWARD-. 7th son of Major-Gen. R. W. H.-V. of Stoke Place, Slough; 1839^{1}–1841^{3}; Ch. Ch. Oxf.; J.P. Essex; Maj.-Gen. (Hon. Lt.-Gen.) 3rd Hussars; *m.* Mary Robinson. *The [illegible], [illegible], Essex.*

Squire (Mrs. P., C.L.) — [illegible] 1840–1843; formerly [illegible] Royals.

Slade (C.J.A.) — W. 1844.

Homfray (Mrs. P., H.D.) — JOHN RICHARDS. Of Penllyn Castle, Cowbridge; eld. son of J. H. of Penllyn Castle; 1839^{1}–1842^{3}; Ch. Ch. Oxf. B.A.; J.P. and D.L. for Glamorganshire; *m.* Mary Elizabeth, *d.* of Sir Glynne Earle Welby-Gregory, Bt., of Denton Hall, Grantham; died Aug. 8, 1882.

Lord Burghley (R.O.) — WILLIAM ALLEYNE CECIL (3rd Marquis of Exeter), P.C. Eld. son of Brownlow, 2nd Marquis of E.; 1839^{3}–1843^{1}; St. John's Coll. Camb. M.A.; Camb. XI. 1847; formerly Capt. of the Hon. Corps of Gentlemen-at-Arms; Treasurer of Her Majesty's household 1866; M.P. for South Lincolnshire 1847–57, Northamptonshire 1857–67; Hon. Col. 3rd and 4th Bn. Northants Regt.; A.D.C. to the Queen; *m.* Lady Georgina Sophia Pakenham, 2nd *d.* of Thomas, 2nd Earl of Longford; died July 14, 1895.

Hyett (Mrs. Ro., J.W.) — WILLIAM HENRY ADAMS. 2nd son of W. H. H. of Painswick House, Stroud; 1839^{3}–1843^{2}; Ball. Coll. Oxf.; died unm. Sept. 1, 1850.

Northcote (Mrs. P., E.C.) — REV. HENRY MOWBRAY. Of Temple Hill, East Budleigh; 3rd son of H. S. N. of Pynes, Exeter; 1839^{3}–1842^{3}; New Coll. Oxf. M.A.; 20 years Rector of Monk Okehampton, Devon; *m.* 1st, Georgina, *d.* of Richard Ford; 2nd, Elinor, *d.* of Hugh Malet of Ash House, Devon, and widow of Rev. Frederick Pitman; died Feb. 6, 1878.

Hulkes (Mrs. P., F.E.D.) — JAMES. Of Little Hermitage, Frindsbury, Rochester; eld. son of J. H. of Little Hermitage; 1840^{1}–1843^{3}; Ch. Ch. Oxf.; J.P. for Kent; *m.* Emma Sarah, *d.* of Laurence Holker Winckworth of Welling; died May 5, 1901.

Lomax (C.L.) — THOMAS. Eld. son of S. L. of Town Head, Rochdale; 1840^{2}–1843^{3}; Opp. Wall. 1841; Tomline Select 1843; Trin. Coll. Camb. M.A.; called to the Bar, Inner Temple, 1849; J.P. and D.L. for Suffolk; *m.* Ann, eld. *d.* of John Chadwick of Broadfield, Rochdale. *Grove Park, Yoxford, Saxmundham.*

Hawthorn (R.O.) — ALEXANDER. . 1840^{2}–1843^{2}.

Salkeld (Mrs. P., C.J.A.) — ROBERT. . 1839^{3}–1842^{3}.

Scarlett (Mrs. Y., C.J.A.) — HON. WILLIAM FREDERICK (3rd Lord Abinger), C.B. Eld. son of Robert Campbell, 2nd Lord Abinger; 1839^{1}–1841^{3}; Trin. Coll. Camb.; Lieut. Col. Scots Gds.; D.L. co. Inverness; *m.* Helen, *d.* of Commodore George Allan Magruder, U.S. Navy; died Jan. 16, 1892.

Spencer (Miss A., W.A.C.) — O. V. 1844.

Loch (Miss Edw., E.H.P.) — JOHN CHARLES. Son of J. L., M.P.; 1840^{2}–1843^{3}; Trin. Coll. Camb. B.A.; President of the Municipal Commission of Madras; *m.* Ruth, *d.* of General John Pennicuik, C.B. 50 *Warwick Road, Earl's Court, S.W.*

Walker (W.G.C.) — CHARLES EDWARD. Son of J. N. W. of Calderstone, Lancs; 1839^{3}–1842^{3}; Capt. Queen's Bays; died unm.

Jones (W.G.C.) — REV. HERBERT WALSINGHAM. 3rd son of Major-Gen. Sir J. T. J., K.C.B., 1st Bt., of Cranmer Hall, Fakenham, Norfolk; 1839^{3}–1842^{3}; Trin. Coll. Camb. M.A. Rector of Sculthorpe, Norfolk; Hon. Canon [illegible] ...e Rachel, *d.* of [illegible] Ructon, King's [illegible]

Woodbridge *mi.* (W.G.C.) — WILLIAM. 1840^{1}–1844^{1}; formerly a Brewer in Whitechapel.

Lord Brownlow Cecil (R.O.) — BROWNLOW THOMAS MONTAGU. 2nd son of Brownlow, 2nd Marquis of Exeter; 1839^{3}–1844^{1}; cox Eton VIII. 1843; Capt. Scots Gds. 1844–9; late Col. 3rd and 4th Bn. Northants Regt.; *m.* 1st, Charlotte Alexandrina Mabella, *d.* of Edward Thompson Curry, British Consul at Ostend; 2nd, Stella, *d.* of Rev. William Randall, D.D. *Cowdray, Reigate.*

Lecky (W.A.C.) — JOHN FREDERICK. Only son of J. J. L. of Ballykealey; 1840^{2}–1843^{1}; Trin. Coll. Dublin; J.P. and D.L. for co. Carlow, High Sheriff 1864; *m.* Frances Margaret Featherstonhaugh, *d.* of John Beauchamp Brady of Myshal, Bagenalstown, co. Carlow. *Ballykealey, Tullow, R.S.O., co. Carlow.*

Moffat (Mrs. Ri., aft. K.S., F.E.D.) — C. W. . 1847.

Mr. Blackwood (W.G.C.) — SIR FREDERICK TEMPLE HAMILTON-TEMPLE-BLACKWOOD, K.P., P.C., G.C.B., G.C.S.I., G.C.M.G., G.C.I.E., F.R.S., D.C.L., LL.D. (1st Marquis of Dufferin and Ava). Only son of Price, 4th Lord Dufferin and Clandeboye; 1839^{3}–1843^{1}; Ch. Ch. Oxf. M.A.; Hon. D.C.L., Hon. LL.D. Camb., Dublin, Harvard, and Laval Univ.; J.P. Middlesex and Westminster; Vice-Adm. of the Province of Ulster; Chanc. of the Royal Univ. of Ireland; Lord Rector of St. Andrew's Univ. 1899–3; Lord Rector of Univ. of Edin. 1899; Hon. Col. 3rd Bn. Royal Irish Rifles; Lord-in-waiting 1848–1852 and 1854–8; Commissioner in Syria 1860–1; Und. Sec. of State for India 1864–6; Und. Sec. of State for War 1866; Chanc. of Duchy of Lancs. and Paymaster-Gen. 1869–72; Gov.-Gen. of Dom. of Canada 1872–8; Amb. at St. Petersburg 1879–81, and at Constantinople 1881–4; H.M. Comm. in Egypt 1882–3; Viceroy of India 1884–8; Amb. Extra. and Plenipo. to King of Italy 1888–91, and to French Republic 1891–6; Lord Warden of Cinque Ports 1891–5; author of 'Letters from High Latitudes,' 'Irish Emigration and the Tenure of Land in Ireland,' and other works on Ireland; *m.* Hariot Georgina, eld. *d.* of Archibald Rowan Hamilton of Killyleagh Castle, co. Down; died Feb. 12, 1902.

Pennington (Mrs. Ri., E.C.) — CHARLES PLUMER. 1839^{1}–1841^{3}; Rifle Bgde.; *m.* *d.* of Rev. Frederick Lomax, Rector of Shere, Guildford, Surrey; died 1853.

Brise-Ruggles (Mrs. Hor., W.A.C.) — COL. SIR SAMUEL BRISE (aft. Ruggles-Brise), K.C.B. Of Spain's Hall, Braintree; only son of J. Ruggles of Spain's Hall (aft. Brise-R.); 1839^{4}–1841^{2}; Magd. Coll. Camb.; J.P. and D.L. for Essex, a Magistrate for Suffolk and Hon. Col. W. Essex Militia; formerly Lieut. 1st Dragoon Gds.; M.P. for E. Essex 1868–83; *m.* Marianne Weyland, *d.* of Sir Edward Bowyer-Smijth, 10th Bt., of Hill Hall, Essex; died 1899.

De Rutzen (C.J.A.) — FREDERICK LEOPOLD SAPIEH MANTEIFLE (Baron De Rutzen). Of Slebech Park, Haverfordwest; son of Baron F. De R. of Slebech; 1839^{1}–1842^{3}; died 1890.

Collings (Mrs. Par., C.J.A.) — D. S. 1844.

Brown *ma.* (W.G.C.) — [illegible]

Mousley *ma.* (Mrs. Y., W.L.E.) — FRANCIS. Son of a Solicitor at Derby; 1839^{1}–1842^{2}; died early.

Mr. Lascelles *ma.* (Mrs. Y., J.W.) — HON. GEORGE EDWIN. 3rd son of Henry, 3rd Earl of Harewood; 1839^{3}–1841^{3}; J.P. for N. and W. Ridings of Yorks, late Registrar of Deeds for W. Riding; formerly Capt. Yorks Hussars; Barrister; *m.* Lady Louisa Nina Murray, *d.* of William David, 4th Earl of Mansfield. *Sion Hill, Thirsk.*

Mr. Stopford (C.J.A.) — HON. BARRINGTON. 3rd son of James Thomas, 4th Earl of Courtown; 1839^{3}–1843^{1}; died Nov. 27, 1845.

Dimsdale (R.O.) — THOMAS ROBERT CHARLES. Eld. son of Thomas Robert, 4th Baron Dimsdale of the Russian Empire, of Essenden Place, Hatfield, Herts; 1839^{4}–1842^{2}; formerly an Officer in the Army; *m.* Jemima Anne, *d.* of Maj.-Gen. Sir James Limond, C.B.; died June 17, 1858.

Fellows *ma.* (Mrs. P., J.W. & W.G.C.) — REV. EDWARD. Son of T. F. of Moneyhill House, Rickmansworth, Herts; 1838^{3}–1842^{4}; Eton VIII. 1841–2; Exeter Coll. Oxf. M.A.; Rector of South Reston; *m.* eld. *d.* of George Pitt Smith. *South Reston Rectory, Louth, Lincs.*

Fellows *mi.* (Mrs. P., J.W., W.G.C.) — HARVEY WINSON. Son of T. F. of Moneyhill House, Rickmansworth, Herts; 1839^{3}–1842^{2}; Eton XI. 1841–2; famous fast bowler; Solicitor; *m.* Harriet Coupland, *d.* of Vice-Adm. James Arthur Murray. *Riverside, Rickmansworth, Herts.*

Codrington (Mrs. P., C.O.G.) — W. W. . 1844.

Clifton (W.E., E.C.) — SIR ROBERT JUCKES, 9th Bt. Of Clifton Hall, Nottingham; 1839^{2}–1841^{3}; M.P. for Nottingham; *m.* Isabel Geraldine, *d.* of Col. O'Meara, K.C.F.; died 1869.

Harkness *mi.* (C.O.G.) — R. . 1844.

Domvile (W.G.C.) — SIR WILLIAM COMPTON, 3rd Bt. 4th son of Sir C. P. D., 1st Bt., of Santry House, co. Dublin; 1839^{2}–1841^{3}; J.P. and D.L.; *m.* Caroline, *d.* of Gen. Hon. Robert Meade; died Sept. 20, 1884.

Wigney (C.J.A.) — CLARENCE WALTER. Son of a Banker at Brighton; 1839^{1}–1841^{2}; Lieut. E.I. Co.'s Service; died at Lahore, 1850.

Butt *mi.* (R.O.) — THOMAS PACKER WALTER. Son of T. P. B. of Arle Court, Cheltenham; 1838^{3}–1841^{3}; *m.* Anna Maria, *d.* of William Lutener; dead.

REMOVE.

Croft (W.E., E.C.) — SIR J. F., Bt. . 1844.

Robins (W.E., W.A.C.) — REV. CHARLES MATTHEW. 1840^{1}–1843^{1}; Oriel Coll. Oxf. B.A.; formerly Curate of St. Clement Danes, London.

Magniac (Mrs. Ri., J.W.) — CHARLES. 1840^{1}–1843^{3}; formerly a Merchant in London.

Rowley *ma.* (Miss Edw., H.D.) — OWSLEY JOHN BICKERTON. 2nd son of G. W. R. of Priory Park, St. Neots; 1839–1843; won School Pulling 1843; left to go to Camb., but died of typhus fever, Dec. 21, 1843.

Thesiger (Mrs. Rl. & E.H.P., E.H.P.) — GENERAL HON. FREDERIC AUGUSTUS, G.C.B. (2nd Lord Chelmsford). Eld. son of the Rt. Hon. Sir Frederic, 1st Lord Chelmsford; 1840^{2}–1843^{3}; entered Army 1844; served before Sebastopol (medal and clasp); Lieut.-Col. 95th Foot 1858; Indian Mutiny; Adj.-Gen. Abyssinian campaign 1867–8; A.D.C. to Queen Victoria 1868–77; commanded forces in Kaffir War 1878; Zulu War 1879; Gen. 1888; Lieut. of the Tower 1884–9; Gen. ret. 1893; Col. 2nd Life Gds. since 1900; *m.* Adria Fanny, *d.* of Maj.-Gen. Heath of the Bombay Army. *5 Knaresboro' Place, S.W.*

Streatfeild *mi.* (R.F.H., C.O.G.) — E. O. . 1844.

Howard (Mrs. Hor., W.A.C.) — G. . 1844.

Heywood *mi.* (Miss A., C.J.A.) — A. H. . 1844.

Peel (R.F.H., C.J.A.) — EDMUND YATES. Of Fern-hill, Carmarthenshire; 3rd son of Rev. G. H. P.; 1840^{1}–1843^{3}; Ch. Ch. Oxf.; *m.* Catherine Anne, *d.* of Major James Hurt, 9th Lancers; died Aug. 29, 1861.

Lord Langford (Mrs. Hor., W.L.E.) — HON. CLOTWORTHY WELLINGTON WILLIAM ROBERT ROWLEY (3rd Lord L.). Eld. son of Hercules Langford, 2nd Lord L., of Summerhill, Enfield, co. Meath; 1840^{1}–1842^{3}; *m.* Louisa Augusta, *d.* of Col. Edward Michael Conolly, M.P., of Castletown; died July 19, 1854.

L'Estrange (Mrs. Ro., J.W.) — GEORGE HENRY. 1840^{3}–1842^{2}; formerly living in Ireland

Yorke (W.A.C.) — PIERCE WYNNE. Of Dyffryn Aled, N. Wales; eld. son of P. W. Y. of Dyffryn Aled; 1839^{3}–1843^{3}; J.P. and D.L., co. Denbigh, High Sheriff 1853; *m.* Lucy Penelope, *d.* of Sir Trevor Wheler, Bt., of Leamington-Hastings, co. Warwick; died Dec. 10, 1891.

Wildman (Mrs. Ro., C.J.A.) — JAMES LUSHINGTON. Of Chilham, Canterbury; 1839^{3}–1844^{1}; was sec. to Lord Harris when Gov. of Trinidad; dead.

Hunter (F.E.D.) — SIR CLAUDIUS STEPHEN PAUL, 2nd Bt. Of Mortimer Hill, Reading; only son of J. H., and grandson of Sir C. S. H., 1st Bt.; 1839^{3}–1842^{3}; St. John's Coll. Oxf. M.A.; J.P. and D.L. for Berks. High Sheriff 1860; *m.* Constance, *d.* of William George Ives Bosanquet; died Jan. 7, 1890.

Mirehouse (E.H.P.) — J. . 1844.

Marsh (Mrs. Hor., W.G.C.) — M. W. J. . 1844.

Ames (Mrs. Ro., J.W.) — G. A. . 1844.

Feilden *ma.* (Miss Edw., H.D.) — REV. WILLIAM LEYLAND. 3rd son of J. F. of Witton Park, Blackburn; 1840^{3}–1843^{3}; Ch. Ch. Oxf. M.A.; Hon. Canon of Liverpool; Rector of Rolleston; Rural Dean of Tutbury; *m.* Jane Elizabeth St. Clair, *d.* of Charles, 12th Lord Sinclair. *Rolleston Rectory, Burton-on-Trent.*

Freeman (C.L.) — J. A. . 1844.

Lyon (W.A.C.) — HENRY D. W. 1839–1843; Scot. Greys, aft. 2nd Life Gds.; A.D.C. to Insp.-Gen. of Cav.; [illegible]

Smith (Mrs. Ro., aft. K.S., W.L.E.) — W. J. . 1847.

Oxenden (Mrs. Hor., J.W.) — CHARLES VERNON. Son of Rev. C. O., Rector of Barham, Kent; 1839–1842; Lieut.-Col. Rifle Bgde.; *m.* Norah Louisa, *d.* of M. R. Gubbins, B.C.S.; died April 26, 1868.

Burton (Mrs. Hor., W.G.C.) — AUGUSTUS FRANCIS PLUNKETT. Eld. son of Adm. R. B.; 1839^{3}–1843^{3}; Ch. Ch. Oxf.; formerly Col. Coldstream Gds.

Mr. Bligh (W.G.C.) — HON. E. V. . 1844.

Gough-Calthorpe (Miss W., F.E.D.) — HON. FREDERICK HENRY WILLIAM (5th Lord Calthorpe). Of Calthorpe, Norfolk; eld. son of Frederick, 4th Lord C.; 1839^{3}–1841^{3}; Trin. Coll. Camb.; D.L., M.P. for East Worcesters 1859–68; died unm. June 26, 1893.

Turton (C.L.) — EDMUND HENRY. Of Upsall Castle, Thirsk; son of E. P. T. of Brasted Park, Kent; 1839^{3}–1842^{3}; J.P. and D.L. for N. Riding of Yorks; Capt. 3rd Dragoon Gds.; *m.* Lady Cecilia Mary Leeson, *d.* of Joseph, 4th Earl of Miltown; died July 30, 1896.

Sutton (Mrs. Y., J.W.) — C. G. . 1844.

Digby (Mrs. D., W.G.C.) — JOHN ALMARUS. Of Chalmington House, Dorchester; 2nd son of Capt. C. G., R.N.; 1839^{3}–1842^{3}; Lieut.-Col. Gren. Gds.; *m.* Diana Alicia, *d.* of the Hon. and Rev. William Hugh Scott, Rector of Maiden Newton, Dorset; died July 13, 1885.

Canning (W.L.E., aft. K.S., W.L.E.) — WILLIAM WALMSLEY. 1838^{3}–1841^{3}; came from near Marlborough, Wilts.

Lord Guernsey (W.G.C.) — HENEAGE FINCH (6th Earl of Aylesford). Eld. son of Heneage, 5th Earl of A.; 1839^{3}–1843^{3}; Opp. Wall 1842; Ch. Ch. Oxf.; *m.* Jane Wightwick, *d.* of John W. Knightley of Offchurch Bury, co. Warwick; died Jan. 10, 1871.

Mr. Finch (W.G.C.) — HON. D. G. . 1844.

Vernon-Smith *min.* (C.J.A.) — HON. C. J. (aft. Vernon). 1844.

Smith *ma.* (Mrs. Rl., W.L.E.) — J. . 1844.

Smith *mi.* (Mrs. Rl., W.L.E.) — DUDLEY ROBERT. Of Glynde Place, Lewes; son of J. A. S. of Dale Park, Sussex; 1840^{3}–1841^{3}; *m.* Emma Margarette, *d.* of Rev. Edward Willes of Astrop; died Sept. 1897.

Lord Grey of Groby (E.C.) — GEORGE HARRY GREY (7th Earl of Stamford). Eld. son of George Harry, 6th Earl of S.; 1840^{3}–1843^{3}; Trin. Coll. Camb.; Master of the Quorn Hunt; Hon. Col. 7th Lancs Rifle Vol.; *m.* 1st, Elizabeth, *d.* of John Billing of Wincanton, Somerset; 2nd, Katherine, *d.* of Henry Cocks; died Jan. 2, 1883.

Pearce *mi.* (C.O.G.) — CHARLES SEROCOLD (aft. Pearce-Serocold). 2nd son of Rev. E. S. P.-S. of Cherry Hinton, Camb.; 1840^{3}–1844^{3}; in Reid's Brewery, London; *m.* Marie, *d.* of Col. George St. Leger Grenfell. *Taplow Hill, Maidenhead.*

Parker *mi.* [illegible] — [illegible]

Close (W.G.C.)	M. C.	. 1844.
Currie (E.H.P.)	B. W.	. 1844.
Jones-Bateman (Miss W., F.E.D.)	P. W.	. 1844.
Molony (Miss W., F.E.D.)	C. A.	. 1844.
Penrhyn (W.E., C.J.A.)	E. H. (aft. Leycester-Penrhyn).	1844.
Kaye (E.B.)	J.	1844.
Dickson (W.L.E.)	A. B.	1844.
Pipe-Wolferstan (E.B.)	F. S.	. 1844.
Blomfield (E.C.)	F.	. 1844.
Mr. Lascelles *mi.* (W.A.C.)	Hon. A. F.	. 1844.
Mr. Hanbury *mi.* (H.D.)	Hon. A. A. (aft. Bateman-Hanbury). 1847.	
James *mi.* (Miss W., aft. K.S., F.E.D.)	C. C.	. 1847.
Alderson (W.E., E.C.)	E. P.	. 1844.
Bankes (W.A.C.)	John Scott. Of Soughton Hall, co. Flint; eld. son of Rev. E. B. of Soughton; 1840^{2}-1843^{2}; J.P. & D.L. co. Dorset, J.P. & Chmn. of Qr. Sessions co. Flint, High Sheriff 1869; *m.* 1st, Anne, *d.* of Sir John Jervis, Chief Justice of the Common Pleas; 2nd, Adelaide Sophia, *d.* of Rev. George Pearson, Rector of Castle Camps, Camb.; died 1894.	
Wayte (Miss W., aft. K.S., F.E.D.)	W.	. 1847.
Gaisford (Mrs. P., C.O.G.)	G.	. 1844.
Babington (R.O.)	W.	. 1844.
Todd (C.L.)	John. 1840^{3}-1842^{3}; Christ's Coll. Camb.; drowned in the Thames in 1851.	
Coltman (W.E., E.C.)	W. B.	. 1844.
Holland (Mrs. Hor., E.H.P.)	I. J.	1844.
Borradaile (R.F.H., aft. K.S., C.L.)	C. B.	. 1847.
Orde (F.E.D.)	Sir John William Powlett (aft. Campbell-Orde), 3rd Bt. Of Kilmorey House, Lochgilphead, N.B.; eld. son of Sir J. P. O., 2nd Bt., of Morpeth, Northumberland; 1840^{1}-1843^{3}: Capt. 42nd Highlanders; *m.* 1st, Alice Louisa, *d.* of Charles Atticus Middleton of the Coldstream Gds.; 2nd, Louisa Charlotte Temple, *d.* of Robert Temple Frere of Harley Street, W.; died Oct. 12, 1897.	
Coleridge (E.C.)	Frederic William. 3rd son of Rt. Hon. Sir J. T. C. of The Chanter's House, Ottery St. Mary; 1840^{1}-1843^{1}; died April 25, 1843.	
Yonge (Mrs. Hor., F.E.D.)	W. W.	. 1844.
Hardinge (E.H.P.)	Hon. Sir Arthur Edward, K.C.B., C.I.E. 2nd son of Henry, 1st Viscount H.; 1840^{3}-1844^{1}; Gen. in the Army, Col. Coldstream Gds., late Col. comm. King's Royal Rifle Corps, Comm.-in-Chief Bombay Army 1881-5; Governor of Gibraltar 1886-90; Knight of the Legion of Honour, and of the Medjidie; Equerry to Queen Victoria; *m.* Mary Georgiana Frances, *d.* of Col. Hon. Augustus Frederick Ellis, M.P.; died July 15, 1892.	
Johnstone (Mrs. Hor., E.H.P.)	C. E.	. 1844.
Sayer (H.D.)	J. R. S.	. 1844.
Burroughes (R.F.H., F.E.D.)	William. 3rd son of H. N. B. of Burlingham Hall, Norwich; 1840^{3}-1842^{3}; died April 1844.	
O'Brien *mi.* (H.D.)	William Edward Freeman. 2nd son of Adm. D. H. O'B., R.N., of Yew House, Hoddesdon, Herts; 1840^{3}-1841^{3}; R.M. Coll. Sandhurst; Capt. 54th Regt. (ret.); *m.* Marianne, *d.* of Henry Bury. 23 *Cheniston Gardens, Kensington, W.*	
Beach (F.E.D.)	Rt. Hon. William Wither Bramston, P.C. Of Oakley Hall, Basingstoke; son of W. H. B. of Oakley Hall; 1840^{3}-1844^{3}; Ch. Ch. Oxf. M.A.; J.P., D.L., and C.Ald. for Hants; formerly Major Hants Yeo. Cav.; M.P. for N. Hants 1857-85 and W. Hants 1885-1901; Director of L. & S.W. Rly. Co.; *m.* Caroline Chichester, *d.* of Col. Augustus Clevland of Tapeley Park, Devon; died Aug. 3, 1901.	
Stuart-Wortley (H.D.)	Hon. Edward Montagu Stuart Granville (aft. Montagu-Stuart-Wortley-Mackenzie) (1st Earl of Wharncliffe). Eld. son of John, 2nd Lord Wharncliffe; 1841^{1}-1843^{3}; Chmn. M. S. and L. Ry. Co.; formerly Lieut. Gren. Gds.; Hon. Col. York and Lancaster Regt., and formerly Lieut.-Col. 1st Yorks Yeo. Cav.; J.P. and D.L. for W. Riding of Yorks and J.P. for co. Forfar; *m.* Lady Susan Charlotte Lascelles, *d.* of Henry, 3rd Earl of Harewood; died May 13, 1899.	
Green (Mrs. Ro., aft. K.S., W.A.C.)	G. C.	. 1847.
Taylor (Miss W., aft. K.S., F.E.D.)	C. H. L.	1844.
Ikin (Mrs. D., W.A.C.)	Thomas Moore. 1839^{3}-1841^{3}	

Jervis (W.A.C.) — HON. WILLIAM MONK. 2nd son of Hon. W. J.; 1842[2]-1844[1]; Trin. Coll. Oxf. B.C.L.; late Capt. King's Own Staffs Militia; J.P., C.A. and D.L. co. Derby; Barrister; *m.* 1st, Harriet Wilmot, *d.* of Robert Sacheverell Sitwell of Stainsby House, co. Derby; 2nd, Mary Maude, *d.* of Hon. Edward Swynfen Parker-Jervis of Aston Hall, co. Warwick; 3rd, Mary, *d.* of Edward Atkinson, D.L., of Seafield and Carrick Brenan, co. Dublin, and widow of Capt. Herbert Stepney, 79th Highlanders. *Quarndon Hall, Derby.*

Clissold (Mrs. D., F.E.D.) — REV. HENRY BAYLEY. Son of Rev. H. C.; 1840[3]-1841[3]; Oriel Coll. Oxf. M.A.; *m.* Frances Elizabeth, *d.* of James Baxter; died April 10, 1879.

Lord Robert Cecil (W.G.C.) — SIR R. A. T. GASCOYNE- (Marquis of Salisbury). 1844.

Mr. Eliot *mi.* (C.J.A.) — HON. G. C. C. . 1844.

Deacon *mi.* (E.H.P.) — W. S. . 1847.

Patteson *mi.* (E.C.) — J. H. . 1844.

Lyall (Miss Edw., F.E.D.) — REV. WILLIAM HEARLE. 3rd son of G. L. of Findon, Worthing; 1840[1]-1844[1]; St. Mary Hall, Oxf. M.A.; formerly Rector of St. Dionis Backchurch, Fenchurch Street, E.C.; *m.* Susan, *d.* of Sir Thomas J. Grant, K.C.B.

Baillie (W.G.C.) — D. J. . 1844.

Oxenden (F.E.D.) — SIR HENRY MONTAGU, 9th Bt. Of Dene, Kent; eld. son of Rev. M. O., Rector of Eastwell, Kent, and nephew of Sir H. C. O., 8th Bt.; 1840[2]-1842[3]; died unm. Sept. 1895.

Peel *ma.* (E.C.) — J. F. . 1844.

Adderley (F.E.D.) — RALPH THOMAS. Of Barlaston Hall, Staffs; 1840[3]-1841[3]; Ch. Ch. Oxf.; J.P. and D.L.; Capt. Staffs Yeo.

Mr. De Ros (W.G.C.) — HON. D. C. F. (Lord De Ros). 1844.

Pott *mi.* (W.A.C.) — EDWARD. Son of W. P. of Bridge St., Southwark; 1840[1]-1842[3]; Merton Coll. Oxf.; *m.* 1st, Ellen, *d.* of Thomas Keen of Croydon; 2nd, Ellen, *d.* of John Bankes Friend of Sussex Sq., Hyde Park, W. *The Cedars, Sunninghill, Ascot.*

Hampden (F.E.D.) — REV. PREB. EDWARD RENN. Of Ewelme, Wallingford; son of Rev. R. D. H., D.D., Bishop of Hereford; 1840[1]-1843[2]; Ch. Ch. Oxf. M.A.; J.P. and C.C. for co. Hereford; Preb. of Hereford; Rural Dean; Rector of Cradley, Malvern; *m.* Catherine Emma, *d.* of Rev. Edward Burdett Hawkshaw, Rector of Weston-under-Penyard, Ross, Herefords; died 1892.

Douglas *mi.* (E.H.P.) — R. A. . 1844.

Thursby (Miss Edw., C.J.A.) — SIR J. H., Bt. . 1844.

Hunt (Mrs. P., C.J.A.) — EDMUND D'ARCY. 1839[3] 1842[3]; Lieut.-Col.; served in 9th Lancers at [illegible], and with the 6th [illegible] Drag. in the Crimea.

Heywood (C.J.A.) — COL. THOMAS. Son of T. H. of Hope End, Ledbury; 1839[3]-1842[3]; Trin. Coll. Camb.; late Capt. 16th Lancers; D.L. co. Hereford, J.P. cos. Hereford and Worcester; Lieut.-Col. comm. 1st Hereford R.V. 1874-93, Hon. Col. of the Bn. from 1893; *m.* 1st, Mary Emily, *d.* of Most Rev. Marcus G. Beresford, D.D., Archbp. of Armagh; 2nd, Sophie Grace, *d.* of Stephen St. George of Headford Castle, co. Galway. *Halley St. George, Malvern.*

Smyth-Pigott *mi.* (Miss W., E.H.P.) — REV. GEORGE OCTAVIUS. 4th son of J. H. S.-P. of Brockley Hall, West Town, Bristol; 1840[3]-1841[3]; St. Mary Hall, Oxf.; Rector of Kingston Seymour, Somerset; *m.* Maria Ricketts; died Jan. 23, 1892.

Mynors (Miss Edw., C.J.A.) — REV. WALTER BASKERVILLE. 3rd son of P. R. M. of Treago, Ross, Herefords; 1840[3]-1843[3]; Oriel Coll. Oxf. B.A.; Rector of Llanwarne, Ross, Herefords; J.P. co. Hereford; *m.* Caroline Elizabeth, *d.* of Henry Clay of Stapenhill, co. Derby; died Feb. 11, 1899.

Myers *ma.* (W.G.C.) — T. B. . 1844.

Bayley (R.F.H., C.L.) — J. A. . 1844.

Dering (Mrs. Hor., C.J.A.) — REV. OSMOND. 2nd son of C. C. W. D. of Ayot St. Lawrence, Welwyn, Herts; 1841[1]-1843[3]; Rector of Edworth, Beds; died Nov. 18, 1860.

Maitland (W.A.C.) — WILLIAM WHITAKER. 2nd son of W. W. M. of Loughton Hall, Loughton, Essex; 1840[3]-1842[3]; Trin. Coll. Camb.; Capt. H.M. 49th Regt.; A.D.C. to Gen. Sir Henry Storks, G.C.B.; died from illness contracted in the Crimea, Nov. 15, 1856.

Balfour (R.O.) — HARRINGTON. 1840[3]-1843[3]; Civil Service, Bengal.

Lewis (J.E.Y.) — J. D. . 1844.

Prinsep (T.H.S., F.E.D.) — JAMES HUNTER. Son of W. P.; 1841[1]-1843[3]; Opp. Wall 1843; Haileybury Coll.; Annuitant, Bengal Civil Service; *m.* Christina Louisa, *d.* of Henry White of Morran, Ross-shire. *46 Thurloe Sq., S. Kensington, S.W.*

Harford (Mrs. P., C.O.G.) — CHARLES JOSEPH. Eld. son of H. C. H. of Frenchay Lodge, Bristol; 1841[1]-1843[3]; Ensign 82nd Regt.; Lieut. 15th Hussars; Capt. 12th Lancers; *m.* Rosa Matilda, *d.* of Robert Scott, R.N., of Oatlands, Devon; died 1872.

Currie (R.O.) — H. W. . 1844.

Stanbrough (Mrs. Hor., aft. K.S., W.L.E.) — M. E. . 1847.

Brown *min.* (W.G.C.) — GEORGE AUGUSTUS. 1838[3]-1841[3]; born at Lydbury, Salop.

Henley — REV. FRANCIS GEORGE. 2nd son of Rt. Hon. J. W. H., M.P., of Waterperry House, Oxf.; 1840[3]-1842[3]; Trin. Coll. Camb. M.A.; Curate of Plumtree, Notts, 1851-2; Vicar of Waterperry 1852-61; Vicar of Cumnor, Oxf., 1861-74; Rector of Lydlinch, Dorset, 1874-98; died unm. June 1898.

Stevenson (F.E.D.) — [illegible] 1844.

Brandreth (Miss Edg., H.D.) — CHARLES. Of St. Osyth, Colchester; son of J. P. B.; 1840^{3}–1842^{3}; Trin. Coll. Camb.; Lieut. 4th Lt. Dragoons; J.P. and D.L. for Essex; *m.* *d.* of W. F. Nassau of St. Osyth Priory, Colchester; died 1892.

Holdsworth (J.E.Y.) — REV. JOHN WILLIAM HOLDSWORTH. 1840^{2}–1843^{1}; Magd. Coll. Camb. B.A.; formerly a Clergyman in London; dead.

Belcher (R.F.H., C.J.A.) — REV. ANDREW HOLMES. 1841^{1}–1841^{3}; Emman. Coll. Camb. B.A.; formerly Curate of Huntspill, Bridgewater, Somerset; aft. Rector of St. Andrews. *St. Andrews Rectory, Fasque, Laurencekirk.*

Headlam (Miss Edw., aft. K.S., E.B.) — F. J. . 1847.

Smith (Mrs. Ro., J.W.) — REV. WILLIAM JOSEPH. 1840^{1}–1843^{2}; Queen's Coll. Oxf.; Consular Chaplain at Fow-choo-foo, Hong Kong.

Abbot (Mrs. D., W.G.C.) — S. T. . 1844.

Luttrell (Mrs. Y. & Mrs. D., C.J.A., & J.E.Y.) — G. F. . 1844.

Oddie (Mrs. Y., F.E.D.) — JOHN. Of Great Cell Barns, near St. Albans; 1840^{3}–1841^{3}.

Myers *mi.* (W.G.C.) — C. . 1844.

Spencer-Stanhope (E.B.) — COL. WALTER THOMAS WILLIAM, C.B. Eld. son of J. S.-S. of Cannon Hall; 1841^{1}–1843^{3}; Ch. Ch. Oxf. M.A.: 1st cl. Math. 1848; J.P., D.L., and C.A. for W. Riding of Yorks: late Capt. 1st W. York Yeo. Cav.; Hon. Col. 2nd Bn. York and Lancaster R.V.; M.P. for S. Div. W. Riding of Yorks 1872–80; *m.* Elizabeth Julia, *d.* of Sir John Jacob Buxton, 2nd Bt., of Shadwell Court, Norfolk. *Cannon Hall, near Barnsley.*

Sibthorpe (R.O.) — ALLEN WILLIAM. . 1838^{3}–1841^{3}.

Peel *mi.* (C.J.A.) — REV. ALFRED LENNOX. 3rd son of L. P. of Brighton; 1840^{1}–1843^{3}; Ball. Coll. Oxf. M.A.; Fellow of All Souls Coll. Oxf.; Rector of St. James, Dunbrody, and Killesk, co. Wexford; died unm. Nov. 4, 1863.

Kendall (Miss Edw., C.L.) — NICHOLAS. Of Pelyn, Lostwithiel; eld. son of N. K., J.P., D.L., M.P., of Pelyn; 1840^{3}–1843^{3}; J.P. and D.L. for Cornwall; Capt. 66th Berks Regt.; *m.* Dora de Havilland, *d.* of Joshua Priaulx of The Mount, Guernsey; died Dec. 21, 1882.

Williamson (E.H.P.) — SIR H., Bt. . 1844.

Lawford (J.W.) — EDWARD MELVILLE. Son of L., Solicitor to the Indian Board; 1840^{3}–1843^{1}; formerly Capt. Madras Light Cav.

Jeddere-Fisher (Mrs. P., C.O.G.) — C. . 1844.

Colquhoun (E.B.) — A. O. . 1844.

Broke (E.B.) — H. . 1844.

Johnstone (W.A.C.) — [illegible] 1844.

Gordon (R.O.) — C. H. W. 1844.

Stanley (E.H.P.) — HON. HENRY EDWARD JOHN (Lord Stanley of Alderley). Eld. son of Edward John, 2nd Lord S. of A.; 1841^{3}–1842^{3}; Trin. Coll. Camb.; entered Foreign Office 1847; Attaché at Constantinople 1851; Sec. of Legation at Athens 1854–9; Sec. to Special Mission to Danubian Provinces 1856–8; *m.* Fabia, *d.* of Don Santiago-Federico San-Roman of Seville. *Alderley Park, Chelford, Cheshire.*

Still (R.F.H., aft. K.S., E.B.) — H. H. . 1847.

Currie (Mrs. Ro., E.H.P.) — M. W. . 1844.

Fullerton (Mrs. Ro., F.E.D.) — THOMAS GREY. Of Thribergh Park, Rotherham; eld. son of J. F. of Thribergh; 1841^{1}–1843^{3}; Ch. Ch. Oxf. M.A.; Barrister; *m.* Euphemia Margaret, *d.* of Rev. Henry Worsley, LL.D.; died June 30, 1881.

Serle (C.L.) — PHILIP. Of The Cliffe, Limpley Stoke, Bath; son of Rev. P. S., Rector of Oddington, Oxfords; 1841^{2}–1843^{3}; Ball. Coll. Oxf.; formerly Lieut. 6th W. York Militia; *m.* Kate Pearson, *d.* of William Patrick Holnett. *22 rue Matignon, Paris.*

Furner (W.L.E.) — WILLIAM CAMPBELL. Son of W. F. of Brighton, Judge of the County Courts of Sussex; 1837^{3}–1841^{3}; formerly High Bailiff of County Courts of Sussex.

Williams (W.L.E., aft. K.S., W.L.E.) — J. S. . 1844.

Helyar (C.O.G.) — CHARLES. 3rd son of W. H. of Coker Court, Somerset; 1840^{1}–1841^{3}; St. John's Coll. Camb.; died of typhus at Great Malvern 1850.

Peel *min.* (E.C.) — ARCHIBALD. 3rd son of Rt. Hon. Gen. J. P. of Marble Hill, Twickenham; 1840^{3}–1842^{3}; Trin. Coll. Oxf. M.A.; J.P. co. Herts and Denbigh; D.L. and C.C.; *m.* 1st, Mary Ellen, *d.* of Sir William Henry Roger Palmer, Bt.; 2nd, Lady Georgiana Adelaide, *d.* of 1st Earl Russell. *Westlea, Broxbourne, Herts.*

Beckwith (Mrs. P., C.O.G.) — T. P. . 1844.

FOURTH FORM.

Calmady (R.F.H., E.H.P.) — VINCENT POLLEXFEN. Of Langdon Hall, Devon; eld. son of C. B. C. of Langdon; 1839^{3}–1841^{3}; J.P. for Devon; *m.* Isabel, *d.* of E. R. C. Sheldon, M.P., of Brailes House, Shipston-on-Stour, Warwicks, and widow of Col. Frederic Granville of Wellesbourn Hall, Warwicks; died March 5, 1896.

Bunny (W.G.C.) — E. J. (aft. St. John). 1844.

Smith *mi.* (Mrs. Ri., J.W.) — ERIC CARRINGTON. Of Ashfold, Crawley, Sussex; 2nd son of O. S. of Blendon Hall, Kent; 1840^{1}–1844^{1}; D.L. for London; *m.* Mary, *d.* of John Maberley. *59 Cadogan Sq., S.W.*

Borrowes (E.H.P.) — ROBERT HIGGINSON. Of Gilltown, Newbridge, co. Kildare; eld. son of R. B. of Gilltown; 1840^{1}–1843^{1}; formerly Capt. 13th Lt. Dragoons, and Major, Kildare Rifles; J.P. and D.L. co. Kildare, High Sheriff 1853; *m.* Hon. Louisa Katherine Browne, *d.* of John Cavendish, 3rd Lord Kilmaine; died Feb. 2, 1901.

Mr. Sidney (Mrs. D., W.G.C.) — HON. PHILIP (2nd Lord De Lisle and Dudley). Eld. son of Philip Charles, 1st Lord De Lisle and Dudley, of Penshurst Place, Tonbridge, Kent; 1840[3]-1844[1]: D.L. Kent; formerly Lieut. Royal Horse Gds.; *m.* 1st, Mary, *d.* of Sir William Foulis, 8th Bt.; 2nd, Emily Frances, *d.* of William Fermor Ramsay; died Feb. 17, 1898.

Fox (W.L.E.) — J. W. 1844.

Luxmoore *mi.* (Mrs. Ro., J.W.) — F. . 1844.

Mousley *mi.* (Mrs. Y., W.L.E.) — C. . 1844.

Wiss *ma.* (Mrs. Hor., W.G.C.) — . 1844.

Rhodes (C.J.A.) — FRANCIS (aft. Darwin). 4th son of W. R. of Bramhope, Leeds; 1840[3]-1842[2]; Christ's Coll. Camb. M.A.; J.P. and D.L. for Notts and W. Riding of Yorks; late Chmn. of Quarter Sessions; Lord of the Manor of Elston; *m.* 1st, Charlotte Maria Cooper, *d.* of William Brown Darwin of Elston Hall, Newark; 2nd, Georgina Huntly, *d.* of Huntly George Gordon Duff of Muirtown, Inverness. *Creskeld Hall, Arthington, Leeds.*

Palmer (Mrs. Ro., J.W.) — HENRY CHARLES. 1840[1]-1841[3].

Tredcroft (Mrs. P., W.G.C.) — E. . 1844.

Tighe (Miss W., E.H.P.) — FREDERICK EDWARD (aft. Bunbury-Tighe). Of Woodstock Park, Inistioge, co. Kilkenny; eld. son of D. T. of Rossanagh, Wicklow; 1840[2]-1842[3]; J.P. co. Wicklow; formerly Ensign 53rd and Capt. 82nd Regts.; Lieut.-Col. comm. Kilkenny Militia; *m.* Lady Kathleen Louisa Georgina Ponsonby, *d.* of John William, 4th Earl of Bessborough; died Jan. 8, 1891.

Ethelston (C.O.G.) — E. (aft. Peel). . 1844.

Fardell (Mrs. Ro., E.H.P.) — HENRY EDWARD. Son of Rev. H. F., Canon of Ely, and Vicar of Wisbech; 1840[2]-1841[3]; dead.

Jenner *ma.* (Mrs. Y., & Mrs. Ri., W.G.C.) — ROBERT FRANCIS LASCELLES. Of Wenvoe Castle, Cardiff; eld. son of R. F. J. of Wenvoe; 1840[2]-1843[3]; Trin. Hall, Camb.; Capt. 41st Regt. and 7th Fusiliers; J.P. and D.L. co. Glamorgan, High Sheriff 1864; *m.* Laura Frances, *d.* of Rev. William S. Birch, Rector of Easton Grey, Malmesbury; died May 8, 1883.

Yorke (H.D.) — JOHN. Of Bewerley Hall, Pateley Bridge, Leeds; eld. son of J. Y. of Bewerley Hall; 1840[2]-1843[2]; St. John's Coll. Camb.; J.P. and D.L. for W. Riding of Yorks; *m.* Alice, *d.* of James Simpson of Westcliffe, Yorks; died Oct. 3, 1883.

Errington *ma.* (W.G.C.) — G. H. . 1844.

Stuart *mi.* (C.O.G.) — C. E. . 1844.

Jackson (C.J.A.) — H. F. . 1844.

St. Aubyn (F.E.D.) — J. . 1844.

Talfourd (Miss A., W.G.C.) — F. . 1844.

Gay (Miss B., W.G.C.) — JOHN. 2nd son of J. G. of Thurning Hall, East Dereham; 1840[2]-1841[3]; J.P. and D.L. for Norfolk and Camb.; Capt. 2nd Norf. Militia; died unm. April 2, 1866.

Thompson (W.E., E.H.P.) — HENRY LANGHORNE, C.B., E.I.C.S. 1840[3]-1842[7]; one of the gallant defenders of Kars; formerly 68th N.I.; died a few days after his return home, June 13, 1856.

Earle *mi.* (Miss W., aft. K.S., F.E.D.) — W. C. . 1844.

Alexander (W.A.C.) — JOSIAS BRACKEN CANNING. Son of A., East India Director; 1840[3]-1843[2]; a Merchant in Manchester; *m.* Agnes Cecilia, *d.* of Sir William Curtis, 2nd Bt., of Caynham Court, Ludlow, Salop; died 1882.

Perceval (F.E.D.) — H. S. . 1844.

Meyrick (C.J.A.) — LIEUT.-GEN. AUGUSTUS WILLIAM HERVEY. Eld. son of Col. W. H. M. of Goodrich Court, Ross, Herefords; 1840[2]-1841[3]; Lieut.-Gen. Scots Gds.; served in the Crimea, and took part in the siege of Sebastopol (ret. 1861); J.P. and D.L. for Herefords; *m.* 1st, Fanny, *d.* of Henry Clifford; 2nd, Elizabeth, *d.* of John Spencer of Stratton Cirencester; died March 26, 1902.

Richards *mi.* (Mrs. Hor., E.H.P.) — H. W. P. . 1844.

Leveson-Gower (Mrs. D., W.G.C.) — JOHN EDWARD. Of Bill Hill, Wokingham; eld. son of J. L.-G. of Bill Hill; 1840[3]-1842[2]; J.P. for Berks; Capt. 69th Foot; *m.* 1st, Harriet Jane, *d.* of Capt. Hunter; 2nd, Katherine Elizabeth, *d.* of Basil Edward Arthur Cochrane; died Jan. 21, 1892.

North (R.O.) — C. . 1844.

Packe (E.H.P.) — CHARLES HUSSEY. Eld. son of Lieut.-Col. G. H. P. of Prestwold Hall, Loughborough; 1840[3]-1842[3]; died of scarlet fever at Eton, Oct. 28, 1842.

Bosanquet (F.E.D.) — H. A. . 1844.

Gurney (Miss W., F.E.D.) — FRANCIS HAY. Of Thorpe, Norwich, J.P. and D.L.; eld. son of D. G. of North Runcton, King's Lynn; 1840[3]-1842[3]; Lieut.-Col. W. Suffolk Yeo. Cav.; *m.* Margaret Charlotte, *d.* of Sir William Browne ffolkes, 2nd Bt., of Hillington, Norfolk; died Dec. 1, 1891.

Wilson *mi.* (E.C.) — H. M. . 1844.

Coleridge (W.E., aft. K.S., E.C.) — A. D. . 1847.

Vivian (W.A.C.) — W. G. . 1844.

Mr. Carew (F.E.D.) — HON. SHAPLAND FRANCIS. 2nd son of Robert Shapland, 1st Lord Carew, of Castle Boro, co. Wexford; 1840[3]-1843[2]; Lieut. 8th Hussars; Lieut.-Col. Wexford Militia; Resident Magistrate at Clonmel; [illegible] Browne, *d.* of [illegible] of Sligo; died [illegible].

Lord Garvagh (W.A.C.)	CHARLES HENRY SPENCER GEORGE (2nd Lord Garvagh). Eld. son of George, 1st Lord G., of Garvagh, co. Londonderry; 1840^{3}-1841^{3}; Capt. 10th Hussars; J.P. and D.L.; *m.* Cecilia Susannah, *d.* of John Ruggles-Brise, of Spains Hall, Braintree, Essex; died May 7, 1871.
Kaye (Mrs. Hor., W.A.C.)	L. LISTER-. . 1844.
Barlow (F.E.D.)	F. M. . 1844.
Arden (E.B.)	FREDERICK. Son of J. A. of Rickmansworth Park, Hertford; 1841^{1}-1843^{3}; St. John's Coll. Oxf.; 12th Lancers; formerly Vice-Consul at St. Sebastian.
Lord Moreton (E.B.)	HENRY JOHN, P.C., F.R.S. (3rd Earl of Ducie). Eld. son of Henry George Francis, 2nd Earl of D.; 1841^{1}-1843^{3}; Lord-Lieut. of Gloucestershire since 1857; J.P. co. Oxford; Hon. Col. 2nd Vol. Bn. Gloucester Regt.; Capt. of the Yeomen of the Guard 1859-66; M.P. for Stroud 1852-3; Lord Warden of the Stannaries in Cornwall from 1888; Member of Council of Prince of Wales; *m.* Julia, *d.* of James Haughton Langston, M.P., of Sarsden, co. Oxf. *Tortworth, Falfield, R.S.O., Glos.*
Hibbert (J.E.Y.)	R. P. . 1844.
Sir C. Smith (C.J.A.)	SIR CHARLES CUNLIFFE, 3rd Bt. Son of Charles Joshua, 2nd Bt., of Suttons, Romford, Essex; 1841^{3}-1841^{3}; Trin. Coll. Camb.; J.P. and D.L. for Essex, High Sheriff 1852; *m.* Agnes Frederica, *d.* of Capel Cure, of Blake Hall, Essex. *Suttons, Romford, Essex.*
Pochin (Mrs. Ro., W.L.E.)	E. N. . 1844.
Dunbar (Mrs. Ro., F.E.D.)	P. J. . 1844.
Chenery (J.E.Y.)	T. . 1844.
Count E. Batthyany (Miss A., W.A.C.)	EDMUND GUSTAVE. 1841^{3}-1843^{3}.
Sadler (J.E.Y.)	J. H. . 1844.
Tremayne *min.* (H.D.)	H. H. . 1847.
Lord St. Lawrence (E.H.P.)	W. U. (Earl of Howth). 1844.
Colvin (W.A.C.)	JAMES HENRY BAYLEY. Son of J. R. C.; 1841^{3}-1841^{3}; was in the Indian Civil Service, retired early on account of bad health; died unm. 1879.
Bowden (E.B.)	J. E. . 1844.
Brown *mi.* (Mrs. D., aft. K.S., W.G.C.)	E. P. . 1844.
Hammond *mi.* (Mrs. Hor., F.E.D.)	R. H. . 1844.
Shaw-Stewart (R.O.)	J. A. . 1844.
Mr. Rowley (Mrs. Hor., W.L.E.)	HON. HERCULES LANGFORD BOYLE. 2nd son of Hercules Langford, 2nd Lord Langford; 1840^{3}-1841^{3}; Hon. Col. 5th Bn. Leinster Regt.; J.P. and D.L. co. Meath, High Sheriff 1856; J.P. co. Dublin; formerly Capt. 6th Dragoons; *m.* Louisa Jane, *d.* of Archibald Campbell of Blythswood, co. Renfrew. *Marlay Grange, Rathfarnham, R.S.O., co. Dublin.*
Warde (Mrs. Ro., W.L.E.)	GEORGE. Of Squerryes Court, Westerham, Kent; 2nd son of Vice-Adm. C. W. of Squerryes; 1840^{3}-1843^{3}; J.P. co. Kent; Capt. 51st Regt.; Lieut.-Col. comm. London Rifle Bgde.; *m.* Lady Harriet North, *d.* of Francis, 6th Earl of Guilford; died Jan. 22, 1877.
Midgley (C.L.)	WILLIAM HOLT. 1840^{3}-1844^{1}.
Rowley *mi.* (Miss Edw., H.D.)	CHARLES PERCEVAL. 3rd son of G. W. R. of Priory Park, St. Neots; 1840^{3}-1843^{3}; Magd. Coll. Camb. M.A.; J.P. for Hunts. *Winteringham Hall, St. Neots, and 61 Pall Mall, S.W.*
Mr. Moore (F.E.D.)	HON. CHARLES WILLIAM (aft. More-Smyth) (5th Earl Mountcashell). 2nd son of Stephen, 3rd Earl M.; 1840^{3}-1841^{3}; J.P. co. Cork, J.P. and D.L. co. Waterford, High Sheriff 1862; *m.* 1st, Charlotte Mary, *d.* of Richard Smyth of Ballynatray, co. Waterford; 2nd, Florence, *d.* of Henry Cornelius of Ross-na-Clonagh, Queen's Co.; died Feb. 20, 1898.
Batchelor *mi.* (W.G.C., aft. K.S., W.G.C.)	C. . 1844.
Gray (Miss Edw., F.E.D.)	REV. HENRY RICHARD. 1840^{3}-1841^{3}; Worc. Coll. Oxf. M.A.; formerly Vicar of Crawley Down, Sussex, and Holt, Denbighshire; died June 1, 1903.
Mayd (Mrs. Hor., W.A.C.)	WILLIAM. 1840^{3}-1842^{3}; a Barrister, Norfolk Circuit.
Smith *mi.* (E.C.)	ARTHUR. Son of R. P. S. of Mortimer, Berks; 1840^{3}-1843^{3}; R. M. Coll. Sandhurst; died early.
Cooper (Mrs. D., W.G.C.)	F. J. . 1844.
Sutherland *ma.* (Mrs. D., W.G.C.)	G. . 1844.
Sutherland *mi.* (Mrs. D., W.G.C.)	F. . 1844.
Vyse *mi.* (W.E., F.E.D.)	FRANCIS HOWARD-. 8th son of Major-Gen. R. W. H.-V. of Stoke Place, Slough; 1840^{3}-1841^{3}; formerly in the Army; died unm. 1891.
Feilden *mi.* (Miss Edw., H.D.)	J. R. . 1844.
Stringer (Mrs. Rl., F.E.D.)	MILES. Of Effingham, Surrey; 1840^{3}-1843^{3}; formerly 6th Inniskilling Dragoons; aft. Capt. 3rd Surrey Militia.
Greene *mi.* (H.D.)	H. A. . 1844.
Mr. Deane (Mrs. D., W.G.C.)	HON. R. T. F. (aft. Deane-Morgan). 1844.

Eden (Mrs. D., E.H.P.) — A. J. . 1844.

Eliott (W.E., E.H.P.) — SIR WILLIAM FRANCIS AUGUSTUS, 8th Bt. Eld. son of Sir W. F. E., 7th Bt., of Stobs; 1841^{1}–1843^{3}; J.P. and D.L. co. Roxburgh; F.R.S.; served several years in the 93rd Highlanders; *m.* 1st, Charlotte Maria, *d.* of Robert Wood; 2nd, Hannah Grissell, *d.* of Holland T. Birkett of Foxbury, Surrey, and widow of Henry Kelsall. *Stobs Castle, Hawick.*

Greene (H.D.) — R. . 1844.

Clissold *mi.* (W.E., W.L.E.) — E. M. . 1844.

Steere (W.E., F.E.D.) — STEERE LEE. Of Jayes Park, Ockley, Dorking; eld. son of L. S. of Jayes Park; 1841^{1}–1843^{3}; Lieut. 88th Foot; *m.* Margaret, *d.* of James Keiro Watson of Hull; died 1900.

Walker (W.G.C.) — H. . 1844.

Balguy (Mrs. Ri., F.E.D.) — C. Y. . 1844.

Preston (R.F.H., F.E.D.) — R. . 1844.

Burton (Mrs. D., W.G.C.) — W. F. . 1844.

Dutton (W.A.C.) — JOHN WILLIAM. Eld. son of James Henry Legge, 3rd Lord Sherborne; 1841^{1}–1841^{3}; Ball. Coll. Oxf. B.A.; killed by accidental discharge of a rifle, Aug. 9, 1850.

Russell (F.E.D.) — SIR CHARLES, 3rd Bt. Of Swallowfield Park, Reading; 2nd son of Sir H. R., 2nd Bt., of Swallowfield; 1841^{1}–1843^{2}; M.P. for Berks 1865–8, and for Westminster 1874–83; Lieut.-Col. Gren. Gds.; V.C. and the Legion of Honour; died unm. April 14, 1883.

Oliver (C.L.) — A. S. (aft. Oliver-Massey). 1844.

Becher (W.E., E.H.P.) — SIR H. WRIXON-, Bt. 1844.

Page (Mrs. Ro., aft. K.S., E.B.) — J. . 1847.

Marshall (J.E.Y.) — J. W. . 1844.

Pye (J.E.Y.) — HENRY JOHN. 2nd son of H. J. P. of Clifton Hall, Tamworth; 1841^{2}–1844^{1}; Trin. Coll. Camb. M.A.; J.P. co. Stafford; Barrister, Inner Temple; *m.* Emily Charlotte, *d.* of Rt. Rev. S. Wilberforce, D.D., Bishop of Winchester. *Clifton Hall, Tamworth.*

Jenner *mi.* (Mrs. Ri., W.G.C.) — A. H. . 1844.

Peel *mi.* (E.C.) — A. W. (Viscount Peel). 1847.

Gordon (W.L.E.) — JOHN (aft. Gordon-Cuming-Skene). Of Pitlurg, Ellon; eld. son of Col. W. G.-C.-S. of Pitlurg; 1841^{2}–1843^{3}; Trin. Coll. Camb.; J.P. and D.L.; *m.* 1st, Maria, *d.* of Capt. William Henry Nares, R.N.; 2nd, Margaret Maria, *d.* of Sir David Brewster, K.H., D.C.L., F.R.S.; died Feb. 1882.

Shuldham *ma.* (J.E.Y.) — EDMUND ANDERSON. Eld. son of Lieut.-Gen. E. W. S. of Coolkelure; 1841^{3}–1844^{1}; Ch. Ch. Oxf. M.A.; J.P. and D.L. co. Cork, High Sheriff 1871; formerly Lieut.-Col. South Cork Militia, and A.D.C. to Lord-Lieut. of Ireland. *Coolkelure, Dunmanway, R.S.O., co. Cork.*

Best (Mrs. Ro., E.H.P.) — THOMAS. Of Red Rice, Andover; son of Rev. T. B. of Red Rice; 1841^{2}–1843^{3}; Magd. Coll. Oxf.; J.P. and D.L. for Hants; Capt. Hants Militia; *m.* Louisa Emily, *d.* of Rev. Sir George Shiffner, 3rd Bt., of Coombe Place, Lewes; died 1886.

Maynard (J.E.Y.) — W. R. . 1844.

Baring (H.D.) — CHARLES. Of Nubia House, West Cowes, I. of Wight; eld. son of H. B. B., M.P. for Marlborough; 1841^{2}–1844^{1}; Lieut.-Gen. Coldstream Gds.; *m.* Helen, *d.* of Rt. Hon. Sir James Robert George Graham, 2nd Bt., G.C.B., of Netherby; died Feb. 7, 1890.

Mr. Curzon *min.* (E.C.) — HON. SIR L., K.C.B., K.C.M.G. (aft. Curzon-Smyth). 1844.

Daniel (Miss Edw., H.D.) — REV. HENRY ARTHUR. 3rd son of T. D. of Stoodleigh, Devon; 1841^{2}–1844^{1}; St. John's Coll. Oxf. M.A.; Vicar of Stockland 1857–83; *m.* Laura Catherine, *d.* of John Were Clarke of Bridwell, Devon. *Manor House, Stockland, Bridgwater.*

Paul (C.O.G.) — C. K. . 1844.

Bryant (W.A.C.) — H. S. . 1844.

Heaviside (C.J.A.) — RICHARD WILLIAM (aft. Spicer). Son of R. H. of Sandhurst Lodge; 1841^{2}–1843^{2}; formerly Capt. 16th Lancers; *m.* Dora Caroline, *d.* of James Scott of Rotherfield Park, Alton, Hants; died 1892.

Clutterbuck (W.A.C.) — D. H. . 1844.

Coke (Miss W., aft. K.S., E.B.) — G. F. . 1847.

Mildmay (C.J.A.) — HENRY BINGHAM. Of Shoreham, Sevenoaks; 2nd son of H. St. J. M. of Shoreham and Flete; 1841^{3}–1844^{1}; Ch. Ch. Oxf.; J.P. and D.L. for Kent; D.L. for Devon, High Sheriff 1886; *m.* Georgiana Frances, *d.* of John Crocker Bulteel of Flete, Devon. *Flete, Ivy Bridge, Devon.*

Fredricks (C.J.A.) — J. J. W. . 1844.

Munro *ma.* (E.B.) — S. C. . 1844.

Munro *mi.* (E.B.) — M. W. . 1844.

Shuldham *mi.* (J.E.Y.) — L. A. F. . 1844.

Lawson (W.A.C.) — JAMES HYLTON DE CARDONNEL. Of Hylton Cottage, Tynemouth, North Shields; 1840[3]-1843[1]: formerly in the 3rd Dragoon Gds.; aft. Capt. W. York Militia.

Lee-Warner *mi.* (Miss B., C.J.A.) — REV. THOMAS HENRY. 9th son of Rev. D. H. L.-W. of Walsingham Abbey, Norfolk; 1841[1]-1843[3]; M.A.; Vicar of St. Paul's, Highmore, Oxfs; *m.* Henrietta, *d.* of Capt. Foley, of Earsham House, Canterbury; died March 16, 1890.

Bax (Mrs. Ri., W.L.E.) — JOHN HENRY, C.B. (aft. Bax-Ironside). Of Houghton-le-Spring; eld. son of J. B. of Preston House, Faversham; 1841[1]-1843[3]; Bengal Civil Service; *m.* Sarah Elizabeth, *d.* of Major-Gen. Robert George Hughes of Plâs Côch, co. Anglesey; died May 12, 1879.

Waddington (W.E., H.D.) — GEORGE HORSEY. 1841[1]-1843[3]; was in the Rifles.

Wilkieson (Mrs. Ri., F.E.D.) — GEORGE HAMPDEN. Son of W. of Woodbury Hall, Cambs; 1841[1]-1844[3]: Capt. 62nd Regt.; died at Kingston, Canada, 1862.

Cooke *ma.* (Miss M., E.B.) — SIR WILLIAM RIDLEY CHARLES, 9th Bt. Of Wheatley Hall, near Doncaster; eld. son of Sir W. B. C., 8th Bt., of Wheatley Hall; 1841[1]-1843[3]; D.L.; Capt. 7th Hussars; D.L. W. Riding of Yorks; *m.* 1st, Harriet Eloise, *d.* of Rev. Jonathan Trebeck, Vicar of Melbourne, co. Camb.; 2nd, Blanche Harriet Juaneta Georgina, *d.* of Sir William Henry Feilden, 2nd Bt., of Feniscowles, Blackburn; died Sept. 27, 1894.

Cooke *mi.* (Miss M., E.B.) — C. E. S. . 1844.

Stratton (C.J.A.) — G. . 1844.

Alexander (Mrs. D., C.O.G.) — L. . 1844.

Errington *mi.* (W.G.C.) — J. L. (aft. Turbutt). 1844

Smyth-Pigott *min.* (Miss W., E.H.P.) — A. C. N. . 1844.

Rudge (J.E.Y.) — E. C. . 1844.

De Salis (Mrs. Ri., W.G.C.) — REV. HENRY JEROME AUGUSTUS FANE. 6th son of Jerome, 4th Count De Salis; 1840[3]-1841[3]; Exeter Coll. Oxf. M.A.; Rector of Fringford, Bicester, 1852-72; *m.* Grace Elizabeth, *d.* of Rt. Hon. Joseph Warner Henley of Waterperry, Oxf. *Portnall Park, Virginia Water, Surrey.*

UNPLACED.

Rolt (Mrs. D., C.O.G.) — H. G. . 1844.

Richards (Miss W., E.B.) — J. R. . 1844.

White (W.E., W.L.E.) — SIR T. W., BT. . 1844.

Hunt *min.* (C.J.A.) — T. H. . 1844.

Boileau (W.E., W.G.C.) — J. E. . 1844.

Coleridge (E.C.) — H. . 1847.

Bashall (Miss Edw., C.L.) — REV. WILLIAM. 1841[2]-1842[3]; St. John's Coll. Camb. M.A.; Vicar of Deane, near Bolton, Lancs; died Aug. 8, 1902.

Pearce *min.* (C.O.G., E.B.) — GEORGE EDWARD SEROCOLD (aft. Pearce-Serocold). 3rd son of Rev. E. S. P.-S. of Cherry Hinton, Camb.; 1841[2]-1841[3]; Lieut. R.N., aft. a Squatter in Queensland; *m.* 1st, Amy, *d.* of John Crow Richardson of Swansea; 2nd, Mary Clarke, *d.* of Jeremiah Clarke Richardson of Derwen Fawr, Swansea. 156 *Sloane Street, S.W.*

Miller (R.F.H., C.O.G.) — SIR C. H., Bt. . 1847.

Barton (W.L.E.) — HARRY FITZGERALD. 2nd son of N. B. of Straffan House, co. Kildare; 1841[2]-1843[3]; died at Bordeaux, May 6, 1848.

Luxmoore (W.L.E.) — E. B. . 1844.

Thellusson (W.A.C.) — A. J. B. . 1844.

LOWER SCHOOL.

THIRD FORM—UPPER GREEK.

Hankin (Mrs. Ro., aft. K.S., W.L.E. & J.E.Y.) — F. G. . 1844.

Edmonds (J.E.Y.) — RICHARD. 1841[2]-1842[3]; formerly in business in London.

Newton (Mrs. Ro., E.H.P.) — H. R. . 1844.

Hankey (Mrs. Ri., C.J.A.) — B. A. . 1844.

Foulkes (W.G.C.) — J. F. . 1844.

Reeve (H.D.) — W. H. . 1844.

Philips (R.O.) — NATHANIEL GEORGE. 2nd son of Lieut. J. P., R.N., of Belle Vue House, near Liverpool; 1840[1]-1841[3]; Capt. 47th Regt.; served in the Crimea, severely wounded at the battle of Alma; Groom of Privy Chamber 1874-1901; Knight of Justice, Order of St. John of Jerusalem; *m.* 1st, Caroline, *d.* of Rev. Samuel Gerrard Fairtlough, Rector of Ahinagh, co. Cork; 2nd, Mary Catherine, *d.* of Alexander Low-Crigie, of Forfarshire, and widow of Col. John Halket Le Couteur of the Coldstream Gds. 85 *Eccleston Square, S.W.*

Leche (R.O.) — JOHN HURLESTON. Of Carden Park, Chester; eld. son of J. H. L. of Carden; 1840[3]-1843[3]; J.P. and D.L. co. Chester, High Sheriff 1851; Capt. 1st Ryl. Cheshire Militia; *m.* 1st, Caroline, *d.* of Edwin Corbett of Darnhall, co. Chester; 2nd, Eleanor Frances, *d.* of Capt. Charles Stanhope Jones of 58th Regt.; died June 21, 1903.

Myers (Miss B., aft. K.S., E.H.P.) — WILLIAM HENRY. 1841[1]-1842[3]; died at Eton in 1842.

Lower Greek.

Hunt (Miss W., W.A.C.) — Richard Elton. 1840-1841.

Chandos-Pole *mi.* (R.O.) — H. (aft. Chandos-Polo-Geil). 1844.

Mr. Nelson (Mrs. Hor., E.H.P.) — Rear.-Adm. Hon. Maurice Horatio. 3rd son of Thomas Bolton, 2nd Earl Nelson; 1839-1841; Ryl. Acad. Gosport; entered Navy 1845, ret. 1873; present at bombardment of Odessa 1854; Crimean and Turkish Medals, Inkerman clasp; 5th class Medjidie; served in Naval Bgde. before Sebastopol 1854-5; in command of a gunboat in the Baltic 1855; *m.* Emily, *d.* of Adm. Sir Charles Burrard, 2nd Bt. *Anglesey, Gosport.*

Milles (C.O.G.) — T. . 1844.

Lonsdale (C.J.A.) — H. H. . 1844.

Flamstead (Home, W.A.C.) — George Ley Wolferstan Dodsley. 1841-1844; Capt. 18th Regt.; Adjt. of Depôt Bn. at Pembroke.

Savage (W.L.E.) — Frederick. 1840-1842.

Thomas *ma.* (J.E.Y.) — Lieut.-Col. Lancelot Francis Charles. 1841-1841; Maj. Madras Artillery, aft. in command of Ordnance at Nagpore; ret. 1878.

SENSE.

Grant (W.L.E.) — Sir Francis William, 8th Bt. Of Monymusk, Aberdeenshire; 2nd son of R. G. of Tillyfourie, Aberdeen, and nephew of Isaac, 6th Bt., of Monymusk; 1841-1844; Capt. 16th Lancers; *m.* Laura, *d.* of John Fraser of Bunchrew, and Netley Park, Surrey; died Dec. 13, 1887.

NONSENSE.

Cookesley (W.G.C.) — A. F. . 1850.

Wiss *mi.* (Mrs. Hor., W.G.C.) — Algernon Philip. 1839-1842.

Branwell (Mrs. Ro., aft. K.S., C.L.) — C. H. . 1844.

SECOND FORM.

Tarver *min.* (Home, W.G.C.) — W. G. . 1844.

Sutton *mi.* (Miss B., W.L.E.) — Augustus Otway. Son of S. of Hertingfordbury, Herts; 1841-1842; Lieut. R.N.; died 1852.

Thomas *mi.* (J.E.Y.) — Alfred Cayley. 1841-1841.

Caley *ma.* (J.E.Y.) — A. J. . 1844.

Caley *mi.* (J.E.Y., aft. K.S., J.E.Y.) — G. A. 1847.

FIRST FORM.

Roberts (Home & Mrs. de R., aft. K.S., E.B.) — J. P. S. . 1850.

De St. Croix (C.L.) — Louis. 1841-1843; died 1858.

Cristall (Home) — H. . 1847.

Unplaced.

Kennedy-Erskine (W.L.E.) — William Henry. Of Dun House, Montrose, N.B.; only son of Hon. J. K.-E. of Dun; 1840-1841; Capt. 17th Lancers; *m.* Catherine, *d.* of John Jones of Henllys, Carmarthenshire; died Sept. 15, 1870.

ELECTION, 1844.

SIXTH FORM.

Drake (K.S., C.O.G.) — BERNARD WILLIAM FRANCIS. 1837[3]-1844[2]; Newc. Select 1841 and 1843; Sch. 1844; Coll. Wall 1843; Capt. of last Montem. 1844; King's Coll. Camb.; Fellow of King's; Editor of 'Demosthenes de Coronâ,' &c.; died 1854.

Brocklebank (K.S.) — REV. THOMAS. 1834[3]-1844[2]; Coll. Wall 1841-3; Sch. of King's Coll. Camb.; Bursar of King's 1852-71, Vice-Provost 1872-8; died July 24, 1878.

Helm *ma.* (K.S.) — JOHN BLACKWELL. 1835[3]-1844[2]; Coll. Wall 1841-3; Christ's Coll. Camb.; formerly a Solicitor in Australia.

Hutton (K.S.) — REV. ROBERT ROSSETER. Son of W. M. H.; 1835[3]-1844[2]; Ensign at last Montem.; Trin. Coll. Oxf. M.A.; Inc. of Ch. Ch. Warminster 1860-6; Rector of Chipping Barnet, Herts, 1866-87; *m.* Sybil Harriett, *d.* of Charles Snell; died at Barnet, Nov. 5, 1887.

Stephens (C.L., aft. K.S., C.L.) — RICHARD. Of Eastington House, Bournemouth; eld. son of Rev. R. S., Vicar of Belgrave-cum-Birstall, Leicester; 1836[1]-1844[2]; Merton Coll. Oxf.; Postmaster at Merton; J.P. for Hants and D.L. for co. Leicester; *m.* Henrietta Maria, *d.* of Rt. Hon. Sir Henry Pottinger, 1st Bt., G.C.B.; died 1898.

Hoskins (Mrs. P., aft. K.S., C.O.G.) — REV. CHARLES THOMAS. Son of Rev. H. H., Rector of North Perrott; 1837[1]-1844[2]; Keeper of Upper Club 1844; Exhib. Ball. Coll. Oxf. M.A.; *m.* Lucy Isabella, *d.* of Rev. John Drake. *North Perrott Rectory, Crewkerne.*

Goertz (K.S.) — FREDERICK LOUIS ALDOUS. 1833[3]-1844[2]; Coll. Wall 1841-3; went out to Ceylon with Bp. of Colombo, aft. went to Australia.

Wright (K.S., E.C.) — REV. JAMES CAMPER. Son of J. C. W.; 1836[3]-1844[2]; Newc. Select 1844; King's Coll. Camb. M.A.; Latin Ode 1845-6; Camden Med. 1846-7; Vicar of Bacton, Norfolk; aft. Rector of Walkern, Stevenage; *m.* Frances Wood, *d.* of Timothy Burstall of Edinburgh; died Jan. 6, 1889.

Wolley (K.S., J.W. & E.H.P.) — REV. CHARLES (aft. Wolley-Dod). Son of Rev. J. W. of Beeston, Nottingham; 1837[3]-1844[3]; Newc. Med. 1844; Pres. Eton Soc. 1844; Coll. Wall 1843; King's Coll. Camb. M.A.; Fellow of King's; Assist. Master at Eton 1850-78; J.P. co. Chester; *m.* Frances Lucy, *d.* of Rev. Pelly Parker, Rector of Hawton, Notts. *Edge Hall, Malpas, Cheshire.*

Day (K.S., R.O.) — WALLACE. Son of Rev. J. D., Rector of Tuddenham, Ipswich; 1837[3]-1845[1]; Coll. Wall 1844; King's Coll. Camb.; formerly a Solicitor at Camb.; died many years ago.

James *ma.* (K.S., C.W., & C.J.A.) — REV. JOHN ACLAND. Son of Rt. Rev. J. T. J., D.D., Bp. of Calcutta; 1835[3]-1845[2]; Eton XI. 1844, Capt. 1845; Coll. Wall 1842-4, Keeper 1844; Keeper of Upper Club 1844; King's Coll. Camb. M.A., Fellow of King's; formerly Rector of Dodington, Chipping Sodbury; aft. Vicar of Wattisham, Suffolk; *m.* Clarissa Catherine, *d.* of [illegible] James Larpent, 7th Baron de Hoche[illegible]; [illegible] Nov. 9, 18[illegible].

Mr. Herbert *ma.* (E.C.) — THE VERY REV. HON. GEORGE, Dean of Hereford. 3rd son of Edward, 2nd Earl of Powis, K.G.; 1837[3]-1844[2]; St. John's Coll. Camb. M.A.; *m.* Elizabeth Beatrice, *d.* of Sir Tatton Sykes, 4th Bt., of Sledmere, Yorks; died Mar. 15, 1894.

Vansittart (C.L.) — FREDERICK. 4th son of Rev. W. V., D.D., Preb. of Carlisle and Rector of White Waltham, Berks; 1838[1]-1844[2]; Eton XI. but did not play at Lord's owing to illness; Opp. Wall 1843; Ch. Ch. Oxf. B.A.; formerly Lieut. 14th Light Dragoons; *m.* Henrietta, *d.* of J. Low; died May 22, 1902.

McNiven *ma.* (Miss W., E.C.) — HENRY. 1838[3]-1844[2]; Barrister, Home Circuit; died 1886.

Mr. Herbert *mi.* (W.E., E.B.) — HON. ROBERT CHARLES. Of Orleton, Wellington, Salop; 4th son of Edward, 2nd Earl of Powis, K.G.; 1838[3]-1845[2]; St. John's Coll. Camb. M.A.; 1st Cl. Class. 1849; called to the Bar Lincoln's Inn 1853; Maj. 2nd Salop Rifle Vol.; D.L., J.P. and C.C. co. Salop, High Sheriff 1878; Chanc. of Diocese of Lichfield 1875-1899; *m.* Anna Maria, *d.* of Edward Cludde of Orleton; died Oct. 31, 1902.

McNiven *mi.* (Miss W., E.C.) — EDWARD. 1839[2]-1845[2]; Newc. Select 1844-5; Eton XI. 1843-5; Opp. Wall 1843-4; Camb. XI. 1846; accidentally killed near Westerham, Kent, by the upsetting of his dog-cart.

Mr. Neville *ma.* (E.H.P.) — HON. AND REV. LATIMER (6th Lord Braybrooke). 4th son of Richard, 3rd Lord B.; 1839[2]-1844[3]; Eton XI. 1844; Sch. of Magd. Coll. Camb. M.A., Fellow of Magd.; 2nd Cl. Class. Trip. 1849; Rector of Heydon since 1851; Master of Magd. Coll. since 1853; Hon. Canon of St. Albans since 1873; Vice-Chanc. Camb. Univ. 1860-1; *m.* Lucy Frances, *d.* of John Le Marchant Thomas Le Marchant. *Magdalene Coll. Cambridge; Heydon Rectory, Royston; and Audley End, Saffron Walden.*

Patteson *ma.* (E.C.) — RT. REV. JOHN COLERIDGE, Bp. of Melanesia. Son of Judge P.; 1838[1]-1845[2]; Newc. Select 1844; Eton XI. 1843-4; Opp. Wall 1844-5; Keeper of Upper Club 1844; Ball. Coll. Oxf. 2nd Cl. Class. 1848; Fellow of Merton; Oxf. XI. 1849; Bp. of Melanesia, South Pacific Isles, 1861-71; killed by natives at Nukapu, Melanesia, Sept. 20, 1871.

Newman Rogers *ma.* (W.E., E.C.) — FRANCIS. Of Rainscombe, near Marlborough, and Foxley Lodge, Worthing; eld. son of F. J. N. R., Q.C., of Rainscombe, Recorder of Exeter; 1839[1]-1845[1]; Exhib. of Ball. Coll. Oxf.; Barrister; died unm. Sept. 2, 1859.

Hunt (C.J.A.) — RT. HON. GEORGE WARD, M.P., P.C., J.P. and D.L. Of Wadenhoe House, Northampton; son of Rev. G. H. of Wadenhoe; 1839[1]-1844[3]; Newc. Select 1844; Ch. Ch. Oxf.; 2nd Cl. Class. 1848; Barrister; Chmn. of Qr. Sessions and M.P. for Northants; Financial Sec. of the Treasury July 1866 to Feb. 1868; Chanc. of the Exchq. Feb. 1868 to Dec. 1868; First Lord of the Admiralty 1874-7; *m.* Alice, *d.* of Rt. Rev. Robert Eden, Bp. of Moray and Ross; died at Homburg July 29, 1877.

Mr. Hanbury *ma.* (H.D.)
HON. WILLIAM BATEMAN BATEMAN-(2nd Lord Bateman). Eld. son of William Hanbury, 1st Lord B. of Shobdon Court, Hereford; 1839^{3}–1844^{2}; Trin. Coll. Camb. M.A.; Lord-Lieut. of Herefords 1852–1901; Lord-in-waiting to Queen Victoria 1858–9; Hon. Col. 4th Bn. King's Shropshire Lt. Inf.; J.P. for Northants; *m.* Agnes Burrell, *d.* of Gen. Sir Edward Kerrison, 1st Bt., K.C.B., K.C.H., of Oakley Park and Brome Hall, Suffolk; died Nov. 30, 1901.

Hornby (R.O.)
REV. JAMES JOHN, D.D., D.C.L., Provost of Eton. Son of Adm. Sir P. H., G.C.B.; 1839^{1}–1845^{3}; Newc. Select 1844–5; Eton XI. 1845; Ball. Coll. Oxf.; 1st Cl. Class.; Oxf. VIII. 1849–51; Fellow of B.N.C. Oxf.; Senior Proctor of Oxf. 1866; Prin. of Bp. Cosin's Hall, Durham, 1853–64; Hon. D.C.L. of Durham; Class. Lec. B.N.C. Oxf. 1864–6; 2nd Master of Winchester 1867; Head Master of Eton 1868–84; Hon. Chaplain to the King; Chairman of Gov. Body of Eton; Provost of Eton since 1884; *m.* Augusta Eliza, *d.* of Rev. J. C. Evans. *The Lodge, Eton College.*

Honywood (Mrs. P., C.O.G.)
ROBERT. 1839^{3}–1844^{2}; Eton XI. 1843–4; Trin. Coll. Oxf.; Oxf. XI. 1845–7; died about 1870.

West *ma.* (Miss A., E.C.)
REV. RICHARD TEMPLE. Son of M. J. W.; 1839^{3}–1845^{1}; Ch. Ch. Oxf. LL.D.; Vicar of St. Mary Magd., Paddington; died unm.

Higginson (C.J.A.)
GENERAL SIR GEORGE WENTWORTH ALEXANDER, K.C.B. Son of Gen. G. P. H., Col. 94th Regt.; of Gyldernscroft; 1839^{3}–1844^{2}; Lieut. Gren. Gds. 1845; Col. 1863; Gen. 1888; retired 1893; Crimean campaign 1854 (medal with four clasps, Legion of Honour, 5th Class Medjidie, Turkish medal); Comm. Home District 1879–84; Lieut.-Gov. of Tower of London 1889–93; Col. Worcs. Regt. 1893; *m.* Hon. Florence Fitzpatrick, *d.* of John, 1st Lord Castletown, of Upper Ossory, Queen's Co. 9 *Wilton Crescent, S.W., and Gyldernscroft, Marlow.*

FIFTH FORM.—UPPER DIVISION.

Brine (K.S., R.O.)
CHARLES CONRAD. 5th son of Maj. J. B. of Claremont, Sidmouth, Devon; 1834^{3}–1844^{2}; Ensign 27th Foot; died unm. Nov. 4, 1849.

Hammond *ma.* (K.S.)
JOHN GEORGE. Son of H., Surgeon in Eton; 1834^{3}–1844^{2}; Coll. Wall 1843; died young.

Batchelor *ma.* (K.S.)
REV. FREDERICK THOMAS. 1834^{3}–1844^{3}; Wadh. Coll. Oxf.; formerly Rector of Calstock, near Tavistock.

Birch *ma.* (Mrs. Ri., aft. K.S., C.J.A.)
REV. AUGUSTUS FREDERICK. 1839^{1}–1844^{2}; Coll. Wall 1844; King's Coll. Camb. M.A.; Fellow 1848–1860; Camden Med. 1848; Assist. Master at Eton 1852–64; aft. Rector of Northchurch, Hants; *m.* Isabella Anne, *d.* of Frederick White Corrance of Parham Hall, Wickham Market; died July 1898.

Bendyshe (Miss Edw., aft. K.S., H.D.)
THOMAS. 4th son of J. B. of Barrington Hall, Camb.; 1837^{1}–1844^{2}; Tomline Select 1844; King's Coll. Camb. M.A.; Fellow of King's; Barrister Norfolk Circuit; died unm. July 1866.

Vance *ma.* (Mrs. P., aft. K.S., W.L.F.)
EDWARD BRENTON. Son of G. V., M.D., of London; 1838–1844; King's Coll. Camb. B.A.; Fellow of King's; died at Camb.

James *mi.* (K.S., C.Wl. & C.J.A.)
FREDERICK ANNESLEY. Son of Rt. Rev. J. T. J., D.D., Bp. of Calcutta; 1836^{1}–1845^{3}; Coll. Wall 1842–4; died at Malta, 1846.

Day (Mrs. Ro., aft. K.S., W.L.F.)
REV. RUSSELL. Son of Rev. H. T. D., LL.D., of Mendlesham, Stowmarket; 1839^{1}–1845^{3}; Newc. Sch. 1845; Coll. Wall 1844; King's Coll. Camb. M.A.; Craven Univ. Sch. 1848; Assist. Master at Eton 1851–74; Rector of Horstead since 1881; *m.* Maria Isabella, *d.* of T. J. Knowlys of Heysham Tower, Morecambe. *Horstead Rectory, Coltishall, Norwich.*

Mackarness (R.F.H., aft. K.S., R.O.)
REV. HENRY SMITH. 1838^{3}–1847^{1}; Coll. Wall 1844–6; King's Coll. Camb.; formerly Vicar of Ash, near Sandwich, Kent; dead.

Stanley (C.J.A.)
EDWARD JAMES. Eld. son of E. S. of Cross Hall, Lancs; 1839^{3}–1844^{3}; Ch. Ch. Oxf. M.A.; M.P. for W. Somerset 1882–5, and for Bridgwater, Somerset, since 1885; J.P., D.L., and C.C., co. Somerset, High Sheriff 1880; D.L. for Lancs; *m.* Hon. Mary Dorothy Labouchere, *d.* of Henry, 1st and last Lord Taunton. *Quantock Lodge, Over Stowey, Bridgwater, and* 29 *Belgrave Sq., S.W.*

Coleridge (W.E., aft. K.S., E.C.)
REV. FREDERICK JOHN. Son of G. F. C.; 1838^{1}–1846^{3}; Newc. Select 1840–1; Pres. Eton Soc. 1845; Eton XI. 1844–6, Capt. 1846; Coll. Wall 1843 and 1845; Keeper of Upper Club 1845; St. Mary Hall, Oxf. M.A.; Oxf. XI. 1847 and 1850; Rural Dean of Cadbury 1873–98; Vicar of Cadbury; *m.* H. Georgiana, *d.* of Rev. J. Honywood Randolph. *Cadbury Vicarage, Tiverton.*

Sartoris (R.O.)
ALFRED URBAN. Of Abbotswood, Stow-on-the-Wold, Glos.; 3rd son of U. S. of Sceaux Park, near Paris; 1839^{3}–1845^{1}; formerly Capt. 7th Hussars; J.P. for Berks and co. Gloucester, High Sheriff 1886; *m.* Hon. Mary, *d.* of William Keppel, 6th Viscount Barrington. 17 *Queen's Gate Place, S.W.*

Speke (Mrs. Hor., C.O.G.)
WILLIAM. Eld. son of W. S. of Jordans, Ilminster; 1838^{3}–1844^{3}; Eton VIII. 1844; Ch. Ch. Oxf.; J.P. for Wilts, J.P. and D.L. for Somerset, High Sheriff 1894; *m.* Eliza Anne, *d.* of Rev. Charles Wicksted Ethelston of Uplyme, Devon, and Wicksted, Cheshire. *Jordans, Ilminster, Somerset.*

Coleridge *ma.* (E.C.)
CHARLES EDWARD. Son of E. C. of Eton and Mapledurham; 1838^{1}–1846^{3}; Eton XI. 1844–6; Keeper of Upper Club 1845; Ball. Coll. Oxf.; Oxf. XI. 1849–50; Barrister; *m.* Georgiana, *d.* of Harris Syne of Llanunwas, Pembrokeshire; died 1876.

Rouse-Boughton (W.G.C.)
ANDREW JOHNES (aft. Rouse-Boughton-Knight). 2nd son of Sir W. E. R.-B., Bt., of Lawford Hall, co. Warwick; 1838^{3}–1845^{3}; Trin. Coll. Camb. B.A.; J.P. and D.L. co. Hereford, High Sheriff 1860; *m.* Eliza, *d.* of John Michael Severne of Wallop Hall, Salop. *Downton Castle, Ludlow.*

Bayley (R.F.H., R.O. & C.L.)
SIR LYTTELTON HOLYOAKE, Kt. 2nd son of Sir J. E. G. B., 2nd Bt.; 1838^{3}–1844^{3}; Eton XI. 1841–4, Capt. 1844; Keeper of Upper Club 1843; Barrister Middle Temple 1850, H.M. Advocate-General, Bombay, 1866–9, Judge of High Court of Justice, Bombay, 1869–95; *m.* Isabella, *d.* of Anthony Mactier of Durris. *Oriental Club, Hanover Sq., W.*

Gully (K.S., C.O.G.)
WILLIAM ALGERNON SLADE. Of Trevennen, St. Austell; son of Rev. — G., Rector of Berrynarber, Ilfracombe; 1837^{3}–1847^{1}; [illegible]; Sch. of King's Coll. [illegible]; Barrister Western [illegible] 1870.

Sir M. Shaw-Stewart (J.W. & R.O.)
SIR MICHAEL ROBERT, 7th Bt. Eld. son of Sir M. S.-S., 6th Bt. of Ardgowan, Greenock; 1838^{3}–1844^{2}; Opp. Wall 1842-3; Ch. Ch. Oxf.; Cornet and Sub-Lieut. 2nd Life Gds. 1845-7; M.P. Renfrewshire 1855-65; Grand Master of Scottish Freemasonry 7 years; Lord-Lieut. of Renfrewshire; *m.* Lady Octavia Grosvenor, *d.* of Richard, 2nd Marquis of Westminster. 11 *Grosvenor Place, S.W.: Ardgowan, Greenock: Duchal, Paisley, N.B.; and Fonthill Abbey, Fonthill Gifford, Salisbury.*

Chandos-Pole *ma.* (R.O.)
EDWARD SACHEVERELL. Of Radbourne Hall, Derby; eld. son of S. C.-P. of Radbourne; 1838^{3}–1844^{2}; J.P. and D.L. co. Derby, High Sheriff 1867; *m.* Lady Anna Caroline Stanhope, *d.* of Leicester, 5th Earl of Harrington; died 1873.

Plumptre (R.O.)
REV. ROBERT WILLIAM. Eld. son of R.B.P.; 1839^{3}–1844^{3}: Univ. Coll. Oxf. M.A.; Rector of Corfe Mullen; *m.* Ellen Blanche, *d.* of John Bingley Garland of Stone Park and Leeson House, Dorset. *Corfe Mullen Rectory, Wimborne, Dorset.*

Simonds (K.S., W.L.E.)
HENRY JOHN. Of Caversham, near Reading; son of H. S. of Reading; 1839^{3}–1846^{1}; Newc. Select 1845; Coll. Wall 1844-5; Sch. of King's Coll. Camb. M.A.; Camb. XI. 1850; Barrister; aft. Brewer at Reading; *m.* Julia, *d.* of Signor Victor Pliati of Brest; died 1896.

Back (R.F.H., J.W.)
REV. JOHN. 1839^{1}–1845^{3}; Newc. Med. 1845; Trin. Coll. Oxf. M.A., 2nd Class 1849; formerly Rector of St. George the Martyr, Queen's Square, Bloomsbury.

Rogers *mi.* (W.E., aft. K.S., W.A.C.)
REV. EDWARD HENRY. Of Rainscombe, near Marlborough; 2nd son of F. N. R. of Rainscombe; 1840^{1}–1846^{3}; Newc. Select 1846; Sch. King's Coll. Camb. M.A.; Fellow of King's; Tyrwhitt's Hebrew Sch. 1853; Vicar of Thames Ditton, 1860-97. *Foxley Lodge, Worthing.*

Dent *ma.* (Miss Edw., H.D.)
JOHN DENT. Of Ribston Hall, Wetherby, Yorks; eld. son of J. D. of Ribston; 1839^{3}–1844^{2}; Trin. Coll. Camb. B.A.; M.P. for Knaresborough 1852-7, for Scarborough 1857-74; Barrister; J.P. and D.L. W. Riding of Yorks; Chmn. N. E. Ry. Co.; *m.* Mary Hebden, *d.* of John Woodall of St. Nicholas House, Scarborough; died Dec. 22, 1894.

Mr. Hanbury *mi.* (H.D.)
HON. CHARLES SPENCER BATEMAN-HANBURY-KINCAID-LENNOX. 2nd son of William, 1st Lord Bateman, of Kelmarsh; 1840^{2}–1845^{3}; B.N.C. Oxf. M.A.; Fellow of All Souls Coll. Oxf.; D.L. and J.P. cos. Hereford and Stirling; formerly Capt. 2nd Life Gds.; A.D.C. to Lord-Lieut. of Ireland 1858-9; M.P. for Herefords 1852-7, Leominster 1858-65; *m.* 1st, Margaret Cuninghame, *d.* of John Lennox Kincaid-Lennox of Lennox Castle, N.B., and widow of George, 7th Viscount Strangford; 2nd, Rose, *d.* of Boyd Alexander Cuninghame, R.N., of Craigends, Renfrew. 63 *Montagu Sq., W.*

Luttrell (Mrs. Y. and Mrs. D., C.J.A.)
HENRY ACLAND FOWNES, C.B. Of Badgworth Court, Axbridge, Somerset; eld. son of Rev. A. F. L., Rector of East Quantoxhead, Bridgwater, Somerset; 1839^{2}–1845^{3}; Eton VIII. 1843-5, Capt. 1845; Opp. Wall 1844; Trin. Coll. Oxf. M.A.; J.P. and D.L. co. Somerset, High Sheriff 1881; Capt. Rifle Bgde.; Hon. Col. 3rd Vol. Bn. Somerset's L.I.; Vol. Dec.; *m.* Mary Anne, *d.* of Joseph Rascombe [illegible]; died Jan. 7, [illegible].

Packe (Mrs. Hor., H.D.)
CHARLES. Of Stretton and Glen, co. Leicester; eld. son of E. P. of Stanhope Place, Hyde Park, W.; 1839^{1}–1845^{3}; Ch. Ch. Oxf. B.A.; Barrister Midland Circuit; J.P. co. Leicester; *m.* Selina Matilda, *d.* of Richard Fox; died July 16, 1896.

Welby (Mrs. P., E.C.)
REV. MONTAGUE EARLE. 4th son of Rev. G. E. W., Rector of Barrowby, Grantham; 1839^{3}–1846^{3}; Newc. Select 1845-6; Magd. Coll. Oxf. M.A.; Fellow of Magd.; formerly Vicar of St. Paul's, Sketty, near Swansea; *m.* Mary, *d.* of L. Dillwyn, M.P. *Tuyncoed, Arthog, Dolgelly.*

Stone *ma.* (Mrs. P., C.J.A.)
REV. ARTHUR. Son of T. A. S. of London; 1839^{2}–1844^{3}; St. Mary Hall, Oxf. M.A.; formerly Vicar of Prestwold, Leicester, aft. a Chaplain in India; *m.* Mary Gill.

Tremayne *ma.* (H.D.)
LIEUT.-COL. ARTHUR. 2nd son of J. H. T. of Heligan, St. Austell, Cornwall; 1839^{3}–1845^{3}; Eton VIII. 1845; Opp. Wall 1844; Ch. Ch. Oxf.; J.P. and D.L. Cornwall; Commanded 13th Lt. Dragoons, took part in the Crimean Campaign, and the Balaclava Charge; Crimean med., 3 clasps; Legion of Honour, Medjidie, &c.; M.P. for Truro 1878-80; *m.* 1st, Lady Frances Margaret Hely-Hutchinson, *d.* of John, 3rd Earl of Donoughmore; 2nd, Emma Penelope, *d.* of Rev. Thomas Phillpotts of Porthgwidden, Cornwall. *Carclew, Perran-ar-Worthal, Cornwall.*

Reynolds (Miss A., C.J.A.)
REV. HENRY REVELL. Son of H. R. R., Barrister, Solicitor to the Treasury, of Harley St., W.; 1840^{1}–1846^{2}; Trin. Coll. Camb. M.A.; Vicar of St. Andrew's, Croydon, aft. Vicar of Markham Clinton, Notts; *m.* Jane Katherine, *d.* of James Baillie of Hill Park, Westerham, Kent; died Sept. 15, 1896.

Earle *ma.* (Miss W., aft. K.S., J.W., and F.E.D.)
A. 1847.

Sir W. Fraser (C.J.A.)
SIR WILLIAM AUGUSTUS, 4th Bt., F.S.A. Of Pilton House, Barnstaple; eld. son of Sir J. J. F., 3rd Bt.; 1839^{3}–1844^{2}; Ch. Ch. Oxf. M.A.; J.P. and D.L. co. Middlesex; one of the Queen's Body-guard for Scotland; Capt. 1st Life Gds.; M.P. for Barnstaple 1852-7, for Ludlow 1863, and for Kidderminster 1874-80; died unm. Aug. 17, 1898.

Smijth-Windham (W.E., E.C.)
WILLIAM GEORGE (aft. Windham), D.L. Of Wawne, near Beverley; eld. son of J. S.-W. of Wawne; 1839^{3}–1844^{2}; Downing Coll. Camb. M.A.; late Capt. Yorks Militia; died Dec. 26, 1887.

Vance *mi.* (Mrs. P., aft. K.S., W.L.E.)
LIEUT.-COL. SIR HORATIO PAGE, Kt. Of 10 Arundel Terrace, Brighton; son of G. V., M.D., of London; 1839^{2}–1845^{2}; served in the Crimea and Indian Mutiny, and attained the rank of Lieut.-Col. in the 38th Regt.; created Kt. Bach. 1897; Lieut. Royal Body-guard of Yeomen; *m.* Mary Emily, *d.* of Thomas Vance, J.P., of Blackrock House, co. Dublin, and widow of Fielding Scovell of Rycroft, Bray; died Nov. 10, 1901.

Cholmeley (C.O.G., aft. K.S., C.O.G.)
REV. JOHN. Son of R. C., Rector of Wainfleet St. Mary, Lincs; 1838^{3}–1844^{2}; St. Cath. Coll. Camb. M.A.; Rector of Waynflete; dead.

Scott (G.O.G.)
REV. JAMES GEORGE (Archdeacon of Dublin). Son of J. S. S., Q.C., of 3 Merrion Sq., Dublin; 1840^{3}–1845^{1}; Tomline Prizeman 1844; Trin. Coll. Dublin, D.D.; 1st Class Math.; Rector of Bray; *m.* Frances Augusta, *d.* of Rev. William Cleaver. *Bray Rectory, co. Wicklow.*

Dugdale (E.C.) — WILLIAM STRATFORD. Of Merevale Hall, near Atherstone; eld. son of W. S. D. of Merevale; 1840[2]-1846[2]; Prince Consort's German Prize 1845; Newc. Select 1846; Ball. Coll. Oxf. M.A.; 1st Cl. Class. 1849; Barrister; J.P. and D.L. co. Warwick, High Sheriff 1876; *m.* Alice Frances, *d.* of Sir Charles Edward Trevelyan, 1st Bt., K.C.B., of Wallington, Cambo, Northumberland; died May 9, 1882, from the effects of injuries received while attempting to rescue a party of his miners.

Johnson (J.W.) — CHARDIN PHILIP. Of Hobarts Hall, Essex; 1840[3]-1844[3]; B.N.C. Oxf.; formerly Capt. and Brevet Major 9th Lancers.

Curtis (R.F.H., aft. K.S., C.L.) — F. H. . 1847.

Wright (R.F.H., E.C.) — LIEUT.-COL. CHARLES ICHABOD, J.P. Of Mapperley Hall, Notts: eld. son of I. C. W. of Mapperley, and Watcombe Park, Torquay; 1840[2]-1845[2]; Ch. Ch. Oxf.; M.P. for Nottingham 1868-9; formerly Banker; aft. Lieut.-Col. Comm. Rob'n Hood Rifles; *m.* Blanche Louisa, *d.* of Henry Gorles Bingham of Wartnaby Hall, Leicester. *Hartondale, Frensham, Surrey.*

Adlington (W.E., C.J.A.) — HENRY SMITH. Of Holm-Hale Hall, Thetford, Norfolk; 1839[3]-1845[2]; Eton VIII. 1845; Trin. Coll. Oxf.; J.P. for Norfolk; Capt. 4th Lt. Dragoons; *m.* Emma Jean, *d.* of Rev. Charles Campbell, Vicar of Weasenham, Norfolk; died 1893.

Pellew (Mrs. Ro., E.C.) — HENRY EDWARD. Only son of Very Rev. G. P., D.D., Dean of Norwich; 1840[2]-1846[1]; Trin. Coll. Camb. M.A.; Camb. VIII. 1849; *m.* 1st, Eliza, *d.* of Hon. Judge William Jay of New York; 2nd, Augusta, *d.* of Hon. Judge William Jay.

Tarver *ma.* (Home, aft. K.S., W.G.C., and C.J.A.) — F. B. C. . 1847.

Venables (W.A.C.) — RT. REV. ADDINGTON ROBERT PEEL. 1839[3]-1845[2]: Exeter Coll. Oxf.; Bp. of Bahamas 1863.

Beckwith (Mrs. P., C.O.G.) — THOMAS PERCIVAL. Son of T. B.; 1839[3]-1844[3]; Ch. Ch. Oxf. M.A.; Barrister; *m.* Frances Maria, *d.* of Henry George Fownes. 14 *Eaton Place, S.W.*

Joynes (Mrs. P., aft. K.S., E.C.) — W. . 1847.

Slade *ma.* (C.J.A.) — WYNDHAM. Of Montys Court, Taunton; 9th son of Gen. Sir J. L., 1st Bt., G.C.H., of Maunsel House, Bridgwater, Somerset; 1840[2]-1844[3]; won School Hurdles 1843; Ball. Coll. Oxf. B.A.; Barrister Western Circuit; J.P. for Somerset; late Recorder of Penzance; Met. Police Magistrate 1877-1901; *m.* Cicely, *d.* of Sir Richard Digby Neave, 3rd Bt., of Dagnam Park, Romford. 88 *Chester Square, S.W.*

Spencer (Miss A., W.A.C.) — REV. CHARLES VERE. Son of Rev. F. C. S. of Wheatfield, Tetsworth; 1840[2]-1845[2]; Opp. Wall 1845; Ch. Ch. Oxf. M.A.; J.P. for Oxfs; Rector of Wheatfield for 46 years; *m.* Emma Frederica, *d.* of John R. A'Court Gray; died May 1898.

Moffat (Mrs. Bl., aft. K.S., F.E.D.) — C. W. . 1847.

Collings (Mrs. P., C.J.A.) — DANIEL STRATTON. 1839[3]-1846[2]; Eton XI. 1846.

Codrington (Mrs. P., C.O.G.) — WILLIAM WYNDHAM. Of Wroughton, Swindon, Wilts; son of W. C. of Wroughton; 1839[3]-1844[2]; Eton VIII. 1842-4, Capt. 1844; Opp. Wall 1842-3; J.P. for Wilts; formerly 17th Lancers; *m.* Cecilia Charlotte, *d.* of Frederick Webb of Westwick, co. Durham.

Harkness (C.O.G.) — REV. ROBERT. 3rd son of Rev. R. H. of Garryfine, co. Limerick, Vicar of East Brent, Somerset; 1837[3]-1844[2]; Opp. Wall 1842-3; St. John's Coll. Camb. M.A.; Camb. VIII. 1845-7; Rector of St. Giles, Wimborne; *m.* Elizabeth, *d.* of William Siddon, of Stoneygate House, co. Leicester, and widow of Dr. Toswill; died Nov. 22, 1881.

Molony (Miss W., F.E.D.) — REV. CHARLES ARTHUR. Son of E. M., H.E.I. Co.'s Secretary to the Government of Bengal; 1841[1]-1845[1]; Lincoln Coll. Oxf. M.A.; Vicar of St. Lawrence, Ramsgate, *m.* Mary Emily Jane, *d.* of R. D. Parker, late H.E.I. Co.'s C.S.; died 1895.

Streatfeild *ma.* (R.F.H., C.O.G.) — EDWARD OGLE. 2nd son of H. S. of Chiddingstone, Edenbridge, Kent; 1840[2]-1844[3]; formerly Capt. 44th Regt.; Crimean and Turkish Medals. *Chiddingstone, Edenbridge, Kent.*

Smith (Mrs. Bl., W.L.E.) — JERVOISE. Of Sandwell, S. Devon; eld. son of J. A. S. of Dale Park, Sussex; 1840[2]-1846[2]; Trin. Coll. Camb.; Banker; M.P. for Falmouth 1866-8; *m.* Hon. Margaret Louisa Verney, *d.* of 9th Lord Willoughby de Broke; died July 21, 1884.

Blomfield (E.C.) — FRANCIS. 4th son of Rt. Rev. C. J. B., Bp. of London; 1841[1]-1845[1]; Trin. Coll. Camb.; drowned off the coast of Newfoundland 1860.

Croft (W.E., E.C.) — SIR JOHN FREDERICK, 2nd Bt. Son of Sir J. C., 1st Bt., of Dodington; 1841[1]-1846[2]; Ball. Coll. Oxf.; J.P. for Kent, High Sheriff 1872; *m.* Emma, *d.* of John Graham. *Dodington, Sittingbourne, Kent.*

Jones-Bateman (Miss W., F.E.D.) — PHILIP WYTHEN. Son of J. J-B. of Pentre-Mawr, Denbighshire; 1841[1]-1846[1]; Opp. Wall 1845; Oxf.; drowned whilst bathing at Abergele, N. Wales, 1849.

Mr. Hanbury *min.* (H.D.) — HON. A. A. (aft. Bateman-Hanbury). 1847.

Pipe-Wolferstan *ma.* (E.B.) — FRANCIS STAFFORD. Of Statfold, near Tamworth; eld. son of S. P-W. of Statfold; 1841[1]-1845[3]; Opp. Wall 1845; Eton XI. 1845; Ball. Coll. Oxf. B.A.; Barrister, Oxf. Circuit; J.P. cos. Derby, Stafford, and Warwick; *m.* Sarah Maria Hill, *d.* of William Hallowes Belli, H.E.I.C.S.; died Nov. 1900.

Mirehouse (E.H.P.) — JOHN. Of Brownslade and Angle, Pembroke; eld. son of J. C. M. of Brownslade and Angle; 1840[2]-1845[3]; Trin. Coll. Camb. M.A.; Barrister, Home Circuit; *m.* Louisa Catherine, *d.* of Leyson O. Lewis; died Jan. 8, 1864.

Marsh (Mrs. Hor., W.G.C.) — MARTIN WILLIAM JAMES. 1840[1]-1844[2]; Merton Coll. Oxf.; died at Athens while an undergraduate at Merton.

Ames *ma.* (Mrs. Ro., J.W.) — GEORGE ACLAND. Of Cote House, Westbury-on-Trym, co. Gloucester; eld. son of G. H. A. of Cote House; 1840[3]-1844[3]; formerly Cornet Glos. Hussars; Musical Composer; *m.* Clara Henrietta Marie, *d.* of Count Maximilian Elbert Alexander von Poletz, of P[illegible], in the Duchy of Altenburg; [illegible] Jan. 5, 18[illegible].

Close (W.G.C.)
MAXWELL CHARLES. Of Drumbanagher, Newry; eld. son of Col. M. C. of Drumbanagher; 1840^{3}–1845^{2}; Prince Consort's Prize, French and Italian 1845; Ch. Ch. Oxf. M.A.; J.P. and D.L. co. Armagh, High Sheriff 1854; M.P. for co. Armagh 1857–64 and 1874–85; *m.* Catherine Deborah Agnes, *d.* of Henry Samuel Close of Newtown Park, co. Dublin; died Jan. 26, 1903.

Penrhyn *ma.* (W.E., C.J.A.)
EDWARD HUGH (aft. Leycester-Penrhyn). Eld. son of E. P. (formerly Leycester); 1840^{3}–1845^{2}; Ball. Coll. Oxf. M.A.; J.P. and D.L. co. Surrey; J.P. for Hants; formerly Chmn. of Qr. Sessions and C.C. for Surrey; and Major 1st Royal Surrey Militia; *m.* Vere, *d.* of Robert Gosling of Botleys Park, Surrey, and of Hassobury, Essex. *East Sheen, Surrey.*

Kaye (E.B.)
JOSEPH. Son of W. K. of Tetworth Hall, Sandy, Beds; 1841^{1}–1846^{1}; Merton Coll. Oxf. M.A.; 3rd Class Lit. Hum.; Postmaster of Merton 1846–50; Barrister Home Circuit; Master of Supreme Court of Judicature; *m.* Mary St. Quintin, *d.* of G. Astell of Ickwell, Biggleswade; died June 27, 1901.

Mr. Lascelles *ma.* (W.A.C.)
HON. ALGERNON FRANCIS. 4th son of Henry, 3rd Earl of Harewood; 1841^{3}–1845^{1}; died of fever at Eton, March 28, 1845.

Howard *ma.* (Mrs. Hor., W.A.C.)
GEORGE. Eld. son of Very Rev. H. E. H., D.D., Dean of Lichfield; 1839^{3}–1844^{3}; Ch. Ch. Oxf. M.A.; Barrister, Inner Temple, 1852; Librarian House of Commons 1867–87; *m.* Marion, *d.* of Edward Southam, M.D., and widow of William Leigh Bennett. *Brighstone, Newport, Isle of Wight.*

Heywood (Miss A., C.J.A.)
ARTHUR HENRY. Of Elleray, Windermere; 3rd son of Sir B. H., 1st Bt. of Claremont, Manchester; 1839^{3}–1844^{3}; Banker; J.P. Lancs and Westmorland; *m.* 1st, Alice, *d.* of William Langton of the Rookery, near Manchester; 2nd, Margaret Helen, *d.* of John Frederic Foster of Alderley Edge, near Manchester; died March 11, 1901.
W. J. . 1847.

Smith (Mrs. Ro., aft. K.S., W.L.E.)
BERTRAM WODEHOUSE. Of Minley Manor, Farnborough, Hants, and Coombe Warren, Surrey; 2nd son of R. C. of Bush Hill, co. Middlesex; 1840^{3}–1845^{1}; Banker; J.P. for Surrey and Hants; High Sheriff of London 1892; *m.* Caroline, *d.* of Sir William Lawrence Young, 4th Bt.; died 1896.

Currie *ma.* (E.H.P.)

Dickson (W.L.E.)
ARTHUR BENSON. Of Abbot's Reading, Haverthwaite, Ulverston; 6th son of G. F. D. of Abbot's Reading; 1841^{1}–1845^{2}; Opp. Wall 1843–4, Keeper 1844; Trin. Coll. Camb. M.A.; Pres. C.U.B.C. 1848; Capt. 3rd Trin. Boat Club 1848; Barrister, Lincoln's Inn; J.P. for Lancs; *m.* Harriett Elizabeth, *d.* of John Barker of Broughton Lodge, Cartmel, Lancs; died Sept. 24, 1901.

Mr. Bligh (W.G.C.)
HON. AND REV. EDWARD VESEY. 2nd son of Edward, 5th Earl of Darnley; 1839^{3}–1845^{2}; Ch. Ch. Oxf. 1848–50; Oxf. Univ. XI. 1850; Downing Coll. Camb. M.A. 1854; Diplomatic Service, 1850–3; Rector of Rotherfield, Sussex, 1856–65; Vicar of Birling, Kent, 1865–75; D.L., J.P. and C.A. for Kent; *m.* Lady Isabel Mary Frances Nevill, *d.* of William, 4th Earl of Abergavenny. *6 Portman Sq., W., and Fartherwell, West Malling S.O., Kent.*

Freeman (C.L.)
JOHN ARTHUR. Only son of J. F. of Gaines, co. Hereford; 1839^{3}–1844^{3}; Capt. Scots Greys; died unm. of cholera in the Crimea, Sept. 29 1854.

Sutton (Mrs. Y., J.W.)
CORNELIUS GRAHAM. Son of S. of Hertingfordbury, Herts; 1839^{3}–1844^{3}; Eton VIII. 1844; Capt. 23rd Fusiliers; died the night the troops landed in the Crimea, Sept. 15, 1854.

Vernon-Smith (C.J.A.)
HON. AND REV. COURTENAY JOHN (aft. Vernon). 3rd son of Robert Vernon, 1st Lord Lyveden, of Farming Woods, Northants; 1839^{3}–1844^{3}; Trin. Coll. Camb. B.A.; Rector of Grafton Underwood, Northants; *m.* Alice Gertrude, *d.* of Rev. Maurice Fitzgerald Stephens Townshend of Castle Townshend, co. Cork; died July 2, 1892.

Robinson (Mrs. Ri., H.D.)
HENRY FREDERICK SAVILE. 1837^{3}–1841^{1}; readmitted from Sandhurst, 1842^{1}–1844^{2}; won Pulling 1843; Trin. Coll. Camb.

Mr. Finch (W.G.C.)
HON. DANIEL GREVILLE. 2nd son of Heneage, 5th Earl of Aylesford; 1839^{3}–1844^{3}; Cox Eton VIII. 1844; Lieut.-Col. 24th Foot; Crimean Med. with three clasps, Medjidie and Turkish Med.; died Feb. 22, 1882.
C. B. . 1847.

Borradaile (R.F.H., aft. K.S., C.L.)

Ranken (Mrs. Hor., E.B.)
GEORGE ELLIOT. 1841^{3}–1845^{1}; Newc. Select 1845; Univ. Coll. Oxf.; 2nd Cl. Class.; formerly Capt. Glamorgan Artillery Militia.
W. . 1847.

Wayte *ma.* (Miss W., aft. K.S., F.E.D.)

Cust (Miss W., H. D.)
SIR R. J., Kt. . 1847.

Chenery (J.E.Y.)
THOMAS. 1841^{3}–1844^{3}; Caius Coll. Camb.; Barrister, Home Circuit; Editor of the 'Times'; died 1884.

Welby *ma.* (C.O.G.)
SIR WILLIAM EARLE (aft. Welby-Gregory), 4th Bt. Of Denton Manor, near Grantham; eld. son of Sir G. E. W.-G., 3rd Bt., of Denton Manor; 1841^{3}–1847^{1}; Newc. Select 1847; Ch. Ch. Oxf. B.A. 1851; M.P. for Grantham 1857–68, and S. Lincs 1868–84; J.P. and D.L. co. Lincoln, High Sheriff 1890; Chmn. of Kesteven C.C.; J.P. co. Leicester; *m.* Hon. Victoria Alexandrina Maria Louisa, *d.* of Hon. Charles Stuart-Wortley; died Nov. 26, 1898.

Luxmoore (Mrs. Ro., J.W.)
FREDERICK. 2nd son of Rev. C. T. C. L., Vicar of Guilsfield, Welshpool; 1840^{3}–1847^{1}; Lieut. 30th Regt.; killed at the Battle of Alma, Sept. 20, 1854.

Gaisford (Mrs. P., C.O.G.)
REV. GEORGE. 5th son of Very Rev. T. G., D.D., Dean of Ch. Ch. Oxf.; 1840^{3}–1845^{3}; Ch. Ch. Oxf. M.A.; formerly Rector of Tangmere, Chichester, and aft. Rector of East Lavant, Sussex; *m.* Agnes, *d.* of Sir Charles Mills, 1st Bt., of Hillingdon Court, Uxbridge; died June 25, 1903.

Lord Robert Cecil (W.G.C.)
SIR ROBERT ARTHUR TALBOT GASCOYNE-CECIL (3rd Marquis of Salisbury), K.G., P.C., G.C.V.O., F.R.S., D.C.L., LL.D. (Hon. Camb.), D.L., J.P. 2nd son of James Brownlow William, 2nd Marquis of Salisbury, K.G.; 1840^{3}–1845^{2}; Ch. Ch. Oxf., B.A.; Hon. Student 1894; Fellow of All Souls 1853; M.P. Stamford 1853–68; Sec. for India and Pres. of Indian Council 1866–7 and 1874–8; Spec. Ambassador for Conf. at Constantinople 1876–7; Plenipotentiary at Congress of Berlin 1878; First Lord of Trea. 1886–7; Sec. of State for For. Affairs 1878–80, 1885–6, 1887–92, and 1895–1900; Prime Min. 1885–6, 1886–92, and 1895–1902; formerly Chmn. Gt. Eastn. Ry.; Lord Privy Seal 1900; High Steward of Westminster 1900–3; Chanc. of Univ. of Oxf. 1869 1903; Member of Council

Lord Robert Cecil —*cont.* — of King's Coll. London; Lord Warden of Cinque Ports, and Constable of Dover Castle 1895–1903; High Steward of Gt. Yarmouth 1888–1903; Elder Bro. of Trin. House 1886–1903; Hon. Col. 4th Bn. Beds Regt. 1868–1903; *m.* Georgina Caroline (V.A., C.I.), *d.* of Hon. Sir Edward Hall Alderson, a Baron of the Exchequer; died Aug. 22, 1903.

James (Miss W., aft. K.S., F.E.D.) — C. C. . 1847.

Colquhoun (E.B.) — ARCHIBALD CAMPBELL. Of Killermont and Garscadden, Dumbarton; eld. son of J. C. C. of Killermont and Garscadden; 1841^{1}–1844^{2}; Dep. Assist. Commissary-General; died 1872.

Sayer (H.D.) — JAMES ROBERT STEADMAN, C.B. Son of R. S., D.L., of Sibton Park, Suffolk; 1840^{3}–1844^{2}; Lieut.-Gen. and Col. 1st King's Dragoon Gds.; *m.* A. S., *d.* of William Blundell. *4 Ovington Gardens, S.W.*

Holland (Mrs. Hor., F.E.D.) — REV. CANON FRANCIS JAMES. 2nd son of Sir H. H., 1st Bt., M.D., of London; 1841^{1}–1845^{3}; Pres. Eton Soc. 1844; Eton XI. 1845; Opp. Wall 1844–5, Capt. 1844; Trin. Coll. Camb. M.A.; Junr. Optime; Vicar of St. Dunstan's, Canterbury, 1853–61; Minister of Quebec Chapel, London, 1861–82; Canon of Canterbury Cath. since 1882; Chaplain to the King; Prior of St. John's Hospital; *m.* Mary Sybilla, *d.* of Rev. Alfred Lyall, Rector of Harbledown. *Precincts, Canterbury; and The Lodge, Harbledown, Canterbury.*

Green *ma.* (Mrs. Ro., aft. K.S., W.A.C.) — G. C. . 1847.

Gordon (R.O.) — CHARLES HENRY WILLIAM. Of Newtimber Place, Hurstpierpoint; eld. son of C. G. of Newtimber Place; 1841^{2}–1845^{2}; Univ. Coll. Oxf.; *m.* Lucy, *d.* of Col. E. F. Grant, R.H.A., of Southend, Eltham; died Feb. 22, 1887.

Gurdon (E.H.P.) — R. T. (Lord Cranworth). 1847.

Jeddere-Fisher (Mrs. P., C.O.G.) — CYRIL. 1841^{3}–1844^{2}; Trin. Coll. Camb. M.A.; a Wrangler 1850.

Johnstone (Mrs. Hor., E.H.P.) — CHARLES EDWARDS. Son of G. J.; 1840^{3}–1844^{2}; Trin. Coll. Camb.; *m.* Elizabeth, *d.* of — Abel; dead.

Deacon (E.H.P.) — W. S. . 1847.

Coltman *ma.* (W.E., E.C.) — WILLIAM BACHELER. Of Blelack, Dinnet, N.B.; son of Sir Thomas C., a Judge of the Court of Common Pleas; 1841^{1}–1845^{3}; Sch. of Trin. Coll. Camb.; 13th Wrangler 1851; Barrister, Inner Temple; Lt.-Col. Inns of Court Rifles; *m.* Bertha Elizabeth Shore, *d.* of Samuel Smith of Embley Park, Hants; died Oct. 22, 1902.

Babington (R.O.) — WILLIAM. Son of Capt. W. B., 6th Madras Cav.; 1840^{2}–1844^{2}; Eton VIII. 1843; Opp. Wall 1842–3; formerly Lt.-Col. 7th Hussars; *m.* Augusta, *d.* of James Moncrief Melville of Hanley. *Brooklands, Sarisbury, Southampton.*

Broke (E.B.) — HORACE. Son of Major-Gen. H. G. B. of Cecil Lodge, Herts; 1841^{3}–1845^{3}; Ch. Ch. Oxf. M.A.; Barrister, Lincoln's Inn; Sec. to Lord Justice Sir G. Mellish 1870–7; J.P. for Essex; *m.* 1st, Charlotte, *d.* of Brampton Gurdon of Letton, Norfolk; 2nd, Georgina M., *d.* of Sir Richard Mayne, K.C.B. *Gladwyns, Harlow, Essex.*

Still (R.F.H., aft. K.S., E.B.) — H. H. . 1847.

Dampier (W.E., F.E.D.) — HENRY LUCIUS, C.I.E. Son of W. D. of the Bengal Civil Service; 1841^{3}–1844^{2}; East India Coll. Haileybury; ent. I.C.S. 1848; Member of Bengal Legislative Council 1874–9; Board of Revenue 1877; Pres. of Rent Law Commission 1881, ret. 1884; *m.* Charlotte Isabella Lindsay, *d.* of Francis Gouldsbury of the Bengal Civil Service. *Fairholme, Parkstone, Dorset.*

Headlam (Miss Edw., aft. K.S., E.B.) — F. J. . 1847.

Lewis (J.E.Y.) — JOHN DELAWARE. Of Westbury House, Petersfield, and Membland, Devonshire; son of J. D. L. of Westbury; 1841^{1}–1844^{2}; Trin. Coll. Camb. M.A.; Barrister, Home Circuit; J.P. for Hants; M.P. for Devonport 1868–74; *m.* Teresa, *d.* of Sir Jervoise Clarke-Jervoise, 2nd Bt., of Idsworth Park, Hants; died July 31, 1884.

Johnstone (W.A.C.) — HARCOURT VANDEN BEMPDE (1st Lord Derwent). Eld. son of Sir J. V. B. J., 2nd Bt., of Hackness; 1841^{3}–1845^{3}; Opp. Wall 1844–5; formerly Lieut. 2nd Life Gds., and Major E. Riding Art. Vol.; J.P. and D.L., N. Riding of Yorks; M.P. for Scarborough 1869–80; *m.* Charlotte, *d.* of Sir Charles Mills, 1st Bart., of Hillingdon, Middlesex. *Hackness Hall, Scarborough.*

Yonge (Mrs. Hor., F.E.D.) — REV. WILLIAM WELLINGTON. Son of Rev. W. J. Y., Rector of Rockbourne, Salisbury; 1840^{2}–1847^{1}; Exeter Coll. Oxf. M.A.; Rector of Shottesbrooke and White Waltham, Berks; died unm. Feb. 27, 1878.

Alderson *ma.* (W.E., E.C.) — EDWARD PAKENHAM. Eld. son of Sir E. H. A., a Baron of the Exchequer; 1840^{1}–1846^{2}; Ball. Coll. Oxf.; formerly a Barrister, aft. a Merchant in London; *m.* Mildred Anne (Lady Scott), *d.* of Sir William Edmund Cradock-Hartopp, 3rd Bt., and widow of Sir Francis Edward Scott, 3rd Bt.; died Dec. 1, 1876.

Bayley (R.F.H., C.L.) — REV. JOHN ARDEN. 1840^{2}–1846^{1}; Oriel Coll. Oxf. B.A.; formerly Curate of Woodford, Northants.

Currie *mi.* (Mrs. Ro., E.H.P.) — REV. MAYNARD WODEHOUSE. 3rd son of R. C. of Bush Hill co. Middlesex; 1841^{2}–1845^{3}; Trin. Coll. Camb. M.A.; formerly Vicar of Mentmore, Bucks; aft. Rector of Hingham, Norfolk; *m.* Lady Charlotte Georgina Mary Cadogan, *d.* of Henry Charles, 4th Earl Cadogan; died 1887.

Baillie *ma.* (W.G.C.) — GENERAL DUNCAN JAMES. Of Loch Loy, Nairn; 3rd son of Col. H. D. B. of Redcastle, and Tarradale, N.B.; 1840^{3}–1845^{1}; formerly Col. Comm. Royal Horse Gds.; J.P. and D.L. co. Nairn, and Convener for the county; *m.* Anna Gleutworth, *d.* of Rev. Gustavus Andrew Burnaby of Somerby Hall, co. Leicester; died 1890.

Taylor (Miss W., aft. K.S., F.E.D.) — CHARLES HENRY LISLE. Of Tor-Cross, Devon; 1839^{2}–1844^{2}; died shortly after leaving Eton.

Ames *mi.* (E.H.P.) — C. H. . 1847.

Stanbrough (Mrs. Hor., aft. K.S., W.L.E.) — M. E. . 1847.

Mr. Eliot *ma.* (C.J.A.) — Hon. Granville Charles Cornwallis. 2nd son of Edward Granville, 3rd Earl of St. Germans, of Port Eliot, St Germans, Cornwall; 1840^{3}–1845^{1}: Capt. Coldstream Gds.; fell in action at the battle of Inkermann, Nov. 5, 1854.

Patteson *mi.* (E.C.) — James Henry. 2nd son of Judge P.; 1840^{3}–1847^{1}; Keeper of Opp. Wall 1844; Barrister; formerly Sec. of the Court of Probate.

Douglas (E.H.P.) — Robert Archibald. Of 14 Cromwell Crescent, S.W.; 2nd son of Rev Canon H. D. of Whickham, Swalwell, co. Durham (Canon of Durham); 1840^{3}–1844^{3}; St. John's Coll. Camb. M.A.; Barrister, Inner Temple; died unm. Nov. 27, 1899.

Mr. de Ros (W.G.C.) — Lieut.-Gen. Hon. Dudley Charles Fitzgerald (24th Lord de Ros), K.P., K.C.V.O. Son of William Lennox Lascelles, 23rd Lord de Ros; 1840^{3}–1844^{2}; entd. 1st Life Gds. 1845; Major and Lieut.-Col. 1859; Comm. 1861–72; Equerry to H.R.H. Prince Consort 1853–61; Equerry to the Queen 1861–74; Lord-in-Waiting 1874–80, 1885–6, and 1886–92; J.P. and D.L. co. Down; m. 1st, Lady Elizabeth Egerton, d. of Thomas, 2nd Earl of Wilton; 2nd, Mary Geraldine, d. of Rev. Sir William Vesey Ross Mahon, 4th Bt. *28 Wilton Crescent, S.W., and Old Court, Strangford, co. Down.*

Currie (R.O.) — Henry William. Son of H. C. of West Horsley Place, Surrey; 1839^{3}–1844^{2}; J.P. for Northants; formerly M.P. for Guildford; m. Flora Caroline, d. of Hon. and Ven. Archdn. Henry Reginald Yorke. *Rushden House, Higham Ferrers.*

Thursby (Miss Edw., C.J.A.) — Sir John Hardy, 1st Bt. Of Ormerod House, Burnley; eld. son of Rev. W. T. of Ormerod House; 1840^{1}–1844^{3}; formerly Lieut. 90th Lt. Inf.; J.P. and D.L. co. Lancaster, High Sheriff 1867; Hon. Col. 3rd Bn. E. Lancs Regt.; m. 1st, Clara, d. of Col. Williams, R.E.; 2nd, Louisa Harriet, d. of John George Smyth of Heath Hall, Wakefield; died March 16, 1901.

Williamson (E.H.P.) — Sir Hedworth, 8th Bt. Of Whitburn Hall, Sunderland; eld. son of Sir Hedworth, 7th Bt., of Whitburn; 1840^{3}–1844^{3}; won Pulling 1844; Ch. Ch. Oxf.; J.P. and D.L. co. Durham, High Sheriff 1877; formerly Capt. Durham Vol. Art.; M.P. for North Durham 1864–74; Attaché at St. Petersburg, and at Paris; m. Lady Elizabeth Liddell, d. of Henry Thomas, 1st Earl of Ravensworth; died August 26, 1900.

Stevenson (F.E.D.) — William George. Of Foxlease, Lyndhurst, Hants; eld. son of G. S. of Batsford Hall, Charlton Kings, Cheltenham; 1840^{3}–1844^{3}; formerly 69th Foot and Scots Gds.; J.P. cos. Hants, Gloucester, and Brecon; m. Maria Anne, d. of Col. Hardress Robert Saunderson of Northbrook House, Hants. *32 First Avenue, Brighton.*

Myers *ma.* (W.G.C.) — Thomas Borron. Of Porters Park, co. Herts; eld. son of W. J. M. of Porters Park; 1840^{3}–1844^{3}; Ch. Ch. Oxf. M.A.; J.P. cos. Herts and Middlesex; formerly Capt. Herts Militia; m. Margaret Storie, d. of Rev. Henry Melvill, B.D., Canon of St. Paul's; died March 3, 1881.

Abbot (Mrs. D., W.G.C.) — Samuel Thomas. Of Chigwell, Essex; 1840^{3}–1844^{3}; Eton xi. 1843–4; dead.

Luttrell (Mrs. Y. and Mrs. D., C.J.A., and J.E.Y.) — George Fownes. Eld. son of Lieut.-Col. F. F. L. of Kilve Court and Wootton House, Somerset; 1840^{3}–1846^{2}; Eton viii. 1845 6, Capt. 1846; Ch. Ch. Oxf. B.A.; J.P. and D.L. co. Somerset, High Sheriff 1874; m. Anne Elizabeth Periam, d. of [illegible]

Myers *mi.* (W.G.C.) — Charles. Of Swanmore, Hants; 2nd son of W. J. M. of Porters Park, Herts; 1840^{3}–1844^{2}; formerly a Merchant in Liverpool and J.P. for Lancs; m. Henrietta, d. of Henry Ashton of Woolton Wood, Lancs, and Poulton Hey, Cheshire; died Sept. 26, 1879.

Williams (W.L.E., aft. K.S., W.L.E.) — John Strahan. Son of a Barrister; 1837^{3}–1846^{1}.

Peel *mi.* (E.C.) — Capt. John Floyd. 4th son of Rt. Hon. Sir R. P., 2nd Bt., M.P., of Drayton Manor, Tamworth; 1840^{3}–1844^{3}; Opp. Wall 1843–4; formerly Capt. 2nd Bn. Scots Fus. Gds.; m. Annie, d. of Edward Jenner of Eccrea. *9 Connaught Sq., Hyde Park, W.*

Middle Division.

Beamont (J.E.Y.) — Rev. William John. 1842^{2}–1846^{2}; Newc. Select 1845, Med. 1846; Prince Consort's French and Italian Prize 1844, and Italian Prize 1844; Trin. Coll. Camb.; 3rd Cl. Classic, Chanc. Med. 1850; Fellow of Trin. Coll.

Boileau *ma.* (W.E., W.G.C.) — John Elliot. Eld. son of Sir J. P. B., 1st Bt., of Tacolnestone Hall, Norwich; 1841^{3}–1845^{1}; Prince Consort's French Prize 1844; formerly Private Sec. to Earl Russell; died at Dieppe, Oct. 8, 1861.

Booth (Mrs. Ri., aft. K.S., H.D.) — C. . 1847.

Fremantle *ma.* (W.E., E.B.) — Hon. T. F. (Lord Cottesloe). 1847.

Wilson (E.C.) — Henry Maitland. 2nd son of H. W. of Stowlangtoft Hall, Bury St. Edmunds; 1840^{3}–1846^{1}; Merton Coll. Oxf.; formerly Capt. W. Suffolk Militia; m. Elizabeth, d. of Charles Wriothesley Digby of Meriden, Coventry; dead.

Stephen *ma.* (Home, E.B.) — Sir James Fitzjames, 1st Bt., K.C.S.I., D.C.L., LL.D. Eld. son of Rt. Hon. Sir J. S., K.C.B., LL.D.; 1842^{3}–1845^{2}; Trin. Coll. Camb. M.A. (Hon. Fellow 1885); Barrister, Inner Temple; Q.C. 1868; Recorder of Newark 1859–69; Legal Member of Council of Governor-Gen. of India 1869–72; Prof. of Common Laws at Inns of Court 1875–9; Judge of High Court of Judicature 1879–91; m. Mary Richenda, d. of Rev. John William Cunningham, Vicar of Harrow; died March 11, 1894.

Nash (C.J.A.) — Rev. George Lloyd. 1841^{3}–1845^{2}; Ch. Ch. Oxf. M.A.; formerly Vicar of Tolpuddle, Dorchester.

Foster *ma.* (Mrs. P., E.C.) — Charles. 2nd son of Sir W. F., 1st Bt., of Thorpe; 1842^{3}–1847^{1}; Opp. Wall 1846; won Steeplechase 1846; Trin. Coll. Camb. B.A.; 2nd Cl. Class.; formerly a Barrister, aft. a Solicitor at Norwich; Clerk of the Peace and Clerk of C.C. for Norfolk; m. 1st, Harriet, d. of Capt. Thomas George Wills, R.N.; 2nd, Georgina Gertrude, d. of Lieut.-Col. Edward George Cubitt. *Thorpe, Norwich.*

Sadler (J.E.Y.) — Col. Sir James Hayes, C.B., K.C.M.G., F.R.G.S. Son of Rev. J. H. S. of 1 Portman Sq., and Keynshambury, Cheltenham; 1841^{3}–1845^{3}; St. Mary Hall Oxf.; Hon. Col. Sussex Militia Art.; Consul at Chicago 1886; Consul-Gen. at Valparaiso 1895–7; m. Sophia Jane, d. of James Taylor, H.E.I.C.S. *73 Queen's Gate, S.W.*

Coleridge *mi.* — H. . 1847.

Whymper (Miss W., J.E.Y.)
F. H. . 1847.

Talfourd *ma.* (Miss A., W.G.C.)
FRANCIS. Son of Judge T. N. T.: 1840[3]-1845[2]; Eton VIII. 1845; Ch. Ch. Oxf.; Barrister Oxf. Circuit; Dramatic Author; died at Mentone, March 9, 1862.

Blore (W.E., E.C.)
E. W. . 1847.

Bowden (E.B.)
REV. JOHN EDWARD. Son of J. W. B. of 17 Grosvenor Place, S.W.: 1841[3]-1847[1]; Trin. Coll. Oxf.; Roman Catholic Priest in The Oratory at Brompton; died Dec. 1874.

Mr. Portman (C.O.G.)
HON. WILLIAM HENRY BERKELEY (2nd Viscount Portman). Eld. son of Edward Berkeley, 1st Viscount P.; 1842[1]-1845[2]; Merton Coll. Oxf.; J.P. and D.L. for Dorset and Somerset; M.P. for Shaftesbury 1852-7, for Dorset 1857-85; Col. W. Somerset Yeo.; Chmn. of Dorset C.C. *Bryanston, Blandford; Wentworth Lodge, Bournemouth; and 22 Portman Sq., W.*

Harford (C.J.A. & W.A.C.)
WILLIAM HENRY. Of Oldown House, Tockington, Glos.; eld. son of W. H. H. of Barley Wood, Wrington, Bristol; 1841[3]-1846[2]; Ball. Coll. Oxf.; Banker at Bristol; J.P. and D.L. for Somerset, J.P. co. Gloucester; *m.* Ellen, *d.* of Rev. William Tower of How Hatch, Essex; died Nov. 2, 1903.

Jackson *ma.* (C.J.A.)
HUGH FREDERICK. 1840[3]-1844[3]; formerly a Solicitor, Lincoln's Inn.

Hamilton (Miss B. & Mrs. Ri., W.A.C.)
ALEXANDER HENRY ABERCROMBY. Son of A. H. H. of The Retreat, Devon; 1842[3]-1846[3]; Ch. Ch. Oxf. B.A.; Author of "Quarter Sessions," "Sir John Northcote," &c; J.P., D.L. and C.C. for Devon; Member of House of Laymen; *m.* 1st, Sophia Anne Adelaide, *d.* of Sir Robert Abercromby, 5th Bt.; 2nd, Flora Henrietta Maria, *d.* of Charles Edward Macdonald, E.I.C.S., and widow of Major G. J. Condy. *Fairfield Lodge, Exeter.*

Hunt *ma.* (C.J.A.)
REV. THOMAS HENRY. Eld. son of Rev. T. H., Rector of West Felton, Salop; 1841[3]-1844[3]; Ch. Ch. Oxf. M.A.; Vicar of Badsey, co. Worcester, and Rural Dean of Evesham; *m.* Charlotte, *d.* of Alexander West Hamilton of Pinmore, co. Ayr; died July, 1896.

St. Aubyn (F.E.D.)
JOHN (1st Lord St. Levan). Eld. son of Sir E. St. A., 1st Bt., of St. Michael's Mount; 1839[3]-1845[2]; Trin. Coll. Camb. M.A.; Special Deputy Warden of the Stannaries; Mayor of Devonport 1890-1 and 1891-2; J.P. and D.L. for Cornwall; M.P. for W. Cornwall 1858-85, Cornwall (St. Ives) 1885-6 and 1886-7; Hon. Col. 3rd Bn. Duke of Cornwall's Lt. Infty.; Commodore of Western Yacht Squadron; *m.* Lady Elizabeth Clementina Townshend, *d.* of John, 4th Marquis Townshend. *St. Michael's Mount, Marazion, Cornwall.*

Perceval (F.E.D.)
HENRY SPENCER. Son of Rev. H. P., Rector of Elmley Lovett, co. Worcester; 1840[3]-1844[3]; formerly in the Paymaster-General's Office; *m.* Fanny, *d.* of Rev. Thomas Taylor; died Jan. 21, 1876.

Lord St. Lawrence (Mrs. Ro., E.H.P.)
WILLIAM ULICK TRISTRAM, K.P. (4th Earl of Howth). Eld. son of Thomas, 3rd Earl of Howth; 1841[3]-1844[3]; J.P. and D.L., co. Dublin, High Sheriff 1854; formerly Capt. 7th Hussars, and Lt.-Col. Dublin [illegible]

Thoyts *ma.* (C.O.G.)
WILLIAM RICHARD MORTIMER. Eld. son of M. G. T. of Sulhamstead; 1841[3]-1846[1]; Univ. Coll. Oxf.; S.C.L. 1850; formerly Major Berks Militia; J.P. for Berks, High Sheriff 1883; *m.* Anne Annabella, *d.* of Col. Sir Richard Puleston, 2nd Bt., of Emral, co. Flint. *Sulhamstead Park, Reading.*

Coleridge (W.E., aft. K.S., E.C.)
A. D. . 1847.

Dunbar *ma.* (Mrs. Ro., F.E.D.)
MAJOR PENROSE JOHN. Eld. son of J. D. of the Bengal Civil Service; 1841[3]-1845[3]; formerly Major 3rd Buffs; served in the Crimea, wounded at the Redan; *m.* 1st, Elizabeth Ann Clarinda, *d.* of W. W. Leigh, M.D.; 2nd, Emma, *d.* of Charles Beddis. *59 Grosvenor Road, N.*

Tremayne *mi.* (H.D.)
H. H. . 1847.

Barlow (F.E.D.)
FRANCIS MOUNT. 1841[1]-1845[3]; Barrister.

Tyler (E.C.)
G. G. (aft. Griffin). . 1847.

Hill (Miss M., E.H.P.)
JOHN DAVID HAY. 1842[1]-1846[3]; Trin. Coll. Camb.; aft. in the Army.

Richards (W.A.C.)
SOLOMON AUGUSTUS. Of Ardamine, Gorey; eld. son of J. G. R. of Ardamine; 1842[1]-1845[3]; Trin. Coll. Oxf. B.A.; formerly Capt. Wexford Militia; J.P. co. Wexford, High Sheriff 1854; *m.* Sophia Mordaunt, *d.* of Rev. Bernard John Ward; died Jan. 13, 1874.

Hibbert (J.E.Y.)
ROGERS PARKER. Son of N. H. of Munden, Watford; 1841[3]-1844[3]; Lieut. 40th Regt.; *m.* Eliza, *d.* of C. McGillewie; died 1864.

Smith (Mrs. Ro., E.H.P.)
P. S. . 1847.

Erskine (E.B.)
REV. THOMAS. Of Dairsie, Cupar, co. Fife; son of E. of Dairsie; 1842[1]-1847[1]; Trin. Coll. Camb. M.A.; 2nd Cl. Class. 1851; Rector of Alderley; *m.* Emmeline Augusta, *d.* of Henry J. Adeane of Babraham, Camb.; died 1878.

Ethelston *ma.* (C.O.G.)
EDMUND (aft. Peel). Of Brynypys, Ellesmere, Salop; eld. son of Rev. C. W. E. of Uplyme Rectory and Wicksted Hall, Cheshire; 1840[3]-1845[3]; Eton VIII. 1844-5; won Sculling and Pulling 1844, Double Sculling 1845; Opp. Wall 1844; Keeper of the Field; Ch. Ch. Oxf.; J.P. cos. Flint, Denbigh, Salop, and Montgomery; High Sheriff of last co. 1858; D.L. co. Flint, High Sheriff 1870; *m.* 1st, Anna Maria, *d.* of Sir John Hesketh Lethbridge, 3rd Bt., of Sandhill; 2nd, Henrietta Margaret, *d.* of Sir Hugh Williams, 3rd Bt., of Bodelwyddan, N. Wales; died March 17, 1903.

Kaye (Mrs. Hor., W.A.C.)
LISTER LISTER-. Eld. son of Sir J. L. L.-K., 2nd Bt., of Denby Grange, Wakefield; 1841[3]-1844[3]; *m.* Lady Caroline Pepys, *d.* of Charles Christopher, 1st Earl of Cottenham; died at Surbiton, Surrey, April 12, 1855.

Richards (Mrs. Hor., E.H.P.)
REV. HENRY WILLIAM PARRY. 3rd son of W. P. R. of Park Cres., W.; 1840[3]-1845[3]; Eton VIII. 1845; Opp. Wall 1843-4; Keeper of the Field and Wall 1845; Ch. Ch. Oxf. M.A.; Vicar of Isleworth, Middlesex; aft. Rector of St. Giles-in-the-Fields, W.C., and [illegible] Jessie Margaret, *d.* [illegible] J.C.; died April 11, [illegible]

Pochin (W.L.E.)
REV. EDWARD NORMAN. 4th son of G. P. of Barkby Hall, co. Leicester; 1841^{3}–1846^{2}: Trin. Coll. Camb. M.A.: formerly Vicar of Sileby, Loughborough; aft. Vicar of Barkby, co. Leicester; *m.* Anna Sarah, *d.* of Rev. Thomas Loveday of Ilsley, Berks; died 1897.

Vivian (W.A.C.)
WILLIAM GRAHAM. Of Clyne Park, Blackpill, Swansea; 2nd son of J. H. V. of Singleton, co. Glamorgan; 1840^{3}–1844^{2}: J.P. and D.L. co. Glamorgan, High Sheriff 1868. *7 Belgrave Square, S.W.*

North (R.O.)
CHARLES. Son of F. N. of Rougham; 1840^{3}–1847^{1}; Trin. Coll. Camb. M.A.; Barrister; J.P. and D.L. for Norfolk; formerly Capt. Norfolk Art. Militia; *m.* Augusta, *d.* of Hon. and Rev. Thomas R. Keppel, Rector of North Creake, Norfolk. *Rougham Hall, Norfolk.*

Stuart (C.O.G.)
CLARENCE ESMÉ. Of Addington House, Reading; 3rd son of W. S. of Tempsford, Sandy, Beds, and Aldenham Abbey, Watford, Herts; 1840^{3}–1845^{2}: St. John's Coll. Camb. M.A.: *m.* Catherine, *d.* of Col. John Cuninghame of Caddel, Ayrshire; died Jan. 8, 1903.

Earle *mi.* (Miss W., aft. K.S., F.E.D.)
WILLIAM CHESELDEN. Son of H. E.; 1840^{3}–1846^{3}.

Bunny (W.G.C.)
LT.-COL. EDWARD JOHN (aft. St. John). Son of E. B. B. of Speen Hill, Berks; 1839^{3}–1846^{2}; Stroke of Eton VIII. 1846; won Sculling 1846; Ch. Ch. Oxf.; J.P. and D.L. for Sussex and J.P. for Berks; Lieut.-Col. (ret.) 4th Bn. R. Sussex Regt.; *m.* Mary St. John, *d.* of Robert Burnett Brander of Belmoredean, W. Grinstead, Sussex. *Slinfold, Horsham, Sussex.*

Fox (W.L.E.)
JOHN WILSON. Of Stratham Lodge, Cheshire, and Girsby Hall, Lincs; 1840^{3}–1844^{2}; formerly 12th Lancers, aft. Capt. Cheshire Yeo.

Bosanquet (F.E.D.)
HENRY ANSTEY. Of Clanville, Minehead, Somerset; son of H. B. of Clanville Lodge, Hants; 1840^{3}–1846^{2}; Opp. Wall 1844, Keeper 1845; Ch. Ch. Oxf. M.A.; Barrister, Home Circuit; J.P. for Somerset; *m.* Mary Anne, *d.* of Lieut.-Col. Luttrell of Kilve Court, Somerset; died Dec. 12, 1901.

Streatfeild *mi.* (R.F.H., C.O.G.)
N. W. . 1847.

Chitty (W.E., W.A.C.)
RIGHT HON. SIR J. W., P.C. 1847.

Munro *ma.* (E.B.)
STUART CARADOC. 3rd son of General J. M. of Teaninich; 1841^{3}–1844^{2}: J.P. co. Ross. *Teaninich, Alness, Ross-shire.*

Munro *mi.* (E.B.)
MAXWELL WILLIAM. 4th son of General J. M. of Teaninich, Alness, Ross-shire; 1841^{3}–1844^{2}: Coffee Planter in Ceylon; died Sept. 1854.

McNaghten (R.F.H., E.B.)
SIR FRANCIS EDMUND WORKMAN-, 3rd Bt. Eld. son of Sir E. C. W.-M., 2nd Bt., of Dundarave; 1842^{3}–1846^{2}; Lord-Lieut. co. Antrim since 1900; ent. Army 1846; served in Eastern Campaign 1854–5; Capt. 8th Hussars 1856; Lieut.-Col. 8th Hussars 1866–71; Hon. Col. 4th Bn. Irish Rifles since 1900: *m.* Alice Mary, *d.* of William Howard Russell, LL.D., of Sumner Place, Brompton. *Dundarave, Bushmills, co. Antrim.*

Herries (W.E., E.B.)
H. C. . 1847.

Wykeham-Martin (W.A.C.)
P. . 1847.

Richards (Miss W., E.B.)
JOHN ROBERT. Son of — R. of Plasnewydd, Cardiff; 1841^{3}–1845^{1}; died at Slough.

Mr. Neville *mi.* (E.H.P.)
HON. GREY. 5th son of Richard, 3rd Lord Braybrooke; 1842^{2}–1847^{1}: Cornet 5th Dragoon Gds.; died of wounds received in the Cav. charge at Balaclava Nov. 11, 1854.

Penrhyn *mi.* (W.E., C.J.A.)
REV. CANON OSWALD HENRY (aft. Leycester-Penrhyn). 2nd son of E. P. (formerly Leycester) of East Sheen, Surrey; 1842^{3}–1845^{2}; Ball. Coll. Oxf M.A.; Rural Dean; Canon of Liverpool; Chaplain to Bishop of Liverpool; Proctor in Convocation, and Rector of Winwick: *m.* Charlotte L. J., *d.* of Edmund G. Hornby of Dalton Hall, co. Lancaster. *Winwick Rectory, Newton-le-Willows, Lanc.*

Yonge (E.B.)
J. B. . 1847.

Hammond (Miss Edw., F.E.D.)
HENRY WALMSLEY. Son of Rev. — H., Rector of Preston, Bath; 1842^{3}–1844^{2}; Bengal Civil Service.

Feilden (Miss Edw., H.D.)
REV. JOHN ROBERT. 4th son of J. F. of Witton Park, Blackburn; 1840^{3}–1845^{2}; Student of Ch. Ch. Oxf., M.A.; Rural Dean of Holt, Norfolk; Hon. Canon of Norwich; Rector of Baconsthorpe, Holt, Norfolk, aft. Vicar of Honingham with E. Tuddenham, Norfolk; and Chaplain to the Marquis of Cholmondeley; *m.* Frances Blanche Anne, *d.* of Frederick, 4th Lord Calthorpe; died Dec. 20, 1891.

Mr. Curzon (E.C.)
GENERAL HON. SIR LEICESTER (aft. Curzon-Smyth), K.C.B., K.C.M.G. 7th son of Richard William Penn, 1st Earl Howe; 1841^{3}–1844^{2}; formerly in the Rifle Bgde.; served under Gen. Cathcart in Kaffir war 1852; Knt. of Legion of Honour and Medjidie; A.D.C. and Assist. Mil. Sec. to Lord Raglan in the Crimea; brought to Eng. the despatches announcing fall of Sebastopol; Mil. Sec. in Ireland 1865–70; Comm.-in-Chief at Cape of Good Hope 1880–5; Gov. and Comm.-in-Chief of Gibraltar 1890–1; comm. troops in Southern District 1889; medals for Zulu War and Crimea; *m.* Alicia Maria Eliza, *d.* of Robert Smyth, of Drumcree, co. Westmeath; J.P. and D.L.; died Jan. 27, 1891.

Bryant (W.E., W.A.C.)
HENRY STRICKLAND. Son of Major-Gen. Sir J. B., C.B.; 1841^{3}–1844^{3}; Trin. Coll. Camb. M.A.; Civil Service, Education Dept.; *m.* Louisa L. E., *d.* of Rev. G. Newcomb, Vicar of Halberton, Tiverton. *Anstey Lodge, Alton, Hants.*

Dickinson (E.H.P., H.D.)
ALEXANDER WEDDERBONE. 1842^{2}–1845^{1}.

Saint (C.J.A., H.D.)
JOHN JAMES HEATH. Of Groombridge Place, Tunbridge Wells; son of Rev. J. J. S. of Groombridge Place; 1841^{3}–1846^{2}; Ch. Ch. Oxf. B.A.; Barrister and Recorder; *m. d.* of Andrew Lynch French; died March 7, 1895.

Marshall (J.E.Y.)
JOHN WILLIAM. Of Patterdale Hall, Penrith; eld. son of W. M. of Patterdale; 1841^{3}–1845^{2}; J. P. co. Westmorland; died unm. Feb. 4, 1881.

Peel *mi.* (E.C.)
A. W. . 1847.

Ansley *ma.* (Mrs. Ro., F.E.D.)
JOHN GILBERT. 1841^{3}–1845^{2}.

Powys *ma.* (Mrs. Ro., E.B.)
CHARLES RICHARD. Son of H. P. P. of Hardwick, Oxf.; 1841^{3}–1846^{2}: Exeter Coll. Oxf. B.A.; St. John's Coll. M.A.; *m.* Mrs. Phillips, *d.* of Thomas Duffield. *Rofford, Wallingford.*

Grenfell *ma.* (W.E., E.B.)
PASCOE DU PRÉ. Of Wilton Park, Beaconsfield; eld. son of P. St. L. G. of Maesteg House, Swansea; 1841^{3}–1846^{3}; formerly one of the firm of Grenfell & Sons, Copper Merchants, near Reading; aft. with Morton, Rose & Co., London; *m.* Sophia, *d.* of Vice-Adml. John Pascoe Grenfell of the Brazilian Service; died Nov. 29, 1896.

Page (Mrs. Ro., aft. K.S., E.B.)
J. . 1847.

Clissold (W.E., W.L.E.)
REV. EDWARD MORTIMER. Son of Rev. S. C., Rector of Wrentham, Wangford, Suffolk; 1841^{3}–1844^{3}; Exeter Coll. Oxf. B.A.; formerly Rector of Wrentham; *m.* Florence Jane Charlotte Giva, *d.* of Sir Edward Sherlock Gooch, 6th Bt., of Benacre Hall, Wangford, Suffolk. *Ravensworth, Cheltenham.*

Maynard (J.E.Y.)
WILLIAM ROPER. 1841^{3}–1845^{3}; formerly a Solicitor in Coleman St., London.

Eden *ma.* (Mrs. D., E.H.P.)
ARTHUR JOHN. Eld. son of A. E.; 1840^{3}–1845^{3}. *19 Bedford Sq., W.C.*

Manley (R.F.H., C.O.G.)
REV. JOHN JACKSON. Son of J. M., M.D., of Barking, Essex; 1842^{2}–1845^{3}; Exeter Coll. Oxf. M.A.; 2nd Class Honours; Vicar of Buckfastleigh, Devon; *m.* Hester Emmeline, *d.* of Robert C. Martin of Dagenham, Romford; died 1886.

Paget (C.J.A.)
REV. EDWARD HENEAGE. 4th son of Rev. F. E. P., Rector of Elford, Tamworth; 1842^{3}–1845^{3}; St. John's Coll. Oxf. M.A.; formerly Rector of Thistleton, Norfolk; aft. Vicar of Hoxne, Eye; *m.* Hon. Emma Mary Eden, *d.* of Robert, 3rd Lord Auckland; died Sept. 29, 1884.

Ford (R.F.H., C.O.G.)
RT. HON. SIR FRANCIS CLARE, G.C.B., G.C.M.G. Son of R. F.; 1842^{2}–1846^{1}; formerly in the 4th Lt. Dragoons; ent. the Diplomatic Service in 1852; H.M.'s Agent at the Commission at Halifax under the Treaty of Washington 1875–7; Envoy-Extraordinary and Minister Plenipotentiary to the Argentine Republic 1878–9; Minister Plen. and Consul-General to Uruguay 1879; Envoy Extr. and Min. Plen. to Brazil 1879–81, and to Greece 1881–4; app. Min. to the King of Spain 1884; Ambassador 1887; Amb. Extr. and Min. Plen. at Rome 1893–8; *m.* Anna, *d.* of Marquis of Garofalo; died 1899.

Thellusson (W.A.C.)
COL. ARTHUR JOHN BETHELL. Of Thellusson Lodge, Aldeburgh, Suffolk; son of Hon. A. T.; 1841^{3}–1844^{3}; J.P. for Suffolk; formerly Major Coldstream Gds.; aft. Hon. Col. Norfolk R.V.; *m.* 1st, Henrietta Frances Elizabeth, *d.* of Frederick William Thomas Vernon-Wentworth of Wentworth Castle, co. York; 2nd, Augusta Mathilde Henriette Louise, *d.* of George Heine of Hanover; died Oct. 18, 1901.

Oliver-Massey (C.L.)
AUGUSTUS SHAKESPEAR (Oliver on entering Eton). Eld. son of R. M. O.-M. of Tickford Abbey, Bucks; 1841^{1}–1844^{3}; Magd. Coll. Oxf.; died 1865.

Coke (Miss W., aft. K.S., E.B.)
G. F. . 1847.

Sidebottom (C.O.G.)
ALEXANDER ROBERT. 1842^{2}–1846^{3}; Trin. Coll. Camb.; Barrister.

Brown (Mrs. D., K.S., W.G.C.)
EDWARD PHILIP. 1840^{2}–1845^{3}.

Burton (Mrs. D., W.G.C.)
WILLIAM FITZWILLIAM. Eld. son of W. F. B. of Burton Hall; 1841^{3}–1844^{3}; formerly in the 4th Lt. Dragoons; J.P. co. Carlow, High Sheriff 1849; *m.* 1st, Coralie Augusta Frederica, *d.* of Henry Lloyd of Farrinrory, co. Tipperary; 2nd, Clara Louisa, *d.* of John Cayley of Bickley, Kent. *Burton Hall, Carlow.*

Jenner (Mrs. Ri., W.G.C.)
REV. ALFRED HERBERT. 2nd son of R. F. J. of Wenvoe Castle, Cardiff; 1841^{3}–1844^{3}; Trin. Hall Camb. M.A.; Rector of Wenvoe; *m.* Everilda, *d.* of George Thornhill of Diddington, co. Huntingdon; died May 8, 1867.

Shaw-Stewart (R.O.)
JOHN ARCHIBALD. Of 48 Chester Sq., S.W., and Dunrod, Torquay; 2nd son of Sir M. S.-S., 6th Bt.; 1840^{3}–1845^{3}; Ch. Ch. Oxf. M.A.; J.P. and D.L. co. Renfrew; J.P. Middlesex; Knt. of Grace of the Order of St. John of Jerusalem in England; member of Canterbury House of Laymen and London Diocesan Conferences; *m.* 1st, Helenora Margaret Angela, *d.* of Boyd Alexander of Ballochmyle; 2nd, Isabella Barbara, *d.* of T. C. Hume, and widow of Capt. J. H. T. Alexander, C.B., R.N., of Southbar; 3rd, Constance Mary, *d.* of Edward Johnston; died May 25, 1900.

Greene (H.D.)
HENRY AYLMER. 3rd son of T. G. of Slyne, Lancaster; 1841^{1}–1845^{3}; formerly in the Colonial Office, aft. War Department; died unm. Aug. 25, 1877.

Clutterbuck (W.A.C.)
DANIEL HUGH. 2nd son of T. C. of Hardenhuish Park, Chippenham; 1841^{2}–1841^{3}; J.P. co. Wilts; formerly Capt. 8th Hussars; Crimean and Turkish Medals, 2 Clasps; ret. Banker; *m.* Sophia Ellen, *d.* of John William Spicer of Esher Place, Surrey. *Middlewick, Corsham, Wilts.*

Walker (W.G.C.)
HENRY. Son of J. N. W. of Calderstone, co. Lancaster; 1841^{1}–1845^{3}; D.L. co. Worcester, High Sheriff 1883; *m.* Georgina Harriett, *d.* of Francis Mostyn Owen of Bryntirion, co. Salop. *Perdiswell Hall, Worcester.*

Hammond *mi.* (Mrs. Hor., F.E.D.)
RICHARD HARVEY. Son of — H., Surgeon at Eton; 1840^{2}–1845^{3}.

Cooper (Mrs. D., W.G.C.)
FREDERICK JOHN. 1840^{2}–1845^{3}; Magd. Coll. Oxf.

Tredcroft (W.G.C.)
EDWARD. Of Warnham Court; eld. son of H. T. of Warnham Court, Horsham; 1840^{2}–1844^{3}; formerly in the 4th Lt. Dragoon Gds.; D.L. for Sussex; *m.* Theodosia Sophia, *d.* of Edward Bligh; dead.

Balguy *ma.* (Mrs. Ri., F.E.D.)
CHARLES YELVERTON. Of Fairfax, Hampton Hill, Middlesex; 3rd son of J. B. of Duffield, Derby; 1841^{1}–1844^{3}; formerly Major 42nd Highlanders; aft. Agent for Life, Fire, Accident and Burglary Insurance; *m.* 1st, Lucy Adela, *d.* of Col. Caulfield of Broomfield, co. Westmeath; 2nd, Ellen Elizabeth, *d.* of Henry Marwood Greaves of Hesley Hall, Notts; died Oct. 1900.

Paul (C.O.G.)
CHARLES KEGAN. Son of Rev. C. P., Vicar of Wellow Bath; 1841^{2}–1846^{3}; Exeter Coll. Oxf. B.A.; Curate of Great Tew, Enstone, Oxf. 1851; Bloxham, Banbury, 1852; Assist. Master at Eton 1855–62, Conduct 1853–61; Vicar of Sturminster Marshall, Wimborne, 1862–74; Publisher 1874–99; *m.* Margaret Agnes, *d.* of Andrew Colvile of Ochiltree, Cumnock, N.B.; died July 19, 1902.

Mr. Deane (Mrs. D., W.G.C.) — Hon. Robert Tilson Fitzmaurice (aft. Deane-Morgan). Eld. son of Matthew Fitzmaurice, 3rd Lord Muskerry; 1840³-1844²; m. Elizabeth Geraldine, d. of H. K. Grogan Morgan of Johnstown Castle; died Feb 28, 1857.

Sutherland *ma.* (Mrs. D., W.G.C.) — George. Of Forse House, Lybster, Wick: 2nd son of J. C. S. of Forse; 1840³-1845²; J.P. and D.L. co. Caithness; m. Mary Elizabeth, d. of William G. Sheppard of Lamogne, co. Waterford.

Sutherland *mi.* (Mrs. D., W.G.C.) — Francis. Of 7 Cranley Gardens, S.W.; 3rd son of J. C. S. of Forse House, Lybster, Wick; 1840³-1845²; J.P. cos. Caithness and Hereford; Capt. 2nd Dragoons (in Crimea); m. Constance, d. of John Freeman of Gaines, Hereford; died Oct. 23, 1901.

Hamond (C.J.A.) — William Parker. Of Haling House, Croydon, and Pampisford Hall, Camb.; son of W. P. H. of Pampisford; 1841¹-1844¹; Trin. Coll. Camb.; Barrister; J.P. and D.L. co. Camb., High Sheriff 1879; died 1884.

Luxmoore (W.L.E.) — Edward Bouverie. Son of Rev. J. H. M. L., Vicar of Marchwiel, Wrexham; 1841³-1845²; Trin. Coll. Camb. M.A.; m. Maria, d. of Capt. Wily; dead.

Wiss (Mrs. Hor., W.G.C.) — Brother of A. P. W. 1839³-1844³.

Becher (W.E., E.H.P.) — Sir Henry Wrixon-, 2nd Bt. Of Ballygiblin, Mallow; eld. son of Sir W. W-B., 1st Bt., of Ballygiblin; 1841¹-1844²; Univ. Coll. Oxf.; D.L. co. Cork; m. Florence Elizabeth Hannah, d. of Frederick John Walker of The Priory, Bath; died Nov. 25, 1893.

Greene (H.D.) — Richard. Son of — G., Banker at Lichfield; 1840³-1844³.

Errington *ma.* (W.G.C.) — George Henry. Of Chadwell Hall, Essex; eld. son of G. H. E. of Chadwell, and Lexden Park, Colchester; 1840³-1844³; Eton viii. 1844; formerly 1st King's Dragoon Gds.; J.P. for Essex; m. Isobel Lannette, d. of John Hopton Forbes of Merry Oak, Southampton; died 1900.

Mousley (Mrs. Y., W.L.E.) — Charles. Son of — M., Solicitor at Derby; 1839³-1844³; Magd. Coll. Camb.; died in New Zealand.

Preston (R.F.H., F.E.D.) — Richard. 1841¹-1844³; formerly Capt. and Brevet-Major 44th Regt.

Lower Division.

Antrobus (R.O.) — R. C. . 1847.

Peel (F.E.D.) — H. R. . 1847.

Mills (R.F.H., E.B.) — C. H. (Lord Hillingdon). 1847.

Palmer *ma.* (W.E., E.H.P.) — Rev. Richard Thomas. 5th son of Sir J. H. P., 5th Bt., of Carlton Park, Rockingham, Uppingham; 1841³-1844³; Univ. Coll. Oxf. M.A.; died Sept. 19, 1861.

Palmer *mi.* (W.E., E.H.P.) — Rev. Francis. 6th son of Sir J. H. P., 5th Bt., of Carlton Park, Rockingham, Uppingham; 1841³-1846³; Merton Coll. Oxf. M.A.; formerly Curate of St. John's Paddington; aft. Incumbent of St. George's Chapel, Albemarle Street, London.

Parker (Miss Edw., F.E.D.) — C. S. . 1847.

Johnson (W.G.C.) — J. G. . 1847.

Luxmoore (R.O.) — J. N. . 1847.

Colvin (W.A.C.) — B. W. . 1847.

Newdigate (W.E., E.C.) — A. . 1847.

Feilden (Miss Edw., H.D.) — Rev. Canon George Ramsay. 2nd son of Rev. R. M. F., Rector of Bebington; 1843³-1846³; Ch. Ch. Oxf. M.A.; Rector of Bebington and Resid. Canon of Chester Cath.; m. Margaret Priscilla, d. of Joseph Feilden of Mytton Park, Blackburn. *Bebington Rectory, Birkenhead.*

Hankey (E.B.) — Arthur. Eld. son of T. H., Banker, of 7 Fenchurch St., E.C.; 1842³-1845³; Banker; died 1865.

Pott (E.C.) — A. S. . 1847.

Ferrers (Mrs. P., F.E.D.) — Rev. Norman Macleod, D.D., F.R.S., LL.D. Son of T. B. F.; 1843³-1846²; Tomline Select 1845; Prizeman 1846; Gonville and Caius Coll. Camb.; Sen. Wrangler and 1st Smith's Prizeman 1851; Fellow Caius Coll. 1852; Tutor Caius Coll. 1865-80; Vice-Chanc. of Camb. 1884-5; Fellow of Eton 1885-96; Master of Gonville and Caius Coll. 1880-1903; m. Emily, d. of Very Rev. John Lamb, D.D., Dean of Bristol; died at Gonville and Caius Lodge, Camb., Jan. 31, 1903.

Shuldham *ma.* (J.E.Y.) — Leopold Arthur Francis. Of Phael Court, co. Cork; 2nd son of Lt.-Gen. E. W. S. of Dunmanway; 1841³-1846³; Ch. Ch. Oxf., B.A.; died unm. Jan. 28, 1887.

Grenfell *mi.* (W.E., E.B.) — St. Leger Murray. 2nd son of P. St. L. G. of Maesteg House, Swansea; 1842³-1846³; Haileybury Coll.; Madras Civil Service; Magistrate at Tanjore; m. Georgiana Currie Wilson Campbell; died at Cuddapah, Feb. 22, 1860.

Board (W.G.C.) — John. Son of Rev. R. B. of Westerham, Kent; 1842¹-1846³; Ch. Ch. Oxf. B.A.; J.P. and D.L. for Kent; Major 1st Bn. Kent R.V., V.D; m. Mary Elizabeth, d. of Rev. W. Masters Pine, Rector of Oxted. *Farley, Westerham, Kent.*

Denison (W.A.C.) — Harry. Of Kilnwick Percy, Beverley; 1842³-1845³; 90th Regt.; died at Lucknow.

Bacon (W.E., W.A.C.) — Charles Anthony. 1842³-1845³.

Oakeley (H.D.) — Sir Charles William Atholl, 4th Bt. Eld. son of Rev. Sir H. O., 3rd Bt., co-Dean of Bocking and Preb. of St. Paul's; 1842¹-1845³; Ch. Ch. Oxf.; formerly Capt. Bengal Cav.; J.P. for Kent; m. 1st, Ellen, d. of John Meeson Parsons of Angley Park, near Cranbrook; 2nd, Elizabeth, d. of Henry W. Tuson, and widow of Hamilton Goodhall. *The Oaks, Frant Road, Tunbridge Wells.*

Thompson (Miss W., F.E.D.) — A. R. . 1847.

Lawford (F.E.D.) — Henry Baring. 1842³-1846³; Civil Service, Bengal; died 1878.

Brodrick *ma.* (C.O.G.) — Hon. W. (Viscount Midleton). 1847.

McCausland (Miss W., E.B.)

CONOLLY THOMAS. Of Drenagh, Limavady; son of M. McC. of Drenagh; 1842[2]-1846[2]; Opp. Wall 1845; Ch. Ch. Oxf. M.A.; formerly in the Diplomatic Service, aft. Capt. Derry Militia; J.P. and D.L. co. Londonderry, High Sheriff 1866; *m.* Hon. Laura St. John, *d.* of St. Andrew, 14th Lord St. John of Bletsoe; died June 25, 1902.

Lyon (W.A.C.)

NASH EDWARDS VAUGHAN. 1842[2]-1846[1]; Trin. Coll. Camb. B.A.; aft. a Solicitor in London.

Hordern (C.L.)

JAMES. 1842[2]-1846[1]; Univ. Coll. Oxf.; died in the Easter Vacation, 1847.

Stuart (Miss W., F.E.D.)

ROBERT RODNEY. Son of Gen. S. of Hillingdon; 1842[2]-1844[3]; formerly Lieut. Madras Lt. Cav.

Greenwood (Mrs. Hor., E.H.P., & H.D.)

J. . 1847.

Watson (R.F.H., C.O.G.)

SIR CHARLES (aft. Watson-Copley). 3rd Bt.; eld. son of Sir C. W. W., 2nd Bt.; 1842[2]-1845[2]; formerly Lieut. 71st Regt.; *m.* Georgina, *d.* of Rev. Robert Tredcroft; died April 5, 1888.

Hopkins (R.O.)

ROBERT JOHN. Of Tidmarsh Manor, Pangbourne, Reading; son of J. H. of Tidmarsh; 1841[3]-1846[2]; Ball. Coll. Oxf. M.A.; J.P. for Berks; *m.* Elizabeth Clara, *d.* of Rev. David Rodney Murray; died April 26, 1899.

Mansfield (Miss Edw., C.O.G.)

COL. SIR CHARLES EDWARD, K.C.M.G. 6th son of J. M. of Diggeswall House, Herts; 1842[1]-1846[2]; Trin. Coll. Camb.; entd. Army 1848, Lieut. 1851, Capt. 1854, Major 1858, Col. 1877; A.D.C. to Sir Colin Campbell; was present at battles of Alma and Balaclava; was in the trenches in the attack on Sebastopol, 1855, and at the fall of the fortress; A.D.C. to Major-Gen. Sir William Mansfield in India 1857; wounded at Cawnpore; Consul-Gen. at Warsaw 1865; Consul-Gen. at Bucharest 1876; Consul-Gen. at Bogotá 1878; Min. Resident at Caracas 1883; Min. Res. and Consul-Gen. at Lima 1884; ret. from Diplomatic Service 1891; Crimean, Turkish, Sardinian, and Indian Medals; *m.* Annie Eliza Margaret, *d.* of Lt.-Col. Hon. Augustus Frederick Ellis, M.P. 6 *Piazza San Lorenzo, Florence.*

Mr. Lascelles *mi.* (W.A.C.)

HON. ALFRED DANIEL. 5th son of Henry, 3rd Earl of Harewood; 1842[1]-1845[1]; died March 20, 1845.

Capper (Mrs. Ro., E.H.P.)

GEORGE COPELAND. Eld. son of S. J. C. of Leyton, Essex; 1843[2]-1845[3]; on the Stock Exchange; died unm. Sept. 14, 1883.

Mr. Campbell (E.C.)

HON. HALLYBURTON GEORGE (3rd Lord Stratheden and Campbell). 2nd son of Lord Chancellor Campbell (1st Lord Stratheden and Campbell); 1842[1]-1845[2]; Trin. Coll. Camb. and East India Coll. Haileybury; Bengal C.S. 1849-55; Associate to Lord Chief Justice 1853; Sec. of Commissions in Court of Chancery 1860-73; Master of Supreme Court of Judicature; Col. 40th Middlesex Rifles 1866-72; J.P. co. Galway and D.L. co. Roxburgh; *m.* Louisa Mary, *d.* of Rt. Hon. A. J. B. Beresford-Hope. 17 *Bruton Street, W.*, and *Hartrigg, Jedburgh.*

Antrobus *mi.* (Mrs. Ro., F.E.D.)

JOHN COUTTS. Eld. son of G. C. A. of Eaton Hall, Congleton; 1843[1]-1846[2]; St. John's Coll. Camb. M.A.; Barrister; J.P. and C.C. co. Chester, High Sheriff 1868; Hon. Lieut.-Col. (ret.) Earl of Chester's Yeo. Cav.; *m.* 1st, Fanny, *d.* of Clement Sweatenham of Somerford Booths, co. Chester; 2nd, Mary Caroline, *d.* of Geoffery Joseph Shakerley; 3rd, Mary Egidia, *d.* of Gen. the Hon. Sir James Lindsay, K.C.M.G. *Eaton Hall, Congleton.*

Platt (W.L.E.)

THEODORE EDWIN HOUGHTON. 1843[1]-1844[2]; formerly in the 49th Regt., aft. Capt. Royal Middx. Rifles.

Leslie (C.J.A., H.D.)

CAPT. THOMAS (aft. Slingsby). 3rd son of Col. C. P. L. of Glasslough, co. Monaghan; 1841[2]-1845[2]; ent. Army 1848; Capt. R. Horse Gds., and A.D.C. to Lord Raglan in the Crimea; wounded at the Alma; J.P. and D.L. for W. Riding of Yorks, High Sheriff 1886; *m.* Emma Louisa Katherine, *d.* of Charles Slingsby of Scriven Park, Knaresborough; died Sept. 6, 1903.

Cator (Miss M., W.A.C.)

JOHN THOMAS. Of Wentbridge House, co. York; 2nd son of Rev. T. C. of Skelbrook Park, Yorks; 1842[2]-1844[3]; formerly 16th Lancers; *m.* Katherine Sarah, *d.* of John Swann of Askham Hall, co. York; died March 29, 1878.

Miller *ma.* (R.F.H., C.O.G.)

SIR C. H., Bt. . 1847.

Fitzgerald (Mrs. Ri., W.G.C.)

LIEUT.-COL. WILLIAM HENRY DOMINIC. Of Graney, co. Kildare; 2nd son of Lord W. C. O'B. F.; 1841[3]-1844[2]; formerly 7th Royal Fusiliers; J.P. for Wilts; *m.* Miss Bettesworth; died Nov. 12, 1901.

Lord North (Mrs. Ro., E.H.P.)

DUDLEY. Eld. son of Francis, 6th Earl of Guilford; 1842[2]-1846[2]; *m.* Charlotte Maria, *d.* of the Hon. and Rev. William Eden of Bishopsbourne, Canterbury; died Jan. 28, 1860.

Errington *mi.* (W.G.C.)

REV. JOHN LAUNCELOT (aft. Turbutt). 2nd son of G. H. E. of Chadwell Hall, Essex, and Lexden Park, Colchester; 1841[3]-1846[1]; B.N.C. Oxf. M.A.; formerly Vicar of Berechurch, Essex; aft. Vicar of Midgham; *m.* Isabella Turbutt, *d.* of Rev. Henry Goodwin of Hinchley Wood, Mapleton, co. Derby. *Midgham Vicarage, Reading.*

Winter (Miss B., F.E.D.)

REV. GEORGE ROBERT. Son of R. W., Barrister, of Calcutta; 1841[3]-1845[2]; Eton VIII. 1844, Stroke 1845; B.N.C. Oxf. M.A.; Oxf. VIII. 1847; Pres. O.U.B.C.; formerly Rector of East Bradenham, Thetford; aft. Vicar of Swaffham and Hon. Canon of Norwich; *m.* Augusta, *d.* of Edward Lawford; died Sept. 27, 18[illegible].

Bidwell (Miss Edw., aft. K.S., H.D.)

G. S. . 1847.

Fredricks (Mrs. Hor., C.J.A.)

JOHN JESTYN WILLIAMS. 1841[1]-1845[1]; formerly 46th Regt., aft. Capt. 2nd Chesham Militia.

Rolt *ma.* (Mrs. D., C.O.G.)

REV. HENRY GEORGE. Eld. son of Lieut.-Gen. J. R., K.C.B., of Sacombe Lodge; 1841[3]-1844[2]; Ball. Coll. Oxf. M.A.; *m.* 1st, Fanny Paulet, *d.* of Col. James Wood; 2nd, Elizabeth Sarah, *d.* of Capt. George Frost, R.A., of Tor Grove, Plymouth. *Sacombe Lodge, Harbledown, Canterbury.*

Childers (W.A.C.)

R. F. WALBANKE- . 1847.

Ellison (Mi[illegible])

NATHANIEL FREDERICK. Formerly of [illegible]; son of — E., Com[illegible] Newcastle; [illegible]

Stratton *ma.* (C.J.A.) — GEORGE. Of Wheler Lodge, co. Leicester; 2nd son of G. S., Member of Council, Madras; 1841^{2}–1845^{3}; St. John's Coll. Oxf. M.A.; Barrister; J.P. co. Leicester; *m.* Ellen, *d.* of Lieut.-Col. William Fane of Wormsley, Oxf.; died 1895.

Rudge (J.E.Y.) — EDWARD CHARLES. Eld. son of E. J. R. of The Abbey Manor House; 1841^{3}–1846^{2}; Trin. Coll. Camb.; J.P. and D.L. co. Worcester, High Sheriff 1866; J.P. co. Gloucester; Lord of the Manor, Evesham; *m.* 1st, Helen Catherine, *d.* of Gen. Middlemore, C.B.; 2nd, Florence, *d.* of — Fox. *Abbey Manor House, near Evesham.*

Naghten (C.L.) — ARTHUR ROBERT. Of Blighmont Lodge, Millbrook, Southampton; son of T. N. of Crofton House, Titchfield, Hants; 1842^{2}–1847^{1}; Worc. Coll. Oxf.; formerly Capt. Hants Artillery; died 1881.

Philips (E.B.) — FREDERICK. Of Rhiial, Mold, Flints: eld. son of Col. F. C. P. of Rhiial; 1841^{3}–1845^{3}; died unm. June 30, 1866.

Hodgson (C.O.G.) — CHRISTOPHER GEORGE. Son of — H. Sec. of Queen Anne's Bounty; 1842^{1}–1844^{2}; Solicitor.

Pott (W.A.C.) — HENRY. Son of W. P. of Beddington, Croydon; 1841^{3}–1845^{3}; on the Stock Exchange; *m.* — *d.* of John Peter Fearon. *81 Cornwall Gardens, South Kensington, S.W.*

Parr *ma.* (Miss W., W.A.C.) — CONRINGTON THOMAS. Of Stonelands, near Dawlish, Devon; 1841^{3}–1846^{1}; dead.

Parr *mi.* (Miss W., W.A.C.) — HENRY DIMSDALE. 1841^{3}–1846^{3}; Exeter Coll. Oxf.; formerly Capt. S. Devon Militia; aft. in business in London.

Rhodes (C.L.) — THOMAS WILLIAM. Of Flore Fields, Weedon; 1841^{3}–1844^{3}; J.P. for Northants; *m.* Elizabeth, *d.* of Rev. Francis William Rhodes, Vicar of Bishop's Stortford, Herts; died 1895.

Davis *ma.* (Mrs. P., C.O.G.) — WILLIAM. Of Cranbrook Park, Leytonstone, Essex; 1841^{3}–1844^{3}; *m.* Miss Stringer of Effingham, Surrey.

Cooke (Miss M., E.B.) — CHARLES EDWARD STEPHEN. Of St. Catherine's, Doncaster; 2nd son of Sir W. B. C., 8th Bt., of Wheatley, Doncaster; 1841^{3}–1845^{3}; St. John's Coll. Camb. B.A.; formerly of the Admiralty; aft. a Banker at Doncaster; J.P. and D.L. for W. Riding of Yorks; Lieut.-Col. Yorks Yeo. Cav.; *m.* Lady Mary Louisa Stewart, *d.* of Randolph, 9th Earl of Galloway; died Oct. 28, 1895.

Batchelor *mi.* (W.G.C., aft. K.S., W.G.C.) — CHARLES. 1838^{3}–1844^{3}; formerly Capt. Bengal Cav.

Alexander (Mrs. D., C.O.G.) — LESLEY. Of Newtownlimavady, co. Londonderry; eld. son of J. A. of Newtownlimavady; 1841^{3}–1844^{3}; Mag. Coll. Oxf.; 11th Hussars; died unm.

Custance (Mrs. Ro., aft. K.S.) — A. F. . 1847.

Bradshaw (Mrs. Ri., F.E.D.) — REV. HENRY HOLDEN. Of Barton Park, Barton Blount, nr. Derby; 2nd son of F. B. of Barton Blount; 1843^{1}–1845^{3}; B.N.C. Oxf. B.A.; formerly Curate of Sudbury, Derby; died 1883.

Pipe-Wolferstan *mi.* (R.F.H., aft. K.S., E.B.) — S. W. . 1847.

Turner (R.F.H., E.B.) — LIEUT.-COL. MANSFIELD. Of Glen View House, Downside, Bath; eld. son of W. T. of Glen View; 1842^{2}–1845^{3}; formerly Capt. 20th Foot, aft. Col. comm. Leicestershire R.V.; J.P. for cos. Leicester and Somerset; Chief of the Stamp Office at Leicester; *m.* Marianne, *d.* of Edward Archer of Trelaske; dead.

Tilghman (Mrs. Ri., W.G.C.) — WILLIAM HUSKISSON (aft. Tilghman-Huskisson). Of Eartham, Chichester; son of R. M. T., Bengal Civil Service; 1842^{2}–1845^{3}; Trin. Coll. Camb. M.A.; called to the Bar 1855; J.P. for Sussex; *m.* Eliza Mary, *d.* of Adml. Rivett Carnac; dead.

Miles *max.* (R.O.) — W. H. . 1847.

Foljambe (H.D.) — F. J. S. . 1847.

Snowden *ma.* (Mrs. P., F.E.D.) — J. H. . 1847.

Stacey (Miss B., aft. K.S., E.B.) — F. E. . 1847.

Holland (F.E.D.) — WILMOT. Of Keston, Beckenham; 1842^{3}–1845^{3}; formerly in business in London.

Barnes (W.L.E.) — R. H. . 1847.

Marshall *ma.* (Miss W., F.E.D.) — W. J. . 1847.

Ross (R.F.H., E.B.) — ALEXANDER HENRY. Son of C. R.; 1843^{1}–1847^{1}; Ch. Ch. Oxf. M.A.; called to the Bar; Major W. Kent Militia; M.P. for Maidstone 1880–88; *m.* Juliana, *d.* of William Moseley of Leaton Hall, Staffs; died Dec. 3, 1888.

Norbury (W.L.E.) — T. C. . 1847.

Martin (Mrs. Hor., E.B.) — G. E. . 1847.

Duckworth *ma.* (Mrs. Hor., E.H.P.) — REV. WILLIAM ARTHUR. 2nd son of W. D. of Orchardleigh Park; 1842^{3}–1846^{3}; Sch. of Trin. Coll. Camb. M.A.; 1st Cl. Class. 1853; Rector of Puttenham, Guildford, 1859–77; J.P. for Somerset; Lord of the Manor of Orchardleigh, Lullington, and Buckland in Somerset and Over Darwin, Lancs; *m.* Hon. Edina Campbell, *d.* of John, 1st Lord Campbell. *Orchardleigh Park, Frome.*

Duckworth *mi.* (Mrs. Hor., E.H.P.) — R. . 1847.

Eden *mi.* (Mrs. D., E.H.P.) — FREDERICK. 2nd son of A. E.; 1841^{3}–1846^{3}; Merton Coll. Oxf.; formerly Commissioner of Fisheries, Home Office; *m.* Caroline, *d.* of E. J. L. Jekyll.

Bagshawe (W.E., E.H.P.) — W. L. G. . 1847.

Mr. Henley (E.C.) — REV. HON. ROBERT. 2nd son of Robert, 2nd Lord Henley; 1842^{3}–1846^{3}; Ball. Coll. Oxf. M.A.; 2nd Class Lit. Hum.; Vicar of Putney, Surrey; *m.* Emily Louisa, *d.* of Robert Aldridge of St. Leonard's Forest, Horsham. *Eden Lodge, Putney, S.W.*

Lord Dungarvan (R.O.) — RICHARD EDMUND ST. LAWRENCE BOYLE (9th Earl of Cork and Orrery), P.C., K.P. Eld. son of Charles, Viscount Dungarvan, and grandson of Edmund, 8th Earl of Cork; 1842^{3}–1846^{2}; Ch. Ch. Oxf. B.A.; A.D.C. to Queen Victoria 1889–99; Lord-Lieut. of co. Somerset and Hon. Col. N. Somerset Yeo.; M.P. for Frome 1854–6; Master of the Buckhounds 1866, 1868–74 and 1880–85; Master of the Horse 1886 and 1894–5; appointed one of the Speakers of the House of Lords 1882; *m.* Lady Emily Charlotte, *d.* of Ulick John, 1st Marquis of Clanricarde. *40 Charles Street, Berkeley Sq., W., and Frome, Somerset.*

Brodrick *mi.* (C.O.G.) — HON. G. C. . 1847.

Walsh (R.F.H., H.D.) — REV. HON. DIGBY. 2nd son of John, 1st Lord Ormathwaite, of Ormathwaite, Keswick, Cumberland; 1842^{3}–1844^{3}; Ball. Coll. Oxf. M.A.; Incumbent of Trinity Church, Trowbridge; *m.* Fanny Matilda, *d.* of Henry Stroud; died April 2, 1869.

Coltman *mi.* (E.C.) — F. J. . 1850.

Shipton (Mrs. Ro., E.H.P.) — REV. PERCEVAL MAURICE. Son of Capt. J. M. S., R.N.; 1841^{3}–1844^{2}; Field XI.; Magd. Coll. Camb. and Exeter Coll. Camb. LL.B.; Rector of Halsham; *m.* 1st, *d.* of Henry Stanley Curwen; 2nd, *d.* of J. Bates. *Halsham Rectory, Holderness, Hull.*

Buller *ma.* (E.C.) — COOTE MANNINGHAM-. 3rd son of Sir E. M.-B., 1st Bt., of Dilhorne Hall, Cheadle, Stoke-on-Trent; 1843^{1}–1846^{2}; Eton VIII. 1846; formerly Capt. and Brevet Major, Rifle Bgde.; died unm. April 5, 1868.

Morgan *ma.* (H.D.) — HON. CHARLES RODNEY. Eld. son of Sir Charles Morgan Robinson, 1st Lord Tredegar; 1842^{1}–1845^{2}; formerly Coldstream Gds.; aft. M.P. for Brecon; died unm. Jan. 14, 1854.

Mr. Ellis (Mrs. Ro., E.B.) — HON. FREDERICK GEORGE (7th Lord Howard de Walden). Eld. son of Charles Augustus, 6th Lord Howard de Walden; 1842^{3}–1846^{2}; Trin. Coll. Camb. M.A.; formerly Major 4th Lt. Dragoons and Attaché at Brussels; *m.* Blanche, *d.* of William Holden of Palace House, co. Lancaster; died Nov. 3, 1899.

Miller *mi.* (Mrs. Ri., C.O.G.) — H. J. . 1847.

Astley *ma.* (E.H.P., C.O.G.) — SIR JOHN DUGDALE, 3rd Bt. Eld. son of Sir F. D. A., 2nd Bt., of Everley, Marlborough; 1842^{3}–1845^{2}; Ch. Ch. Oxf.; formerly Lieut.-Col. Scots Fusilier Gds.; served in the Crimea, Medal with two Clasps and the Turkish Order of the Medjidie; M.P. for N. Lincs 1874–80; J.P. for Wilts and Lincs; *m.* Eleanor Blanche Mary, *d.* of Thomas E. Corbett of Elsham Hall, Lincs; died Oct. 10 1894.

Travers-Clarke (C.L.) — WILLIAM HENRY (aft. Clarke-Travers.) Eld. son of Sir W. H. St. L. C.-T., 2nd Bt., of Rossmore, co. Cork; 1842^{3}–1845^{3}; Capt. 14th Lt. Dragoons; served in Indian Mutiny (ret. 1867); died unm. in Natal, Mar. 12, 1868.

Battiscombe (Mrs. Ro., W.L.E.) — ROBERT WILLIAM PERCIVAL. Eld. son of Rev. — B., Vicar of Barkway, Royston, Herts; 1843^{3}–1845^{1}.

Cockerell *ma.* (W.A.C.) — A. P. 1847.

Lyon (F.E.D.) — CARRISBROOK JAMES. 1843^{1}–1845^{1}.

Hogg (R.O.) — FERGUSSON FLOYER. 3rd son of Rt. Hon. Sir J. W. H., 1st Bt., Barrister, of Calcutta; 1842^{3}–1845^{2}; E. I. Coll. Haileybury; Bengal Civil Service; *m.* Elizabeth Helen, *d.* of Hon. Laurence Parsons; died Dec. 19, 1862.

Foulkes (W.G.C.) — JOHN FORTESCUE. 1841^{1}–1845^{2}.

Christie (Mrs. Ro., J.W.H.) — CHARLES PETER. Of Hoddesdon House, Hoddesdon, Herts; son of P. C.; 1842^{3}–1846^{1}; Brewer; *m.* Isabel Constance, *d.* of John Perkins.

Evans *ma.* (W.E., W.A.C.) — SAMUEL THOMAS GEORGE, R.W.S. Son of W. E.; 1842^{3}–1845^{2}; won School Pulling 1845; Drawing Master at Eton 1854–1903; *m.* Susan, *d.* of T. Bros. *Eton College.*

Horne (Mrs. Ro.) — HENRY JAMES DAVISON. Of Ponfield, Herts; son of a former Master in Chancery; 1842^{3}–1847^{1}; Trin. Coll. Camb.; formerly Lieut. Herts R.V.

French (Mrs. Ro., W.A.C.) — ROBERT CHARLES. 1842^{3}–1844^{1}.

Amos (Miss M., W.A.C.) — REV. JAMES. 1841^{3}–1844^{2}; Sch. of Clare Coll. Camb.; formerly Incumbent of St. Stephen's, Southwark.

Russell (F.E.D.) — SIR GEORGE, 4th Bt. Of Swallowfield, Reading; 3rd son of Sir H. R., 2nd Bt., of Swallowfield; 1842^{3}–1847^{1}; Exeter Coll. Oxf. M.A.; Barrister and Recorder of Wokingham; Judge of County Court (Circuit No. 49) 1874–85; M.P. for East Berks 1885–98; J.P. for Kent and co. Derby; J.P. and D.L. for Berks; Chmn. S.E. Ry. Co.; *m.* Constance Charlotte Elisa, *d.* of Lord Arthur Lennox; died Mar. 7, 1898.

Crawley *ma.* (R.O.) — PHILIP SAMBROOK. 4th son of S. C. of Stockwood, Beds; 1841^{3}–1846^{2}; formerly Lieut.-Col. Coldstream Gds.

Arnaud (Miss Edw., W.A.C.) — HENRY BRUCE. Of Padbury, Buckingham; eld. son of E. A., Collector of Customs at Liverpool; 1842^{1}–1844^{2}; Ch. Ch. Oxf. M.A.; Barrister; J.P. for Bucks; dead.

Murchison (Miss Edw., F.E.D.) — KENNETH ROBERT, F.R.G.S. Of Tarradale, Ross-shire; son of — M. of Tarradale; 1842^{3}–1844^{2}; J.P. for Somerset; J.P. and D.L. for Sussex; *m.* Harriet Isabella, *d.* of Major James C. Travers, K.H., Rifle Bgde.; died 1897.

Moore *ma.* (R.O.) — EDWARD GEORGE AUGUSTUS HARCOURT (6th Earl of Mountcashell). Eld. son of Hon. and Rev. E. G. M., Canon of Windsor; 1842^{3}–1846^{3}; St. John's Coll. Camb. M.A.; called to the Bar, Lincoln's Inn, 1854. *Beryl, Wells, Somerset.*

Miles *ma.* (R.O.) — EDWARD PEACH WILLIAM. Of Stainsbridge House, Malmesbury; 7th son of P. J. M. of Leigh Court, Bristol; 1842^{3}–1846^{2}; Ch. Ch. Oxf.; Merchant; J.P. co. Gloucester; *m.* 1st, Olivia Caroline, *d.* of William Cave of Brentry, near Bristol; 2nd, Annie, *d.* of Gen. Conyngham; died 1889.

Hibbert (W.L.E.) — HUGH ROBERT. Of Birtles Hall, co. Chester; eld. son of T. H. of Birtles Hall; 1842^{3}–1846^{2}; Col. 7th Royal Fusiliers; ent. the Army 1847; served throughout Crimean War; four Medals and mentioned in despatches; J.P. and D.L. co. Chester, High Sheriff 1885; J.P. co. Brecon; *m.* Sarah [illegible], *d.* of Frederick R. Lee of Broadgate House, Barnstaple; died Sept. 12, [illegible].

Halford *ma.* (W.E., E.C.) — HENRY ST. JOHN. Of Manor House, Newton Harcourt, Leicester; son of Sir — H., Bt., of Newton Harcourt; 1842^{1}–1845^{3}; Merton Coll. Oxf.; formerly Lieut.-Col. Leicester R.V.; *m.* Miss Bagshawe; died 1893.

Arnold (Miss W., F.E.D.) — G. H. . 1847.

Oldfield *ma.* (W.G.C.) — SIR RICHARD CHARLES, Kt. Eld. son of H. S. O.; 1842^{3}–1845^{2}; Haileybury Coll.; ent. B.C.S. 1848; served with the Vol. Horse raised at Agra during the Indian Mutiny 1857; dangerously wounded in action at Agra (Medal); Addn. Judge of High Court of Judicature N.W. Provinces of India 1874–81; Puisne Judge 1881–87 (ret.); *m.* Maria, *d.* of Major Frederick Angelo. *2 Harewood Place, Hanover Sq., W.*

Newton (Mrs. Ro., E.H.P.) — HARRY ROBERT. 1841^{3}–1844^{2}; formerly living in Argyle Place, Regent St., W.

Lewin (Mrs. Ri., C.O.G.) — GRANVILLE FREDERICK JOHN. Son of Sir G. L.; 1842^{3}–1845^{3}; formerly Capt. Staff Corps, Madras, and Asst. Comm. of the Punjab.

Praed (R.O.) — WILLIAM BACKWELL (aft. Tyringham). Of Tyringham, Bucks, and Trevethoe, Cornwall; eld. son of J. B. P. of Tyringham and Trevethoe; 1842^{1}–1845^{3}, Ch. Ch. Oxf.; J.P. and D.L. for cos. Bucks and Cornwall; High Sheriff for Bucks 1869; *m.* Fanny Adela, *d.* of Col. W. Wilby; died Nov. 29, 1870.

Hankey (Mrs. Ri., C.J.A.) — BLAKE ALEXANDER. Of Balcombe Place, Haywards Heath; eld. son of J. A. H. of Balcombe; 1840^{3}–1844^{2}; Trin. Coll. Camb.; J.P. for Sussex; High Sheriff for Rutland 1883; died unm. Mar. 10, 1899.

Foley (E.B.) — HENRY JOHN WENTWORTH (aft. Hodgetts-Foley). Of Prestwood House, Stourbridge; son of J. H. H.-F. of Prestwood; 1842^{3}–1846^{1}; Ch. Ch. Oxf. M.A.; M.P. for S. Staffs 1857–68; J.P. and D.L. for cos. Stafford and Worcester; and J.P. for Hereford; High Sheriff co. Stafford 1877; *m.* Hon. Jane Frances Anne, *d.* of Richard Hussey, 1st Lord Vivian; died April 23, 1894.

White (W.E., W.L.E.) — SIR THOMAS WOOLLASTON, 3rd Bt. Eld. son of Col. Sir T. W. W., 2nd Bt., of Wallingwells; 1841^{3}–1844^{3}; served in the 16th Lancers 1847–73; J.P. for Notts. *Wallingwells, Worksop.*

Milles (C.O.G.) — MAJOR-GEN. THOMAS. Of the Kraal, Sidmouth, Devon; son of Major T. P. M. of 14th Lt. Dragoons; 1841^{3}–1845^{1}; Eton VIII. 1844; Col. 75th Regt.; ret. 1875; *m.* Harriet, *d.* of Rev. Francis J. Burlton; died June 6, 1903.

Stephens (J.E.Y.) — HENRY JOHN TOWNSHEND (aft. Townshend). Son of Rev. M. F. S. T. of Castle Townshend, Skibbereen; 1841^{3}–1844^{2}; formerly 2nd Life Gds.; *m.* Jane Adeliza Clementina, *d.* of John Hamilton Hussey de Burgh of Kilfinnan Castle, co. Cork; died Sept. 7, 1869.

Markham (Miss W., H.D.) — W. T. . 1847.

Hankin (Mrs. Ro., aft. K.S., W.L.E., & J.E.Y.) — COL. FREDERICK GEORGE. Son of D. H. of Stanstead, Herts; 1840^{3}–1847^{1}; won Lower Boy Steeplechase; Indian Army (ret.); H.M. Inspector of Prisons, England and Wales; *m.* 1st, Lucy, *d.* of Benjamin Travers, President, College of Surgeons; 2nd, Kathleen, *d.* of William Halls. *Kel-[illegible], West Kirby, Birkenhead.*

Reeve (H.D.) — WILLIAM HENRY. 2nd son of J. R. of Leadenham House, Lincoln; 1841^{3}–1846^{1}; formerly Lieut.-Col. Coldstream Gds.; died 1868.

Maule (R.F.H., F.E.D.) — GEORGE NORMAN. Son of J. M. of Bath; 1841^{3}–1846^{2}; St. John's Coll. Oxf. M.A.; Barrister Western Circuit (ret.); J.P. co. Devon. *1 Hillsborough Terrace, Ilfracombe.*

Vaughan (Mrs. Ri., W.G.C.) — HERBERT MILLINCHAMP. 1841^{3}–1845^{3}; 95th Regt.; wounded and taken prisoner in attack on Redan; died in hospital, Sept. 13, 1855.

Sykes *ma.* (C.L.) — REV. EDWARD JOHN. Son of Rev. W. S. of The Grotto, Basildon, Berks; 1841^{3}–1844^{2}; Worc. Coll. Oxf. M.A.; formerly Vicar of Basildon; *m.* Constance Mary, *d.* of Edward Brown; died Dec. 24, 1891.

Phillimore (W.L.E.) — WILLIAM BROUGH. Formerly of Newberries, Herts; 1841^{3}–1844^{2}; formerly in the Carabineers, aft. Capt. in the Gds.

Bankes (J.E.Y.) — HENRY HYDE NUGENT, M.A. Of Wraysbury, Bucks; 2nd son of Rt. Hon. G. B. of Kingston Lacy, Wimborne; 1842^{3}–1845^{3}; Barrister, Lincoln's Inn; *m.* Hon. Lalage Letitia Caroline, *d.* of Richard Hussey, 1st Lord Vivian; died Mar. 26, 1883.

Buchanan *ma.* (C.L.) — WILLIAM. 3rd son of Rev. A. H. B. of Hales Hall, Market Drayton; 1842^{1}–1845^{3}; died at Madeira.

Johnson (W.A.C.) — JOHN ALLEN. 1843^{2}–1847^{1}.

Barnard (H.D.) — SIR H., Kt. . 1847.

Holden *ma.* (C.L.) — CHARLES JAMES. 1843^{1}–1846^{2}; won Pulling 1846; Camb. VIII. 1848–9.

Colthurst (E.H.P., F.E.D.) — LIEUT.-COL. DAVID LA TOUCHE. 3rd son of Sir N. C. C., 4th Bt., of Ardrum, Inniscarra; 1841^{3}–1845^{3}; 29th Regt. (ret.) Crimean and Turkish Medals; M.P. for co. Cork 1879–85; *m.* Frances, *d.* of William Douglas Dick of Pitkerrow. *Ardrum Lodge, Bournemouth.*

Soley (H.D., aft. K.S., H.D.) — T. L. . 1847

Sir J. Marjoribanks (R.O.) — SIR J., Bt. . 1847.

Knatchbull *ma.* (E.B.) — EDWARD HUGESSEN (aft. Knatchbull-Hugessen). 1st Lord Brabourne, P.C.; 6th son of Rt. Hon. Sir E. K., 9th Bt., of Mersham Hatch, Ashford, Kent; 1841^{3}–1847^{1}; Magd. Coll. Oxf. M.A.; M.P. for Sandwich 1857–80; a Lord of the Treasury 1859–66; Under-Sec. of the Home Dept. 1866 and 1868–71, and for the Colonies 1871–74; J.P., D.L., and Chmn. of East Kent Qr. Sessions; *m.* 1st, Anna Maria Elizabeth, *d.* of Rev. Marcus Richard Southwell, Vicar of St. Stephen's, St. Albans; 2nd, Ethel Mary, *d.* of Col. Sir George Gustavus Walker, K.C.B. of Crawfordton, co. Dumfries; died Feb. 6, 1893.

REMOVE.

Grover (Mrs. Ro., aft. K.S., E.B.) — H. . 1847.

Lloyd-Mostyn (W.A.C.) — HON. T. E. . 1847

Thackeray (R.F.H., aft. K.S., E.B.)	C. . 1850.
Coleridge *mi.* (E.C., aft. K.S., E.C.)	A. J. . 1850.
Prest (R.F.H., H.D.)	E. B. . 1847.
Bernal (Miss Edw., H.D.)	FREDERIC, C.M.G. Son of R. B., many years Chmn. of House of Commons; 1843^{1}-1845^{2}; Supernumerary Committee Clerk, House of Commons, 1847-8; H.B.M. Consul at Madrid 1854-8, Carthagena, S. America, 1858-60, Baltimore 1860-66, Havre 1866-83, and Consul-Gen. Havre 1883-96; *m.* Charlotte Augusta, *d.* of J. Brewster Cozens of Woodham Mortimer Lodge, Maldon. 94 *Cheriton Road, Folkestone.*
Welby *mi.* (C.O.G.)	H. G. E. . 1847.
Hale (E.B.)	CHARLES CHOLMELEY. Of The Bury, King's Walden, Hitchin; 2nd son of W. H. of King's Walden; 1843^{2}-1846^{3}; formerly in the Army; J.P. Herts, High Sheriff 1880; *m.* 1st, Augusta Mary, *d.* of Edward Fearnley Whittingstall of Langleybury, Herts; 2nd, Emily Rebecca, *d.* of William Comerford Casey; died Dec. 1884.
Roberts (C.J.A. & E.B.)	W. W. . 1847.
Buchanan *mi.* (W.L.E.)	REV. ALEXANDER. 4th son of Rev. A. H. B. of Hales Hall, Market Drayton; 1843^{1}-1847^{1}; Opp. Wall 1846; formerly Incumbent of Hales, Market Drayton; *m.* Ann Alice, *d.* of Richard Fort, M.P., of Read Hall, Lancs.
Blackett (E.H.P.)	SIR E. W., Bt. . 1847.
Anderdon (C.J.A.)	JOHN EDMUND. 1843^{1}-1847^{1}; Ball. Coll. Oxf.; formerly Director of the Bank of London.
Lygon *ma.* (R.O.)	HON. H. (Earl Beauchamp). 1847.
Procter (C.J.A., aft. K.S., C.J.A.)	C. T. . 1847.
Dent *mi.* (H.D.)	REV. CANON JOSEPH JONATHAN DENT. 2nd son of J. D. of Ribston Hall, Wetherby; 1843^{1}-1846^{2}; Trin. Coll. Camb. M.A.; Vicar of Hunsingore; Rural Dean; *m.* Laura Manning, *d.* of James William Freshfield of The Wilderness, Reigate. *Hunsingore Vicarage, Wetherby.*
Campbell (R.F.H., E.H.P.)	SIR GEORGE. 4th Bt.; 2nd son of J. C. and grandson of Sir A. C., 2nd Bt., of Succoth, Dumbartonshire; 1842^{3}-1844^{2}; formerly Capt. 1st Dragoons; D.L. for Lanark; *m.* Margaret Annie Maria, *d.* of Sir Edward Borough, 2nd Bt.; died Feb. 17, 1874.
Currey (E.H.P.)	BENJAMIN SCOTT. 1843^{1}-1846^{2}; formerly a Solicitor at Derby.
Tinling (W.A.C.)	W. P. . 1847.
Hunt *mi.* (R.F.H., C.J.A.)	CHARLES JOHN. 2nd son of Rev. T. H., Rector of West Felton, co. Salop; 1842^{3}-1844; 4th Bengal Cav.; shot by his own men in Indian Mutiny, June 12, 1857.

Evelyn (C.J.A.)	JAMES. 5th son of G. E. of Wotton, Dorking, Surrey; 1841^{2}-1845^{3}; formerly Capt. Grenadier Gds.; *m.* Annie Davis; died 1874.
Parker (H.D.)	CHARLES JOHN BULLIVANT. 2nd son of W. P. of Hanthorpe House, Bourne, Lincs; 1842^{3}-1845^{2}; Exeter Coll. Oxf. B.A.; J.P. co. Lincoln; Lieut.-Col. R.S. Lincoln Militia; *m.* Martha, *d.* of John Hardy of Stone Bridge House, Grantham. *Stone Bridge, Grantham.*
Mr. Eliot *mi.* (C.J.A., & W.A.C.)	HON. WILLIAM GORDON CORNWALLIS (4th Earl of St. Germans). 3rd son of Edward Granville, 3rd Earl of St. G., of Port Eliot, St. Germans, Cornwall; 1842^{3}-1846^{2}; M.P. for Devonport; Sec. of Legation at Rio de Janeiro, Athens, and Lisbon; died unm. Mar. 19, 1881.
Farrer (E.C.)	FREDERICK WILLIS. 3rd son of T. F. of 66 Lincoln's Inn Fields, W.C.; 1842^{3}-1846^{3}; Ball. Coll. Oxf. B.A.; Solicitor; *m.* Mary, *d.* of George Richmond R.A. 16 *Devonshire Place, Portland Place, W.*
Boothby (Miss W., F.E.D.)	ROBERT TOD. 1843^{3}-1846^{3}.
Randall (R.F.H., aft. K.S., E.B.)	E. . 1847.
Dashwood (W.L.E.)	H. W. . 1847.
Aitken *ma.* (R.F.H., F.E.D.)	J. . 1847.
Hammond (Mrs. Rl., E.B.)	H. A. . 1847.
Aitken *mi.* (R.F.H., F.E.D.)	H. M. . 1847.
Wayte *mi.* (Miss W., aft. K.S., F.E.D.)	G. H. . 1850.
Peile (C.J.A., aft. K.S., C.J.A.)	REV. ARTHUR LEWIS BABINGTON. Son of Rev. B. P.; 1842^{3}-1846^{3}; Jesus Coll. Camb. M.A.; Master of St. Katharine's, Regent's Park; Hon. Chaplain to the King; *m.* Ellen Olivia, *d.* of G. W. Sheppard. 39 *Fitzroy Road, Regent's Park, N.W.*
Molony *ma.* (Miss W., F.E.D.)	REV. FRANCIS WHELER. 3rd son of J. M. of Kiltanon, near Tulla, Limerick; 1843^{3}-1846^{1}; St. Mary Hall Oxf. M.A.; *m.* Harriet, *d.* of Capt. G. Baker, R.N.; died 1860.
Tillbrook (Mrs. P., E.H.P.)	PHILIP LIMBORCH. Of Greylands, Ashburton, Devon; son of Rev. S. T., B.D., of Freckenham, Soham; 1843^{3}-1846^{1}; Major 50th Regt.; served at Sebastopol during the Crimea; Standard Bearer Royal Bodyguard of late Queen Victoria; *m.* Ada Byng, *d.* of Maj.-Gen. M. R. S. Whitmore; died Jan. 24, 1902.
Mure (C.J.A.)	COL. WILLIAM. Of Caldwell by Glasgow, N.B.; son of Col. W. M. of Caldwell; 1843^{1}-1846^{1}; Lieut.-Col. Scots Guards; served in Kaffir war 1852, and Crimea; J.P. and D.L. cos. Ayr and Renfrew; M.P. for Renfrewshire 1873-80; *m.* Hon. Constance Elizabeth Wyndham, *d.* of George, 1st Lord Leconfield; died 1880.
Haviland (C.O.G.)	A. C. . 1847.
Biddulph (H.D.[illegible])	[illegible] T. W., Bt. . 1847.

Peel (C.J.A., & F.E.D.) LIEUT.-COL. CECIL LENNOX. 4th son of L. P.; 1842[3]-1846[1]; formerly in 52nd Regt., aft. Lieut.-Col. Scots Guards; *m.* Caroline Susan Mary, *d.* of Wellington Henry, 2nd Lord Combermere. *Easthampstead Cottage, Wokingham.*

Brinckman (W.A.C.) SIR THEODORE HENRY, 2nd Bt. Eld son of Sir T. H. L. B., 1st Bt.; 1843[1]-1844[2]; Ensign of 17th Foot 1849; Capt. (ret.) 1855; Dep.-Lieut. of the Tower Hamlets; M.P. for Canterbury 1868-74; *m.* Lady Cecilia Augusta, *d.* of Francis Nathaniel, 2nd Marquis Conyngham, K.P. *St. Leonard's, Windsor, and 34 Grosvenor St., W.*

Bateson *ma.* (C.O.G.) LIEUT.-GEN. RICHARD, C.V.O. 6th son of Sir R. B., 1st Bt., of Belvoir Park, Belfast; 1843[3]-1846[3]; Trin. Coll. Camb.; served in and commanded 1st Life Gds.; A.D.C. and Equerry to H.R.H. Duke of Cambridge; Dep. Ranger of Hyde Park since 1886. *Ranger's Lodge, Hyde Park, W.*

Bedford *ma.* (R.F.H., aft. K.S., W.G.C.) C. R. . 1847.

Manning (E.C.) CHARLES DOWNES. 1843[3]-1847[1]; formerly 1st Royal Dragoons.

Cooper (Mrs. Ro., H.D.) LIEUT.-COL. RT. HON. EDWARD HENRY, P.C. Of Markree Castle, Collooney, Sligo; eld. son of R. W. C. of Longford Lodge, Kingstown, co. Dublin; 1842[3]-1844[3]; formerly Capt. 7th Hussars; aft. Lieut.-Col. Grenadier Guards; ret. 1863; M.P. for co. Sligo 1865-8; Lord-Lieut. co. Sligo 1877-1902, J.P., High Sheriff 1871; *m.* Charlotte, *d.* of Edward Wheler Mills; died Feb. 26, 1902.

Chandos-Pole *mi.* (R.O.) HENRY (aft. Chandos-Pole-Gell). Of Hopton Hall, Wirksworth, Derbys; 2nd son of E. S. C.-P. of Radbourne Hall, Derby; 1841[3]-1845[3]; St. Mary Hall, Oxf.; J.P. co. Derby; High Sheriff 1886; Member of the Council of the R.A.S., and Founder of the Shire Horse Society; *m.* 1st, Henrietta Auriol, *d.* of Edward William Auriol Drummond-Hay, Chargé d'Affaires in Morocco; 2nd, Teresa Charlotte, *d.* of Sir Edward Manningham-Buller, 1st Bt., of Dilhorn Hall, Stoke-on-Trent; died Oct. 31, 1902.

Lonsdale (C.J.A.) HENRY HEYWOOD. Son of Rev. H. G. L., Vicar of St. Mary's, Lichfield; 1841[3]-1845[1]; Capt. 3rd Dragoon Guards; died unm. at Market Harborough by a fall from his horse, Jan. 15, 1860.

Arden (E.H.P., E.B.) HENRY. Son of J. A. of Rickmansworth Park, Hertford; 1842[3]-1845[3]; went abroad.

Gordon *ma.* (H.D.) WEBSTER THOMAS. 1843[3]-1845[3]; formerly Major 66th Regt.

Watkins (C.O.G.) CHARLES WILLIAM. Of Badby House, Daventry; son of W. W. of Badby; 1842[3]-1845[3]; formerly Lieut. 88th Regt.; aft. Capt. Northants Militia; J.P. for Northants; *m.* Mary Mitchell, *d.* of Richard John Uniacke, Judge of the Supreme Court of Nova Scotia; died Dec. 10, 1857.

Bushby (Miss A., F.E.D.) GEORGE. Son of G. A. B., Bengal Civil Service; 1842[3]-1845[1]; formerly Capt. Bengal Cav.; dead.

Moody (Mrs. P., aft. K.S., C.O.G.) H. . 1850.

Sharp (Miss B., C.L.) WILLIAM JAMES. 1842[3]-1845[2]; formerly Capt. 2nd Surrey Militia.

King (F.E.D.) HENRY WILLIAM. 1843[3]-1845[1]; Ball. Coll. Oxf.

Boileau *mi.* (W.G.C.) SIR F. G. M., Bt. . 1847.

Evans (Mrs. Hor., aft. K.S., C.J.A.) C. J. . 1847.

Marlay (R.O.) CHARLES BRINSLEY. Of Belvedere House, Mullingar; 2nd son of Lieut.-Col. G. M., C.B., of Cavendish Sq., W.; 1843[3]-1845[1]; Trin. Coll. Camb. M.A.; J.P. and D.L. for co. West Meath, High Sheriff 1853; High Sheriff co. Louth 1863, and of co. Cavan 1885. *St. Katharine's Lodge, Regent's Park, N.W.*

Drake (Miss M., aft. K.S., E.C.) H. . 1850.

Alexander (W.A.C.) MAJ.-GEN. SIR C., Bt. 1847.

Hand (Mrs. Ro., aft. K.S., C.J.A.) T. M. . 1847.

Barton (Mrs. Ro., E.H.P.) CHARLES HASTINGS. Eld. son of C. C. B. of Rosse Hill, near Lymington; 1843[3]-1846[3]; Ch. Ch. Oxf. B.A.; Journalist and Schoolmaster at Maryborough, Queensland, Australia; *m.* 1st, Catherine Basedow; 2nd, Elizabeth Basedow; died June 16, 1902.

Grenfell *min.* (W.E., E.B.) A. R. . 1847.

Lygon *mi.* (R.O.) HON. F. (aft. Earl Beauchamp). 1847.

Ashworth (C.L.) FREDERICK CHARLES. 1844[1]-1847[1]; formerly Major of a Dragoon Regt.

Lord Pevensey (W.A.C.) H. N. (aft. Earl of Sheffield). 1847.

Arnold (R.F.H., E.H.P.) KERCHEVER WILLIAM. Son of T. K. A.; 1844[1]-1846[3]; Ball. Coll. Oxf. B.A.

Rust (F.E.D.) G. J. . 1847.

Mr. Legge (F.E.D.) HON. G. B. . 1847.

Jackson *mi.* (E.H.P.) W. H. . 1847.

Buller *mi.* (E.C.) R. J. (aft. Manningham-Buller). 1847.

Thoyts *mi.* (C.O.G.) NEWMAN BURFOOT. 2nd son of M. G. T. of Sulhamstead Park, near Reading; 1844[1]-1844[3]; ent. Indian Army 1849; ret. Col. Indian Staff Corps 1875; served through Indian Mutiny 1857; J.P. co. Gloucester; *m.* Louisa, *d.* of Staff-Surg. Colquhoun Grant. *The Abbots, Cheltenham.*

Fremantle *mi.* (W.E., E.B.) W. H. . 1847.

Birch *mi.* (Miss A., H.M.B.) — ERNEST GEORGE. Son of Rev. H.W.R.B.; 1844[2]-1846[3]; Haileybury Coll.; Bengal Civil Service (ret.); Judge H.M. High Court, Calcutta; *m. d.* of J. T. Darcy Hutton. *Villa Negri, Florence, Italy.*

Herbert (E.C.) — SIR R. G. W., G.C.B. . 1850.

Lord Porchester (Miss M., E.C.) — H. G. H. M. (Earl of Carnarvon). 1847.

Moore *mi.* (R.O.) — CHARLES ROBERT. 2nd son of Hon. and Rev. E. G. M., Canon of Windsor; 1844[3]-1847[1]; died unm. Feb. 2, 1853.

Sir John Ramsden (Miss M., E.H.P.) — SIR J. W., Bt. . 1847.

Ansley *mi.* (Mrs. Ro., F.E.D.) — J. F. . 1847.

Ethelston *mi.* (C.O.G.) — R. P. . 1847.

Johnson (R.F.H., H.D.) — F. W. . 1847.

Wynne (Miss A., E.B.) — W. G. . 1847.

Mr. Harris (R.F.H., E.B.) — HON. R. T. (aft. Harris-Temple). 1847.

Smyth-Pigott (Miss W., E.H.P.) — ALFRED CONSTANTINE NORMAN. 5th son of J. H. S.-P. of Brockley Hall, West Town, Somerset; 1841[2]-1844[3]; went to Rome and entered one of the Colleges there; died May 5, 1870.

Mr. Boyle (R.O.) — HON. W. G. . 1847.

Tovey (Mrs. Ro., W.L.E.) — JAMES. 1842[3]-1846[1]; was a short time at Oxford; aft. in the 87th Regt.; dead.

Elphinstone (Mrs. Hor., C.J.A.) — SIR HOWARD WARBURTON, 3rd Bt. Son of Sir H. E., 2nd Bt.; 1844[1]-1846[1]; Sch. Trin. Coll. Camb. M.A.; 17th Wrangler 1854; Barrister, Lincoln's Inn, 1862; Lecturer to Incorpd. Law Society 1869-71; Prof. of Real Property Law to Inns of Court 1889-92; Reader of the Law of Real Property 1892-6; Conveyancing Counsel to the Court 1895; J.P. for Sussex; *m.* Constance Mary Alexander, *d.* of John Alexander Hankey of Balcombe Place, Sussex. *2 Stone Buildings, W.C., and Struan, Wimbledon Park, S.W.*

Bankes (W.A.C.) — REV. CANON ELDON SURTEES. 2nd son of Rev. Canon E. B. of Soughton Hall, co. Flint; 1843[2]-1846[2]; Univ. Coll. Oxf. M.A.; 3rd Cl. Class.; formerly Rector of Corfe Castle; Canon Res. of Salisbury; *m.* Lady Charlotte Elizabeth Scott, *d.* of John, 2nd Earl of Eldon. *The Close, Salisbury.*

Bernard (Miss A., J.E.Y.) — DAVID WILLIAMS. Eld. son of Sir T. T. B., 6th Bt., of Nettleham, Lincoln; 1843[1]-1846[2]; Postmaster of Merton Coll. Oxf.; 1st Cl. Lit. Hum. 1852; Craven Sch. 1853; died unm. Dec. 29, 1853.

Alderson *mi* (E.C.) — C. H. . 1847.

Elwyn *ma.* (R.F.H., J.W.H.) — HENRY SEPTRANS. 1842[3]-1846[3]; formerly Sec. of the Ottoman Bank, London.

Barnett (W.R., W.L.E.) — W. E. . 1847.

Green *mi.* (Mrs. Ro., aft. K.S., W.A.C.) — W. C. . 1850.

Howman (Miss M., H.D.) — REV. EDWARD JAMES. 1843[2]-1847[1]; Univ. Coll. Oxf. M.A.; formerly Vicar of Exhall, Coventry; aft. Rector of Chinnor, Wallingford, 1876-1902.

Coleridge (E.C.) — W. R. . 1847.

Dowdeswell (W.G.C.) — GEORGE FRANCIS. Eld. son of G. D. of Down House, Redmarley, Gloucester; 1843[2]-1846[3]; Magd. Coll. Camb.; formerly an officer in 83th Foot; died Oct. 1891.

Norton *ma.* (E.C.) — FLETCHER CAVENDISH CHARLES CONYERS. Eld. son of Hon. G. C. N., Recorder of Guildford; 1843[3]-1846[2]; Attaché to the British Embassy at Paris; died at Paris Oct. 13, 1863.

Cobbold (W.E., E.C.) — J. P. . 1847.

Arkwright (W.C., C.O.G.) — LOFTUS WYGRAM. Of Parndon Hall, Little Parndon, Harlow, Essex; 4th son of Rev. J. A. of Mark Hall, Harlow; 1844[1]-1845[3]; *m.* Elizabeth, *d.* of Rowland John Reynolds of Bruton Street, London; died 1889.

Learmonth (F.E.D.) — A. . 1847.

Bradshaw (Miss A., aft. K.S., W.G.C.) — H. . 1847.

Goodall (E.H.P., aft. K.S., E.H.P.) — W. . 1850.

Nind (E.C.) — P. H. . 1850.

Duffield (W.E., E.H.P.) — C. P. . 1847.

Jolliffe (R.F.H., F.E.D.) — HEDWORTH HYLTON (2nd Lord Hylton). 2nd son of Rt. Hon. Sir W. G. H. J., Bt., 1st Lord Hylton, of Merstham House, Redhill, Surrey; 1844[1]-1846[2]; Oriel Coll. Oxf.; formerly Capt. 4th Lt. Dragoons; served in Crimea at Alma and Inkerman, and in Lt. Cav. charge at Balaclava; M.P. for Wells 1855-68; J.P. and D.L. for Somerset, and J.P. Sussex, Cornwall, and Surrey; Capt. N. Somerset Yeo.; *m.* 1st, Lady Agnes Mary Georgiana, *d.* of George Stevens, 2nd Earl of Strafford; 2nd, Anne, *d.* of Henry Lambert, and widow of Edwin, 3rd Earl of Dunraven, of Carnagh, co. Armagh; died Oct. 31, 1899.

Wrangham (R.O.) — WALTER FRANCIS. Of the Rocks, Gloucester; 1844[1]-1846[2]; Barrister W. Circuit; Lieut. Glouc. Yeo.; dead.

Cotterell — SIR JOHN HENRY GEERS, 2nd Bt. Eld. son of J. H. C. and grandson of Sir J. G. C., 1st Bt., of Garnons, near Hereford; 1844[1]-1847[2]; died at Eton, Feb. 17, 1847.

Ferguson *ma.* (W.A.C.) — SIR JOHN DAVIE (aft. Ferguson-Davie), 2nd Bt. 2nd son of Sir H. R. F.-D., 1st Bt., of Creedy Park; 1843[2]-1846[2]; formerly Capt. Gren. Gds.; served in Crimea 1855-6, aft. Col. 1st Devon Militia 1858-69; M.P. for Barnstaple 1859-65; J.P. and D.L. cos. Devon and Carmarthen; J.P. co. Somerset; High Sheriff co. Carmarthen 1874; *m.* E[illegible] [illegible] Augusta, *d.* of Sir James [illegible] Williams, 3rd Bt., of Edwinsford [illegible] *Park, Crediton.*

Crosse (F.E.D.) T. R. . 1847.

Buckley *ma.* (J.E.Y.) A. . 1847.

Atcherley (Miss W., C.J.A.) W. A. . 1847.

Naper (H.D.) LIEUT.-COL. WILLIAM DUTTON. 2nd son of J. L. W. N. of Loughcrew, Oldcastle, co. Meath; 1843–1845; Major 11th Foot; Devons Regt. 1849–77; *m.* Jane, *d.* of Richard Wyatt Edgell of Milton Place, Surrey. *26 Dawson Place, Princes Sq., W.*
SIDNEY HENRY. 1843–1847.

Cornish (E.H.P.)

Christie (J.E.Y.) W. L. . 1847.

Lambert (Miss A., J.E.Y.) C. H. . 1847.

Newton (Miss Edw., C.L.) GEORGE ONSLOW. Of Croxton Park, St. Neots; eld. son of G. N. of Croxton; 1843–1846; Trin. Coll. Camb. B.A.; J.P. and D.L. for cos. Cambridge and Huntingdon; High Sheriff for co. Camb. 1864; *m.* 1st, Mary, *d.* of Wyndham Berkeley Portman of Ham Park; 2nd, Cecilia Florence, *d.* of Edwyn Burnaby of Baggrave Hall, Leicester; 3rd, Lady Alice Sophia Cochrane, *d.* of Thomas, 11th Earl of Dundonald; died 1900.

Halford *mi.* (E.H.P., E.C.) SIR J. F., Bt. . 1847.

Maugham (Mrs. Ri., C.J.A.) H. . 1847.

Praed (Mrs. Hor., E.B.) W. MACKWORTH-. . 1847.

Jones (J.E.Y.) ERNEST. Eld. son of H. T. J.; 1842–1844; died unm.

Bouverie (E.H.P.) HENRY MONTOLIEU. Son of Lieut.-Gen. Sir H. F. B., G.C.B., G.C.M.G., Governor of Malta; 1843–1846; Capt. Coldstream Guards; killed in action at Battle of Inkerman Nov. 5, 1854.

Legge (W.E., W.A.C.) H. E. . 1847.

Morris-Reade WILLIAM. Son of — M.-R. of Rossenarra, Kilkenny; 1843–1847.

Fennell (Miss W., F.E.D.) ROBERT SPENCER. 1843–1845.

Buckston (Mrs. Ri., F.E.D.) REV. ROWLAND GERMAN. Of Bradbourne, Ashbourne; son of Rev. G. B. of Bradbourne, and Vicar of Sutton-on-the-Hill, Derby; 1843–1846; B.N.C. Oxf. M.A.; Vicar of Sutton-on-the-Hill 1861–1903; *m.* Ada Letitia, *d.* of Rev. Henry White; died June 10, 1903.

Burder *ma.* (Miss P., E.B.) C. S. . 1847.

Fletcher (E.H.P., F.E.D.); EDWARD PHILIP. Son of C. P. F.; 1842–1845; went abroad.

Coney (Miss P., E.B.) W J . 1847.

Lord Ribblesdale (R.F.H., E.B.) THOMAS (3rd Lord). Son of Thomas, 2nd Lord R.; 1843–1844; Ch. Ch. Oxf.; formerly Lieut. Royal Horse Gds. Blue; *m.* Emma, *d.* of Col. William Mure of Caldwell; died at Geneva, Aug. 1876.

Aytoun (W.L.E.) JAMES. 2nd son of J. A. of Inchdairnie, Kirkcaldy; 1843–1845; Major 85th Regt; formerly 7th Hussars; served in the Indian Mutiny.

Walpole (W.G.C.) H. A. . 1847.

Cust (W.E., H.D.) HORACE WILLIAM. 3rd son of Lieut.-Col. Hon. P. F. C.; 1843–1845; Capt. Coldstream Gds.; killed at battle of Alma, Sept. 20, 1854.

Mount (E.C.) F. J. . 1847.

Pretyman (E.H.P.) A. C. . 1847.

Walker (W.G.C.) REV. JOSEPH. Son of J. N. W. of Calderstone, Lancs; 1842–1846; B.N.C. Oxf. M.A.; Rector of Averham-cum-Kelham; *m.* *d.* of Rev. John Drake Becher. *Averham Rectory, Newark.*

Law (H.D.) HENRY TOWRY. 3rd son of Hon. C. E. L., Q.C., Recorder of London; 1843–1845; was in the Army; died Nov. 7, 1855.

Templer (Mrs. Hor., W.A.C.) J. G. J. . 1847.

Onslow (C.L.) ANDREW GEORGE. Of Oxenhall, Newent, Gloucester; eld. son of R. F. O. of Staurdene, co. Gloucester; 1843–1845; J.P. and D.L. co. Gloucester; formerly Capt. 97th and 13th Regts.; *m.* Mary, *d.* of Sir John Owen, 1st Bt.; died Aug. 26, 1894.

Adeane (Mrs. Hor., E.B.) R. J. . 1847.

Baillie *mi.* (Mrs. Ro., W.G.C.) A. W. . 1847.

Mr. Massey (J.E.Y.) HON. EYRE CHALLONER HENRY (4th Lord Clarina). Eld. son of Eyre, 3rd Lord C.; 1843–1844; Col. Durham L.I.; General in the Army, comm. Dublin district 1881–6; Knight of the Legion of Honour; died unm. Dec. 16, 1897.

Snowden *mi.* (F.E.D.) E. . 1850.

Tryon *ma.* (Miss A., J.E.Y.) THOMAS. Of Bulwick Park, Wansford, Northants; eld. son of T. T. of Bulwick; 1842–1846; served in the Crimea; Lieut.-Col. 7th Royal Fusiliers; J.P. for Northants, High Sheriff 1875; *m.* Alice, *d.* of Rev. Samuel Vere Dashwood of Stanford Hall, Notts; died Dec. 19, 1888.

Oakeley (H.O.) WILLIAM EDWARD. Son of W. O. of Glanwilliam, Merionethshire; 1841–1845; Ch. Ch. Oxf.; formerly Capt. Staffs Yeo.; J.P. & D.L. co. Merioneth, High Sheriff 1874; *m.* Hon. Mary Russell, *d.* of Sophia Baroness de Clifford. *Plâs Tan-y-Bwlch, N. Wales, and Cliff House, Atherstone.*

Molony *min.* (Miss W., F.E.D.) EDMUND WELDON, H.E.I.C.S. 4th son of J. M. of Kiltanon, near Tulla, Limerick; 1843–1846; Bengal Civil Service; *m.* Frances Selina, *d.* of A. Edward Gayer, LL.D., Q.C.; died Jan. 30, 1888.

Blundell (C.J.A. & H.D.) H. (aft. Blundell-Hollinshead-Blundell). . 1847.

Taylor (H.D.) W. F. . 1847.

Stephen *mi.* (Home, E.B.) — SIR LESLIE, K.C.B. 2nd son of Rt. Hon. Sir J. S., K.C.B., Under Sec. of State for the Colonies; 1842[3]-1845[3]; Trin. Hall, Camb. M.A.; 20th Wrangler 1854, Fellow and Tutor of Trin. Hall, Camb.; Clark Lecturer in English Literature; Pres. of Ethical Socy.; Editor of 'Cornhill' Mag. 1871-82; Dictionary of Nat. Biography 1882-91; formerly in Holy Orders; *m.* 1st, Harriet Marion, *d.* of William Makepeace Thackeray, the celebrated novelist; 2nd, Julia Prinsep, *d.* of John Jackson, M.D., and widow of Herbert Duckworth, Barrister. *22 Hyde Park Gate, S.W.*

Powys *mi.* (Mrs. Ro., E.B.) — F. A. . 1847.

Ramsden (H.D.) — FREDERICK HENRY. Eld. son of H. J. R. of Oxton Hall, Tadcaster; 1843[1]-1847[2]; entd. Rifle Bgde. 1847; Capt. Coldstream Gds. 1851; killed at Inkerman Nov. 5, 1854.

Hamilton (W.E., W.A.C.) — HON. GUSTAVUS RUSSELL (aft. Hamilton-Russell). 8th Viscount Boyne, son of Gustavus Frederick, 7th Viscount B.; 1843[3]-1846[2]; J.P. and D.L. co. Durham & J.P. co. Meath; *m.* Lady Katharine Frances Scott, *d.* of John, 2nd Earl of Eldon.

Prendergast (Miss A., E.H.P.) — L. . 1847.

Tugwell (W.A.C.) — G. . 1847.

Lewis (Miss A., H.M.B.) — W. L. . 1847.

Mangles (F.E.D.) — WILLIAM HENRY. Son of — M. of Whitmore Lodge, Sunninghale; 1844[1]-1846[1]; formerly Capt. 56th Regt.

Helm *mi.* (Mrs. Ro., aft. K.S.) — C. O. . 1847.

Watson (W.E., F.E.D.) — SIR A. T., Bt. . 1847.

Rolt *mi.* (Mrs. D., C.O.G.) — THOMAS FRANCIS. 2nd son of Gen. Sir J. R., K.C.B.; 1842[3]-1845[1]; formerly Capt. Coldstream Gds.; *m.* 1st, Miss Boot; 2nd, Miss Garnett; died Oct. 23, 1901.

Hamilton (F.E.D.) — JOHN GLENCAIRN CARTER (1st Lord Hamilton of Dalzell). Of Dalzell House, Motherwell; son of A. J. H. of Dalzell; 1842[3]-1845[3]; J.P., D.L. and Vice-Lieut. of Lanarkshire; formerly Capt. 2nd Life Gds.; aft. Col. Queen's Own Glasgow and Lanarks Yeo.; M.P. for Falkirk Burghs 1857-9, for S. Lanarks 1868-74 and 1880-6; a Lord-in-waiting to Queen Victoria 1892-4; *m.* Lady Emily Eleanor Leslie-Melville, *d.* of David, 8th Earl of Leven and Melville; died Oct. 15, 1900.

Staunton (H.D.) — GEORGE WILLIAM MALGER. 1843[1]-1845[1]; St. Catherine's Hall, Camb.

Webb (W.G.C.) — WILLIAM FREDERICK. Of Newstead Abbey, Notts; eld. son of F. W. of Westwick, co. Durham; 1843[3]-1845[3]; formerly Lieut. 17th Lancers; J.P. and D.L. for N. Riding, Yorks, and Notts; High Sheriff of Notts 1866; *m.* Emilia Jane, *d.* of Thomas Mills Goodlake of Wadley, Shellingford, Faringdon; died Feb. 24, 1899.

Sparke (Mrs. Ro., E.H.P.) — HENRY ASTLEY. Eld. son of Rev. Canon J. H. S. of Gunthorpe Hall, East Dereham; 1842[3]-1845[3]; Lieut. 4th Lt. Dragoons; medal and clasps, Alma and Balaclava; killed in the charge at Balaclava, Oct. 25, 1854.

Wood (C.O.G.) — V. (aft. Stuckey). . 1847.

Yonge *max.* (W.G.C., aft. K.S., W.G.C.) — H. . 1847.

Yonge *ma.* (W.G.C., aft. K.S., W.G.C.) — F. L. . 1847.

Dimsdale (R.O.) — HENRY FRASER. 2nd son of Thomas Robert, 4th Lord Dimsdale; 1842[3]-1844[3]; an officer in 11th Hussars; died Jan. 16, 1857.

Price (J.E.Y.) — JOHN GRIFFITH. 1842[1]-1844[3]; Major Queen's Bays; died at Cawnpore 1857.

Hough (Miss W., W.A.C.) — COL. LEWIS. Son of Rev. J. H. of Ham, Richmond, Surrey; 1842[1]-1845[3]; Trin. Coll. Camb. M.A.; Col. 5th Bn. Royal Fusiliers (ret.); *m.* Francesca Mary, *d.* of Woodcock Hayward. *4 San Remo, Hove, Sussex.*

Zwilchenbart (C.L.) — RODOLPH. 1843[3]-1845[1]; a Merchant in Liverpool, of the firm of Zwilchenbart, Forrer & Co.

Wilmot (Miss Edw., F.E.D.) — R. E. E. . 1847.

Bevan (C.O.G.) — ROBERT. 3rd son of R. B. of Rougham Rookery, Rougham, Bury St. Edmunds; 1842[3]-1846[3]; Trin. Coll. Camb.; *m.* Isabella Crapp; died June 6, 1875.

Bligh (Mrs. Ro., W.G.C.) — FREDERICK CHERBURGH. Of Brittas, Nobber, co. Meath; son of E. B. of Brittas; 1842[3]-1844[3]; formerly Major 41st Foot; wounded at Inkerman; J.P. co. Meath; *m.* Emily Matilda, *d.* of Hinton East; died Nov. 30, 1901.

FOURTH FORM.

Stileman (Mrs. Ro., J.W.H., & J.E.Y.) — MAJ.-GEN. WILLIAM CROUGHTON. Son of R. S. of The Friars, Winchelsea, Rye; 1842[3]-1844[3]; served in the H.E.I.C. 1845-75 (ret.); *m.* Fanny, *d.* of John Gibbard of Sharnbrook House, Bedford. *21 Lewes Crescent, Brighton.*

Atkin (W.E., W.A.C.) — WALTER ROBERT. 1841[3]-1844[3]; formerly at the Irish Bar.

Kavanagh (W.A.C.) — THOMAS. Of Borris House, Borris, co. Carlow; eld. son of T. K. of Borris; 1842[3]-1844[3]; emigrated to Australia and died there unm. March 1852.

Marshall (W.L.E.) — LIEUT.-GEN. SIR FREDERICK, K.C.M.G. Of Broadwater, Godalming; 3rd son of G. M. of Broadwater; 1844[3]-1846[1]; Lieut.-Gen., 2nd Life Gds. (ret. 1881); A.D.C. to Sir J. Y. Scarlett in the Crimea; med., clasp, and Turkish med.; served in the Zulu War; Col. 1st R. Dragoons 1890; formerly A.D.C. to H.R.H. the Commander-in-Chief; Master of Chiddingfold Foxhounds; J.P. for Surrey; *m.* Adelaide Laura, *d.* of Edward Howard; died June 8, 1900.

Fursdon (W.E., W.A.C.) — C. . 1847.

Chichester — CHARLES. Eld. son of R. C. of Hall; 1842[3]-1845[3]; Magd. Coll. Oxf.; J.P. and D.L. for Devon; formerly Lieut. Devon Mounted Rifles; *m.* Beatrice, *d.* of Sir Arthur Chichester, 8th Bt. of Raleigh. *Hall, Bishop's Tawton, Barnstaple.*

Hamilton (J.E.Y.) — Hugh. Son of Col. A. W. H. of Pinmore: 1843^{1}–1845^{1}; J.P. and D.L. co. Ayr; formerly Capt. King's Dragoon Gds.; *m.* 1st, Selina Mary, *d.* of Sir George Burdett L'Estrange: 2nd, Georgina Hay, *d.* of James Campbell of Craigie, Ayr, and widow of Lieut.-Col. W. Brewster. *Pinmore, Daljarrock, S.O., Ayrshire.*

Parks *ma.* (Miss W., E.H.P. & F.E.D.) — John Charles. Son of — P. of Woodside, Old Windsor; 1840^{2}–1840^{3}; readmitted 1843^{1}–1844^{3}.

Dickson (W.L.E.) — Lieut.-Gen. William Thomas. Son of Major-Gen. W. D., C.B., of Croom Castle, Limerick; 1843^{2}–1846^{3}; Lieut.-Gen. (ret.) and Col. 16th Lancers. 26 *Portman Square, W.*

Nicholls (Mrs. Ro., J.W.H.) — Howel Arthur. 1842^{3}–1847^{1}.

Fellows *ma.* (Mrs. P., W.G.C.) — Herbert William. Son of T. F. of Moneyhill House, Rickmansworth, Herts: 1843^{2}–1845^{3}; Partner in Salter & Co., Brewers, Rickmansworth; *m.* Marion, *d.* of William Stephens of Bedford Row, London; died 1883.

Lord Russborough (Miss M., W.G.C.) — Joseph Henry (5th Earl of Milltown). Eld. son of Joseph, 4th Earl of M.: 1843^{2}–1844^{2}; Capt. Dublin Militia, formerly 68th Regt. and A.D.C. to H.E. Lord-Lieut. of Ireland; died unm. April 8, 1871.

Angell (Mrs. Rl., W.G.C.) — J. B. . 1847.

Shuckburgh (J.E.Y.) — Sir George Thomas Francis. 9th Bt. Son of Sir F. S., 8th Bt., of Shuckburgh, Daventry; 1843^{2}–1844^{2}; Maj. 1st Bn. Scots Fusilier Gds.; Kt. of Legion of Honour and of the Medjidie; Crimean Medal; present at battles of Alma and Balaclava, served in the trenches before Sebastopol, severely wounded at Inkerman March 20, 1857; J.P. and D.L. for Warwickshire; *m.* Ida Florence Geraldine, *d.* of Rev. Frederick William Robertson of Brighton; died Jan. 12, 1884.

Villers *ma.* (R.F.H., aft. K.S.) — Edward William Basevi. 1843^{2}–1844^{2}.

Villers *mi.* (R.F.H., aft. K.S.) — R. J. . 1847.

Lucas (Miss M., W.G.C.) — Eward Thomas. 1843^{2}–1847^{1}.

Shuldham *mi.* (Miss A., aft. K.S., J.E.Y.) — N. L. . 1847.

Penruddocke (E.H.P.) — Charles. Of Compton Park, Compton Chamberlayne, Salisbury, and Bratton Lodge, Wincanton, Somerset; eld. son of C. P. of Compton Park; 1843^{2}–1845^{2}; Barrister; sometime Maj. Comm. 14th Wilts R.V. and Capt. Melksham troop Royal Wilts Yeo. Cav.; J.P. and D.L. for Wilts, High Sheriff 1861; *m.* Flora Henrietta, *d.* of Walter Long, M.P., of Rood Ashton, Wraxall; died Oct. 30, 1899.

Maxwell (C.L.) — W. . 1847.

Morgan *mi* (H.D.) — Hon. G. C. (Lord Tredegar). 1847.

Davis *mi.* (Mrs. P., C.O.G.) — J. C. . 1847.

Marquis of Bath (E.C.) — J. A. . 1847.

Halford (C.O.G.) — C. A. D. . 1847.

Wyndham (Mrs. Hor., C.J.A.) — Hon. Henry (2nd Lord Leconfield). 2nd son of George, 1st Lord L. of Petworth House, Sussex: 1843^{1}–1846^{3}; Ch. Ch. Oxf.; J.P. and D.L. for Sussex; formerly Capt. 1st Life Gds., and Lieut. Yorks Yeo. Hussars; M.P. for W. Sussex 1854–69; Vice-Chmn. and Aldmn. W. Div. of Sussex C.C.; M.F.H. of the Leconfield Hunt; Vice-Pres. of St. George's Hospital, London; *m.* Hon. Constance Evelyn, *d.* of Archibald, Lord Dalmeny; died Jan. 6, 1901.

Cockerell *mi.* (W.A.C.) — H. A. . 1847.

Melville (E.H.P.) — John Rererson. 1843^{2}–1845^{1}.

Carr (E.H.P.) — E. D. . 1847.

Stone *mi.* (Mrs. P., C.J.A.) — Charles. Son of T. A. S. of London; 1843^{2}–1845^{2}; studied Medicine, aft. went to India as a Civil Engineer and died there.

Hardinge (W.E., E.H.P.) — Sir H. C., Bt. . 1847.

Stratton *mi.* (R.F.H., C.J.A.) — J. . 1847.

Mr. Hely-Hutchinson (W.E., E.H.P.) — Hon. John William. 2nd son of John, 3rd Earl of Donoughmore: 1843^{2}–1846^{2}; Capt. 13th Lt. Dragoons; died of illness at Scutari, July 16, 1855.

Carew (C.O.G.) — Charles Hallowell. Formerly of Beddington Park, Surrey; 1842^{2}–1846^{1}.

Wigram (R.F.H., E.C.) — R. J. . 1847.

Forbes (R.F.H., C.O.G.) — Lachlan. Of Shillingstone, near Blandford: son of J. F.: 1844^{1}–1847^{1}; formerly Major 31st Foot; J.P. for Dorset; *m.* Julia, *d.* of Capt. A. Wyndham; died Oct. 31, 1895.

Paget (Mrs. P., C.O.G.) — Arthur John Snow. Eld. son of J. M. P. of Cranmore Hall, Shepton Mallet; 1844^{1}–1846^{2}; died April 1863.

Waterfield (R.F.H., aft. K.S., C.J.A.) — O. C. . 1847.

Harper (Mrs. Hor., aft. K.S., C.J.A., & H.D.) — H. W. . 1850.

King (Mrs. Ro., W.A.C.) — R. M. . 1847.

Thesiger (E.H.P.) — Hon. C. W. . 1847.

Halton (Mrs. Ro., F.E.D.) — Lancelot. 1844^{1}–1846^{3}; formerly Major 16th Lancers.

Tryon *mi.* (J.E.Y.) — Sir G., K.C.B. . 1847.

Pottinger (Miss M., E.B.) — SIR FREDERICK WILLIAM, 2nd Bt. 2nd son of Rt. Hon. Sir H. P., 1st Bt.; 1844^{2}–1847^{1}; formerly Gren. Gds.; aft. Chief Commissioner of Mounted Police in New South Wales; died at Sydney, N.S.W., April 9, 1865.

Wollaston (R.F.H., aft. K.S., C.J.A., & C.Wo.) — W. M. . 1850.

Turner (R.F.H., E.B.) — C. H. . 1847.

Cheales (Mrs. Ro., aft. K.S., C.J.A.) — H. J. . 1847.

Babington (Home, J.E.Y.) — FRANCIS EVANS. Eld. son of M. B. of Rothley, Banker at Leicester; 1844^{2}–1846^{2}; formerly in the War Office; J.P. for Suffolk; *m.* Margaret Susan, *d.* of Rev. W. B. Dunbar of Glencairn, co. Dumfries. *South Lodge, Halesworth.*

Foster *mi.* (Miss A., H.M.B.) — FRANCIS GOSTLING. 3rd son of Sir W. F., 1st Bt., of Thorpe, Norwich; 1844^{2}–1846^{1}; Solicitor; *m.* 1st, Lucy, *d.* of Capt. William Gwyn, R.N., of Tasburg Lodge, Norfolk; 2nd, Bertha, *d.* of Timothy Steward of Heigham Lodge, Norfolk; died March 20, 1894.

Dawson *ma.* (J.E.Y.) — GEORGE. Son of — D. of Yaldhurst House, Lymington; 1843^{3}–1846^{1}; Barrister.

Coote (Miss A., E.B.) — CHIDLEY DOWNES. 5th son of Sir C. H. C., 9th Bt., of Ballyfin, Mountrath; 1843^{3}–1846^{2}; 52nd Foot; *m.* Theresa, *d.* of Capt. John Anthony Reinbod of Nice; died March 10, 1872.

Croft (E.H.P.) — G. A. H. . 1847.

Irlam (C.L.) — G. . 1847.

Barton *ma.* (W.L.E.) — D. F. . 1847.

Hunt (C.J.A.) — ROWLAND. Of Boreatton Park, Shrewsbury, and Kibworth Hall, Leicester; eld. son of R. H. of Boreatton; 1843^{3}–1845^{2}; Ch. Ch. Oxf.; *m.* Florence Marianne, *d.* of R. B. Humfrey of Stoke Albany House, Market Harborough; died Dec. 5, 1878.

Lennox (C.L.) — J. K. . 1847.

Fraser (Mrs. Hor., E.H.P.) — SIR CHARLES CRAUFORD, K.C.B., V.C. 2nd son of Sir J. J. F., 3rd Bt.; 1843^{3}–1845^{1}; Lieut.-Gen. in the Army; Col. 8th Hussars; M.P. for Lambeth 1885–92; formerly Inspector-Gen. of Cav. in England and Comm. of Cav. at Aldershot; prev. Insp.-Gen. of Cav. in Ireland; Col. 11th Hussars and A.D.C. to F.-M. Commanding-in-Chief; highly distinguished in India during the Mutiny and in the Abyssinian War; died unm. June 7, 1895.

Cookesley *ma.* (W.G.C.) — A. F. . 1850.

Balguy *mi.* (Miss Edw., F.E.D.) — FRANCIS ST. JOHN. 4th son of J. B. of Duffield, co. Derby; 1843^{3}–1844^{3}; B.N.C. Oxf.; Merchant in the City; *m.* Caroline Georgiana, *d.* of Thomas Hawkesworth of Stoke-under-Ham, Somerset; died 1863.

Bedford *mi.* (R.F.H., aft. K.S., W.G.C.) — F. R. . 1847.

Lawrence (H.D.) — HUGH ALLAN. 1842^{3}–1846^{1}.

Mariette *ma.* (Home) — A. DE V. . 1847.

Court (Miss M., J.E.Y.) — DAVID ALEXANDER. 1842^{3}–1845^{1}.

Shaw (Mrs. Ro., E.B.) — J. M. . 1847.

Hardisty (Mrs. Ro., H.D.) — R. R. . 1847.

Caley *ma.* (J.E.Y.) — ALBERT JARMAN. Son of J. C. of Windsor; 1841^{1}–1844^{1}; formerly Chemist at Norwich, aft. Mfr. of Mineral Waters; *m.* Elizabeth, *d.* of James Bain of 1 Haymarket, St. James's, S.W.; died 1895.

Caley *mi.* (J.E.Y., aft. K.S., J.E.Y.) — G. A. . 1847.

Umphelby (Mrs. D.) — ARTHUR. 1842^{3}–1844^{3}.

Slade *mi.* (C.J.A. & H.D.) — G. F. . 1847.

Holden *mi.* (C.L.) — J. G. . 1847.

Wyatt (R.F.H., W.A.C.) — MAJOR CHARLES EDWYN. 1842^{3}–1845^{1}; served with 14th Lt. Dragoons in Persian expedn. 1857, and in Central India Field Force, under Sir Hugh Rose, in 1858; one of H.M.'s Hon. Corps of Gentlemen-at-Arms 1869–95.

Purvis (Mrs. Hor., F.E.D.) — VICE-ADMIRAL JOHN CHILD. Son of Rev. R. P., Vicar of Whitsbury, Hants; 1842^{3}–1845^{2}; Vice-Adml. (ret.). *16 Hanover Sq., W.*

Hunt *ma.* (E.H.P.) — FREDERICK WHATELY. Son of — H., Parliamentary Agent; 1842^{3}–1846^{3}; died young.

Haywood *ma.* (W.G.C.) — E. W. . 1847.

Boynton (J.E.Y.) — GEORGE HEBBLETHWAITE LUTTON. 4th son of Sir H. B., 9th Bt., of Barmston, Hull; 1842^{3}–1844^{3}; formerly Lieut. 11th Hussars; aft. Capt. 17th Lancers; *m.* 1st, Elizabeth Laura, *d.* of Thomas Henry Keeling; 2nd, Elizabeth Anne, *d.* of Thomas Prickett of the Avenue, Bridlington; died May 18, 1888.

Branwell (Mrs. Ro., aft. K.S., C.L.) — CHARLES HENRY. Born at Penzance, Cornwall; 1840^{3}–1844^{3}.

Wallis (E.B.) — JOHN RICHARD SMYTH. Of Drishane Castle, Millstreet, co. Cork; son of H. W. of Drishane; 1842^{3}–1845^{1}; Trin. Coll. Dublin; formerly 4th Dragoon Gds.; J.P. co. Cork, High Sheriff 1857; *m.* Octavia Willoughby, *d.* of Lord Middleton; died Oct. 27, 1868.

Philips *ma.* (C.L.) — F. . 1847.

Philips *mi.* (C.L.) — G. H. . 1847.

West *mi.* (Miss A., E.H.P.) — [illegible] G.C.B. . 1847.

Kinloch (C.J.A. & H.M.B.) — SIR ALEXANDER, 10th Bt. Son of Sir D. K., 9th Bt., of Gilmerton; 1844^{1}-1846^{2}; formerly Capt. Gren. Gds.; served in the Crimea, med. with four clasps and Turkish med.; J.P. and D.L. East Lothian; *m.* Lucy Charlotte, *d.* of Sir Ralph Abercromby Anstruther, 4th Bt., of Balcaskie, co. Fife. *Gilmerton House, Drem, Haddingtonshire.*

Browne (Mrs. Ri., E.B.) — ARTHUR HERBERT. 1844^{1}-1845^{2}.

Caulfeild (H.D.) — ST. G. F. R. . 1847.

Marshall *mi.* (Miss W., F.E.D.) — J. B. . 1847.

Suttie (W.L.E.) — SIR J. GRANT-, Bt. . 1847.

Gordon-Cumming (W.L.E.) — WILLIAM GORDON. 5th son of Sir W. G. G.-C., 2nd Bt.; 1844^{1}-1845^{3}; Lieut.-Col. Bombay Staff Corps (ret.); D.L. for Banff; *m.* 1st, Alexa Angelina Harvey, *d.* of James Brand of Bedford Hill, Balham, Surrey; 2nd, Hon. Lettice Hermione Violet Willoughby, *d.* of Henry, 8th Lord Middleton. *Forres House, Forres.*

Bayly (W.L.E.) — JOHN. Son of — B. of Desborough, co. Tipperary; 1844^{1}-1844^{3}; Trin. Coll. Camb.; formerly Capt. 1st Lancs Militia.

Drummond (H.D.) — CAPT. ALFRED MANNERS. 3rd son of A. R. D. of Cadland, Fawley, Southampton; 1844^{1}-1846^{2}; formerly Capt. Rifle Bgde.; served in Crimea, Sebastopol; medal and clasp and Turkish medal; *m.* Augusta, *d.* of Robert Verschoyle of Kilberry, co. Kildare. *54 Fitzjohn's Avenue, Hampstead, N.W.*

Neave *ma.* (Miss M., E.H.P.) — SIR ARUNDELL, 4th Bt. Of Dagnam Park, Romford; eld. son of Sir R. D. N., 3rd Bt., of Dagnam Park: 1844^{1}-1846^{2}; Capt. 3rd Dragoon Gds.; D.L. for Essex; *m.* Hon. Gwen Gertrude Hughes, *d.* of William Lewis, 1st Lord Dinorben; died Sept. 21, 1877.

Neave *mi.* (Miss M., E.H.P.) — EDWARD DIGBY. 2nd son of Sir R. D. N., 3rd Bt., of Dagnam Park, Romford; 1844^{1}-1845^{2}; Bombay Civil Service; died unm. at Mulligawne, July 1, 1858.

Howard *mi.* (W.A.C.) — EDWARD HENRY. 3rd son of Very Rev. H. E. J. H., D.D., Dean of Lichfield; 1844^{1}-1845^{3}; Vice-Adm. R.N.; formerly A.D.C. to Queen Victoria; *m.* Sophia Caroline Lucille, *d.* of Francis Robertson Lynch of Spanish Town, Jamaica; died Jan. 18, 1890.

Mr. Quin (W.E., E.C.) — HON. W. H. WYNDHAM-. 1847.

Janvrin (Miss M., F.E.D.) — F. W. . 1847.

Mr. Talbot (Miss M., E.H.P.) — HON. CHARLES JOHN CHETWYND (19th Earl of Shrewsbury and Talbot). Eld. son of Henry John Chetwynd, 18th Earl of S. and T.; 1844^{1}-1844^{2}; Merton Coll. Oxf.; formerly 1st Life Gds.; M.P. for S. Staffs and Stamford; Capt. of Hon. Corps of Gentlemen-at-Arms; *m.* Anna Theresa, *d.* of Richard Howe Cockerell, Comm. R.N.; died May 11, 1877.

Bradley (W.L.E.) — J. H. . 1847.

Christie (C.L.) — W. J. . 1847.

Talfourd *mi.* (Miss A., W.G.C.) — REV. WILLIAM WORDSWORTH. Son of Judge T. N. T.; 1842^{3}-1847^{1}; New. Coll. Oxf. M.A.; formerly Rector of Winceby, Lincs, aft. Rector of Mundersley, Essex; died unm. Dec. 8, 1900.

Ferguson *mi.* (W.A.C.) — W. A. (aft. Ferguson-Davie). 1850.

Thomson (W.E., C.L.) — COL. SIR ROBERT THOMAS (aft. White-Thomson), K.C.B. Eld. son of R. T. of Camphill, Renfrewshire; 1844^{2}-1846^{3}; formerly Major King's Dragoon Gds. and Hon. Col. Comm. 4th Bn. Devon Regt. 1867-93; J.P. for Kent, J.P. and D.L. for Devon; Aldmn. Devon C.C.; Member of House of Laymen, Prov. of Canterbury; *m.* Fanny Julia, *d.* of Sir Henry Robert Ferguson-Davie, 1st Bt., of Creedy Park, Crediton. *Broomford Manor, Exbourne, N. Devon.*

Tighe (J.E.Y.) — J. S. . 1847.

Oldfield *mi.* (W.G.C.) — MAJ.-GEN. HENRY THOMAS. Of Orchardmains House, Peebles-shire; 2nd son of H. S. O. of Bengal Civil Service; 1844^{2}-1847^{1}; Military Coll. Addiscombe; Maj.-Gen. (ret.) Bengal Staff Corps; Comm. 6th Bengal Cav.; *m.* Matilda Douglas, *d.* of Charles Lionel Maitland-Keirwan of Gilston Castle, Castle Douglas; died Dec. 6, 1902.

Astley *mi.* (C.O.G.) — H. F. L. . 1847.

Wheatley (Miss A., H.M.B.) — W. . 1847.

Heygate (Mrs. Ri., E.B.) — ROBERT HENRY JOHN. Of Oaklands, Leominster; 4th son of Sir W. H., 1st Bt., of Roecliffe Hall, Loughborough; 1844^{2}-1847^{2}; Trin. Coll. Camb. M.A.; J.P. for cos. Hereford and Essex; *m.* Isabella Dorothy, *d.* of George Gill Mounsey of Castletown, Cumberland; died Jan. 7, 1890.

Tolley (C.O.G.) — HENRY. Son of Lieut.-Gen. Sir H. D. T., C.B.; 1844^{2}-1847^{1}; died unm. in Italy in 1851.

Jervoise (C.O.G.) — SIR H. CLARKE-, Bt. . 1847.

Pearson (R.F.H., E.B.) — RICHARD LYONS OTWAY. 1844^{2}-1844^{3}; formerly Capt. Gren. Gds.; was A.D.C. to Sir G. Brown in the Crimea.

Robinson (C.O.G.) — SIR J. B., Bt. . 1847.

Hampson (E.H.P.) — W. S. . 1847.

Ogle (W.L.E.) — S. J. . 1847.

Pares (W.L.E.) — THOMAS HENRY. Of Hopwell Hall, near Derby; eld. son of T. P. of Hopwell; 1844^{2}-1846^{3}; Trin. Coll. Camb.; formerly Leicesters Yeo., aft. Capt. 48th Northants Militia; *m.* Mary Louisa, *d.* of Rev. Richard Stephens, Vicar of Belgrave-cum-Birstall, Leicester; died May 9, 1878.

Fellows *mi.* (Mrs. P. & Mrs. Vav., W.G.C.) — COL. ROBERT BRUCE, C.B. Son of T. F. of Moneyhill House, Rickmansworth, Herts; 1844^{2}-1847^{1}; Christ's Coll. Camb.; Col. Comm. 4th Beds. Regt. 1878-92; ent. Privy Council Office 1858; Dep. Clerk of the Council 1894-5; J.P. for Herts; *m.* Emily Ann, *d.* of John Fellows of Eynsford, Kent. *Stanborough Cottage, Hatfield.*

Shaw (W.B., F.E.D.) — Sir J. C. K., Bt. . 1847.

White (Mrs. Ro., F.E.D.) — Hon. Luke (2nd Lord Annaly), K.P. Eld. son of Henry, 1st Lord A. of Woodlands, co. Dublin; 1844^{2}-1844^{3}; Lieut.-Col. Rifle Bgde., formerly Capt. 13th Lt. Dragoons; a Lord of the Treasury 1868-74; State Steward to H.E. Earl Spencer Lord-Lieut. of Ireland; M.P. for Longford 1861-2, and Kidderminster 1862-5; *m.* Emily, *d.* of William Stuart; died March 17, 1888.

Pole (R.O.) — Cecil Charles (aft. Van Notten-Pole). Eld. son of Sir P. V. N.-P., 3rd Bt., of Todenham, Moreton-in-Marsh; 1844^{2}-1846^{2}; *m.* Frances Emma, *d.* of Hon. and Rev. Henry Rice, Rector of Gt. Rissington, Glos.; died Sept. 17, 1876.

Hall (Mrs. Ri., F.E.D.) — Marshall. 1844^{2}-1844^{3}; Magd. Coll. Camb.; a Barrister.

Uniacke (R.O.) — H. T. . 1847.

Crawley (Miss A. & Miss Edg., H.M.B.) — R. T. . 1847.

Montgomery (W.L.E.) — Major-Gen. Hugh Parker. Son of A. H. M. of Tyrella, Clough, co. Down; 1844^{2}-1847^{1}; formerly in 60th Rifles, aft. Lieut.-Col. comm. Rifle Depôt at Winchester. 35 *Southgate Street, Winchester.*

Green (H.D.) — H. Egerton-. . 1847.

Meade-King (Miss Edw., H.D.) — R. . 1847.

Morris (W.L.E.) — Charles John. Of Wood Eaton Manor, Stafford; son of J. M. of Wood Eaton; 1844^{2}-1847^{1}; Ch. Ch. Oxf. B.A.; J.P. cos. Stafford and Salop; High Sheriff co. Salop, 1884; *m.* Constance Lingen, *d.* of Robert Burton of Longner Hall, Salop; died Aug. 29, 1899.

Bateson *mi.* (C.O.G.) — J. . 1847.

Mr. Colborne (W.E., E.C.) — Major Hon. John. 5th son of John, 1st Lord Seaton, of Seaton, Devon; 1844^{2}-1846^{3}; served in Crimea, India and China; Lieut.-Col. Egyptian Army, served on Gen. Hicks Pasha's Staff Soudan Field Force; present at battle of Marabea Senna; recd. 3rd Class Order Medjidie; died unm. Feb. 13, 1890.

Wilder (Mrs. Ro. & C.O.G., C.O.G. & W.W.) — H. B. . 1850.

Shirley (Mrs. Ro., aft. K.S.) — H. H. . 1850.

Hunt *mi.* (E.H.P.) — A. . 1847.

Buckley *mi.* (J.E.Y.) — D. F. B. . 1847.

Gibbs *mi.* (J.E.Y.) — Rev. John Lomax. 8th son of G. H. G. of Aldenham House, Elstree, Herts; 1843^{3}-1845^{2}; Exeter Coll. Oxf. M.A.; Vicar of Clifton Hampden, Berks, 1864-74, of Exwick, Devon, 1878-85, and Rector of Clyst-St.-George, Exeter, 1885-97; *m.* Isabell Marianne, *d.* of Robert Bright of Abbotsleigh, Bristol. *Speen House, Newbury, Berks.*

Mitford (R.F.H., aft. K.S.) — H. R. . 1847.

Richards (Miss W., aft. K.S., C.J.A.) — Charles James. Son of Rev. — R., Rector of Sampford Courtenay, N. Devon; 1843^{3}-1845^{3}.

Norris (Miss A., aft. K.S.) — W. A. . 1847.

Way (Mrs. Ri., W.G.C.) — B. H. W. . 1847.

Crawley *mi.* (R.O.) — R. S. . 1847.

Tremlett (Mrs. Ro., aft. K.S., W.L.E.) — T. D. . 1850.

Baring (H.D.) — Capt. Henry. 2nd son of H. B. B. of 23 Eaton Sq., S.W.; 1844^{1}-1844^{3}; formerly Capt. 17th Lancers; *m.* Harriette Emily, *d.* of Edward George Cubitt of Honing Hall, Norfolk. 5 *Clanricarde Gardens, Tunbridge Wells.*

Unplaced.

Lysley (W.L.E.) — W. G. . 1847.

Knatchbull *mi.* (E.B.) — R. B. (aft. Knatchbull-Hugessen). 1847.

Miles *mi.* (R.O.) — H. C. W. . 1850.

Miles *min.* (R.O.) — C. J. W. . 1850.

Warren — E. L. . 1847.

Brocas (Miss W., aft. K.S., C.J.A.) — Reginald. 1844^{2}-1846^{1}; formerly Lieut. 75th Regt.

Mathias (H.D., aft. K.S., H.D.) — G. H. D. . 1850.

Holt (Home. C.J.A.) — H. . 1847.

Norton *mi.* (E.C.) — T. B. (Lord Grantley). 1847.

Pilcher (Miss Edw., W.G.C.) — G. L. . 1847.

Gordon *mi.* (H.D.) — Russell Manners. 1844^{2}-1845^{1}.

Burnaby (E.H.P.) — MAJ.-GEN EDWYN SHERARD. Of Baggrave Hall, Leicester; son of E. B. of Baggrave; 1844^{2}-1846^{2}; formerly Maj.-Gen. Comm. Gren. Gds., aft. M.P. for N. Leicesters; *m.* Louisa Julia Mary, *d.* of Sir Willoughby Wolstan Dixie, 8th Bt., of Bosworth Park, Leicester; died May 13, 1583.

Forshall (C.J.A., aft. K.S., C.J.A.) — E. V. . 1850.

Sothern (Mrs. Ri., W.G.C.) — 1844^{2}-1846^{2}.

Gibbs *ma.* (J.E.Y.) — WILLIAM LLOYD. 7th son of G. H. G. of Aldenham House, Elstree, Herts; 1843^{2}-1845^{3}; Exeter Coll. Oxf.; died unm. Aug. 27, 1860.

LOWER SCHOOL.

THIRD FORM—UPPER GREEK.

Tarver *mi.* (Home, W.G.C.) — WILLIAM GIFFORD. Son of J. C. T., French Master at Eton; 1840^{3}-1845^{2}; Clerk in the Bank of England; *m.* Catherine, *d.* of S. Finney; died April 27, 1889.

Haywood *mi.* (W.G.C.) — RUSSELL. Son of F. H. of Liverpool; 1843^{1}-1846^{3}; Lieut. 82nd Regt.; died at Liverpool, Feb. 1855, while embarking his men for the Crimea.

Browne (Miss A., F.E.D.) — ALEXANDER. 1843^{1}-1845^{3}.

Lukin (E.B.) — COL. FREDERICK WINDHAM. 1841^{3}-1846^{1}; formerly with the 17th Regt. in the Crimea and Indian Mutiny; aft. Paymaster 2nd Dragoon Gds.

Lavie (J.E.Y.) — R. C. . 1847.

Parks *mi.* (Miss M., F.E.D.) — F. C. . 1847.

Paul *ma.* (R.F.H., C.L.) — W. H. . 1847.

Evans *mi.* (W.E., W.A.C.) — RICHARD GEORGE. Son of W. E., Drawing Master at Eton; 1842^{2}-1846^{1}; in the Navy; died at Rangoon, 1853.

Burder *mi.* (Mrs. P., E.B.) — T. H. C. . 1847.

Godman *ma.* (W.L.E.) — JOSEPH. Of Park Hatch, Godalming; eld. son of J. G. of Park Hatch; 1844^{1}-1846^{3}; Emmanuel Coll. Camb.; J.P. and D.L. co. Surrey and J.P. co. Sussex and London; *m.* 1st, Gertrude Henrietta Eliza, *d.* of N. Weekes of Mangrove, Barbados; 2nd, Bertha Marion, *d.* of H B. W. Williams-Wynn of Howberry Park, co. Oxford; died Sept. 18, 1896.

Leigh (W.A.C.) — JAMES MOSLEY. 2nd son of J. H. L. of Belmont Hall, Northwich, co. Chester; 1844^{1}-1845^{1}; *m.* Susan Mary, *d.* of Capt. Wynyard, R.N.; died Jan. 14, 1858.

Drewe (R.F.H., E.H.P.) — MAJOR-GEN. FRANCIS EDWARD. Of Grange, Honiton; eld. son of E. S. D. of Grange; 1844^{1}-1845^{3}; formerly Capt. 23rd R. Welsh Fusiliers; Knt. of Legion of Honour and of the Sardinian and Turkish Orders; *m.* 1st, Louisa Anne, *d.* of Rev. Sir Frederick Vincent, 11th Bt., Rector of Slinfold, Sussex; 2nd, Katharine Cecilia, *d.* of Adolphus Shelly and widow of James Bontein, Gentleman Usher to the Queen; died Feb. 20, 1891.

LOWER GREEK.

Chandos-Pole *min.* (Miss W., J.W.H.) — W. . 1850.

Roberts (Home & Mrs. de R., aft. K.S., E.B.) — J. P. S. . 1850.

Dunbar *mi.* (Mrs. Ro., F.E.D.) — R. L. . 1850.

Dupuis (H.D., aft. K.S., H.D., C.O.G. & A.F.B.) — G. R. . 1850.

Mr. Rowley (Mrs. Ro. & Mrs. Vav., J.W.H. & W.L.E.) — HON. HUGH. 3rd son of Hercules, 2nd Lord Langford, of Summer Hill House, Meath; 1842^{3}-1846^{2}; R.M. Coll. Sandhurst; formerly in the 16th Lancers; *m.* 1st, Theresa Caroline, *d.* of John Bishop of Sunbury House, Middlesex; 2nd, Caroline Frances, *d.* of John Green of Ormiston Lodge. *46 Silwood Road, Brighton.*

Mr. Keith (J.W.H.) — HON. CHARLES JAMES (aft. Keith-Falconer). 3rd son of Anthony Adrian, 7th Earl of Kintore; 1844^{1}-1844^{3}; served three years in the Navy, aft. in the 10th and 4th Hussars during Crimean War; ret. as Maj. and appointed Commiss. of Inland Revenue in 1875; *m.* Caroline Diana, *d.* of Robert Aldridge of St. Leonards Forest, Sussex; died Jan. 7, 1889.

Charlton (Mrs. Ri.) — ST. JOHN WILLIAM. Eld. son of St. J. C. C. of Apley Castle, Wellington, Salop; 1843^{1}-1844^{3}; Capt. 1st Rl. Dragoons; served in the Crimea, present at the Charge of Balaclava; died unm. Oct. 30, 1864.

SENSE.

Godman *mi.* (W.L.E.) — FREDERICK DU CANE, D.C.L., F.R.S. 3rd son of J. G. of Park Hatch, Godalming; 1844^{2}-1846^{3}; Trin. Coll. Camb.; Hon. D.C.L. Oxf.; *m.* 1st, Edith Mary, *d.* of J. H. Elwes of Colesborne, Glos.; 2nd, Alice Mary, *d.* of Major Percy Chaplin, 60th Rifles, of 5 Eaton Place, S.W. *7 Carlos Place, Grosvenor Sq., W., and South Lodge, Horsham.*

Ford (Mrs. P., C.J.A.) — M. W. . 1850.

Pugh — W. B. . 1850.

Cherry (J.W.H.) — JOHN HECTOR. Son of Rev. — C. of Burghfield, Reading; 1843^{2}-1846^{3}; Merchant at Valparaiso; died on his return home 1862.

Dawson *mi.* (J.E.Y.) — PELSANT HENRY. Son of — D. of Yaldhurst, Lymington; 1843^{2}-1844^{2}; died about 1859 from the effects of an accident.

Kay (J.W.H.) — W. . 1850.

Cockerell *min.* (J.W.H. & W.A.C.) — R. V. . 1847.

Alderson *min.* (W.J.) — F. J. . 1850.

Yonge *mi.* (W.G.C.) — C. W. . 1847.

Bousfield (Mrs. D., J.W.H.) — EDWARD HOLROYD. Son of W. C. B., Barrister; 1842^{3}–1845^{3}; Surveyor; *m.* Mary Helen, *d.* of J. Davenport. 201 *Cromwell Mansions, Cromwell Road, S.W.*

NONSENSE.

Graham — G. B. . 1847.

Paul *mi.* (J.W.H. & Mrs. Edw., C.L.) — F. B. . 1847

Theobald (Miss W., aft. K.S.) — J. S. . 1850.

SECOND FORM.

Elwyn *mi.* (R.F.H., J.W.H.) — ALFRED JOHN. 1843^{3}–1847^{1}.

Sykes *mi.* (C.L.) — REV. JOHN HEATH. 5th son of Rev. W. S. of the Grotto, Basildon, Berks, and Vicar of Cullompton, Devon: 1844^{2}–1845^{3}; Oxf. M.A.; Rector of Billesley, and Vicar of Haselor; *m.* Frances Amelia, *d.* of Rev. Philip Henry Nind. *Haselor, Alcester, Warwks.*

Cristall (Home) — H. . 1847.

Yonge *min.* (W.G.C., aft. K.S., W.G.C.) — D. N. . 1850.

Mariette *mi.* (aft. K.S.) — J. C. . 1850.

Seymour (W.G.C.) — W. H. . 1847.

Barton *mi.* (W.L.E.) — C. T. H. . 1850.

Moore (Home, J.W.H.) — THOMAS CHARLES. Son of — M. of Windsor; 1844^{1}–1845^{3}.

FIRST FORM.

Harington (J.W.H.) — ROBERT EDWARD STUART (aft. Harington-Stuart). Eld. son of Major R. H. of Crutherland; 1844^{1}–1847^{1}; formerly Capt. Rifle Bgde.; aft. Col. 2nd Vol. Bn. Cameronians; J.P. and D.L. co. Lanark; *m.* Louisa Alice, *d.* of Hon. Robert Arthur Arundell. *Torrance, East Kilbride, Glasgow.*

Mariette *min.* — G. . 1850.

UNPLACED.

Cookesley *mi.* (W.G.C., J.E.Y.) — F. J. . 1850.

Yonge *quintus* (W.G.C.) — G. L. . 1850.

INTERMEDIATE LIST.

Names of Boys entered between Election 1841 and 1844, who left Eton before Election 1844, and are therefore not included in the foregoing list.

Amos (Miss M., W.A.C.) — REV. WILLIAM. 1841^{3}–1844^{1}; Trin. Coll. Camb. B.A.; formerly Rector of Braceborough, near Stamford.

Hurt *ma.* (Miss Edw., F.E.D.) — JAMES THOMAS (aft. Edge). Of Strelley Hall, Nottingham; eld. son of Major J. H. of Wirksworth, Derbys; 1841^{3}–1842^{1}; Ch. Ch. Oxf.; formerly Capt. Rl. Sherwood Foresters; J.P. and D.L. co. Notts, High Sheriff 1870; *m.* 1st, Julia Frances, *d.* of Samuel Trehawke Kekewich of Peamore, Devon; 2nd, Emily Mary, *d.* of Robert Holden of Nuthall Temple, Notts; died 1894.

Hurt *mi.* (Miss Edw., F.E.D.) — REV. JOHN FRANCIS. 2nd son of Major J. H. of Wirksworth, Derbys: 1841^{3}–1842^{1}; Trin. Coll. Camb. B.A.; Rector of Bilborough and Strelley, co. Notts; *m.* Cecilia Isabella, *d.* of Francis Hurt of Alderwasley, Wirksworth; died Oct. 25, 1868.

Marryat (Miss Edw., W.A.C.) — VERY REV. CHARLES. Dean of Adelaide. Son of C. M., Merchant, of Regent's Park, London; 1841^{3}–1843^{1}; Queen's Coll. Oxf. M.A.; Ellerton Theological Prize 1851; Curate of Ide Hill, Kent, 1850–2; Chaplain to penal establishment at Darlinghurst and Cockatoo Island, N.S.W., 1852–3; Curate of Trin. Ch., Adelaide, 1853–7; Incumbent of St. Paul's, Port Adelaide, 1857–68; Archdn. of Adelaide, 1868–87; Dean of Adelaide since 1887; Member of Ch. Ch. N. Adelaide since 1868; Vicar-Gen. and Commissary; *m.* Grace Montgomery, *d.* of Rev. C. B. Howard, 1st Colonial Chaplain of S. Australia. *The Deanery, Palmer Place, N. Adelaide, Australia.*

Dimsdale (W.A.C.) — ROBERT (6th Baron Dimsdale), of the Russian Empire. Son of Charles John, 5th Baron D., of Essendon Place, Hatfield, Herts; 1841^{3}–1841^{3}; Corpus Christi Coll. Oxf. M.A.; M.P. for Hertford 1867–74, and N. Herts 1884–92; J.P. and D.L. for Herts, and J.P. for Middlesex and Westminster; *m.* Cecilia Jane, *d.* of Rev. Marcus Richard Southwell, Rector of St. Stephens, St. Albans; died May 2, 1898.

Holdsworth (E.H.P., W.L.E.) — ROBERT. 1841^{3}–1843^{3}.

Jary (Miss Edw., F.E.D.) — WILLIAM HEATH. Of Burlingham House, Norwich; eld. son of W. H. J. of Blofield Lodge, Norfolk; 1841^{3}–1842^{2}; formerly Capt. 18th Norfolk Rifle Vol.; J.P. for Norfolk; died unm. Sept. 1888.

Balfour (R.O.) — REAR-ADMIRAL CHARLES JOHN. Of 74 Madeley Road, Ealing; 1841^{3}–1842^{3}; formerly Comm. of H.M.S. 'Talent' in the Mediterranean; died Jan. 19, 1902.

Peel (R.F.H., H.D.) — WILLIAM YATES. 4th son of R. P. of Dotshill Lodge, Warwick; 1841^{3}–1842^{1}.

Buller (E.C.) — MAJ.-GEN. EDMUND MANNINGHAM-. Of Brockton Lodge, Staffs; 2nd son of Sir E. M.-B., 1st Bt., of Dilhorn Hall, Cheadle, Stoke-on-Trent; 1841^{3}–1843^{3}; formerly Maj.-Gen. 1st Bn. Rifle Bgde.; *m.* Lady Anne Coke, *d.* of Thomas William, 3rd Earl of Leicester; died Feb. 14, 1897.

Lord Bangor (J.E.Y.) — [illegible] (4th Viscount B.). Eld. son of [illegible] 3rd Visct. B., of [illegible] Ward, Downpatrick; 1841^{3}–1842^{2}; [illegible] Sept. 14, 1881.

Cole (Miss M., W.G.C.)

EDWARD CAMPBELL STUART. Of Stoke Lyne, Exmouth; eld. son of E. H. C. of Stoke Lyne: 1841^{3}–1843^{1}; went to Rugby: formerly Capt. Oxfs. Militia: J.P. for co. Devon; D.L. co. Oxf.: *m.* Olivia Anne, *d.* of Rev. Joseph Stevenson; dead.

ARTHUR. 1841^{3}–1842^{2}.

Lloyd-Davies (Mrs. Ri., W.G.C.)

Wise (C.O.G.)

HENRY CHRISTOPHER. Eld. son of H. C. of Woodcote, co. Warwick; 1842^{1}–1843^{3}; 40th Regt.; killed at Ballarat, S. Australia, Dec. 21, 1854.

Clayton-East (R.F.H., E.H.P.)

FREDERICK RICHARD. 4th son of Sir E. G. C.-E., 1st Bt., of Hall Place, Maidenhead; 1842^{1}–1842^{3}; formerly Capt. 8th Madras Cav.; *m.* Caroline Louisa, *d.* of Thomas Spooner Palmer of Bayview, co. Sligo; died in Madras Sept. 15, 1860.

Churchill (W.E.)

CHARLES HENRY SPENCER-. Eld. son of Lord C. S.-C.; 1842^{1}–1844^{1}; Lieut.-Col. 60th Rifles; *m.* Rosalie, *d.* of Rev. Gorges Paulin Lowther, Rector of Orcheston St. George, Wilts; died April 3, 1877.

Lyon (Mrs. Ro., F.E.D.)

EDMUND DAVID. 1842^{1}–1844^{1}.

Hodgson *ma.* (R.F.H., E.B.)

CECIL. 6th son of Rev. E. H., Vicar of Rickmansworth, Herts; 1842^{1}–1843^{3}; Trin. Coll. Oxf.: died unm. 1895.

Hodgson *mi.* (R.F.H., E.B.)

PERCEVAL. 7th son of Rev. E. H., Vicar of Rickmansworth, Herts; 1842^{1}–1843^{3}; Major, Indian Army; died in India 1870.

Crawley (E.H.P., C.O.G.)

CHARLES EDWARD. Of Littlemore, Oxf.; son of C. C. of Littlemore; 1842^{1}–1842^{3}; Exeter Coll. Oxf. M.A.; formerly Lieut. in Oxfs. Militia; *m.* 1st, Maria Walter Scott, *d.* of William Wilson; 2nd, Marion, *d.* of George Karop of Copenhagen; died 1893.

Payn (Mrs. Ro., W.G.C.)

JAMES. 1842^{2}–1842^{3}; Trin. Coll. Camb.: Novelist and Journalist; died Mar. 25, 1898.

Donne (Miss A., E.B.)

JAMES. 1842^{2}–1844^{1}.

Cator (Miss W., W.A.C.)

THOMAS WILLIAM. Of Ollerton House, Notts; 3rd son of Rev. T. C. of Skelbrook Park, Yorks; 1842^{2}–1843^{1}; formerly Lieut.-Col. 76th Foot: *m.* Jane Louisa, *d.* of Rear-Adml. Charles Sotheby; died Jan. 14, 1900.

Wilson (Mrs. Ro., W.G.C.)

FRANCIS JOHN COLQUHOUN. 1842^{2}–1843^{2}.

Currie (C.O.G.)

MICHAEL PARNTHER. 2nd son of J. C. of Essendon, Hatfield, Herts; 1842^{2}–1842^{3}; died June 25, 1882.

Scarlett (Miss M., C.J.A.)

HON. JAMES HENRY LAWRENCE. 2nd son of Robert Campbell, 2nd Lord Abinger; 1842^{2}–1843^{1}; died June 15, 1845.

Van Tole (R.F.H.)

HENRY DELMAR. Son of a Merchant at Cape of Good Hope; 1842^{2}–1843^{3}.

Salmon (R.F.H., W.L.E.)

THOMAS WILLIAM. 1842^{2}–1842^{3}.

Cooper (Miss M.)

LOVICK HENRY. Son of B. C., Surgeon; 1842^{2}–1842^{3}; formerly 1st Bengal Eur. Fus.; died at Meerut 1852.

Bedford (R.F.H., aft. K.S., W.G.C.)

COL. RICHARD BISSE RILAND. 3rd son of Rev. W. R. B., Rector of Sutton Coldfield, Birmingham; 1842^{2}–1844^{1}; B.N.C. Oxf.; served in 79th Cameron Highl., aft. Ajt. Staffs Vol. 18 *Bore Street, Lichfield.*

Lane (W.E., E.B.)

JOHN HENRY BAGOT. Of King's Bromley Manor, Lichfield; eld. son of J. N. L. of King's Bromley; 1842^{2}–1843^{3}; Ch. Ch. Oxf. M.A.; formerly Lieut.-Col. Coldstream Gds.; served all through Crimea; J.P. and D.L. co^{s}. Staffs and Berks; *m.* Susan Anne, *d.* of Henry William Vincent of Lily Hill, Bracknell; died March 22, 1886.

Batthyany (C.J.A., W.A.C.)

COUNT GUSTAVE EMILE. Son of Count Batthyany; 1842^{2}–1843^{2}; was killed in the Hungarian Revolt 1848–50.

Bertie (Mrs. Ro., J.E.Y.)

CHARLES MCDONNELL. Eld. son of Rev. F. B., Rector of Albury, co. Oxf.; 1842^{2}–1843^{3}; died Sept. 8, 1884.

Brownlow (W.G.C.)

HON. C. (2nd Lord Lurgan). See Intermediate List 1847.

Gage (J.E.Y.)

WILLIAM HENRY. Son of T. W. G.; 1842^{2}–1843^{1}; died unm. 1846.

Bell (H.D.)

REV. WILLIAM GILLISON. Son of — B. of Melling Hall, Lancs; 1843^{1}–1843^{1}; formerly Curate of Braunston, Leicester.

Assheton (W.A.C.)

RALPH. Eld. son of W. A. of Downham Hall; 1843^{1}–1843^{1}; Trin. Coll. Camb. M.A.; Jun. Opt. Math. Trip.; J.P. and D.L. co. Lancaster, and J.P. W. Riding of Yorks; M.P. for Clitheroe 1868–80; *m.* Emily Augusta, *d.* of Joseph Feilden of Witton Park, Blackburn, Lancaster. *Downham Hall, Clitheroe.*

Wingfield (Mrs. Hor., F.E.D.)

JOHN. 1843^{2}–1843^{3}.

MeeGwire (Miss M., E.B.)

WILLIAM RICHARD BERMINGHAM. Eld. son of W. J. MeeG. of Carrigbawn, Rostrevor, co. Down; 1843^{2}–1843^{3}; *m.* Caroline Sophia Newall; died July 13, 1896.

Rodney (F.E.D.)

WILLIAM POWELL. Son of W. P. of Llanvihangel Court, Abergavenny; 1843^{2}–1843^{3}; *m.* Diana Hotham, *d.* of Sir John William Lubbock, 3rd Bt.; died June 19, 1868.

Cholmeley (C.O.G.)

MONTAGUE AUBREY. Eld. son of Sir M. J. C., 2nd Bt., of Easton Hall, Grantham; 1843^{2}–1844^{1}; died at Eton, after measles, Mar. 1844.

ELECTION, 1847.

SIXTH FORM

Earle *ma.* (Miss W., aft. K.S., J.W. & F.E.D.)
RT. REV. ALFRED, Bishop of Marlborough. Son of H. E.; 1838[3]-1847[2]: Eton XI. 1847; Coll. Wall 1844-5; Keeper of Upper Club 1846; Hertford Coll. Oxf. D.D. (Lusby Sch.); Curate of St. Edmund, Sarum, 1858-63; Rector of Monkton-Farleigh, Wilts, 1863-5; Vicar of W. Alvington, St. Huish, St. Mellon, and Marlborough; joint Vicarage, Devon, 1865-87; Rural Dean 1867-72; Archdn. of Totnes, 1872-87; Preb. of Exeter Cath. 1872-85; Examining Chaplain to Bishops Temple and Bickersteth; Canon Resid. of Exeter Cath. 1886-88; Rector of St. Michael's, Cornhill, 1888-96; Bp. of Marlborough 1888-1900; Rector of St. Botolph's, Bishopsgate, and Preb. of St. Paul's Cath.; Dean of Exeter since 1900. *The Deanery, Exeter.*

Tarver (Home, aft. K.S., W.G.C. & C.J.A.)
FRANCIS BATTEN CRISTALL. Son of J. C. T. of Eton Coll.; 1834[3]-1848[2]; Coll. Wall 1845-7; Merton Coll. Oxf., Postmaster of Merton; French Master at Eton 1864-95; *m.* Sara Elizabeth, *d.* of Principal Tulloch of St. Andrews. *The Links, Walton-on-Thames.*

Moffat (Mrs. Ri., aft. K.S., F.E.D.)
CHARLES WILLIAM. 1840[3]-1847[2]; Coll. Wall 1845-6; Queen's Coll. Oxf.; died immediately after leaving Coll.

Mr. Hanbury (H.D.)
HON. and REV. ARTHUR ALLEN (aft. Bateman-Hanbury). 3rd son of William, 1st Lord Bateman; 1841[2]-1847[2]; Ch. Ch. Oxf. M.A.; Fell exhibitioner 1850; Rector of Shobdon, and Preb. Hereford Cath.; *m.* Mary Ward, *d.* of John Davenport of Foxley, Herefords. *Shobdon Rectory, R.S.O., Herefords.*

Cust *ma.* (Miss W. & H.D., H.D.)
SIR REGINALD JOHN, Kt. 3rd son of Hon. and Rev. H. C. C., Canon of Windsor; 1841[3]-1847[4]; Sch. of Trin. Coll. Camb., M.A.; 15th Wrangler, and 2nd Cl. Class. Trip. 1852; Barrister; Asst. Commissioner, W. Indian Incumbered Estates Court, 1865-87; Chief Comm. 1887-92; *m.* Lady Elizabeth Caroline Bligh, *d.* of Edward, 5th Earl of Darnley. *13 Eccleston Square, S.W.*

Curtis (R.F.H., aft. K.S., C.L.)
REV. FRANCIS HENRY. 1840[3]-1848[1]; Newc. Select 1848; formerly Sub-Master of Grammar Sch., Norwich.

Smith (Mrs. Ro., aft. K.S., W.L.E.)
WILLOUGHBY JOHN. 1840[1]-1848[2]; Coll. Wall 1843-7, Keeper 1845-7; Lieut. H.M.S. 'Daring'; was blown out of the rigging in a gale and drowned 1853.

Gurdon (E.H.P.)
ROBERT THORNHAGH (1st Lord Cranworth). Of Letton Hall, Thetford, Norfolk; eld. son of B. G. of Letton; 1841[1]-1848[2]; Trin. Coll. Camb. M.A.; Sen. Opt. Camb.; called to the Bar, Lincoln's Inn, 1856; Norfolk Circuit; J.P. and D.L. for Norfolk; Chmn. Qr. Sessions and Chmn. C.C.; M.P. S. Norfolk 1880-86, Mid-Norfolk 1886-92 and 1895; Hon. Col. 4th Vol. Bn. Norfolk Regt.; *m.* 1st, Harriott Ellin, *d.* of Sir William Miles, 1st Bt., of Leigh Court; 2nd, Emily Frances, *d.* of Rev. Robert Boothby Heathcote of Friday Hill, Chingford, Essex; died Oct. 13, 1902.

Deacon (E.H.P.)
WILLIAM SAMUEL. Of Poynters, Cobham, Surrey; son of J. D. of Mabledon, Tonbridge; 1840[3]-1847[3]; Eton XI. 1845-7; Opp. Wall 1845-6; Trin. Coll. Camb.; Camb. XI. 1848-50; Banker; *m.* Mary Sophia, *d.* of Raikes Currie of Bush Hill, co. Middlesex; died Mar. 4, 1903.

Headlam (Miss Edw., aft. K.S., E.B.)
FRANCIS JOHN. 7th son of Ven. Archdn. J. H. of Gilmonby Hall, Yorks; Rector of Wycliffe; 1841[3]-1848[4]; Sch. of Univ. Coll. Oxf.; 2nd Class Lit. Hum. 1852; Fellow 1854; Bursar 1863-71; Assist. Master Westminster 1855-6; Barrister; Stipendiary Magist. of Manchester since 1869; *m.* Matilda Ann, *d.* of S. Pincoff of Polygon, Ardwick, Manchester. *Dalefield, Chelford, Crewe.*

Still (R.F.H., aft. K.S., E.B.)
REV. HENRY HUGHS. Son of Rev. P. S., Rector of Cattistock, Dorchester, Dorset; 1841[3]-1848[3]; Exeter Coll. Oxf., M.A.; Rector of Cattistock; *m.* Agnes F., *d.* of Rev. C. M. Mount; died Oct. 9, 1859.

Ames (E.H.P.)
CHARLES HERBERT. Of Remenham Place, Henley-on-Thames; 2nd son of G. H. A. of Cote House, Westbury-on-Trym, Bristol; 1841[2]-1847[3]; Haileybury Coll.; Madras Civil Service; *m.* Eliza Scott, *d.* of Rev. William Scott Robinson, Rector of Dyrham, Chippenham; died Jan. 20, 1876.

Stanbrough (Mrs. Hor., aft. K.S., W.L.E.)
REV. MORRIS EDGAR. 1839[2]-1847[2]; Coll. Wall 1844-6; Caius Coll. Camb.; formerly Curate of Redgrave, Suffolk.

Booth (Mrs. Ri., aft. K.S., H.D.)
CHARLES. 1841[2]-1848[1]; Newc. Select 1847-8; Coll. Wall 1845-7; Fellow King's Coll. Camb.; Barrister.

Joynes (Mrs. P., aft. K.S., E.C.)
REV. WILLIAM. Son of Rev. — J., Rector of Gravesend; 1839[2]-1847[2]; Trin. Coll. Camb. M.A.; formerly Vicar of Chalk, Gravesend.

Wayte *ma.* (Miss W., aft. K.S., F.E.D.)
REV. WILLIAM. Son of W. W. of Highlands, Calne; 1840[2]-1848[2]; Newc. Select 1845, Sch. 1846; Sch. of King's Coll. Camb., M.A.; Craven Univ. Sch. 1852; Brown's Medal; Fellow of King's, 1852; Asst. Master at Eton 1853-75; Prof. of Greek at Univ. Coll. London 1876-9; Greek Examiner to London Univ.; *m.* Mary L., *d.* of Rev. J. Lovett-Cameron, Vicar of Shoreham, Sevenoaks; died 1898.

Fremantle *ma.* (W.E., E.B.)
HON. THOMAS FRANCIS (2nd Lord Cottesloe). Eld. son of Thomas Francis, 1st Lord C.; 1842[2]-1848[2]; Newc. Select 1846-7; Med. 1848; Pres. Eton Soc. 1847; Eton XI. 1848; Field XI. 1847; Ball. Coll. Oxf. M.A.; Hertford Sch. 1849; 1st Cl. Lit. Hum. 1852; M.P. for Bucks 1876-85; Barrister; J.P. and D.L. for Bucks; Chmn. Bucks Qr. Sessions; Chmn. and Ald. Bucks C.C.; *m.* Lady Augusta Henrietta Scott, *d.* of John, 2nd Earl of Eldon. *Swanbourne House, Winslow, and 44 Eaton Sq., S.W.*

Coleridge (E.C.)
HERBERT. Son of H. N. C. of Downshire Hill, Hampstead; 1841[3]-1848[2]; Newc. Med. 1847, Sch. 1848; Prince Consort's Italian Prize 1847; Sch. of Ball. Coll. Oxf.; [illegible] First 1852; Class. Barrister; Sec. [illegible]; *m.* [illegible] Penhouse, *d.* of [illegible] died 1861.

Whymper (Miss M., J.E.Y.)
FREDERICK HAYES. 1842^{3}–1847^{3}; Newc. Select 1846; Sch. 1847; Prince Consort's French and German Prize 1843; Eton XI. 1846–7; Opp. Wall 1845–6; Sch. Trin. Coll. Camb.; Craven Sch. and 1st Cl. Class. 1851; Camb. XI. 1849; formerly Inspector of Factories.

Blore (W.E., F.C.)
REV. EDWARD WILLIAM. 1842^{3}–1847^{3}; Newc. Select 1846–7; Tomline Prizeman 1845 and 1847; Eton XI. 1845–7; Fellow of Eton 1880–85; Trin. Coll. Camb., M.A. 37th Wrangler and 1st Cl. Class. 1851; Camb. XI. 1848–51; Fellow, Tutor and Dean of Trin. Coll. Camb.; died 1886.

Tremayne (H.D.)
HENRY HAWKINS, J.P. 3rd son of J. H. T. of Heligan, St. Austell, Cornwall; 1841^{3}–1848^{2}; Eton VIII. 1847–8; Capt. 1848; Opp. Wall 1846–7; Keeper of the Field 1847; Ch. Ch. Oxf. B.A.; Oxf. VIII. 1848; in the Bank of England; m. Charlotte Jane, d. of John Buller of Morval, Sandplace, Cornwall; died May 19, 1894.

Tyler (E.C.)
GEORGE GRIFFIN (aft. Griffin). Son of Rev. J. E. T., Rector of St. Giles-in-the-Fields, London, and Canon of St. Paul's; 1842^{1}–1847^{3}; Newc. Select 1847; Ch. Ch. Oxf. M.A.; 2nd Class Lit. Hum. 1851; formerly Major Rl. Monmouth Militia; J.P. cos. Monmouth and Hereford; D.L. co. Monmouth; m. 1st, Maria Louisa, d. of Rev. Allen Cooper, Vicar of St. Mark's, N. Audley Street, W.; 2nd, Mary Octavia, d. of John E. W. Rolls, of The Hendre, Monmouth. *Newton Court, Monmouth.*

FIFTH FORM—UPPER DIVISION.

Borradaile (R.F.H., aft. K.S., C.L.)
CUTHBERT BLIZARD. Son of the Rev. B., Vicar of Wandsworth; 1840^{2}–1848^{1}; Newc. Select 1848 and 1848; Sch. of Ch. Ch. Oxf. and Lincoln Coll. Oxf.; aft. a writer for the London Press; died 1867.

James (Miss W., K.S., F.E.D.)
REV. CHARLES CALDECOTT. Son of Rev. E. J. of Alton, Winchester; 1839^{1}–1848^{3}; Newc. Select 1846–8; Prince Consort's Italian prize 1848; Coll. Wall 1847–8; Sch. of King's Coll. Camb., M.A.; 1st Cl. Class. 1853; Fellow of King's; Assist. Master at Eton 1855–84; Curate at Papworth St. Agnes, nr. St. Neots, 1884–8; Rector of Wortham, Diss, 1888–1903; m. Katharine Caroline, d. of William Hopkins of Camb.; died April 10, 1903.

Green *ma.* (Mrs. Ro., aft. K.S., W.A.C.)
REV. GEORGE CLARK. Son of Rev. G. B. G., Fellow of Eton and Rector of Everdon, Northants; 1839^{3}–1848^{3}; Coll. Wall 1848; Sch. of King's Coll. Camb., M.A.; Vicar of Modbury; m. Emma Elizabeth Helen, d. of Francis Hall, solicitor. *Modbury Vicarage, Ivybridge, S. Devon.*

Coleridge (W.E., aft. K.S., E.C.)
ARTHUR DUKE. 1840^{3}–1848^{3}; Eton XI. 1847–8; Pres. Eton Soc. 1848; Coll. Wall 1847–8; Field XI. 1848; Keeper of Upper Club 1847; Sch. of King's Coll. Camb.; Barrister; Clerk of the Crown, Midland Circuit. *12 Cromwell Place, South Kensington, S.W.*

Smith (Mrs. Ro., E.H.P.)
CAPT. PERCY SHAWE. Son of J. B. S.; 1842^{1}–1847^{2}; formerly Capt. 13th Lt. Dragoons; served in the Crimea; Crimean Med. 4 Clasps; Turkish Med.; Sardinian Med.; 5th Class, Medjidie; m. Annette, d. of Willson Yeates.

Streatfeild (R.F.H., C.O.G.)
REV. NEWTON WILLIAM. 3rd son of H. S. of Chiddingstone, Edenbridge, Kent; 1841^{3}–1847^{3}; Eton XI. 1844–7; M.A. Oxf.; formerly Incumbent of Lamorbey, Bexley, Kent; m. Flora, d. of Rev. W. E. Hoskins, [illegible] of Chiddingstone; [illegible] June 2[illegible], [illegible].

Chitty (W.E., W.A.C.)
RT. HON. SIR JOSEPH WILLIAM (Lord Justice C.), P.C., Q.C. 2nd son of T. C. of the Inner Temple; 1842^{1}–1847^{3}; Pres. Eton Soc. 1845–6; Eton XI. 1844–7, Capt. 1847; Opp. Wall 1846; Keeper of Upper Club 1846; Ball. Coll. Oxf. M.A.; 1st Class Lit. Hum. 1851; Vinerian Sch. 1852; Oxf. XI. 1848–9; Oxf. VIII. 1848–9, Stroke 1851–2; Fellow of Exeter Coll. Oxf.; called to the Bar, Lincoln's Inn, 1856; appointed a Q.C. 1874; M.P. for Oxf. City 1880; a Judge in the Chanc. Div. of High Court of Justice 1881; a Lord Justice of the Court of Appeal 1897; 23 years Umpire at the Univ. Boat Race; formerly Major Inns of Court R.V.; m. Clara Jessie, d. of Rt. Hon. Sir Frederick Pollock, 1st Bt.; died Feb. 15, 1899.

Herries (W.E., E.B.)
HERBERT CROMPTON. Of Frimley Park, Farnborough, Hants; son of Lieut.-Gen. Sir W. L. H. of Glenlyn, Lynmouth, Barnstaple; 1842^{2}–1848^{3}; Eton VIII. 1848; Trin. Coll. Camb. M.A.; 26th Wrangler 1852; called to the Bar, Inner Temple, 1856; m. Leonora Emma, d. of Henry Louis Wickham, Chmn. of Board of Stamps and Taxes; died Mar. 19, 1870.

Wykeham-Martin *ma.* (W.A.C.)
PHILIP. Of Leeds Castle; eld. son of C. W.-M. of Leeds Castle; 1842^{2}–1847^{3}; Ball. Coll. Oxf. B.A.; M.P. for Rochester 1856–78; J.P. and D.L. for cos. Kent and Warwick; m. Elizabeth, d. of John Ward; died suddenly in the Library of House of Commons, May 31, 1878.

Yonge (E.B.)
JULIAN BARGUS. Of Otterbourne House, Winchester; son of W. C. Y. of Otterbourne; 1842^{2}–1848^{1}; Ball. Coll. Oxf. M.A.; formerly Lieut. in Rifle Brgde.; J.P. for Hants; m. Emma Frances, d. of Col. Edward Walter, 3rd Bombay Lt. Cav.; died 1891.

Peel (E.C.)
ARTHUR WELLESLEY (1st Visct. Peel), P.C., D.C.L. 5th son of Rt. Hon. Sir R. P., 2nd Bt., of Drayton Manor, Staffs; 1841^{2}–1848^{1}; Ball. Coll. Oxf. M.A.; 2nd Cl. Class. 1852; Visitor of Ball.; Hon. D.C.L. 1887; M.P. for Warwick 1865–85, Warwick and Leamington 1885–95; Parliamentary Sec. to Poor Law Board 1868–71, to Board of Trade 1871–3; Patronage Sec. of the Treasury 1873–4; Under Sec. to Home Office 1880; Speaker of the House of Commons 1884–95; J.P. Beds; J.P. and D.L. co. Warwick; Chmn. of Trustees of Nat. Portrait Gallery and a Trustee of the British Museum; m. Adelaide, d. of William Stratford Dugdale of Merevale Hall and Blyth Hall, co. Warwick. *The Lodge, Sandy.*

Page (Mrs. Ro., aft. K.S., E.B.)
JOHN. 1841^{3}–1849^{2}; Exeter Coll. Oxf.

Coke (Miss W., aft. K.S., E.B.)
REV. GEORGE FRANCIS. Of Lemore House, Eardisley, Hereford; son of Rev. G. C. of Lemore; 1841^{2}–1849^{2}; Exeter Coll. Oxf. B.A.; Vicar of Titley, Herefords; J.P. co. Hereford; m. Frances, d. of Henry Hide Seymour, R.N., of Wells, Somerset; died Feb. 13, 1885.

Antrobus (R.O.)
ROBERT CRAWFURD. 3rd son of Sir E. A., 2nd Bt., of Antrobus Hall, Chester; 1842^{3}–1847^{3}; Eton XI. 1846–7; Partner with Lindsay & Co., China Merchants at Shanghai; m. Emily, d. of Col. Ireland Blackburn of Hale Hall, co. Lancs, and widow of W. J. Hope Edwardes of Netley, co. Salop. *16 Buckingham Palace Gardens, S.W.*

Peel
REV. HERBERT RICHARD. 2nd son of Very Rev. J. P., D.D., Dean of Worcester; 1843^{1}–1847^{3}; Ch. Ch. Oxf.; Oxf. XI. 1851–2; formerly Rector of Handsworth, Birmingham; m. Georgiana Maria, d. of Rev. Thomas Baker; died June 2, 1865.

Mills (R.F.H., E.B.)
CHARLES HENRY (1st Lord Hillingdon). Son of Sir C. M., 1st Bt., of Camelford House, Park Lane, W.; 1843[3]–1847[3]; Ch. Ch. Oxf. M.A.; M.P. for Northallerton 1866, and W. Kent 1868–85; J.P. and D.L. for Middlesex and Kent; Banker in Lombard Street, London (Glyn, Hallifax & Co.); m. Lady Louisa Isabella Lascelles, d. of Henry, 3rd Earl of Harewood; died April 3, 1898.

Parker (Miss Edw., F.E.D.)
CHARLES STUART. Eld. son of C. S. P. of Aigburth, Liverpool, and Fairlie, co. Ayr; 1842[3]–1848[1]; Newc. Select 1847–8; Prince Consort's German Prize 1846; Univ. Coll. Oxf. M.A.; 1st Class Lit. Hum.; 2nd Class Math.; Fellow and Tutor of Univ. Coll.; Private Sec. at Colonial Office 1864–6; M.P. for Perthshire 1868–74, for Perth 1878–92; J.P. co. Ayr; formerly Maj. Univ. Vol.; Member of Royal Commns. on Public Schools, Military Education, and Endowments of Scotland. *Fairlie, Ayrshire, and 32 Old Queen St., S.W.*

Johnson (W.A.C.)
JOHN GEORGE. Of Winkleigh Court, N. Devon; son of Rev. P. J. of Winkleigh, Preb. of Exeter; 1843[1]–1848[2]; B.N.C. Oxf. M.A.; J.P. and D.L. co. Devon, High Sheriff 1872; Capt. N. Devon Hussars 1859–80; M.P. for Exeter 1874–80; m. Frances Grace, d. of Sir Theodore Henry Lavington Brinckman, 1st Bt.; died May, 1896.

Luxmoore (R.O.)
JOHN NICHOLL. Son of the Very Rev. C. S. L., Dean of St. Asaph; 1843[1]–1848[3]; Newc. Select 1847; Trin. Coll. Camb.; was thrown from his horse and killed at Camb., May 30, 1849.

Colvin (W.A.C.)
BAZETT WETENHALL. Son of J. R. C.; 1843[2]–1847[2]; Haileybury Coll.; Bengal Civil Service (ret.); m. Mary, d. of Maj.-Gen. J. Graham. *The Manor House, Lexden, Colchester.*

Newdigate *ma.* (W.E., E.C.)
REV. ALFRED. 6th son of F. N. of West Hallam, Derby; 1843[1]–1848[2]; Ch. Ch. Oxf. M.A.; formerly Vicar of Kirk Hallam, Derby; became a Roman Catholic in 1875; m. Selina C., d. of Rev. Griffith Boynton. *27 Clarendon Sq., Leamington.*

Pott (..)
REV. ARTHUR SIDNEY. Son of C. P. of Freeslands, Kent; 1843[1]–1847[3]; Ball. Coll. Oxf. M.A.; Rector of Northill, Biggleswade; m. Gladys, d. of Howell Jones Williams; died 1866.

Thompson (Miss W., F.E.D.)
SIR AUGUSTUS RIVERS. 1842[2]–1848[1]; Eton VIII. 1846–7; Opp. Wall 1845–7; Keeper of the Field 1847; Bengal Civil Service; served 35 years in India; Lieut.-Gov. of Bengal 1884; died at Gibraltar Nov. 27, 1890.

Brodrick *ma.* (C.O.G.)
HON. WILLIAM (8th Visct. Midleton). Eld. son of the Very Rev. William John, 7th Visct. M., Dean of Exeter; 1843[1]–1847[2]; Ball. Coll. Oxf. M.A.; Barrister 1855; High Steward of Kingston-on-Thames 1875–93; M.P. for Mid-Surrey 1868–70; Lord-Lieut. of Surrey; J.P. co. Cork; m. Hon. Augusta Mary, d. of Thomas, 1st Lord Cottesloe. *18 Eaton Sq., S.W., and Peper Harow, Godalming, Surrey.*

Greenwood (Mrs. Hor., E.H.P. & H.D.)
JOHN. Of Swarcliffe Hall, Ripley, Leeds; son of F. G. of Knowle House, Keighley; 1842[1]–1847[2]; won Sculling 1845; Double Sculling 1846; Cox of Eton VIII. 1847; Ch. Ch. Oxf. M.A.; J.P. and D.L. for W. Riding of Yorks; M.P. for Ripon 1853–65; formerly Maj. Yorks Hussars Yeo. Cav.; m. Louisa Elizabeth, d. of Nathaniel Clarke Barnardiston of the Ryes, Suffolk; died Feb. 21, 1874.

Miller *ma.* (R.F.H., C.O.G.)
SIR CHARLES HAYES, 7th Bt. Of Froyle Place, Alton, Hants; eld. son of Rev. Sir T. C. M., 6th Bt., Vicar of Froyle; 1841[3]–1847[1]; Eton VIII. 1846–7; Capt. of the Boats 1847; Opp. Wall 1846; formerly Cornet 2nd Life Gds.; m. Katherine Maria, d. of James Winter Scott of Rotherfield Park, Hants; died Jan. 12, 1868.

Bidwell (Miss Edw., aft. K.S., H.D.)
REV. GEORGE SHELFORD. Son of G. B., Rector of Stanton, Bury St. Edmund's; 1841[3]–1843[3]; St. John's Coll. Camb. B.A.; Rector of Simpson, Bletchley, 1871–90; m. d. of R. Prall, Solicitor, Rochester; died 1891.

Childers (W.A.C.)
ROWLAND FRANCIS WALBANKE. 3rd son of J. W.-C. of Cantley, nr. Doncaster; 1842[2]–1848[2]; Ch. Ch. Oxf.; formerly Scots Fusilier Gds.; m. Susan Anne, d. of Gen. Bourchier of Lavant House, Chichester; died 1855.

Brodrick *mi.* (C.O.G.)
HON. GEORGE CHARLES, D.C.L., F.R.G.S. 2nd son of William John, 7th Visct. Midleton; 1843[1]–1848[2]; Newc. Select 1847–8; Ball. Coll. Oxf. M.A., D.C.L., 1st Cl. in Mods. 1852, 1st Cl. in final Class. Schools 1853, 1st Cl. Lit. Hum. 1853, and Law and History School 1854; Arnold Historical Prize and English Essay Prize, Oxf. 1855; Barrister, Lincoln's Inn; Fellow of Merton Coll. Oxf. 1855; Fellow of Eton 1884–1903; Member of the Governing Body of Eton; Warden of Merton Coll. Oxf. 1881–1903; J.P. Oxfs.; died at Merton College, Oxford, Nov. 8, 1903.

Custance (Mrs. Ro., aft. K.S., C.O.G.)
ARTHUR FREDERICK. Eld. son of Rev. F. C., Rector of Colwell, Herefs; 1842[2]–1847[1]; died at Eton Oct. 16, 1847.

Bagshawe (W.E., E.H.P.)
WILLIAM LEONARD GILL. Of Oakes, Norton by Sheffield; eld. son of W. J. B. of Oakes and Wormhill Hall, nr. Buxton; 1842[2]–1847[2]; won Pulling 1845 and 1847, Sculling and Double Sculling 1846; Eton VIII. 1846–7; Trin. Coll. Camb.; Camb. VIII. 1848–9; died unm. July 20, 1854.

Duckworth *ma.* (Mrs. Hor., E.H.P.)
RUSSELL. 3rd son of W. D. of Orchardleigh Park, Frome; 1842[3]–1848[2]; Newc. Select 1848; Trin. Coll. Camb. B.A.; 1st Cl. Class. Trip. 1853; called to the Bar; J.P. for co. Somerset; m. Janette, d. of Rev. Preb. Henry Clutterbuck. *The Cloisters, Bath.*

Stacey (Miss B., aft. K.S., E.B.)
FRANCIS EDMUND. 1841[3]–1850[1]; Eton XI. 1848–9; Pres. Eton Soc. 1849; Coll. Wall 1845–9, Keeper 1849; Sch. of King's Coll. Camb. M.A.; Camb. XI. 1853; Barrister, Lincoln's Inn, 1857; S. Wales Circuit; died Oct. 3, 1885.

Pipe-Wolferstan *ma.* (R.F.H., aft. K.S., E.B.)
STANFORD WILLIAM. 2nd son of S. P.-W. of Statfold, nr. Tamworth; 1842[3]–1849[1]; Fellow of King's Coll. Camb.; m. Blanche, d. of S. S. Jervis of Darlaston Hall, co. Stafford; died Dec. 1863.

Martin *ma.* (Mrs. Hor., E.B.)
GEORGE EDWARD. Eld. son of Rev. Canon G. M., Chanc. of the Diocese of Exeter and Vicar of Harberton; 1842[2]–1848[2]; Tomline Select 1848; Merton Coll. Oxf. B.A.; 2nd Cl. Math.; J.P. and D.L. co. Worcester, High Sheriff 1882; formerly Major Q.O. Worcs. Yeo. Cav.; Barrister; Lord of the Manor of Upton; Banker, Old Bank, Worcester; m. Maria Henrietta, d. of Benjamin Cherry of Brickendon Grange, co. Hertford. *Ham Court, Upton-on-Severn.*

Coltman (E..)
[illegible] 1850.

Foljambe (H.B.)
Rt. Hon. Francis John Savile, P.C. Eld. son of G. S. F. of Osberton; 1847–1849; Ch. Ch. Oxf. M.A.; High Steward of Borough of E. Retford; M.P., E. Retford and Hundred of Bassetlaw 1857–85; Capt. Notts Yeo. 1871–9; J.P. and D.L. for Notts, High Sheriff 1889; J.P. for W. Riding of Yorks; m. Lady Gertrude Emily Acheson, d. of Archibald, 3rd Earl of Gosford, K.P. *Osberton, Worksop.*

Snowden ma. (Mrs. P., F.E.D.)
Rev. John Hampden. Son of J. S.; 1847–1847; Univ. Coll. Oxf. M.A.; Rector of St. Vedast, London, E.C.; Preb. of St. Paul's; m. d. of George Scovell. *25 Carlton Road, Putney Hill, S.W.*

Miles ma. (E.C.)
William Henry. Of Ham Green, Bristol; 2nd son of Sir W. M., 1st Bt., of Leigh Court, Somerset; 1847–1849; Ball. Coll. Oxf.; Partner in Prescott & Dimsdale's Bank; m. Mary Frances, d. of Rev. John Kynaston Charleton, Vicar of Elberton, co. Gloucester; died Jan. 25, 1888.

S-ley (H.B., aft. K.S., H.B.)
Rev. Thomas Lewis. Son of R. A. S., Surgeon, of Windsor; 1847–1849; Sch. of King's Coll. Camb., M.A.; Curate of St. Edward's, Camb., 1860–64; Curate of Prior's Portion, Tiverton, 1864–7; Vicar of Lois Weedon, Towcester, 1867–87; m. Miss Austen of Canterbury; died Sept. 7, 1897.

Barnes (W.L.E.)
Bernard Hawkesworth. 1847–1847; Eton viii. 1846; won School Pulling 1847; Fellow of Trin. Coll. Camb.; 36th Wrangler 1853; went to live on his property in Ceylon.

Miller mi. (Mrs. H., C.O.G.)
Hon. Sir Henry John, Kt. 2nd son of Rev. Sir T. C. M., Vicar of Froyle, Alton, Hants; 1847–1847; Eton viii. 1847; Camb. viii. 1849; Member of Prov. Govt. of Otago 1863–4, of New Zealand Govt. 1872; Chmn. for eight years of Waitaki High School Bd.; J.P., M.L.C. New Zealand since 1865; Speaker of Leg. Council since 1892; Chmn. of Westport Coal Co.; m. Jessie, d. of John Orbell of Hawksbury, Waikouaiti, New Zealand. *Fernbrook, Oamaru, Otago, New Zealand.*

Cockerell ma. (W.A.C.)
Andrew Pepys. Son of J. C.; 1847–1847; Ch. Ch. Oxf.; A.D.C. to Lord-Lieut. of Ireland; dead.

Norbury (W.L.E.)
Col. Thomas Coningsby, C.B. Of Sherridge, Malvern; eld. son of T. N. of Sherridge; 1847–1847; formerly Capt. 6th Dragoon Gds. and Hon. Col. Worcs. Militia; J.P. and D.L. co. Worcester and J.P. co. Hereford; m. Hon. Gertrude O'Grady, d. of Standish, 2nd Visct. Guillamore; died Oct. 16, 1898.

Sir J. Marjoribanks (E.C.)
Sir John, 3rd Bt. Of Lees, Coldstream; eld. son of Sir W. M., 2nd Bart., of Lees; 1847–1849; Ch. Ch. Oxf. M.A.; formerly Lieut.-Col. Berwicks R.V.; m. Charlotte Athole Mary, d. of Richard Trotter of Morton Hall, Edinburgh; died Nov. 18, 1884.

Barnard (H.D.)
Sir Herbert, Kt., F.S.A. Son of J. B. of Ham, Richmond, Surrey; 1847–1849; Tomline Select 1849; Banker; J.P. for Surrey, Middlesex and London; Chmn. of the Public Works Loan Commission; m. Ellen, d. of William Wyndham of Dinton, Salisbury. *Burrows Lea, Shere, Guildford, and 22 Portland Place, W.*

Marshall ma. (Miss V., F.E.D.)
William Julius. 1847–1847; Eton viii. 1846; Opp. Wall 1845–6; formerly Capt. W. Suffolk Militia.

Markham (Miss V., E.D.)
William Thomas, J.P. Of Becca Hall, Yorks; son of W. M. of Becca Hall; 1847–1847; Cox Eton viii. 1846; served in the Rifle Brigade and Coldstream Gds. in the Crimea; aft. Capt. Yorks Hussars and Lieut.-Col. 7th W. Riding Vol.; m. [illegible]

Arnold ma. (Miss W., F.E.D.)
George Henry. 1847–1847; went to Camb.; aft. lived at Bath.

Lord Porchester (Miss M., E.C.)
Henry George Howard Molyneux Herbert (4th Earl of Carnarvon), P.C., D.C.L., F.S.A., LL.D. Eld. son of Henry John George, 3rd Earl of C.; 1847–1849; Ch. Ch. Oxf. M.A.; 1st Class Lit. Hum. 1852; Lord-Lieut. of Southampton; High Steward of the Univ. of Oxf., 1859, and Constable of Carnarvon Castle; Under-Sec. of State for Colonies 1858; Sec. of State for Colonies 1866–7 and 1874–8; Lord-Lieut. of Ireland 1885–6; D.L. for Notts; Hon. Col. 2nd Vol. Bn. Hants Regt.; Pres. of the Society of Antiquaries; m. 1st, Evelyn Stanhope, d. of George, 6th Earl of Chesterfield; 2nd, Elizabeth Catharine, d. of Henry Howard of Greystoke Castle, Cumberland; died June 28, 1890.

Herbert (E.C.)
Hon. Sir R. G. W., G.C.B. . 1850.

Boileau (W.G.C.)
Sir Francis George Manningham, F.S.A., 2nd Bt. 2nd son of Sir J. P. B., 1st Bart., of Tacolnestone, Norwich; 1847–1848; Prince Consort's Italian prize 1846; Ch. Ch. Oxf. B.A.; called to the Bar, Lincoln's Inn, 1855; J.P., D.L. and C. Ald. for Norfolk; formerly Lieut.-Col. 3rd Norfolk R.V.; Vol. Officers' Decoration; Knt. of the Order of St. John of Jerusalem in England; m. Lady Henrietta, d. of Sir George Nugent, 2nd Bart.; died Dec. 2, 1900.

Drake (Miss M., aft. K.S., E.C.)
E. . 1850.

Lloyd-Mostyn (W.A.C.)
Hon. Thomas Edward. Eld. son of Edward, 2nd Lord Mostyn; 1847–1849; Eton xi. 1848; Ch. Ch. Oxf.; M.P. for Flints; m. Lady Henrietta Augusta Nevill, d. of William, 4th Earl of Abergavenny; died May 8, 1861.

Thackeray (R.F.H., aft. K.S., E.B.)
C. . 1850.

Coleridge (E.C., aft. K.S., E.C.)
A. D. . 1850.

Prest ma. (E.P.H., H.D.)
Edward Bailey. Son of S. P. of Stapleford Lodge, Camb.; 1847–1849; Trin. Coll. Camb. M.A.; Camb. xi. 1850; Barrister; District Auditor Local Govt. Board 1863–1900; m. Margaret Anne Pelham, d. of Thomas Papillon of Crowhurst Park, Sussex; died June 8, 1902.

Buller (E.C.)
Reginald John Manningham-. 4th son of Sir E. M.-B., 1st Bt., of Dilhorn Hall, Cheadle, Stoke-on-Trent; 1844–1849; Eton viii. 1849; Opp. Wall 1847–8, Keeper 1848; Field xi. 1849; Ball. Coll. Oxf.; Oxf. viii. 1852–3; formerly Col. Gren. Gds.; m. Marianne Henrietta, d. of William Davenport of Maer, Newcastle, Staffs; died Aug. 2, 1888.

Procter (C.J.A., aft. K.S., C.J.A.)
Rev. Canon Charles Tickell. 1847–1849; Newc. Select 1850; Fellow of King's Coll. Camb.; Assist. Master at Eton 1855–58; aft. Curate of All Saints, Dorchester, [illegible] mond, Surrey, 1867– [illegible] of Rochester Cath.; [illegible]

Fremantle *mi.* (W.R., E.B.) — VERY REV. HON. WILLIAM HENRY, D.D., Dean of Ripon. 2nd son of Thomas Francis, 1st Lord Cottesloe, of Swanbourne, Winslow; 1844–1849; Newc. Med. 1849; Field XI. 1849; Ball. Coll. Oxf. M.A.; 1st Cl. Lit. Hum. 1850; 1st Cl. final Class. Schools; Chanc. English Essay Prize 1854; Fellow of All Souls 1854–64; Fellow and Theo. Tutor of Ball. Coll. 1882–94; Select Preacher 1879–80; Bampton Lecturer 1883; Chaplain to Bishop of London 1861–4, and to Archbishop of Canterbury 1868–82; Rector of St. Mary's, Marylebone, 1866–82; Canon of Canterbury 1882–95; Dean of Ripon since 1895; m. 1st, Isabella Maria, d. of Sir Culling Eardley, 3rd Bt., of Bedwell Park, Hatfield, Herts; 2nd, Sophie F., d. of Major Stuart. *The Deanery, Ripon.*

Eden (M.F.H., E.B.) — FREDERICK MORTON. Son of Rt. Rev. R. E., D.D., Bishop of Moray and Ross; 1844–1847; Opp. Wall 1847; Field XI. 1847; Ch. Ch. Oxf. M.A.; Fellow of All Souls; Oxf. XI. 1850–1; Count of the Holy Roman Empire; Barrister; m. 1st, Louisa Anne, d. of Vice-Adml. Hyde Parker, C.B.; 2nd, Fanny Helen, d. of Edward Pomeroy Barrett-Lennard of St. Leonard's, Middle Swan, W. Australia. *63 Warwick Road, S.W.*

Mr. Harris (R.F.H., E.B.) — HON. ROBERT TEMPLE (aft. Harris-Temple). Of Waterston, Athlone; 3rd son of William George, 2nd Lord Harris, of Belmont, Faversham; 1844–1849; Ch. Ch. Oxf. B.A.; J.P. and D.L. cos. Kent and Westmeath, High Sheriff 1866; died unm. Feb. 24, 1892.

Welby *ma.* (C.O.G.) — HENRY GLYNNE EARLE. 2nd son of Sir G. E. Welby-Gregory, 3rd Bt.; 1842–1849; formerly Capt. 48th Regt.; died July 2, 1876.

Sir John Ramsden (Miss M., E.H.P.) — SIR JOHN WILLIAM, 5th Bt. 2nd son of J. C. R. of Byram, Ferrybridge, Normanton; 1844–1849; Trin. Coll. Camb. M.A.; M.P. for Taunton 1853–7; for Hythe 1857–9; Under Sec. of State for War 1857–8; M.P. for W. Riding, Yorks, 1859–65, Monmouth 1868–74, East Div. of W. Riding, Yorks, 1880–5, Osgoldcross Div. 1885–6; Hon. Col. 1st W. Riding Yorks Art. since 1862; J.P. and D.L. for W. Riding, Yorks, High Sheriff 1868; D.L. Inverness; m. Lady Helen Gwendolen, d. of Edward Adolphus, 12th Duke of Somerset, K.G. *Byram, Ferrybridge, Normanton; Longley Hall, Huddersfield; and Bulstrode Park, Gerrard's Cross, Bucks.*

Tinling (W.A.C.) — WILLIAM PATTISON. 1843–1847; formerly Maj. and Brevet Lieut.-Col. 90th Regt.

Roberts (C.J.A. & E.B.) — REV. WILLIAM WALTER. Son of Capt. J. W. R., R.N.; 1842–1848; Merton Coll. Oxf.; m. Ann Shannon, d. of James Cairns. *74 Kensington Gardens Sq., W.*

Wayte *mi.* (Miss W., aft. K.S., F.E.D.) — G. H. [illegible] 1850.

Johnson (R.F.H., H.D.) — FREDERICK WILLIAM. 1844–1849; Trin. Coll. Camb.; Camb. VIII. 1851–2 and 4, Stroke 1851–2; Minister of St. John's, Great Yarmouth; died there 1860.

Grover *ma.* (Mrs. Ro., aft. [illegible] E.B.) — [illegible]

Blackett (E.H.P.) — SIR EDWARD WILLIAM, 7th Bt. Eld. son of Sir E. B., 6th Bt., of Matfen Hall; 1842–1849; Staff Coll. Camberley; Maj.-Gen. Rifle Brig. (ret.); served in the Crimea 1854–5; severely wounded at Redan; Knt. of Legion of Honour; J.P. Northumberland, High Sheriff 1888; m. Hon. Julia Frances, d. of Kenelm, 17th Lord Somerville. *Matfen Hall, Corbridge, Northumberland.*

Lord Pevensey (W.A.C.) — HENRY NORTH HOLROYD (2nd Earl of Sheffield). 2nd son of George Augustus Frederick Charles 2nd Earl of S., of Sheffield Park; 1844–1849; Field XI. and Opp. Wall 1849; attaché to the Embassy at Constantinople 1851–2 and 1852–4; Attaché at Copenhagen 1855; M.P. for E. Sussex 1857–65; J.P. and D.L. for Sussex. *Sheffield Park, Uckfield.*

Rust (F.E.D.) — GEORGE JOHN. Son of G. R., of Cromwell House, Huntingdon; 1844–1849; Univ. Coll. Oxf. B.A.; J.P. and D.L. for Hunts; m. Agnes Caroline, d. of William Henry Desborough of Hartford House, co. Huntingdon. *Alconbury House, Huntingdon.*

Mr. Legge *ma.* (F.E.D.) — HON. AND REV. GEORGE BARRINGTON. 2nd son of William, 4th Earl of Dartmouth; 1844–1848; formerly Capt. Rifle Brig.; served in the Kaffir War 1852–3 (Med.); Crimea 1854–5; Medal and 4 Clasps; 5th Class Medjidie; Vicar of Packington, co. Warwick, 1860–4, and Vicar of Whittington 1878–93; m. Sophia Frances Margaret, d. of John Levett of Wichnor Park, Lichfield; died Dec. 3, 1900.

Wynne (Miss A., E.B.) — WILLIAM GRIFFITH. Son of — W. of Voelas, co. Denbigh; 1844–1849; Trin. Hall, Camb.; Capt. Coldstream Gds.; died 1862.

Dashwood (W.L.E.) — HENRY WORKHOUSE. 2nd son of T. J. D., Remembrancer of Bengal; 1843–1847; Bengal Civil Service; died unm. June 11, 1862.

Aitken *ma.* (R.F.H., F.E.D.) — REV. JAMES. Son of J. A. of Radley, Herts; 1842–1847; Eton XI 1846–7; Field XI. 1847; Wall XI. 1847; Exeter Coll. Oxf. M.A.; Oxf. XI. 1848–50; Capt. 1850; Oxf. VIII. 1849 and 1851; Vicar of Chorley Wood, Rickmansworth, Herts, 1857–89; Chaplain of the Royal Memorial Church, Cannes, since 1889; m. Ellen, d. of William Parr. *Cannes, France.*

Jackson *ma.* (E.H.P.) — REV. WILLIAM HUTCHINSON. Son of J. J. of Hampstead, and of Hambleton Manor House, Rutland; 1844–1847; Trin. Coll. Camb. B.A.; formerly Curate of Hambleton, Rutland; Vicar of Stagsden since 1879. *Stagsden Vicarage, Bedford.*

Haviland (C.O.G.) — REV. ARTHUR COLES. 5th son of J. H., M.D., Regius Prof. of Medicine, Camb.; 1843–1847; St. John's Coll. Camb. M.A.; 26th Wrangler 1852; Fellow of St. John's; Rector of Lilley; m. d. of Rev. Charles Kegwin, Rector of Emberton. *Lilley Rectory, Luton.*

Alexander (W.A.C.) — MAJ.-GEN. SIR CLAUD, 1st Bt. Of Ballochmyle, Mauchline; eld. son of B. A. of Ballochmyle; 1842–1847; Ch. Ch. Oxf.; formerly Maj.-Gen. Gren. Gds.; served in the Crimea, including Siege of Sebastopol (Crimean and Turkish Medals and 5th Cl. Medjidie); M.P. for S. Ayrshire 1874–85; J.P. and D.L. cos. Ayr and Renfrew; m. Eliza, d. of Alexander Speirs of Elderslie, N.B.; died May 22, 1899.

Evans (Mrs. Hor., aft. K.S., C.J.A.) — CHARLES JOHN. Son of the Chancellor of Norwich; 1842–1849; Newc. Select 1849; Fellow of King's Coll. Camb.; 2nd Cl. Class. Trip.; died Dec. 29, 1862.

[illegible] Son of a Solicitor at [illegible] Oxf. B.A.; [illegible] St. Mary [illegible]

Moody (Mrs. P., aft. K.S., C.O.G.)
H. . 1850.

Ansley (Mrs. Ro., F.E.D.)
JOHN FREDERICK. 1844–1847; died 1852.

Ethelston (C.O.G.)
ROBERT PEEL. 2nd son of Rev. C. W. E., Rector of Uplyme, Lyme Regis; 1844–1849; Field XI. 1848–9, Keeper 1849; Opp. Wall 1849; Ch. Ch. Oxf.; J.P. for Salop; Chmn. of Whitchurch Bd. of Guardians 37 years; *m.* 1st, Louisa Phillppa, *d.* of Thomas Perry of Moor Hall, Essex; 2nd, Mabel, *d.* of Rev. William Henry Egerton, Rector of Whitchurch. *Hinton Hall, Whitchurch, Salop.*

Hand (Mrs. Ro., aft. K.S., C.J.A.)
THOMAS MORE. 1843–1849; Emm. Coll. Camb.: formerly Lieut. 51st N. I. Bengal; shot by a party of hill tribes, near the Khyber Pass, 1857.

Lygon *ma.* (R.O.)
HON. HENRY (5th Earl Beauchamp). 2nd son of Henry, 4th Earl B., of Madresfield Court, Malvern: 1843–1847; formerly Capt. 1st Life Gds. and M.P. for W. Worcs.; died unm. Mar. 4, 1866.

Lygon *mi.* (R.O.)
HON. FREDERICK (6th Earl Beauchamp), P.C., D.C.L., F.S.A. 3rd son of Henry, 4th Earl B., of Madresfield Court, Malvern; 1844–1843: Ch. Ch. Oxf. M.A.: Fellow of All Souls Coll. Oxf. 1852; Hon. D.C.L. 1870; Lord-Lieut. co. Worc.; M.P. for Tewkesbury 1857–63, and for W. Worcs. 1863–6; a Lord of the Admiralty 1859; Lord Steward of the Household 1874–80; Paymaster-Genl. 1886–7; formerly Capt. Worcs. Yeo. Cav.; *m.* 1st, Lady Mary Catherine Stanhope, *d.* of Philip Henry, 5th Earl Stanhope; 2nd, Lady Emily Annora Charlotte Pierrepont, *d.* of Sydney William, 3rd Earl Manvers; died Feb. 19, 1891.

Aitken *mi.* (R.F.H., F.E.D.)
HENRY MORTLOCK. Son of J. A. of Hadley, Herts; 1843–1849; Eton XI. 1846–49, Capt. 1848–49: Field XI. and Opp. Wall 1848; Keeper of Upper Club 1847–8; Exeter Coll. Oxf. B.A.; Oxf. XI. 1853; formerly a Merchant in Calcutta. 9 *Gilston Road, W. Brompton, S.W.*

Biddulph (H.D.)
SIR THEOPHILUS WILLIAM, 7th Bt. Son of Sir T. B., 6th Bt., of Westcombe, Kent; 1842–1847; Trin. Coll. Oxf.; J.P. and D.L. co. Warwick; formerly Major 2nd Warwicks Militia; *m.* Mary Agnes, *d.* of Kenelm, 17th Lord Somerville; died Mar. 1, 1883.

Hammond (Mrs. Ri., E.B.)
HENRY ANTHONY. 4th son of W. O. H. of St. Albans Court, Wingham, Dover; 1841–1847; Merton Coll. Oxf. M.A.; Curate of Middle and E. Claydon, Bucks, and Southborough, Kent, aft. Incumbent of Holy Trinity, Dover; withdrew from Church of England; *m.* Catherine Charlotte, *d.* of John Deacon of Mabledon, Tonbridge, Kent. *Sundridge House, Bournemouth.*

Grenfell (W.E., E.B.)
ARTHUR RIVERSDALE. Of Butler's Court, Beaconsfield; 3rd son of P. St. L. G. of Maesteg House, Swansea; 1843–1847; travelled in India, China, Palestine, &c., aft. a Farmer near Maidenhead; J.P. for Bucks; died Nov. 1, 1895.

Bedford *ma.* (R.P.H., aft. K.S., W.G.C.)
CAMPBELL RILAND. Son of Rev. W. R. B., *Rector of Sutton Coldfield, Birmingham*; 1842–1849; formerly Major 3rd Scottish Borderers Militia; *m.* Harriet M., *d.* of Rev. T. Beach Whitehurst. *Woodburn, ... S.B.*

Marquis of Lothian (Miss A., E.B.)
WILLIAM SCHOMBERG ROBERT (8th Marquis of Lothian). Eld. son of John William Robert, 7th Marquis of L.; 1844–1848; Ch. Ch. Oxf. B.A.; 1st Cl. Lit. Hum. 1854, 1st Cl. Modern History 1854; *m.* Lady Constance Harriet Mahonesa Talbot, *d.* of 18th Earl of Shrewsbury; died July 4, 1870.

Adair (C.L.)
COL. ALEXANDER WILLIAM. Of Heatherton Park, Taunton; son of A. A. of Heatherton Park; 1844–1848; Eton VIII. 1848; Ch. Ch. Oxf.; formerly Coldstream Gds., aft. 52nd Regt.; J.P. for Somerset; *m.* Caroline, *d.* of J. G. Turnbull, Accountant-Gen. at Madras; died 1889.

Taunton (Mrs. Ri.)
REV. CHARLES EDWARD. 1844–1848; formerly Curate at Frome, aft. Head of the Ladies' College at Fulham.

Lewis (Miss A., H.M.B.)
REV. WILLIAM LEMPRIERE. 1844–1849; Newc. Select 1848, Newc. Sch. 1849: Fellow of Trin. Coll. Oxf.; 2nd Cl. Lit. Hum.; formerly Curate of Hardwicke, Cambs.

Alderson *ma.* (E.C.)
CHARLES HENRY, C.B. 2nd son of Hon. Sir E. H. A., a Baron of the Exchequer; 1843–1849; Trin. Coll. Oxf. M.A.; 1st Cl. in Mods., 2nd Cl. in Final Class. Schs.; Fellow of All Souls Coll.; Barrister Inner Temple 1855; Senior Inspector of Schools 1882–5: 2nd Charity Commissioner 1885–1900; Chief Charity Comm. for England and Wales since 1900. 40 *Beaufort Gardens, S.W.*

Byng *ma.* (Mrs. Hor., H.M.B.)
HON. GEORGE HENRY CHARLES (3rd Earl of Strafford). Eld. son of George Stevens, 2nd Earl of S.; 1844–1848; Prince Consort's French prize 1846, German prize 1847; Ch. Ch. Oxf. M.A.; M.P. for Tavistock 1852–7, for Middx. 1857–74; Parliamentary Sec. to Poor Law Bd. 1865–6, Under Sec. for Foreign Affairs 1870–4, Under Sec. for India 1880–3; Lord-Lieut. of Middx.; J.P. for Surrey and Herts; 1st Civil Service Commissioner; Hon. Col. 17th Middx. R.V.; *m.* Lady Alice Harriet Frederica Egerton, *d.* of Francis, 1st Earl of Ellesmere, K.G.; died Mar. 28, 1898.

Atcherley (Miss W., C.J.A.)
WILLIAM ATCHERLEY. 1843–1848; formerly Lieut. 84th Regt., aft. Cornet 14th Lt. Dragoons.

Rogers (W.E., W.A.C.)
WALTER LACY. 3rd son of F. J. N. R. of Rainscombe, Marlborough; 1844–1849; Ball. Coll. Oxf. M.A.; 2nd in Math.; Barrister; J.P. for Wilts; *m.* 1st, Hermione Lucy, *d.* of J. J. E. Hamilton; 2nd, Sophia Mary Coore, *d.* of George Paton; died April 18, 1885.

Mr. Lascelles (E.B.)
HON. AND REV. CANON JAMES WALTER. 6th son of Henry, 3rd Earl of Harewood; 1844–1847; Exeter Coll. *Oxf.* M.A.; Rector of Goldsborough, Knaresborough, and Canon of Ripon; *m.* Emma Clara, *d.* of Sir William Miles, 1st Bt.; died Nov. 24, 1901.

Bradshaw (Miss A., aft. K.S., W.G.C.)
HENRY. Son of J. H. B.; 1843–1849; Newc. Select 1849; Sch. of King's Coll. Camb., M.A.; 2nd Cl. Class. Trip. 1854; Dean of Coll. 1857–8 and 1863–5; Univ. Librarian 1867–86; died Feb. 11, 1886.

Goodall (E.H.P., aft. K.S., E.H.P.)
W. . 1850.

Cobbold (W.E., E.C.)
JOHN PATTESON. Eld. son of J. C. C. of the Holywells, Ipswich; 1843–1850; J.P. for Suffolk, M.P. for Ipswich; Solicitor at Ipswich; *m.* Adela Harriette, *d.* of Rev. George John Dupuis, Vice-Provost of Eton; died Dec. 9, 1875.

Halford (E.H.P., E.C.) — REV. SIR JOHN FREDERICK, 4th Bt. Of Wistow Hall, Leicester; 2nd son of Sir Henry Halford, Bt., of Wistow; 1843^{3}–1848^{2}; Trin. Coll. Camb. B.A.; formerly Curate of Wistow; *m.* Ismene, *d.* of J. S. Andrews; died 1897.

Barnett (W.E., W.L.E.) — WILLIAM EDWARD. 1843^{3}–1848^{2}; Eton XI. 1847–8; Field XI. 1847; Trin. Coll. Camb.; Camb. XI. 1849–50; Banker at Newcastle (Hodgkin, Barnett, Pease & Co.); dead.

Nind (E.C.) — P. H. . 1850.

Coleridge (E.C.) — WILLIAM RENNELL. Son of Rt. Rev. W. H. C. of Salston, Bp. of Barbados; 1843^{1}–1849^{3}; Eton VIII. 1849; Keeper Opp. Wall 1849; Field XI. 1849; Ch. Ch. Oxf.; J.P. and D.L. for Devon; formerly Major S. Devon Militia; *m.* Katherine Frances, *d.* of Capt. Robert Cutts Barton, R.N. *Salston House, Ottery St. Mary.*

Keppel (E.H.P.) — FREDERICK CHARLES. Eld. son of Rev. W. A. W. K. of Lexham Hall, Swaffham, Norfolk, Rector of Haynford, Norfolk; 1844^{2}–1847^{2}; Col. Gren. Gds. and Equerry to H.R.H. the Prince of Wales 1858–60; died Mar. 2, 1876.

Buckley *ma.* (J.E.Y.) — ALFRED. Of New Hall, Bodenham, Salisbury; eld. son of Gen. E. P. B. of New Hall; 1843^{2}–1848^{2}; Eton XI. 1848; Trin. Coll. Camb. B.A.; in the Admiralty; aft. Sec. to Duke of Somerset; 13 years Chmn. of Board of Governors of Salisbury Infirmary; Director of Wilts and Dorset Banking Co., Chmn. 1898; J.P., D.L. and C.C. for Wilts; *m.* Geraldine Mary, *d.* of Capt. George William St. John Mildmay, R.N.; died Dec. 15, 1900.

Tugwell (W.A.C.) — REV. CANON GEORGE. 1844^{2}–1847^{2}; Oriel Coll. Oxf. M.A.; formerly Curate of Ilfracombe; Rector of Bathwick with Woolley since 1871; Preb. and Canon of Wells Cath. *Bathwick Rectory, Bath.*

Adeane (Mrs. Hor., E.B.) — ROBERT JONES. Of Babraham, Camb.; eld. son of H. J. A. of Babraham; 1843^{2}–1848^{2}; Trin. Coll. Camb.; died unm. Dec. 7, 1853.

Blundell *ma.* (C.J.A. & H.D.) — COL. HENRY BLUNDELL HOLLINSHEAD, C.B. Son of R. B. B. H. B. of Deysbrook; 1843^{2}–1849^{3}; Eton VIII. 1848–9; Capt. of the Boats 1849; won Pulling and Sculling 1848; Opp. Wall 1847–8; Field XI. 1847–8, Keeper 1848; Ch. Ch. Oxf. B.A.; entered Army 1855; served in the Crimea aft. fall of Sebastopol 1855–6; passed Staff Coll. 1864; Assist. Adjt.-Gen. Home District 1877–82; Nile Expedition 1884–5; J.P. and D.L. for Lancs; Col. Gren. Gds. (ret. 1889); M.P. S.W. Lancs (Ince Div.) 1885–92 and since 1895; Col. Comm. Manchester Vol. Bgde.; *m.* Hon. Beatrice, Maid of Honour to Queen Victoria, *d.* of Vice-Adm. Hon. Henry Dilkes Byng. 10 *Stratton St., W.; Ashurst Lodge, Sunninghill, Berks; and Deysbrook, W. Derby, Liverpool.*

Green *mi.* (Mrs. Ro., aft. K.S., W.A.C.) — W. O. . 1850.

Heneage (E.B.) — MAJ. CLEMENT WALKER, V.C. Of Compton Basset, Calne; eld. son of G. H. W. H. of Compton Basset; 1844^{2}–1849^{3}; Ch. Ch. Oxf.; formerly Maj. 8th Hussars; served in Crimea 1854–5 (rode in the Charge of the Lt. Bgde. at Balaclava), and in Indian Mutiny; awarded V.C. for gallantry at Battle of Gwalior; J.P. and D.L. for Wilts, High Sheriff 1887; *m.* Henrietta Letitia Victoria, *d.* of John Henry Vivian, M.P., of Singleton, co. Glamorgan; died Dec. 9, 1901.

Mr. Boyle (R.O.) — LIEUT.-COL. HON. WILLIAM GEORGE. 2nd son of Charles, Viscount Dungarvan, and grandson of Edmund, 8th Earl of Cork; 1844^{2}–1848^{2}; formerly Lieut.-Col. Coldstream Gds., aft. Lieut.-Col. 2nd Somerset Militia; served in Crimea 1854, inc. Alma, Inkerman and Sebastopol (medal with 3 clasps, Turkish med., 5th class Medjidie); M.P. for Frome 1856–7.

Helm (Mrs. Ro., aft. K.S.) — CHARLES ORLANDO. 1844^{2}–1848^{1}; Worc. Coll. Oxf.

Mount (E.C.) — VEN. ARCHDN. FRANCIS JOHN. 3rd son of W. M. of Wasing Place, Reading; 1843^{1}–1850^{1}; Oriel Coll. Oxf. M.A.; Curate at Horsham 1855–71; Vicar of Firle 1871–7; Vicar of Cuckfield 1877–87; Examining Chaplain to Bp. of Chichester 1870; Preb. of Sutton 1875–87; Canon of Chichester 1887–1900; Vicar of Burpham, Arundel, 1899–1903; Archdn. of Chichester 1887–1903; died May 5, 1903.

Christie (J.E.Y.) — WILLIAM LANGHAM. Son of L. C. of Preston Deanery, Northants; 1844^{1}–1848^{2}; Trin. Coll. Camb. M.A.; J.P. for Northants; J.P. and D.L. for Sussex; formerly Capt. Northants Militia; M.P. for Lewes 1874–85; *m.* Agnes Hamilton, *d.* of Col. Augustus Saltren Clevland of Tapeley Park, Instow, N. Devon. 117 *Eaton Sq., S.W., and Glyndebourne, Lewes.*

Maugham (Mrs. Ri., C.J.A.) — HENRY. 1843^{3}–1847^{2}.

Learmonth (F.E.D.) — ALEXANDER. Son of J. L. of Dean, Edinburgh; 1843^{2}–1847^{2}; Univ. Coll. Oxf.; Lieut.-Col. 17th Lancers; served in the Crimea and Indian Mutiny; M.P. for Colchester 1870–80; *m.* Charlotte, *d.* of Gen. Lyons; died Mar. 12, 1887.

Crosse *ma.* (F.E.D.) — THOMAS RICHARD. Of Shaw Hill, Chorley, Lancs; eld. son of T. B. C. of Shaw Hill; 1843^{2}–1848^{2}; Trin. Coll. Camb. M.A.; Col. Comm. 3rd and 4th Bns. N. Lancs Regt. 1874–92, and Hon. Col. from 1892; *m.* Lady Mary Stuart, *d.* of Charles Knox, 4th Earl of Castle Stewart; died Nov. 27, 1897.

Lambert *ma.* (Miss A., J.E.Y.) — CHARLES HENRY. 5th son of Sir H. J. L., 5th Bt.; 1843^{1}–1847^{2}; formerly Capt. 19th Foot, ret. 1861; died at Queensland July 4, 1872.

Praed (Mrs. Hor., E.B.) — WINTHROP MACKWORTH. Of Mickleham Downs, Dorking; eld. son of B. J. M.-P. of Owsden Hall, Suffolk; 1843^{2}–1849^{2}; Banker in London (Praed & Co.); *m.* Louisa, *d.* of James Ewing; died Feb. 11, 1896.

Legge (W.E., W.A.C.) — HENRY EDWARD. Eld. son of Rev. H. L. of Mareland, Surrey, and Rector of East Lavant, Chichester; 1843^{2}–1847^{2}; died at Algiers Dec. 15, 1861.

Pretyman (E.H.P.) — ARTHUR CHARLES. Of Haughley Park, Stowmarket; 4th son of Rev. G. T. P., Chancellor of Lincoln; 1843^{3}–1848^{2}; formerly Capt. 74th Highlanders and 25th Regt. K.O.B.; Capt. Warwicks Yeo. Cav.; J.P. for Suffolk and co. Warwick; *m.* Mary, *d.* of Henry Baxter of Idvies, co. Forfar; died June 21, 1898.

Snowden *mi.* (F.E.D.) — E. . 1850.

Taylor (H.D.) — WILLIAM FRANCIS. Of Moor Green, co. Worcester; 3rd son of J. T. of Moseley Hall and Moor Green; 1843^{2}–1848^{2}; Trin. Coll. Camb. B.A.; J.P. cos. Derby, Worcester [illegible]; *m.* Augusta Charlotte, [illegible] of Lincoln's Inn, [illegible]

Powys (Mrs. Ro., E.B.)
REV. FRANCIS ARTHUR. Of Tettenha'l, Branksome, Dorset; son of H. P. P. of Hardwick, Oxfs; 1843^{3}-1850^{1}; Eton VIII. 1850; Winner of Sculling Sweepstakes 1849; St. John's Coll. Oxf.; Fellow of St. John's 1851-70; formerly Vicar of St. Giles, Oxf.; aft. Rector of Winterslow, Salisbury; died May 13, 1902.

Watson (W.E., F.E.D.)
SIR ARTHUR TOWNLEY, 2nd Bt., K.C. Son of Sir T. W., 1st Bt., M.D., LL.D., Pres. of the Royal Coll. of Physicians; 1841^{1}-1847^{2}; St. John's Coll. Camb. M.A.; Barrister Lincoln's Inn, 1856; Q.C. 1885; Bencher 1888; *m.* Rosamond, *d.* of Charles Powlett Rushworth of Queen Anne St., Marylebone. *39 Lowndes Sq., S.W., and Reigate Lodge, Reigate.*

Wood (C.O.G.)
VINCENT (aft. Stuckey). Of Hill House, Langport, Somersets; eld. son of Rev. W. W. of Staplegrove, Taunton; 1842^{1}-1847^{3}; Trin. Coll. Camb.; Banker; formerly Capt. W. Somerset Yeo.; J.P. and D.L. co. Somerset, High Sheriff 1883; *m.* Mary, *d.* of Rev. Thomas Prowse Lethbridge; died Jan. 20, 1902.

Prendergast (Miss A., E.H.P.)
COL. LENOX. Son of G. L. P.; 1843^{3}-1847^{3}; Ch. Ch. Oxf.; Col. in Scots Greys; severely wounded at Balaclava Oct. 25, 1854; J.P. for co. London and Middlesex; *m.* Marion, *d.* of Neil Malcolm of Poltalloch. *14 Thurloe Sq., S. Kensington, S.W.*

MIDDLE DIVISION.

Cheales (Mrs. Ro., aft. K.S., C.J.A.)
REV. HENRY JOHN. 2nd son of Rev. J. C., Vicar of Skendleby, Spilsby; 1844^{2}-1849^{2}; Eton XI. 1848-9; Coll. Wall 1846-8, Keeper of Wall and Upper Club 1848; Pres. of Eton Soc. 1848; Exeter Coll. Oxf. M.A.; Oxf. VIII. 1850; Vicar of Friskney (ret.) and Rural Dean; *m.* Edith Maria, *d.* of the Rev. T. W. Booth, Vicar of Friskney. *The Vicarage, Friskney, Lincs.*

Atkinson (Mrs. P., F.E.D.)
REV. CANON JAMES AUGUSTUS, D.C.L. Son of J. A., of Bengal Medical Service; 1844^{1}-1847^{3}; Wall XI. 1847; Sch. of Exeter Coll. Oxf., M.A.; 1st Cl. Mods; 3rd Cl. Lit. Hum.; Rector of St. John's, Longsight, Manchester, 1861-87; Rural Dean of Ardwick 1880-7; Vicar and Rural Dean of Bolton 1887-96; Vicar of Gedney, Holbeach, 1896-1900; Vicar of St. Michael's, Coventry, and Hon. Canon of Manchester since 1884; *m.* Hon. Charlotte Adelaide, *d.* of Richard Walter, 6th Viscount Chetwynd. *St. Michael's Vicarage, Coventry.*

Martin *mi.* (Mrs. Hor., E.B.)
H. A. . 1850.

King (Mrs. Ro., W.A.C.)
ROBERT MOSS. Of Ashcott Hill, Bridgwater; son of Rev. W. M. K., Rector of Long Crichel, Wimborne; 1841^{3}-1850^{1}; Field XI. and Opp. Wall 1849; Merton Coll. Oxf., 1st Cl. Mods 1852; 2nd Cl. Lit. Hum.; Postmastership; served 25 years Bengal Civil Service; Indian Mutiny Med.; J.P. and D.L. co. Somerset; *m.* Elizabeth Augusta, *d.* of Rev. John Egerton of Hextable, Swanley Junction, Kent; died July 7, 1903.

De Rutzen *ma.* (Miss M., W.L.E.)
BARON RUDOLPH WILLIAM HENRY ERHARD. 2nd son of Baron F. De R. of Slebech; 1844^{2}-1847^{3}; Trin. Coll. Camb. B.A.; Barrister Inner Temple; High Sheriff co. Pembroke 1895. *Slebech Park, Haverfordwest.*

Ferrand (E.B.)
WILLIAM BUSFIELD. Son of W. B. F. of St. Ives, Bingley; 1844^{3}-1849^{1}; Univ. Coll. Oxf.; J.P. and D.L. W. Riding, Yorks; died unm. Sept. 1, 1865.

Egerton (F.E.D.)
HON. WILBRAHAM (1st Earl Egerton), P.C. Eld. son of William Tatton, 1st Lord Egerton of Tatton; 1845^{1}-1850^{1}; Ch. Ch. Oxf. M.A.; 2nd Cl. Law and Mod. Hist.; M.P. for N. Cheshire 1858-68, Mid-Cheshire 1868-73; Chmn. of the Manchester Ship Canal 1887-94; Pres. of the Royal Agricultural Soc.; Shire Horse Soc.; Hackney Horse Soc.; formerly Major, Earl of Chester's Yeo. Cav.; Chmn. of Qr. Sessions co. Chester 1883-9; Prov. Grand Master, Cheshire, 1885-1900; Chmn. of Royal Commission on the Port of London 1900; Lord-Lieut. of Cheshire; Chanc. of the Order of the Hospital of St. John of Jerusalem; Eccl. Comm. for England; *m.* 1st, Lady Mary Sarah, *d.* of William, 2nd Earl Amherst; 2nd, Alice Anne, *d.* of Sir Graham Graham-Montgomery of Stanhope, 3rd Bt., and widow of Richard, 3rd Duke of Buckingham and Chandos. *7 St. James' Sq., S.W., and Tatton Park, Knutsford.*

Kington (H.D.)
THOMAS LAURENCE (aft. Kington-Oliphant), F.S.A. Of Gask Auchterarder; son of T. K. of Charlton House, Wraxall, Bristol; 1845^{2}-1849^{1}; Ball. Coll. Oxf. M.A.; called to the Bar, Inner Temple, 1858; J.P. and D.L. for Perthshire; *m.* Frances Dorothy, *d.* of Henry Jebb of Boston, co. Lincoln; died July 8, 1902.

Mathias (H.D., aft. K.S., H.D.)
G. H. D. . 1853.

Bosanquet (Mrs. Hor., E.B.)
S. C. . 1850.

Smith (Mrs. Hor., W.A.C.)
REV. CANON FREDERICK GEORGE HUME. Son of R. S. of Richmond, Surrey; 1841^{3}-1848^{2}; Eton VIII. 1848; Trin. Coll. Camb. M.A.; Sen. Opt. Camb. 1852; Vicar of Armley; Hon. Canon of Ripon since 1893. *Armley Vicarage, Leeds.*

Paynter (R.F.H., C.O.G.)
REGINALD HEARLE. Of Boskenna, St. Buryan, Cornwall; eld. son of T. P. of Boskenna; 1845^{1}-1847^{3}; *m.* Mary Davies, *d.* of Rev. Preb. J. O. W. Haweis, Rector of Slaugham, Sussex; died Feb. 16, 1878.

Waterfield *ma.* (R.F.H., aft. K.S., C.J.A.)
OTTIWELL CHARLES. Son of C. W., a Registrar of the Court of Bankruptcy; 1844^{1}-1850^{1}; Coll. Wall 1849; King's Coll. Camb. M.A.; Assist. Master at Eton 1856-8, aft. Principal of Temple Grove Sch., East Sheen, Surrey; died 1898.

Norton (E.C.)
THOMAS BRINSLEY (4th Lord Grantley). 2nd son of Hon. G. C. N. of Kettlethorpe Hall, Wakefield, and nephew of Fletcher, 3rd Lord G.; 1844^{2}-1848^{2}; *m.* Maria Chiara Eliza, *d.* of Signor Federigo of Casa Federigo, Capri, Italy; died at Capri, July 24, 1877.

Maxwell (C.L.)
WELLWOOD. Of Glenlee, New Galloway, Kirkcudbrightshire; 1843^{3}-1848^{2}; Trin. Coll. Camb.; Barrister.

Hole (Mrs. Ri., H.M.B.)
WILLIAM ROBERT. Of Parke, Bovey Tracey, S. Devon; son of W. H. of Parke; 1845^{1}-1848^{1}; Univ. Coll. Oxf.; J.P., D.L. and C.C. for Devon; *m.* Emily Letitia, *d.* of Rev. John Hall Parlby of Manadon, Crown Hill, Devon; died Feb. 7, 1903.

Carr (E.H.P.)
REV. EDMUND DONALD. Son of Rev. E. C., Rector of Quatt Malvern, Salop; 1843^{3}-1848^{2}; Emm. Coll. Camb. B.A.; formerly Incumbent of Ratlinghope, Shrewsbury, aft. Rector of Wolstaston, Salop; *m.* Elizabeth, *d.* of Rev. John Edmund Carr of Outwoods, co. Derby; dead.

Wollaston (R.F.H., aft. K.S., C.J.A. & C. Wo.)
W. M. . 1850.

Carter (Mrs. Ro., aft. K.S., E.H.P.)
E. . 1850.

Porter (Mrs. Hor., H.M.B.)
REV. CANON CHARLES FLEETWOOD. Son of Rev. C. P.; 1844[3]–1848[3]; Caius Coll. Camb. M.A.; Vicar of Banbury, Rural Dean of Deddington; Dioc. Inspector of Schools and Hon. Canon of Ch. Ch. Oxf.: *m.* Emily, *d.* of Rev. Canon Lawrence Ottley. *The Vicarage, Banbury.*

Harper (Mrs. Hor., aft. K.S., C.J.A. & H.D.)
H. W. . 1850.

Cust *mi.* (Miss W., F.E.D.)
SIR LEOPOLD, 2nd Bt. Son of Hon. Sir E. C., K.C.H., 1st Bt.; 1845[1]–1850[1]; Eton VIII. 1849; Gentleman-Usher to Her Majesty; *m.* Charlotte Sobieski Isabel, *d.* of Vice-Adml. Hon. Charles O. Bridgeman; died Mar. 3, 1878.

Shuldham (Miss A., aft. K.S., J.E.Y.)
REV. NAUNTON LEMUEL. Eld. son of M. S., Comm. R.N., of Melton, Woodbridge; 1843[2]–1850[1]; Coll. Wall 1849; Demy of Magd. Coll. Oxf.; M.A. Fellow of Magd.; Master in College at Eton 1862–7; Conduct 1863–7; aft. Vicar of Scawby, Lincolns; *m.* Sophia Frances, *d.* of John Mathew Quantock of Norton Manor, Somerset; died July 24, 1874.

Fursdon *ma.* (W.E., W.A.C.)
CHARLES. Eld. son of G. F. of Fursdon, Tiverton; 1842[2]–1848[1]; formerly Capt. 1st Devon Militia; J.P. for Devon; *m.* Eliza, *d.* of Henry Willis of Hill Street, Berkeley Sq., S.W. *Fursdon, Tiverton.*

Halford (C.O.G.)
CHARLES AUGUSTUS DRAKE. Son of C. D. H. of West Lodge, East Bergholt; 1843[2]–1849[1]; served as Capt. in 5th Dragoon Gds. during the Crimea; *m.* Hon. Geraldine Frances, *d.* of Charles Henry, 14th Visct. Dillon. *West Lodge, East Bergholt, Colchester, and 50 Princes Gate, S.W.*

Taylor (Mrs. Ri., E.H.P.)
FREDERICK JAMES. 1844[3]–1849[1].

Ogle (W.L.E.)
SCOTT JAMES. Of Oakenwood, Kent; 1844[2]–1847[3]; Trin. Coll. Camb.; formerly W. Kent Yeo.

Jefferyes (Mrs. P., H.M.B.)
ST. JOHN GEORGE. Of Blarney Castle, Ireland; 1844[2]–1847[3].

Villers (R.F.H., aft. K.S.)
REV. ROBERT JOHN. 1843[2]–1847[3]: Coll. Wall 1846; formerly Incumbent of King's Heath, Birmingham.

Cockerell *mi.* (W.A.C.)
HORACE ABEL, C.S.I. Son of J. C.; 1843[3]–1847[3]; E. I. Coll. Haileybury; Bengal Civil Service (ret.); formerly Sec. to Govt. of Bengal in Judicial and Political Dept., and Member of Council of Lieut.-Gov.; *m.* Julia Mary, *d.* of Hon. Sir Edmund Drummond, K.C.B. 27 *Beaufort Gardens, S.W.*

Portman (Mrs. P., C.O.G.)
WYNDHAM BERKELEY. Son of W. B. P. of Hare Park, Newmarket; 1844[3]–1848[1]: Magd. Coll. Camb.; Coffee Planter in Ceylon, aft. Newspaper Prop.; *m.* Emily Charlotte, *d.* of George Newton of Croxton Park, St. Neots; died Sept. 18, 1890.

Duffield (W.E., E.H.P.)
CHARLES PHILIP. Of Marcham Park, near Abingdon; son of T. D. of Marcham; 1843–1847[3]; J.P. for Berks, High Sheriff 1859; *m.* Penelope, *d.* of William Graham of Fitzharris, Bucks; died 1880.

Thesiger (E.H.P.)
LIEUT.-GEN. HON. CHARLES WEMYSS. 2nd son of Rt. Hon. Sir Frederick, 1st Lord Chelmsford; 1844[3]–1848[1]; ent. Army (6th Inniskilling Drag.) 1853; Lieut.-Gen. 1891; served in China 1860, inc. capture of Pekin (Med. with two clasps); A.D.C. to Lord-Lieut. of Ireland 1858; Insp. for Auxil. Cav. 1878–83; Insp.-Gen. of Cav. in Ireland, and in command Curragh Camp 1885–90; ret. 1895; Col. 14th Hussars since 1896; *m.* Charlotte Elizabeth, *d.* of Hon. George Handcock; died July 29, 1903.

Lysley *ma.* (W.L.E.)
WILLIAM GERARD. Of Pewsham, Chippenham; eld. son of W. J. L. of Pewsham; 1844[3]–1847[3]; Trin. Coll. Camb. M.A.; Barrister; Col. Inns of Court R. Vol.; J.P. for Wilts; *m.* Frances Elizabeth, *d.* of Sir Charles Hugh Lowther, 3rd Bt., of Swillington, Leeds; died Oct. 6, 1887.

De Rutzen *mi.* (Miss M., W.L.E.)
SIR ALBERT RICHARD FRANCIS MAXIMILIAN, Kt., J.P., D.L. 3rd son of Charles Frederick Baron De R. of Slebech Park, Haverfordwest; 1844[3]–1847[3]; Eton VIII. 1847; Opp. Wall 1846–7, Keeper 1847; Field XI. 1847; Trin. Coll. Camb. B.A.; Camb. VIII. 1848–9; Barrister Inner Temple 1857; Met. Police Mag. Marylebone 1876–91, Westminster 1891–7, aft. at Marlborough Street and Bow Street; Chief Mag. of Met. Police Courts since 1901. 90 *St. George's Sq., S.W.*

Mr. Bridgeman (Miss M., H.M.B.)
REV. HON. JOHN ROBERT ORLANDO. 2nd son of George, 2nd Earl of Bradford; 1844[3]–1849[1]; Trin. Coll. Camb. M.A.; Rural Dean and Rector of Weston-under-Lizard, Shifnal, 1859–97; *m.* Marianne Caroline, *d.* of Ven. William Clive, Archdn. of Montgomery; died Nov. 26, 1897.

Angell (Mrs. Ri., W.G.C.)
JOHN BENEDICT. 1843[3]–1847[3]; Magd. Coll. Oxf.: formerly living near Market Harborough.

Baillie (Mrs. Ro., W.G.C.)
ALFRED WILLIAM. 4th son of Col. H. D. B. of Redcastle, Londonderry; 1841[3]–1847[3]; Eton VIII. 1847; Trin. Coll. Camb.; Sec. of the M.C.C.; died 1857.

Morgan (H.D.)
HON. GODFREY CHARLES (2nd Lord Tredegar). 2nd son of Charles Morgan Robinson, 1st Lord T.; 1843[2]–1848[1]; Lord-Lieut. of co. Monmouth since 1899; J.P. and D.L. co. Brecon; M.P. for co. Brecon 1858–75; formerly Capt. 17th Lancers; ret. 1855; served in the Crimea and rode with his regt. in Balaclava Charge 1854, med. with 4 clasps; aft. Major R. Glos. Yeo. Hussars; Vice Chmn. and Ald. Monmouth C.C. 39 *Portman Sq., W., and Tredegar Park, Newport, Mon.*

Burder *ma.* (Mrs. P., E.B.)
REV. CHARLES SUMNER. 1843[3]–1848[3]; St. Mary Hall Oxf.; formerly Rector of Ham, Hungerford.

Caley (J.R.Y., aft. K.S., J.E.Y.)
REV. GEORGE AUGUSTUS. Son of J. C. of Windsor; 1841[3]–1843[3]; St. John's Coll. Camb. M.A.; formerly Curate of Hitcham, Ipswich; *m.* Fanny, *d.* of Rev. Thomas Dry; dead.

Stratton (R.P.H., C.J.A.)
JOHN. 3rd son of G. S., Member of Council, Madras; 1843[3]–1847[3]; formerly 38th Regt., and Capt. 2nd Warwick Militia; died unm. Aug. 1868.

Hardinge (W.E., E.H.P.)
SIR HENRY CHARLES, 3rd Bt. Eld. son of Rev. Sir C. H., 2nd Bt.; 1843[3]–1847[3]; died unm. Nov. 13, 1873.

Evered *ma.* (Miss M., H.M.B.)
CAPT. JOHN GUY COURTENAY, R.N. 2nd son of R. G. E. of Hill House, Otter[illegible]; 1844[3]–1848[3]; *m.* [illegible] of Thomas Hay Nem[illegible] *Bar[illegible]ard Park, Sparton, B[illegible]*

Wigram (R.F.H., E.C.)
ROBERT JAMES. 2nd son of Rt. Hon. Sir J. W., P.C., Vice-Chanc.; 1844^{3}-1848^{1}; E.I. Civil Service in Bengal Presidency; *m.* Leonora Jane, *d.* of Henry Alexander, E.I.C.S.; died Oct. 6, 1886.

Templer (Mrs. Her., W.A.C.)
JAMES GEORGE JOHN. Of Lyndridge, Bishop's Teignton, Teignmouth; son of Rev. J. A. T. of Puddlstown, Dorset; 1842^{3}-1847^{3}; Ch. Ch. Oxf. B.A.; J.P. co. Devon; Lieut.-Col. comm. 3rd Bn. Devon R.V.; *m.* Frances Mary, *d.* of Joseph Mortimer; died Feb. 10, 1883.

Walpole (W.G.C.)
HORATIO ANDREW. Son of F. W.; 1843^{3}-1847^{3}; Magd. Coll. Camb.; died Jan. 20, 1855.

Wilmot (Miss Edw., F.E.D.)
ROBERT EDWARD EARDLEY. Eld. son of Sir H. S. W., 4th Bt.; 1843^{3}-1847^{3}; died unm. Oct. 22, 1861.

Davis (Mrs. P., C.O.G.)
JOHN COOPE. 1843^{3}-1848^{1}; Trin. Coll. Camb.; Lieut.-Col. R.V., Ilford, Essex; formerly in business in London.

Turner (R.F.H., E.B.)
CHARLES HAMPDEN. Of Rook's Nest, Godstone, Surrey; son of C. H. T. of Rook's Nest; 1844^{1}-1849^{1}; J.P. for Surrey; formerly in Gren. Gds.; dead.

Tryon (J.E.Y.)
VICE-ADMIRAL SIR GEORGE, R.N., K.C.B. 3rd son of T. T. of Bulwick Park, Wansford, Northants; 1844^{1}-1847^{3}; ent. R.N. 1848; served with Naval Bgde. before Sebastopol; wounded in the trenches (Crimean Med., Inkerman and Sebastopol Clasps, Turkish Med., and 3rd Cl. Medjidie); Director of Transports, Abyssinian Expdn. 1868; Med. and mentioned in despatches; Sec. to Admiralty; Comm.-in-Chief on Australian Station; Comm.-in-Chief Med. 1891; *m.* Hon. Clementina Charlotte Heathcote, *d.* of Gilbert John, 1st Lord Aveland; drowned in his Flagship 'Victoria' whilst comm. the Med. Fleet, June 22, 1893.

Yonge *max.* (W.G.C., aft. K.S., W.G.C.)
HENRY. Son of Rev. F. L. Y. of Torrington; 1841^{3}-1848^{3}; Clerk in Public Record Office; *m.* *d.* of W. Long; died Jan. 31, 1863.

Yonge *ma.* (W.G.C., aft. K.S., W.G.C.)
FREDERICK LANGFORD. Son of Rev. F. L. Y. of Torrington; 1841^{3}-1848^{3}; Coll. Wall XI. 1846-8; Lieut. 16th Bombay N. Inf., and Adjt. Kolapore Lt. Inf.; *m.* *d.* of Gen. Duff of the Bombay Army; died at Kolapore June 1856.

Earl of Dalkeith (E.B.)
WILLIAM HENRY WALTER, K.G., K.T., P.C. (6th Duke of Buccleuch). Eld. son of Walter Francis, 5th Duke of B., K.G.; 1843^{1}-1847^{3}; Ch. Ch. Oxf.; Lieut.-Col. Midlothian Yeo. 1856-72; M.P. for Midlothian 1853-68 and 1874-80; Lord-Lieut. of Dumfriesshire since 1858; J.P. and D.L. for co. Selkirk; J.P. for Midlothian; Capt.-Gen. of Royal Company of Scottish Archers; *m.* Lady Louisa Jane Hamilton, *d.* of James, 1st Duke of Abercorn, K.G. *Dalkeith Palace, Dalkeith, and Montagu House, Whitehall, S.W.*

Coney *ma.* (Mrs. P., E.B.)
WALTER JOHN. Eld. son of J. J. C. of Braywick Grove, Maidenhead; 1843^{3}-1848^{3}; Major 1st Dl. Dragoons; served in Eastern Campaign 1854-5; Med. and [illegible] 1888.

Marquis of Bath (E.C.)
JOHN ALEXANDER (4th Marquis of B.) Eld. son of Henry Frederick, 3rd Marquis of B.; 1843^{3}-1848^{1}; Ch. Ch. Oxf.; despatched on special mission to Lisbon to invest King of Portugal with the Order of the Garter 1858; received Grand Cross of Portuguese Order of the Tower and Sword; and spel. miss. to Vienna 1867; received Grand Cross of Austrian Order of Leopold; Chmn. of Wilts Qr. Sessions 1880; app. Trustee of British Museum 1884; Lord-Lieut. of Wilts 1889; Hon. Col. Wilts Yeo. Cav.; Chmn. Wilts C.C.; J.P. and D.L. for Wilts and Somerset; *m.* Hon. Frances Isabella Catherine Vesey, *d.* of Thomas, 3rd Viscount de Vesci; died at Venice, April 20, 1896.

Ridler (Miss Edg., aft. K.S., J.E.Y.)
W. E. . 1850.

Reynolds (Miss Edg., aft. K.S., E.C.)
H. J. . 1850.

Smijth-Windham *ma.* (R.F.H., E.B.)
ASHE (aft. Windham). 2nd son of J. S.-W. of Wawne; 1845^{1}-1847^{3}; Trin. Coll. Camb. M.A.; Cape of Good Hope Univ. M.A.; formerly a Magist. at Natal, S. Africa; *m.* Juliet, *d.* of Col. Hugh Maclean of Coll, Oban. *2 St. Helen's Road, Norbury, Surrey.*

Bramley-Moore (Miss Edw., C.J.A.)
REV. WILLIAM JOSEPH. Eld. son of J. B.-M. of Langley Lodge, Gerrard's Cross, Bucks; 1845^{1}-1848^{3}; Trin. Coll. Camb. M.A.; Incumbent of St. James, Gerrard's Cross, Bucks, 1859-69; Author; *m.* Ella, *d.* of Swinfen Jordan of Clifton. *26 Russell Sq., W.C.*

Knatchbull (E.B.)
REV. REGINALD BRIDGES (aft. Knatchbull-Hugessen). 7th son of Rt. Hon. Sir E. K., 9th Bt., of Mersham Hatch, Ashford, Kent; 1844^{3}-1848^{3}; Ball. Coll. Oxf. B.A.; Rector of West Grinstead; *m.* 1st, Maria, *d.* of Rev. Tatton Brockman of Beachborough, Hythe, Kent; 2nd, Rachael Mary, *d.* of Adm. Sir Alexander Leslie Montgomery, 3rd Bt., of The Hall, co. Donegal. *West Grinstead Rectory, Horsham.*

Fitzwygram (E.C.)
LOFTUS ADAM. 5th son of Sir R. F., 2nd Bt. Of Leigh Park, Havant; 1845^{3}-1850^{1}; Univ. Coll. Oxf. S.C.L.; 1st Cl. Law and Hist. 1856; Barrister; *m.* Lady Frances Georgina Danvers, *d.* of Capt. Charles Augustus Butler, and sister of 6th Earl of Lanesborough. *77 Eaton Place, S.W.*

Forshall (C.J.A., aft. K.S., C.J.A.)
E. V. . 1850.

Capper (E.H.P.)
WILLIAM COPELAND. Son of S. J. C. of Leyton, Essex; 1845^{3}-1849^{3}; Bengal Civil Service; *m.* Sarah, *d.* of William Taylor Copeland, M.P., Ald. of London; died July 8, 1902.

Lambton (C.L.)
F. W. . 1850.

Rous (H.M.B.)
W. J. . 1850.

Whitting *ma.* (R.F.H., aft. K.S., E.H.P.)
W. H. . 1850.

Thackeray (Mrs. Bo., aft. K.S., [illegible])
F. St. J. . 1850.

Keate (E.C.)

MAJ.-GEN. EDWARD. Son of R. K., Serj. Surg.; 1845[2]-1848[3]; Maj.-Gen. Royal Art.; *m.* Florence, *d.* of Gen. Bacon. *High Croft, Winchester.*

Stone (K.S., C.O.G.)

E. D. . 1850.

Garry (R.F.H., J.E.Y.)

REV. CANON NICHOLAS THOMAS. Son of N. G., Founder of Fort Garry, now City of Winnipeg, Canada; 1845[1]-1849[3]; Queen's Coll. Oxf. M.A.; 3rd Cl. Lit. Hum.; Rector of Taplow and Hon. Canon Christ Church Cath., Oxf.; *m.* Marian, *d.* of John Murray of Whitehall Place, S.W. *The Rectory, Taplow.*

Evered *mi.* (Miss M., aft. K.S., H.M.B.)

J. J. G. . 1850.

Cutler (Mrs. P. & J.L.J., H.M.B. & J.L.J.)

EDWARD, J.P., K.C. Son of E. C., Surgeon, of New Burlington St., W.; 1844[3]-1849[3]; Eton XI. 1849; Ball. Coll. Oxf.; 2nd Cl. Mods., 2nd Cl. Class.; Barrister and Musical Composer; *m.* Ellen Mona, *d.* of Maj. Larkins. 12 *Old Sq., Lincoln's Inn, W.C., and Edgware House, Edgware.*

Bathurst (H.M.B.)

ALLEN ALEXANDER (6th Earl Bathurst). Son of Lieut.-Col. T. S. B. and nephew of William Lennox, 5th Earl B.; 1845[2]-1849[3]; Trin. Coll. Camb. M.A.; Hon. Lieut.-Col. N. Glouc. Militia; M.P. for Cirencester 1857-1878; J.P. and C.C. for co. Gloucester; *m.* 1st, Meriel Leicester, *d.* of George, 2nd Lord de Tabley: 2nd, Evelyn Elizabeth, *d.* of George James Barnard Hankey of Fetcham Park, Leatherhead; died Aug. 1, 1892.

Pilcher *ma.* (Miss Edw., W.G.C.)

GEORGE LOAT. Son of J. P. of Worthing, Sussex; 1844[3]-1848[3]; Pemb. Coll. Oxf.; living in Australia.

Philips *ma.* (C.L.)

FRANCIS. Of Lee Priory, Wingham, Dover; eld. son of F. A. P. of Bank Hall, Stockport; 1844[1]-1848[3]; Ch. Ch. Oxf. M.A.; J.P. and D.L. for Kent, High Sheriff 1871; Barrister Inner Temple; Commissioner of Income Tax; Capt. R. E. Kent Yeo. Cav.; *m.* 1st, Caroline Mary, *d.* of Rev. Charles Kenrick Prescot, Rector of Stockport; 2nd, Constance, *d.* of Edward William Bonham of Bramling House, Kent; died Mar. 7, 1898.

Lord Stanhope (H.M.B.)

GEORGE PHILIP CECIL ARTHUR (7th Earl of Chesterfield). Son of George, 6th Earl of C., P.C.; 1845[2]-1847[3]; Lieut. in the Blues, aft. M.P. for S. Notts; died unm. Dec. 1, 1871.

Lord Muncaster (W.A.C.)

GAMEL AUGUSTUS (4th Lord M.). Eld. son of Lowther Augustus John, 3rd Lord M., of Muncaster Castle, Ravenglass, Cumberland; 1845[2]-1849[3]; Trin. Coll. Camb. B.A.; *m.* Lady Jane Louisa Octavia, *d.* of Richard, 2nd Marquis of Westminster; died of gastric fever at Castellamare, near Naples, June 13, 1862.

Bayley (R.F.H., C.L.)

JOHN ARTHUR. Son of F. B., Judge of Westminster County Court; 1845[1]-1849[1]; Eton XI. 1848; Major 52nd Oxfs. Lt. Infantry; served at the siege of Delhi; aft. High Bailiff, Westminster County Court; *m.* Elizabeth, *d.* of Samuel Sterling of Belfast; died Feb. 4, 1903.

Shaw-Lefevre (R.O.)

RT. HON. GEORGE JOHN, P.C., L.C.C., F.R.G.S. Son of Sir J. G. S.-L., K.C.B., Clerk of the Parliaments; 1845[1]-1849[3]; Trin. Coll. Camb. M.A.; Barrister 1855; J.P. & D.L. for Kent, J.P. for Berks; Civil Lord of the Admiralty 1856; Member of Sea Fisheries Commission 1862; M.P. for Reading 1863-85; Sec. Board of Trade 1869-71; Under-Sec. Home Office 1871; Sec. to Admiralty 1871-4 and in 1880; 1st Commissioner of Works 1880-4 and 1892-4; Postmaster-Gen. 1884-5; M.P. Central Bradford 1885-95; Chmn. of Royal Commission on Loss of Life at Sea 1885; Member of Cabinet 1892-3; Pres. of Local Gov. Board 1894-5; Chmn. of Royal Comm. on Agricultural Depression 1893-6; Pres. Statistical Soc. 1878-9; *m.* Lady Constance Emily Moreton, *d.* of Henry John, 3rd Earl of Ducie. 18 *Bryanston Sq., W., and Abbotsworthy House, Kingsworthy, Winchester.*

Cayley (W.G.C.)

SIR GEORGE ALLANSON, 8th Bt., D.L. Eld. son of Sir D. C., 7th Bt.; 1844[3]-1849[3]; Coll. Wall 1848; Trin. Coll. Camb.; formerly Lieut. Yorks Hussars; J.P. and D.L. for N. Riding of Yorks, and J.P. for cos. Denbigh and Flint; High Sheriff co. Denbigh 1863; *m.* Catherine Louisa, *d.* of Sir William Worsley, 1st Bt., of Hovingham Hall, York; died Oct. 10, 1895.

Suttie (W.L.E.)

SIR JAMES GRANT-, 6th Bt. Eld. son of Sir G. G.-S., 5th Bt., of Preston Grange and Balgone, Prestonpans, co. Haddington; 1844[1]-1848[3]; Eton VIII. 1848; Opp. Wall 1847-8; Field XI. 1847-8, Keeper 1848; Merton Coll. Oxf.; D.L. for Berwick; Lieut.-Col. East of Scotland Garrison Art. Militia; *m.* Lady Susan Harriet Innes-Ker, *d.* of James Henry Robert, 6th Duke of Roxburghe; died Oct. 30, 1878.

Wilson (Miss Edw., H.M.B.)

SIR CHARLES RIVERS, G.C.M.G., C.B. Son of M. W.; 1845[2]-1848[3]; Prince Albert's French Prize 1847; Ball. Coll. Oxf. M.A.; entd. Treasury 1856; Compt.-Gen. National Debt Office 1874-94; on Council, Suez Canal Co. 1876-95; Finance Minister, Egypt 1877-9; Royal Commr. Paris Exhibn. 1878 and 1900; Pres. Grand Trunk Rly., Canada, since 1895; 1st Class Order of the Medjidie; *m.* 1st, Caroline, *d.* of R. Cook; 2nd, Hon. Beatrice Violet Mary, *d.* of Hon. George Charles Mostyn and sister of 7th Lord Vaux of Harrowden. 21 *Pont Street, S.W.*

Hoskins (F.E.D.)

REV. EDGAR. Son of S. E. H., M.D., F.R.S., of Guernsey; 1844[1]-1849[3]; Opp. Wall 1848; Exeter Coll. Oxf. M.A.; Rector of St. Martin's, Ludgate, E.C. 16 *Godliman St., E.C.*

West (Miss A., E.H.P.)

RT. HON. SIR ALGERNON EDWARD, G.C.B., P.C. Son of M. J. W., Recorder of Lynn; 1844[1]-1849[3]; Ch. Ch. Oxf.; was a Clerk in the Admiralty; Asst. Sec. to Sir C. Wood and Duke of Somerset; Sec. to Sir C. Wood at India Office, and Mr. Gladstone when Prime Minister; Chmn. of Board of Inland Rev.; served on Prison Commission, and was Vice-Chmn. of the Licensing Comm.; Dep.-Governor of Union Bank of London; Ald. L.C.C. since 1898; *m.* Mary, *d.* of Capt. Hon. George Barrington, M.P. 1 *Mount St., W., and Wanborough Manor, Guildford.*

Hare *ma.* (R.F.H., F.E.D.)

FRANCIS GEORGE. Of Gresford, co. Denbigh; eld. son of F. G. H. of Herstmonceaux, Hailsham, Sussex, and Gresford; 1845[1]-1847[3]; Downing Coll. Camb.; Officer in 1st Life Gds.; died at Pisa, Nov 1868.

Lord Grey de Wilton (H.M.B.)

A. E. H. . 1850.

Lubbock (Miss A., H.M.B.) — RT. HON. SIR JOHN, 4th Bt. (1st Lord Avebury), P.C., D.C.L., LL.D., F.R.S., D.L. Eld. son of Sir J. W. L., 3rd Bt. of High Elms; 1845^{3}-1848^{3}; M.P. Maidstone 1870-1880; Chmn. Public Accounts Committee 1888-9; Member of Royal Commissions on Advancement of Science, on Public Schools, on International Coinage, on Gold and Silver, on Education; Pres. British Assoc. 1881; Pres. Entomological Socy., Ethnological Socy., Linnean Socy., Anthropological Institute, Ray Socy., Statistical Socy.; Vice-Pres. Royal Socy.; 1st Pres. Interml. Institute of Sociology 1894; Pres. Interml. Assocn. of Prehistoric Archæology, Pres. Interml. Assocn. of Zoology, Pres. Interml. Library Assocn.; Hon. Mem. of many foreign Scientific Societies; Vice-Chanc. Univ. of London 1872-80; Principal, London Working Men's Coll.; Pres. London Univ. Extension Socy.; Sec. London Bankers, 25 years; 1st Pres. Inst. of Bankers; Pres. London Chamber of Commerce 1888-93; Vice-Chmn. L.C.C. 1889-90, Chmn. 1890-2; Chmn. London Bankers and Pres. Central Assocn. of Bankers; M.P. London Univ. 1880-1900; Hon. D.C.L. of Oxf. and Hon. LL.D. of Cambridge, Dublin, and Edinburgh; Banker (Robarts, Lubbock & Co.); one of H.M.'s Lieuts. for City of London; J.P. and D.L. Kent. *m.* 1st, Ellen Frances, *d.* of Rev. Peter Hordern of Chorlton-cum-Hardy; 2nd, Alice Augusta Laurentia Lane, *d.* of Gen. Augustus Henry Lane Fox-Pitt-Rivers of Rushmore, Wilts. *6 St. James' Sq., S.W., and High Elms, Farnborough, Kent.*

Astley (C.O.G.) — HUGH FRANCIS LETHBRIDGE. 2nd son of Sir F. D. A., 2nd Bt., of Everley, Marlborough; 1844^{3}-1848^{3}; Univ. Coll. Oxf.; formerly in the Foreign Office, and Major Royal Wilts Yeo. Cav.; *m.* Augusta Ellen, *d.* of R. Cockburn. *Arthur's Club, 69 St. James's Street, S.W.*

Bastard (E.C.) — REV. WILLIAM POLLEXFEN. 3rd son of E. P. B. of Kitley, Yealmpton, Plymouth; 1845^{1}-1849^{3}; Ball. Coll. Oxf. M.A.; formerly Rector of Lezant, Cornwall; *m.* Caroline, *d.* of Adml. Woollcombe of Hemerdon, Devon. *Cofflete, Torquay.*

Cotton (E.B.) — A. B. . 1850.

Ferguson-Davie (W.A.C.) — W. A. . 1850.

Warren — EDWARD LEWIS. Of Lodge Park, Freshford, co. Kilkenny; son of P. A. W. of Lodge Park; 1844^{2}-1848^{3}; Trin. Coll. Dublin; J.P. and D.L. co. Kilkenny, High Sheriff 1861; *m.* Marianne Emilie, *d.* of Col. Charles Garraway, H.E.I.C.S.; died 1898.

Philips *mi.* (C.L.) — GEORGE HENRY. Of Abbey Cwmhir, Penybont, co. Radnor; son of F. A. P. of Bank Hall, Stockport, and Abbey Cwmhir; 1844^{1}-1849^{3}; Eton XI. 1849; Ch. Ch. Oxf. M.A.; J.P. and D.L. co. Radnor; *m.* Anna Theophila, *d.* of Rev. Charles Kenrick Prescot, Rector of Stockport; died Oct. 22, 1886.

Hampson (E.H.P.) — REV. WILLIAM SEYMOUR. 2nd son of Sir G. F. H., 8th Bt., of Bolton St., Mayfair, W., and Lincoln's Inn, W.C.; 1844^{3}-1847^{3}; Ch. Ch. Oxf. M.A.; Rector of Stubton, Newark 1857-68; *m.* Julia Jane, *d.* of Charles Franks of Cumberland Place, N.W.; died June 8, 1868.

Mr. Quin (W.E., E.C.) — HON. WINDHAM HENRY WYNDHAM-, 2nd son of Windham Henry, 2nd Earl of Dunraven; 1844^{1}-1847^{3}; Capt. Gren. Gds.; served in the Crimea; *m.* Caroline, *d.* of Vice-Adml. Sir George Tyler, K.H., of Cotterell, co. Glamorgan; died Oct. 24, 1865.

Bradley (W.L.E.) — JOHN HENRY. 1844^{1}-1848^{3}.

Molesworth (Miss Edw., H.D.) — J. . 1850.

Mr. Legge *mi.* (F.E.D.) — HON. E. H. . 1850.

Newdigate *mi.* (W.E., E.C.) — LIEUT.-GEN. SIR HENRY RICHARD LEGGE, K.C.B. Son of F. N., D.L., of Byrkley Lodge, Burton-on-Trent; 1845^{3}-1849^{2}; Lieut.-Gen. Rifle Bgde.; served in the Crimea 1854 (medal with clasp); in Indian Mutiny 1857-8 (medal with 2 clasps); in Afghan Campaign 1878-9 (medal and clasp, C.B.); Comm. Inf. Bgde. at Gibraltar 1888-93 (ret. 1898); J.P. and D.L. co. Warwick; *m.* Phillis, *d.* of Rev. Arthur Shirley, Vicar of Stinsford, Dorchester. *Allesley, Coventry.*

Wheatley (Miss A., H.M.B.) — WILLIAM. 1844^{3}-1848^{1}; formerly Lieut.-Col. Scots Fusilier Gds.

Morrison (C.O.G.) — HENRY. 4th son of J. M. of Basildon Park, Reading; 1844^{3}-1847^{3}; died 1849.

Norman (H.M.B. & Mrs. Dr., H.M.B. & E.H.P.) — C. L. . 1850.

Bedford *mi.* (R.F.H., aft. K.S., W.G.C.) — FRANCIS RILAND. Son of Rev. W. R. B., Rector of Sutton Coldfield, Birmingham; 1842^{3}-1848^{1}; Solicitor (ret.). *Kenilworth, Warwicks.*

Hardisty (Mrs. Ro., H.D.) — ROBERT RICHARD. Son of E. S. H., Solicitor, of 48 Gt. Marlborough St., W.; 1841^{3}-1847^{3}; formerly in the Charity Commission Office; died Sept. 15, 1869.

Davies *ma.* (R.O.) — ARTHUR HENRY SAUNDERS. Of Pentre, Boncath, Pembrokes; eld. son of D. A. S. D. of Pentre; 1844^{3}-1850^{1}; Ch. Ch. Oxf.; Lieut.-Col. Carmarthens R.V.; J.P. and D.L. co. Pembroke, High Sheriff 1861; *m.* Frances, *d.* of Grismond Phillpps of Cwmgwilly, co. Carmarthen; died June 8, 1873.

Tighe (J.E.Y.) — LIEUT.-COL. JAMES STUART. 2nd son of D. T. of Rossana; 1844^{3}-1847^{3}; Lieut.-Col. 8th Madras Cav. (ret.); formerly Assist. Commissioner at Mooltan; J.P. and D.L. co. Wicklow, High Sheriff 1876; *m.* Charlotte, *d.* of Very Rev. Thomas John de Burgh, Dean of Cloyne. *Rossana, Ashford, co. Wicklow.*

Gottwaltz (R.F.H., C.L.) — JOHN FRANCIS. Of Eastbourne; 1844^{3}-1847^{3}; Ch. Ch. Oxf.; formerly Lieut. Sussex R.V.

Lord Henry Scott (E.B.) — HENRY JOHN DOUGLAS-SCOTT-MONTAGU (1st Lord Montagu of Beaulieu), F.R.G.S. 2nd son of Walter Francis, 5th Duke of Buccleuch and Queensberry, K.G.; 1845^{3}-1848^{3}; M.P. for co. Selkirk 1861-8, S. Hants 1868-84; Official Verderer of New Forest 1890-2; J.P. and D.L. for Hants and co. Selkirk; J.P. Midlothian; C.A. for Hants; Hon. Col. 4th Bn. Hants R.V. since 1885; *m.* Hon. Cecily Susan, *d.* of John, 2nd Lord Wharncliffe. *3 Tilney Street, Park Lane, W., and Palace House, Beaulieu, Brockenhurst, Hants.*

Janvrin (Miss M., F.E.D.) — FREDERICK WILLIAM. 1844^{1}-1848^{3}.

Gosling (E.B.) — Robert. Of Hassobury, Bishop's Stortford; eld. son of R. G. of Hassobury; 1844[3]–1849[2]; formerly Capt. 13th Lt. Infantry; served in the Crimea; J.P. for Essex and Herts; D.L. for Essex, High Sheriff 1871; *m.* 1st, Cecil Mary, *d.* of Alexander Park; 2nd, Eleanor Spencer, *d.* of Spencer Smith of Brooklands, Hants; died Aug. 23, 1895.

Prest *mi.* (R.F.H., H.D.) — W. P. . 1850.

Holden (C.L.) — John George. 1843[3]–1847[2]; Eton VIII. 1847; won Pulling 1846.

Crosse *mi.* (W.E., F.E.D.) — Lieut.-Col. Charles Kenrick. 2nd son of T. B. C. of Shaw Hill, Chorley; 1845[3]–1849[3]; Field XI. 1847; Opp. Wall 1848; ent. Army, 52nd Lt. Infantry, 1850; served in Indian Mutiny 1857; mentioned in despatches, med. and clasp (ret. 1869). 61 *Pall Mall, S.W.*

Irlam (C.L.) — George. 1843[3]–1848[2]; Eton VIII. 1848.

Lennox (C.L.) — John Kincaid. 1843[3]–1847[2]; served with the 12th Lancers at Cape of Good Hope; died of consumption in Egypt.

Fane (Miss W. & T.H.S., F.E.D.) — Major John Augustus. Eld. son of Col. J. W. F. of Wormsley; 1844[3]–1848[3]; formerly Capt. 46th Regt.; served in the Crimea; med. and clasp for Sebastopol; ret. Maj. and Adjt. 2nd Bn. Oxfs R.V.; J.P. co. Oxf.; *m.* Eleanor, *d.* of Thomas Thornhill of Woodleys, Woodstock. *Wormsley, Stokenchurch, Wallingford.*

Mariette *ma.* (Home) — Albert de Villeblin. 1843[3]–1847[2]; Trin. Coll. Camb.; travelled over the greater part of the world and settled in Jamaica.

Slade (C.J.A. & H.D.) — Rev. George FitzClarence. 11th son of Sir J. S., 1st Bt., of Mansel House, Bridgwater, Somerset; 1843[3]–1848[2]; Eton VIII. 1848; won School Pulling 1848; Wall and Field XI's 1847; Ball. Coll. Oxf. M.A.; Fellow of All Souls' Coll. Oxf.; 2nd Class Hist.; Rector of Buckland; *m.* Eleanor Frances, *d.* of Henry Warre of Bindon, Somerset. *Buckland Rectory, Betchworth, Surrey.*

Caulfeild *ma.* (H.D.) — St. George Francis Robert. Eld. son of St. G. F. C. of Donamon Castle, Roscommon; 1844[1]–1847[2]; formerly in the 1st Life Gds.; *m.* Louisa Ann, *d.* of Thomas Russell Crampton; died Mar. 9, 1875.

Shaw (Mrs. Ro., E.B.) — John Monson. Son of Rev. Hon. Canon R. W. S., Rector of Cuxton, Rochester; 1842[2]–1847[2]; *m.* Sarah, *d.* of Thomas Franklyn of Cob Tree, near Maidstone. 322 *South Cliffe, Lowestoft.*

Marshall *mi.* (Miss W., F.E.D.) — John Barry. 1844[1]–1848[2]; Capt. 4th Lt. Dragoons; died of fever in the Crimea, Sept. 20, 1855.

Robinson (C.O.G.) — Sir John Blencowe, 8th Bt. 2nd son of Rev. Sir G. S. R., 7th Bt., of Cranford Hall, Kettering; 1844[2]–1847[2]; Trin. Coll. Oxf.; J.P. Northants; *m.* Winifred, *d.* of Rev. Edward Stewart, Rector of Lainston, Hants; died Aug. 10, 1877.

Atherley (Miss A., H.M.B.) — Francis Henry. Of Landguard Manor, Shanklin, I. of W.; 2nd son of Rev. A. A., Rector of Heavitree, Devon; 1844[3]–1847[2]; formerly Major Rifle Bgde. and Col. Comm. I. of W. Vol. Bn.; J.P. for Hants; *m.* Lady Isabel Julia Elizabeth Howard, *d.* of Charles John, 17th Earl of Suffolk; died 1897.

Nicholl (R.O.) — Rev. Edward Powell. 3rd son of Rt. Hon. J. N., M.P., of Merthyr Mawr, Glamorgan; 1844[2]–1849[3]; B.N.C. Oxf. M.A.; Rector of Llandough, Cardiff; Vicar of Ascott-under-Wychwood, Oxf.; Curate-in-charge of St. Luke's, Pembiza Crossing, Manitoba, 1885–1902; *m.* Sarah, *d.* of John Jenkins of Llanblethian; died April 12, 1902.

Croft (E.H.P.) — George Arthur Hutton. Of Aldborough Hall, Boroughbridge, York; son of Rev. Canon T. H. C. of Aldborough, Canon of York and Vicar of Hutton Bushel, West Ayton, Yorks; 1843[3]–1847[2]; Trin. Coll. Camb.; Lieut. Yorks Hussars; J.P. N. and W. Riding of Yorks; *m.* Catherine Mary, *d.* of Griffith Richards, Q.C.; died April 8, 1889.

Christie (C.L.) — William John. 1843[3]–1847[2].

Haywood (W.G.C.) — Edward Waldron, LL.B. Son of F. H. of Liverpool; 1843[3]–1847[2]; Christ's Coll. Camb.; called to the Bar, Inner Temple 1854; Barrister Northern Circuit, ret.; formerly Capt. and Hon. Major Worcs. Yeo. Cav.; J.P. and D.L. co. Worc., High Sheriff 1872; *m.* Hon. Ada Katherine, *d.* of Henry, 1st Lord Hindlip. *Sillins, Redditch.*

Welby (W.E., E.C.) — Sir R. E., G.C.B. (Lord Welby). 1850.

Lower Division.

Walford (Miss Edg., aft. K.S., C.J.A.) — J. T. . 1850.

Pipe-Wolferstan *mi.* (Miss Edg., aft. K.S., E.B.) — Edward. 3rd son of S. P.-W. of Statfold, Tamworth; 1845[3]–1849[3]; Solicitor. 45 *Lincoln's Inn Fields, W.C.*

Bent *ma.* (Mrs. Ro., aft. K.S., C.J.A. & J.E.Y.) — J. O. . 1850.

Tremlett *ma.* (Mrs. Ro., aft. K.S., W.L.E.) — T. D. . 1850.

Cookesley *ma.* (W.G.C.) — A. F. . 1850.

Kekewich (Mrs. P. & J.L.J., H.M.B. & J.L.J.) — Hon. Sir A., Kt. . 1850.

Mitchell (E.H.P.) — Alexander. 1844[3]–1847[2]; formerly Capt. 31st Regt.

Russell (Mrs. Vav., E.C.) — C. H. . 1850.

Palk *ma.* (W.G.C.) — A. . 1850.

Snow (Miss A. & Miss Edg., J.E.Y.) — W. R. (aft. Andre). . 1850.

Peareth (W.G.C.) — William. Of Usworth House, Gateshead; eld. son of W. P. of Usworth; 1845[3]–1847[2]; Trin. Coll. Camb.; formerly Capt. 4th Lt. Dragoons; J.P. co. Durham, High Sheriff [illegible]; *m.* Cecilia, *d.* of John Lennox-Kincaid-Lennox of Lennox Castle, N.B.; died Ju[illegible] 15, 18[illegible].

White (Mrs. Ro., F.E.D.)
HON. GEORGE FREDERICK. 3rd son of Henry, 1st Lord Annaly, of Luttrellstown, Clonsilla, co. Dublin; 1845^{3}-1849^{1}; killed by the bursting of his gun, 1849.

Wilder (Mrs. Ro. & C.O.G., C.O.G., & W.W.)
H. B. . 1850.

Buller (W.E., H.D.)
JAMES HORNBY. Of Down Hall, Epsom; eld. son of Rev. R. B., Rector of Lanreath, Liskeard; 1845^{3}-1849^{3}; Col. 57th Regt., served in Crimea; *m.* 1st, Catherine Ann, *d.* of Sir William Williams, 1st Bt. of Tregullow, Cornwall; 2nd, Emily Augusta, *d.* of Major Henry Dashwood, R.H.A.; died Aug. 7, 1895.

Walters (R.O.)
W. . 1850.

Bateson (C.O.G.)
JOHN. 7th son of Sir R. B., 1st Bt., of Belvoir Park, Belfast; 1844^{3}-1850^{1}; Cox Eton VIII. 1849; Trin. Coll. Camb.; Barrister; *m.* Edith Elizabeth, *d.* of Charles John Pearse; died Mar. 1900.

Earle
T. H. . 1850.

Hebden (Miss Edw., E.H.P.)
ARTHUR HENRY. 1845^{3}-1848^{3}; Trin. Coll. Camb.

Keppel (F.E.D.)
WILLIAM COUTTS (7th Earl of Albemarle), P.C., K.C.M.G. Son of George Thomas, 6th Earl of A.; 1846^{1}-1848^{3}; Lieut. Scots Gds., A.D.C. to the Queen; M.P. for Norwich 1857-9, for Wick 1860-5, Berwick 1868-74; Treas. of the Household 1859-66; Under-Sec. for War 1878-80; Hon. Col. 2nd Vol. Bn. Manchester Regt., and Col. comm. 5th Vol. Bn. King's Royal Rifles (Vol. Officer's Decoration); *m.* Sophia Mary, *d.* of Hon. Sir Alan Napier Macnab, 1st and last Bt., of Dundurn Castle, co. Wentworth, W. Canada, Prime Minister of Canada; died Aug. 28, 1894.

O'Hara (C.O.G.)
LIEUT.-COL. JAMES. Of Lenaboy, Galway; eld. son of J. O'H. of Lenaboy; 1845^{3}-1847^{3}; Trin. Coll. Dublin; formerly Capt. 2nd Dragoon Gds., aft. Lieut.-Col. comm. Galway Art.; J.P. and D.L. for Galway, High Sheriff 1863 and 1879; *m.* Blanche, *d.* of Rev. Sebastian Gambier, Vicar of Sandgate; died Aug. 14, 1902.

Puller *ma.* (E.C.)
A. G. GILES+. . 1850.

Paynter *ma.* (J.E.Y.)
REV. WILLIAM CAMBOURNE. 2nd son of W. P. of Cambourne House, Richmond, Surrey; 1845^{1}-1848^{3}; formerly Curate of Redbourne, Herts; *m.* Helen Mary, *d.* of Henry Toulmin of Childwickbury, St. Albans.

Blackwood (Miss A., H.M.B.)
SIR STEVENSON ARTHUR, K.C.B.; son of A. J. B. of Upper Brook Street, W.; 1845^{1}-1848^{3}; Trin. Coll Camb.; app. Financial Sec. to G.P.O. 1874, Princ. Sec. to Gen. Post Office 1880-93; *m.* Harriet Sydney, *d.* of Conway R. Dobbs of Castle Dobbs, co. Antrim, and widow of George, 6th Duke of Manchester; died Oct. 2, 1893.

Marillier (Miss Edg., aft. K.S., C.J.A.)
C. H. . 1850.

Yorke (Mrs. Vav., W.A.C.)
THOMAS EDWARD. Son of J. Y. of Bewerley; 1845^{3}-1849^{1}; St. John's Coll. Camb. B.A.; J.P. W. Riding, Yorks, High Sheriff 1889; *m.* 1st, Augusta Margaret, *d.* of Hon. and Rev. Canon John Baillie, Rector of Elsdon, Otterburn, Northumberland; 2nd, Fanny, *d.* of Sir John Walsham, 1st Bt., of Knill Court, Hereford. *Beverley Hall, Pateley Bridge, Leeds.*

Meade-King *ma.* (Miss Edw., H.D.)
RICHARD. Of North Petherton, Bridgwater; eld. son of R. K. M.-K. of Walford, Taunton; 1844^{3}-1848^{3}; Trin. Coll. Camb. B.A.; called to the Bar; J.P. co. Somerset; *m.* Flora Evelyn, *d.* of Rev. W. C. Kinglake; died 1870.

Denne *ma.* (Mrs. P. & W.E., C.J.A.)
HENRY. Son of D. D. of Elbridge House, near Canterbury; 1845^{1}-1849^{3}; Univ. Coll. Oxf. B.A.; Oxf. VIII. 1852-3; called to the Bar, Lincoln's Inn, 1856; formerly Capt. East Kent Mounted Rifles; *m.* Annie Murray, *d.* of C. F. Berkeley of Halliford House, Shepperton, Middlesex. *The Field, Minchinhampton, Stroud, Glos.*

Thackeray (Miss Edg., H.M.B.)
CAPT. FREDERICK RENNELL, J.P. Son of Gen. F. R. T., R.E., C.B.; 1844^{3}-1848^{3}; Opp. Wall 1847; won Steeplechase 1847; Capt. 74th Highl. (ret.); *m.* Elizabeth, *d.* of W. Ayton of Alphaton, Fort Beaufort, Cape of Good Hope. *Yarrow House, East Dereham, Norfolk.*

Arbuthnot *ma.* (F.E.D.)
SIR WILLIAM WEDDERBURN, 3rd Bt. Eld. son of Sir R. K. A., 2nd Bt.; 1845^{3}-1847^{3}; Major 18th Hussars; *m.* Alice Margaret, *d.* of Rev. Matthew Carrier Tompson, Vicar of Alderminster, Stratford-on-Avon; died June 5, 1889.

Basset (Mrs. Ro., C.J.A.)
REV. ARTHUR CRAWFURTH DAVIE, M.A., J.P. Son of A. D. B. of Watermouth Castle, Ilfracombe; 1845^{1}-1849^{1}; Preb. of Endellion, Cornwall; died unm. April 23, 1880.

Knowlys (Miss A., H.M.B.)
CULLING EARDLEY. Son of T. J. K. of Heysham, Morecambe, Lancs; 1844^{3}-1847^{3}; Trin. Coll. Oxf.; Surgeon; dead.

Walters (C.O.G.)
R. . 1850.

Robertson *ma.* (W.A.C.)
G. M. . 1850.

Pemberton (Mrs. Ro., C.O.G.)
LOFTUS LEIGH. 4th son of E. L. P. of Torry Hill, Sittingbourne; 1844^{3}-1849^{1}; Registrar of the Supreme Court since 1875. 29 *Rutland Gate, S.W.*

Lane (J.E.Y.)
H. C. . 1850.

Labouchere (E.B.)
HENRY DU PRÉ. Eld. son of J. L. of Broome Hall, Dorking; 1844^{3}-1847^{3}; Diplomatic Service 1854-64, having been attached successively to British Embassies at Washington, Munich, Stockholm, Frankfort, St. Petersburg, Dresden, and Constantinople; Journalist; Propr. and Editor of 'Truth'; M.P. for Windsor 1866, Middlesex 1867, Northampton since 1880; *m.* Henrietta, *d.* of William Hodson. 5 *Old Palace Yard, Westminster, S.W., and Pope's Villa, Twickenham.*

Herbert (Mrs. P., H.M.B.)
GEORGE WILLIAM. 1845^{1}-1848^{3}.

Longbourne (Mrs. Ro., H.M.B.)
JOHN VICKERMAN. Of Langley Rogate, Sussex; eld. son of W. T. L., Solicitor; 1845^{3}-1849^{3}; Tomline Select 1849; Solicitor; Taxing Master in the Chanc. Div. of the High Court of Justice; J.P. for Sussex; *m.* Mary Fanny Sarah, *d.* of Rev. John Harrison Bell of Kirkley, Suffolk; dead.

Shirley (Mrs. Ro., aft. K.S.)
H. H. . 1850.

Lloyd (Miss Edg., aft. K.S., C.J.A. & F.E.D.)
A. O. . 1850.

Byng *mi.* (Mrs. Hor., H.M.B.) — HON. HENRY WILLIAM JOHN (4th Earl of Strafford), K.C.V.O., C.B. 2nd son of George Stevens, 2nd Earl of S.; 1844^{3}–1847^{3}; Lieut.-Col. Coldstream Gds.; Equerry in ordinary to Her Majesty; Hon. Col. 7th Bn. King's Royal Rifles; *m.* 1st, Countess Henrietta, *d.* of H. E. Count Christian Danneskiold Samsoe; 2nd, Cora, widow of Samuel Colgate of Uplands, New-Hamburg-on-Hudson, U.S.A.; killed by the Cambridge Express at Potter's Bar Rly. Stn., May 16, 1899.

Bell (Mrs. Ro., E.H.P.) — MATTHEW. 1845^{2}–1847^{2}.

Shaw (W. E., F.E.D.) — SIR JOHN CHARLES KENWARD, 7th Bt. Eld. son of Capt. C. S., R.N., and nephew of Sir J. K. S., 6th Bt.; 1843^{3}–1848^{1}; Merton Coll. Oxf.; Lieut. W. Kent Yeo. Cav. 1852–8; J.P. Kent; *m.* 1st, Maria, *d.* of Henry Sparkes of Summerberry, Guildford; 2nd, Sophia Emma Anna Maria, *d.* of Capt. John William Finch, R.N., of Knight's Place, Pembury, Tunbridge Wells. *Kenward, Tunbridge, Kent.*

Barker (Mrs. Rk., C.O.G.) — J. E. . 1850.

Ellison (E.H.P.) — COL. RICHARD GEORGE, C.V.O. Eld. son of Col. R. E. of Boultham; 1845^{2}–1847^{3}; Col. 47th Regt. (ret.); served in the Crimea (at Alma, Inkerman and Sebastopol) as A.D.C. to Sir J. Pennefather, C.C.B.; Ensign King's Body-guard; J.P. and D.L. co. Lincoln, High Sheriff 1886; *m.* Amelia, *d.* of John Todd of West Newton, Aspatria, Cumb. 23 *Queen's Gate, S.W., and Boultham Hall, Lincoln.*

Lord Balgonie (E.H.P.) — ALEXANDER. Eld. son of David, 8th Earl of Leven and Melville; 1845^{2}–1848^{1}; Major Gren. Gds.; Knt. of the Legion of Honour; died Aug. 20, 1857.

Phillips (F.E.D.) — W. P. T. . 1850.

Green (H.D.) — HENRY EGERTON-. Son of J. W. E.-G., of Colchester; 1844^{3}–1848^{3}; Banker at Colchester (Round, Green & Co.); J.P. for Essex; *m.* Caroline Frances, *d.* of George Green of Harley St., and widow of Capt. E. C. W. Fulcher; died Sept. 12, 1882.

Jackson *mi.* (E.H.P.) — HERBERT INNES. Son of J. J. of Hampstead and of Hambleton Manor House, Rutland; 1846^{1}–1849^{1}; Second Chancery Registrar of the Supreme Court; *m.* Elizabeth Rolanda, *d.* of Rev. William Wollaston Pym, Rector of Willian, Hitchin. 26 *Talbot Sq., Hyde Park, W.*

Macan (F.E.D.) — REV. TURNER ARTHUR. Of Carriff, co. Armagh; son of Major T. M. of Carriff; 1844^{2}–1849^{2}; *m.* Florence, *d.* of Henry Lawes Long of Hampton Lodge, Hants; died 1889.

Lindsay *ma.* (E.H.P.) — LIEUT.-COL. HENRY GORE. 2nd son of G. H. L. of Glasnevin; 1844^{3}–1847^{3}; formerly Capt. Rifle Bgde.; served in Crimea and Indian Mutiny; Lieut.-Col. Brecknock R.V.; J.P. and D.L. cos. Brecknock and Dublin; *m.* Hon. Ellen Sarah Morgan, *d.* of Charles, 1st Lord Tredegar. *Glasnevin House, Dublin.*

Miles *mi.* (R.O.) — H. C. W. . 1850.

Miles *min.* (R.O.) — CHARLES JOHN WILLIAM. 3rd son of Sir W. M., 1st Bt., of Leigh Court, Bristol; 1844^{3}–1849^{3}; Cox Eton VIII. 1848; Merton Coll. Oxf.; Capt. 5th Fusiliers; *m.* Elizabeth Maria, *d.* of Rev. Henry Lloyd of Selattyn, Oswestry; [illegible] June 2, 1874.

Hunt (E.H.P.) — AUGUSTUS. Son of — H., Parliamentary Agent; 1843^{1}–1848^{1}; Capt. 3rd Dragoon Gds.; died at Torquay, 1861.

Mitford (R.F.H., aft. K.S.) — HENRY REVELEY. Son of — M. of Exbury Park, Southampton; 1843^{2}–1849^{1}.

Crawley (Miss A., & Miss Edg., H.M.B.) — REV. ROBERT TOWNSEND. Son of G. A. C. of Fitzroy Farm, Highgate; 1844^{3}–1848^{3}; Ch. Ch. Oxf. M.A.; Rector of N. Ockendon and Rural Dean of Chafford; *m.* *d.* of Rev. James Charles Clutterbuck. *N. Ockendon Rectory, Romford.*

Browning (F.E.D.) — H. B. . 1850.

Buckley *mi.* (J.E.Y.) — DUNCOMBE FREDERICK BATT. 3rd son of Gen. E. P. B. of New Hall, Bodenham, Salisbury; 1844^{3}–1848^{3}; Opp. Wall 1848; Capt. Scots Fus. Gds.; killed in the trenches before Sebastopol Sept. 6, 1855.

Crawley (R.O.) — RICHARD SAMBROOK. 5th son of S. C. of Stockwood, Luton; 1843^{3}–1849^{1}; Magd. Coll. Camb.; Capt. Beds Militia; *m.* Henrietta, *d.* of E. Dickson; dead.

Smith (Mrs. Rl., W.L.E.) — MARTIN RIDLEY. Eld. son of M. T. S. of Shirley, Croydon; 1845^{3}–1849^{1}; Trin. Coll. Camb.; Banker; High Sheriff of London 1891; Lieut. for City of London; *m.* Emily Catherine, *d.* of Henry Stewart of Crosbie, Galloway. 9 *Wilbraham Place, Sloane Street, S.W., and Hayes, Kent.*

Uniacke (R.O.) — CAPTAIN HENRY TURNER. 2nd son of J. U. of Kermincham and Boughton House, Cheshire; 1844^{3}–1847^{3}; Ch. Ch. Oxf.; Capt. 19th Foot; present at the battle of Alma, siege of Sebastopol, and storming of the Redan; *m.* Isabel, *d.* of George Fortescue of Newton Abbot. 35 *Earl's Court Sq., S.W.*

Parks *ma.* (Miss M., F.E.D.) — FREDERICK CALDWELL. Son of — P. of Woodside, Old Windsor; 1843^{3}–1847^{3}; formerly Lieut. E. York Militia.

West (J.E.Y.) — FREDERICK MYDDELTON. Of Ruthin Castle, Ruthin; eld. son of F. R. W. of Ruthin; 1844^{3}–1847^{3}; formerly 7th Lt. Dragoons, aft. Capt. Denbighs Yeo.; died unm. Aug. 13, 1868.

Morris (W.G.C.) — GEORGE BARBAR. 1845^{1}–1848^{1}; Ch. Ch. Oxf.; Master of Salop Foxhounds. *Lydbury, Salop.*

Way — 1847^{2}–1847^{3}.

Mr. Pellew *ma.* (E.B.) — HON. FLEETWOOD JOHN. 4th son of Pownoll Bastard, 2nd Viscount Exmouth; 1844^{3}–1848^{3}; *m.* Emily Sarah, *d.* of Thomas Ferguson of Greenville, Down, Ireland; died Aug. 2, 1866.

Tower (R.O.) — LIEUT.-COL. HARVEY, J.P. Son of Rev. W. T. of The Hatch, Brentwood, Essex; 1845^{1}–1848^{1}; Lieut.-Col. Coldstream Gds.; served in the Crimea (Alma, Inkerman and siege of Sebastopol); Knt. of the Legion of Honour; died unm. Nov. 17, 1870.

Barton *ma.* (W.L.E.) — BERTRAM FRANCIS. 3rd son of N. B. of Straffan; 1843^{3}–1847^{3}; J.P. and D.L. co. Kildare; *m.* Fannie Annie, *d.* of Frank Cutler, Comm. R.N., of Upton Lodge, Brixham, S. Devon. *Straffan House, Straffan Station, co. Kildare.*

Whittingstall (Mrs. Rl. & W.G.C., W.G.C.) — MAJOR GEORGE FEARNLEY-. Son of E. F.-W. of Langleybury and Watford, Herts; 1844^{3}–1847^{3}; formerly Maj. Herts Yeo. Cav. and Capt. 12th Lancers; J.P. for Herts; *m.* Anne Mary, *d.* of William Joseph Myers of Porters, Shenley, Barnet. 105 *Queen's Gate, S.W.*

Norris (Miss A., [illegible]) — REV. WILLIAM ARTHUR. 1842^{3}–1849^{3}; Eton XI. 1848–9; Coll. Wall 1847–8; Trin. Coll. Camb. M.A.; Camb. XI. 1851; Camb. VIII. [illegible]; Rector of Oaksey, [illegible]

Packe (R.F.H., H.D.) — W. J. . 1850.

Grover *mi.* (Mrs. Ro., aft. K.S., E.B.) — C. C. . 1850.

Haworth (W.A.C.) — EDWARD LUMLEY. 1845^3-1847^3; joined 28th Regt.; died 1856.

Mr. Herbert (Miss M., W.J.) — HON. W. H. . 1850.

Owen (J.E.Y.) — JOHN. 1845^3-1849^1; Jesus Coll. Camb.

Phillips (Mrs. Vav., C.L.) — L. GUY. . 1850.

Pemberton (W.E., F.E.D.) — R. L. . 1850.

Watson (J.E.Y.) — W. . 1850.

Scott *ma.* (E.C.) — G. A. J. . 1850.

Twisleton (Mrs. P., E.C.) — HON. I. DE V. E., C.B. (aft. Twisleton-Wykeham-Fiennes). . 1850.

Malcolm *ma.* (E.H.P.) — J. W. (Lord Malcolm of Poltalloch). 1850.

Foulkes *ma.* (W.G.C.) — PETER EVERARD. Son of Rev. — F., Vicar of Shebbear, Highampton, N. Devon; 1845^1-1848^3; went to reside at the Cape of Good Hope.

Harford (W.A.C.) — E. J. . 1850.

Moseley (H.D.) — WALTER. Of Buildwas Park, Shrewsbury; eld. son of W. M. of Buildwas; 1846^1-1847^3; Trin. Coll. Oxf.; J.P. and D.L. for Salop; *m.* Maria Katherine, *d.* of Rev. Richard Anderson of the Grange, Bedale; died July 11, 1887.

Mr. Annesley (J.E.Y.) — HON. HUGH (5th Earl Annesley). 2nd son of William Richard, 3rd Earl A.; 1845^1-1848^3; Trin. Coll. Dublin. B.A.; Lieut.-Col. Scots Gds. (ret.); served in Kaffir war 1851-3, and Crimea 1854; M.P. Cavan 1857-74; J.P. and D.L. co. Down; *m.* 1st, Mabel Wilhelmina Frances, *d.* of Col. William Thomas Markham of Cufforth Hall, Yorks; 2nd, Priscilla Cecilia, *d.* of William Armitage Moore of Arnmore, co. Cavan. *Annesley Lodge, Sussex Place, Regent's Park, N.W., and Castlewellan S.O., co. Down.*

Stone *ma.* (Mrs. P. & Miss Edg., C.J.A. & F.E.D.) — H. . 1850.

Duckworth *mi.* (Mrs. Hor., E.H.P.) — H. . 1850.

Webb (Mrs. Hor., H.M.B.) — COL. RICHARD FREDERICK. Of Donnington; eld. son of R. W. of Donnington Hall, Ledbury; 1845^3-1848^3; Ch. Ch. Oxf. M.A.; formerly Col. comm. 4th Bn. King's Shrops. Regt.; J.P. and D.L. cos. Hereford, Middlesex, and London; *m.* Hon. Isabella Catherine Wykeham-Fiennes, *d.* of Frederick, 13th Lord Saye and Sele. *6 West Cromwell Road, S.W.*

Wethered (Mrs. P., H.D.) — THOMAS OWEN. Eld. son of O. W. of Remnantz and Seymour Court, Bucks; 1846^3-1848^3; Ch. Ch. Oxf.; M.P. for Gt. Marlow 1868-80; J.P. for Bucks; formerly Capt. Bucks R.V.; *m.* Edith Grace, *d.* of Rev. Hart Ethelston, Rector of St. Marks, Cheetham Hill, Manchester. *Seymour Court, Gt. Marlow, Bucks.*

Barnard (W.E., H.M.B.) — ANDREW. 1846^1-1848^3; formerly in the Bengal Civil Service.

Welby *mi.* (C.O.G.) — W. H. E. . 1850.

Wykeham-Martin *mi.* (W.A.C.) — MAJOR FIENNES (aft. Cornwallis). Of Linton Place, Maidstone; 2nd son of C. W.-M. of Leeds Castle, Maidstone; 1845^3-1849^3; won School Pulling 1849; Major 4th Hussars (in Balaclava charge); *m.* Harriet Elizabeth, *d.* of John Thomas Mott of Barningham Hall, Norfolk; died April 24, 1867.

Verner (Mrs. P., H.M.B.) — SIR EDWARD WINGFIELD, 4th Bt. Of Corke Abbey, Bray, Ireland; 2nd son of Sir W. V., 1st Bt., of Corke Abbey; 1845^1-1848^3; Ch. Ch. Oxf.; M.P. for Lisburn 1863-73, and co. Armagh 1873-80; J.P. and D.L. co. Dublin, High Sheriff 1866; J.P. co. Wicklow; *m.* Selina Florence, *d.* of Thomas Vesey Nugent; died June 21, 1899.

Leigh (W.A.C.) — J. . 1850.

Lyall (K.S., C.J.A. & C.Wo.) — RT. HON. SIR A. C., K.C.B. 1850.

Sparke (Mrs. de R., E.H.P.) — E. B. . 1850.

De Winton (F.E.D.) — CAPT. WALTER. Of Maesllwch Castle, Glasbury, Brecons; eld. son of W. W. De W. of Maesllwch; 1845^3-1848^3; Capt. 1st Life Gds.; J.P. and D.L. co. Radnor, High Sheriff 1854 and 1862; *m.* Frances Jessie, *d.* of Hon. and Rev. Arthur Talbot, Rector of Ingestre and Church Eaton, Stafford; died May 24, 1878.

Lord Schomberg Kerr (H.M.B.) — SCHOMBERG HENRY (9th Marquis of Lothian), K.T., P.C., LL.D. 2nd son of John William Robert, 7th Marquis of L.; 1845^3-1847^3; New Coll. Oxf.; Hon. LL.D. Edinburgh Univ. 1882; Diplomatic Service 1858-65; Sec. of State for Scotland and Keeper of Privy Seal 1887-92; Lord Rector of Edin. Univ. 1887-8; Hon. Col. 3rd Bn. Royal Scots Lothian Regt. 1878-89; Capt.-Gen. of Royal Company of Archers and Gold Stick of Scotland; P.R.S.A. Scotland; Kt. of Grace of the Order of St. John of Jerusalem in England; *m.* Lady Victoria Alexandrina, *d.* of Walter Francis, 5th Duke of Buccleuch, K.G.; died Jan. 17, 1900.

Gipps (Miss Edw., H.D.) — GENERAL SIR REGINALD RAMSAY, G.C.B. Son of Sir G. G., R.E., K.C.B., Governor of Australia; 1845^1-1847^3; ent. Scots Gds. 1849; served in the Crimea 1854-5; Alma and Inkerman med. and 4 clasps; Comm. 1878-81; Major-Gen. 1881; Lieut.-Gen. 1889; Comm. Home district 1884-9; D.A.G. Aux. Forces 1891-2; Military Sec. 1892-6; Kt. of Legion of Honour (France); *m.* Evelyn Charlotte, *d.* of Col. Fielden of Dulas Court, co. Hereford. *11 Chester Street, Grosvenor Place, S.W., and Sycamore House, Farnborough, Hants.*

Hinrich (R.F.H., E.H.P.) — HENRY DENT. 1845^3-1849^3; St. John's Coll. Camb. M.A.

Marshall (H.D.) — T. H. . 1850.

Byng *min.* (Mrs. Hor. & Miss G., H.M.B. & J.L.J.) — Hon. F. E. C. (Earl of Strafford). 1850.

Lord Clinton (W.E., E.C.) — H. P. A. (Earl of Lincoln). . 1850.

Praed (R.O.) — C. T. . 1850.

Palmer (R.O.) — Lieut.-Gen. Sir Roger William Henry, 5th Bt. Son of Sir W. H. R. P., 4th Bt., of Kenure Park; 1845^{3}–1849^{3}; Ch. Ch. Oxf.; served in 11th Hussars through Crimea; charged in Lt. Bgde. at Balaclava; med. and 4 clasps; 2nd Life Gds. 1858-70; Col. 20th Hussars; M.P. co. Mayo 1867-75; J.P. and D.L. co. Sligo; J.P. for Berks and cos. Camb., Denbigh, Mayo (High Sheriff 1888), and Dublin (High Sheriff 1875); *m.* Gertrude Millicent, *d.* of Rev. Plumer Rooper of Abbots Ripton, Huntingdon. *Kenure Park, Rush, Dublin; Cefn Park, Wrexham; and Glenisland, Maidenhead.*

Hole (Mrs. P., W.G.C.) — Richard Aram. 1845^{3}–1848^{3}.

Waterfield *mi.* (Miss Edw., aft. K.S., C.J.A.) — W. G. . 1850.

Beresford (Miss Edw., H.D.) — George De la Poer. Of Awbawn, co. Cavan and Armagh; eld. son of Most Rev. M. G. De la P. B., D.D., Archbp. of Armagh; 1845^{3}–1849^{2}; Univ. Coll. Oxf.; J.P. and D.L. co. Cavan, High Sheriff 1867; J.P. co. Armagh, High Sheriff 1887; M.P. for Armagh 1875-85; *m.* Mary Annabella, *d.* of Rev. Canon William Vernon Harcourt of Nuneham Park, Oxf. and Canon of York. *Ovenden House, Sundridge, Sevenoaks.*

Sir Henry Vane (W.L.E.) — Sir Henry Ralph Fletcher-, 4th Bt. Eld. son of Sir R. F.-V., 3rd Bt.; 1844^{3}–1847^{3}; Ch. Ch. Oxf.; J.P. and D.L. for Westmorland and Cumberland; High Sheriff of Cumberland 1856; Hon. Col. Westm and Cumb. Yeo. Cav.; *m.* Margaret, *d.* of Thomas Steuart Gladstone of Capenoch, Dumfries-shire. *Hutton-in-the-Forest, Penrith, and Scarness Cottage, Bassenthwaite, Keswick.*

Gore-Booth (Miss Edw., H.D.) — R. N. . 1850.

Cookesley (W.G.C.) — H. S. . 1850.

Newman (Mrs. Ro., H.M.D.) — Alured. 4th son of Sir R. W. N., 1st Bt., of Mamhead Park, Kenton, Exeter; 1845^{1}–1848^{1}; *m. d.* of Abert E. Arlington. *London and Co. Bank, Winchester.*

Cocks (Mrs. Ro., W.L.E.) — Rev. Henry Bromley. Eld. son of Rev. H. S. C. of Leigh Vicarage, Worcester; 1844^{3}–1849^{2}; Exeter Coll. Oxf. M.A.; Vicar of Leigh, Worc.; aft. Vicar of Sydenham, Christ Church, New Zealand; *m.* Harriett Elizabeth, *d.* of Col. Philip Wodehouse; died 1894.

Mr. Ponsonby (F.E.D.) — Hon. Ashley George John. Of Heatherfield, Ascot; 2nd son of William, 1st Lord De Mauley, of Hatherop Castle, Fairford, Glos.; 1845^{1}–1847^{3}; Trin. Coll. Camb.; formerly Capt. Gren. Gds.; M.P. for Cirencester 1852-7 and 1859-65; J.P. and D.L. for Berks, Middlesex, London, and co. Glos.; C.C. for Central Finsbury; *m.* Hon. Louisa Frances Charlotte (Maid of Honour to Queen Victoria), *d.* of Lord Henry Gordon; died Jan. 12, 1898.

Mr. Fermor (C.O.G.) — Hon. Thomas Hatton George. Brother of Earl of Pomfret; 1845^{3}–1848^{3}; in 2nd Life Gds.; died 1864.

Rycroft (F.E.D.) — Sir Nelson, 4th Bt. Of Calton, co. York; eld. son of Sir R. H. C. R. of Basingstoke; 1845^{3}–1847^{3}; 85th Lt. Infantry and Col. 3rd Bn. Hants Regt.; J.P. and D.L. for co. Southampton, High Sheriff 1881; *m.* Juliana, *d.* of Sir John Ogilvy, 9th Bt., of Inverquharity, co. Forfar; died Mar. 30, 1894.

Dawson-Damer (Miss M., H.M.B.) — Lionel Seymour William (4th Earl of Portarlington), D.L. Son of G. L. D.-D. and cousin of Henry, 3rd Earl of P.; 1845^{1}–1847^{3}; Capt. Scots Fusilier Gds.; M.P. for Portarlington 1857-65 and 1868-80; *m.* Hon. Harriet Lydia Montagu, *d.* of Gen. Lord Rokeby, G.C.B.; died Dec. 17, 1892.

Sheffield (H.D.) — Henry Digby. 2nd son of Sir R. S., 4th Bt., of Normanby Park, Doncaster; 1846^{3}–1848^{3}; Trin. Coll. Camb.; *m.* Evelyn Diana Turnour, *d.* of Vicomtesse D'Lardio; died Oct. 22, 1888.

Jervoise (C.O.G.) — Lieut.-Col. Sir Henry Clarke-, 4th Bt. 2nd son of Sir J. C.-J., 2nd Bt., of Idsworth Park, Horndean, Hants; 1844^{3}–1847^{3}; Lieut.-Col. Coldstream Gds. (ret.); served in Eastern Campaign 1854-5 (Alma, Balaclava, and siege of Sebastopol); med. with 3 clasps; Sardinian and Turkish Meds., 5th Class Medjidie; High Sheriff co. Rutland 1898. 33 *Charles Street, Berkeley Sq., W., and Langham House, Oakham.*

Burder *mi.* (Mrs. P., E.B.) — Thomas Henry Carr. 1844^{1}–1849^{3}; Opp. Wall 1848; died at Camb.

Dickins *ma.* (W.L.E.) — Col. Compton Alwyne Scrase-. 2nd son of C. S.-D. of Coolhurst, Horsham; 1845^{3}–1847^{3}; Col. 28th Regt.; Knt. of the Legion of Honour; died unm. Feb. 11, 1884.

Dickins *mi.* (W.L.E.) — Maj.-Gen. William Drummond Scrase-. 3rd son of C. S.-D. of Coolhurst, Horsham; 1845^{2}–1847^{3}; Maj.-Gen. 31st Regt. (ret.); Indian and Crimean Meds.; J.P. for Kent; *m.* Anna Matilda Catherine, *d.* of Gen. Sir George Townshend Walker, 1st Bt., G.C.B., and widow of Maj. Henry William Paget, A.Q.M.G. *Collingwood, Hawkhurst.*

Lambert *mi.* (J.E.Y.) — W. H. . 1850.

Lyon *ma.* (C.O.G.) — Charles. 3rd son of T. L. of Appleton Hall, Warrington; 1846^{1}–1849^{3}; died of brain fever 1849.

Swann (W.J.) — R. . 1850.

Williams (W.G.C., aft. K.S., W.G.C.) — M. S. . 1850.

Montgomerie ([illegible]) — [illegible] M. . 1850.

Ward (Miss Edw., aft. K.S., W.J.) — J. M. . 1850.

Hopkins (Miss Edw., W.J.) — T. H. T. . 1850.

Luxmoore (W.L.E.) — P. B. . 1850.

Sterry (Miss Edg., aft. K.S., E.H.P.) — W. . 1850.

Heathcote (E.H.P.) — J. M. . 1850.

Fremantle *min.* (W.E., E.B.) — Hon. Sir C. W., K.C.B. . 1850.

Lord Granard (E.O.) — George Arthur Hastings Forbes (7th Earl of Granard), K.P. Eld. son of George John, Visct. Forbes, and grandson of George, 6th Earl of G.; 1846^{3}-1850^{1}; Lieut.-Col. comm. and Hon. Col. 9th Bn. Rifle Bgde.; one of the Senate of the Royal Univ. of Ireland; Vice-Adml. of the Province of Connaught; Knt. of the Order of Malta and Knt. Grand Cross of the Order of St. Gregory-the-Great; *m.* 1st, Jane Colclough, *d.* of Hamilton Knox Grogan Morgan, M.P., of Johnstown Castle, co. Wexford; 2nd, Hon. Frances Mary Petre, *d.* of William Bernard, 12th Lord Petre; died Aug. 25, 1889.

Arbuthnot *mi.* (F.E.D.) — W. . 1850.

Fraser (R.F.H., E.H.P.) — J. K. . 1850.

Arnold *mi.* (Mrs. Hor., E.H.P.) — C. T. . 1850.

Dering (R.O.) — Edward Cholmeley. Eld. son of Sir E. C. D., 8th Bt., of Surrenden-Dering, Ashford, Kent; 1846^{1}-1848^{3}; in the 85th and 44th Regts.; *m.* 1st, Harriet Mary, *d.* of Hon. Adolphus Capell, and widow of Viscount Forth; 2nd, Fanny Mary, *d.* of Francis Wilby Whitehead; died Nov. 17, 1874.

Way — Benjamin Henry Walpole. Of Denham Place, Uxbridge; son of B. W. of Denham Place; 1842^{3}-1847^{1}; *m.* Eleanor Isabella Eliza, *d.* of Rev. Henry Hugh Way of Alderbourne Manor, Gerrard's Cross, Bucks, and Vicar of Henbury; died Jan. 8, 1891.

Paul *ma.* (R.F.H., C.L.) — Col. William Henry. Son of W. P. of Southleigh, Truro; 1844^{1}-1847^{3}; formerly in 36th Regt., aft. Capt. and Adjt. Depôt Bn. Belfast, and late Head Constable, Isle of Man; *m.* Mary, *d.* of Major Weiman of Tasmania.

REMOVE.

Dupuis (H.D., aft. K.S., H.D., C.O.G. & A.P.B.) — G. R. . 1850.

Harington (J.W.H., R.O., and C. Wo.) — Sir R., Bt. . 1850.

White (C.O.G.) — Lieut.-Col. Raymond Herbert. 1846^{3}-1848^{1}; Lieut.-Col. Scots Fusilier Gds.

Mallory (C.L.) — G. . 1850.

Puller *mi.* (E.C.) — C. Giles-. . 1850.

Mr. Marsham (Miss A. & E.B., E.B.) — Hon. R. (aft. Marsham-Townshend). . 1850.

Foulkes *mi.* (K.S.) — S. W. . 1850.

Northey (C.O.G.) — E. W. . 1850.

Ramsay (C.O.G.) — John. Of Barra Castle, Old Meldrum, Aberdeen; son of J. R. of Barra; 1845^{1}-1848^{3}; Trin. Coll. Camb. M.A.; formerly Major Royal Aberdeens Highlanders, and Lieut.-Col. Aberdeens R.V.; J.P. and D.L. co. Aberdeen, and D.L. co. Banff; *m.* Leonora Sophia, *d.* of Rev. Nathaniel Bond of Creech Grange, Dorset; died May 29, 1895.

Mayne *ma.* (R.F.H., E.B.) — Carvick Cox. Eld. son of Sir R. M., K.C.B., Chief Commnr. of Police; 1845^{3}-1848^{2}; died Sept. 23, 1851.

Sutton (F.E.D.) — R. . 1850.

Meade-King *mi.* (Miss Edw. & W.E., H.D.) — W. O. . 1850.

Currie (E.H.P.) — Sir P. H. W., P.C., G.C.B. (1st Lord Currie). . 1850.

Fosbery (Mrs. Vav., C.J.A. & F.E.D.) — G. V. . 1850.

Nevile (C.O.G.) — G. . 1851.

Younger (K.S., C.J.A.) — H. W. . 1850.

Dunbar (Mrs. Ro., F.E.D.) — R. L. . 1850.

Dudding *ma.* (Mrs. Ro., W.A.C.) — Rev. Henry Swan. Son of J. D.; 1845^{1}-1849^{1}; Magd. Coll. Oxf. M.A.; Rector of Stanton; *m.* Hannah Eliza, *d.* of William Markham. *Stanton Rectory, Bury St. Edmunds.*

Chandos-Pole (Miss W., J.W.H.) — W. . 1850.

Palmer (R.F.H., F.E.D.) — Rev. James Nelson. 1845^{3}-1849^{3}; St. John's Coll. Oxf. M.A.; formerly Curate of Breamore, Hants.

Dorrien-Magens (H.M.B.) — Frederick. Eld. son of — D.-M. of Hammerwood Lodge, Sussex; 1845^{3}-1849^{1}; formerly Capt. 1st Life Gds.

Wentworth (W.A.C.)
THOMAS FREDERICK CHARLES VERNON-. Of Wentworth Castle, Barnsley, and Aldeburgh Lodge, Suffolk; son of F. W. T. V.-W. of Wentworth; 1845^{3}–1847^{3}; Trin. Coll. Camb. M.A.; formerly Lieut. 1st W. Yorks Militia; elected M.P. for Aylesbury 1859, unseated on petition; J.P. W. Riding of Yorks, Bucks, Suffolk, and co. Perth; *m.* Lady Harriet Augusta de Burgh, *d.* of Ulick John, 1st Marquis of Clanricarde, K.P.; died Jan. 1, 1902.

Mytton (W.J.)
D. H. . 1850.

Lyon (Mrs. Vav., W.A.C.)
COL. FREDERICK LEE HOPKINSON. Son of J. W. L. of Miserden Park, Cirencester; 1846^{2}–1847^{3}; formerly Capt. Royal Horse Art.; J.P. for Sussex; *m.* Rosabelle, *d.* of William Peters of Ashfold, Sussex. *Harwood House, Horsham.*

Coney *mi.* (Mrs. P., E.B.)
PHILIP GEORGE. 2nd son of J. J. C. of Braywick Grove, Maidenhead; 1846^{2}–1848^{1}; Capt. 7th Fusiliers; severely wounded at battle of Alma (medal and clasps); went to India 1857; died unm., of fever, at Mean Meer 1858.

Ford (Mrs. P., C.J.A.)
M. W. . 1850.

Roberts (Home and Mrs. de R., aft. K.S., E.B.)
J. P. S. . 1850.

Denne *mi.* (W.E., W.J.)
R. H. . 1850.

Mr. Pellew *mi.* (E.B.)
HON. BARRINGTON REYNOLDS. 5th son of Pownoll Bastard, 2nd Visct. Exmouth; 1845^{2}–1848^{3}; Major Rifle Bgde. and A.D.C. to Gen. Sir C. Van Straubenzee, K.C.B.; served with distinction in the Kaffir war, at the siege of Sebastopol, storming of Canton, and at the assault and capture of Lucknow; died of dysentery at Lucknow Dec. 6, 1858.

Fursdon *mi.* (W.E., aft. K.S., C.J.A.)
W. . 1850.

Gervis (Mrs. Ro., J.E.Y.)
AUGUSTUS TAPPS-. 3rd son of Sir G. W. T.-G., 2nd Bt., of Christchurch, Hants; 1845^{3}–1849^{1}; in the 52nd Lt. Infantry; *m.* Maria Catherina Hortensia; died April 17, 1884.

Ryan (Mrs. Vav., C.O.G.)
SIR CHARLES LISTER, C.B., K.C.B. 5th son of Rt. Hon. Sir E. R.; 1845^{3}–1849^{2}; ent. Civil Service 1851; Clerk in the Treasury 1852-65; Priv. Sec. to Mr. Disraeli when Chanc. of Exchq., to Sir Stafford Northcote, and to Mr. Gladstone 1859-65; Sec. to Board of Audit, Asst. Compt., and Compt. and Auditor-General 1887-96; a Commr. of the Exhib. of 1851; Gov. of Wellington and Royal Holloway Colls.; J.P. for Berks; *m.* Jane Georgiana, *d.* of Sir John Shaw-Lefevre, K.C.B. *Burley Bushes, Ascot.*

Russell (J.E.Y.)
GILES BANGER. 1845^{3}–1849^{3}; Trin. Coll. Oxf.; died at Oxf.

Moore (W.L.E.)
GENERAL SIR ALEXANDER GEORGE, K.C.B. (aft. Montgomery-Moore). Son of A. J. M.-M. of Garvey House, Aughnacloy, co. Tyrone; 1845^{3}–1849^{3}; won Double Sculling with R. Swann 1849; Col. 18th Hussars; Comm. Belfast and S.E. Districts 1886-91, troops in Canada 1893-8, Aldershot 1899; J.P. Belfast and D.L. co. Tyrone; *m.* Hon. Jane C[illegible], *d.* of Field-Marshal Sir John, 1st Lord Seaton G.C.B. *Gipsy Lodge, Norwood, S.E.*

Holt *ma.* (Home, C.J.A.)
HARVEY. Son of R. F. H. of Eton; 1845^{3}–1849^{1}; won Steeplechase 1848; settled in Australia.

Mr. Campbell (H.M.B.)
HON. H. W. . 1850.

Congreve (Mrs. Ro., E.H.P.)
AMBROSE. Of Mount Congreve, Kilmeaden, Waterford; son of J. C. of Mount Congreve; 1845^{3}–1849^{1}; Field XI. 1848; formerly Lieut. 2nd Life Gds.; J.P. and D.L. co. Waterford, High Sheriff 1871; *m.* Alice Elizabeth Dillon, *d.* of Robert, 3rd Lord Clonbrock; died Mar. 15, 1901.

Johnston (W.J.)
WILLIAM HENRY. Son of W. J. of 51st King's Own Yorks Regt.; 1846^{1}–1848^{3}; Football XI.; Trin. Coll. Dublin B.A.; Civil Servant, Home Office (ret.); *m.* Fanny Lewis, *d.* of Rev. Edmund Antrobus. 13 *Kent Gardens, Ealing, W.*

Bridges (Mrs. Vav., W.A.C.)
J. A. . 1850.

Dorington (W.L.E.)
RT. HON. SIR JOHN EDWARD, 1st Bt., P.C. Son of J. E. D. of Lypiatt Park; 1846^{1}–1850^{1}; Trin. Coll. Camb. M.A.; formerly Hon. Maj. Gloucs. Yeo. Cav.; M.P. for Stroud 1873-4 and for N. Gloucs. since 1886; Chmn. Qr. Sessions 1878-89; Commr. in Lunacy since 1892; Chmn. of Gloucs. C.C. since 1889; J.P. and D.L. co. Glouc.; *m.* Georgina Harriet, *d.* of William Speke of Jordans, Ilminster. 30 *Queen Anne's Gate, S.W., and Lypiatt Park, Stroud.*

Northcote (Mrs. P., E.B.)
LEWIS STAFFORD. Son of Rev. S. C. N., Rector of Upton Pyne, Exeter; 1845^{3}–1848^{2}; formerly Capt. 39th Regt.; *m.* Isabella, *d.* of Capt. J. O. R. Weguelin; died Sept. 21, 1882.

Wilberforce *ma.* (W.E., aft. K.S., C.J.A. & J.L.J.)
W. F. . 1850.

Chapman (E.C.)
G. H. J. . 1850.

Neville (E.C.)
W. W. . 1850.

Blaauw (E.B.)
H. W. G. . 1850.

Knight (H.D.)
MAJOR-GEN. LEWIS EDWARD. Of Millgate, Maidstone; son of Major H. K.; 1846^{2}–1849^{2}; formerly Lieut.-Col. 17th Lancers; J.P. for Kent; *m.* Belinda, *d.* of Charles Knight; dead.

Mr. Dillon (E.H.P.)
HON. L. G. (Lord Clonbrock). 1850.

Lyon *mi.* (C.O.G.)
COL. FRANCIS. 4th son of T. L. of Appleton Hall, Warrington; 1846^{2}–1847^{3}; R.M.A. Woolwich; Col. Royal Horse Art.; *m.* Flora, *d.* of Hon. Arthur Annesley; killed at Shoeburyness, Feb. 26, 1885.

Warre (Mrs. Vav. & F.V., C.J.A., E.C. & W.B.M.)
F. . 1850.

Lysley *mi.* (W.L.E.)
WARINE BAYLEY MARSHALL. 2nd son of W. J. L. of Pewsham, Chippenham; [illegible] 849; Ch. Ch. Oxf. M.A.; [illegible]; *m.* Lavinia, *d.* of Col. [illegible] *Grosvenor Square, S.W.*

Gore (J.E.Y.)
SIR CHARLES JAMES KNOX- (2nd and last Bt.). Of Belleek Manor, Ballina: eld. son of Sir F. A. K.-G., 1st Bt., of Belleek; 1846^{3}–1849^{3}: ent. Army, 27th Inniskilling Fusiliers, aft. in the 66th Berks Regt.; Comm. the Sligo Rifles Militia; J.P. and D.L. for cos. Mayo and Sligo; died unm. 1890.

Beck (Mrs. Ro., C.L.)
RICHARD EDWARD. 1847^{1}–1850^{3}.

Whitting *mi.* (Miss Edg., aft. K.S., E.H.P.)
F. . 1850.

Giles (W.J.)
J. . 1850.

Arkwright (R.O. & C.Wo.)
J. H. 1850.

Norman (Mrs. Ro. & C.O.G., H.M.B. & C.O.G.)
H. J. . 1850.

Smijth-Windham *mi.* (E.B.)
GEORGE. 4th son of J. S.-W. of Wawne, Beverley: 1847^{3}–1849^{3}; formerly Major 2nd Bn. Rifle Bgde.; served in the Crimea and Indian Mutiny: *m.* Hon. Clarissa Elizabeth, *d.* of Lieut.-Col. Lord Charles James Fox-Russell, 52nd Regt. *Bembridge, Isle of Wight.*

Paynter *mi.* (J.E.Y.)
MAJOR GEORGE. 3rd son of W. P. of Camborne House, Richmond, Surrey: 1845^{1}–1848^{3}; formerly Major 1st King's Dragoon Gds.; served in the Crimea (Turkish med. and clasps): J.P. co. Leicester: *m.* Frances Maria Janetta, *d.* of Lord Amelius Wentworth Beauclerk. *21 Belgrave Square, S.W., and Eaton Grange, Grantham.*

Beaumont (R.O.)
HENRY FREDERICK. Son of H. R. B. of Bretton Hall, Wakefield: 1845^{1}–1849^{3}; Trin. Coll. Camb.: M.P. S. Div. of W. Riding of Yorks 1865–74, and Colne Valley Div. 1885–92; J.P. and D.L. W. Riding of Yorks, and J.P. N. Riding, and co. Lincoln; Hon. Col. W. Riding Yorks Vol.: *m.* Maria Johanna, *d.* of Capt. William Garforth, R.N., of Wiganthorpe, York. *Whitley Beaumont, Huddersfield.*

Clagett (Miss Edw., C.J.A.)
FREDERICK BARNARD. 1845^{1}–1847^{3}; formerly in the Madras Army; died 1851.

Lavie (J.E.Y.)
MAJOR-GEN. ROBERT COMYN. Son of Lieut.-Col. T. L., R.A.: 1843^{2}–1847^{2}; formerly Lieut. 3rd Madras Lt. Infantry; aft. attached to Malabar Police Corps: ret. 1885; *m.* C. E. Gertrude, *d.* of A. H. Langston of Lostwithiel; dead.

Yonge *mi.* (W.G.C.)
COL. CHARLES WILLIAM. Son of Rev. F. L. Y. of Torrington; 1843^{3}–1849^{3}; Col (ret.) 16th Bombay Regt.; served at the suppression of the Mutiny of Native Art. a Shakirpur 1857 (med.); Derajat Frontier 1858–61; in China 1862–3, and with the Abyssinian Expedition 1867–8 (med.). *Cayuton, Torrington.*

Lord Dunglass (H.M.B.)
C. A. D. H. (Earl of Home). . 1850.

Marjoribanks (R.O.)
SIR WILLIAM (4th and last Bt.). 2nd son of Sir W. M., 2nd Bt.; 1845^{3}–1847^{3}; formerly Capt. Herts Militia; *m.* Frances Anne, *d.* of Baldwin Duppa-Duppa of Hollingbourne, Maidstone; died Feb. 22, 1888.

Lord Walter Scott (E.B.)
WALTER CHARLES MONTAGU-DOUGLAS-, 3rd son of Walter Francis, 5th Duke of Buccleuch: 1845^{3}–1849^{1}: formerly Capt. 15th Hussars and A.D.C. to Comm.-in-Chief in India; *m.* Anna Maria, *d.* of Sir William Edmund Cradock-Hartopp, 3rd Bt.; died Mar. 3, 1895.

Bathurst (H.M.B.)
SIR F. T. A. HARVEY-, 4th Bt. . 1850.

Woodmass (Miss Edg., H.M.B.)
M. . 1850.

Mr. Vivian (Miss Edg., H.M.B.)
HON. HUSSEY CRESPIGNY (3rd Lord Vivian), P.C., G.C.M.G., C.B. Eld. son of Charles Crespigny, 2nd Lord V.: 1847^{3}–1849^{1}: ent. Foreign Office 1851: Agent and Consul.-Gen. in Moldavia and Wallachia 1874–6; Consul-Gen. in Egypt 1876–9; H.M. Res. Min. at Swiss Confederation 1879–81; H.M. Envoy Extra. and Plen. to Belgium 1884–91: H.M. Ambassador at Rome 1891–3; *m.* Louisa Alice, *d.* of Robert George Duff of Ryde, Isle of Wight; died at the Embassy in Rome, Oct. 21, 1893.

Williams-Freeman (W.E., H.M.B.)
W. P. . 1850.

Mr. Vernon (F.E.D.)
HON. W. J. BORLACE-WARREN-VENABLES- . 1850.

Clark (W.J.)
J. W. . 1850.

Lloyd (R.O. & C.Wo.)
A. P. . 1850.

Blundell *mi.* (H.D.)
T. B. H. . 1850.

Stuart-Wortley (W.A.C.)
ARCHIBALD HENRY PLANTAGENET. Son of C. S. S.-W.: 1845^{3}–1847^{3}: Lieut.-Col., served in the Kaffir war 1850–53; D.A.Q.M.G. in Crimea; M.P. for Honiton 1857–9; Chevalier of Legion of Honour, Medjidie, St. Maurice, and St. Lazarus; *m.* Lavinia Rebecca, *d.* of Samuel Gibbins; died April 30, 1890.

Hare *mi.* (R.F.H., F.E.D.)
WILLIAM ROBERT. 2nd son of F. G. H. of Hurstmonceaux, Hailsham, Sussex; 1845^{1}–1847^{3}: Camb.: formerly an Officer in the Blues: *m.* Edith, *d.* of C. Adamson of Clifton; died Mar. 18, 1867.

Lonsdale (E.B.)
A. P. (aft. Heywood Lonsdale). . 1850.

Mr. Trefusis. (Miss M., H.M.B. & J.L.J.)
HON. C. H. R. HEPBURN-STUART-FORBES- (Lord Clinton). . 1850.

Gladstone (W.J.)
R. . 1850.

Scott *mi.* (E.C.)
W. J. . 1850.

Wilberforce *mi.* (E.C.)
EDWARD. 2nd son of Ven. R. I. W., Archdn. of E. Riding of Yorks: 1846^{3}–1848^{1}; Trin. Coll. Oxf.: Barrister, and Master of Supreme Court of Judicature; *m.* Fannie, *d.* of Alexander Flash of New Orleans. *34 Elvaston Place, S.W.*

Hayter (H.M.B. & Mrs. Dr., H.M.B. & J.L.J.)
A. D. . 1850.

Mr. Wodehouse (E.H.P.) — HON. H. . 1850.

Clarke (Mrs. Vav.) — 1846^{1}–1849^{3}.

Lord Charles Bruce (H.M.B.) — C. W. B. . 1850.

Graham (Mrs. Vav., W.J.) — M. R. . 1850.

Spalding (W.E., C.J.A.) — JOHN HENRY UPTON. Eld. son of J. E. S. of Holme and Skirmers, Kircudbrightshire; 1847^{1}–1847^{3}; ent. Royal Navy in 1848, landed with Naval Bgde. from H.M.S. 'London,' and was killed in the trenches before Sebastopol Jan. 21, 1855.

Pearson (W.A.C.) — CHARLES. Of Bryn Sciont, Carnarvon; 1847^{1}–1849^{2}; Capt. 4th Dragoon Gds.; died 1879.

Gould (J.W.H.) — A. R. N. . 1850.

Jervis (Mrs. Ro. and Mrs. de R., E.H.P.) — GEORGE FREDERICK ROBINSON. Of Eccleshall Castle, Staffs; son of Col. G. R. J. of the Bombay Army; 1845^{3}–1850^{1}; Eton VIII. 1849; Capt. of the Boats Easter 1850; Field XI. and Opp. Wall 1849; won Steeplechase 1849; Exeter Coll. Oxf. M.A.; Lieut. 9th Bombay Native Infantry 1850–8; Barrister-at-Law, Middle Temple; J.P. for Staffs; *m.* Justine Wilhelmine Gertrude Léonie, *d.* of Baron von Rosen of Rukamois, Esthonia, Russia. *Common Room, Middle Temple, E.C.*

Maynard (W.E., E.H.P.) — A. J. . 1850.

Watson (Mrs. P., C.L.) — COL. WILLIAM HENRY. Of Minsted, Midhurst; son of Hon. Sir W. H. W., Baron of the Exchequer; 1846^{3}–1848^{2}; R.M.A. Woolwich; served with the R.A. in the Crimea; J.P. for Sussex; *m.* Amy, *d.* of Nathaniel Weekes of Guillard's Oak; died 1899.

Johnston (R.F.H., C.J.A.) — HENRY ROEBUCK. Of Howick Grange; 1845^{3}–1849^{2}.

Stone *mi.* (Mrs. P., C.J.A.) — W. . 1850.

Vesey (R.F.H., J.E.Y.) — A. C. . 1850.

Clive (Miss M., W.J.) — HON. G. H. W. WINDSOR-. 1850.

Steuart — A. J. H. . 1850.

Furnivall (J.W.H., aft. K.S., W.J.) — E. T. 1850.

L'Estrange (R.F.H., W.G.C.) — A. G. K. ; 1850.

Puxley (C.O.G.) — H. L. . 1850.

Grove-Price (C.J.A.) — LETTSOM. Eld. son of — G.-P., M.P. for Sandwich; 1846^{1}–1848^{2}.

Mitford *ma.* (W.E., F.E.D.) — PERCY. Eld. son of H. R. M. of Exbury, Southampton; 1846^{3}–1849^{1}; formerly in 43rd Regt., aft. in Scots Fusilier Gds.; Barrister-at-Law; 2nd Sec. Leg. at Berlin; *m.* Hon. Emily Marianne Egerton, *d.* of William Tatton, 1st Lord Egerton of Tatton; died June 27, 1884.

Mitford *mi.* (W.E., F.E.D.) — HENRY. 2nd son of H. R. M. of Exbury, Southampton; 1846^{3}–1849^{3}.

Pepys (J.E.Y) — E. . 1850.

Pugh (Aft. K.S.) — W. B. . 1850.

Fitzgerald (H.D.) — T. K. . 1850.

Henley (J.E.Y.) — A. . 1850.

Bernard (Mrs. Ro., W.J.) — HENRY NORRIS. 1846^{3}–1847^{3}.

Foster (Mrs. Hor., W.A.C.) — FREDERICK WILMOT. 3rd son of A. F. of Warmwell House, Dorchester, Dorset; 1846^{3}–1849^{1}; served through Crimea in 39th Regt., aft. Capt. 72nd Highlanders; died 1860.

Shawe (Mrs. Ro., W.J.) — H. C. . 1850.

Fletcher *ma.* (E.B.) — H. C. . 1850.

Mr. Portman (Mrs. P., C.O.G.) — HON & REV. WALTER BERKELEY. 4th son of Edward Berkeley, 1st Viscount Portman, of Bryanston, Blandford; 1846^{3}–1847^{3}; Ch. Ch. Oxf. M.A., Ordained 1861; formerly Curate of Sandbach, aft. Rector of Corton Denham, Sherborne, for 42 years; *m.* Alice, *d.* of Sir John Mordaunt, 9th Bt.; died March 22, 1903.

Mr. Jocelyn (E.H.P.) — HON. WILLIAM NASSAU, C.B. 3rd son of Robert, 3rd Earl of Roden; 1846^{3}–1849^{3}; Sec. of Leg. at Constantinople 1874–8; Chargé d'Affaires at Hesse-Darmstadt 1878, and Res. Min. to Grand Dukes of Baden and Hesse-Darmstadt 1892; *m.* Cecilia Mary, *d.* of Adml. Hon. Sir George Elliot, K.C.B.; died Nov. 11, 1892.

Curtis (F.E.D.) — WILLIAM EDMUND. Eld. son of Sir W. C., 3rd Bt.; 1846^{3}–1849^{3}; formerly Lieut. 1st Royal Dragoons; *m.* Ariana Emily, *d.* of Col. William Chester Master, of Knole Park, co. Gloucester; died May 11, 1860.

Kay (J.W.H.) — W. . 1850.

Hebeler (Mrs. Vav., W.A.C.) — BERNARD RICHARDSON. 1846^{1}–1848^{3}; formerly Prussian Consul-Gen. in London.

Blane (Mrs. Vav., W.J.) — LIEUT.-GEN. SIR SEYMOUR JOHN, C.B., 3rd Bt. Eld. son of Sir H. S. B., 2nd Bt.; 1846^{3}–1850^{1}; Oppidan Wall 1849; Capt. Fusilier Gds. 1854, served throughout the siege of Sebastopol and at Inkerman, wounded at Inkerman; Col. Rifle Bgde. 1869, Bgde.-Major to Sir Neville Chamberlain, and subsequently to Gen. Nicholson during siege and at storming of Delhi; Bgde.-Major Calcutta 1859; A.D.C. and Military Sec. to Governors-Gen. of India, Lords [illegible], [illegible], Lawrence, and Mayo; mentioned 4 times in despatches; ret. 1881. [illegible] Club, 37 *St. James's St., S.W.*

Mayne *mi.* (Mrs. Hor., E.P.) — ADML. RICHARD CHARLES, C.B. 2nd son of Sir R. M., K.C.B., Chief Commr. of Police; 1846^{3}–1847^{3}; served in the Baltic, Crimea, and New Zealand war; M.P. for Pembroke 1886–92; Comm. H.M.S. 'Eclipse'; author of 'Four Years in British Columbia'; *m.* Sabine, *d.* of Thomas Dent; died May 1892.

Barclay (R.O.) — DAVID. 1845^{3}–1848^{2}; formerly Capt. 16th Lancers.

Dawson (H.D.) — THOMAS. 1845^{3}–1849^{3}.

Cockerell *min.* (J.W.H. & W.A.C.) — ROWLAND VINER. Son of J. C.; 1845^{3}–1848^{3}; E. I. Col. Haileybury; Bengal Civil Service; d ad.

Bright (Miss W., H.M.B.) — R. . 1850.

Martyn (Mrs. Yav.) — REV. WILLIAM WADDON. Of Tonacombe; son of W. W. M. of Tonacombe; 1846^{3}–1849^{3}; Trin. Coll. Oxf. B.A.; Rector of Lifton, Devon, 1863–1900; *m.* Maria Andrew, *d.* of Northmore Herle Pierce Lawrence; died April 15, 1900.

Dymoke (W.J.) — H. L. . 1850.

Moon — 1846^{1}–1849^{3}.

Law (Miss W., W.J.) — W. H. . 1850.

Jemmett (W.J.) — CHARLES EDWARD. Son of W. T. J., Commr. of Bankruptcy at Manchester; 1846^{3}–1849^{3}; Exeter Coll. Oxf. B.A.; Barrister; Revising Barrister for Sussex. *12 Old Square, Lincoln's Inn, W.C.*

Temple (W.J.) — WILLIAM JOHN. Eld. son of W. T. of Bishopstrow House, Warminster; 1846^{3}–1849^{3}; died Dec. 7, 1849.

Packe (Mrs. Yav., E.B.) — VERE. 5th son of Lieut.-Col. H. P. of Twyford Hall, Norfolk; 1847^{2}–1847^{3}; dead.

Pottinger (W.L.E.) — SIR H., Bt. . 1850.

Musgrave (Miss A., H.M.B.) — PHILIP. Eld. son of Sir G. M., 10th Bt., of Edenhall, Langwathb., Cumberland; 1847^{3}–1848^{3}; died May 16, 1859.

Luttrell (Mrs. D., C.J.A., & J.E.Y.) — E. F. . 1850.

Cunliffe (R.O.) — CAPT. ELLIS BROOKE. Eld. son of E. W. C.; 1845^{3}–1848^{3}; formerly Capt. 6th Dragoon Gds.; J.P. for Chester; *m.* Emma Florence, *d.* of Rev. John Sparling of Petton Park. *Petton Park, Shrewsbury.*

Goodlake (W.L.E.) — LIEUT.-COL. GERALD LITTLEHALES, V.C. Son of T. M. G. of Wadley, Berks; 1846^{1}–1848^{3}; Field XI. 1848; Lieut.-Col. Coldstream Gds.; *m.* Margaret, *d.* of R. Ewing Curwen; died April 5, 1890.

Hutchinson (R.F.H., H.M.B.) — LIEUT.-GEN. COOTE SYNGE-. 2nd son of F. S.-H.; 1845^{3}–1848^{3}; formerly Lieut.-Gen. 2nd Dragoon Gds. (Indian med. and clasp); Hon. Col. 19th Hussars; *m.* Emily, *d.* of Charles James Jeeks, and widow of W. Wright-Broughten; died Feb. 13, 1902.

Carlyon (Mrs. P., W.L.E.) — H. . 1850.

King (Mrs. Ro.) — ISAAC. 1845^{3}–1847^{3}; formerly 41st Regt., aft. Capt. and Adj. Surrey Rifle Vol.

Alderson *mi.* (W.J.) — F. J. . 1850.

Burgoyne (W.E., W.J.) — LIEUT.-COL. SIR JOHN MONTAGU, 10th Bt. Son of Sir J. M. B., 9th Bt., of Sutton Park; 1846^{1}–1849^{1}; ent. Gren. Gds. 1850; served in the Crimea and wounded at Alma; ret. Lieut.-Col. 1861; Hon. Col. 3rd Bn. Beds Regt.; J.P. and D.L. co. Bedford, High Sheriff 1868; J.P. co. Camb.; *m.* Amy, *d.* of Capt. Henry Neilson Smith, R.E. *Sutton Park, Sandy.*

Clarke (W.J.) — HENRY LADBROOKE WELLER. Son of H. D. C. of Swakeleys, near Uxbridge; 1846^{3}–1849^{1}; formerly Capt. 23rd Fusiliers; dead.

Johnston *mi.* (W.L.E.) — HARRY. 1846^{1}–1848^{3}.

Seale-Hayne (Home, H.M.B. & J.L.J.) — C. . 1850.

Peyton (R.F.H., H.M.B.) — SIR A. W., Bt. . 1850.

Hogg (R.O.) — SIR STUART SAUNDERS, Kt. 4th son of Rt. Hon. Sir J. W. H., 1st Bt.; 1846^{3}–1847^{3}; E.I. Coll., Haileybury; ent. Indian Civil Service 1853; served in Political Dept. N.W. Provinces; Asst. Commr. in Punjab during time of Mutiny; served as Civil Officer attached to Flying Column under Gen. John Nicholson (mentioned in despatches); transferred to Oude, aft. Magis. and Coll. of Burdwan, Bengal, Inter Chief Comm. of Police and Chmn. of the Municipality, Calcutta; Director of Prov. Bank of Ireland and General Steam Navigation Co.; *m.* Selina Catherine, *d.* of Sir Thomas Erskine Perry. *Villa Céline, Beaulieu-sur-Mer, France.*

Wombwell (Mrs. Yav., W.A.C.) — SIR GEORGE ORBY, 4th Bt. Eld. son of Sir G. W., 3rd Bt.; 1846^{3}–1849^{3}; formerly Cornet 17th Lancers, promoted for gallantry, having taken part in Ba a-clava Charge; ret. 1855; Master of York and Ainsty Hounds for several years; J.P. and D.L. for N. Riding of Yorks, High Sheriff 1861; *m.* Lady Julia Sarah Alice Villiers, *d.* of George Augustus Frederick, 6th Earl of Jersey. *20 Wilton Crescent, S.W., and Newburgh Priory, Easingwold.*

Collins *ma.* (Mrs. P., W.J.) — E. . 1850.

FOURTH FORM.

Egerton (W.A.C.) — SIR P. LE B. GREY- . 1850.

Maskelyne (Mrs. Ro.) — WILLIAM V. 1846^{3}–1849^{3}.

Ede *ma.* (Miss Edw., aft. K.S.) — EDWARD LEE. 1845^{3}–1849^{3}; formerly living in Southampton.

Sir Lionel Smith (W.L.E.) — SIR LIONEL ELDRED (aft. Smith-Gordon), 2nd Bt. Eld. son of Lt.-Gen. Sir L. S., 1st Bt., G.C.B.; 1846^{1}–1848^{3}; formerly Capt. 71st Lt. Infantry; served in Crimea and Indian Mutiny (med. and clasps); *m.* Fanny, *d.* of Thomas Pottinger of Mount Pottinger, Belfast. *Richmond House, Caterham Valley, S.O., Surrey.*

Lindsay (F.E.D.)
COL. SIR ROBERT JAMES (aft. Loyd-Lindsay) (1st and only Lord Wantage), K.C.B., V.C. Of Lockinge House, Wantage; 2nd son of Lieut.-Gen. J. L. of Balcarres, Colinsburgh, co. Fife; 1846^{1}–1850^{1}; Col. Scots Gds.; served in the Crimea; Extra Equerry to H.R.H. Prince of Wales; Brig.-Gen. of Vol.; Lieut.-Col. comm. Vol. Bn. R. Berks Regt.; Hon. Col. London Art. Co.; M.P. for Berks 1865–85; Financial Sec. to War Office 1877–80; Lord-Lieut. of Berks; *m.* Hon. Harriet Sarah Loyd, *d.* of Samuel, 1st and last Lord Overstone; died June 10, 1901.

Sutton (Mrs. Hor., W.L.E.)
F. H. . 1850.

Garden (R.F.H., W.J.)
J. L. . 1850.

Hutton (Mrs. Vav.)
ANTHONY. Of Court Garden, Bucks; son of W. M. H. of Clapham, S.W.; 1844^{3}–1849^{2}; J.P. for Cheshire; *m.* 1st, *d.* of Sir Peter Coats of Auchendrane, co. Ayr; 2nd, Maria Louisa, *d.* of Rev. Frederick Bennett; died 1898.

Theobald (Miss W., aft. K.S.)
J. S. 1850.

Davies *mi.* (R.O.)
OWEN GWYN SAUNDERS. 2nd son of D. A. S. D. of Pentre, Boncath, Pembrokes; 1844^{3}–1847^{2}; Lieut. 38th Regt.; killed in Crimea, June 18, 1855.

Paul *mi.* (J.W.H. & Mrs. Edw., C.L.)
REV. FREDERIC BATEMAN. Son of W. P. of Southleigh, Truro; 1843^{2}–1850^{1}; Univ. Coll. Durham, L.Th.; formerly Rector of Lanivet, Bodmin. *Hoe Villa, 11 Elliot Street, Plymouth.*

Graham
GEORGE BRISCO. 1843^{3}–1848^{3}.

Bassat (Mrs. Vav., W.G.C.)
ARTHUR. Of Tehidy Park, Camborne; 2nd son of J. B. of Tehidy; 1846^{2}–1848^{1}; died. unm. May 7, 1870.

Marquis of Hastings (Miss M.)
PAULYN REGINALD SERLO (3rd Marquis of H.). Eld. son of George Augustus Francis, 2nd Marquis of H.; 1846^{3}–1848^{1}; ent. the Army; died unm. Jan. 17, 1951.

Palk *mi.* (W.G.C.)
W. H. . 1850.

Spearman (W.J.)
ALEXANDER YOUNG. Of Holmer, Hereford; eld. son of Rt. Hon. Sir A. Y. S., 1st Bt., P.C.; 1846^{2}–1848^{2}; J.P. cos. Hereford and Brecon; *m.* 1st, Mary Anne Bertha, *d.* of Sir Joseph Bailey, 1st Bt., of Glanusk; 2nd, Louisa Ann Caroline Amelia, *d.* of Edward Pellew Mainwaring; died Aug. 14, 1865.

Lindsay *mi.* (E.H.P.)
REV. WILLIAM JOHN COUSSMAKER. Son of G. H. L. of Glasnevin, Dublin; 1846^{3}–1849^{1}; Trin. Coll. Dublin, M.A.; Rector of Llanvair since 1872; Rural Dean of Raglan, Newport, Mon.; *m.* Rosamond Emily, *d.* of Frederick Clinton Mundy. *Llanvair Rectory, Abergavenny.*

Reay (Miss Edg., aft. K.S., C.J.A. & J.E.Y.)
T. O. . 1850.

Lord Ennismore (E.H.P.)
WILLIAM HARE (3rd Earl of Listowel), K.P., P.C. Eld. son of William, 2nd Earl of L.; 1846^{3}–1849^{3}; formerly Lieut. Scots Gds.; severely wounded at the Alma (ret. 1856); Lord-in-waiting to Queen Victoria 1880; J.P. co. Cork; Vice-Adm. of the Province of Munster; *m.* Lady Ernestine Mary, *d.* of Ernest Augustus Charles, 3rd Marquis of Ailesbury. *Kingston House, Princes Gate, S.W., and Convamore, Ballyhooly, co. Cork.*

Lord Hervey (E.B.)
F. W. J. (Marquis of Bristol). . 1850.

Sutherland (Mrs. Hor. & Miss G., W.J.)
W. S. . 1850.

Mr. Nelson (R.F.H., H.M.B.)
HON. E. P. . 1850.

Mr. Nevill (C.O.G.)
HON. R. P. . 1850.

Bayley *ma.* (R.O.)
EDWARD HENRY. Son of W. B. B.; 1846^{3}–1847^{2}; Christ's Coll. Camb. B.A.; *m.* Amelia, *d.* of William Emmett; died 1893.

Lord Boyle (E.H.P.)
HENRY BENTINCK (5th Earl of Shannon). Eld. son of Richard, 4th Earl of S.; 1846^{3}–1848^{3}; Hon. Col. 2nd Bgde. S. Irish div. Royal Art.; *m.* Lady Blanche Emma Lascelles, *d.* of Henry, 3rd Earl of Harewood; died Feb. 8, 1890.

Lord Edw. H. Cecil (R.O.)
EDWARD HENRY. 3rd son of Brownlow, 2nd Marquis of Exeter; 1846^{3}–1848^{3}; Comm. R.N.; died Sept. 12, 1862.

Murray (W.A.C.)
CHARLES FREDERICK. Son of W. M., M.P. for Newcastle-under-Lyme; 1847^{1}–1849^{3}; Senior partner in Murray, Hutchins, Stirling & Murray, Solicitors; *m.* Kate Georgiana, *d.* of T. B. Jauquerary Willaume of Chester Terrace, Regent's Park, N.W. *11 Birchin Lane, E.C., and Woodcote Hall, Epsom.*

Farquharson (C.O.G.)
J. R. . 1850.

Caulfeild *mi.* (H.D.)
ALFRED HENRY. 2nd son of St. G. F. C. of Donamon Castle, co. Roscommon; 1847^{1}–1848^{3}; *m.* 1st, Augusta, *d.* of Arthur, 1st Lord Templemore, and widow of Robert Edward, 7th Earl of Kingston; 2nd, Rosamond, *d.* of Thomas Bowker and widow of Lord Alan Spencer Churchill. *Yewden Manor, Henley-on-Thames.*

Godfrey (W.A.C.)
T. S. . 1850.

Wodehouse (E.B.)
E. R. . 1850.

Prodgers (W.J.)
E. . 1850.

Brandreth (Miss Edw. & T.H.S., H.D. & R.D.)
H. . 1850.

Chamberlayne (Miss Edw., H.D.)
DENZIL THOMAS. Eld. son of T. C. of Cranbury Park, Winchester; 1847^{3}–1850^{1}; formerly Capt. 13th Lt. Dragoons; *m.* Frances Selina, *d.* of Thomas Bourke; died April 16, 1873.

Barton (E.B.)
J. H. . 1850.

Irvine (W.J.)
E. T. . 1850.

Dudding *mi.* (Mrs. Ro., W.A.C.)
REV. JOHN. Son of J. D. of Lincoln; 1846^{3}–1847^{2}; Trin. Hall Camb. M.A.; for[illegible] Naughton, Suffolk; [illegible] W[illegible]gborough, Wash[illegible] [illegible], L[illegible]coln.

Hall (Miss Edw., C.J.A.) — SEYMOUR GILBERT. 1846^{3}-1847^{3}.

Vernon (F.E.D.) — THOMAS BOWATER. Of Hanbury Hall, Droitwich; eld. son of T. T. V. of Hanbury Hall; 1846^{3}-1847^{3}; Ch. Ch. Oxf.; formerly Lieut. Queen's Worcester Yeo.; J.P. co. Worc.; died unm. Sept. 22, 1853.

Vane (W.L.E.) — FREDERICK FLETCHER FLETCHER-. 2nd son of Sir F. F.-V., 3rd Bt., of Hutton-in-the-Forest, Penrith; 1846^{3}-1849^{2}; Major 23rd Fusiliers, served in the Crimea and was severely wounded at the Redau; died Dec. 7, 1865.

Hargreaves (Miss Edw., E.H.P.) — CAPT. THOMAS. Of Arborfield Hall, Reading; eld. son of J. H. of Hall Barn, Beaconsfield; 1846^{3}-1848^{3}; Trin. Coll. Camb.; formerly Capt. 3rd Royal Lancs. Militia; Hon. Lieut. R.N.R.; J.P. for Berks. High Sheriff 1867; *m.* Sarah, *d.* of Washington Jackson of Liverpool; died 1891.

King (W.G.C.) — EDWARD RALEIGH. Of Chad's Hunt, Kineton, Warwick; son of E. B. K. of Chad's Hunt; 1846^{3}-1848^{2}; formerly Capt. 4th Lt. Dragoons, aft. Major Warwicks Yeo.; J.P. co. Warwick; *m.* Susanna Octavia, *d.* of Sir John Hesketh Lethbridge, 3rd Bt.; died March 14, 1900.

Harrison (H.D.) — E. SLATER- . 1850.

Jenner (W.G.C.) — E. . 1850.

Johnstone — . 1850.

Bayley *mi.* (J.W.H., aft. K.S., W.J.) — SIR S. C., K.C.S.I., C.I.E. . 1850.

Yonge *min.* (W.G.C., aft. K.S., W.G.C.) — D. N. . 1850.

Mariette *mi.* — J. C. . 1850.

Markham (Miss W., H.D.) — REV. CHARLES WARREN. Son of Lieut.-Col. C. M., 60th Rifles; 1846^{3}-1848^{3}; Magd. Coll. Camb. M.A.; Rector of Aughton, co. Lancaster; *m.* 1st, Margaret, *d.* of John Watson Barton of Stapleton Park, Pontefract; 2nd, Elizabeth Harriett, *d.* of Col. John Barnett; died July 5, 1896.

Earle — EDWARD SEPTIMUS. 1845^{3}-1847^{3}.

Pemberton (Mrs. Ro., C.O.G.) — H. L. . 1850.

Pilcher *mi.* (J.W.H. & W.J., W.J.) — H. D. . 1850.

Buckley *min.* (E.B.) — F. J. . 1850.

Rolt (W.E.) — J. . 1850.

Seymour (W.G.C.) — WILLIAM HENRY. Son of Capt. H. S.; 1844^{3}-1847^{3}; dead.

Blakiston (J.E.Y.) — ARTHUR TYTON. 1845^{3}-1850^{3}; St. John's Coll. Oxf. 58 *Great Pulteney Street, Bath.*

Hatherell (W.L.E.) — LIEUT.-COL. JAMES ABRAHAM. Of Radford House, Leamington; son of Rev. J. W. H., D.D., Vicar of St. James's, West-end, Sonthampton; 1845^{3}-1849^{3}; Major and Hon. Lieut.-Col. 3rd Bn. Royal Scots Fusiliers; J.P. co. Warwick; *m.* Eliza Emily, *d.* of Hon. Charles Lennox Butler; died Dec. 25, 1887.

Knox — G. W. . 1850.

Henning (R.F.H., C.L.) — WILLIAM WALTER. Of Woodhill, Shamley Green, Guildford; son of W. L. H. of Frome Whitfield, Dorchester; 1847^{1}-1849^{3}; Oriel Coll. Oxf.; J.P. for Surrey; died unm. March 3, 1903.

Williams-Bulkeley (W.A.C.) — SIR RICHARD MOSTYN LEWIS, 11th Bt. Of Baron Hill, Beaumaris; eld. son of Sir R. B. W.-B., 10th Bt., of Baron Hill; 1847^{1}-1849^{3}; formerly Capt. Royal Horse Gds.; *m.* 1st, Mary Emily, *d.* of Henry Bingham Baring; 2nd, Margaret Elizabeth, *d.* of Col. Peers Williams of Temple House, Marlow; died Jan. 27, 1884.

Fletcher (E.B.) — PHILIP SHORE. 2nd son of E. C. F. of Kenward, Yalding, Maidstone; 1847^{1}-1847^{2}; formerly a Merch nt in the City; *m.* Lucy, *d.* of J. Pickering of Brighton; died Sept. 30, 1882.

Drummond (H.D.) — VICTOR ARTHUR WELLINGTON, C.B. 4th son of A. R. D. of Cadland, Sonthampton; 1846^{3}-1848^{1}; Ch. Ch. Oxf.; Attaché to Embassy, Paris, 1852; Sec. of Embassy, Vienna, 1882; Min. Res. to King of Bavaria and King of Wurtemberg 1885; Min. Res. at Courts of Munich and Stuttgart since 1890; *m.* Elizabeth, *d.* of Charles Lamson of New York. *British Legation, Munich, Bavaria.*

Athorpe (C.O.G.) — J. . 1850.

Lempriere *ma.* (W.J., W.J. & H.M.B.) — CAPT. AUDLEY. Eld. son of Adml. G. O. L. of Pelham, Hants; 1847^{1}-1849^{1}; R. M. Coll. Sandhurst; Capt. 77th Regt.; served in the Crimea (Ahnn and Inkerman), medal, mentioned in despatches; killed before Sebastopol, April 19, 1855.

Lempriere *mi.* (Miss Edg. & W.J., W.J. & H.M.B.) — A. T. . 1850.

Ashford (E.B.) — W. . 1850.

Starky (W.L.E.) — J. B. . 1850.

Holford (W.A.C.) — J. P. W. (aft. Gwynne-Holford). . 1850.

Hamond (E.B.) — A. . 1850.

Gambier (E.H.P.) — EDWARD PARRY. 1847^{2}-1850^{1}; formerly Madras Engineers, aft. Lieut. R.E.

Thompson (F.E.D.) — P. . 1850.

Crawfurd (W.J.) — J. O. F. . 1850.

Marindin (W.E., E.B.) — H. C. . 1850.

Mr. Amherst (E.B.) — HON. W. A. (Earl Amherst). . 1850.

Vivian (W.J.) — SIR A. P., K.C.B. . 1850.

Hamilton (Mrs. Vav.) — LIEUT.-COL. ROBERT WILLIAM. Of Holyfield Hall, Essex; eld. son of W. J. H., F.R.S., M.P.; 1846^{1}–1850^{1}; Lieut. Col. Gren Gds.; *m.* Charlotte Maria, *d.* of Col. George Palmer of Nazing Park; died Oct. 3, 1883.

Barton *mi.* (W.L.E.) — C. T. H. . 1850.

Tremlett *mi.* (Mrs. Ro., aft. K.S., W.L.E.) — E. J. . 1850.

Collins *mi.* (Mrs. P., W.J.) — C. . 1850.

Parks *mi.* (F.E.D.) — YNYR DEANE HAWTREY. Son of — P. of Woodside, Old Windsor; 1847^{2}–1847^{3}; formerly an Asst. School Master.

Robertson *mi.* (W.A.C.) — J. C. . 1850.

Cristall (Home) — HARRY. 1841^{2}–1849^{3}; formerly a Clerk in Barclay, Bevan & Co.'s London Bank.

Nesfield — WILLIAM EDEN. Eld. son of — N., the eminent Landscape Gardener; 1844^{3}–1849^{3}; an Architect.

Warter — H. DE G. . 1850.

Usborne (J.W.H.) — T. S. . 1850.

Ewart — JOHN WILLIAM CHENEY. Of Loddington Hall, Leicester; 1845^{3}–1847^{3}; Ch. Ch. Oxf.; formerly Lieut. Leic. Yeo.

Cuninghame *ma.* — JOHN WILLIAM HERBERT. Eld. son of J. C. of Lainshaw; 1846^{1}–1849^{3}; Ch. Ch. Oxf.; formerly Capt. 2nd Life Gds.; J.P. co. Ayr; *m.* Emily, *d.* of Major George Graham, Indian Regt. *Lainshaw, Ayr.*

Holt *mi.* (Home, C.J.A.) — HENRY FARQUHAR. Son of R. F. H. of Eton; 1847^{3}–1848^{2}; a Sailor.

Hayne — REV. LEIGHTON GEORGE. Son of Rev. R. H., D.D., of Bradfield, Manningtree; 1845^{2}–1847^{3}; Queen's Coll. Oxf.; Mus. Doc.; Precentor and Organist at Eton 1868–72; Rector of Mistley, Manningtree, 1872–83; *m.* Agnes, *d.* of Lieut.-Col. Pickering, R.A.; died March 3, 1883.

Moore *ma.* — . 1845^{2}–1847^{2}.

UNPLACED.

Mitford *min.* (W.E., aft. K.S., F.E.D.) — A. B. FREEMAN- (Lord Redesdale). . 1850.

Nanney (W.E., W.A.C.) — JOHN, J.P. Of Maes-y-Neuadd, co. Merioneth; son of — N. of Maes-y-Neuadd; 1847^{2}–1850^{1}; died 1868.

Bent *mi.* (Mrs. Ro., aft. K.S., C.J.A. & J.E.Y.) — S. W. . 1850.

Malcolm *mi.* (E.H.P.) — LEONARD NEILL. 2nd son of J. M. of Poltalloch, Lochgilphead; 1847^{3}–1849^{3}; Lieut. Rifle Bgde.; killed at Inkerman Nov. 5, 1854.

Mills (W.L.E.) — R. B. . 1850.

Way (R.F.H., H.D.) — G. A. . 1850.

Thompson (W.E., W.G.C.) — A. D. C. . 1850.

Reeve (R.F.H.) — . 1850.

LOWER SCHOOL.

THIRD FORM.—UPPER GREEK.

Edgar (Miss Edg.) — R. . 1850.

Ede *mi.* (Miss Edw., aft. K.S.) — GEORGE MATTHEWS. 1845^{3}–1847^{3}; formerly living in Southampton.

Shilleto (Mrs. P., H.M.B.) — R. . 1850.

Pryor — J. E. . 1850.

Willats — W. H. . 1850.

Clerk (J.W.H.) — MAJ.-GEN. MALCOLM GEORGE. Eld. son of Rev. D. M. C., Preb. of Warminster; 1844^{1}–1847^{3}; Maj.-Gen. Indian Army (ret.), medal and clasps for relief and defence of Lucknow; *m.* Marietta, *d.* of William Robert Forrest. 3 *Neville Terrace, Onslow Gardens, S.W.*

Yonge *quintus* (W.G.C.) — G. L. . 1850.

Cuninghame *mi.* — R. D. B. . 1850.

Phipps (R.F.H.) — PAUL ANDREW LEWIS. 1847^{1}–1849^{3}; formerly Capt. 90th Lt. Infantry.

Hoare — H. N. (aft. Hamilton-Hoare). . 1850.

LOWER GREEK.

Irby — HON. F. G. H. (Lord Boston). . 1850.

Judd (W.L.E.) — H. J. . 1850.

Watkins — J. G. . 1850.

Graham — JAMES AUGUSTUS. 1846^{3}–1849^{1}.

Mariette *min.* — G. . 1850.

Llewelyn (R.O.) — SIR JOHN TALBOT DILLWYN-, 1st Bt. Son of J. D.-L. of Penllergaer; 1846^{3}–1850^{1}; Ch. Ch. Oxf. M.A.; was Chmn. Qr. Sessions of Glamorgans; aft. Ald. of the C.C.; J.P. and D.L. co. Glamorgan, High Sheriff 1878; J.P. co. Carmarthen; late Capt. 5th Glams. R.V.; M.P. for Swansea 1895–1900; Director Gt. Western Rly.; *m.* Caroline Julia, *d.* of Sir Michael Hicks-Beach, 8th Bt. 39 *Cornwall Gdns., S.W.*, [illegible] *Swansea.*

Jones (W.L.)[illegible] — R. [illegible] . 1850.

Buckley (Miss M., F.E.D.) — C. E. . 1850.

Down — RICHARD WELLESLEY. 1845^{3}–1847^{2}.

SENSE.

Wynne *ma.* — HENRY JOHN LLOYD. Eld. son of J. L. W. of Trofarth and Coed Coch, Abergele, co. Denbigh: 1846^{3}–1849^{3}; Capt. 2nd Life Gds.; died unm. Oct 15, 1874.

Gregson — J. . 1850.

Vidal *ma.* — F. F. . 1850.

Prosser — F. W. . 1850.

Wynne *mi.* — MAJOR-GEN. E. W. . 1850.

Gledstanes (W.L.E.) — W. E. . 1850.

Angelo (Miss A.) — ARTHUR. Son of — A., Fencing-master: 1847^{1}–1848^{1}; formerly Lieut. 74th Highlanders.

Shadwell — LANCELOT ÆMILIUS. 1846^{3}–1849^{2}; formerly an Officer in the 29th Regt.; aft. a Stockbroker in London.

Proby (Miss G., W.A.C.) — HON. W. (Earl of Carysfort). . 1850.

Nugent — WALTER RUTHVEN. 1846^{3}–1849^{2}.

Cookesley *mi.* (W.G.C. & J.E.Y.) — F. J. . 1850.

Moore *mi.* — GEORGE PILCHER. 1845^{3}–1847^{3}.

King-Harman — E. R. . 1850.

NONSENSE.

Pigott (Mrs. Do., H.M.B.) — SIR CHARLES ROBERT, 3rd Bt. Son of Sir T. P., 2nd Bt.: 1846^{3}–1850^{1}: Lieut. 90th Foot; served in the Crimea; wounded before Sebastopol; Crimean med. and clasp and Turkish med. (ret. 1856); aft. in Middlesex Yeo.; J.P. and D.L. for Bucks; *m.* 1st, Mary Louisa, *d.* of Capt. Hallowell Carew, R.N., of Beddington Park, Surrey; 2nd, Margaret Mary Pole, *d.* of Sydney Cosby of Stradbally Hall, Queen's Co., and widow of Capt. John Chidley Coote, 43rd Regt. *Wexham Park, Slough.*

Cleland (J.W.H.) — J. . 1850.

Vidal *mi.* (W.J., J.W.H.) — CHARLES JOHNSON. Son of Rev. F. V. of Sutton Vicarage, Woodbridge: 1846^{3}–1847^{3}: Capt. R.N.: *m.* Margaret Catharine Lascelles-Lloyd; dead.

Maynard — J. M. . 1850.

Lord Powerscourt (J.L.J.) — M. E. (7th Visct. P.) . 1850.

Dymock — F. D. . 1850

SECOND FORM.

Smith — S. H. . 1850.

Fox (F.E.D.) — G. S. F. LANE-. . 1850.

Barton *min.* (W.L.E.) — F. S. . 1850.

FIRST FORM.

Holford — H. P. . 1850.

Mr. Wingfield — HON. M. R. . 1850

Stevens — T. C. . 1850.

INTERMEDIATE LIST.

Names of Boys entered between Election 1897 and 1899, who left Eton before Election 1899 and are therefore not included in the foregoing list.

Loughborough (W.G.C.) — JAMES ALEXANDER, LORD. Eld. son of James Alexander, 3rd Earl of Rosslyn: 1844^{3}–1846^{3}; in the 2nd Life Gds.; died unm. at New Orleans, Dec. 28, 1851.

Turner (Miss A.) — 1844^{3}–1844^{3}.

Tredcroft (Miss M., W.G.C.) — GEORGE. 2nd son of H. T. of Warnham Court, Horsham; 1844^{3}–1847^{1}. 34 *Halsey Street, Lennox Gardens, S.W.*

Hutchinson (R.F.H., H.M.B.) — SIR EDWARD SYNGE-, 4th Bt. Eld. son of F. S.-H. and grandson of Rev. Sir S. S.-H., 3rd Bt., of Castle Sallah, co. Wicklow; 1844^{3}–1846^{3}; formerly Lieut. 5th Dragoon Gds.; served in the Crimea (med. and clasp). *Army and Navy Club, 36 Pall Mall, S.W.*

White (F.E.D.) — HON. HENRY. 2nd son of Henry, 1st Lord Annaly, of Luttrellstown, Clonsilla, co. Dublin; 1844^{3}–1845^{3}; Capt. 68th Foot; died unm. 1860.

Clarke-Jervoise (Mrs. Ri., W.L.E.) — JERVOISE. Eld. son of Sir J. C.-J., 2nd Bt., of Idsworth Park, Horndean, Hants; 1844^{3}–1845^{1}; Major 23rd Fusiliers; served in the Crimea and Indian Mutiny; *m.* Sophia Horatia Churchill, *d.* of Henry Lawes Long of Hampton Lodge, Surrey; died April 22, 1878.

Penruddocke (W.L.E.) — REV. JOHN HUNGERFORD. 2nd son of C. P., Barrister; 1844^{3}–1845^{2}; Clare Hall, Camb. M.A.; formerly Vicar of South Newton, near Salisbury; aft. Rector of Baverstock, Wilts; *m.* Emma, *d.* of John Powys of Crickhowell.

Arkwright (W.E., C.O.G.) — ARTHUR WILLIAM. Son of Rev. J. A. of Mark Hall, Harlow, Essex; 1841^{3}-1845^{1}; J.P. and D.L. co. Leicester; *m.* Emma, *d.* of William John Wolley of Beeston, Nottingham. 107 *Oakwood Court, Kensington, W.*

Bullock (W.G.C.) — GEORGE (aft. TROYTE-BULLOCK) (aft. Troyte-Chafyn-Grove). Son of G. B. of North Coker; 1844^{3}-1845^{2}; Ch. Ch. Oxf.; J.P. and D.L. for cos. Somerset and Dorset; High Sheriff 1888; J.P. for Wilts; *m.* 1st, Emily Lucy, *d.* of Henry William Berkeley Portman; 2nd, Alice, *d.* of Sir Glynne Earle Welby-Gregory, 3rd Bt. *North Coker House, Yeovil.*

Evered (Miss M., H.M.B.) — ANDREW ROBERT GUY. Eld. son of R. G. E. of Hill House: 1845^{1}-1846^{1}; formerly Capt. 54th Regt.; J.P. for Somerset; *m.* Emily Louisa, *d.* of Rev. Henry Townend, Rector of Lifton, Devon. *Hill House, Bridgwater.*

Coote (C.O.G.) — EYRE. Of West Park, Damerham, Salisbury; son of E. C. of West Park; 1844^{3}-1845^{2}; formerly in the 11th Hussars, aft. Lieut. Wilts Yeo.; *m.* Jessie Mary, *d.* of Gen. Henry Lechmere Worrall, I.C.S., of The Cottage, Clifton; died at Ischl in Austria, Aug. 23, 1864.

Barton (F.E.D.) — THOMAS ERSKINE. Of Glendalough House, Greystones; eld. son of T. J. B. of Glendalough; 1844^{3}-1846^{2}; died unm. 1874.

Antrobus (R.O.) — JOHN EDWARD. 4th son of Sir E. A., 2nd Bt., of Amesbury Abbey, Salisbury; 1844^{3}-1845^{1}; died April 21, 1845, at Cheam, Sutton, Surrey.

Rocheid (W.A.C.) — CHARLES FREDERICK. 1844^{3}-1845^{3}; formerly an Officer in the Prussian service.

Venables (W.A.C.) — HENRY PARES. 1844^{3}-1847^{1}; formerly Govt. Inspector of Schools in Australia.

Battiscombe (R.F.H., C.O.G.) — REAR-ADMIRAL ALBERT HENRY WILLIAM. Son of Rev. R. B. of Hactons, Upminster, Romford; 1844^{3}-1845^{3}; Rear-Adml. in the Navy (ret.). *Eastwood, Weston-super-Mare.*

Low (Mrs. D.) — HENRY JOHN REVELL. Son of Major J. H. L. of the Indian Army and Lowville, co. Galway; 1844^{3}-1846^{1}; Capt. 40th Bengal Lt. Infantry; served throughout the Burmese war and with the Turkish contingent at Sebastopol; *m.* 1st, Hon. Juliet Sugden, *d.* of Edward Burtenshaw, 1st Lord St. Leonards, and widow of Kennett Dickson; 2nd, Juliana Mary, *d.* of Rev. Ellis Walford, Rector of Dallinghoo, Wickham Market, Suffolk; killed in a carriage accident at Barnard Castle, 1901.

Gilly (R.F.H., H.M.B.) — FREDERICK DAWSON. Son of Rev. Canon G. of Durham: 1844^{3}-1846^{2}; formerly in the Home Office.

Swinfen (R.F.H., F.E.D.) — FREDERICK HAY. 1844^{3}-1846^{2}; formerly Major 5th Dragoon Gds.; wounded at Balaclava.

White (Mrs. Ro., F.E.D.) — FRANCIS (aft. Popham). Of Shanklin and Wotton Lodge, Isle of Wight; son of Rev. R. W. W., Rector of Wotton; 1844^{3}-1845^{3}; Univ. Coll. Oxf. M.A.; J.P. for Hants and D.L. for Isle of Wight; *m.* Margaret Emma, *d.* of Rev. Nathan Hubbersty of Wirksworth, co. Derby; died Feb. 18, 1894.

Stonehewer (R.F.H., H.M.B.) — WILLIAM SCOTT. Of Brighton; 1844^{3}-1845^{1}; formerly a Farmer near Shoreham.

Prendergast (Miss M., E.H.P.) — REYNOLDS STEPHEN JAMES. Son of G. L. P.; 1845^{1}-1846^{2}; Capt. 2nd Madras Lt. Cav.; died Aug. 18, 1887.

Ashworth (Miss M., C.O.G.) — THOMAS RAMSDEN. 1845^{1}-1847^{1}; Jesus Coll. Camb.

Smith (Mrs. Ri., W.G.C.) — HENRY. 1845^{1}-1847^{1}.

Jelly (Mrs. Vav., W.L.E.) — REV. HARRY RICHARDSON. 1845^{1}-1846^{2}.

Mr. Brownlow (W.G.C.) — HON. CHARLES (2nd Lord Lurgan). 1842^{3}-1842^{3} (see Intermediate List 1814); 2nd entry 1845^{1}-1846^{3}; formerly in the 43rd Regt.; Lord-Lieut. co. Armagh; Lord-in-Waiting to Queen Victoria; *m.* Hon. Emily Anne Browne, *d.* of John Cavendish, 3rd Lord Kilmaine; died Jan. 15, 1852.

Maxse (Mrs. Vav., W.A.C.) — LIEUT.-COL. SIR HENRY FITZHARDINGE BERKELEY, K.C.M.G. Son of J. M.; 1845^{1}-1846^{3}; Lieut.-Col. Coldstream Gds.; served in the Crimea, aft. Gov. of Heligoland and later Gov. of Newfoundland; *m.* Augusta, *d.* of Herr von Rudloff, of Austria; died 1883.

Goodlake (W.L.E.) — EDWARD WALLACE. Son of T. M. G. of Wadley, Berks; 1845^{1}-1847^{1}; Ball. Coll. Oxf.; Barrister; Stipendiary Mag. in the Falkland Islands; *m.* Cecilia, *d.* of Comm. C. Ellice, R.N.; died Nov. 1881.

Puxley (C.O.G.) — JOHN SIMON LAVALLIN. Of Dunboy Castle, Berehaven, co. Cork; eld. son of J. L. P. of Dunboy; 1845^{1}-1846^{3}; B.N.C., Oxf.; Capt. 6th Dragoons; died at Cheltenham, 1869.

Aldridge (W.L.E.) — JOHN. Of St. Leonard's Forest, Horsham, eld. son of R. A. of St. Leonard's Forest; 1845^{1}-1847^{1}; Major Royal Scots Fusiliers and Col. Comm. 3rd and 4th Bns. Royal Sussex Regt.; J.P. and D.L. for Sussex; *m.* Mary Alethea, *d.* of Samuel Matthews, and widow of Thomas Broadwood of Holmbush, Sussex; died Feb. 23, 1888.

Starkie (Miss Edw., H.M.B.) — JOHN PIERCE CHAMBERLAIN, LL.B. Of Ashton Hall, co. Lancaster; 2nd son of Le G. N. S. of Huntroyde, Burnley; 1845^{1}-1846^{2}; Trin. Hall Camb. B.A.; M.P. for North-East Lancs. 1868-80; J.P. co. Lancaster; *m.* Anne Charlotte Amelia, *d.* of Harrington George Frederic Hudson of Bessingby, co. York; died June 12, 1888.

Kaye (E.B.) — JAMES. Of Potter's Bar, Middlesex; son of W. K., formerly of Ampney, Cirencester, aft. of Tetworth Hall, Sandy, Beds; 1845^{1}-1846^{3}; Univ. Coll. Oxf.; Barrister, Middle Temple: practising at the Chancery Bar; *m.* Elizabeth, *d.* of Rev. Levett Edward Thoroton; died June 30, 1886.

STEPHENSON SIMON. 1845^{1}-1846^{3}.

Bristowe (Mrs. P., H.M.B.)

Mr. Plunkett (Mrs. Ri., W.G.C.) — HON. RANDAL PERCY OTWAY (13th Lord Louth). Eld. son of Thomas Oliver, 12th Lord L.; 1845^{1}-1845^{1}; formerly in 79th Regt.; *m.* 1st, Anne Maria MacGeough, *d.* of Walter MacGeough Bond of Drumsill, co. Armagh; 2nd, Elizabeth Lily, *d.* of John Black of Ceylon; died July 19, 1883.

Rhodes (Mrs. Ri., H.M.B.) — FREDERICK RHODES. 1845^{1}-1846^{2}; formerly Capt. 98th Regt.

Smith (Miss A., E.H.P.) — NORBORNE GILPIN. 1845^{1}-1847^{1}; formerly Paymaster 17th Regt.

Townshend *ma.* — JOHN VILLIERS STUART (5th Marquis Townshend). Eld. son of John, 4th Marquis T.; 1845^{1}-1845^{3}; in Foreign Office 1850-4; M.P. for Tamworth 1856-63; J.P. and D.L. Norfolk and Middlesex; High Steward of Tamworth; *m.* Lady Anne Elizabeth Clementina Duff, *d.* of James 5th Earl of Fife; died Oct. 26, 1899.

Townshend *mi.* — LORD JAMES DUDLEY BROWNLOW STUART. 2nd son of John, 4th Marquis Townshend; 1845^{3}–1846^{2}; in the Navy; killed by a fall from the mast, Aug. 11, 1846.

Boileau (W.G.C.) — EDMUND WILLIAM POLLEN. 3rd son of Sir J. P. B., 1st Bt.; 1845^{2}–1845^{3}; *m.* Bridget, *d.* of James Walsh; was drowned in Corio Bay, July 9, 1881.

Basset (Mrs. Vav., W.A.C.) — JOHN FRANCIS. Of Tehidy Park, Camborne; eld. son of J. B. of Tehidy; 1845^{3}–1846^{3}; *m.* Hon. Emily Henrietta Vereker, *d.* of John Prendergast, 2nd Visct. Gort; died Feb. 9, 1869.

Lloyd-Mostyn (Mrs. Vav., W.A.C.) — LIEUT.-COL. HON. ROGER. 2nd son of Edward, 2nd Lord Mostyn; 1845^{3}–1846^{2}; formerly Lieut.-Col. Scots Gds.; *m.* Adeline Frances Brereton, *d.* of James Ashley; died Feb. 27, 1899.

Devon (H.M.B.) — FREDERICK WILLIAM. 1845^{2}–1845^{3}; went to Harrow.

Hurt (Miss Edw., F.E.D.) — FRANCIS RICHARD. Eld. son of F. H. of Alderwasley, Wirksworth, co. Derby; 1845^{3}–1846^{3}; Lieut. 34th Foot; killed at the attack on the Redan, Sebastopol, June 18, 1855.

Miller (Mrs. Ri., C.O.G.) — MAJOR THOMAS EDMUND. 3rd son of Rev. Sir T. C. M., 6th Bt., Vicar of Froyle, Alton, Hants; 1845^{3}–1847^{1}; served with 12th Regt. in Zulu war (med.); ret. 16 *Brockman Road, Folkestone.*

Mirehouse (E.H.P.) — EVELYN. 2nd son of J. C. M. of Brownslade and Angle, Pembroke; 1845^{3}–1847^{1}; Capt. 71st Highlanders; J.P. co. Pembroke; died at Brighton from the effects of an accident, 1862.

Willes (W.E., C.J.A.) — AUGUSTUS. Son of E. W. of Newbold Comyn, co. Warwick; 1845^{3}–1847^{1}; Officer in 2nd European Fusiliers, Indian Army, 1859; ret. Major in 104th Foot, 1870; died 1896.

Stoddart — GEORGE. Son of Rev. G. H. S. of Eton, Editor of sundry Elementary Latin Books; 1845^{3}–1846^{1}.

Wilberforce (E.C.) — HERBERT WILLIAM. Eld. son of Rt. Rev. S. W., Bishop of Winchester; 1845^{3}–1846^{1}; Lieut. R.N.; died at Torquay, Feb. 20, 1856, on his return from the Baltic.

Browning — OSCAR. 1845^{3}–1845^{3}; entered again 1851^{1}.

Roberts (Mrs. Ro., J.E.Y.) — FIELD-MARSHAL FREDERICK SLEIGH (1st Earl Roberts), K.G., P.C., K.P., G.C.B., G.C.S.I., G.C.I.E., V.C., D.C.L., LL.D., Lit.D., Order of Merit. 2nd son of Gen. Sir A. R., G.C.B., of the Indian Army; 1845^{3}–1846^{2}; R.M. Coll. Sandhurst and Addiscombe; 2nd Lieut. Bengal Art. 1851; Lieut. 1857; Capt. 1860; Bre. Maj. 1860; Brev. Lieut.-Col. 1868; Brev. Col. 1875; Maj.-Gen. 1878; Lieut.-Gen. 1883; Gen. 1890; Field-Marshal 1895; D.A.Q.M.G. throughout Indian Mutiny; A.Q.M.G. (Bengal) 1863–8; 1st A.Q.M.G. 1869–72; D.Q.M.G. 1872–5; Q.M.G. in India 1875–8; Comm. Kuram Field Force Nov. 1878 to Sept. 1879; Comm. Kabul F.F. Sept. 1879 to April 1880; Comm. Kabul-Kandahar F.F. Aug.–Sept. 1880; Comm. in S. Afghanistan Sept.–Oct. 1880; Comm.-in-Chief (Madras) Nov. 1881 to Aug. 1885; Comm.-in-Chief in India Nov. 1885 to April 1893; Comm. of Forces in Ireland 1895–9; served throughout siege and capture of Delhi (wounded July 14, horse shot Sept. 14, 1857); actions of Bulandshahr (horse shot), Aligarh, Agra, Kanauj (horse wounded), and Bantharra; throughout operations connected with relief of Lucknow; battle [illegible] in defeat of Gwalior [illegible], action of Khudaganj and reoccupation of Fatgarh; storming of

Roberts—*cont.* Mianganj; operations connected with siege of Lucknow; storming of Laloo; capture of Umbeyla and destruction of Malka; Abyssinian expedition 1867–8; Lushai expedition 1871–2; capture of Kholel villages and attack on Murtlang range; Comm. Kuram F.F. at capture of Peiwar Kotal; reconnaissance to summit of the Shutargardan Pass; attack by Mongols in Sapari Pass; occupation of Khost and reconnaissance up Kuram river; Comm. Kabul F.F. at battle of Charasia; capture of city of Kabul, and throughout operations in and around Sherpur between Dec. 8 and 24, 1879; Comm. Kabul–Kandahar F.F. specially detailed to proceed from Kabul to relief of Kandahar, and Southern Afghanistan F.F. at battle of Kandahar, Sept. 1, 1880; Comm. army, Burma 1886; Mutiny med. with clasps for Delhi, relief of Lucknow and siege of Lucknow; Indian Frontier med. with clasps for Umbeyla, Lushai, and Burma; Abyssinian med.; Afghan War med., with clasps for Peiwar Kotal, Charasia, Sherpur, and Kandahar; Kabul-Kandahar bronze star; received thanks of both Houses of Parliament Aug. 4, 1879, and May 5, 1881; thanked on several occasions by Govt. of India, and mentioned twenty-three times in despatches before the campaign in Afghanistan; Comm.-in-Chief South Africa, 1899–1900; relieved Kimberley Feb. 1900; took Comm. Cronje and the Western Army prisoners Feb. 27, 1900; Comm.-in-Chief since Oct. 1901; D.C.L. Oxford 1881; LL.D. Dublin 1880, Camb. 1893, and Edinburgh 1893; D.C.L. Durham 1903; Freedom of London, Edinburgh, Glasgow, Newcastle-on-Tyne, Dundee, Waterford, Cardiff, and Chesterfield, and Royal Boroughs of Inverness, Wick, Windsor, and Dunbar; Col. Irish Gds.; Col. Comm. R. Art.; Hon. Col. City of London Imp. Vol.; Hon. Col. 3rd Bn. Sherwood Foresters, the Waterford Art. (Militia), 3rd Bn. Loyal N. Lancs Regt., 2nd Vol. Bn. Gloucestershire Regt., 10th Vol. Bn. King's Royal Rifle Corps, 1st Newcastle-on-Tyne Art. Vol., 2nd Hants Vol. Art., and Royal Canadian Art.; Knt. of Justice of Order of St. John of Jerusalem; has the Prussian Order of the Black Eagle; *m.* Nora Henrietta, *d.* of Capt. John Bews, 73rd Foot. 47 *Portland Place, W.*

Elphinstone (H.M.B.) — HON. EDWARD CHARLES BULLER-FULLERTON-[illegible]. 2nd son of Lieut.-Col. J. D. B.-F.-E.; 1845^{3}–1846^{1}; formerly Capt. 92nd Highlanders; *m.* Elizabeth Harriette, *d.* of Rt. Hon. Sir George Clerk 7th Bt., of Penicuik. *Inveresk Lodge, Musselburgh.*

Brandling (E.H.P.) — CHARLES. 1845^{3}–1847^{1}; formerly in the Foot Gds.

Knapp (Mrs. Vav.) — MATTHEW GRENVILLE SAMWELL. Of Little Linford, Newport Pagnell; son of M. K. of Linford; 1845^{3}–1846^{3}; J.P. for Bucks and Northants; D.L. for Bucks; *m.* Catharine Eliza Spottiswoode, *d.* of Capt. Robert Robertson Bruce of the Bengal H. Art.; died 1896.

Mr. Eliot (W.A.C.) — HON. HENRY CORNWALLIS (5th Earl of St. Germans). 5th son of Edward Granville, 3rd Earl of St. G., of Port Eliot; 1845^{3}–1847^{1}; served in the R.N. 1848–53; Foreign Office 1855–81; J.P. and D.L. for Cornwall; *m.* Hon. Emily Harriet Labouchere, *d.* of Henry, 1st and last Lord Taunton. *Port Eliot, St. Germans, R.S.O., Cornwall,* and 13 *Grosvenor Gardens, S.W.*

St. Clair-Erskine (W.G.C.)
HON. ROBERT FRANCIS (4th Earl of Rosslyn), P.C. 2nd son of James Alexander, 3rd Earl of R.; 1846^{1}–1847^{1}; Merton Coll. Oxf. M.A.; Capt. Hon. Corps of Gentlemen-at-Arms; H.M. High Commr. 1874 and 1878–80 to the Gen. Assembly of Church of Scotland, and H.M. special Ambassador at marriage of King of Spain, 1878: *m.* Blanche Adeliza, *d.* of Henry Fitzroy of Salcey Lawn, Northampton, and widow of Hon. Charles Maynard; died Sept. 6, 1890.

Robbins (W.G.C.)
REV. JOHN, D.D., F.S.A. Son of J. R. of Batramsley, Hants: 1846^{1}–1847^{1}; Ch. Ch. Oxf. M.A., D.D.; formerly British Chaplain at Wiesbaden: *m.* Annie Dunbar, *d.* of Samuel Abbot. 14 *Norfolk Sq., Hyde Park, W.*

Porter (J.E.Y.)
REV. REGINALD. Son of — P. of Winslade, Devon: 1846^{1}–1846^{2}; Exeter Coll. Oxf. and Cuddesdon Theo. Coll.: formerly Rector of Kenn, Exeter; *m.* Miss Hole; dead.

Dudley (H.D.)
WILLIAM HORACE. 1846^{1}–1846^{3}.

Parr (Miss Edg., F.E.D.)
JOHN. 1846^{1}–1846^{2}.

Stephens (R.F.H., C.L.)
CAPT. HENRY EUSEBY, R.N. 3rd son of Rev. R. S., D.D., Vicar of Belgrave-cum-Birstall, Leicester; 1846^{3}–1847^{1}; Capt. R.N. (ret.). *Army and Navy Club, 36 Pall Mall, S.W.*

Mr. O'Grady (W.G.C.)
1846^{3}–1846^{3}.

King (Mrs. Ro., W.A.C.)
WILLIAM. 1846^{3}–1846^{3}.

Ramsden (H.D.)
JOHN CHARLES FRANCIS. Son of H.J.R. of Oxton Hall, co. York; 1846^{3}–1846^{3}; formerly Capt. Royal Art.; served in Crimea (med. and clasp for Sebastopol) and in Indian Mutiny (med. and clasp for Lucknow): J.P., D.L. and C. Ald. for Surrey; D.L. for W. Riding of Yorks; *m.* Emma Susan, *d.* of Rev. Edward Duncombe, Rector of Barthomley, Crewe, and widow of Ellis Gosling of Busbridge Hall, Godalming. *Willinghurst, Guildford.*

Bethell
HENRY SLINGSBY. Eld. son of J. B.; 1846^{3}–1847^{1}; *m.* Minnie, *d.* of Rev. Arthur Maclaine.

Stanley *ma.* (Miss Edg.)
AUGUSTUS GEORGE. 1846^{3}–1846^{3}.

Stanley *mi.* (Miss Edg.)
WILLIAM HENRY. 1846^{3}–1847^{1}.

Stanley *min.* (Miss Edg.)
HORACE. 1846^{3}–1847^{1}.

Joy (Miss Edg., W.J.)
ALGERNON PURLING. Son of H. H. J., Q.C., of Inner Temple, and Hartham Park, Wilts; 1846^{3}–1847^{1}; R.M. Academy, Woolwich; formerly in the Royal Art.; aft. a Civil Engineer; *m.* Janet Mary, *d.* of John Marshall, and widow of Stair Douglas. 20 *Wilton Place, S.W.*

Baillie (W.G.C.)
COL. JAMES WILLIAM. Son of D. B. of 14 Belgrave Square, S.W.; 1846^{3}–1846^{3}; served with the Royal H. Gds. in the Crimea; Crimean and Turkish meds.; Col. Leicesters Imp. Yeo.; J.P. co. Leicester; *m.* Elizabeth Florence, *d.* of Frederick R. Magenis. *Ilston Grange, Leicester.*

Berrington (C.O.G.)
ARTHUR VENDIGAID DAVIES. Son of J. D. B. of Woodland Castle, co. Glamorgan; 1846^{3}–1846^{3}; Exeter Coll. Oxf.; J.P. and D.L. cos. Glamorgan and Monmouth; High Sheriff 1868; formerly Chmn. of Qr. Sessions for co. Monmouth; Assist. Sec. to the Board of Trade for Fisheries Dep., and Chief Inspector of Fisheries for England and Wales; *m.* 1st, Frances Lennox Heneage, *d.* of Rev. Charles Lane, Rector of Wrotham, Kent; 2nd, Ada Barbara, *d.* of John Lane of Leyton Grange, Essex. *Pant-y-Goitre, Abergavenny.*

Wykeham-Martin (W.A.C.)
CORNWALLIS. Of The Hill, Purton, Swindon, Wilts; 2nd son of C. W.-M. of Leeds Castle, Maidstone; 1846^{3}–1846^{3}; Lieut. R.N. 1846–61; served in the Baltic during the Crimean war (med.); J.P. for Wilts; *m.* Anne Katherine, *d.* of John Etherington Welch Rolls of the Hendre, Monmouth; died April 28, 1903.

WILLIAM. 1846^{3}–1847^{1}; formerly a Lieut. in the R.N.

Howorth (Miss Edg., W.J.)

Sandeman (W.L.E.)
ALBERT GEORGE. Eld. son of G. G. S. of Westfield, Hayling Island, Havant; 1847^{1}–1847^{1}; one of H.M.'s Lieuts. for City of London; D.L. for co. London; High Sheriff of Surrey 1872; Gov. of the Bank of England 1895–7; Pres. of the London Chamber of Commerce 1898; formerly Major 21st Middlesex R.V.; a commendador of the Order of Christ of Portugal and Grand Cross of the Royal Mil. Order of our Lady of the Conception of Villa Viçosa; Commr. of Income Tax, City of London; J.P. for Herts; Merchant; *m.* Maria Carlota Perpetua de Moraes Sarmento, *d.* of Viscount da Torre de Moncorvo, Portuguese Ambassador in England. *Presdales, Ware, and 20 St. Swithin's Lane, E.C.*

ELECTION, 1850.

SIXTH FORM.

Ridler (Miss E.lg., aft. K.S., J.E.Y.)

WILLIAM EDWARD. Son of W. R., Banker of Cheltenham; 1845^{3}–1850^{2}; Newc. Select 1848–50; King's Coll. Camb. M.A.; Fellow of King's and a Classical Examiner at Degree Exams.; died 1860.

Drake (Miss M., aft. K.S., E.C.)

HENRY. 1843^{3}–1850^{3}; Newc. Select 1849–50; Eton XI. 1850; Coll. Wall 1848–9; formerly Barrister, Norfolk circuit.

Whitting *ma.* (R.F.H., aft K.S., E.H.P.)

REV. WILLIAM HENRY. Son of W. W. of Thorney Abbey, co. Camb.; 1845^{3}–1851^{1}; Coll. Wall 1849–50; Sch. of King's Coll. Camb. M.A.; Fellow of King's; formerly Vicar of Broad Chalk, Salisbury; aft. Rector of Stour Provost, Gillingham, Dorset; *m.* Elizabeth Frances, *d.* of Rev. F. Le Grice; died at Bournemouth, Sept. 1896.

Moody (Mrs. P., aft. K.S., C.O.G.)

HARRY. Son of Rev. H. R. M., Rector of Chartham, Canterbury, and Hon. Canon of Canterbury; 1843^{3}–1851^{1}; Newc. Select 1851; Coll. Cricket and Football XI.'s; Coll. Wall XI. 1849–50; Pres. Eton Soc. 1850; King's Coll. Camb. M.A.; Fellow of King's; Capt. Oxf. Militia 1857–66; various staff appointments, Canada and Trinidad; Sec. in London of Canadian Pacific Railway; *m.* Florence, *d.* of Hon. Nevile Parker, Master of the Rolls. *Fleet, R.S.O., Hants.*

Wayte (Miss W., aft. K.S., F.E.D.)

REV. GEORGE HODGSON. Son of W. W. of Highlands, Calne; 1842^{3}–1851^{1}; Newc. Select 1851; King's Coll. Camb. M.A.; Fellow of King's; Private Chaplain to G. Inge of Thorpe, Staffs; *m.* Annie, *d.* of Sir Joseph Paxton, M.P.; died in the Tyrol, Dec. 28, 1881.

Forshall (C.J.A., aft. K.S., C.J.A.)

EDWARD VAUGHAN. 1844^{3}–1851^{2}; Exeter Coll. Oxf.; aft. Christ's Coll. Camb. M.A.; Assist. Master at Rossall 1856–63; aft. Master at the Royal School, Armagh; died June 2, 1891.

Thackeray (R.F.H., aft. K.S., E.B.)

LIEUT.-COL. CHARLES. Son of F. T., M.D., of Camb.; 1843^{4}–1851^{3}; Eton XI. 1849–51; Capt. 1851; Coll. Wall 1849–50; Keeper of Upper Club 1849–50; Emmanuel Coll. Camb. B.A.; Lieut.-Col. 28th N. Gloucester Regt.; J.P. for Essex; *m.* Katharine Minnie Elise, *d.* of Richard P. Drew. *Chapple, Earl's Colne, R.S.O., Essex.*

Coleridge *ma.* (E.C., aft. K.S., E.C.)

REV. ALFRED JAMES. Son of E. C. of Eton and Mapledurham, Reading; 1843^{3}–1851^{3}; Newc. Select 1851; Eton XI. 1850–1; Coll. Wall 1847–50; Univ. Coll. Oxf.; Demy. of Magd. Coll.; 2nd Cl. Class. Mods. 1853; formerly Rector of Rokeby, Yorks; *m.* Agnes, *d.* of Rev. Philip Henry Nind of Woodcote, Reading; dead.

Goodall (K.S., J.E.Y.)

REV. WILLIAM. Son of W. G. of London; 1841^{3}–1851^{3}; Coll. Wall 1849–50; Clare Coll. Camb. B.A.; formerly Curate of Middleton, Manchester; Vicar of Woodside since 1876; *m.* Harriette, *d.* of John Walker. *Woodside Vicarage, Horsforth, Leeds.*

Wollaston (R.F.H., aft. K.S., C.J.A. & C.Wo.)

REV. CANON WILLIAM MONRO. 6th son of H. S. H. W.; 1844^{3}–$185.^{3}$; Newc. Select 1851; Tomline Select 1851; Coll. Wall 1847–50, Keeper 1850; Sch. of Trin. Coll. Oxf. 1851–5; M.A.; 1st Cl. Class. Mods. 1853; 1st Class Lit. Hum. 1855; Fellow of Exeter Coll. Oxf. 1855–64; Conduct at Eton 1863; formerly Tutor of Exeter Coll. and Vicar of Merton, co. Oxf., aft. Chaplain of St. Paul's, Cannes, and Canon of Gibraltar; *m.* 1st, Constance Sophia, *d.* of James MacGregor of Merton; 2nd, Mary Arabella, *d.* of Rev. William Brodie. *Villa des Cygnes, Cannes, and 3 The Common, Chislehurst.*

Coltman (E.C.)

FRANCIS JOSEPH. Son of Sir T. C., Judge of the Court of Common Pleas; 1843^{1}–1850^{3}; Tomline Prizeman 1848; Newc. Select 1850; Eton XI. 1850; Field XI. 1848–9, Keeper 1849; Opp. Wall 1849; Sch. of Trin. Coll. Camb.; 22nd Wrangler and 2nd Cl. Class. 1854; Barrister. 9 *Atherstone Terrace, Gloucester Road, S.W.*

Herbert (E.C.)

SIR ROBERT GEORGE WYNDHAM, G.C.B., D.C.L., LL.D., J.P., D.L. Eld. son of Hon. A. H., Barrister; 1844^{3}–1850^{3}; Newc. Select 1849, Sch. 1850; Sch. of Ball. Coll. Oxf. D.C.L.; 1st Cl. Mods. 1852; Hertford, Ireland, and Eldon Sch.; Chanc. Latin Verse Prize 1852; Fellow of All Souls' Coll. 1854; Private Sec. to W. E. Gladstone, Chanc. of the Exchequer, 1855; Barrister, Inner Temple, 1858; Colonial Sec. Queensland 1859; Member of Legislative Assembly and Premier of Queensland 1860–5; Assist. Sec. Board of Trade 1868; Assist. Under-Sec. Colonial Office 1870; Permanent Under-Sec. of State for the Colonies 1871–92; Agent-Gen. for Tasmania 1893–6; High Sheriff of London 1899; Knt. (1st Class) of the Order of the Crown of Johore; Chanc. of the Order of St. Michael and St. George since 1892. 3 *Whitehall Court, S.W., and Ickleton, Great Chesterford, Essex.*

Nind (E.C.)

PHILIP HENRY. Of Lashlake House, Thame; eld. son of Rev. P. H. N. of Woodcote House, and Vicar of Southstoke and Woodcote, Reading; 1844^{1}–1850^{3}; Eton VIII. 1850; Opp. Wall 1849–50, Keeper 1850; Pres. Eton Soc. 1850; Ch. Ch. Oxf. M.A.; in the Oxf. VIII. 1852–5; won Stewards' Cup at Henley 1853 and 1855 in Oxf. IV.; sometime Gold Commissioner in Vancouver Island, British Columbia; *m.* Elizabeth Frances, *d.* of J. Sivewright; died at Thame, Mar. 8, 1896.

Snowden (F.E.D.)
REV. CANON EDMUND. Son of J. S.; 1843^{3}–1850^{3}; Univ. Coll. Oxf. B.A.; Rector of Kirkby Overblow, Pannal, Yorks, and Hon. Canon of Wakefield; *m. d.* of Preb. Toogood; died 1894.

Martin (Mrs. Hor., E.B.)
REV. HENRY ARTHUR. 2nd son of Rev. Canon G. M.; Chanc. of the Diocese of Exeter and Vicar of Harberton, Totnes; 1845^{1}–1850^{3}; Tomline Select 1849–50; Ch. Ch. Oxf. M.A.; Vicar of Laxton, Newark, 1858–98. *Tintern House, Abbey Road, Gt. Malvern.*

Bosanquet (Mrs. Hor., E.B.)
SAMUEL COURTHOPE. Eld. son of S. R. B. of Forest House and Dingestow Court, Monmouth; 1845^{1}–1850^{3}; Tomline Prizeman 1849; Newc. Select 1849–50; Ch. Ch. Oxf. M.A.; 1st Cl. Math. Mods., 2nd Cl. Mods. 1852; 1st Cl. Math., 2nd Cl. Lit. Hum. 1854; Senior Math. Sch. and Johnson's Math. Sch. 1855; Barrister; J.P., D.L., and Chmn. of Qr. Sessions for co. Monmouth, High Sheriff 1898; *m.* Mary, *d.* of John Arkwright of Hampton Court, Hereford. *Dingestow Court, Monmouth.*

Lambton *ma.* (C.L.)
MAJOR-GEN. FREDERICK WILLIAM. 2nd son of W. H. L. of Biddick Hall, Durham; 1845^{3}–1850^{3}; Prince Consort's German Prize 1850; Opp. Wall and Field XI.'s 185 ; served with the 71st Highland Lt. Infantry in the Crimea and Indian Mutiny; ret. Maj.-Gen. after 32 years' service; died, unm. May 1, 1901.

Rous (H.M.B.)
WILLIAM JOHN. Son of W. R. R. of Worstead; 1845^{3}–1851^{2}; formerly Lieut.-Col. Scots Gds.; served in the Crimea, 1854 (med. with clasp and Turkish med.). *Worstead House, Norwich.*

Lord Grey de Wilton (H.M.B.)
ARTHUR EDWARD HOLLAND GREY (3rd Earl of Wilton). Eld. son of Thomas Grosvenor, 2nd Earl of W.; 1845^{3}–1850^{3}; Prince Consort's French prize 1848; Lieut. 1st Life Gds. 1854–9; Hon. Col. 5th Bn. Prince Consort's Rifle Bgde.; Hon. Col. Duke of Lancaster's Yeo. Cav.; M.P. successively for Weymouth and Bath; *m.* Lady Elizabeth Charlotte Louisa Craven, *d.* of William, 2nd Earl of Craven; died Jan. 18, 1885.

Cotton (E.B.)
REV. ARTHUR BENJAMIN. Son of W. C. of Leytonstone, Essex; 1845^{3}–1850^{3}; Tomline Prizeman 1850; Ch. Ch. Oxf. M.A.; 1st Cl. Math. 1854; *m.* Clare Elizabeth, *d.* of Rev. Thomas Pelham Dale. *Shepbourne Grange, Tonbridge.*

Ferguson-Davie *ma.* (W.A.C.)
WILLIAM AUGUSTUS, C.B. (Ferguson on entering Eton). 3rd son of Sir H. R. F.-D., 1st Bt., of Creedy Park; 1844^{1}–1850^{3}; Trin. Coll. Camb. M.A.; formerly principal clerk Public Bill Office, House of Commons, and Clerk of the Fees; *m.* Frances Harriet, *d.* of Sir William Miles, 1st Bt., of Leigh Court, Somerset. *Creedy Park, Crediton.*

FIFTH FORM.—UPPER DIVISION.

Green (Mrs. Ro., aft. K.S., W.A.C.)
REV. WILLIAM CHARLES. Son of Rev. G. R. G.; Fellow of Eton and Rector of Everdon, Northants; 1843^{3}–1851^{3}; Newc. Select 1850–1; King's Coll. Camb. M.A.; 2nd in 1st Cl. Class. Trip., Senior Opt. Math. 1855; Craven Univ. Sch.; Epigrams 1852–3–4; Rector of Hepworth. *Hepworth Rectory, Diss.*

Mathias (H.D., aft. K.S., H.D.)
REV. GEORGE HENRY DUNCAN. 1844^{3}–1852^{3}; Newc. Select 1852; Sch. of King's Coll. Camb., M.A.; 1st Cl. Class. Trip. 1856, Fellow of King's; Curate of Lambourn Woodlands, Berks; Incumbent of East Molesey, Surrey; aft. had a private school at Cowes, Isle of Wight; died June 7, 1863.

Carter (Mrs. Ro., aft. K.S., E.H.P.)
CAPT. EDWARD. Son of T. S. C. of Moor Place, Herts; 1844^{3}–1852^{3}; Coll. Wall 1850–1, Keeper 1851; Trin. Hall, Camb.; formerly in the 90th Regt.; *m.* Eleanor, *d.* of Thomas Frewen of Brickwall, Northiam, Sussex. *7 Marlborough Buildings, Bath.*

Harper (Mrs. Hor., aft. K.S., C.J.A. & H.D.)
VEN. ARCHDN. HENRY WILLIAM. Son of Rt. Rev. H. J. C. H., Bp. of Christ Church, New Zealand; 1844^{1}–1852^{3}; Newc. Select 1851–2; Merton Coll. Oxf. M.A.; 2nd Cl. Lit. Hum.; Merton Postmastership 1852; Archdn. of Timaru and Westland, and Canon of Christ Church Cath., New Zealand. *Timaru, Canterbury, New Zealand.*

Reynolds (Miss Edg., aft. K.S., E.C.)
HERBERT JOHN, C.S.I. Son of S. R.; 1845^{3}–1851^{3}; Newc. Select 1849, Med. 1850–1; Coll. Wall 1850–1; Sch. of King's Coll. Camb. B.A.; English Poem 1853–4; Members' Prize, Epigrams, and Fellow of King's, 1855; 3rd Indian C.S.; Browne's Med., Chanc.'s Eng. Med., 1853–4; formerly Vice-Chanc., Calcutta Univ.; ent. I.C.S. 1855; Member of Bengal Leg. Council and Board of Rev. (ret. 1889); J.P. for Middlesex; *m.* Margaretta Catherine, *d.* of H. F. Waring of Lyme Regis. *51 Severn Square, London, S.W.*

Thackeray (Mrs. Ro., aft. K.S., C.O.G.)
REV. FRANCIS ST. JOHN, F.S.A., F.G.S. Son of Rev. F. T., author of the 'Life of Lord Chatham'; 1845^{1}–1852^{3}; Newc. Select 1851–2; Merton Coll. Oxf. 1852–7; M.A., Postmaster 1852; 1st Class Mods. 1854; 1st Class Lit. Hum. 1856; Librarian of Oxf. Union Society 1857; Fellow of Lincoln Coll. Oxf. 1857–61; Assist. Master at Eton 1858–83; Vicar of Mapledurham since 1883; *m.* Louisa Katharine, *d.* of Rev. Andrew Irvine, Vicar of St. Margaret's, Leicester. *Mapledurham Vicarage, Reading.*

Stone (K.S., C.O.G.)
REV. EDWARD DANIEL. Son of J. S. of Dorchester, Dorset; 1845^{3}–1852^{3}; Newc. Select 1849–51; Newc. Sch. 1852; Sch. of King's Coll. Camb. M.A.; 4th in Class. Trip., and Fellow of King's 1856; Assist. Master at Eton 1857–84; *m. d.* of Rev. Francis Vidal. *Helensbourne, Abingdon.*

Evered (Miss M., aft. K.S., H.M.B.)
JOHN JEFFERY GUY. Of Clifford Lodge, Bridgwater; 3rd son of R. G. E. of Hill House, Otterhampton, Bridgwater; 1844^{1}–1852^{3}; Newc. Select 1851–2; Sch. of Magd. Coll. Oxf. M.A.; 1st Cl. Mods. and Demy. at Magd. 1854; ent. at Lincoln's Inn for the Bar; J.P. for co. Somerset; *m.* Mary, *d.* of Rev. John Jeffery, D.D., Rector of Otterhampton, Bridgwater; died 1880.

Molesworth (Miss Edw., H.D.)
JAMES. 5th son of Rev. W. M. of St. Breoke, Cornwall; 1845^{3}–1850^{3}; Lieut. 7th Fusiliers; served in the Crimea; died at Malta of the Varna fever on his return from the Crimea, Oct. 5, 1854.

Mr. Legge (F.E.D.)
LIEUT.-COL. HON. EDWARD HENRY. Of Holmwood Lodge, Dorking; 3rd son of William, 4th Earl of Dartmouth; 1845^{3}–1851^{3}; Ch. Ch. Oxf. M.A.; Assist. Serjeant-at-Arms in the House of Commons; formerly Lieut.-Col. Coldstream Guards; *m.* Cordelia Twysden, *d.* of Walter Hele Molesworth; died Aug. 16, 1900.

Norman (H.M.B., & Mrs. Dr., H.M.B. & E.H.P.)
CHARLES LOYD. Of the Rookery, Bromley Common, Kent; son of G. W. N. of Bromley Common; 1845^{1}–1850^{3}; Eton XI. 1848–50, Capt. 1850; Field XI. and Opp. Wall 1849; Keeper of Upper Club 1849; Trinity Coll. Camb.; Camb. XI. 1852–3; J.P. and D.L. for Kent; Partner in Baring Bros. & Co., Merchants, 8 Bishopsgate Street, E.C.; *m.* 1st, Julia, *d.* of Charles Hay [illegible] ...er, Isle of Wight; [illegible] ...s Donelly Mangles; [illegible] ...17, 1883.

Welby (W.E., E.C.)
SIR REGINALD EARLE (1st Lord Welby), G.C.B. 5th son of Rev. J. W., Rector of Hareston, co. Leicester: 1845^{3}–1851^{2}: Newc. Select 1851; Opp. Wall and Field XI.'s 1850; Trin. Coll. Camb. B.A.; ent. Treasury 1856; Assist. Financial Sec. of the Treas. 1880; Permanent Sec. of the Treas. 1885–92; Commr. of Patriotic Fund; Chairman of London C.C. 1899–1900. 15 *Stratton Street, Piccadilly, W.*

Walford (Miss Edg., aft. K.S., C.J.A.)
REV. JOHN THOMAS. 1845^{3}–1852^{3}; Newc. Select 1851, Med. 1852; Sch. of King's Coll. Camb. M.A.; 13th in Class. Trip. and Fellow of King's 1857; Assist. Master at Eton 1861–5; became a Roman Catholic 1865; Assist. Master at Edgbaston under Cardinal Newman; ent. Jesuit Order and was employed by them educationally at Malta, Liverpool, and Holywell College, N. Wales; died Jan. 9, 1894.

Bent *ma.* (Mrs. Ro., aft. K.S., C.J.A. & J.E.Y.)
REV. JOHN OXENHAM. Son of Major J. B. of Wexham Lodge, Slough; 1845^{2}–1851^{2}; Newc. Select 1851; Coll. Wall XI. 1849–50; Sch. of Pembroke Coll. Oxf. M.A.; Rector of St. John's, Woolwich 1868–91; *m.* Elizabeth Standen, *d.* of Henry Austen Harrison. 17 *Drayton Gardens, S.W.*

Tremlett *ma.* (Mrs. Ro., aft. K.S., W.L.E.)
THOMAS DANIEL. Son of Rev. D. T. of Rodney Stoke, Cheddar, co. Somerset; 1843^{3}–1852^{3}; Eton XI. 1850–2, Capt. 1852; Coll. Wall 1850–2, Keeper 1852; Keeper of Upper Club 1851; Sch. of King's Coll. Camb.; Fellow of King's; Camb. XI. 1854; Barrister (Chancery); *m.* Laura, *d.* of Count Gustave De Costain; died Feb. 1897.

Cookesley *ma.* (W.G.C.)
AUGUSTUS FOULKES. Son of W. G. C., Assist. Master at Eton 1830–54; 1840^{2}–1852^{3}; Opp. Wall 1851–2, Keeper 1852; Field XI. 1852; served in the Crimea and in the Chinese War; Dep. Assist. Commissary Gen. in China; died at Shanghai, July 16, 1863.

Kekewich (Mrs. P. & J.L.J., H.M.B. & J.L.J.)
SIR ARTHUR, Kt. (Hon. Mr. Justice K.). Son of S. T. K. of Peamore, Exeter; 1845^{3}–1850^{2}; Ball. Coll. Oxf. M.A.; 1st Cl. Lit. Hum.; 2nd Cl. Math. and Fellow of Exeter Coll. Oxf. 1853; Barrister Lincoln's Inn 1858; Q.C. 1877; Master of Lincoln's Inn Library to 1902; elected a Bencher 1881; Judge of the Chanc. Div. of High Court of Justice since 1886; Treas. of Linc.'s Inn since 1902; *m.* Marianne, *d.* of James William Freshfield. 7 *Devonshire Place, Portland Place, W.*

Russell (Mrs. Vav., E.C.)
CECIL HENRY. Son of G. L. R.; 1846^{1}–1851^{1}; Opp. Wall XI. 1850; Trin. Coll. Camb. M.A.; Barrister-at-Law; Bencher of Lincoln's Inn; Col. Inns of Court R. Vol.; Vol. Dec; *m.* Katharine, *d.* of Henry Porter of Winslade, Devon. 44 *Ennismore Gardens, S.W.*

Palk *ma.* (W.G.C.)
ASHLEY. Eld. son of R. J. M. P., Barrister; 1846^{1}–1852^{2}; died 1861.

Snow *ma.* (Miss A. & Miss Edg., J.E.Y.)
WILLIAM ROGER (aft. André). Son of R. S., of 6 Chesterfield St., Mayfair, W.; 1846^{2}–1850^{2}; St. John's Coll. Camb.; Gold Med. (Water Colour Drawing) Int. Exhibn. 1873; Artist and Author; *m.* 1st, Christine Louise Warden, *d.* of Robert Luard; 2nd, Clara, *d.* of William S. Foote. *Melrose, Bushey, Watford.*

Wilder (Mrs. Ro. & C.O.G., C.O.G. & W.W.)
REV. HENRY BEAUFOY, L.S.A., M.R.C.S. 2nd son of Rev. H. W. W. of Purley Hall, Reading, and Rector of Sulham; 1843^{3}–1852; Ball. Coll. Oxf. M.A.; Rector of Sulham; *m.* Augusta, *d.* of Langham Christie of Preston Deanery, Northampton. *Sulham Rectory, Reading.*

Walters (R.O.)
VEN. ARCHDN. WILLIAM. Son of J. W. W.; 1846^{1}–1850^{2}; Ch. Ch. Oxf. M.A.; Vicar of Oldham 1864–73; Vicar of Pershore 1873–94; Hon. Canon of Worcester 1881–9; Archdn. of Worcester since 1889; Rector of Alvechurch since 1894; *m.* Louisa Mary, *d.* of Rev. G. St. John. *Alvechurch Rectory, S.O., co. Worcester.*

Earle (K.S., F.E.D.)
THOMAS HUGHES. Of Enham Place, Andover; 2nd son of H. E. of Enham; 1846^{1}–1852^{3}; Coll. Wall 1851–2; Sch. of King's Coll. Camb. M.A.; 28th Wrangler and Fellow of King's 1857; Barrister, Lincoln's Inn; Clerk of the Peace for Hants 1865–91; *m.* Isabel, *d.* of William Francis of Blackheath; died Feb. 3, 1891.

Puller *ma.* (E.C.)
ARTHUR GILES GILES-. Of Youngsbury, Ware; eld. son of C. W. G.-P. of Youngsbury; 1845^{3}–1851^{2}; Tomline Select 1850, Prizeman 1851; Sch. of Trin. Coll. Camb. M.A.; 16th Wrangler 1855; called to the Bar, Lincoln's Inn, 1861; Lieut. Herts Yeo.; J.P. co. Herts; died unm. Mar. 31, 1885.

Marillier (Miss Edg., aft. K.S., C.J.A.)
CHARLES HENRY. 1845^{2}–1853^{2}; Newc. Select 1852; Prince Consort's French Prize 1849; Eton XI. 1853; King's Coll. Camb.; Fellow of King's; formerly in the Cape Mounted Rifles and Garrison Adjt. at Grahamstown, S. Africa; died at Gibraltar 1875.

Walters (C.O.G.)
ROBERT. Son of R. W., Barrister of Lincoln's Inn; 1845^{2}–1850^{3}; Ball. Coll. Oxf. M.A.; Barrister, Inner Temple; J.P. for Herts; *m.* Florence Serena, *d.* of Stephen Collins of Theale, Cheddar, co. Somerset. *Ware Priory, Ware.*

Robertson *ma.* (W.A.C.)
GILBERT METCALFE. Son of T. C. R.; 1845^{2}–1850^{3}; Eton VIII. 1849–50; Capt. of the Boats 1850; Merton Coll. Oxf.; formerly Capt. 1st Royal Dragoons; served through Crimean campaign; horse shot under him at Balaclava. 47 *Lennox Gardens, Pont Street, S.W.*

Lane (J.E.Y.)
HENRY CHARLES. Son of H. T. L. of Middleton; 1844^{3}–1850^{2}; Ch. Ch. Oxf.; Lieut. 2nd Life Gds., ret. 1858; J.P. for Sussex; *m.* Katharine, *d.* of Rev. Anthony Lewis Lambert, Rector of Chilbolton, Stockbridge, Hants. *Middleton, Hassocks, R.S.O., Sussex.*

Phillips (F.E.D.)
WILLIAM PAGE THOMAS. Son of B. P., F.R.S., F.R.C.S., of Hasketon and Melton Grange, Woodbridge; 1846^{2}–1851^{2}; Exeter Coll. Oxf. M.A.; Barrister (ret.); J.P. and D.L. for Suffolk; *m.* Clara Matilda, *d.* of Henry Browning of Grosvenor Street, S.W. *Pyrford Croft, Pyrford, Woking.*

Shirley (Mrs. Ro., aft. K.S.)
HORATIO HENRY. Eld. son of Rev. J. S., Rector of Frettenham, Norwich; 1843^{3}–1853^{1}; Fellow of King's Coll. Camb.; Barrister; died unm. Jan. 9, 1900.

Lloyd *ma.* (Miss Edg., aft. K.S., C.J.A. & F.E.D.)
ALEXANDER OGILVIE. 4th son of G. L. of Cowesby Hall, Thirsk; 1845^{3}–1851^{2}; Trin. Coll. Oxf. M.A.; a Sheep Farmer in Queensland from 1864; died unm. Oct. 24, 1865.

Barker (Mrs. Ri., C.O.G.)
JOHN EDWARD, K.C. Son of E. B. of West Don House, Sheffield; 1845^{3}–1850^{2}; Exeter Coll. Oxf. M.A.; Barrister, Inner Temple, 1862; Q.C. 1871; Recorder of Leeds 1880–96; Chmn. of Derbys Qr. Sessions 1894–7; *m.* Susan Marianne, *d.* of Rowley Wynyard, R.N., and widow of James Mosley Leigh of Davenham, Northwich. *Brooklands, Bakewell.*

Miles (R.O.)
HENRY CRUGER-WILLIAM. 8th son of P. J. M. of Leigh Court, Bristol; 1844^{3}–1850^{2}; Ch. Ch. Oxf.; Merchant; died April, 1888.

Browning *ma.* (F.E.D.)

HENRY BAINBRIDGE. Son of H. B.; 1848^{3}–1850^{2}; Merchant in Mark Lane, E.C. 9 *Cadogan Square, S.W.*

Sterry (Miss Edg., aft. K.S., E.H.P.)

WASEY. Son of W. S. of Upminster: Romford; 1846^{2}–1852^{2}; King's Coll. Camb., Fellow of King's; died unm. July 4, 1858.

Montgomerie (Mrs. Vav., E.C.)

FREDERICK BUTLER MOLINEUX. Son of F. M. M.: 1846^{2}–1851^{2}; Newc. Select 1850, Sch. 1851: Ball. Coll. Oxf. M.A.: 1st Class Mods. 1853; Hertford Sch. and Craven Sch. 1854; Barrister; *m.* Isabella, *d.* of Hon. Colin Lindsay. 1 *Cromwell Place, S.W.*

Pemberton (W.E., F.E.D.)

RICHARD LAURENCE. Of Hawthorn Tower, Seaham Harbour, Sunderland; son of R. P. of Hawthorn Tower; 1845^{3}–1851^{2}; Eton VIII. 1851; Wall XI. 1850; ran dead-heat for Mile; Pembroke Coll. Oxf.; formerly Capt. N. Durham Militia; J.P. and D.L. co. Durham, High Sheriff 1861; *m.* 1st, Jane Emma, *d.* of Rev. Martin Stapylton, Rector of Barlborough, Chesterfield; 2nd. Elizabeth Jane, *d.* of Rev. James Watson Stote Donnison of Mendham, Harleston; died June 21, 1901.

Heathcote *ma.* (E.H.P.)

JOHN MOYER. Eld. son of J. M. H. of Conington; 1846^{3}–1852^{2}; Trin. Coll. Camb. M.A.; called to the Bar, Lincoln's Inn, 1859; J.P. and D.L. for co. Huntingdon; J.P. for Sussex; Hon. Col. 3rd Bn. Cambs R.V. 1873–80; V.D.; Amateur Tennis Champion; Chmn. Hants Qr. Sessions; *m.* Louisa Cecilia, *d.* of Norman MacLeod of Dunvegan Castle, Isle of Skye. *Conington Castle, Peterborough.*

Prest (R.F.H., H.D.)

WILLIAM PITT. Son of S. P. of Stapleford Lodge, Camb.; 1844^{3}–1850^{3}; Eton XI. 1849–50; Caius Coll. Camb.; Capt. Camb. City R.V.; aft. in the Army, 6th Foot; *m.* Maria, widow of Commr. William Lloyd, R.N.; died at Molesey 1878.

Fremantle (W.E., E.B.)

HON. SIR CHARLES WILLIAM, K.C.B. 3rd son of Thomas Francis, 1st Lord Cottesloe, of Swanbourne, Winslow; 1846^{2}–1851^{2}; Cox Eton VIII. 1851; Private Sec. to Rt. Hon. B. Disraeli 1866–8; Dep. Master of the Mint 1868–94; J.P. for Middlesex and Westminster; *m.* Sophia, *d.* of Abel Smith of Woodhall Park, Hertford. 4 *Lower Sloane Street, S.W.*

Arnold (Mrs. Hor., E.H.P.)

CHARLES THOMAS. Son of Rev. T. K. A., Rector of Lyndon in Rutland and Fellow of Trin. Coll Camb.; 1846^{3}–1850^{3}; Corpus Christi Coll. Oxf. M.A.; 1st Cl. Mods. 1854; 1st Cl. Lit. Hum. 1856; Solicitor; *m.* Annie Jane, *d.* of Hugh Jackson of Ewell, Epsom. 3 *Arlington Street, St. James's, S.W., and Stamford House, Wimbledon Common, S.W.*

Hopkins (Miss Edw., W.J.)

REV. THOMAS HENRY TOOVEY. 1846^{2}–1850^{4}; formerly Fellow and Tutor of Magd. Coll. Oxf.; M.A.

Lyall (K.S., C.J.A., & C.Wo.)

RT. HON. SIR ALFRED COMYNS, P.C., K.C.B., G.C.I.E., K.C.S.I., D.C.L., LL.D. Son of Rev. A. L.; 1845^{3}–1852^{3}; Newc. Select 1852; E.I. Coll. Haileybury; ent. Bengal Civil Service 1856; Lieut.-Gov. North-West Provinces of India 1882–7; Hon. D.C.L. Oxf. and LL.D. Camb.; Member of Council of India since 1888; *m.* Cora, *d.* of P. Cloete. 18 *Queen's Gate, S.W.*

Luxmoore (W.L.E.)

PHILIP BOUVERIE. Son of Rev. J. H. M. L., Vicar of Marchwiel, Wrexham; 184[illegible]–185[illegible]; Trin. Coll. Camb.; *m.* Mary, *d.* of Richard Fen[illegible]; dead.

Watson *ma.* (J.E.Y.)

WILLIAM. 1845^{2}–1851^{2}; Opp. Wall and Field XI.'s 1850; formerly in the 17th Lancers.

Scott *ma.* (E.C.)

GEORGE ARTHUR JERVOISE. Of Rotherfield Park, Alton, Hants; eld. son of J. W. S. of Rotherfield; 1846^{2}–1852^{2}; Ch. Ch. Oxf. M.A.; 1st Cl. Mod. Hist. and Fellow of All Souls, Oxf. 1856; J.P., D.L., and C.A. for Hants; *m.* Lady Mary Angela, *d.* of Gen. Lord Charles Wellesley of Conholt Park, Hants; died at sea off Aden March 4, 1895.

Grover (Mrs. Ro., aft. K.S., E.B.)

CHARLES CHAPLYN. Son of — G., Solicitor, of Hemel Hempstead; 1846^{1}–1850^{2}.

Arbuthnot *ma.* (F.E.D.)

WILLIAM. Of The Ham Manor, Newbury; eld. son of J. A. A. of Coworth Park, Old Windsor; 1846^{1}–1851^{2}; Trin. Coll. Camb. B.A.; Banker and Merchant at Madras; J.P. and D.L. for Berks; *m.* 1st, Adolphine Eliza Macleod, *d.* of Edward Lecot, French Consul at Madras; 2nd, Margaret Rosa, *d.* of John Campbell of Kilberry, Tarbert, N.B.; died February 9, 1896.

Harford (W.A.C.)

REV. CANON EDWARD JOHN. 2nd son of W. H. H. of Barley Wood, Wrington, Bristol; 1845^{3}–1850^{3}; Oriel Coll. Oxf. M.A.; 2nd Cl. Law and Hist.; formerly Lecturer and Curate at Henbury, Bristol; Rector of Marston Bigott with Gaer Hill since 1892; Preb. of Combe since 1889; Canon Res. of Wells; *m.* Gertrude Emma, *d.* of Rev. Sir Thomas Pym Bridges, 7th Bt., Rector of Danbury, Chelmsford. *Marston Rectory, Frome.*

Mr. Herbert (Miss M., W.J.)

MAJOR-GEN. HON. WILLIAM HENRY. 5th son of Edward, 2nd Earl of Powis, K.G.; 1845^{2}–1852^{1}; ent. Army 1852; served in the Crimea with 46th Regt. 1855 (med. with clasp and Turkish med.); Maj.-Gen. 1885 (ret.); Mayor of Shrewsbury 1889–90; J.P. for Salop and Northants; *m.* Sybella Augusta, *d.* of Mark William Vane Milbank of Thorp Perrow, Bedale. *Prestfelde, Shrewsbury*

Lambert (J.E.Y.)

REV. WILLIAM HENRY. 6th son of Sir H. J. L., 5th Bt.; 1846^{2}–1852^{2}; Newc. Select 1852; Merton Coll. Oxf. M.A.; Postmaster of Merton 1852; Rector of Stoke Edith, and Preb. of Hereford Cath.; *m.* Georgiana Joyce, *d.* of Robert Biddulph of Ledbury. *Stoke Edith Rectory, Hereford.*

Guy-Phillips (Mrs. Vav., C.L.)

LEWIS (Phillips on ent.). 1845^{2}–1850^{2}; Prince Consort's German Prize 1848; Eton XI. 1850; Field and Opp. Wall XI.'s 1849–50; Keeper of Field 1850; Ch. Ch. Oxf.; formerly Capt. Gren. Gds.

Mr. Byng (Mrs. Hor., & Miss G., H.M.B. & J.L.J.)

REV. HON. FRANCIS EDMUND CECIL (5th Earl of Strafford). 3rd son of George Stevens, 2nd Earl of S.; 1845^{3}–1852^{2}; Prince Consort's French and Italian Prizes 1851; Ch. Ch. Oxf. M.A.; 3rd Cl. Law and Mod. Hist.; Rector of Little Casterton, Rutland, 1859–62; Vicar of Holy Trinity, Twickenham; Chaplain at Hampton Court 1862–7; Hon. Chap. to Queen Victoria 1867; Chap. in Ordinary 1872; Chap. to the Speaker 1874–89; Vicar of S. Peter's, S. Kensington, 1867–89; Grand Chap. of Freemasonry in England 1889; *m.* 1st, Florence Louisa, *d.* of Sir William Miles, 1st Bt., of Leigh Court, Bristol; 2nd, Emily Georgina, *d.* of Vice-Admiral [illegible] Kerr. *Wrotham* [illegible] *St. James's Square,* [illegible]

Mr. Fiennes *ma.* (Mrs. P., E.C.)
Hon. Ivo De Vesci Edward, C.B. (aft. Twisleton-Wykeham-Fiennes). 3rd son of Rev. Frederick Benjamin, 16th Lord Saye and Sele, D.C.L.; 1845[1]-1850[3]: Eton VIII. 1850; Field XI. and Opp. Wall 1849; formerly in 7th Hussars, aft. Col. 9th Lancers; served in Indian Mutiny; *m.* Isabella Emily, *d.* of Capt. Charles Francis Gregg of the Inniskilling Dragoons; died Nov. 23, 1875.

Duckworth (Mrs. Hor., E.H.P.)
Herbert. 4th son of W. D., formerly of Beechwood, New Forest, aft. of Orchardleigh Park, Frome; 1845[3]-1851[2]: Trin. Coll. Camb. B.A.; Barrister: *m.* Julia Prinsep, *d.* of Dr. Jackson; died Sept. 19, 1870.

Stone *ma.* (Mrs. P., & Miss Edg., C.J.A. & F.E.D.)
Rev. Henry. Son of T. A. S.; 1845[3]-1850[3]: Exeter Coll. Oxf. M.A.; Rector of Croydon and Rural Dean of Shingay; *m.* Charlotte Decima, *d.* of George Treweeke. *Croydon Rectory, Royston, Herts.*

Waterfield (Miss Edg., aft. K.S., C.J.A.)
Col. William Garrow, C.S.I. Son of C. W., a Registrar of the Court of Bankruptcy; 1845[3]-1850[3]; Barrister, Middle Temple 1872; formerly 23rd N. Infantry; served in Indian Mutiny 1857-8, Afghan Campaign 1878-9, and on N.W. Frontier; A.D.C. to Gen. Wilson at Delhi; Lieut. Staff Corps, and Assist. Commr. of Punjab, 1878-88; *m.* Rosa Helen, *d.* of Rev. Sir Charles Clarke, 2nd Bt., of Worlingham, Beccles; died Feb. 3, 1897.

Lord Clinton (W.E., E.C.)
Henry Pelham Alexander (6th Duke of Newcastle). Eld. son of Henry Pelham, 5th Duke of N., K.G.; 1846[1]-1850[3]: Ch. Ch. Oxf.; M.P. for Newark; *m.* Henrietta Adela, *d.* of Henry Thomas Hope of Deepdene, Dorking; died Feb. 22, 1879.

Ward (Miss Edw., aft. K.S., W.J.)
John Martyr. Son of Rev. — W., Rector of East Clandon, Guildford; 1846[2]-1853[1]: King's Coll. Camb.; Fellow of King's; formerly Lieut. 2nd Surrey Militia; Barrister.

Welby (C.O.G.)
Rev. Walter Hugh Earle. 3rd son of Sir G. E. Welby-Gregory, 3rd Bt.; 1846[1]-1851[3]: Ch. Ch. Oxf. M.A.; formerly Rector of Harston, Grantham; J.P. co. Leicester; *m.* 1st, Frances, *d.* of Rt. Rev. Dr. Ollivant, Bp. of Llandaff; 2nd, Florence Laura, *d.* of Rev. G. Sloane-Stanley, Rector of Branstone. *St. George's Lodge, Ryde, Isle of Wight.*

Fraser (R.F.H., E.H.P.)
Lieut.-Gen. James Keith, C.M.G. 3rd son of Sir J. J. F., 3rd Bt.; 1846[2]-1850[3]; Military Attaché at Vienna and Col. 1st Life Gds.; Lieut.-Gen. Comm. Dublin Dist. 1890; Insp.-Gen. of Cav. in Gt. Britain and Ireland 1891; *m.* Amelia Alice Julia, *d.* of Hon. Humble Dudley Ward; died July 30, 1895.

Gore-Booth (Miss Edw., H.D.)
Robert Newcomen. Eld. son of Sir R. G.-B., 4th Bt., of Lissadell, Sligo; 1845[1]-1850[3]; formerly Lieut. 4th Lt. Dragoons; *m.* Mary, *d.* of Rowland Eyles Egerton-Warburton of Arley Hall, Northwich; died Oct. 29, 1861.

Malcolm (E.H.P.)
John Wingfield (1st Lord Malcolm), C.B. Of Poltalloch, Lochgilphead; eld. son of J. M. of Poltalloch; 1845[2]-1850[3]; Eton VIII. 1850; Ch. Ch. Oxf. M.A.; formerly Capt. Kent Art. Militia, aft. Lieut.-Col. comm. and Hon. Col 5th V.B. Argyll and Sutherland Highl.; M.P. for Boston 1860-78, and Argyle 1886-92; J.P. and D.L. co. Argyll, J.P. Kent; *m.* 1st, Hon. Alice Frederica, *d.* of George Ives, 4th Lord Boston; 2nd, Marie Lilian, widow of H. Gardner Lister of U.S.A.; died Mar. 6, 1902.

Marshall (H.D.)
Col. Thomas Horatio, C.B. Son of T. M., Barrister, of Hartford Beach, Northwich; 1846[1]-1850[3]; Eton VIII. 1850; won School Pulling 1850: Exeter Coll. Oxf. M.A.; Cox of Oxf. VIII. 1853-5; Earl of Chester's Yeo. Cav. 1852-62; 3rd Bn. Cheshire Regt. (Mil.) 1862-88; ret. as Major and Hon. Lieut.-Col. 3rd Vol. Bn. Cheshire Regt. 1860-98 (Lieut.-Col. comm. 1885-98); Hon. Col. 1898; J.P. for cos. Cheshire, Anglesey, and Carnarvon; Vol. Dec.; *m.* 1st, Laura Anne, *d.* of Rev. Martin Stapylton; 2nd, Lucy Martina, *d.* of Rev. Edward Nugent Bree. *Bryn-y-Coed, Bangor.*

Swann (W.J.)
Robert. Of Askham Hall, co. York; 1846[2]-1850[3]; Eton VIII. 1850; won Double Sculling 1849; formerly a Banker at York; *m.* Blanche Maria, *d.* of Sir John Johnstone, 2nd Bt., of Hackness Hall, Scarborough; dead.

Williams (W.G.C., aft. K.S., W.G.C.)
Montagu Stephen. Of Freshford, Bath; 1846[3]-1852[1]; formerly Barrister and Dramatic Author; Stipendiary Magistrate at Worship St.; died 1893.

Leigh (W.A.C.)
Joseph. Of Belmont Hall, Northwich; eld. son of J. H. L. of Belmont; 1844[3]-1850[3]: formerly Major, Chester Yeo. Cav.; *m.* Fanny Penelope, *d.* of Rev. James Streynsham Master, Rector of Chorley and Canon of Manchester; died July 23, 1869.

Sparke *ma.* (Mrs. de R., E.H.P.)
Edward Bowyer. 2nd son of Rev. J. H. S. of Gunthorpe Hall, and Canon of Ely; 1845[3]-1851[1]; Trin. Coll. Camb. M.A.; J.P. and D.L. for Norfolk, High Sheriff 1877; *m.* Annie, *d.* of Lieut.-Col. John Marcon of Wallington Hall, Downham Market, Norfolk. *66 Eaton Square, S.W., and Gunthorpe Hall, East Dereham, Norfolk.*

Packe (R.F.H., H.D.)
Rev. William James. Of Stretton Hall, Leicester; 3rd son of Capt. E. P. of Stanhope Place, Hyde Park, W.; 1844[3]-1851[3]; Ch. Ch. Oxf. M.A.; Vicar of Feering since 1873; *m.* Margaret Lucy, *d.* of Alexander Pym of the Firs, Ampthill. *Feering Vicarage, Kelvedon, Essex.*

Praed (R.O.)
Charles Tyringham. Of Edgecombe Hall, Wimbledon; 2nd son of J. B. P. of Tyringham, Bucks, and Trevethoe, Cornwall; 1845[3]-1850[3]; Banker; M.P. for St. Ives 1874-80; *m.* Jane, *d.* of Ralph W. Munuel of Brighton; died 1895.

Cookesley *ma.* (W.G.C.)
Henry Slingsby. Son of Rev. H. P. C. of Wimborne; 1845[3]-1850[3]; died Jan. 1851.

Wilberforce (W.S., aft. K.S., C.J.A. & J.L.J.)
Rev. William Francis. Eld. son of Ven. R. I. W., Archdn. of E. Riding of Yorks; 1846[3]-1852[3]; Newc. Select 1851-2; Sch. of Univ. Coll. Oxf.; 3rd Cl.; Vicar of St. John's, York, aft. Vicar of Brodsworth; *m.* Elizabeth, *d.* of Charles Hope Maclean, Barrister. *Brodsworth Vicarage, Doncaster.*

Whitting *mi.* (Miss Edg., aft. K.S., E.H.P.)
Frederick. Son of W. W. of Thorney Abbey, co. Camb.; 1847[1]-1854[3]: Newc. Select 1852, Sch. 1853; Coll. Wall 1852-3; Sch. of King's Coll. Camb.; M.A.; Latin Ode 1854; 1st Cl. Class. Trip. and Fellow of King's 1858; Members' Prize 1860; Browne's Medal; Bursar of King's and Financial Sec. of Univ.; Vice-Provost of King's. *King's Coll. Camb.*

Chapman (E.C.)
George Henry James. 1846[3]-1850[3]; formerly Capt. 5th Regt.

Dupuis *ma.* (H.D., aft. K.S., H.D., C.O.G. & A.F.B.)
Rev. George Richard. Son of the Rev. G. J. D., Assist. and Lower Master, Fellow, Bursar, and Vice-Provost of Eton; 1844[3]-1853[3]; Eton XI. 1852-3; Coll. Wall XI. 1851-3, Keeper 1853; Keeper of Upper Club 1852; King's Coll. Camb.; Fellow of King's; Camb. XI. 1857; Assist. Master at Eton 1858-75; Rector of Sessay; *m.* Amelia Letitia, *d.* of Capt. John Kyffin Lloyd of the 14th Regt. *Sessay Rectory, Thirsk.*

Neville (E.C.)

William Wyndham. 6th son of Hon. and Very Rev. G. N.-Grenville of Butleigh Court, Glastonbury; 1846[3]-1852[2]; Magd. Coll. Camb.; 2nd Cl.; died at Torquay Dec. 1858.

Lambert (K.S., W.L.E.)

Anthony. Son of Rev. A. L. L., Rector of Chilbolton, Stockbridge, Hants; 1847[3]-1853[1]; Newc. Select 1852-3; Sch. of King's Coll. Camb.; died 1858.

Clark (W.J.)

John Willis. Son of Rev. W. C., M.D., of Trinity Coll. Camb.; 1847[3]-1851[3]; Trin. Coll. Camb. M.A.; Br. 12th Class., and Fellow of Trin. 1856; formerly Auditor of Trin.; Registrar of Univ. of Camb. since 1891; *m.* Frances Matilda, *d.* of Rt. Hon. Sir Andrew Buchanan, 1st Bt., of Dunburgh, co. Stirling. *Scroope House, Cambridge.*

Puller *mi.* (E.C.)

Charles Giles. Of Youngsbury, Ware; 2nd son of C. W. G.-P. of Youngsbury; 1845[3]-1853[3]; Tomline Select 1852-3; Sch. of Trin. Coll. Camb.; 15th Wrangler and Fellow of Trin. 1857; formerly Vicar of Standon; in Holy Orders till 1874; J.P. and D.L. co. Herts; *m.* Emmeline Maria, *d.* of William Longman of Ashlyns, Herts; died May 3, 1892.

Younger (K.S., O.J.A.)

Henry William. Formerly of Old Windsor; 1845[3]-1852[1]; Eton XI. 1851; Coll. Wall 1850-1.

Newnham (E.H.P.)

William Heurtley. Son of Rev. G. W. N.; 1847[3]-1851[3]; Prince Consort's German Prize 1851; Ball. Coll. Oxf. M.A.; 1st Cl. Mods. 1854; 2nd Cl. Greats; Hon. 4th Math.; Barrister Inner Temple; late Bombay Civil Service. *Moston, St. George's Hill, Weybridge.*

Currie (E.H.P.)

Sir Philip Henry Wodehouse (1st Lord Currie), P.C., G.C.B. 4th son of R. C. of Bush Hill, Middlesex, and Minley Manor, Hants; 1846[3]-1852[3]; Junior Clerk, Foreign Office, 1854; attached to Legation at St. Petersburg 1856; Précis Writer to Earl of Clarendon (Sec. of State for Foreign Affairs 1857-8); attached to Lord Wodehouse's Special Mission to King of Denmark 1863; appointed Acting Second Sec. in Diplomatic Service; assisted Julian Fane, Protocolist, at Conferences in London on affairs of Luxemburg 1867; Assist. Clerk 1868; Sen. Clerk 1874; Sec. to Lord Salisbury's Special Embassy to Constantinople 1876; Priv. Sec. to Lord Salisbury (Sec. of State for Foreign Affairs 1878-80); Sec. to Special Embassy Congress at Berlin 1878; in charge of correspondence respecting affairs of Cyprus 1878-80; Sec. to Lord Northampton's Special Mission to invest King Alfonso XII. of Spain with Order of Garter 1881; Assist. Under Sec. of State for Foreign Affairs, Joint Protocolist to Conference in London on Egyptian Finance 1884; Permanent Under-Sec. of State for Foreign Affairs 1889; Ambassador at Constantinople 1893-8; Ambassador at Rome since 1898; *m.* Mary Montgomerie, *d.* of Charles James Savile Montgomerie Lamb, and widow of Henry Sydenham Singleton of Mell, co. Louth. 1 *Connaught Place, W.; Hawley House, Blackwater, S.O., Hants; and British Embassy, Rome.*

Warre *ma.* (Mrs. Vav., & F.V., C.J.A., E.C., & W.B.M.)

Rev. Francis. Eld. son of H. W. of Bindon House, Langford Budville, Wellington, Som.; 1846[3]-1852[1]; Newc. Select 1852; Opp. Wall 1851; Field XI. 1851; Ball. Coll. Oxf. M.A.; formerly Rector of Bere Regis, Dorset, aft. Rector of Bemerton, and Preb. of Sarum; *m.* Ellin Jane, *d.* of Rev. James Jarvis P[illegible], Rector of Holm Pierrepoint, Notts. *B[illegible] Rectory, Salisbury.*

Mr. Dillon (E.H.P.)

Hon. Luke Gerald, K.P., P.C. (4th Lord Clonbrock). 2nd son of Robert, 3rd Lord C.; 1846[3]-1852[3]; Ball. Coll. Oxf.; 2nd Cl. Law and Mod. Hist. 1855; Attaché, Berlin 1856; Paid Attaché, Vienna 1859; 2nd Sec. at Vienna 1862; Priv. Sec. to Lord-Lieut. of Ireland 1866-8 and 1874-6; Lord-Lieut. of co. Galway, High Sheriff 1865; *m.* Hon. Augusta Caroline, *d.* of Edward, 2nd Lord Crofton. *Clonbrock, Ahascragh, Ballinasloe.*

Lloyd (R.O., & C.Wo.)

Arthur Philip. Of Leaton Knolls, Shrewsbury; son of Rev. H. J. L., Rector of Selattyn, Oswestry; 1847[3]-1851[3]; Ch. Ch. Oxf. B.A.; J.P. and D.L. cos. Salop and Montgomery; formerly Capt. Salop Yeo. Cav.; *m.* Leila Katharine Selina, *d.* of Vice-Adml. Hon. Charles Orlando Bridgeman; died Feb. 9, 1893.

Snow *mi.* (Miss Edg., J.E.Y.)

Rev. Canon Herbert (aft. Kynaston), D.D. Son of R. S. of 6 Chesterfield St., Mayfair, W.; 1847[3]-1853[1]; Newc. Select 1853; Field and Opp. Wall XI.'s 1852; Sch. of St. John's Coll. Camb.; Porson Sch. 1855; Latin Ode and Camden Med. 1856; Br. Sen. Class. and Fellow of St. John's 1857; Browne Med.; Camb. VIII. 1856, Stroke 1857; Assist. Master at Eton 1858-74; Princ. of Cheltenham Coll. 1874-88; Vicar of St. Luke's, Kentish Town, 1888-9; Canon of Durham and Prof. of Greek and Class. Lit. in Durham Univ. since 1889; *m.* 1st, Mary Louisa Anne, *d.* of Thomas Bros, Barrister; 2nd, Charlotte, *d.* of Rev. John Cordeaux, Rector of Hooton Roberts, Rotherham. *The College, Durham.*

Arkwright *ma.* (R.O., & C. Wo.)

John Hungerford. Eld. son of J. A. of Hampton Court; 1847[3]-1852[1]; Opp. Wall and Field XI.'s 1851; Ch. Ch. Oxf. M.A.; J.P. and D.L. co. Hereford, High Sheriff 1862; Capt. Leominster (No. 6) Herefords Vol. 1861; M.F.H. Herefords Hounds 1858-68, and North Herefords 1869-74; Gov. Christ's Hospital and Foundlings' 1856; Chief Steward, Leominster Borough 1889; Herefords C.C. 1889; Ald. 1902; Lord-Lieut. co. Hereford 1902; *m.* Charlotte Lucy, *d.* of John Davenport of Foxley, Hereford. *Hampton Court, Leominster.*

Mr. Holroyd (W.A.C.)

Hon. Douglas Edward. 2nd son of George Augustus Frederick Charles, 2nd Earl of Sheffield; 1847[3]-1851[3]; Barrister; died Feb. 9, 1882.

Harington

His Honour Sir Richard, 11th Bt., Judge of County Court. Eld. son of Rev. R. H., D.D., Princ. of B.N.C. Oxf.; 1844[3]-1853[3]; won School Pulling 1852; Ch. Ch. Oxf. M.A.; B.C.L.; Slade Sch. 1853; 2nd Cl. Class. 1856; 1st Cl. Law and Mod. Hist. 1857; Vinerian Sch. 1858; called to the Bar, Lincoln's Inn, 1858; Police Magis. of Hammersmith and Wandsworth 1871; J.P. and D.L. co. Hereford; J.P. cos. Warwick and Worcester; Chmn. of Herefords Qr. Sessions and Co. Ald.; Judge of County Courts since Jan. 1872; *m.* Frances Agnata, *d.* of Rev. Robert Biscoe, Preb. of Hereford, and Rector of Whitbourne. *Whitbourne Court, Worcester.*

Mr. Marsham (Miss A., & E.B., E.B.)

Hon. Robert, F.S.A., F.R.G.S., F.G.S. (aft. Marsham-Townshend). 2nd son of Charles, 2nd Earl of Romney; 1846[3]-1852[3]; Ch. Ch. Oxf. M.A.; formerly in Diplomatic Service; J.P. and D.L. for Kent; J.P. for London; *m.* Clara Catherine, *d.* of Rev. [illegible] Paley, Rector of Frecken[illegible] [illegible]erfield Street, W., and F[illegible] S.O., Kent.

Mr. Campbell (H.M.B.)
LIEUT.-COL. HON. HENRY WALTER. 3rd son of John Frederick, 1st Earl Cawdor; 1845^{2}–1851^{2}; served in the Crimea 1854–5 (Alma, Inkerman, and siege and fall of Sebastopol): twice mentioned in despatches; med. with 3 clasps: Knt. of Legion of Honour; 5th Cl. Medjidie; Turkish med.; Lieut.-Col. Coldstream Gds. (ret.): J.P. co. Carmarthen; Chmn., L. and S. W. R'y; *m.* Fanny Georgina, *d.* of Col. George Campbell. 44 *Charles Street, Berkeley Square, W.*

Norman (Mrs. Ro., & C.O.G., H.M.B., & C.O.G.)
HENRY JOHN. Son of H. N., Banker, of Oakley, Bromley, Kent; 1847^{1}–1852^{2}; Trin. Coll. Camb.; Director of London and Westminster Bank and other Co.'s; *m.* Anne Hewitt, *d.* of Col. C. J. Coote. 21 *Cadogan Square, Chelsea, S.W., and Gadsden, Hayes, Beckenham, Kent.*

Dunbar (Mrs. Ro., F.E.D.)
ROTHES LENOX. 3rd son of J. D of the Bengal Civil Service; 1842^{3}–1850^{2}; Capt. 42nd Highlanders; died unm. Feb. 1, 1857.

Giles (W.J.)
JAMES. 1847^{1}–1851^{2}; Field XI. 1850; Trin. Coll. Camb.; formerly Lieut. 7th Hussars.

Woodmass (Miss Edg., H.M.B.)
MONTAGU. Of Green Hill, Compstall, Stockport; eld. son of C. W. of Avonhurst, co. Warwick; 1847^{2}–1852^{1}; Trin. Coll. Camb. M.A.: called to the Bar, Inner Temple, 1861; J.P. co. Chester; *m.* Edith Alice, *d.* of George Andrew of Ernecroft, Compstall. 7 *Southwell Gardens, S.W.*

Blaauw (E.B.)
HENRY WILLIAM GILLMAN. Eld. son of W. H. B. of Beechland, Newick, Cooksbridge, Sussex; 1846^{3}–1852^{2}; Ch. Ch. Oxf. 1st Cl. Mod. Hist. 1856; formerly W. Sussex Militia; died unm. at Cairo, Mar. 25, 1857.

Williams-Freeman (W.E., H.M.B.)
WILLIAM PEERE. Of Clapton, Thrapston; eld. son of W. P. W.-F., formerly of Fawley Court, Henley, aft. of Pylewell Park, Lymington; 1847^{2}–1852^{1}; Trin. Coll. Camb.; formerly Sec. H.M. Diplomatic Service; *m.* Isabella Frances Sophia, *d.* of Herman Merivale, C.B., Permanent Under-Sec. of State for India; died Sept. 18, 1884.

Foulkes (K.S.)
STEPHEN WESTON. Son of Rev. — F., Vicar of Shebbear, Highampton, N. Devon; 1844^{2}–1853^{1}; Coll. Wall 1852.

Nevile (C.O.G.)
GEORGE. Of Thorney, Newark; eld. son of Rev. C. N. of Thorney and Rector of Wickenby, Lincoln; 1846^{2}–1850^{3}; won School Sculling 1850; Magd. Coll. Camb. M.A.; Capt. Magd. Coll. Boat 1854; J.P. for Notts; *m.* Sarah, *d.* of Edward Williamson of Scarborough. *Prestatyn, Rhyl.*

Sutton (F.E.D.)
VEN. ARCHDN. ROBERT. Son of R. S., J.P. Bucks; 1846^{1}–1850^{3}; Exeter Coll. Oxf. M.A.; Chichester Theo. Coll.; Assist. Curate of St. Botolph, Aldgate, E., 1856–8; Incumbent of St. Leonard's, Aston Clinton, Bucks, 1858–61; Vicar of Westhampnett, Chichester, 1861–8; Canon-Preb. of Chichester 1866; Rector of Slinfold, Horsham, 1868–75; Vicar of Pevensey since 1875; Proctor in Convocation for Clergy of Archdeaconry of Chichester 1874–9; Rural Dean of Pevensey, Div. I., since 1881; Archdn. of Lewes since 1888; Surrogate for Archdeaconries of Chichester and Lewes; *m.* Lucy, *d.* of Rt. Rev. Ashurst T. Gilbert, D.D., Bp. of Chichester. *Pevensey Vicarage, Hastings.*

Fosbery (Mrs. Vav., C.J.A. & F.E.D.)
LIEUT.-COL. GEORGE VINCENT, V.C. Eld. son of Rev. T. V. F.; 1846^{3}–1850^{2}; joined Bengal Army 1852, ret. 1877.

Mallory (C.L.)
REV. GEORGE. Eld. son of Rev. G. M. (formerly Leigh), Rector of Mobberley, Knutsford; 1846–1850; B.N.C. Oxf. M.A.; died unm. at the Manor House, Mobberley, Mar. 8 1864.

Mr. Venables-Vernon (F.E.D.)
HON. WILLIAM JOHN BORLASE-WARREN-. 2nd son of George, 5th Lord Vernon; 1847^{3}–1852^{2}; Prince Consort's Italian Prize 1850; won School Steeplechase 1851; Ch. Ch. Oxf. M.A.; Accademico Corrispondente della Crusca at Florence; a Cavaliere of the Italian Order of San Maurizio e Lazzaro, and a Knight of the Order of St. Olaf in Norway; J.P. for cos. Stafford and Derby; D.L. co. Stafford; *m.* 1st, Agnes Lucy, *d.* of Sir John Peter Boileau, 1st Bt., of Ketteringham Park, Wymondham, Norfolk; 2nd, Annie Georgiana, *d.* of Charles Eyre of Welford Park, Newbury. 47 *Courtfield Gardens, South Kensington, S.W.*

Fursdon (W.E., aft. K.S., C.J.A.)
REV. WALTER. 2nd son of G. F. of Fursdon, Tiverton; 1845^{3}–1852^{1}; Coll. Wall 1851; Pembroke Coll. Oxf. B.A.; Rector of Berrynarbor, Ilfracombe; *m.* Sarah Anna, *d.* of Rev. Francis Hole, Rector of Georgeham, Braunton, N. Devon; died at Berrynarbor, Mar. 2, 1876.

Northey *ma.* (C.O.G.)
REV. EDWARD WILLIAM. Eld. son of E. R. N. of Woodcote House; 1845^{3}–1851^{2}; Field XI. 1849–50; Keeper of the Field 1850; C.C.C. Oxf. M.A.; formerly Vicar of Chaddesden, Derby; J.P. and C.A. Wilts; *m.* Florence Elizabeth, *d.* of Sir John Edward Honywood, 6th Bt., of Evington, Ashford, Kent. *Woodcote House, Epsom.*

Blundell *ma.* (H.D.)
REV. CANON THOMAS BLUNDELL HOLLINSHEAD. Son of R. B. B. H. B. of Deysbrook, West Derby, Liverpool; 1847^{3}–1851^{3}; Eton VIII. 1848–51; Capt. of the Boats 1851; Opp. Wall 1850; Ch. Ch. Oxf.; Oxf. VIII. 1854; formerly Curate of Handsworth, Birmingham, Rector of Halsall since 1863; Hon. Canon of Liverpool; Hon. Chap. to the King; *m.* Adelaide Fanny Ashworth, *d.* of Sir Francis Astley, 2nd Bt., of Everley, Marlborough. *Halsall Rectory, Ormskirk.*

Denne *ma.* (W.E., W.J.)
REV. RICHARD HENRY. Son of D. D. of Elbridge, near Canterbury; 1846^{1}–1851^{3}; Field XI. and Capt. Opp. Wall XI. 1851; Univ. Coll. Oxf. M.A.; Oxf. VIII. 1855; Rector of Brimpsfield; *m.* Katherine, *d.* of Rev. W. Evans of Shipston-on-Stour. *Brimpsfield Rectory, Gloucester.*

Mytton (W.J.)
CAPT. DEVEREUX HERBERT. Eld. son of R. H. M. of Garth; 1846^{1}–1850^{3}; Wall and Field XI.'s 1850; formerly Capt. 85th Regt.; J.P. and D.L. co. Montgomery, High Sheriff 1873; J.P. for Salop; Chmn. of Montgomerys Qr. Sessions; *m.* Emma Lydia, *d.* of Edmund Story of the Madras Civil Service. *Garth, Welshpool.*

Roberts (Home & Mrs. de R., aft. K.S., E.B.)
JOHN PRETYMAN SLINGSBY. Son of J. R; 1840^{3}–1851^{1}; Solicitor (ret.); *m.* Sarah Mary, *d.* of Frederick Schönerstedt, German Master at Eton. 3 *Powis Villas, Brighton.*

Chandos-Pole (Miss W., J.W.H.)
REV. WILLIAM. 4th son of E. S. C.-P. of Radbourne Hall, co. Derby; 1842^{2}–1852^{3}; won School Pulling 1852; Ch. Ch. Oxf.; formerly Rector of Trusley, near Derby; aft. Rector of Radbourne; *m.* Christina, *d.* of Capt. Christopher Crackenthorpe Askew, R.N.; died Mar. 3, 1895.

Meade-King (Miss Edw. & W.E., H.D.)
WILLIAM OLIVER. 2nd son of R. K. M.-K. of Walford; 1846^{3}–1851^{3}; Eton VIII. 1850–1; won School Pulling 1850; Sculling 1851; Pemb. Coll. Oxf.; Pres. O.U.B.C.; Oxf. VIII. 1852–4, Stroke 1853–4; formerly one of H.M.'s Sup. Insp. of Factories; Major and Hon. Lieut.-Col. 3rd Bn. Somerset Lt. Infantry (ret.); J.P. for Somerset; *m.* Mary Musgrave, *d.* of William Beadon of Otterhead, Honiton. *Walford House, Taunton.*

Ford (Mrs. F., C.J.A.)
REV. MORTIMER WILLIAM. 1844^{3}–1852^{2}; Opp. Wall and Keeper of the Field 1851; Camb. B.A.; formerly Curate of Hilton St. Ives, Hunts.

Bridges (Mrs. Vav., W.A.C.)

JOHN AFFLECK. Son of J. T. B. of St Nicholas Court, Isle of Thanet; 1846^{1}-1851^{2}; Eton VIII. 1851; Ch. Ch. Oxf.; J.P. co. Worcester; Member of Council of National Union; Chmn. for 20 years of E. Div. of Worc.; Literature and Politics; *m.* Henrietta, *d.* of T. R. Philippi of Belfield Hall, Rochdale. 2 *Avenue Elmers, Surbiton, Surrey.*

Lord Dunglass (H.M.B.)

CHARLES ALEXANDER DOUGLAS HOME (12th Earl of Home), K.T. Eld. son of Cospatrick Alexander, 11th Earl of H.; 1845^{3}-1850^{3}; Trin. Coll. Camb. M.A.; Lord-Lieut. of co. Berwick 1879-90; Lord-Lieut. of co. Lanark since 1890; D.L. co. Berwick and Glasgow; Brig.-Gen. in Royal Archers and Hon. Col. Lanarks Yeo. (Vol. Dec.); A.D.C. to Queen Victoria 1887-97; *m.* Maria, *d.* of Capt. Charles Conrad Grey, R.N. 6 *Grosvenor Square, W.*; *Douglas and Bothwell Castles, co. Lanark, and The Hirsel, Coldstream.*

Bathurst (H.M.B.)

SIR FREDERICK THOMAS ARTHUR HERVEY-, 4th Bt. Of Clarendon Park, Salisbury; eld. son of F. H. H.-B., 3rd Bt., of Clarendon; 1846^{1}-1850^{3}; Eton XI. 1849-50; Lieut.-Col. Gren. Gds.; served in the Crimea (Alma, Balaclava, and Inkerman); med. with four clasps, Turkish med., and 5th Cl. Medjidie; ret. 1861; M.P. for S. Wilts 1861-5; *m.* Ada, *d.* of Sir John Sheppy Ribton, 3rd Bt., of Woodbrook, co. Dublin; died May 20, 1900.

Marindin (W.E., E.B.)

HENRY COLVILE. Eld. son of Rev. S. M., Capt. 2nd Life Guards, aft. Rector of Buckhorn Weston, Bath; 1847^{2}-1853^{2}; Newc. Select 1852-3; Ball. Coll. Oxf.; 2nd Cl. Class.; Barrister, formerly practising in Calcutta; *m.* Mary Elizabeth, *d.* of John Gregory Watkins of Woodfield, Ombersley, Droitwich; died of fever at Calcutta, May 7, 1872.

Yorke (E.B.)

JOHN REGINALD. Son of J. Y. of Forthampton; 1848^{2}-1854^{1}; Newc. Select 1853-4; Prince Consort's French Prize 1852; Eton XI. 1852-3; Opp. Wall 1852-3; Field XI. 1852, Keeper 1853; Ball. Coll. Oxf. M.A.; 1st Cl. Mods. 1856; formerly Capt. Tewkesbury R. Vol.; M.P. for Tewkesbury 1864-8, E. Gloucester 1872-85, and N. Div. Gloucester 1885-6; J.P. co. Gloucester, High Sheriff 1892; J.P. and D.L. co. Worcester; *m.* 1st, Augusta Emmeline, *d.* of Lieut.-Gen. Sir Thomas Monteith Douglas, K.C.B., of Stonebyres, co. Lanark; 2nd, Sophia Matilda, *d.* of Baron Vincent de Tuyll de Serooskerken. 2 *Chesham Street, S.W., and Forthampton Court, Tewkesbury.*

Lonsdale (E.B.)

ARTHUR PEMBERTON (aft. Heywood-Lonsdale). Of Shavington, Market Drayton, and Cloverley, Whitchurch, Salop; 2nd son of Rev. H. G. L. of Wakefield; 1847^{1}-1853^{1}; Eton VIII. 1852; Field XI. 1851-2; Opp. Wall 1852; Ball. Coll. Oxf. B.A.; Oxf. VIII. 1856-7; Barrister-at-Law, Lincoln's Inn; J.P., D.L., C.A. and Vice-Chmn. of C.C. for co. Salop, High Sheriff 1868; J.P. co. Flint; High Sheriff co. Louth 1877; *m.* Frances Elizabeth, *d.* of Daniel Neilson of Hundhill, Pontefract; died Feb. 24, 1897.

Scott *mi.* (E.C.)

WALTER JERVOISE. 2nd son of J. W. S. of Rotherfield Park, Alton, Hants; 1847^{1}-1853^{1}; Newc. Med. 1853; Sch. of Merton Coll. Oxf., B.A.; 1st Cl. Mods. 1856; Postmaster of Merton; Sec. to Gov. of Mauritius, aft. settled in Queensland; J.P. for Queensland; died unm. June 1890.

Wodehouse (E.B.)

RT. HON. EDMOND ROBERT, P.C. Son of Sir P. E. W., G.C.S.I., K.C.B., Gov. of Bombay; 1847 [illegible] 1854; Newc. Select 1854; Eton XI. 1852-3; Opp. Wall 1851-3, Keeper 1853; Field XI. 1852-3, Keeper; [illegible]

Wodehouse—*cont.*

Hurdle Race; Pres. of Eton Soc. 1853; Ball. Coll. Oxf. M.A.; 1st Cl. Mods. 1856; 1st Cl. Greats; 1st Cl. Lit. Hum. 1858; called to the Bar, Lincoln's Inn, 1861; Priv. Sec. to Earl of Kimberley 1864-74, and to his father 1875-6; M.P. for Bath since 1880; *m.* Adela Harriet Sophia, *d.* of Rev. Charles Walter Bagot, Chanc. of Bath and Wells and Rector of Castle Rising, King's Lynn. 56 *Chester Square, S.W., and Minley Grange, Farnborough, Hants.*

Gould (W.A.C.)

CAPT. ARTHUR ROBERT NUTCOMBE. Son of Rev. R. J. G., Vicar of Stratfield Mortimer, Berks; 1845^{3}-1853^{2}; Exeter Coll. Oxf.; Capt. 97th Regt.; served through the Indian Mutiny, inc. Siege of Lucknow; died June 1, 1867.

Gladstone (W.J.)

ROBERT. Eld. son of T. S. G. of Capenoch, co. Dumfries; 1847^{1}-1851^{1}; Edinburgh Univ; J.P. co. Dumfries; Chmn. Mersey Docks and Harbour Board; *m.* Mary, *d.* of Robertson Gladstone of Court Hey, co. Lancaster. *Woolton Vale, near Liverpool.*

Mr. Wodehouse (E.H.P.)

HON. HENRY. 2nd son of H. W., and brother of 1st Earl of Kimberley; 1847^{1}-1851^{2}; *m.* Mary Livingstone, *d.* of J. P. King of Sand Hills, Georgia, U.S.A.; died Aug. 20, 1873.

L'Estrange (R.F.H., W.G.C.)

REV. ALFRED GUY KINGAN. Son of H. F. L'E., Barrister; 1846^{1}-1851^{2}; Keeper of the Hockey Club at Eton; Exeter Coll. Oxf. M.A.; Author. 26 *Cumberland Terrace, Regent's Park, N.W.*

Gregory (W.E., H.M.B.)

FRANCIS BACON. 1847^{3}-1851^{3}; died at Eton, 1851.

Hayter (H.M.B., & Mrs. Dr., H.M.B., & J.L.J.)

RT. HON. SIR ARTHUR DIVETT, 2nd Bt., P.C. Son of Rt. Hon. Sir W. G. H., 1st Bt., of South Hill Park; 1847^{1}-1853^{3}; Eton XI. 1851-3; Field XI. 1851; Pres. Eton Soc. 1852; winner of 100 yds. race; Ball. Coll. & Sch. of B.N.C. Oxf. M.A.; Class. Hon., Mods. and Greats; Capt. Gren. Gds., ret. 1866; Lieut.-Col. London Rifle Bgde. 1872-81; M.P. for Wells 1865-8, Bath 1873-85, Walsall 1893-5 and since 1900; a Lord of the Treasury 1880-2; Financial Sec. at War Office 1882-5; Chmn. Public Accounts Committee 1901-2; J.P. and D.L. for Berks and J.P. for Somerset; Member of the Executive Comm. of the R. Patriotic Fund; *m.* Henrietta, *d.* of Capt. Adrian John Hope. 9 *Grosvenor Square, W., and South Hill Park, Bracknell.*

Vesey *ma.* (R.F.H., J.E.Y.)

ARTHUR CYRIL. 1846^{3}-1853^{3}; Eton VIII. 1853; Ch. Ch. Oxf.; formerly Princp. Clerk in Audit Office; died 1896.

Furnivall (J.W.H., aft. K.S., W.J.)

EDWARD THOMAS. Son of G. F. F., Surgeon, of Egham, Surrey; 1845^{1}-1851^{3}; formerly Surgeon at St. Barth. Hospital, London; died Oct. 2, 1875.

Mr. Trefusis *ma.* (Miss M., H.M.B., & J.L.J.)

HON. CHARLES HENRY ROLLE HEPBURN-STUART-FORBES- (20th Lord Clinton). Son of Charles Rodolph, 19th Lord C.; 1846^{3}-1852^{3}; Eton VIII. 1851-2; Capt. of the Boats 1852; Opp. Wall 1851; Pres. Eton Soc. 1851; Ch. Ch. Oxf. M.A.; 1st Cl. Law and Mod. Hist. 1856; M.P. for N. Devon 1857-66; Chmn. of Qr. Sessions 1863-99; Under-Sec. for India 1867-8; Charity Comm. for England and Wales 1874-80; Lord-Lieut. and Chmn. of C.C. of Devon; D.L. for co. Kincardine; formerly Lieut.-Col. N. Devon Yeo. Cav.; *m.* 1st, Harriet Williamina, *d.* of Sir John Stuart Forbes, 8th Bt.; 2nd, Margaret, *d.* of Sir John Walrond Walrond, 1st Bt. 41 *Portland* [illegible] *Satchville, Lolton,* [illegible]

Fletcher (E.B.) — HENRY CHARLES, C.M.G. Eld. son of E. C. F. of Kenward, Yalding, Maidstone; 1846^{1}-1850^{3}; Col. Scots Gds.; J.P. for Kent; *m.* Lady Harriet Marsham, *d.* of Charles, 3rd Earl of Romney; died Aug. 31, 1879.

Hope (J.E.Y.) — HENRY. 1847^{3}-1852^{1}.

Pottinger (W.L.E.) — SIR HENRY, 3rd Bt. 3rd son of Rt. Hon. Sir H. P., 1st Bt.; 1847^{2}-1851^{1}; Merton Coll. Oxf. B.A.; Barrister, Inner Temple 1861; J.P. and D.L. co. Durham; *m.* Mary Adeline, *d.* of Rev. Edmund Hector Shipperdson of Hermitage, co. Durham. *The Pines, Queen's Road, Richmond, Surrey.*

Stone *mi.* (Mrs. P. & Miss Elg., C.J.A. & F.E.D.) — WILLIAM. Son of T. A. S.; 1845^{3}-1851^{3}; Exeter Coll. Oxf. M.A.; Solicitor (ret.); *m.* Catherine Fleetwood, *d.* of Park Nelson, Solicitor. *Park End, Guildford.*

Graham (Mrs. Vav., W.J.) — REV. MALISE REGINALD, M.A. 2nd son of Rt. Hon. Sir J. R. G. G., 2nd Bt; 1846^{3}-1851^{3}; Rector of Arthuret, Cumberland; *m.* Agnes, *d.* of Sir George Musgrave, 10th Bt., of Edenhall, Langwathby, Cumberland; died Nov. 18, 1895.

Maynard (W.E., E.H.P.) — ANTHONY JEFFERSON. 1846^{3}-1850^{2}; died soon after leaving Eton.

Puxley *ma.* (C.O.G.) — HENRY LAVALLIN. 2nd son of J. L. P. of Dunboy; 1845^{3}-1851^{3}; B.N.C. Oxf. M.A.; J.P. co. Cork, High Sheriff 1865; J.P. co. Carmarthen, High Sheriff 1864; *m.* 1st, Katherine Ellen, *d.* of Rev. William Waller of Castletown Manor, co. Limerick; 2nd, Adeline, *d.* of Gen. Charles W. Nepean, and widow of Col. William Fergusson Hutchinson. *Dunboy Castle, Castletown, Berehaven, Bantry.*

Pugh (K.S.) — WALTER BARNES. 1844^{2}-1852^{3}; Coll. Wall 1851; formerly Lieut. and Adjt. 90th Regt.; aft. Adjt. St. George's Rifles.

Lord Chas. Bruce (H.M.B.) — RT. HON. CHARLES WILLIAM BRUDENELL, P.C. 3rd son of Charles, 2nd Earl & 1st Marquis of Ailesbury; 1846^{3}-1850^{2}; formerly Capt. 1st Life Gds. and Hon. Major Royal Wilts Yeo.; M.P. N. Wilts 1865-74, and for Marlborough 1878-85; Vice-Chamberlain to Queen Victoria 1880-5; *m.* Augusta Georgina Sophia, *d.* of Frederick Charles William Seymour; died April 16, 1897.

Clive (Miss M., W.J.) — LIEUT.-COL. HON. GEORGE HERBERT WINDSOR WINDSOR-. 2nd son of Hon. R. H. C. and Baroness Windsor; 1846^{3}-1851^{3}; in the 52nd Lt. Inf. 1852-60; Lieut.-Col. Coldstream Gds. 1860-70; M.P. for Ludlow 1860-85; *m.* Hon. Gertrude Albertina Trefusis, *d.* of Charles Rodolph, 19th Lord Clinton. 12 *Stratford Place, Oxford Street, W.*

Fitzgerald (R.D.) — THOMAS KEANE. Of Shalstone Manor, Buckingham; eld. son of T. F. of Shalstone; 1846^{3}-1851^{3}; Merton Coll. Oxf.; formerly Capt. 1st Rl. Dragoons; Lord of the Manor of Mortlake, co. Surrey; *m.* Marianne, *d.* of Hon. Richard Cavendish of Thornton Hall, Stratford, Bucks; died Aug. 27, 1887.

Law (Miss W., W.J.) — WILLIAM HENRY. 1846^{3}-1851^{3}.

Dymoke (W.J.) — HENRY LIONEL. Of Scrivelsby Court, Horncastle; son of Rev. J. D. of Scrivelsby; 1846^{3}-1850^{3}; Capt. N. Lincoln Militia; J.P. and D.L. co. Lincoln; *m.* Anne Louisa, *d.* of Henry Gilmore; died 1875.

Seale-Hayne (Home, H.M.B., & J.L.J.) — RT. HON. CHARLES, P.C. Son of C. H. S.-H. of Fuge House, Dartmouth; 1846^{1}-1853^{2}; Wall XI. 1852; Capt. of Upper Hockey XI.; Barrister, Lincoln's Inn, 1857; Hon. Col. 3rd Devon Regt.; Paymaster-Gen. 1892-5; M.P. for Mid. Div. of Devon since 1885; Chmn. of the Dartmouth Harbour Commission and the Dartmouth and Torbay Ry.; Chmn. of Buenos Ayres Northern Ry. and Texas Land and Mortgage Co.; J.P. for Devon and Middlesex. 6 *Upper Belgrave Street, S.W.; Pitt, Chudleigh, R.S.O., S. Devon; and Kingswear Castle, Dartmouth.*

Carlyon *ma.* (Mrs. P., W.L.E.) — HORATIO. Of Caldwell, Devon; 7th son of E. C. of Tregrehan, Par Station, Cornwall; 1845^{2}-1851^{1}; Trin. Coll. Oxf. M.A.; *m.* Jane, *d.* of John Lomas, M.D.; died June 20, 1896.

Kay (J.W.H.) — WILLIAM. 1843^{3}-1850^{3}; formerly of Hill Street, Berkeley Square, W.; Lord of the Manor of Tring, Herts.

Bright (Miss W., H.M.B.) — REGINALD. Of Melbourne, Victoria; 7th son of R. B. of Abbots Leigh, Bristol; 1846^{1}-1850^{2}; formerly a Merchant at Melbourne.

Alderson *ma.* (W.J.) — FRANCIS JOHN. Son of Hon. Sir E. H. A., a Baron of the Exchequer; 1844^{1}-1850^{3}; Eton XI. 1849-50; Field and Opp. Wall XI.'s 1850; formerly in the Admiralty, aft. Civil Service in Borneo, and later a Sheep Farmer in New Zealand; *m.* Jane, *d.* of Dr. Black of Melbourne, Victoria; dead.

Pepys *ma.* (J.E.Y.) — EDMUND. Son of E. P. of 20 Portland Place, W.; 1845^{2}-1851^{1}; formerly Lieut. 1st Rl. Dragoons. 115 *Sloane Street, S.W.*

Shawe (Mrs. Ro., W.J.) — HENRY CUNLIFFE. Son of S. P. S. of Maple Hayes, Lichfield; 1846^{3}-1851^{3}; Opp. Wall 1851; Ch. Ch. Oxf.; J.P. for Notts and J.P. co. Warwick; High Sheriff 1895; *m.* Georgina Wilmot, *d.* of Rev. Sir William Nigel Gresley, 9th Bt., of Netherseale Hall, co. Leicester. *Weddington Hall, Nuneaton.*

Henley (J.E.Y.) — CAPT. ARTHUR. 4th son of Rt. Hon. J. W. H. of Waterperry, Oxf.; 1846^{3}-1851^{1}; served with the 52nd Regt. in the Indian Mutiny as A.D.C. to Sir Charles Windham and Sir Robert Walpole; aft. Priv. Sec. to Sir William Denison at Madras; J.P. co. Carlow; *m.* Margaret, *d.* of Joseph John Gore of Derrymore, co. Clare. *Eastwood, Bagenalstown.*

Luttrell (Mrs. D., C.J.A. & J.E.Y.) — EDWARD FOWNES. Son of Col. F. F. L. of Kilve Court, Bridgwater; 1845^{2}-1851^{1}; Opp. Wall 1846 and 1848-50; Field XI. 1849-50; Ch. Ch. Oxf.; died 1865.

UNPLACED.

Steuart — AUGUSTUS JAMES HENRY. Son of Rev. C. A. S. of Sunningdale; 1845^{3}-1850^{1}.

MIDDLE DIVISION.

Peyton (R.F.H., H.M.B.) — SIR ALGERNON WILLIAM, 4th Bt. 2nd son of Sir H. P., 3rd Bt.; 1845^{3}-1850^{3}; formerly Capt. 1st Life Gds.; High Sheriff co. Oxf. 1870; *m.* Laura Sarah, *d.* of Daniel H. Webb of Wykham Park, co. Oxf.; died Mar. 25, 1872.

Wigram *ma.* (W.J.) — ARTHUR JAMES. 3rd son of Rt. Hon. Sir J. W., P.C.; 1847^{3}-1851^{3}; Eton XI. 1851; Keeper of Upper Club 1850; Barrister; died unm. Nov. 5, 1874.

Godfrey (W.A.C.) — THOMAS SPRAGGING. Son of — G. of Balderton, Newark; 1847^{1}-1851^{3}; Trin. Coll. Camb.; formerly a Banker at Newark; dead.

Dugdale *ma.* (E.C.)

JOHN STRATFORD, K.C. 3rd son of W. S. D. of Merevale Hall, Atherstone, and Blythe Hall, Coleshill, Birmingham; 1847^{2}–1853^{3}; Newc. Select 1853; Sch. of Merton Coll. Oxf., M.A.; Barrister, Inner Temple, 1862; Recorder of Grantham 1874; Recorder of Birmingham since 1877; M.P. for Nuneaton Div. of Warwicks 1886–92; Chmn. of Warwicks Qr. Sessions since 1883; Chmn. of Warwicks C.C.; Chanc. of Diocese of Worcester, and a Trustee of Rugby School; J.P. and D.L. co. Warwick; *m.* Alice, *d.* of Gen. Henry Alexander Carleton, C.B., R.A., of Clare, co. Tipperary. 29 *Eaton Square, S.W.*

Johnson (H.D., & F.E.D.)

RT. REV. HENRY FRANK, Bp. of Colchester. Son of Col. J. J. of Walbury, Hallingbury, Essex; 1848^{1}–1853^{2}; Eton VIII. 1852–3; won Steeplechase 1852; Trin. Coll. Camb. LL.B., D.D.; Camb. VIII. 1855; Pres. C.U.B.C. 1855; Cornet 1st Rl. Dragoons 1855–6; Ordained 1858; Curate at Richmond, Surrey; Curate at Sawbridgeworth, Herts, 1860–2; 1st Vicar of High Wych, Sawbridgeworth, 1862–80; Rector of Chelmsford 1880–94; Archdn. of Essex 1885–94; Archdn. of Colchester 1894; Suffragan Bp. in the Diocese of St. Albans; *m.* Emily Ann, *d.* of Thomas Perry of Moor Hall, Harlow. *The Rectory, Chelmsford.*

Adlercron (F.E.D.)

GEORGE ROTHE LADEVEZE. Son of J. L. A. of Moyglare, co. Meath, and Woodville, co. Dublin; 1848^{2}–1850^{3}; *m. d.* of Baron de Blonay; died May 1884.

Maxwell (C.L.)

GEORGE. 1848^{1}–1851^{3}; died 1895.

Mr. Wellesley (E.H.P.)

HON. WILLIAM HENRY (2nd Earl Cowley). Eld. son of Henry Richard, 1st Earl C., K.G.; 1847^{3}–1851^{1}; Lieut.-Col. Coldstream Gds.; served in the Crimea; Knt. of the Medjidie; A.D.C. to Lord Clyde in India 1858, ret. 1860; *m.* Emily Gwendolen, *d.* of Col. Thomas Peers-Williams, M.P., of Temple House, Marlow; died Feb. 28, 1895.

Reay (Miss Edg., aft. K.S., C.J.A., & J.E.Y.)

REV. THOMAS OSMOTHERLEY. Son of J. R. of Cumberland; 1846^{2}–1852^{3}; Eton XI. 1850–2; Coll. Wall 1851; Exeter Coll. Oxf. M.A.; Rural Dean of Canewdon, Rochford, Essex; Vicar of Prittlewell and Chaplain 1st Essex Vol. Art.; *m.* Alice, *d.* of John Borradaile of Shanklin, Isle of Wight. *Prittlewell Vicarage, Southend-on-Sea.*

Lambton *mi.* (C.L.)

LIEUT.-COL. FRANCIS WILLIAM. 3rd son of W. H. L. of Biddick Hall, Durham; 1848^{1}–1850^{3}; Lieut.-Col. Scots Gds. (ret.); served in the Crimea; J.P. for co. Pembroke, High Sheriff 1896; *m.* Lady Victoria Alexandrina Elizabeth, *d.* of John Frederick, 2nd Earl of Cawdor. *Brownslade, Pembroke.*

Barton (E.B.)

JOHN HOPE. Of Stapleton Park, Pontefract, and Saxby Hall, Barton-on-Humber, Hull; son of J. W. B. of Stapleton Park and Saxby Hall; 1847^{3}–1851^{3}; Ch. Ch. Oxf. M.A.; Master of Badsworth Hounds 1869–76; J.P. and D.L. co. York. High Sheriff 1863; *m.* Florence Mary Annabella, *d.* of Henry James Ramsden of Oxton Hall, co. York; died Mar. 20, 1876.

Brandreth (Miss Edw., & T.H.S., H.D., & R.D.)

REV. HENRY. Son of T. S. B.; 1847^{3}–1853^{3}; Tomline Select 1851, Prizeman 1852; Field and Wall XI.'s 1852; Sch. of Trin. Coll. Camb., M.A.; 11th Wrangler 1857; Fellow of Trin. 1858–71; Lecturer and Asst. Tutor Trin. Coll. Camb.; Math. Master at Eton 1860–4; Math. Master at Rugby 1865; J.P. for Norfolk; late Rector of Dickleburgh, Scole, Norfolk; *m.* Louisa Victoria, *d.* of Col. Henry Augustus Jackson. 72 *Hills Road, Cambridge.*

Buckley (Mrs. Ro., aft. K.S., H.M.B.)

REV. WILLIAM BURTON. 1848^{1}–1853^{3}; Coll. Wall 1852; Sch. of Trin. Coll. Camb.; 21st Wrangler 1858; formerly Curate of Tarvin, Chester.

Prodgers *ma.* (W.J.)

EDWIN. Eld. son of Rev. E. P., Rector of Ayot St. Peter, Welwyn; 1847^{3}–1851^{3}; Ch. Ch. Oxf. M.A.; J.P. for Herts; *m.* Elizabeth Ellen, *d.* of Henry E. Surtees of Redworth House, co. Durham. *Ayot Bury, Welwyn.*

Thompson (F.E.D.)

PENTON. Son of G. P. T. of the Indian Civil Service; 1847^{3}–1850^{2}; Capt. Royal Art. (ret.); med. for Indian Mutiny with clasps for Delhi and Lucknow; *m.* Emily, *d.* of Gen. George Whish of the Indian Army. 15 *Grosvenor Park, Tunbridge Wells.*

Mr. Nelson *ma.* (R.F.H., H.M.B.)

HON. AND REV. EDWARD FOYLE, M.A. 4th son of Thomas Bolton, 2nd Earl Nelson; 1846^{3}–1850^{3}; died Sept. 8, 1853.

Mr. Nevill (C.O.G.)

HON. RALPH PELHAM. 2nd son of William, 4th Earl of Abergavenny; 1846^{3}–1851^{2}; Cox of Eton VIII. 1850; Field XI. 1850; Merton Coll. Oxf.; 30 years Master W. Kent Foxhounds; formerly W. Kent Yeo. Cav.; J.P. and D.L. for Kent, High Sheriff 1896; *m.* Louisa Marianne, *d.* of Sir Charles Fitzroy Maclean, 9th Bt. 38 *Lowndes Square, S.W., and Birling Manor, Maidstone.*

Nugent (J.E.Y.)

LIEUT.-GEN. ANDREW. Eld. son of Col. P. J. N. of Portaferry; 1848^{1}–1850^{3}; Trin. Coll. Camb.; Lieut.-Gen. (ret.); Col. Royal Scots Greys; served in the Crimea, med. with clasps for Balaclava, Inkerman, and Sebastopol; J.P. and D.L. co. Down, High Sheriff 1882. *Portaferry, S.O., co. Down.*

Sutherland (Mrs. Hor. & Miss G., W.J.)

WILLIAM STEWART. Son of J. W. S. of Coombe, near Croydon; 1846^{3}–1852^{2}; Ch. Ch. Oxf. M.A.; Barrister. 139 *Sloane Street, S.W.*

Theobald (Miss W., aft. K.S.)

JOHN SHADWELL. Son of — T. of Hyde Abbey, Winchester; 1843^{3}–1853^{3}; Coll. Wall 1851–2; formerly Lieut. 18th Regt.; died of cholera in India, 1860.

Palk *mi.* (W.G.C.)

WILMOT HENRY. 2nd son of R. J. M. P., Barrister; 1846^{3}–1854^{1}; formerly Clerk in the House of Lords; *m.* Elizabeth Alexandrina Greig, *d.* of William Mackenzie of Aberdeen; died June 13, 1876.

Egerton (W.A.C.)

SIR PHILIP LE BELWARD GREY-, 11th Bt. Of Oulton Park, Tarporley; eld. son of Sir P. de M. G.-E., 10th Bt., of Oulton; 1846^{3}–1850^{3}; joined Rifle Bgde. 1852; served in the Crimea (Alma and siege of Sebastopol) (Turkish and Crimean Meds.) and Indian Mutiny; exchanged to Coldstream Gds. 1857; ret. 1861; Hon. Lieut.-Col. 4th Bn. Cheshire Regt. (1869–83); J.P. and D.L. for Cheshire; *m.* Hon. Henrietta Elizabeth Sophia, *d.* of Albert, 1st Lord Londesborough; died Sept. 1, 1891.

Lord Hervey (E.B.)

FREDERICK WILLIAM JOHN (3rd Marquis of Bristol). Eld. son of Frederick William, 2nd Marquis of B.; 1846^{3}–1852^{2}; winner of Pulling and Double Punting 1851; Trin. Coll. Camb. M.A.; M.P. for W. Suffolk 1859–64; Lord-Lieut. of Suffolk since 1886; Hereditary Steward of Bury St. Edmunds; Hon. Col. 3rd Bn. Suffolk Militia; *m.* Geraldine Georgiana Mary, *d.* of Gen. Hon. George Anson, M.P. *Ickworth Park, Bury St. Edmunds, and 19 Sussex Square, Kemp Town, Brighton.*

Garden (R.F.H. W.J.)

JOHN LEWIS. Of Redisham Hall, Suffolk; [illegible]; Trin. Coll. Camb.; *m.* [illegible] M[illegible]at; dead.

Farquharson (C.O.G.)
JAMES ROSS. Of Invercauld, Ballater, co. Aberdeen; eld. son of J. R. F. of Invercauld; 1847[1]-1850[2]; Lieut.-Col. Scots Fusilier Gds.; served in the Crimea; J.P. and D.L. co Aberdeen; m. Elizabeth Louisa, d. of Alexander Haldane Oswald of Auchincruive; died March 19, 1888.

Sutton (Mrs. Hor., W.L.E.)
REV. CANON FREDERICK HEATHCOTE. 8th son of Sir R. S., 2nd Bt., of Norwood Park, Nottingham; 1846[1]-1850[3]; Magd. Coll. Oxf. M.A.; Canon of Lincoln and Rector of Brant Broughton, Newark; died unm. March 2, 1888.

Buckle (K.S., F.E.D.)
REV. GEORGE MANLEY. 5th son of Rev. W. L. B. of Burgh, Banstead, and Vicar of Banstead, Epsom; 1848[3]-1855[1]; Newc. Select 1855; Coll. Wall 1853-4; Mixed Wall 1854; Fellow of King's Coll. Camb.; Incumbent of East Molesey, Surrey; died 1876.

Hartopp (E.H.P.)
GEORGE. Son of E. B. H. of Dalby Hall, Melton Mowbray; 1847[3]-1852[1]; died abroad 1855.

Coldham (F.V., aft. K.S., E.H.P.)
REV. JAMES CHARLES. 1848[3]-1854[1]; Newc. Select 1854; Coll. Wall 1853; Fellow of King's Coll. Camb., M.A.; formerly Curate of East Walton and Gayton Thorpe, Norfolk; died 1870.

Farquhar (W.E., E.B.)
SIR ERIC ROBERT TOWNSEND-, 3rd Bt. Eld. son of Sir W. M. T.-F., 2nd Bt., M.P.; 1848[3]-1854[1]; Diplomatic Service; Sec. of Legation at Pekin; died unm., of fever, at Pekin, June 1867.

Smijth-Windham (E.B.)
STEUART. 5th son of J. S.-W. of Wawne, Beverley; 1848[1]-1853[1]; Eton XI. 1852; Field XI. 1852; formerly Capt. Rifle Bgde.; died unm. Sept. 1872.

Rendel (W.E., W.A.C.)
STUART (1st Lord Rendel). 3rd son of J. M. R., F.R.S., Civil Engineer; 1848[3]-1852[3]; Oriel Coll. Oxf. M.A.; Hon. 4th Class.; called to the Bar, Inner Temple, 1861; formerly member of Sir W. Armstrong & Co., Engineers; M.P. for co. Montgomery 1880-94; J.P. co. Montgomery; Pres. of Univ. Coll. of Wales since 1895; m. Ellen Sophy, d. of William Egerton Hubbard of Leonardslee, Horsham. *23 Prince's Gate, S.W., and Hatchlands, Guildford, Surrey.*

Evans (R.F.H., aft. K.S.)
GEORGE HENRY. Son of the Chanc. of Norwich; 1848[3]-1853[2]; Fellow of King's Coll. Camb.; Ensign in the St. Helena Rifles 1861; died 1883.

Heathcote *mi.* (E.H.P.)
WILLIAM GEORGE. 2nd son of J. M. H. of Conington Castle, Peterborough; 1848[3]-1854[2]; Eton XI. 1854; Trin. Coll. Camb.; died at Camb. 1857.

Shaw (K.S., H.D.)
GEORGE JOHN. Son of Rev. — S., Vicar of Stoke Poges, Bucks; 1848[3]-1853[2]; Coll. Wall 1851-2; formerly a Clerk in the Admiralty, aft. went to live in Australia.

Tremlett *mi.* (Mrs. Ro., aft. K.S., W.L.E.)
COL. EDMUND JOHN. Son of Rev. D. T. of Rodney Stoke, Cheddar, co. Somerset; 1846[1]-1854[1]; Eton XI. 1853-4; Coll. Wall 1852-4, Keeper 1854; Keeper of Mixed Wall 1854; Keeper of Upper Club 1853; joined Royal Art. 1855; served in the Zulu War 1879 (Med. and clasp); ret. 1882; died June 28, 1903.

Bent *mi.* (Mrs. Ro., aft. K.S., O.J.A. & J.E.Y.)
STEPHEN WESTON. Son of Major J. B. of Wexham Lodge, Slough; 1847[2]-1853[3]; Coll. Wall 1852; formerly in 66th Regt., aft. Capt. 19th Regt.; died at the Cape 1880.

Pinney (C.O.G.)
REV. JOHN CHARLES. 2nd son of C. P. of Camp House, Clifton, Bristol; 1847[3]-1854[2]; Eton XI. 1853-4; Opp. Wall 1852-3; Keeper of the Field 1851-2, Field XI. 1853; Caius Coll. Camb. M.A.; Vicar of Coleshill; m. Harriet Margaretta, d. of Rev John Digby Wingfield-Digby, Vicar of Coleshill. *Coleshill Vicarage, Birmingham.*

Mr. Amherst *ma.* (E.B.)
HON. WILLIAM ARCHER (3rd Earl Amherst). Eld. son of William Pitt, 2nd Earl A.; 1847[2]-1852[2]; formerly Capt. Coldstream Gds.; served in the Crimea 1854-5, wounded at Inkerman; aft. Capt. Kent R.V.; M.P. for W. Kent 1859-68, for Mid-Kent 1868-80; Pro Grand Master English Freemasons since 1898; P.G.M. Kent since 1860; J.P. and D.L. Kent; A Knt. of Justice of St. John of Jerusalem; m. 1st, Mary Julia Cornwallis, d. of 1st Earl Cornwallis; 2nd, Alice D'Alton, d. of Edmund Probyn of Huntley Manor, Gloucester, and widow of Ernest Augustus Malet, 5th Earl of Lisburne. *3 Wilton Terrace, S.W., and Montreal, Sevenoaks.*

Sparks (H.M.B., R.O., & C.Wo.)
COL. ROBERT WATSON. Son of J. S. of West Lodge, Byfleet, Weybridge; 1848[3]-1853[2]; Opp. Wall 1853; served 26 years in the 7th Royal Fusiliers; J.P. for Surrey; m. Jenella, d. of Capt. J. Douglas, R.N., of Seafield, Walmer, Deal. *16 Dynevor Gardens, Richmond, Surrey.*

Bosanquet (E.B.)
CHARLES BERTIE PULLEINE. Eld. son of Rev. R. W. B. of Rock Hall; 1847[3]-1853[1]; Ball. Coll. Oxf. M.A.; 3rd Cl. Class.; Hon. 4th Mod. Hist. and Law; called to the Bar, Lincoln's Inn, 1862; J.P. for Northumberland; m. Eliza Isabella, d. of Ralph Carr-Ellison of Dunston Hall, co. Durham. *Rock Hall, Alnwick.*

Goldney (T.H.S., aft. K.S., W.J.)
REV. SAMUEL. Son of S. A. G. of Langley, Slough; 1848[3]-1853[2]; Pembroke Coll. Oxf. M.A.; sometime Headmaster of Lichfield Grammar School; m. Grace, d. of Capt. Peel, R.N. *Priory Park, Kew, S.W., Surrey.*

Pemberton (Mrs. Ro., C.O.G.)
HENRY LEIGH. 6th son of E. L. P. of Torry Hill, Sittingbourne; 1844[3]-1852[3]; formerly a Solicitor in Whitehall Place, S.W.; m. Mary, d. of Sir Richard Garth, P.C.; died Mar. 29, 1895.

Hamond (E.B.)
ANTHONY. Of Westacre High House, Swaffham; eld. son of A. H. of Westacre; 1847[1]-1852[1]; Opp. Wall 1851; Trin. Coll. Camb.; J.P. and D.L. for Norfolk; Lord of the Manor of Westacre and Swaffham; m. Mary Leigh, d. of Sir Thomas Hare, 2nd Bt., of Stow Hall, Downham; died March 30, 1895.

Booth (C.O.G.)
THOMAS. Son of Rev. T. B. of Friskney, co. Lincoln; 1847[3]-1851[3]; Univ. Coll. Oxf.; formerly Lieut. 5th Dragoon Gds.

Colvin *ma.* (W.A.C.)
RUSSELL PAKENHAM. Son of J. R. C.; 1848[1]-1850[2]; formerly a Merchant in Calcutta; m. E. Mary, widow of B. L. Heriott; died 1892.

Mynors (W.E., H.M.B.)
THOMAS BASKERVILLE. Of Penhony, Builth, co. Brecon; 4th son of P. R. M. of Treago, Ross, co. Hereford; 1848[3]-1851[2]; J.P. co. Radnor; m. Constance Mary, d. of Sir Richard Green-Price, 1st Bt.

Pegge-Burnell *ma.* (E.H.P.)
COL. EDWARD STRELLEY. Eld. son of E. V. P.-B. of Beauchief and Winkburn; 1848[1]-1852[3]; Ch. Ch. Oxf.; Col. Coldstream Gds. (ret.); J.P. for Notts. *Winkburn Hall, Southwell, and Beauchief Abbey, Sheffield.*

Bayley (J.W.H., aft. K.S., W.J.)
SIR STEUART COLVIN, K.C.S.I., C.I.E. Son of W. B. B., Director H.E.I.C.S.; 1846[3]-1851[3]; Haileybury Coll.; Bengal Civil Service; Commr. of Patna 1873-4; Sec. to Govt. of Bengal 1877; Sec. to Govt. of India (Home Dept.) and Chief Commr. at Assam 1878; Res. at Hyderabad 1881; Member of the Council of the Gov.-Gen. of India 1882-7; Lieut.-Gov. of Bengal 1887-90; Sec. Political Dept. India Office 1890-5; Member of Indian Council since 1890; m. Anna, d. of Robert Nesham Farquharson, Bengal C.S. *2 Barkston Gardens, S.W.*

Blackmore (Mrs. Ro., aft. K.S., H.D.) — ARTHUR. Of Fulham; 1848^{3}–1853^{2}; formerly in the Commissariat; died on his way home from China.

Ashford (E.B.) — WILLIAM. 1847^{2}–1853^{1}; formerly in the War Dept.

Fardell (Mrs. Ro., & Mrs. de R., E.H.P.) — SIR THOMAS GEORGE, Kt. Son of Rev. H. F., Canon of Ely, and Vicar of Wisbech; 1847^{2}–1850^{2}; Ch. Ch. Oxf. B.A.; Barrister, Lincoln's Inn. 1862; formerly Norfolk Circuit, aft. Registrar in Bankruptcy at Manchester; Member of L.C.C. for S. Paddington 1889–98; J.P. and Chmn. of Qr. Sessions for Isle of Ely; M.P. for S. Paddington since 1895; *m.* Lethia Anne, *d.* of Henry Swann Oldfield, Bengal C.S. 28 *Hyde Park Street, W.*

Gwynne-Holford (W.A.C.) — JAMES PRICE WILLIAM. Eld. son of J. P. G.-H. of Buckland; 1847^{3}–1851^{2}; Ch. Ch. Oxf.; formerly Cornet 16th Lancers; M.P. for co. Brecon 1870–80; J.P., D.L., and C.C. for co. Brecon; J.P. co. Carmarthen, High Sheriff 1857; *m.* Mary Eleanor, *d.* of P. R. Gordon Cumming of Hartpury, Gloucester. *Buckland, Bwlch, R.S.O., Brecon, and Cilgwyn, co. Carmarthen.*

Knox — GEORGE WILLIAM. 1846^{2}–1851^{3}.

Davies (Mrs. P., W.J.) — REV. THOMAS LEWIS OWEN. 1847^{3}–1852^{1}; Exeter Coll. Oxf. M.A.; Vicar of St. Mary Extra. *Pear Tree Vicarage, Southampton.*

Vivian *ma.* (W.J.) — LIEUT.-COL. SIR ARTHUR PENDARVES, K.C.B. 3rd son of J. H. V. of Singleton, Swansea; 1847^{2}–1851^{1}; Trin. Coll. Camb., and Mining Academy at Freiberg in Saxony; M.P. for W. Cornwall 1868–85; Lieut.-Col. comm. 2nd Vol. Bn. Welsh Regt. 1872–95 (Vol. Dec.); Member of Glamorgan C.C. 1892–8; Ald. of Cornwall C.C. since 1898; J.P. and D.L. for co. Glamorgan; J.P. for Cornwall, High Sheriff 1889; Col. comm. S. Wales Vol. Infantry Bgde. 1895–1902; Commr. of S. Wales Border Bgde. since 1902; *m.* 1st, Lady Augusta Emily, *d.* of Edwin, 3rd Earl of Dunraven; 2nd, Lady Jane Georgina, *d.* of John Hamilton, 10th Earl of Stair. 23 *Buckingham Gate, S.W.*, *and Bosahan, St. Martin, R.S.O., Cornwall.*

Edwardes (J.E.Y.) — HON. WILLIAM (4th Lord Kensington). Eld. son of William, 3rd Lord K.; 1848^{3}–1852^{3}; Lord-Lieut. of co. Pembroke; formerly Lieut.-Col. Coldstream Gds.; M.P. for Haverfordwest 1868–85; a Groom-in-Waiting to Queen Victoria 1873–4; Compt. of the Household 1880–5; a Lord-in-Waiting Feb.–July 1886; Capt. of H.M.'s Bodyguard of Yeomen of the Guard 1892–5; *m.* Grace Elizabeth, *d.* of Robert Johnstone-Douglas of Lockerbie; died Oct. 7, 1896.

Athorpe (C.O.G.) — CAPT. JOHN. Eld. son of J. C. A. of Dinnington, Rotherham; 1847^{1}–1850^{3}; Capt. 85th Regt.; *m.* Avice, *d.* of Capt. Hayden; died in Natal March 3, 1861.

Jenner (W.G.C.) — REV. EDMUND. 4th son of R. F. J. of Wenvoe Castle, Cardiff; 1846^{3}–1851^{1}; Trin. Hall, Camb.; formerly Curate of Powerstock, Melplash, co. Dorset; *m.* Ellen, *d.* of Rev. James Greenwood; died Sept. 2, 1878.

Ewart (F.E.D.) — LIEUT.-COL. WILLIAM SALISBURY. Eld. son of Rev. P. E., Rector of Kirklington, Bedale; 1847^{3}–1851^{2}; Eton VIII. 1851; Lieut.-Col. Gren. Gds.; served with the 93rd Highl. in the Crimea; *m.* Selina, *d.* of Capt. Thomas Bulkeley, 1st Life Gds.; died 1890.

Mariette *ma.* (Home) — JOHN CHARLES. 1844–1850; formerly Ensign 6th R[illegible].

Moore (R.F.H., E.H.P.) — WILLIAM PRICE. 1848^{3}–1850^{2}; Solicitor (Moore & Currey); Proctor and Notary; Registrar of the Faculty Office of the Archbp. of Canterbury and Registrar of the Commissary Court of Surrey and the Archdeaconries of Surrey (Southwark and Kingston). 23 *Knightrider Street, E.C.*

Lempriere (Miss Edg. & W.J., W.J. & H.M.B.) — ALGERNON THOMAS. 2nd son of Adml. G. O. L. of Pelham, Hants; 1847^{3}–1851^{1}; Trin. Coll. Oxf. M.A.; Barrister, Inner Temple; Capt. Hants Militia; Priv. Sec. and A.D.C. to Sir George Fergusson Bowen, Gov. of Queensland (2 years) and aft. New Zealand (1 year); J.P. for Hants; died unm. Nov. 13, 1874.

Forster (R.F.H., E.H.P.) — JOHN PHILIP BOHUN. 1847^{3}–1850^{2}.

Pilcher *ma.* (J.W.H. & W.J., W.J.) — HENRY DRAYSON, F.R.G.S. Son of J. P. of Worthing; 1845^{1}–1850^{1}; *m.* *d.* of W. Banks. 21 *Ennismore Gardens, S.W.*

Crawfurd (W.J.) — JOHN OSWALD FREDERICK, C.M.G. Son of J. C., Gov. of Singapore; 1847^{2}–1851^{1}; Oxf.; formerly Clerk in the Foreign Office; aft. H.M.'s Consul at Oporto 1867–91; served through the troubles in Portugal 1889–90; Chmn. London Gen. Publishing Co.; *m.* 1st, Margaret, *d.* of Richard Ford; 2nd, Lita Browne, *d.* of Hermann von Flesch Brunningen. *Queen Anne's Mansions, S.W.*

Barton *ma.* (W.L.E.) — CHARLES THOMAS HUGH. Of Bordeaux; 4th son of N. B. of Bordeaux and Straffan House, co. Kildare; 1844^{3}–1851^{2}; Eton VIII. 1851; Merchant at Bordeaux; *m.* Clara Sophia, *d.* of Frank Cutler, R.N., of Upton Lodge, Brixham, S. Devon; died at Bordeaux Sept. 11, 1871.

Yonge *ma.* (W.G.C., aft. K.S., W.G.C.) — REV. DENYS NELSON. Son of Rev. F. L. Y.; 1843^{3}–1854^{2}; Coll. Wall 1853; Christ's Coll. Camb. B.A.; formerly Diocesan Insp. of Schools; Vicar of Boreham; *m.* Mary Isabel, *d.* of Rev. John Eyre Yonge of Eton. *Boreham Vicarage, Chelmsford.*

Buckley *ma.* (E.B.) — REV. CANON FELIX JOHN. 4th son of Gen. E. P. B. of New Hall, Bodenham, Salisbury; 1845^{2}–1851^{1}; Merton Coll. Oxf. M.A.; Rector of Stanton St. Quintin; *m.* Augusta Frederica, *d.* of Sir Frederick Hutchinson Hervey-Bathurst, 3rd Bt. *Stanton St. Quintin Rectory, Chippenham.*

Rolt (W.E.) — JOHN. Of Ozleworth Park, Wotton-under-Edge; son of — R. of Ozleworth; 1846^{3}–1852^{2}; Barrister; died 1876.

Collins *ma.* (Mrs. P., W.J.) — EDWARD. Of Truthan, Truro, and Newton Ferrers, Callington, Cornwall; eld. son of E. C. of Truthan and Newton Ferrers; 1846^{3}–1852^{2}; Opp. Wall 1851; formerly Capt. Cornwall Rangers; J.P. and D.L. for Cornwall; died unm. 1870.

LOWER DIVISION.

Johnstone — 1846^{3}–1851^{1}; Field XI. 1850.

Witt (F.V., aft. K.S., F.E.D.) — JOHN GEORGE, K.C. Son of J. W. W.; 1848^{2}–1856^{1}; Newc. Select 1856; Eton XI. 1855; Coll. Wall. 1853–5, Keeper 1855; Mixed Wall 1854–5, Keeper 1855; Keeper of Upper Club 1854; Sch. of King's Coll. Camb.; 1st Cl. Class. Trip.; Hulsean Prize and Fellow of King's 1860; Barrister-at-Law; *m.* Emily Anne, *d.* of James Taylor. 1 *King's Bench Walk, Temple, E.C.*, *and B[illegible], [illegible]pstead, Wokingham.*

Tottenham (E.C.) — Col. Charles George. Eld. son of C. T. of Ballycurry; 1848^{3}–1854^{1}; Newc. Select 1853; Prince Consort's French and German Prizes 1852; served with Scots Fusilier Gds. in the Crimea (5th Cl. Medjidie and Turkish Med.); M.P. for New Ross 1863-8 and 1878-80; Hon. Col. Wicklow Militia Art.; J.P. for co. Wexford, High Sheriff 1874; J.P. and D.L. co. Wicklow, High Sheriff 1881; *m.* Catherine Elizabeth, *d.* of Hon. and Rev. Sir Francis Jarvis Stapleton, 7th Bt., Rector of Mereworth, Maidstone. *Ballycurry, Ashford, R.S.O., co. Wicklow.*

Mr. Warren (E.C.) — Hon. John Byrne Leicester (3rd and last Lord De Tabley). Eld. son of George, 2nd Lord De T.; 1847^{3}–1851^{2}; Ch. Ch. Oxf. M.A.; called to the Bar, Lincoln's Inn, 1860; formerly Lieut. Chester Yeo.; died unm. Nov. 22, 1895.

Warner (F.V., W.A.C.) — Sir Joseph Henry, Kt. 1847^{1}–1855^{1}; Newc. Select 1853; Med. 1854; Sch. 1855; Ball. Coll. Oxf.; 1st Cl. Mods and Gaisford Greek verse 1857; Chanc. Latin Prize 1858; 1st Cl. Lit. Hum. 1859; Master of the Grocers' Co. and Counsel to Chmn. of Committees, House of Lords; Lieut.-Col. comm. 2nd Bn. Middlesex R.V. (V.D.); *m.* Mary Wilelmina, *d.* of James Carson of Spinfield, Marlow; died 1897.

Burnaby *ma.* (F.V., aft. K.S., E.C. & W.B.M.) — Rev. Henry Fowke. Of Brampton Manor House, Huntingdon; eld. son of T. F. A. B. of Brampton; 1848^{3}–1854^{2}; Coll. Wall 1852; King's Coll. Camb. M.A.; Fellow of King's; Rector of Buckland, Buntingford, Herts, 1872–94; *m.* Louisa Jane, *d.* of George Thomas Davy of Colston Basset Hall, Nottingham. 29 *Kensington Gardens Sq., W.*

Tyssen (W.A.C.) — William Amhurst (aft. Tyssen-Amherst) (1st Lord Amherst of Hackney). Eld. son of W. G. T.-A. of Didlington; 1849^{1}–1850^{3}; Ch. Ch. Oxf.; M.P. for W. Norfolk 1880–5, and for S.W. Norfolk 1885–92; J.P. for Norfolk, High Sheriff 1866; J.P. and D.L. for Middlesex; Knt. of Justice of St. John of Jerusalem; *m.* Margaret Susan, *d.* of Adml. Robert Mitford of Mitford Castle, Morpeth. 8 *Grosvenor Sq., W., and Didlington Hall, Brandon, Norfolk.*

Kindersley (W.L.E.) — Edward Molesworth. Of the Old Clock House, Wanstead, Essex; 1848^{3}–1851^{1}; Field XI. 1853; formerly Capt. 19th Regt.; J.P. for Essex.

Moore (K.S.) — Rev. Denis Times. 1849^{1}–1854^{1}; Exhib. of Exeter Coll. Oxf.; Vicar of Woolton Hill, Newbury, 1878–84, aft. living at Brighton.

Jones (J.L.J.) — Edward Talbot Day (aft. Foxcroft). Eld. son of T. J. of Hinton House; 1849^{2}–1855^{2}; Newc. Select 1855; Ball. Coll. Oxf. M.A.; Barrister, Inner Temple, 1866; formerly Capt. N. Somerset Yeo. Cav.; J.P., D.L., and C.C. for Somerset; High Sheriff 1890; *m.* Wilhelmina Colquhoun, *d.* of Robert Robertson-Glasgow of Montgreenan, Irvine. *Hinton House, Hinton Charterhouse, Bath, and Halsteads, Ingleton, co. York.*

Barter (E.C.) — Rev. Henry. Son of Rev. C. B., Rector of Sarsden, co. Oxf.; 1849^{1}–1853^{3}; Tomline Prizeman 1853; Merton Coll. Oxf. M.A.; Postmaster at Merton 1853; 1st Cl. Math. Mods. and 2nd Cl. Mods. 1855; 3rd Cl. Lit. Hum.; formerly Vicar of Lambourn, Berks; aft. Vicar of Shipton-under-Wychwood, Oxf., and later Vicar of Sonning, Reading; *m.* Elsbett Catherine, *d.* of Dr. Moberley, Head Master of Winchester, after Bp. of Salisbury; died May 24, 1901.

Mitford (W.E., aft. K.S., F.E.D.) — Algernon Bertram Freeman- (1st Lord Redesdale), C.B., C.V.O. 3rd son of H. R. M. of Exbury, Southampton, and Newton Park, Northumberland; 1846^{3}–1854^{2}; Ch. Ch. Oxf.; 2nd Cl. Mods.; ent. Foreign Office 1858; 3rd Sec. of Embassy at St. Petersburg 1863; appointed to Pekin 1865; 2nd Sec. of Legation in Japan 1868; Sec. to H.M.'s Office of Works 1874–86; M.P. for S.W. Warwicks 1892–5; Member of Royal Comm. on Civil Services 1887; J.P., D.L. and C.C. co. Gloucester; *m.* Lady Clementine Gertrude Helen Ogilvy, *d.* of David, 7th Earl of Airlie. 29 *Piccadilly, W., and Batsford Park, Moreton-in-the-Marsh, Glos.*

Mr. Bertie (E.B.) — Hon. Montagu Arthur (7th Earl of Abingdon). Eld. son of Montagu, 6th Earl of A.; 1847^{3}–1852^{2}; Hon. Col. 3rd Bn. Berks Regt.; J.P. and D.L. for Oxfs and Berks; *m.* 1st, Caroline Theresa, *d.* of Charles Towneley of Towneley, co. Lancaster; 2nd, Gwendeline Mary, *d.* of Lieut.-Gen. Hon. Sir James Charlemagne Dormer, K.C.B. *Wytham Abbey, Oxford.*

Lloyd (C.L. & Miss G., C.L. & J.L.Y.) — Robert Lewis-. Son of T. L.-L. of Nantgwillt, Rhayader; 1847^{3}–1855^{3}; Eton VIII. 1853–5; Capt. of the Boats 1855; Wall XI. 1853–4; Field XI. 1853–4, Keeper 1854; Mixed Wall 1854; Sch. of Magd. Coll. Camb.; Capt. Camb. VIII. 1856–9; Barrister, Inner Temple 1865; J.P. and D.L. for cos. Brecon and Radnor; High Sheriff co. Radnor 1872; *m.* Mary Anne Jane, *d.* of Capt. Lewes of Llanlear, co. Cardigan. *Bryntirion, Rhayader, and Otterhead, Honiton.*

Morrison (C.O.G.) — Walter. 5th son of J. M. of Basildon Park, Reading; 1849^{1}–1852^{2}; Ball. Coll. Oxf. M.A.; 1st Cl. Lit. Hum. 1857; M.P. for Plymouth 1861–74, Skipton Div. 1886–92 and 1895–1900; Hon. Col. 3rd Bn. Duke of Wellington's W. Riding Regt.; J.P. for W. Riding of Yorks, High Sheriff 1883. *77 Cromwell Road, S.W., and Malham Tarn, Langcliffe, Settle.*

Arkwright *mi.* (R.O. & C.Wo.) — Rev. George. 3rd son of J. A. of Hampton Court, Leominster; 1849^{2}–1853^{3}; Merton Coll. Oxf. M.A.; Curate of Barthomley, Cheshire, aft. Rector of Pencombe, co. Hereford; *m.* Elizabeth, *d.* of Lloyd, 3rd Lord Kenyon, of Gredington, Flint; died Oct. 5, 1877.

Parr (F.E.D.) — Thomas Philip. Of Kilillechronan, co. Argyll, and Ashton Hayes, Chester; eld. son of T. P. of Grappenhall Heyes, Warrington; 1847^{3}–1850^{3}; Capt. Scots Greys; J.P. for Cheshire; *m.* Agnes, *d.* of Major George Darby Griffith; died Oct. 29, 1891.

Fitton (Mrs. Vav., E.B.) — Rev. Frederick Chambers. 1847^{3}–1852^{1}; Emman. Coll. Camb. B.A.; formerly Curate of Freshwater, Isle of Wight.

Clifford (H.D.) — Henry Somers Morgan. Son of Col. M. C. of Llantilio, co. Monmouth; 1849^{2}–1854^{3}; Merton Coll. Oxf.; died at Merton.

Smith (Mrs. Ro., E.H.P.) — John Graham. 1848^{3}–1853^{3}; formerly 2nd Life Gds.

Gambier (E.H.P.) — 1848^{3}–1852^{3}.

Patten (F.E.D.) — Hon. Eustace John Wilson-. Eld. son of John, 1st and only Lord Winmarleigh, of Winmarleigh, co. Lancaster; 1849^{1}–1852^{3}; Capt. 1st Life Gds.; *m.* Emily Constantia, *d.* of Rev. Lord John Thynne; died Dec. 17, 1873.

Chapman *ma.* (E.B.) — Arthur George. 3rd son of D. B. C. of Roehampton, Surrey; 1848^{1}–1851^{3}; *m.* Sophia Georgina, *d.* of Capt. John Davidson, 2nd Life Gds.; died Nov. 27, 1867.

Cornish (W.E., H.M.B.) — REV. CHARLES JOHN. Of Salcombe Regis, Devon; son of C. J. C. of Salcombe Regis; 1848^{2}-1851^{3}; C.C.C. Oxf. M.A.; formerly Vicar of Debenham, Suffolk, aft. Rector of Childrey. *Childrey Rectory, Wantage.*

Whitley (F.E.D.) — HENRY JACKSON. Of the Close, Biggleswade; son of J. W. of Ashton; 1849^{2}-1853^{3}; Trin. Coll. Camb. B.A.; *m.* Elizabeth Catharine, *d.* of John Micklethwait of Ardsley, Barnsley; died 1888.

Peach (W.G.C.) — HENRY PEACH KEIGHLY-. Eld. son of H. P. Keighly of Idlicote; 1848^{3}-1852^{2}; Eton VIII. 1852; Trin. Coll. Oxf.; formerly Capt. Royal Horse Gds. Blue; J.P. cos. Warwick and Worcester; *m.* Lucy Isabella, *d.* of William Selby-Lowndes of Whaddon Hall, Stony Stratford. *Idlicote House, Shipston-on-Stour, and Alderminster Lodge, Stratford-on-Avon.*

Robertson *mi.* (W.A.C.) — JAMES CASAMAJOR. Son of T. C. R.; 1845^{3}-1851^{2}; E. I. Coll. Haileybury; Bengal Civil Service (ret.); *m.* Eleanor, *d.* of Col. R. T. Sandeman; died July 31, 1903.

Colvin *mi.* (W.A.C.) — ELLIOT. Son of J. R. C.; 1849^{2}-1853^{1}; E. I. Coll. Haileybury; Bengal Civil Service; *m.* Edith, *d.* of Peter Cunningham; died 1883.

Hankey (J.L.J.) — RODOLPH ALEXANDER. 2nd son of J. A. H. of Balcombe Place, Hayward's Heath; 1849^{2}-1855^{2}; Field, Opp. and Mixed Wall XI.'s 1854; Eton VIII. 1855; Trin. Coll. Camb.; Senr. Opt. 1859; West India Merchant in London; D.L. for Middlesex; *m.* Clara Johanna Beata, *d.* of Emil von Collani of Breslau, Silesia. *54 Warwick Sq., S.W.*

Puxley *mi.* (C.O.G.) — REV. EDWARD LAVALLIN. 3rd son of J. L. P. of Dunboy Castle, Castletown, Berehaven; 1848^{1}-1852^{2}; Opp. Wall and Field XI.'s 1851; formerly Lieut. 4th Dragoons; served in the Crimea; aft. B.N.C. Oxf.; later Vicar of Steep; *m.* Maria Winifred, *d.* of Henry Leader of Clonmoyle. *Steep Vicarage, Petersfield.*

Usborne (J.W.H.) — THOMAS STARLING. Of Mardley-Bury Manor, Therfield, Royston, and Loddenden, Staplehurst, Kent; son of T. H. U. of Mardley-Bury; 1845^{1}-1851^{2}; formerly in the 7th Dragoon Gds.; died Jan. 5, 1903.

Hoblyn (W.G.C.) — THOMAS HALLAM. Of White Barns, Buntingford, Herts; 1847^{2}-1851^{3}; formerly Lieut. Herts R.V.; *m.* Miss Usborne.

Collins *mi.* (Mrs. P., W.J.) — CHARLES. 2nd son of E. C. of Truthan, Truro, and Newton Ferrers, Callington, Cornwall; 1847^{2}-1854^{2}; Merton Coll. Oxf.; killed by a fall from his horse in S. America.

Harding (W.J. & F.V., W.J.) — REV. CANON JOHN TAYLOR. Son of J. H. of Henbury Hill, near Bristol; 1847^{3}-1853^{2}; Eton VIII. 1851-3; Capt. of the Boats 1853; Field XI. 1851; Wall XI. 1852; Merton Coll. Oxf. M.A.; Vicar of Rockfield, Monmouth, and Preb. of St. Nicholas in Llandaff Cath.; *m.* Patty, *d.* of John Etherington Welch Rolls of the Hendre, Monmouth. *Pentwyn, near Monmouth.*

Thorold (Mrs. Hor., H.M.B., & J.L.J.) — HENRY. Son of H. T. of Cuxwold, Lincoln; 1847^{3}-1851^{3}; Lieut. 33rd Duke of Wellington's Regt.; killed at battle of Inkerman Nov. 5, 1854.

Shilleto (Mrs. P., H.M.B.) — RICHARD. Son of Rev. R. S. of Cambridge; 1847^{2}-1852^{1}.

Thompson (W.E., W.G.C.) — REV. ARCHIBALD DOUGLAS CAVENDISH. 1847^{2}-1851^{1}; formerly Curate of Sigglesthorne, Hull.

Sheffield *ma.* (H.D.) — JOHN CHARLES. Of Carradoyne, Claremorris; 3rd son of Sir R. S., 4th Bt., of Normanby Park, Doncaster; 1848^{1}-1851^{1}; formerly Capt. 21st Fusiliers; J.P. co. Mayo; *m.* 1st, Mary Sarah, *d.* of Thomas Butler Stoney of Portland Park, co. Tipperary; 2nd, Marie Louise Westcott, *d.* of L. J. A. Papineau of the Manor of Monte Bello, Quebec, Canada; died Nov. 12, 1903.

Reeve (R.F.H.) — 1847^{2}-1851^{1}.

White (W.E., E.H.P.) — WILLIAM KNIGHT HAMILTON RAMSAY. Of Lealhurst, Tickhill, Rotherham; 2nd son of Sir T. W. W., 2nd Bt., of Wallingwells, Worksop; 1847^{3}-1851^{2}; Trin. Coll. Camb.; *m.* Edith Laura, *d.* of Rev. Archibald Paris, Rector of Ludgvan, Long Rock, Cornwall; died June 11, 1900.

Warter — LIEUT.-COL. HENRY DE GREY. Son of H. de G. W. of Cruck Meole House, Shrewsbury; 1846^{2}-1850^{2}; formerly a Solicitor in London; died Aug. 1, 1903.

Sir C. Honywood (C.O.G.) — SIR COURTENAY, 7th Bt. Of Evington, Ashford, Kent; son of Sir J. E. H., 6th Bt., of Evington; 1847^{3}-1851^{2}; Capt. E. Kent Rifles; D.L. for Kent; *m.* Annie Maria, *d.* of William Paynter of Camborne House, Richmond, Surrey; died April 17, 1878.

Starky (W.L.E.) — JOHN BAYNTUN. Of Spye Park, Devizes; son of J. B. A. S. of Spye Park; 1847^{2}-1851^{2}; *m. d.* of Rev. James Hunt Grubbe; died at Singleton, N.S. Wales, 1872.

Irvine (W.J.) — EDWARD TOTTENHAM. Son of Major G. St. G. I. of Newtownbarry, co. Wexford; 1846^{2}-1850^{2}; formerly Capt. 16th Lancers; J.P. and D.L. co. Wexford, High Sheriff 1861; *m.* Elizabeth Beatrice, *d.* of Edward Gonne Bell of Streamstown, Moate. *St. Aidan's, Ferns.*

Waud *mi.* (Miss Edg., aft. K.S., C.O.G.) — BRIAN WILKES. Son of E. W. of Manston Hall, Leeds; 1848^{3}-1855^{2}; Eton XI. 1855; Coll. Wall 1853-4, Mixed Wall 1854; Univ. Coll. Oxf.; Oxf. XI. 1857-60; formerly Barrister, Northern Circuit.

Cowell (W.E., H.M.B. & J.L.J.) — SIR EMILE ALGERNON ARTHUR KEPPEL (aft. Cowell-Stepney), 2nd Bt., F.R.G.S., 3rd son of Lieut.-Col. Sir J. S. C.-S., 1st Bt., of Llanelly; 1848^{3}-1852^{2}; Prince Consort's German and Italian Prizes 1849; French Prize 1850; Clerk in Foreign Office for 20 years; M.P. for Carmarthen 1876-8 and 1886-92; J.P. and D.L. co. Carmarthen, High Sheriff 1884; *m.* Hon. Margaret Leicester, *d.* of George, 2nd Lord De Tabley. *The Dell, Llanelly, and Wood End, Sunninghill, Ascot.*

Prodgers *mi.* (W.J.) — HERBERT. 2nd son of Rev. E. P., Rector of Ayot St. Peter, Welwyn; 1848^{3}-1851^{2}; Ch. Ch. Oxf.; J.P. for Wilts; *m.* Emily Sibella, *d.* of Rev. Canon Thomas Phillpotts of Porthgwidden, Truro. *Kington St. Michael, Chippenham.*

Field *ma.* (F.E.D.) — GEORGE HANBURY. Of Ashurst Park, Tunbridge Wells; eld. son of G. F. of Ashurst; 1849^{1}-1854^{2}; Univ. Coll. Oxf. M.A.; Banker; J.P. and D.L. for Kent; *m.* 1st, Lady Georgiana Turnour, *d.* of Edward, 4th Earl of Winterton; 2nd, Hon. Emily Maude, *d.* of Charles Stewart, 2nd Visct. Hardinge; died July 7, 1901.

Knatchbull-Hugessen *ma.* (E.B.) — HERBERT THOMAS. Of Lynsted, Sittingbourne; 9th son of Rt. Hon. Sir E. Knatchbull, 9th Bt., of Mersham Hatch, Ashford, Kent; 1849^{2}-1853^{2}; Trin. Coll. Oxf. M.A.; Barrister 1860; M.P. for N.E. Kent 1868-85. *Carlton Club, 94 Pall Mall, S.W.*

St. Aubyn *ma.* (F.E.D.) — REV. WILLIAM. 3rd son of Sir E. St. A., 1st Bt., of St. Michael's Mount, Marazion, Cornwall; 1849^{1}-1853^{1}; Opp. Wall 1852; Oriel Coll. Oxf. M.A.; Rector of Stoke Damerell and Preb. of Exeter; *m.* Edith Emily, *d.* of Edward Johnston, of Silwood Lodge, Berks; died July 5, 1891.

Sanderson (E.C.) — RICHARD MANNERS. 1848^{3}-1850^{2}; formerly a Merchant in King William Street, E.C.

Tyler (E.C.) — WILLIAM ROBERTSON. Son of Rev. J. E. T., Canon of St. Paul's; 1848^{3}-1853^{2}; won School Sculling 1853; Capt. 15th Regt.; died Nov. 10, 1863.

Tyrrell (W.E., E.H.P.) — GEORGE. Son of Capt. T. of Fordhook, Middlesex: 1848^{3}-1853^{2}; Trin. Coll. Camb. M.A.; Barrister; died 1887.

Parish (Mrs. P., F.E.D.) — HENRY. 1848^{3}-1851^{2}; Ch. Ch. Oxf.

Bowden (E.B.) — REV. HENRY GEORGE. Son of H. B; 1848^{3}-1852^{2}; Eton XI. 1852; Field XI. 1851; Capt. Scots Gds. 1855-67; Roman Catholic Priest at the Oratory since 1867. *The Oratory, S. Kensington, S.W.*

Antrobus (F.E.D.) — EDWARD CRAWFURD. Son of G. C. A. of Eaton Hall, Congleton; 1848^{3}-1851^{2}; Capt. 50th Regt.; died 1864.

Knox (Miss G., W.J.) — HENRY GEORGE AUGUSTUS. Son of Rev. H. C. K., Vicar of Lechlade, co. Gloucester; 1848^{3}-1854^{2}; Exeter Coll Oxf. M.A.; J.P. and C.C. for Berks; Chmn. Wokingham R.D. Council; *m.* Elizabeth Anne, *d.* of T. S. Carter of Moor Place, Much Hadham, Herts. *Sonning, Reading.*

Mr. Clinton (E.C.) — COL. LORD EDWARD WILLIAM PELHAM-CLINTON, G.C.V.O., K.C.B. 2nd son of Henry Pelham, 5th Duke of Newcastle, K.G.; 1848^{3}-1854^{1}; Cox. Eton VIII. 1853; Ensign Rifle Bgde. 1854: served in the Crimea after the fall of Sebastopol; Capt. 1857; in Canada 1861-5; Lieut.-Col. 1878; ret. 1880; in India 1880; M.P. for N. Notts 1865-8; Sherwood Rangers Yeo. Cav. 1865-8; Comm. London Rifle Vol. Bgde. 1881-90; Groom-in-Waiting to Queen Victoria 1881-94; Master of Queen Victoria's Household 1894-1901; G.C. Saxe-Ernestine Order 1897: G.C. Crown of Prussia 1901; D.L. for Notts; Groom-in-Waiting to the King since 1901; *m.* Matilda Jane, *d.* of Sir William Edmund Cradock-Hartopp, 3rd Bt. 81 *Eccleston Square, S.W. and The Heights, Witley, Godalming.*

Arbuthnot *mi.* (F.E.D.) — COL. GEORGE. 2nd son of J. A. A. of Coworth Park, Old Windsor; 1848^{3}-1852^{1}; Trin. Coll. Camb.; Lieut.-Col. and Hon. Col. R.A. (ret.): served in Indian Mutiny; special messenger on Staff in Abyssinian War; mentioned in despatches; M.P. for Hereford 1871-4 and 1878-80; J.P. and D.L. for co. Hereford and J.P. for co. Gloucester; *m.* Caroline Emma Nepean, *d.* of Capt. Andrew Nepean Aitchison, H.E.I.C. *Norton Court, Gloucester.*

Lord Vaughan (H.M.B.) — ERNEST AUGUSTUS MALET (5th Earl of Lisburne). Eld. son of Ernest Augustus, 4th Earl of Lisburne; 1848^{3}-1852^{2}; Ch. Ch. Oxf.; *m.* 1st, Gertrude Laura, *d.* of Edwyn Burnaby of Baggrave Hall, Leicester; 2nd, Alice D'Alton, *d.* of Edmund Probyn of Huntley Manor, Gloucester; died March 31, 1888.

Hicks (Miss Edg., aft. K.S., C.J.A.) — REV. GEORGE GRISDALE, B.A. 1848^{3}-1855^{2}; formerly Curate of Cubberley, Cheltenham; died 1882.

Watkins (aft. K.S.) — JOHN GREGORY. Eld. son of J. G. W. of Woodfield, Ombersley, Droitwich; 1846^{2}-1856^{2}; Ch. Ch. Oxf.; Barrister, Lincoln's Inn (Oxf. Circuit); died unm. Nov. 5, 1869.

Waud *ma.* (Miss Edg., C.O.G.) — EDWARD WILKES. Son of E. W. of Manston Hall, Leeds; 1818^{3}-1853^{2}; Trin. Coll. Camb; formerly Capt. 4th W. York Militia; J.P. for W. Riding of Yorks; *m.* Hon. Elizabeth, *d.* of William, 2nd Lord Heytesbury.

Lane (T.H.S., E.B.) — REV. JOHN REYNOLDS. 3rd son of C. L. of Badgemore, co. Oxf.; 1848^{3}-1854^{2}; Trin. Coll. Oxf. M.A.; formerly Rector of Tattersett with Tatterford, Norfolk; Rector of Hampnett with Stowell since 1895; *m.* Nura Norman, *d.* of Sir William Holmes. *Hampnett Rectory, Northleach, R.S.O., Glos.*

Willats — WILLIAM HALL. Of Denton Court, Canterbury; son of — W. of Denton Court; 1845^{3}-1853^{2}; Opp. Wall 1853; Field XI. 1852, Keeper 1853; Ch. Ch. Oxf.; Barrister; formerly Lieut. E. Kent Mounted Rifles; J.P. for Kent; *m.* Julia Ruperta, *d.* of Col. Charles Gostling-Murray; died 1893.

Campion (W.J. & F.V., W.J.) — COL. WILLIAM HENRY, C.B. Eld. son of W. J. C. of Danny; 1848^{3}-1852^{2}; 72nd Highl. 1854-61 (served in the Crimea and Indian Mutiny); 53rd Regt. 1861-3; aft. Lieut.-Col. and Hon. Col. 2nd Vol. Bn. Royal Sussex Regt.; J.P. for Sussex; *m.* Hon. Gertrude Brand, *d.* of Henry, 1st Visct. Hampden. *Danny, Hassocks, R.S.O., Sussex.*

Peacock (E.H.P.) — FREDERICK BARNES. Son of Rt. Hon. Sir B. P., Kt., Chief Justice at Calcutta; 1848^{3}-1853^{2}; Bengal Civil Service; Sec. Board of Revenue, Calcutta; died on board ship in the Mediterranean on passage home, 1894.

Godman (W.L.E.) — PERCY SANDEN. 4th son of J. G. of Park Hatch, Godalming; 1849^{1}-1853^{2}; Trin. Coll. Camb. B.A.; J.P. for Sussex; *m.* Isabel Fredericа, *d.* of Frederick Smithe. *Muntham, Horsham.*

Ferguson-Davie *mi.* (W.A.C.) — REV. CHARLES ROBERT. 4th son of Sir H. R. F.-D., 1st Bt., of Creedy Park, Crediton; 1848^{3}-1850^{2}; Trin. Hall, Camb. M.A.; formerly Rector of Exhall with Wixford, Coventry, aft. Rector of Yelverton, Norfolk; *m.* Anne Clarissa, *d.* of Biggs Andrews, Q.C., of Heavitree House, Exeter; died April 6, 1897.

Ruddell-Todd (F.E.D.) — JAMES ARCHIBALD. 1848^{3}-1850^{2}; formerly Capt. 87th Regt.

Hayward (R.O.) — FRANCIS JAMES. 1848^{3}-1851^{2}.

Abbott (E.H.P.) — CHARLES STUART AUBREY (3rd Lord Tenterden), K.C.B. Son of C. A., and nephew of John Henry, 2nd Lord T.; 1848^{3}-1852^{2}; Permanent Under-Sec. of State for Foreign Affairs; *m.* 1st, Penelope Mary Gertrude, *d.* of Lieut.-Gen. Sir John Rowland Smyth, K.C.B.; 2nd, Emma Mary, *d.* of Charles Bailey of Lee Abbey, Ilfracombe, and widow of Henry Howcliffe, Q.C.; died Sept. 22, 1882.

Cox (Mrs. For., H.M.B. & E.B.) — FREDERICK. Son of F. W. C.; 1848^{3}-1851^{2}; Ch. Ch. Oxf.; Banker (Cox & Co.); formerly Hon. Col. Middlesex Yeo. Cav.; J.P. and D.L. for Middlesex; *m.* Mabel, *d.* of Arthur Eden, Assist. Compt. of the Exchequer. 3 *Grosvenor Crescent, S.W., and Harefield Place, Uxbridge.*

Vivian *mi.* (W.J.) — RICHARD GLYNN. 4th son of J. H. V. of Singleton, co. Glamorgan; 1848[3]-1852[2]; Trin. Coll. Camb. M.A.; formerly a Copper Merchant at Swansea; *m.* Laura Hermione Beatrice, *d.* of Henry Craigie Halkett, Bengal Civil Service. 24 *Eaton Square, S.W., and Sketty Hall, Swansea.*

Taylor (Mrs. Ri., E.H.P.) — WARINGTON. 1848[1]-1850[3].

Berners (H.D.) — HERBERT JOHNES. 1849[1]-1853[1]; formerly Capt. 43rd Regt.

Pryor *ma.* — REV. JOHN EADE. Eld. son of J. P. of Baldock, Herts; 1846[3]-1854[2]; Newc. Select 1854; Magd. Coll. Oxf. M.A.; Rector of Bennington, Stevenage; *m.* Mary Gertrude, *d.* of Alfred Pett, M.D.; died July 5, 1884.

Filmer (H.D.) — SIR EDMUND, 9th Bt. Of East Sutton Park, Staplehurst, Kent; eld. son of Sir E. F., 8th Bt., of East Sutton; 1848[3]-1853[2]; Capt. Gren. Gds.; M.P. for W. Kent 1859-65, for Mid Kent 1880-84; D.L. for Kent, High Sheriff 1870; *m.* Hon. Mary Georgiana Caroline, *d.* of Arthur Marcus Cecil, 2nd Lord Sandys; died Dec. 17, 1886.

Hoare — HAMILTON NOEL (aft. Hamilton-Hoare). Eld. son of Rev. W. H. H. of Oakfield; 1847[3]-1853[3]; Eton XI 1851-53, Capt. 1853; Keeper of Upper Club 1851 and 1852; Banker (Hoare's Bank). 3 *Draycott Place, Chelsea, S.W., and Oakfield Lodge, Three Bridges, Sussex.*

Beresford *ma.* (R.O.) — LIEUT.-GEN. MOSTYN DE LA POER. Eld. son of Right Hon. W. B. of Hampton Court Palace; 1849[1]-1852[3]; formerly Lieut.-Col. 72nd Highl.; served in the Crimea and Indian Mutiny; ret. 1887. 76 *Jermyn Street, S.W.*

Edgar (Miss Edg.) — ROBERT. 1844[3]-1853[3]; formerly employed on the London Press.

Harcourt (R.O. & C.Wo.) — JOHN SIMON CHANDOS. Of Ankerwycke Priory, Wraysbury, Staines; son of G. S. H. of Ankerwycke; 1848[1]-1852[1]; formerly Capt. 30th, 31st, 50th (King's Own), and 2nd Bn. 20th Regt.; served in the Crimea and Chinese War; *m.* Harriet Emma Elizabeth, *d.* of Adml. Sir J. H. Plumridge, K.C.B., R.N.; died Feb. 12, 1890.

Lovett (Mrs. Hor. & Miss G., F.E.D.) — JOHN HENNIKER. Eld. son of T. L. of Fernhill; 1848[3]-1853[3]; Eton VIII. 1853; formerly Capt. 2nd Life Gds.; J.P. and D.L. for Salop, High Sheriff 1872; *m.* Laura, *d.* of Philip Morier, H.M.'s Minister at Dresden. *Fernhill, Oswestry.*

Davy (C.O.G.) — JOHN WILLIAM. Of Ingoldsthorpe and Kilverstone Hall, Thetford; 1849[1]-1852[3]; Exeter Coll. Oxf.; J.P. for Norfolk; *m.* Wilhelmina Louisa, *d.* of Rev. Thomas Gerard Ferrand, Rector of Tunstall, Suffolk; died Feb. 22, 1903.

Clough *ma.* (Mrs. Vav., H.D.) — WILLIAM. Eld. son of — C. of Clifton House, York; 1848[1]-1852[2].

Beresford *mi.* (R.O.) — MAJOR-GEN. EDWARD MARCUS. 2nd son of Rt. Hon. W. B.; 1849[1]-1852[3]; in the Scots Fusilier Gds.; died Jan. 14, 1896.

Clough *mi.* (Mrs. Vav., H.D.) — JOHN. Son of — C. of Clifton House, York; 1848[1]-1852[2]; was killed in the Indian Mutiny.

Innes (J.E.Y.) — ARTHUR CHARLES (aft. Innes-Cross). Son of A. I. of Dromantine; 1848[2]-1851[1]; M.P. for Newry 1865-68; J.P. and D.L. co. Down; *m.* 1st, Louisa Letitia Henrietta, *d.* of James Brabazon of Mornington House, co. Meath; 2nd Jane B[illegible], *d.* of Col. W[illegible] Cro[illegible] of Darton, co. Armagh. [illegible] N[illegible]y.

Holland *ma.* (Mrs. Hor., W.J.) — EDWARD THURSTAN. Son of E. H. of Dumbleton Hall, Evesham; 1849[2]-1853[3]; Trin. Coll. Camb. M.A.; Barrister, Lincoln's Inn; *m.* Marianne, *d.* of William Gaskell; died Sept. 27, 1884.

Swinburne (W.J.) — ALGERNON CHARLES. Son of Adml. C. H. S., R.N.; 1849[2]-1853[3]; Prince Consort's French and Italian Prizes 1853; Ball. Coll. Oxf.; Taylor Sch. 1858; Poet. *The Pines, Putney.*

Assheton (W.A.C.) — REV. RICHARD ORME. 2nd son of W. A. of Downham Hall, Clitheroe; 1849[2]-1853[3]; Ch. Ch. Oxf. M.A.; Rector of Bilton, 1862-95; *m.* Charlotte Emma Willoughby, *d.* of Joseph Feilden of Witton Park, Lancaster. *The Gable House, Bilton, Rugby.*

West (F.E.D.) — COL. WILLIAM CORNWALLIS, V.D. 2nd son of F. R. W. of Ruthin Castle; 1849[2]-1854[1]; called to the Bar, Lincoln's Inn, 1862; Lord-Lieut. of co. Denbigh since 1872, High Sheriff 1872; J.P. and C.C. for Hants; Hon. Col. 3rd Bn. Royal Welsh Fusiliers; M.P. for W. div. of co. Denbigh 1885-92; *m.* Mary Adelaide Virginia Eupataria, *d.* of Rev. Frederick Fitzpatrick, Rector of Cloone, Drumod, co. Leitrim. 55 *Jermyn Street, S.W.; Newlands Manor, Lymington, and Ruthin Castle, North Wales.*

Sir Brydges P. Henniker (R.O.) — SIR BRYDGES POWELL, 4th Bt. Eld. son of Rev. Sir A. B. H., 3rd Bt., of Newton Hall, Essex; 1849[2]-1851[1]; Ensign 68th Foot 1852; Cornet Royal H. Gds. 1854, Lieut. 1855, Capt. 1858; ret. 1859; Capt. W. Essex Yeo. 1861-3; Assist.-Inspector Local Govt. Board 1874-80; Registrar-Gen. of Births, Deaths and Marriages for England and Wales 1880-1900; J.P. and D.L. for Essex; *m.* Justina Louisa, *d.* of Thomas Hughan of Airds, N.B. *Montpellier Hall, Brighton.*

Dawson *ma.* (E.C.) — EDWARD FINCH. Of Launde Abbey, Leicester; eld. son of E. D. of Whatton, Nottingham; 1849[2]-1853[3]; formerly Capt. Inniskilling Dragoons; served in the Crimea; J.P. and D.L. co. Leicester, High Sheriff 1857; *m.* Emily Sarah, *d.* of Thomas Fowke Andrew Burnaby of Brampton Manor, Huntingdon; died Aug. 21, 1892.

De la More (Mrs. de R., C.O.G.) — ARTHUR GEORGE JAMES. 1849[2]-1850[3].

Wigram *mi.* (J.L.J.) — MAJOR-GEN. GODFREY JAMES, C.B. 4th son of Rt. Hon. Sir J. W., Vice-Chanc.; 1849[2]-1853[1]; ent. Army 1854; served in the Crimea 1854 (despatches, med. with clasp, 5th Cl. Medjidie, Turkish Med.); Egypt 1882 (despatches, med. with clasp, 3rd Cl. Medjidie, Khedive's Star, C.B.); Maj.-Gen. 1889; Col. Comm. Coldstream Gds.; ret. 1893. 82 *Albany, Piccadilly, W.*

Mills (W.L.E.) — RICHARD BRIDGEMAN. 1847[3]-1850[3]; Ch. Ch. Oxf.

Morse (J.E.Y.) — THOMAS. Son of T. M. of Ashmead; 1847[3]-1851[2]; Queen's Coll. Oxf.; formerly Capt. S. Glouc. Militia; J.P. for co. Glouc.; *m.* Sarah Jane, *d.* of Arthur John Goldney. *Ashmead House, Dursley.*

Radclyffe (H.D.) — CHARLES EDWARD. Son of Rev. C. E. R. of South Sydenham, Devon; 1848[1]-1852[2]; Eton VIII 1852; Ch. Ch. Oxf.; J.P. for [illegible], *d.* of Col. Harfress [illegible] Park, Wickham, Fare-

Fletcher (B.O. & C.Wo.) — RT. HON. SIR HENRY. 4th Bt., C.B., P.C. (aft. Aubrey-Fletcher). Eld. son of Sir H. F., 3rd Bt.; 1848^{1}–1852^{2}: Ensign 69th Regt. 1853; Lieut. Gren. Gds. 1855; ret. 1859; Maj. Surrey Rifle Vol. 1859–65, aft. in Northants and Sussex R. Vols. (Vol. Dec.); M.P. for Horsham 1880–5; Groom-in-Waiting to the Queen 1885–6; Brig.-Gen. Sussex Vol. Infantry Bgde.; M.P. for Lewes Div. of Sussex since 1885; J.P. and D.L. for Sussex; J.P. for Surrey; *m.* Agnes, *d.* of Col. Sir John Morillyon Wilson, K.H., C.B., of the Royal Hospital, Chelsea. 1 *Upper Belgrave Street, S.W., and Ham Manor, Angmering, Sussex.*

Page (W.E., W.A.C.) — HERBERT WILLIAM COBBOLD. Son of Rev. L. F. P. o Woolpit, Bury St. Edmund's; 1849^{2}–1850^{2}; Ch. Ch. Oxf. B.A.; *m.* Susanna E., *d.* of Rev. J. Spencer Cobbold; dead.

Turner (K.S., W.A.C.) — HENRY. Of Seaforth, Liverpool; 1849^{2}–1850^{3}; formerly Capt. 58th Regt.

Patteson (K.S., E.H.P.) — THOMAS CHARLES. Son of Rev. — P., Vicar of Hambleton; 1849^{2}–1854^{3}; Coll. Wall 1854; Merton Coll. Oxf.; Postmaster 1855; Barrister, practising in New Brunswick.

Huddleston (K.S., C.L. & J.L.J.) — LIEUT.-COL. GEORGE CROFT. Of Upwell, Isle of Ely, co. Camb.; eld. son of Rev. G. J. H. of Upwell, and Rector of Tunworth, Basingstoke; 1849^{2}–1854^{2}; Coll. Wall XI. 1853; Ball. Coll. Oxf.; Lieut.-Col. 13th Hussars; J.P. co. Camb.; *m.* Emily Henrietta, *d.* of Rt. Hon. William N. Massey, M.P.; died Mar. 18, 1896.

Moore (E.B.) — JOHN CROFT. 1849^{2}–1854^{2}; Eton VIII. 1852–4; Capt. of the Boats 1854; Opp. Wall 1853; formerly Capt. Rifle Bgde.; served in the Crimea and Indian Mutiny.

Wharton (Mrs. Hor. & Miss G., J.L.J.) — ROBERT. Son of R. W., Barrister, Judge of the County Court, N. Riding of Yorks; 1849^{2}–1855^{1}; Cox, Eton VIII. 1854; Field XI. 1853, Keeper 1854; Sch. of Magd. Coll. Camb., M.A.; Cox of Camb. VIII. 1857–8. *Surrey House, Victoria Embankment, W.C., and Hurley, Marlow.*

Warre *mi.* (Mrs. Vav., F.V. & W.B.M., E.C. & W.B.M.) — REV. EDMOND, D.D., M.V.O. 2nd son of H. W. of Bindon House, Langford Budville, Wellington, Som.; 1849^{2}–1854^{2}; Newc. Sch. 1854; won School Pulling 1854; Sch. of Ball. Coll. Oxf. 1855; 1st Cl. Mods. 1856; 1st Cl. Lit. Hum. 1859; Fellow of All Souls 1859; Oxf. VIII. 1857–8; Pres. O.U.B.C. 1859; founded Rifle Corps at Oxf.; Hon. Fellow of Ball. 1896; Ass't. Master at Eton 1860–84, Head-Master since 1884; Hon. Col. 2nd Bucks (Eton Coll.) R.V. 1884 (Vol. Dec.); Hon. Chaplain to Queen Victoria; Hon. Chaplain to the King; Preb. of Wells since 1899; *m.* Florence Dora, *d.* of Lieut.-Col. Charles St. Lo Malet of Fontmell Parva, Dorset. *Eton College, and Baron's Down, Dulverton, R.S.O., co. Somerset.*

Lambton *min.* (C.L.) — MAJOR-GEN. ARTHUR, C.B. 4th son of W. H. L. of Biddick Hall, Durham; 1849^{2}–1853^{2}; ent. Army 1854; Capt. 1860; Lieut.-Col. Comm. Coldstream Gds. 1882–6; Maj.-Gen. 1890 (ret. 1892); served in Crimea 1854–6 (mentioned in despatches, med. with clasp, 5th Class Medjidie, Turkish med.); Egyptian war 1882 (med. with clasp, 4th Class Osmanieh, Khedive's [illegible]); Suakin 1885 (mentioned in despatches, [illegible] clasp); *m.* [illegible], *d.* of Robert [illegible] *[illegible], Heath, [illegible].*

Smith (W.L.E.) — HUGH COLIN. 3rd son of J. A. S. of Dale Park, Sussex; 1849^{2}–1854^{2}; Trin. Coll. Camb.; a Director of the Bank of England, Gov. 1897–9; one of H.M. Lieuts. for City of London; *m.* Constance Maria Josephine, *d.* of Henry John Adeane, of Babraham, Camb. 71 *Prince's Gate, S.W., and Mount Clare, Roehampton, S.W.*

REMOVE.

Mozley (K.S., J.L.J.) — HERBERT NEWMAN. Son of J. M. of Derby; 1849^{2}–1857^{1}; Newc. Select 1856–7; Coll. Wall XI. 1856; Sch. of King's Coll. Camb., M.A.; 19th Wrangler; 2nd Cl. Class. Trip. and Fellow of King's 1861; Chanc. Legal Med. 1864; Barrister, Lincoln's Inn; *m.* Lucy Martha, *d.* of Louis Buchanan. *East View, Murray Road, Northwood, R.S.O., Middlesex.*

Salting (E.C.) — GEORGE. Son of an Australian Merchant; 1848^{2}–1853^{3}. 86 *St. James's Street, S.W.*

Gregson — JOHN. Eld. son of J. G. of Burdon, Sunderland; 1846^{2}–1851^{3}; Univ. Coll. Oxf. B.A.; died Aug. 17, 1877.

Howorth (K.S., W.J.) — THOMAS ORTON. Son of Rev. — H., Rector of Whitton, Ipswich; 1848^{2}–1853^{2}; formerly Capt. 44th Regt.; severely wounded in the Crimea; died at sea.

Kirby (E.C.) — THOMAS FREDERICK. Son of T. K. of Inhurst House, Hants; 1848^{2}–1855^{2}; Newc. Select 1855; Trin. Coll. Camb. M.A.; 5th Class. Trip. and Fellow of Trin. 1859; Barrister and Bursar of Winchester Coll.; *m.* Helen, *d.* of W. John Hunter. *The College, Winchester.*

Cuninghame — RICHARD DUNNING BARRÉ. Of Duchrae, co. Kirkcudbright; 2nd son of J. C. of Lainshaw, Ayr, and Duchrae; 1846^{1}–1850^{2}; formerly Capt. 2nd Life Gds.; J.P. and D.L. for co. Kirkcudbright. *Hensol, New Galloway Station, R.S.O., co. Kirkcudbright.*

Otley (Mrs. Ro., F.E.D.) — HENRY LEONCE. Son of — O., Publisher in Conduit Street, W.; 1848^{2}–1851^{1}; died in Paris.

Bradshaw (W.E., F.E.D.) — ROBERT WILMOT. Of Barton Park, Barton Blount, Derby; 3rd son of F. B. of Barton Blount; 1849^{2}–1851^{2}; Barrister, Midland Circuit; died 1884.

Fraser (F.V., W.J.) — HUGH. Son of Sir J. F.; 1849^{1}–1854^{2}; formerly Sec. of Legation and Consul-Gen. in Chili, Rome, and Vienna.

Standish (E.H.P.) — WILLIAM STANDISH CARR-. Of Duxbury Park, co. Lancaster, and Cocken Hall, Durham; son of W. Standish-Standish of Duxbury; 1849^{1}–1851^{2}; formerly an Officer in the 7th Hussars; J.P. for cos. Lancaster and Durham; died Feb. 21, 1878.

Waldy (W.E., W.L.E.) — EDWARD GARMONSWAY. Eld. son of T. W. W. of Egglescliffe, Yarm; 1849^{2}–1851^{1}; formerly Capt. 76th Foot; served in the Crimea; J.P. for Durham and N. Riding of Yorks; *m.* Cecily Jane, *d.* of Rev. John Garvey; died July 30, 1887.

King-Harman (C.O.G.) — RT. HON. EDWARD ROBERT, P.C. Of Rockingham, co. Roscommon, and Newcastle, Ballymahon, Mullingar; eld. son of Hon. L. H. K.-H. of Newcastle and Rockingham; 1846^{2}–1853^{1}; served in the 60th Rifles; aft. Capt. Royal Longford Militia; M.P. co. Sligo 1877–80, co. Dublin 1883–5, and for Isle of Thanet 1885–93; Parliamentary Under-Sec. for Ireland 1887–8; J.P. cos. Longford, Sligo, and Westmeath; H.M.'s Lieut. co. Roscommon; *m.* Emma Frances, *d.* of Sir William Worsley, 1st Bt., of Hovingham, York; died May 10, 1893.

Hamilton (E.B.) — HANS JAMES. Eld. son of — H. of Abbotstone; 1848^{3}–1855^{2}; dead.

Pinckney (F.E.D.) — WILLIAM. 4th son of R. P. of Amesbury, Salisbury; 1848^{3}–1853^{3}; Eton VIII. 1852–3, Stroke 1853; Field XI. 1852, Wall XI. 1853; Exeter Coll. Oxf. M.A.; Oxf. VIII. 1854–5; formerly Major 1st Wilts R.V.; Banker; J.P. for Wilts; *m.* Frances C., *d.* of Rev. George F. Everett. *Milford Hill House, Salisbury.*

Goldney (F.E.D.) — ARTHUR CHARLES NELSON. Son of A. J. G. of Egham, Staines; 1848^{3}–1851^{3}; Capt. Royal S. Gloucs. Militia 1860; Silver Med. Charing Cross Hospital 1878; L.S.A. London 1879; M.R.C.S. (Eng.) 1882; Legacy Duty Office, Somerset House; *m.* Ann Sarah, *d.* of William Guest of Gloucester; died Nov. 1899.

Russell (F.V., W.A.C.) — DAVID NEVILLE GRAY WATTS-. Son of J. D. W.-R. of Biggin Grange, Oundle; 1849^{1}–1853^{1}.

Hensley (C.O.G.) — ARTHUR PLATT. 1849^{2}–1852^{3}.

Craven (C.O.G.) — WILLIAM GEORGE. Eld. son of Hon. G. A. C., brother of William, 2nd Earl of Craven; 1848^{3}–1851^{3}; formerly in the 1st Life Gds.; Member of the Jockey Club since 1860, Steward 1864–6 and 1873–81; J.P. for Middlesex, London, Suffolk, and co. Camb.; *m.* Lady Mary Catherine Yorke, *d.* of Charles Philip, 4th Earl of Hardwicke. 63 *Curzon Street, Mayfair, W.*

Macaulay (T.H.S., aft. K.S., W.G.C.) — HENRY GEORGE. 1849^{2}–1855^{2}; formerly in the Treasury Office; dead.

Holmes-A'Court (C.O.G.) — HON. WILLIAM LEONARD. Eld. son of William Henry Ashe, 2nd Lord Heytesbury; 1848^{3}–1852^{3}; St. John's Coll. Camb. M.A.; D.L. Isle of Wight; *m.* Isabella Sophia, *d.* of Rev. Richard A'Court Beadon, Vicar of Cheddar, Somerset; died Dec. 16, 1885.

Cator (W.L.E.) — CHARLES OLIVER FREDERICK. Of the Hall, Beckenham; 5th son of the Rev. T. C. of Skelbrook Park, Doncaster, and Rector of Kirby Smeaton, Yorks; 1849^{2}–1850^{2}; Trin. Coll. Camb. M.A.; Barrister; *m.* Isabella Maria, *d.* of Sir George Baker, 3rd Bt.; died Dec. 10, 1876.

West (Mrs. Vav., W.A.C.) — REV. HENRY. 1849^{1}–1852^{1}; formerly Curate of Wraysbury, Staines.

Shaw-Stewart (R.O., H.D. & J.E.Y.) — ROBERT FARQUHAR. 3rd son of Sir M. Shaw-Stewart, 6th Bt.; 1848^{3}–1853^{2}; Ch. Ch. Oxf.; *m.* Isabella Jane, *d.* of Hon. Charles William Warner, C.B. *Redholm, North Berwick.*

Yeo (F.V., W.L.E.) — WILLIAM ARUNDELL. Of Fremington House, Barnstaple, and Dinham House, St. Minver, Wadebridge, Cornwall; son of W. A. Y. of Fremington; 1849^{2}–1854^{3}; Field XI. 1853; Eton XI. 1854; Oriel Coll. Oxf.; Barrister, Western Circuit; died unm. Sept. 1880.

Blundell *mi.* (H.D. & C.O.G.) — MAJOR-GEN. RICHARD BLUNDELL HOLLINSHEAD. Son of R. B. B. H. B. of Deysbrook, West Derby, Liverpool; 1848^{3}–1852^{2}; Ch. Ch. Oxf.; Major-Gen. 3rd K.'s O. Hussars (ret.); *m.* Henrietta Frances, *d.* of Richard Andrew Hyacinth Kirwan of Baunmore, co. Galway. 12 *Lennox Gardens, S.W.*

Wade-Browne (C.O.G.) — CAPT. EDWARD PENNEFATHER. Of Monkton Farleigh Manor, Bradford-on-Avon; 1849^{1}–1852^{2}; formerly Capt. Scots Fusilier Gds. 28 *Ashburn Place, Cromwell Road, S.W.*

Lea Smith (W.A.C.) — FERDINANDO DUDLEY. Eld. son of Col. F. S. of Halesowen; 1848^{3}–1850^{3}; Ch. Ch. Oxf.; called to the Bar, Inner Temple, 1858; formerly Capt. Queen's Own Worcesters Yeo.; J.P. and D.L. for co. Worcester, High Sheriff 1860; J.P. for Staffs; *m.* Amy Sophia, *d.* of James Heath Leigh of Belmont Hall, Northwich. *Halesowen Grange, Birmingham.*

Wicksted *ma.* (F.V., W.J.) — GEORGE EDMUND. Of Betley Hall, Crewe; eld. son of C. W. of Betley; 1849^{2}–1854^{2}; Ch. Ch. Oxf.; Barrister; J.P. for Salop and Cheshire; *m.* Margaret Mary Theresa, *d.* of Sir Edward Blount, 8th Bt., of Sodington, co. Worcester; died 1895.

Heneage (E.B.) — LIEUT.-COL. MICHAEL WALKER. 2nd son of G. H. W. H. of Compton Basset, Calne; 1849^{2}–1852^{2}; formerly Lieut.-Col. Coldstream Gds.; *m.* Florence Margaret Isabella, *d.* of Sir John Andrew Cathcart, 5th Bt. *Carleton House, Ayr.*

Waddington (Mrs. Vav., C.O.G.) — GEORGE. Son of Major-Gen. C. W., C.B., H.E.I.C., Bombay Engineers; 1848^{3}–1853^{2}; Bombay Civil Service; Collector and Political Agent Bombay Presidency (ret. 1896); died April 28, 1902.

Way (Mrs. Hor., H.D.) — GEORGE AUGUSTUS, C.B. Of Spaynes Hall, Great Yeldham, Halstead; eld. son of Rev. C. J. W. of Spaynes Hall and Rector of Boreham, Chelmsford; 1847^{2}–1853^{3}; formerly Lieut.-Col. Bengal Staff Corps; J.P. for Essex; *m.* Catherine, *d.* of Rev. W. E. Warren, Rector of Tacolneston, Norwich; died Oct. 19, 1899.

Wise (F.V., W.A.C.) — CHARLES JOHN. 2nd son of M. W. of Shrubland Hall, Leamington; 1849^{2}–1853^{2}; Ch. Ch. Oxf. B.A.; *m.* Louisa Caroline, *d.* of Richard Malone Sneyd; died July 19, 1896.

Brougham (W.E., C.O.G. & R.D.) — HON. HENRY CHARLES (3rd Lord Brougham and Vaux). Eld. son of William, 2nd Lord B. and V.; 1849^{2}–1853^{3}; Trin. Coll. Camb.; Clerk in House of Lords 1857–86; J.P. and D.L. for Cumberland and Westmorland; *m.* Adora Frances Olga, *d.* of Peter Wells of Forest Farm, Windsor Forest, and widow of Sir Richard Courtenay Musgrave, 11th Bt., of Edenhall, Langwathby, Cumberland. 36 *Chesham Place, S.W.; Brougham Hall, Penrith; and Château Eléonore, Cannes, France.*

Boughey *ma.* (F.V., W.A.C.) — SIR THOMAS FLETCHER, 4th Bt. Eld. son of Sir T. F. F. B., 3rd Bt., of Aqualate; 1848^{3}–1854^{2}; won Steeplechase 1854; Ch. Ch. Oxf.; formerly Capt. 2nd Stafford Militia; D.L. for co. Stafford, High Sheriff 1898; J.P. for co. Salop; *m.* Sarah Annabella, *d.* of Harold Littledale of Liscard Hall, Birkenhead. *Willaston Cottage, Nantwich, and Aqualate, Newport, Salop.*

Edgell (W.E., E.C.) — ARTHUR WYATT-, F.G.S. Son of R. W.-E. of Milton Place, Surrey; 1848^{3}–1851^{3}; Trin. Coll. Camb. B.A.; formerly Lieut. 10th Hussars and W. Somerset Yeo.; aft. Lieut.-Col. 1st Devon Bgde. Vol. R.A.; J.P. and D.L. for Devon; *m.* Frances Albinia Gresham, *d.* of William Leveson-Gower of Titsey Park, Surrey.

Ogle (W.E., B.H.P.) — JOHN SAVILE. 2nd son of Rev. E. C. O. of Kirkley Hall, Newcastle; 1849^{2}–1852^{2}; Ch. Ch. Oxf.; J.P. and D.L. for Northumberland; died unm. Jan. 15, 1892.

Irby — HON. FLORANCE GEORGE HENRY (5th Lord Boston). Son of George Ives, 4th Lord B.; 1846^{3}–1852^{3}; formerly Capt. [illegible]; *m.* Augusta Caroline, *d.* of [illegible] 3rd Lord De Saumarez; [illegible] 4, 1877.

Sir Wm. Forbes (W.A.C.)
SIR WILLIAM (Forbes-Sempill), 8th Bt. (16th Lord Sempill). Eld. son of Sir J. F., 7th Bt., and cousin of Selkirk, 15th Lord S.; 1848^{3}–1853^{2}; formerly Lieut. Coldstream Gds.; served in the Crimea; aft. Hon. Col. 4th V. Bn. Gordon Highl. (Vol. Dec.); J.P. and D.L. co. Aberdeen; *m.* 1st, Caroline Louisa, *d.* of Sir Charles Forbes, 3rd Bt., of Castle Newe, Gartly, co. Aberdeen; 2nd, Frances Emily, *d.* of Sir Robert Abercromby, 5th Bt., of Birkenbog, co. Banff; 3rd, Mary Beresford, *d.* of Henry Sherbrooke of Oxton Hall, Southwell. *Craigievar Castle, Whitehouse, Aberdeen, and Fintray House, Fintray, Aberdeen.*

Lloyd *mi.* (Mrs. Vav. & T.H.S., aft. K.S., F.E.D.)
ALFRED HART. 5th son of G. L. of Cowesby Hall, Thirsk; 1849^{1}–1855^{2}; Coll. Wall 1853–4; Mixed Wall 1854; Merton Coll. Oxf. B.A.; Jackson Sch.; settled in Queensland (1859–95), Squatter 10 years, Sugar Planter 20 years; *m.* Maria, *d.* of William Walker of Dumbleton, co. Gloucester; died at Wahroonga, Sydney, N.S.W., June 30, 1902.

Clayton (F.E.D.)
COL. FITZROY AUGUSTUS TALBOT. Son of Rev. A. P. C. of Coombe Bank, Sevenoaks; 1848^{1}–1851^{2}; Lieut.-Col. Gren. Gds. (ret.); served in the Crimea; med. and clasp for Sebastopol; *m.* Lady Isabella Frances Taylour, *d.* of Thomas, 3rd Marquis of Headfort. *Fyfield House, Maidenhead.*

Hamilton (E.H.P.)
ARTHUR (aft. Hamilton-Scrope), adopted son of G. Poulett-Scrope; 1849^{2}–1851^{1}; Ch. Ch. Oxf.; formerly in the 7th Hussars and 12th Lancers.

Story (R.O.)
JOHN BAINBRIDGE. Son of — S. of Lockington, Loughborough; 1848^{1}–1851^{2}; Eton XI. 1851; formerly 53rd Regt., aft. Cornet Leicesters Yeo.; dead.

Munn (E.B.)
HENRY OLDHAM. Son of — M. of Throwley House, Faversham, Kent; 1848^{2}–1852^{2}; formerly Capt. 13th Lt. Dragoons.

Couper (Mrs. P., H.M.B.)
HENRY EDWARD. 5th son of Sir G. C., 1st Bt.; 1849^{1}–1851^{2}; formerly Capt. 70th Foot; died June 6, 1876.

Dickens (W.E., W.G.C.)
CHARLES BOZ. Son of C. D., the Novelist; 1850^{1}–1852^{3}; Journalist; *m.* Elizabeth, *d.* of F. Evans; died July 20, 1896.

Hudson (T.H.S., E.H.P. & F.E.D.)
REV. ROBERT. Son of R. H., F.R.S., of Clapham Common, Surrey; 1850^{1}–1853^{2}; Tomline Select 1852–3; Sch. of Trin. Coll. Camb., M.A.; 40th Wrangler 1858; Math. Master at Eton 1858–60; formerly Tutor and Math. Lecturer at Selwyn Coll. Camb.; *m.* Marian, *d.* of George Fisher of the Leys, Camb. *Houghton, 9 The Drive, Brighton.*

Beaumont (R.O.)
RICHARD. Son of Capt. R. B., R.N., of Bossall House, Yorks; 1850^{1}–1855^{2}; Trin. Coll. Camb.; formerly a Sheep Farmer in New Zealand; dead.

Browne (Mrs. Vav., C.Wo.)
HERBERT FREDERICK LOUIS. 1850^{1}–1850^{2}.

Yonge *mi.* (Day-boy, W.G.C.)
GEORGE LANGFORD. Son of Rev. F. L. Y. of Torrington; 1844^{2}–1853^{2}; Merchant in Madras; *m.* May, *d.* of J. Dalziel of Ceylon.

Bushby (F.E.D.)
CHARLES METCALF. Son of G. A. B., Bengal Civil Service; 1847^{3}–1852^{3}; Bengal Staff Corps; *m.* Caroline Elizabeth, *d.* of George Hawes Morland; died Feb. 27, 1879.

Peacock (E.H.P.)
MARK BEAUCHAMP. 1848^{3}–1852^{2}; Barrister, Home Circuit.

Blofeld (Mrs. Hor. & Miss G., F.E.D.)
THOMAS CALTHORPE. Eld. son of Rev. T. J. B. of Hoveton; 1850^{2}–1855^{2}; Eton VIII. 1854–5, Stroke 1855; Pres. of Eton Soc. 1854; Opp. W. XI. 1851; Keeper

Blofeld—*cont.*
1854; Field XI. 1853–4; Mixed Wall 1854; Trin. Coll. Camb. M.A.; Barrister, Lincoln's Inn, 1862, South-Eastern Circuit; Recorder of Ipswich since 1877; Chanc. of the Diocese of Norwich; Pres. of Norwich Union Life Insurance Soc.; J.P. for Norfolk; *m.* Fanny Elizabeth, *d.* of Rev. John Anthony Partridge, Rector of Baconsthorpe, Holt, Norfolk. *Hoveton House, Norwich.*

Dawson *mi.* (E.C.)
CHARLES ALFRED. 2nd son of E. D. of Whatton, Nottingham; 1850^{2}–1855^{1}; Ball. Coll. Oxf.; Barrister, Midland Circuit; Inspector, Local Govt. Board; *m.* Edith, *d.* of Philippe de Broca, Capt. French Navy; died 1901.

Leighton (R.O.)
SIR BALDWYN, 8th Bt. Of Loton Park, Shrewsbury; eld. son of Sir B. L., 7th Bt., of Loton Park; 1850^{2}–1853^{2}; Ch. Ch. Oxf. M.A.; formerly S. Salop Yeo.; M.P. for S. Salop 1877–85; J.P. and D.L. for Salop; *m.* Hon. Eleanor Leicester Warren, *d.* of George, 2nd Lord de Tabley; died Jan. 22, 1897.

Wharton (Mrs. Hor. & Miss G., J.L.J.)
RT. HON. JOHN LLOYD, P.C. Of Dryburn, Durham; son of J. T. W. of Dryburn; 1850^{2}–1855^{2}; Trin. Coll. Camb. B.A.; called to the Bar, Inner Temple, 1862; M.P. for Durham 1871–4, and for Ripon Div. W. Riding of Yorks since 1886; J.P., D.L., C.C. and Chmn. of Qr. Sessions for co. Durham; Hon. D.C.L. of Durham 1887; Director N.E. Railway; Knt. of Grace, St. John of Jerusalem; J.P. for W. Riding of Yorks; *m.* Susan Frances, *d.* of Rev. Arthur Duncombe Shafto, Rector of Brancepeth, co. Durham. 1c *King Street, St. James's, S.W., and Bramham, Tadcaster, Yorks.*

Egerton (J.L.J.)
GEORGE MARK LEYCESTER. Of North Muskham, Newark; eld. son of Rev. T. E., Rector of Middle, Shrewsbury; 1850^{2}–1854^{1}; formerly Capt. Rifle Bgde.; aft. Hon. Major 4th Vol. Bn. Sherwood Foresters; J.P. for Notts; *m.* Mary Elizabeth, *d.* of Sir Edward Blackett, 6th Bt.; died Sept. 2, 1898.

Nelson (Mrs. de R., aft. K.S., C.O.G.)
JAMES HENRY. 1850^{2}–1856^{2}; Newc. Select 1856; Eton XI. 1856; Coll. Wall 1854–5; Mixed Wall 1855; King's Coll. Camb.; Fellow of King's; 2nd Cl. Class.; District and Sessions Judge, Madras Presidency (ret. 1887); died 1898.

Hicks-Beach (F.E.D.)
RT. HON. SIR MICHAEL EDWARD, 9th Bt., P.C. Eld. son of Sir M. H. H.-B., 8th Bt.; 1850^{2}–1855^{2}; Newc. Select 1855; Ch. Ch. Oxf. M.A.; 1st Cl. Law and Mod. Hist. 1858; Hon. D.C.L. 1878; Capt. N. Gloucs. Militia 1862–76; M.P. East Gloucesters 1864–85; Under Sec. Home Dept. and Sec. of Poor Law Board 1868; Chief Sec. for Ireland 1874–8 and 1886–7; Sec. for the Colonies 1878–80; Chanc. of the Exchequer 1885–6 and 1895–1902; Pres. of Board of Trade 1888–92; Church Estates Commr. 1892–5; M.P. W. Bristol 1885–1900 and since 1900; J.P. and D.L. co. Gloucester; High Steward of Glouc.; Prov. Grand Master co. Glouc. since 1880; *m.* 1st, Caroline Susan, *d.* of John Henry Elwes of Colesbourne Park, Andoversford, co. Glouc.; 2nd, Lady Lucy Catherine Fortescue, *d.* of Hugh, 3rd Earl Fortescue. *Coln St. Aldwyns, Fairford, co. Glouc.*

Harrison (H.D.)
EDWARD SLATER-. Son of J. H. S.-H. of Shellswell Park; 1846^{3}–1850^{3}; formerly Capt. Oxf. Militia and Lieut.-Col. Oxfs Yeo.; J.P. and C.C. co. Oxf., High Sheriff 1882; *m.* 1st, Cecilia, *d.* of Col. H. R. Saunderson of Northbrook House, Hants; 2nd, Emma Cecilia, *d.* of Richard Aubrey Cartwright of Edgcote, near Banbury. *Shellswell Park, Bicester.*

Boughey *mi.* (W.A.C.)
REV. GEORGE. 2nd son of Sir T. F. F. B., 3rd Bt., of Aqualate, Newport, Salop; 1849^{3}–1855^{2}; Ch. Ch. Oxf. M.A.; Rector of Forton; *m.* Theodosia Mary, *d.* of Rev. Charles Smith Royds of Haughton, Stafford. *Forton Rectory, Newport, Salop.*

Radcliff (J.E.Y.)
JOSEPH. 1849^{3}–1855^{3}; Trin. Coll. Camb.; Barrister, Lincoln's Inn; dead.

Hewett (W.E., J.E.Y.)
EDWARD HYDE. 1849^{3}–1851^{1}.

Grant (H.D.)
HERBERT. 1849^{3}–1854^{2}; formerly 64th Regt.; dead.

Sir Mountstuart Jackson (Mrs. Vav., W.A.C.)
SIR MOUNTSTUART GOODRICKE, 3rd Bt. Eld. son of Sir K. A. J., 2nd Bt.; 1849^{3}–1853^{2}; E. I. Coll. Haileybury; ent. Bengal Civil Service 1855; perished in the massacre at Lucknow during the Indian Mutiny, Nov. 16, 1857.

Sir George Young (Home, J.L.J.)
3rd Bt. Eld. son of Capt. Sir G. Y., 2nd Bt., R.N., of Formosa; 1849^{3}–1856^{2}; Newc. Select 1855–6; Trin. Coll. Camb. M.A.; Le Bas Prize 1861; Fellow of Trin. 1862; Barrister, Lincoln's Inn, 1864; Royal Commr. on Coolie Immigration, British Guiana, 1870; exploration of the Kaieteur Waterfall, river Potaro, 1870; Assist.-Commr Friendly Soc. Comm. 1871–3; Sec. Factory and Workshop Acts Comm. 1875, and Irish Land Acts Comm. 1881; Pres. of the Senate Univ. Coll. London 1881–6; Charity Commr. since 1882; J.P. for Berks; *m.* Alice Eacy, *d.* of Evory Kennedy, M.D., of Belgard, co. Dublin, and widow of Sir Alexander Hutchinson Lawrence, 1st Bt. *Formosa Place, Cookham, Berks.*

Burnaby *mi.* (F.V., E.C. & W.B.M.)
THOMAS FREDERICK (aft. Burnaby-Atkins). 2nd son of T. F. A. B. of Brampton Manor House, near Huntingdon; 1849^{3}–1854^{2}; Trin. Hall, Camb. M.A.; formerly Solicitor at Newark; J.P. and D.L. for Kent; *m.* Elizabeth, *d.* of John Francklin of Gonalston Hall, Nottingham. *Orgreave Hall, Lichfield, and Halstead Place, Sevenoaks.*

Wethered (H.D., C.O.G. & W.B.M.)
COL. OWEN PEEL. 2nd son of O. W. of Remnantz and Seymour Court, Marlow; 1850^{1}–1854^{2}; Ch. Ch. Oxf. M.A.; Chmn. of Thomas Wethered & Sons, Ltd. Marlow Brewery; Hon. Col. 1st Bucks R.V. Corps (Vol. Dec.); *m.* Frances Alice, *d.* of George T. Ellison of Seymour Street, W. *El Robado, Puerto Orotava, Teneriffe.*

Hills (J.L.J.)
HERBERT AUGUSTUS. Son of J. H. of Walmer, Deal; 1849^{3}–1852^{2}; Ball. Coll. Oxf. B.A.; 2nd Cl. Lit. Hum.; Barrister, Inner Temple, 1864; Judge of Tribunals in Egypt 1875–82, and Court of Appeal 1882; *m* Anna *d.* of Rt. Hon. Sir William R. Grove, Kt., P.C. *Highhead Castle, Carlisle.*

Pearson (W.A.C.)
WILLIAM CHARLES. Son of — P. of Tempsford Hall, St. Neots; 1849^{3}–1852^{2}; won Steeplechase 1850; formerly Capt. 88th Regt.

Smith (T.H.S., aft. K.S., F.E.D.)
REV. GRAHAM. Son of Rev. J. S. of Holybourne, Alton, Hants, and Vicar of Irchester, Wellingboro; 1849^{3}–1857^{2}; Mixed Wall 1854–6, Keeper 1856; Coll. Wall 1854–6, Keeper 1856; Clare Coll. Camb. M.A.; Curate of Kirkby, Fleetham, Bedale; died October 20, 1868.

Congreve (W.E., F.E.D.)
REV GEORGE. 2nd son of Capt. W. W. C. of Congreve, co. Stafford, and Burton Hall, Neston, Chester; 1849^{3}–1854^{2}; Exeter Coll. Oxf. M.A.; Missionary of the Socy. o St. John Evangelist at Cowley. *Mission House, Chapel Street, Cape Town, S Africa*

St. Aubyn *mi.* (F.E.D.)
EDWARD. 4th son of Sir E. St. A., 1st Bt., of St. Michael's Mount, Marazion, Cornwall; 1849^{3}–1854^{1}; Trin. Coll. Camb. B.A.; Barrister, Lincoln's Inn; formerly Col. Comm. 3rd Bn. Duke of Cornwall's Lt. Infantry; a Dep. Warden of the Stannaries; J.P. for Devon; J.P. and D.L. for Cornwall; *m.* 1st, Edith, *d.* of Vice-Adml. Hon. Keith Stewart, C.B.; 2nd, Eugenia Susannah, *d.* of David Barclay Chapman, and widow of George Henry Fitzroy; 3rd, Ada Mary, *d.* of Col. Sir Robert Thomas White-Thomson of Broomford Manor, Exbourne, N. Devon. *Gipna, near Bodmin.*

Wickham (H.D.)
WILLIAM WICKHAM. Son of L. W. W., of Chestnut Grove; 1849^{3}–1852^{2}; formerly Capt. Yorks Hussars Yeo. Cav.; J.P. for W. Riding of Yorks; *m.* Katharine Henrietta, *d.* of Thomas Fairfax. *Chestnut Grove, Boston Spa, R.S.O., Yorks.*

Malet *ma.* (Mrs. Vav., F.V. & W.G.C., W.G.C.)
LIEUT.-COL. SIR HENRY CHARLES EDEN, 3rd Bt. Eld. son of Sir A. M., 2nd Bt., K.C.B., of Wilbury; 1849^{3}–1852^{2}; ent. Gren. Gds. 1854 (served in the Crimea at Sebastopol); ret. Lieut.-Col. 1870; late in command of 20th Middlesex Rifles; J.P. for Wilts; *m.* Laura Jane Campbell, *d.* of John Hamilton of Hilston Park, Monmouth. *Wilbury House, Salisbury.*

Browning *mi.* (F.E.D.)
COL. MONTAGUE CHARLES, C.B. 3rd son of H. B. of 73 Grosvenor Street, W.; 1849^{3}–1854^{2}; Eton VIII. and Wall XI. 1854; served in the 89th Regt. and 87th Royal Irish Fusiliers 1855–69; Crimean Campaign, Siege and Fall of Sebastopol (med. and clasp and Turkish med.); Indian Mutiny 1857–8; Staff Officer to a Field Force at attack of Tarnigha Hills and at attack and capture of Mondetti; mentioned in despatches 1858; served in 3rd Bn. Suffolk Regt. 1870–97, late Lieut.-Col. and Hon. Col.; J.P. for Suffolk; *m.* Fanny Allen, *d.* of Rev. E. Hogg of Fornham St. Martin, Suffolk. *73 Grosvenor Street, W., and Brantham Court, Manningtree.*

Northey *mi.* (C.O.G. & W.B.M.)
FRANCIS VERNON. 3rd son of E. R. N. of Woodcote House, Epsom; 1850^{1}–1854^{2}; Eton XI. 1851–4, Capt. 1854; Keeper of Upper Club 1853; Major 60th Rifles; meds. for Indian Mutiny, Red River Expedition, and Zulu War 1879; *m.* Charlotte Belinda, *d.* of Casimir S. Gzowski of Toronto, Canada; died of a wound received at battle of Gingilova, S. Africa, April 6, 1879.

Mr. Hervey (E.B.)
LORD AUGUSTUS HENRY CHARLES. 2nd son of Frederick William, 2nd Marquis of Bristol; 1848^{3}–1855^{1}; Trin. Coll. Camb. M.A.; formerly in the Diplomatic Service, aft. M.P. for W. Suffolk; *m.* Mariana, *d.* of William P. Hodnett, and widow of Ashton Benyon of Stetchworth Park, Newmarket; died May 28, 1875.

Denne *mi.* (W.E., E.B.)
HERBERT HENRY. Son of D. D. of Elbridge House, near Canterbury; 1849^{3}–1854^{1}; formerly Cornet E. Kent Yeo.; Barrister. *The Firs, Fordwich, Canterbury.*

Mr. Fiennes *mi.* (W.E., E.C.)
HON. FREDERICK NATHANIEL (aft. Twisleton-Wykeham-Fiennes). 5th son of Rev. Frederick Benjamin, 16th Lord Saye and Sele, D.C.L.; 1849^{3}–1852^{2}; Capt. 23rd Royal Welsh Fusiliers; served with distinction in Crimean War, in the attack on the Redan, and aft. in India; aft. Military Knt. of Windsor; *m.* Isabella Margaret, *d.* of Thomas Martinson Richardson of Hibaldstow Cliff, Brigg; died Sept. 26, 1896.

Bullock (Mrs. H[illegible], W.G.C.)
EDWARD. Eld. son of E. B. Common Serjeant, London; 1849^{3}–1851^{3}, called to the Bar 1858, formerly Northern Circuit; Recorder of B[illegible]ngham since 1884. [illegible]

Bagge (E.H.P. & Mrs. Dr., E.H.P.) — RICHARD SALISBURY. Of Gaywood Hall, King's Lynn; e'd. son of R. B. of Gaywood; 1849^{1}–1853^{3}; Eton XI. 1852–3; Field XI. 1853; Ensign 66th Regt. 1854; Capt. 10th Foot 1862 (ret. 1864); Queen's Foreign Service Messenger 1867–70; died Dec. 18, 1886.

WILLIAM. 1849^{1}–1852^{3}; formerly Capt., 15th Lt. Dragoons.

Atkinson (E.H.P.)

Askew (W.A.C.) — WATSON (aft. Robertson). Son of Capt. C. C. A., R.N., of Broadland, Petersfield; 1848^{3}–1852^{3}; Ch. Ch. Oxf.; J.P. and D.L. for Northumberland and Berwickshire; High Sheriff for Northumberland 1863; Chmn. of Qr. Sessions and Vice-Chmn. of C.C. for Northumberland; *m.* Hon. Sarah, *d.* of David Robertson, Lord Marjoribanks, of Ladykirk. *Pallinsburn, Cornhill, Northumberland, and Ladykirk, Norham, R.S.O., Northumberland.*

Hanning Lee (C.O.G.) — VAUGHAN (aft. Vaughan-Lee). Of Dillington Park, Ilminster; eld. son of J. L. L. of Dillington; 1849^{3}–1852^{1}; formerly Capt. 21st Regt.; served in the Crimea, aft. Glamorgan Militia and W. Somerset Yeo.; M.P. for W. Somerset 1874–82; J.P. and D.L. cos. Somerset and Glam.; High Sheriff co. Glam. 1871; *m.* Clara Elizabeth, *d.* of George Moore of Appleby Hall, Atherstone; died July 7, 1882.

Voules *ma.* (W.G.C.) — CHARLES STUART. Son of C. S. V., Solicitor, of Windsor; 1848^{3}–1851^{3}; formerly in the Army; dead.

Fletcher (C.O.G.) — WILLIAM FREDERICK HAMILTON. Son of W. F., D.C.L., Barrister; 1849^{1}–1852^{1}; Trin. Coll. Oxf.; *m.* Ida Wilton; died Feb. 16, 1879.

Burton (W.E.) — ROBERT LINGEN. Of Longner Hall, Shrewsbury; eld. son of R. L. B. of Longner; 1849^{3}–1854^{1}; Opp. Wall 1853; Ch. Ch. Oxf. B.A.; formerly in S. Staffs Yeo.; J.P. and D.L. co. Salop; *m.* Catherina Sophia, *d.* of Richard Francis Cleaveland, Comm. R.N.; died Nov. 17, 1881.

Miers (Mrs. Hor., C.L.) — RICHARD HANBURY. Of Cadoxton Lodge, Barry, Glamorgan; eld. son of R. H. M. of Cadoxton; 1849–1852^{1}; *m.* Elizabeth Ann, *d.* of George Penrose of Clyn-y-bont, Neath; died May 17, 1870.

Cooke (W.E., W.G.C.) — CHARLES RUSSELL. 1849^{3}–1852^{3}.

Jones (W.L.E.) — HIS HONOUR JUDGE HERBERT RIVERSDALE MANSEL. Son of H. G. J., Serjeant-at-Law, Judge of Clerkenwell County Court; 1846^{3}–1853^{3}; Eton VIII. 1853; won School Pulling 1853; Trin. Coll. Camb.; 1st Cl. Law; Stroke Camb. VIII. 1855–6; Barrister, Home Circuit, and Capt. Hants Militia, aft. Judge of C.C. Circuit XIII.; *m.* 1st, Emelia, *d.* of John Davis of Cranbrook Park, Essex; 2nd, Fanny, *d.* of J. R. Baker of Cooling, Kent. *County Court, Sheffield.*

Gledstanes *ma.* (W.L.E.) — WALTER EVANS. Son of J. H. G. of Cheshunt, Waltham Cross; 1847^{3}–1853^{3}; formerly Partner in Messrs. Gledstanes, E.I. Merchants in the City. *Hawkstone, The Avenue, Southampton.*

Fane (W.E., E.B.) — HENRY JOHN. 1849^{3}–1850^{3}; formerly in the 81st Regt.

Pickering (E.H.P., & C.Wo.) — EDWARD HENRY UMFREVILLE. Son of Rev. E. H. P., Assist.-Master at Eton 1830–52; 1849^{3}–1855^{2}; formerly in Sec.'s Dept. G.P.O., and Manager 'Sporting Life' Newspaper; *m.* Dora, *d.* of John Seldons of Egham. *Pelham Lodge, St. Lawrence, Isle of Wight, and Brotton Hall, Brotton, R.S.O., [illegible].*

Chapman *mi.* (E.B.) — PETER GODFREY. Of Devon House, Surrey; 4th son of D. B. C. of Roehampton; 1849^{3}–1852^{3}; formerly in the Surrey Militia; *m.* Henrietta Sophia, *d.* of Rev. Edward Hamer Ravenhill.

Bowyer (F.V., W.A.C.) — HENRY. Of Steeple Aston, Oxf.; eld. son of H. A. B. of Steeple Aston; 1849^{3}–1854^{3}; Capt. 10th Hussars; J.P. and D.L. co. Oxf.; *m.* Lizzie, *d.* of Lieut.-Col. Vernon of the Coldstream Gds.; died May 6, 1882.

Mr. Trefusis *mi.* (Miss M. & Mrs. Vo., H.M.B., & J.L.J.) — HON. MARK GEORGE KERR (aft. Rolle), 2nd son of Charles Rodolph, 19th Lord Clinton; 1848^{1}–1854^{2}; Eton XI. 1853–4; formerly Capt. N. Devon Yeo.; J.P. and D.L. co. Devon, High Sheriff 1864; High Steward of Barnstaple; *m.* Lady Gertrude Jane Douglas, *d.* of George Sholto, 19th Earl of Morton. *St. Leonards, Torrington, and Bicton, East Budleigh, Budleigh Salterton, S.O., Devon.*

Mills (Miss G., E.B.) — JOHN. Of Bisterne, Ringwood; eld. son of J. M. of Bisterne; 1848^{3}–1854^{2}; Ch. Ch. Oxf.; J.P. and D.L. for Hants; *m.* Louisa Frances, *d.* of Thomas Entwisle of Woolhayes, Christchurch, Hants; died Feb. 24, 1899.

Maynard — JAMES MACDONNEL. 1847^{3}–1851^{3}; formerly in the War Dept.

Secker (C.L.) — JOHN HERBERT. Of Hangmoor, Virginia Water, Surrey; son of J. S. of Windsor; 1848^{3}–1856^{1}; St. John's Coll. Camb.; Barrister, Oxf. Circuit; died Mar. 1, 1903.

Lord Molyneux (E.B.) — WILLIAM PHILIP (4th Earl of Sefton), K.G. Eld. son of Charles William, 3rd Earl of S.; 1848^{3}–1853^{3}; formerly Capt. Gren. Gds.; Lord-Lieut. of Lancashire; *m.* Hon. Cecil Emily, *d.* of William George, 1st Lord Hilton; died June 27, 1897.

Handley (F.V., E.B.) — HENRY EDWARDES. Of Culverthorpe Hall, co. Lincoln; eld. son of H. H. of Culverthorpe; 1848^{3}–1850^{3}; formerly Lieut. Scots Greys; died 1892.

Burn (W.E., E.H.P.) — HENRY DAVID. 1848^{3}–1852^{3}.

Allfrey *ma.* (W.L.E.) — GOODRICH HOLMSDALE. Of Wokefield Park, Reading; eld. son of R. A. of Wokefield; 1848^{3}–1853^{3}; formerly Major 2nd Dragoon Gds.; J.P. for Berks. High Sheriff 1881; *m.* Helen Clara, *d.* of William Little; died April 9, 1898.

Judd (W.L.E.) — HARRY JOHNSTON. Son of J. P. J. of Maces Place, Rickling, Essex; 1846^{3}–1851^{1}; 8th Madras Cav.; died 1870.

Platt (Mrs. Hor., E.H.P.) — HENRY ALBERT. 1849^{3}–1852^{3}; formerly Lieut. 69th Regt.

Wilkinson (Miss Edg., J.L.J.) — BATHURST EDWARD. Of Potterton Hall, Barwick-in-Elmet, Leeds; son of J. E. W. of Potterton Hall; 1848^{3}–1850^{3}; formerly Lieut. 4th Dragoon Gds.; served in the Crimea (Crimean med., Turkish med., and 3rd Cl. Medjidie); J.P. for W. Riding of Yorks; *m.* Jane Annie, *d.* of George Breary; died May 1, 1901.

Dearden (W.A.C.) — JOHN. Of Holmstead, Crawley; son of J. D. of the Hollins, Halifax; 1848^{3}–1850^{3}; formerly Capt. 13th Lt. Dragoons; served in the Crimea; J.P. for Sussex and W. Riding of Yorks; *m.* Henrietta Maria, *d.* of Sir Henry Edwards, 1st Bt., of Pye Nest, Halifax; died Feb. 1901.

Collins *min.* (Mrs. P., W.J.) — DIGBY. 3rd son of E. C. of Truthan and Newton Ferrers; 1848^{3}–1855^{2}; Opp. Wall 1854; Eton VIII. 1855; Trin. Hall. Camb.; J.P. and D.L. for Cornwall, High Sheriff 1887; *m.* Jane Arabella, *d.* of Rev. William Vaughan, Rector of Pontesbury, Shrewsbury, and widow of W. Tatham of Heppington, Kent. *Netton Ferrers, Plymouth, and Truthan, Truro.*

Melville (E.H.P. & W.G.C.) — HON. RONALD RUTHVEN LESLIE- (11th Earl of Leven and Melville), P.C. 3rd son of John Thornton, 9th Earl of L. and M.; 1848^{3}–1852^{2}; Ch. Ch. Oxf. M.A.; formerly Director of the Bank of England; Repr. Peer for Scotland since 1892; Keeper of the Privy Seal of Scotland since 1900; Lord High Commr. to General Assembly of Church of Scotland 1898–1901; D.L. co. Nairn; Lieut. for City of London; Head of Banking House of Melville, Evans & Co.; *m.* Hon. Emma Selina, *d.* of William Henry, 2nd Visct. Portman. *Roehampton House, Roehampton, S.W.; Hintwood House, Grove Road, East Bournemouth; and Glenferness, Dunphail, N.B.*

Sir Charles Mordaunt (J.L.J.) — 10th Bt. Of Walton Hall, Warwick; eld. son of Sir J. M., 9th Bt., of Walton Hall; 1849^{2}–1854^{3}; Ch. Ch. Oxf.; M.P. for S. Warwick 1859–68; Hon. Lieut.-Col. Warwicks Yeo.; D.L. co. Warwick; *m.* 1st, Harriet Sarah, *d.* of Sir Thomas Moncreiffe, 7th Bt., of Moncreiffe House, Bridge of Earn, co. Perth; 2nd, Mary Louisa, *d.* of Hon. and Rev. Canon Henry Pitt Cholmondeley, Rector of Adlestrop, Chipping Norton; died Oct. 15, 1897.

Lord Powerscourt (J.L.J.) — MERVYN EDWARD WINGFIELD (7th Visct. P.), K.P., P.C. Eld. son of Richard, 6th Visct. P.; 1847^{2}–1852^{2}; Member of the Royal Irish Academy of Science; 1st Life Gds. 1853–62; elected Repr. Peer for Ireland 1865; formerly Pres. Royal Dublin Soc.; J.P. and D.L. for co. Wicklow; J.P. co. Dublin; Chmn. of Dublin Hospital Board; Lord-Justice of Ireland 1900; *m.* Lady Julia Coke, *d.* of Thomas William, 2nd Earl of Leicester, K.G. 51 *Portland Place, W., and Powerscourt, Enniskerry, co. Wicklow.*

Wynne — MAJ.-GEN. EDWARD WILLIAM. Of Trofarth and Coed Coch, Abergele, co. Denbigh; 2nd son of J. L. W. of Trofarth and Coed Coch; 1846^{3}–1851^{3}; Col. Gren. Gds. and Maj.-Gen. in the Army; J.P. and D.L. co. Denbigh, High Sheriff 1893; *m.* Anne Gwendolyn, *d.* of Hugh Robert Hughes of Kinmel, Abergele; died Nov. 4, 1893.

Vidal *ma.* (H.D.) — REV. FRANCIS FURSE. Son of Rev. F. V. of Sutton Vicarage, Woodbridge; 1846^{3}–1851^{3}; Trin. Hall, Camb. M.A.; Rector of Creeting; *m.* Lucy Mary, *d.* of Sir Robert Henry Cunliffe, 4th Bt. *Creeting Rectory, Needham Market, R.S.O., Suffolk.*

Battiscombe (C.L.) — ARTHUR. Of Woodlands, Glasbury, co. Radnor; son of Rev. W. B.; 1847^{3}–1853^{2}; Trin. Coll. Camb.; J.P. co. Radnor; *m.* Jane Elizabeth, *d.* of George Hayne. *Hinton Court, Hereford.*

Watson (J.E.Y.) — ROBERT. Of North Seaton, Morpeth; 1850^{2}–1851^{3}.

Lascelles (J.L.J.) — COL. WALTER RICHARD. Son of Hon. A. L. of Norley; 1850^{2}–1854^{3}; Assist. Adjt. and Q.M.G. in Egypt 1883; Assist. Mil. Sec. at Headqrs. 1885–6; A.-A.-G. 1886–91, and D.A.G. in Ireland 1891–4; Col. Rifle Brigade (ret.); J.P. and D.L. for Cheshire; *m.* Ellen, *d.* of Charles Kane Sivewright. 55 *Hans Road, Brompton Road, S.W., and Norley, Frodsham, Warrington.*

Ward (J.L.J.) — LAMBERT HOULTON. Of Calverley Manor, Tunbridge Wells; eld. son of A. W. W. of Calverley; 1850–1852; formerly Capt. 2nd Life Gds. *Arthur's Club, 69 St. [illegible] St[illegible], S.W.*

Scott *min.* (E.C.) — REV. CHARLES JAMES. Of Rotherfield Park, near Alton, Hants; 3rd son of J. W. S. of Rotherfield; 1850^{3}–1855^{2}; Merton Coll. Oxf. M.A.; Postmaster of Merton 1855; 1st Cl. Nat. Science 1858; 2nd Cl. Hist.; Rector of East Tisted, Alton, Hants; *m.* Ruth, *d.* of Robert Caldwell of Charleston, S. Carolina, U.S.A.; died at Cannes May 10, 1899.

Hall (C.O.G.) — JOHN. Of Scorborough Hall and Walkington Lodge, Beverley; son of J. H. of Scorborough; 1848^{3}–1853^{1}; Magd. Coll. Camb.; Stroke of Camb. VIII. 1858–61; Banker at Beverley; *m.* Mary Amelia, *d.* of William Bradley Wainman of Carhead, Crosshills, co. York; died 1868.

Carlyon *mi.* (Mrs. Hor., W.L.E.) — ARTHUR HOOKER. 8th son of E. C. of Tregrehan Par Station, Cornwall; 1849^{3}–1851^{1}; Midshipman; died on his way home from India.

UNPLACED.

Lear (W.E., E.B.) — REV. EDWARD WILLIAM. Son of Very Rev. F. L., B.D., Dean of Salisbury; 1849^{2}–1859^{2}; New Coll. Oxf. 9 *Goldsmith Street, Exeter.*

De Vidil (W.G.C.) — ALFRED JOHN. 1849^{3}–1850^{2}; Trinity Coll. Camb. B.A.

FOURTH FORM.

Pegge-Burnell *mi.* (E.H.P.) — HUGH D'ARCY. 2nd son of E. V. P.-B. of Winkburn Hall, Southwell, and Beauchief Abbey, Sheffield; 1848^{1}–1851^{1}; Col. 7th Hussars; died Dec. 18, 1883.

Wyndham (E.B.) — HON. PERCY SCAWEN. 3rd son of G. W., 1st Lord Leconfield; 1848^{2}–1850^{2}; formerly in the Coldstream Gds.; M.P. for W. Cumberland 1860–85; Chmn. Cumberland Qr. Sessions 1870–86; J.P. for Sussex and Cumberland; J.P., D.L., C.C. (and Vice-Chairman C.C.) for Wilts, High Sheriff 1896; *m.* Madeline Caroline Frances Eden, *d.* of Gen. Sir Guy Campbell, 1st Bt., C.B. *Clouds, East Knoyle, Salisbury, and 44 Belgrave Square, S.W.*

Mariette *mi.* (Home) — GEORGE. 1844^{2}–1851^{2}; formerly in the War Dept., Pall Mall, S.W.

Mr. Poulett (R.O.) — HON. AMIAS. 3rd son of John, 5th Earl Poulett; 1849^{1}–1851^{3}; Lieut. Grenadier Gds.; died Feb. 20, 1857.

Thompson (W.J.) — EDWARD PERCY. 1849^{2}–1850^{3}; served in the Crimea; after at Trin. Coll. Camb.

Alderson *mi.* (W.J., Miss M. & Mrs. Vo., W.J.) — REV. CANON FREDERICK CECIL. 5th son of Hon. Sir E. H. A., a Baron of the Exchequer; 1849^{2}–1854^{2}; Eton VIII. 1854; Trin. Coll. Camb. M.A.; Camb. VIII. 1856; Curate of Ampthill 1861–3; Curate of Hursley, Winchester 1863–5; Rector of Holdenby, Northampton, 1865–93; Canon of Peterborough since 1891; Rector of Lutterworth since 1893; Chaplain-in-Ordinary to Queen Victoria 1869–1901; Hon. Chaplain to the King; *m.* Katharine Gwladys, *d.* of Sir Josiah John Guest, 1st Bt., of Dowlais. *The Precincts, Peterborough, and the Rectory, Lutterworth.*

Clarke (E.C.) — STANLEY AUGUSTUS. 2nd son of H. D. C. of Swakeleys, near Uxbridge; 1849^{3}–1851^{1}; in the G.P.O.; dead.

Hallifax (H.D.) — GODFREY THOMAS. 1848^{3}–1852^{2}; died young.

Brown ([illegible]) — [illegible] 1849^{1}–1851^{3}; Eton XI. [illegible]

Mr. Nelson *mi.* (R.F.H., E.B.) — HON. HENRY. Of Sandford House, Plastford, Wilts; 5th son of Thomas Bolton, 2nd Earl Nelson; 1849[3]–1851[2]; killed by a fall from his horse Nov. 28, 1863.

Williams (W.E., W.A.C.) — DERING. 1849[3]–1850[2]; formerly in the Civil Service, Madras.

Harkness (C.O.G.) — REV. JAMES CLARKE. 5th son of Rev. R. H. of Garryfine, Bruree, co. Limerick; 1849[3]–1852[3]; Field XI. 1851, Keeper 1852; St. John's Coll. Camb. M.A.; Rector of West Clandon, Guildford; aft. Vicar of Hawkley, West Liss, Hants; *m.* 1st, Constance Susan, *d.* of G. W. Franklin of Poole: 2nd, Edith Charlotte, *d.* of Charles Steuart Smyth of Bayswater. *Hawkley, West Cliff Road, Bournemouth.*

Prosser — FRANCIS WILLIAM. Son of the Lieut.-Gov. of the R. M. Coll. Sandhurst; 1847[1]–1851[1].

Buckley (Miss M., F.E.D.) — CHARLES EDWARD. Son of Rev. H. W. B., Rector of Hartshorne, Burton-on-Trent; 1846[1]–1851[2]; formerly Capt. in the Rifle Bgde.; died Nov. 17, 1868.

Davies (W.J.) — FRANCIS BYAM. Eld. son of Gen. F.J.D., of Danehurst, Sussex; 1848[3]–1852[3]; Lieut. Gren. Gds.; died at sea Nov. 10, 1854, from a wound received in the trenches before Sebastopol, Oct. 22, 1854.

Lord Worsley (E.C.) — CHARLES MAUD WORSLEY ANDERSON-PELHAM (3rd Earl of Yarborough). Eld. son of Charles Anderson Worsley, 2nd Earl of Y.; 1848[3]–1850[2]; M.P. for Gt. Grimsby 1857–62; *m.* Lady Victoria Alexandrina, *d.* of William, 2nd Earl of Listowel; died Feb. 6, 1875.

Dymock — FRANCIS DOUGLAS. 1846[3]–1851[2].

Lubbock *ma.* (J.L.J.) — HENRY JAMES. 2nd son of Sir J. W. L., 3rd Bt., of High Elms, Down, Farnborough, Kent; 1848[3]–1852[2]; Partner in Robarts, Lubbock & Co., Bankers, 15 Lombard St., E.C.; J.P. and D.L.; High Sheriff co. of London 1894 and 1897; *m.* Frances Mary, *d.* of Rev. Henry Turton, Incumbent of Betley, Crewe. *Newberries Park, St. Albans, and 15 Lombard Street, E.C.*

Baynes (B.O.) — GEORGE HENRY. 1849[3]–1851[2].

Dupuis *mi.* (H.D.) — REAR-ADMIRAL ARTHUR EDWARD. Son of Rev. G. J. D., Assist. and Lower Master, Fellow, Bursar, and Vice-Provost of Eton; 1849[3]–1852[2]; ent. Royal Navy 1852; served in the Crimea and Chinese War 1857; on active service in Egypt 1884–6; *m.* Agnes, *d.* of Rev. P. Williams, Rector of Rewe, Exeter; died Jan. 1897.

Wilson *ma.* (Home, aft K.S., C.O.G. & W.J.) — WILLIAM KNYVET. Eld. son of Rear-Adml. G. K. W., R.N., of 3 Brunswick Place, Windsor; 1849[3]–1858[2]; Newc. Select 1857–8; Coll. Wall 1856–7; Sch. of Trin. Coll. Camb., M.A.; 4th in Class. Trip.; Chanc. Med. and Fellow of Trin. 1862; Sen. Opt. Math.; formerly Assist. Master at Wellington Coll.; aft. at Rugby; killed on the Riffelhorn, July 17, 1865.

Cleland *ma.* (J.W.H.) — JOHN. Of Stormont Castle, Dundonald, co. Down; eld. son of S. J. C.; 1845[3]–1850[3]; Col. 9th Lancers; J.P. and D.L. co. Down, High Sheriff 1866; *m.* Therese Maria, *d.* of Capt. Thomas Leyland of Haggerston Castle, Beal, Northumberland; died 1893.

Lindsay (C.O.G. & W.B.M.) — ROBERT WEBBER. Son of R. L. of Glanafon, Taibach, Port Talbot; 1849[3]–1853[3]. *Barford, Warwick.*

Clive *mi.* (Miss M., W.J.) — HON. WILLIAM WINDSOR WINDSOR-. 3rd son of Hon. H. C. and the Baroness Windsor-Clive of Oakly Park, Bromfield, Salop; 1849[3]–1855[2]; Eton VIII. 1854–5; St. John's Coll. Camb.; killed in a railway accident near Tuxford, Newark, Sept. 24, 1857.

Ernwin (E.B.) — HAROLD AUGUSTUS. 1849[3]–1854[3]; Opp. Wall 1853; Eton VIII. 1854; Trin. Coll. Camb.; aft. in India; dead.

Heaton (T.H.S., C.O.G.) — FREDERICK LUXMOORE. 5th son of J. H. of Plas Heaton, nr. Trefnant co. Denbigh; 1849[3]–1855[2]; Opp. Wall 1854; Jesus Coll. Oxf. M.A.; M.B.; 1st Cl. Nat. Science 1859; Physician and Surgeon; *m.* Eleanor, *d.* of Very Rev. Richard Bonnor Maurice Bonnor, Dean of St. Asaph. *53 Argyle Road, West Ealing.*

Gosling (H.D. & J.E.Y.) — FRANCIS. Son of F. G. of the Manor House, Sutton, Surrey; 1849[3]–1854[3]; Partner in Barclay & Co., Bankers, Fleet Street, E.C. *Wellbury House, near Hitchin, Herts.*

Caulfeild (W.A.C.) — HENRY MURRAY. 3rd son of Lieut.-Gen. J. C., C.B., M.P.; 1849[3]–1853[1]; Capt. Bengal Cav.; served through Indian Mutiny; *m.* Susan, *d.* of Gen. George Campbell; was lost in the s.s. 'Persia,' which foundered on her way home Oct. 5, 1864.

Ramsden (H.D. & J.E.Y.) — REV. HENRY JAMES. 2nd son of H. J. R. of Oxton Hall, Tadcaster; 1849[3]–1854[1]; Trin. Coll. Camb. B.A.; aft. Wells Theo. Coll.; Curate at Handsworth, Birmingham; died unm., of Syrian fever, Dec. 8, 1862.

Dugdale *mi.* (E.C.) — COL. HENRY CHARLES GEAST. 4th son of W. S. D. of Merevale Hall, Atherstone, and Blythe Hall, Coleshill, Birmingham; 1849[3]–1854[3]; served for 30 years in the Rifle Bgde. (ret. as Col.); *m.* Edith Cecilia, *d.* of Hugh Montgomery of Grey Abbey, co. Down. *Hill House, Winchester.*

Hunter (Miss Edg., C.O.G.) — HENRY LANNOY. Son of H. H. of Beech Hill; 1849[3]–1855[2]; Ch. Ch. Oxf. B.A.; Lieut. Hants Yeo. 1858–69; aft. Lieut.-Col. Royal Berks Vol.; J.P. for Berks; *m.* Anna, *d.* of Sir James Carter. *Beech Hill, Reading.*

Gregory (E.C.) — FRANCIS HOOD. 2nd son of A. F. G. of Styvechale; 1849[3]–1851[3]; Ch. Ch. Oxf. M.A.; formerly Major 15th Hussars; A.D.C. to Duke of Abercorn, K.G., when Lord-Lieut. of Ireland, and aft. to Lord Strathnairn, Gen. Comm.-in-Chief in Ireland; A.D.C. to Lord Mayo, Viceroy of India, 1870–2, and to Lord Napier of Magdala, Comm.-in-Chief in India, 1874–6; J.P. co. Warwick. *Styvechale, Coventry.*

Parr (W.E., W.J.) — LIEUT.-COL. THOMAS ROWORTH. Son of T. C. P. of Clifton, Bristol; 1849[3]–1854[3]; formerly in the Rifle Bgde., aft. 3rd Somerset Regt.; *m.* 1st, *d.* of Sir A. Downie; 2nd, *d.* of Rev. George Acklom. *10 Sumner Terrace, Onslow Square, S.W.*

Sparke *mi.* (Mrs. de R., E.H.P.) — JOHN FRANCIS. 3rd son of Rev. J. H. S. of Gunthorpe Hall, East Dereham, and Canon of Ely; 1849[3]–1851[1]; served with the 68th Regt. in the Crimea (med. and clasps); aft. in the 84th Regt.; later Major and Adjt. Oxfs Militia; *m.* 1st, Mary Adela, *d.* of George Edwin Taunton of The Marfords, Bromborough, Birkenhead; 2nd, *d.* of — Foster; died Feb. 27, 1888.

Follett (F.C.) — GEORGE. Eld. son of Sir W. W. F., Attorney-Gen., of Culm Davy, Cullompton; 1850[1]–1855[2]; Ball. Coll. Oxf.; 1st Cl. Mods. 1857; 2nd Cl. Class. 1859; Barrister, Western Circuit; died 1866.

Routledge (K.S., C.Wo.)
REV. CANON CHARLES FRANCIS. Son of Rev. W. R., D.D., Rector of Cotleigh, Honiton; 1850^{1}–1858^{1}; Newc. Select 1857; Coll. and Mixed Wall 1855-7; Sch. of King's Coll. Camb. M.A.; 11th in Class. Trip. and Fellow of King's 1862; one of H.M.'s Inspectors of Schools and Hon. Canon of Canterbury; *m.* 1st, Dorothy Hester, *d.* of Bishop Blomfield of London; 2nd, Ellen, *d.* of Col. Bruce, R.A. *St. Martin's, Canterbury.*

Blacker (E.H.P.)
WILLIAM. Son of Lieut.-Col. St. J. B. of the Madras Army; 1850^{1}–1852^{2}; Ch. Ch. Oxf.; formerly Lieut. 12th Lancers.

Murdoch (W.E., E.H.P.)
CHARLES TOWNSHEND. Of Buckhurst, Wokingham; eld. son of J. G. M. of Frognal and Great Berkhamsted; 1850^{1}–1850^{2}; formerly in the Rifle Bgde.; served in the Crimea; aft. Partner in Barclay's Bank; M.P. for Reading 1885-92 and 1895-98; J.P. and D.L. for Berks; *m.* Sophia, *d.* of William Speke of Jordans, Ilminster; died July 7, 1898.

Stewart (Miss M., W.A.C.)
ROBERT. Of Culgruff, Crossmichael, co. Kirkcudbright; son of M. H. S. of Southwick, Dumfries; 1849^{3}–1852^{2}; formerly Lieut. Cameron Highlanders; served in the Indian Mutiny; med. and clasp; aft. a Squatter in Queensland for 10 years; J.P. and D.L. co. Kirkcudbright; *m.* Georgina Eleanor, *d.* of Sir William Maxwell, 3rd Bt., of Cardonnes, Gatehouse, co. Kirkcudbright; died Dec. 27, 1902.

Hall (F.E.D.)
HENRY JOHN. 4th son of Sir J. H., 5th Bt., F.R.S., of Dunglass, Dunbar; 1849^{3}–1854^{3}; Opp. Wall and Field XI.'s 1853; B.N.C. Oxf.; formerly in the 9th Lancers.

Hussey (F.E.D.)
AMBROSE DENIS (aft. Hussey-Freke). Son of A. H. of the Hall, Salisbury; 1849^{3}–1854^{1}; Ch. Ch. Oxf. M.A.; J.P., D.L. and C.C. for Wilts, High Sheriff 1866; *m.* Florence Mary Spencer, *d.* of Col. Henry John Freke, C.B., of Hannington Hall. *Hannington Hall, Highworth, Swindon, Wilts.*

Burnand (F.E.D. & W.G.C.)
SIR FRANCIS COWLEY, Kt. Son of F. B.; 1850^{1}–1853^{3}; Trin. Coll. Camb. B.A.; Barrister, Lincoln's Inn; Editor of 'Punch'; Dramatic Author. 27 *The Boltons, S.W.*, *and* 18 *Royal Crescent, Ramsgate.*

Willes (W.E., E.B.)
JOHN WILLIAM SHIPPEN. Of Astrop House, Banbury; eld. son of W. W. of Astrop House; 1850^{1}–1853^{3}; Merton Coll. Oxf.; 4th Cl. in Law and Mod. Hist. 1858; Clerk in the Admiralty; J.P. for North Hants; *m.* Katherine, *d.* of Emanuel Wills. *Manor House, King's Sutton, Banbury.*

Vyner (W.J.)
HENRY FREDERICK CLARE. Of Gautby Hall, Lincoln; eld. son of H. V. of Newby Hall, Ripon; 1850^{1}–1852^{2}; J.P. for N. Riding of Yorks; died unm. Nov. 11, 1883.

Biddulph (E.H.P. & W.G.C.)
RICHARD MYDDELTON- (aft. Myddelton). Eld. son of R. M.-B. of Chirk Castle; 1850^{1}–1853^{3}; formerly Lieut. 1st Life Gds.; J.P. co. Denbigh, High Sheriff 1879; *m.* Catherine Arabella, *d.* of Edward Giles Howard. *K* 1 *Albany, Piccadilly, W.*, *and Chirk Castle, Chirk, co. Denbigh.*

Cunliffe *ma.* (R.O.)
ARTHUR. 2nd son of E. W. C.; 1850^{1}–1854^{2}; Ch. Ch. Oxf.; died unm. May 29, 1876.

Gatty (J.E.Y.)
CHARLES HENRY, LL.D. Son of G. G. of Fellbridge Place; 1850^{1}–1850^{3}; Trin. Coll. Camb. M.A.; LL.D. St. Andrews; J.P. for Sussex. *Fellbridge Place, East Grinstead.*

Turner (C.O.G.)
HENRY SCOTT. 1850^{2}–1853^{3}; formerly Capt. 68th Regt.; dead.

Malet *mi.* (F.V. & W.G.C., W.G.C.)
RT. HON. SIR EDWARD BALDWIN, P.C., G.C.B., G.C.M.G. 2nd son of Sir A. M., 2nd Bt., K.C.B., of Wilbury House, Monmouth; 1850^{2}–1853^{3}; C.C.C. Oxf.; Attaché at Frankfort Oct. 10, 1854, aft. Argentine Confederation, Washington, Constantinople, Paris, Pekin, Athens, Rome, Cairo, Brussels, and Berlin; in charge of the Embassy at Paris during the Commune; Min. Plen. at Constantinople 1878-9, and at Cairo 1882; H.M.'s Ambassador at Berlin 1884-95; Member of the International Court of Arbitration at The Hague 1900; *m.* Lady Ermyntrude Sackville Russell, *d.* of Francis Charles, 9th Duke of Bedford, K.G. 85 *Eaton Square, S.W.*; *Château Malet, Monaco*; *and Wrest Wood, Bexhill-on-Sea, Sussex.*

Gem (H.D. & F.V., H.D. & W.J.)
REV. SAMUEL HARVEY. Son of H. G. of Brandwood End House, King's Norton, Birmingham; 1850^{2}–1854^{2}; Prince Consort's German Prize 1852; Univ. Coll. Oxf. M.A.; Ellerton Theo. Essay 1861; shot in Oxf. VIII. at Wimbledon against Camb. 1861; Rector of Aspley Guise, Beds, 1869-78; *m.* Louisa, *d.* of Rev. Newton Smart, Preb. of Salisbury. 2 *Keble Road, Oxford.*

Mr. North (E.B.)
HON. WILLIAM HENRY JOHN (11th Lord North). Son of Rt. Hon. John Sidney Doyle, P.C., D.C.L. (aft. North), and Susan, Baroness North; 1850^{2}–1852^{2}; Ch. Ch. Oxf.; formerly Lieut. 1st Life Gds., aft. Major Queen's Own Oxfs. Hussars and Hon. Col. 2nd Vol. Bn. Oxfs. Lt. Infantry; J.P. for Suffolk, Oxfs., Middlesex, co. Camb. and Westminster; C.C. for Oxfs.; Knt. of the Order of Malta. *Kirtling Tower, Newmarket, and Wroxton Abbey, Banbury.*

Broadbent (W.E., F.E.D.)
DAVENPORT CORNELIUS. 1849^{3}–1852^{2}; St. John's Coll. Oxf.; formerly Lieut. Rifle Bgde.

Disney (Mrs. de R., J.E.Y.)
EDGAR JOHN. Of The Hyde, Ingatestone, Essex; eld. son of E. D. of The Hyde; 1849^{3}–1851^{1}; formerly Capt. Royal Fusiliers, aft. Hon. Col. 3rd Bn. Essex Regt.; J.P. and D.L. for Essex; *m.* 1st, Lilias Charlotte, *d.* of Rev. H. W. Buckley, Rector of Hartshorne, Burton-on-Trent; 2nd, Ellen Louisa, *d.* of Edward Thomas Bainbridge of Croydon Lodge, Surrey; died Jan. 16, 1903.

Smith (H.D.)
HENRY MEUX. Of Hockliffe Grange, Leighton Buzzard; 1849^{3}–1852^{1}; Capt. Beds Militia; dead.

Voules *mi.* (W.G.C.)
FREDERICK LOUIS. Son of C. S. V., Solicitor, of Windsor; 1849^{3}–1852^{1}; formerly in the Navy; dead.

Burke (C.L.)
EDMUND HAVILAND. 1849^{3}–1853^{3}; Barrister, Oxf. Circuit; dead.

Darvill (W.G.C.)
HENRY. Son of — D., Solicitor, of Windsor; 1849^{3}–1852^{1}.

Mr. Trefusis *min.* (J.L.J.)
HON. WALTER RODOLPH. 3rd son of Charles Rodolph, 19th Lord Clinton, of Heanton Satchville, Dolton, N. Devon; 1849^{3}–1854^{2}; Lieut.-Col. Comm. 2nd Bn. Scots Fusilier Gds.; *m.* Lady Mary Charlotte Montagu-Douglas-Scott, *d.* of Walter Francis, 5th Duke of Buccleuch; died [illegible], 1888.

Buck (J.L.J.)
LIEUT.-COL. SIR WILLIAM LEWIS STUCLEY (aft. Stucley), 2nd Bt. Eld. son of Sir G. S. B. (aft. Stucley), 1st Bt.; 1849^{3}-1852^{1}; ent. Army 1854; served in the Crimea; Lieut.-Col. Gren. Gds. (ret.); J.P. and D.L. for Devon; *m.* 1st, Rosamond Head, *d.* of Head Pottinger Best of Donnington Grove, Newbury; 2nd, Mary Elizabeth, *d.* of Col. Henry Edward Hamlyn Fane of Clovelly Court, Devon, and Avon Tyrell, Hants. *Hartland Abbey, Bideford, and Affeton Castle, Morchard Bishop, R.S.O., N. Devon.*

Benyon (Mrs. Hor., W.J.)
ASHTON SAMUEL YATE. Eld. son of — B. of Stetchworth Park, Camb.; 1849^{3}-1850^{3}; Lieut. 53rd Regt.; died in England from exposure in the Crimea, May 22, 1855.

Vandeleur (W.L.E.)
CAPT. HECTOR STEWART. Of Kilrush House, co. Clare; eld. son of C. M. V. of Kilrush; 1849^{3}-1851^{3}; formerly Capt. Rifle Brgde.; J.P. and Lord-Lieut. of co. Clare, High Sheriff 1873; *m.* Charlotte, *d.* of William Orme Foster of Apley Park, Salop. *Cahiracon House, Ennis, co. Clare.*

Wilson *mi.* (Home, aft. K.S., C.O.G. & W.J.)
SIR ROLAND KNYVET, 2nd Bt. 2nd son of Rear-Adml. G. K. W., R.N., of 3 Brunswick Place, Windsor, and nephew of Major-Gen. Sir A. W., 1st Bt., G.C.B.; 1849^{3}-1859^{1}; Newc. Select 1856-7, Sch. 1858; Sch. of King's Coll. Camb., M.A. and LL.M.; Craven Sch. 1861; Sen. Class. and Fellow of King's 1863; Barrister 1867; Reporter for the 'Weekly Reporter' and 'Law Journal' 1867-71; Class. and Hist. Lecturer for Walter Wren 1871-8; Reader in Indian Law to the Univ. of Camb. 1878-91; *m.* Christiana Whiting, *d.* of Richard Phillips, F.R.S. *86 Church Road, Richmond, Surrey.*

Proby (Miss G., W.A.C.)
HON. WILLIAM (5th Earl of Carysfort), K.P. 4th son of Granville Leveson, 3rd Earl of C.; 1847^{3}-1855^{3}; Trin. Coll. Camb. M.A.; formerly Capt. Wicklow Militia; H.M.'s Lieut. co. Wicklow; J.P. and D.L. for Hunts; J.P. for Northants; *m.* Charlotte Mary, *d.* of Rev. Robert Boothby Heathcote of Friday Hill, Chingford, Essex. *10 Hereford Gardens, W.; Elton Hall, Peterborough; and Glenart Castle, Arklow, Ireland.*

Mr. de Montmorency (J.E.Y.)
MAJ.-GEN. HON. RAYMOND HERVEY (3rd Visct. Frankfort de Montmorency), K.C.B. Son of Lodge Raymond, 2nd Visct. F. de M.; 1848^{3}-1850^{3}; ent. Army 1854; served in Crimea, Indian Mutiny, and Abyssinian wars; Capt. 33rd Foot; exchanged to 32nd Lt. Infantry; Col. 1881; Comm. Frontier Field Force in Egypt 1886; Alexandria 1887-9; expedition on Frontier 1889; Maj.-Gen. 1889; Comm. a District in Bengal 1890-5; Dublin 1895-7; ret. 1897; *m.* Rachael Mary Lumley Godolphin, *d.* of F.-M. Rt. Hon. Sir John Michel, G.C.B., P.C., of Dewlish, Dorchester; died May 7, 1902.

Lubbock *mi.* (J.L.J.)
SIR NEVILE, K.C.M.G. 3rd son of Sir J. W. L., 3rd Bt., of High Elms Down, Farnborough, Kent; 1848^{3}-1853^{3}; Sub.-Gov. of Royal Exchange Assurance Corporation; one of the Merchant Assessors of the Admiralty Court; Director of the Colonial Bank, New Colonial Co., Ltd., New Trinidad Lake Asphalt Co., Ltd., London and India Dock Co., Ltd.; Chmn. W. India Committee; West India Merchant; *m.* 1st, Harriet Charlotte, *d.* of Western Wood of North Cray Place, Foots Cray, Kent; 2nd, Constance Ann, *d.* of Sir John Frederick William Herschel, 1st Bt. *65 Earl's Court Square, S. Kensington, S.W.*

Lane-Fox *ma.* (F.E.D.)
GEORGE SACKVILLE FREDERICK. Eld. son of G. L.-F. of Bramham Park, Boston Spa, York; 1847^{3}-1856^{2}; Eton VIII. 1855-6; Capt. of the Boats 1856; Ch. Ch. Oxf.; formerly Lieut. Yorks Hussars; J.P. W. Riding of Yorks; *m.* 1st, Fanny Maule, *d.* of Lieut.-Gen. Marcus John Slade; 2nd, Annette Mary, *d.* of Thomas Weld-Blundell of Ince Blundell, co. Lancaster. *81 Cadogan Gardens, S.W.*

Upton (W.L.E.)
SIR JOHN HENRY GREVILLE (aft. Smyth), 1st and only Bt. Of Ashton Court, Bristol; son of T. U. of Ingmire Hall, Westmorland; 1848^{3}-1851^{3}; Ch. Ch. Oxf.; J.P. for Somerset, High Sheriff 1865; *m.* Emily Frances, *d.* of Rev. Henry Hugh Way of Alderbourne, Bucks, and widow of George Oldham Edwards of Redland Court, Bristol; died Sept. 27, 1901.

Holford
HENRY PRICE. 1847^{3}-1852^{1}; formerly Lieut. 10th Hussars; served with the 79th Highl. at Lucknow.

Prendergast (W.L.E.)
MAJOR-GEN. MAUNSELL MARK. Son of G. L. P.; 1849^{3}-1852^{1}; ent. Bengal Cav.; served in the Indian Mutiny 1857-8, against the tribes in Googaria district 1857, siege and capture of Lucknow, affair of Barree (wounded), actions of Simree, Nawabgunge, and Barabanki; mentioned in despatches, 'London Gazette'; med. with clasp Afghan War 1879-80; expeditions to Wazir and Hisarak, mentioned in despatches (med.); Hon. Maj.-Gen. ret.; *m.* Eliza Anne, *d.* of Col. J. Aubert of the Bengal Army. *Arington, London Road, Guildford.*

Barton *mi.* (W.L.E.)
FRANCIS SAVILE. 5th son of N. B., formerly of Bordeaux, aft. of Straffan House, co. Kildare; 1847^{3}-1852^{1}; died at Rome, Jan. 3, 1860.

Browne (E.H.P.)
WILLIAM CLAYTON (aft. Browne-Clayton). Eld. son of R. C. B. of Browne's Hill; 1849^{3}-1853^{1}; Ch. Ch. Oxf.; J.P. and D.L. co. Carlow, High Sheriff 1859; *m.* Caroline, *d.* of John Watson Barton of Stapleton Park, Pontefract. *Browne's Hill, co. Carlow.*

Lumsden (J.E.Y.)
HARRY GREY. 1849^{3}-1852^{2}; died just after leaving Eton.

Ferrand (Mrs. Hor., F.E.D.)
GERARD THOMAS WORTHINGTON. 1849^{3}-1853^{1}; Emmanuel Coll. Camb.

Wagner (J.L.J.)
JOSHUA WATSON. Son of Rev. H. M. W. Vicar of Brighton; 1850^{1}-1853^{3}; Oriel Coll. Oxf. B.A.; died unm. Aug. 8, 1898.

Coleridge *mi.* (E.C.)
CAPT. FRANCIS GEORGE. Son of E. C. of Eton and Mapledurham; 1850^{1}-1854^{3}; Eton XI. 1854; formerly Capt. 42nd Royal Highl. and 25th King's Own Borderers; Artist; *m.* Anne Jane, *d.* of Pierce Taylor of Ogwell, Newton Abbott. *The Hermitage, Twyford, R.S.O., Berks.*

Sheffield *mi.* (H.D.)
GEORGE. 4th son of Sir R. S., 4th Bt.; 1850^{1}-1853^{1}; Oxf. M.A.; served in Diplomatic Service 1859-88; Private Sec. to Lord Lyons, H.B.M. Ambassador at Paris, 1867-87; died Oct. 10, 1898.

Pepys *mi.* (J.E.Y.)
JOHN ALFRED. Son of E. P. of 20 Portland Place, W.; 1850^{1}-1856^{2}; Opp. Wall 1854-5, Keeper 1855; Mixed Wall 1854, Keeper 1855; Field XI. 1854-5; Eton XI. 1855-6; Ch. Ch. Oxf.; Oxf. XI. 1861. *16 York Terrace, Regent's Park, N.W.*

Mr. Egerton (E.B.)
HON. SEYMOUR JOHN GREY (4th Earl of Wilton). 2nd son of Thomas Grosvenor, 2nd Earl of W.; 1850^{1}-1854^{1}; formerly Capt. 1st Life Gds.; *m.* Laura Caroline, *d.* of William Russell; died Jan. 3, 1898.

Bulkeley (W.A.C.)
ROBERT STANLEY WILLIAMS-. 2nd son of Sir R. B. W.-B, 10th Bt., of Baron Hill, nr. Beaumaris, Anglesey; 1850^{1}–1851^{4}; Capt. 9th Hussars; died from the effects of a fall in India, Feb. 1, 1861.

Mr. Hare (E.H.P.)
REAR-ADML. HON. RICHARD. 2nd son of William, 2nd Earl of Listowel, K.P.; 1850^{1}–1850^{3}; ent. R.N. 1850; served in the Baltic 1854 (med.), Crimea 1855 (Crimean and Turkish meds. with clasps), China 1857–9 (med. with clasp); ret. 1894; *m.* Caroline Acland, *d.* of Capt. George Rideout Pinder, of the Madras Army; died July 16, 1903.

Barrett *ma* (W.G.C.)
CHARLES JOHN. Son of C. P. B., Solicitor, of Eton; 1850^{1}–1851^{3}; Solicitor; *m.* Mary, *d.* of James Burnett of Norwood, S.E.; died Oct. 8, 1900.

Barrett *mi.* (W.G.C.)
ALFRED EDWARD, M.R.C.S.Eng., L.S.A. Son of C. P. B., Solicitor, of Eton; 1850^{1}–1852^{1}; *m.* Henrietta, *d.* of Hon. and Rev. Thomas Robert Kepple, Hon. Canon of Norwich and Rector of North Creak, Fakenham. 123 *Holland Park Avenue, W.*

Kershaw (J.L.J.)
ARTHUR. 1850^{1}–1853^{2}; died young.

Williams (J.L.J.)
LIEUT.-GEN. OWEN LEWIS COPE. Son of Col. T. P. W. of Temple House, Gt. Marlow; 1850^{1}–1852^{2}; ent. Royal Horse Gds. 1854; Lieut.-Col. 1866; Col. 1871; Maj.-Gen. 1882; Lieut.-Gen. 1887; M.P. for Marlow 1880–5; Equerry to H.R.H. the Prince of Wales during his Indian Tour, 1875–6; J.P. for Anglesey, Bucks, Flint, and Carnarvon; *m.* 1st, Fanny Florence, *d.* of St. George Francis Robert Caulfeild of Donamon Castle, co. Roscommon; 2nd, Nina Mary Adelaide, *d.* of Sir John George Tollemache Sinclair, 3rd Bt., of Ulbster, co. Caithness. 24 *Hill Street, Berkeley Square, W.; Craig-y-don, Anglesey; and Temple House, Gt. Marlow, Bucks.*

Waller (J.W.H., H.D. & Mrs. de R., J.W.H., H.D. & W.A.C.)
LIEUT.-COL. ROBERT. Son of Rev. R. W.; 1849^{3}–1853^{3}; served in the 33rd, 53rd, and 76th Regts.; 1861–86. *Bourton-on-the-Water, R.S.O., Glos.*

Holland *mi.* (Mrs. Hor., O.Wo.)
REV. FREDERICK WHITMORE. Son of E. H. of Dumbleton Hall, Evesham; 1850^{3}–1856^{2}; Eton VIII. 1856; won Steeplechase 1854; Trin. Coll. Camb.; formerly Assist. Min. Quebec Chapel, London; died in Switzerland.

Field *mi.* (F.E.D.)
BARCLAY. Of Beechy Lees, Kemsing, Sevenoaks; 2nd son of G. F. of Ashurst Park, Tunbridge Wells; 1850^{2}–1856^{2}; Eton XI. 1856; Univ. Coll. Oxf. M.A.; Hop Merchant; J.P. for Kent; died Nov. 7, 1892.

Wicksted *mi.* (F.V. & W.J., W.J.)
CHARLES WIGLEY. 2nd son of C. W. of Betley and Shakenhurst; 1850^{2}–1855^{2}; Eton VIII. 1855; Trin. Coll. Camb.; J.P. for Salop; *m.* Emily, *d.* of Anthony Hamond of Westacre, Norfolk. *Shakenhurst, Cleobury Mortimer, S.O., Salop, and Betley Hall, Crewe.*

Pennant *ma.* (J.L.J.)
HON. GEORGE SHOLTO GORDON DOUGLAS- (2nd Lord Penrhyn). Eld. son of Edward Gordon, 1st Lord P.; 1850^{2}–1852^{3}; Ch. Ch. Oxf.; M.P. co. Carnarvon 1866–8, and 1874–80; Hon. Col. 4th Bn. Royal Welsh Fusiliers since 1895; J.P. and D.L. co. Carnarvon; *m.* 1st, Pamela Blanche, *d.* of Sir Charles Rushout, 2nd Bt.; 2nd, Gertrude, *d.* of Rev. Henry Glynne, Rector of Hawarden, Chester. *Mortimer House, Halkin Street, Grosvenor Place, S.W.; Penrhyn Castle, Bangor, N. Wales; and Wicken Park, Stony Stratford.*

Butler (W.A.C.)
LINDSEY HOLLAND. Eld. son of Hon. C. L. B. of Coton House, Rugby; 1850^{2}–1853^{2}; formerly in 7th Fusiliers; died July 13, 1887.

Tarratt (C.L.)
DANIEL FOX. Of Ellary, co. Argyll; 3rd son of J. T. of Ellary; 1850^{2}–1851^{3}; Oriel Coll. Oxf.; formerly in the 63rd Regt.; *m.* Mary, *d.* of John Lorn Stewart of Coll, co. Argyll; died April 20, 1888.

Franks (F.E.D.)
ROBERT CHARLES. 1850^{2}–1851^{2}; formerly Lieut. 88th Regt.; aft. settled in Australia.

Thesiger (E.H.P. & W.J.)
HON. ALFRED HENRY. 4th son of Frederick, 1st Lord Chelmsford; 1850^{2}–1855^{2}; Cox of Eton VIII. 1855; Ch. Ch. Oxf. M.A.; Lord Justice of Appeal; Attorney-Gen. to H.R.H. the Prince of Wales; *m.* Henrietta, *d.* of Hon. George Handcock; died Oct. 20, 1880.

Divett (W.L.E.)
EDWARD ROSS. 1850^{2}–1856^{2}; Trin. Coll. Camb.

Madden (J.E.Y.)
JOHN. Of Hilton Park, Clones; eld. son of Col. J. M. of Hilton Park; 1850^{2}–1851^{3}; J.P. for Monaghan, Fermanagh Cavan, and Leitrim; D.L. for Monaghan (High Sheriff 1863) and Fermanagh (High Sheriff 1859); *m.* Lady Caroline, *d.* of Rev. Hon. Francis Nathaniel Clements and sister of Robert, 4th Earl of Leitrim; died July 24, 1902.

Wilbraham (J.L.J.)
EDWARD BOOTLE- (Lord Skelmersdale), aft. 1st Earl of Lathom, G.C.B., P.C. Son of Hon. R. B. W. and grandson of Edward, 1st Lord S.; 1850^{2}–1854^{3}; Eton VIII. 1854; Opp. and Mixed Wall 1854; Ch. Ch. Oxf.; Lord-in-waiting 1866–8; Capt. of Yeomen of the Guard 1874–80; Lord Chamberlain of H.M.'s Household 1885–6, 1887–92, and 1895; Hon. Col. Lancs Hussars; J.P. and D.L. for Lancs; *m.* Lady Alice, *d.* of George William Frederick, 4th Earl of Clarendon, K.G.; died Nov. 19, 1898.

Rolls (R.O. & C. Wo.)
JOHN ALLAN (1st Lord Llangattock), F.S.A. Eld. son of J. E. W. R. of The Hendre; 1849^{3}–1854^{3}; Opp. Wall and Field XI. 1854; Ch. Ch. Oxf.; M.P. for co. Monmouth 1880–5; Prov. Grand Master of Freemasons E. Div. of S. Wales 1894; Mayor of Monmouth 1887–8; formerly Capt. Royal Gloucs. Hussars; aft. Hon. Col. 1st Monmouths Vol. Art.; J.P. and D.L. co. Monmouth, High Sheriff 1875; *m.* Georgiana Marcia, *d.* of Sir Charles Fitzroy Maclean, 9th Bt., of Morvaren. *South Lodge, Rutland Gate, S.W., and The Hendre, Monmouth.*

Wilkinson (H.M.B.)
MAJOR CHRISTOPHER BRICE, J.P. 1848^{3}–1850^{3}; Ch. Ch. Oxf.; formerly Lieut. Gloucs. Hussars; aft. Capt. 68th Regt.; served in the Crimea; ret. 1858. 29 *Cleveland Square, Hyde Park, W.*

Pigott (W.E., W.A.C.)
FRANCIS PAYNTON (aft. Pigott-Carleton). Son of F. P. P., Governor of the Isle of Man; 1849^{3}–1852^{3}; served 10 years in the 16th Lancers; J.P. for Hants; *m.* Hon. Henrietta Anne Carleton, *d.* of Guy, 3rd Lord Dorchester; died April 7, 1883.

Paynter (J.E.Y.)
JOHN. 5th son of W. P. of Camborne House, Richmond, Surrey; 1850^{1}–1852^{3}; Capt. Scots Guards; *m.* Margaret, *d.* of Henry Farquharson of Langton, co. Dorset; died Nov. 16, 1881.

Mr. Harbord (W.G.C.)
HON. HARBORD. 8th son of Edward, 3rd Lord Suffield; 1850^{1}–1851^{3}; Hon. Lieut.-Col. Norfolk Art. Militia; *m.* 1st, Constance Adelaide, *d.* of Sir Henry Josias Stracey, 5th Bt.; 2nd, Barbara Sophia Harriot, *d.* of Edgar Disney of The Hyde, Ingatestone, Essex, and widow of Major Philip Bennet of Rougham Hall, Bury St. Edmunds; died Feb. 11, 1894.

Mr. Hogg (R.O.) — SIR FREDERICK RUSSELL, K.C.I.E., C.S.I. 5th son of Rt. Hon. Sir J. W. H., 1st Bt.; 1849^{3}–1851^{3}; E. I. Coll., Haileybury: Bengal Civil Service; Postmaster-General, Punjab, 1863, Bombay 1867, Bengal 1868; Dep. Director-Gen. Post Office of India 1869, Director-Gen. 1880; ret. 1889; formerly partner in Hogg, Curtis, Campbell & Co.: *m.* 1st, Emily, *d.* of Gen. Eckford; 2nd, Harriett Venn, *d.* of William Stephens Dicken. *Oriental Club*, 18 *Hanover Square, W.*

Withington (J.L.J.) — REV. EDWARD. Of Fringford Lodge, Bicester; 3rd son of T. E. W. of Culcheth, Warrington; 1849^{3}–1854^{2}; Ch. Ch. Oxf. M.A.; J.P. co. Oxf.; *m.* Mary Ann Elizabeth, *d.* of Sir Andrew Armstrong of Gallen Priory, Ferbane, King's County; died June 7, 1901.

Curtis (F.V., W.A.C.) — COL. FRANCIS GEORGE SAVAGE, C.M.G. Son of G. S. C. of Teignmouth; 1850^{1}–1854^{2}; joined Carabineers 1854; served in the Crimea 1853, Indian Mutiny 1858–9, and Boer War in S. Africa 1881; Comm. Inniskilling Dragoons in Bechuanaland Expedn. under Sir Charles Warren 1885; D.A.G. at Cape of Good Hope 1886–8; was Ch. of Staff, Zululand, 1888; Comm. troops in Natal 1888–91; Cav. A.A.G. Headquarters 1892–3; Crimean, Indian Mutiny, and Turkish meds.; C.M.G. for S. Africa; *m.* Philadelphia Mary Grace, *d.* of Col. William Stuart-Menteth of the Bengal Army. *Army and Navy Club*, 36 *Pall Mall, S.W.*

Faulkner (W.E., F.E.D.) — GEORGE. 1849^{3}–1853^{1}; a Law Student.

Harvey (W.G.C.) — CHARLES REANETH. 1850^{1}–1851^{4}.

Allfrey *mi.* (W.L.E.) — COL. IRVING STENING. 2nd son of R. A. of Wokefield Park, Mortimer, Berks; 1850^{2}–1853^{3}; joined the 6th Regt.; Col. Comm. 13th Somerset Lt. Infantry; *m.* 1st, Mary Elizabeth, *d.* of Major Talbot; 2nd, Florence Foot. *Army and Navy Club*, 36 *Pall Mall, S.W.*

Radford (W.E., C.Wo.) — JOHN. Eld. son of J. R. of Smalley Hall, Derby; 1850^{2}–1850^{3}; Lieut. 1st Derby Militia; died 1855.

Cookesley *mi.* (W.G.C., J.E.Y.) — REV. FREDRICK JOHN. Son of Rev. W. G. C., Assist. Master at Eton 1830–54; 1844^{3}–1850^{3}; St. Augustine's Coll. Canterbury; aft. in Canada in connection with the S. P. G.; died May 28, 1867.

Park — 1850^{2}–1853^{3}.

Seddon *ma.* (Mrs. de R., E.H.P.) — STRETTELL. Formerly of Swinton Grove, near Chorlton-on-Medlock; 1850^{2}–1852^{3}.

Buckley *mi.* (E.B.) — VICTOR. 5th son of Gen. E. P. B. of New Hall, Bodenham, Salisbury; 1850^{2}–1855^{1}; Clerk in Foreign Office; *m.* Mary, *d.* of Adml. Sir James Stirling; died June 10, 1882.

Mr. Amherst *mi.* (W.E., E.B.) — HON. FREDERICK. 2nd son of William Pitt, 2nd Earl Amherst; 1850^{2}–1851^{2}; formerly in the Royal Navy; aft. Capt. 14th Hussars; died Mar. 15, 1895.

Cunliffe (C. Wa.) — SIR ROBERT ALFRED, 5th Bt. Eld. son of R. E. C. of H.E.I.C. Service, and grandson of Sir R. H. C., 4th Bt., C.B.; 1847^{2}–1854^{3}; Lieut. Scots Fusilier Gds. 1857, Capt. 1862 (ret.); Lieut.-Col. 3rd Bn. Royal Welsh Fusiliers 1872; M.P. for Flint 1872–4, and Denbigh 1880–5; J.P., D.L., and C.C. co. Denbigh, High Sheriff 1868; *m.* 1st, Eleanor Sophia Egerton, *d.* of Col. Egerton Leigh of Jodrell Hall, Chester; 2nd, Cecilie Victoria, *d.* of Col. Hon. William Edward Sackville-West, of Gren. Gds. *Acton Park, Wrexham.*

Seddon *mi.* (Mrs. de R., E.H.P.) — THOMAS. 1849^{3}–1855^{3}.

Mildred — DANIEL MILDRED. 1849^{3}–1855^{3}; Trin. Coll. Camb.; Brewer at Cirencester; dead.

Smith — SEYMOUR HENRY. 1846^{3}–1855^{3}; Magd. Coll. Camb.; Barrister; died 1864.

Law (F.V.) — ROBERT. 1849^{1}–1851^{3}.

Hay (R.O.) — HENRY HIRD. Of Houghton Lodge, Stockbridge, Hants; 1849^{1}–1851^{3}; formerly Capt. 5th Dragoon Gds.

Luxmoore (Miss G., J.L.J.) — REV. CHARLES CORYNDON. Son of C. L., Fellow of Eton; 1850^{2}–1858^{3}; Pembroke Coll. Oxf. M.A.; Vicar of Great Milton; *m.* Janet Lambert Penrose, *d.* of William Penrose Marle, H.B.M. Consul at Malaga. *Great Milton Vicarage, Wallingford.*

Mr. Wingfield (J.W.H.) — HON. MAURICE RICHARD. 2nd son of Richard, 6th Visct. Powerscourt; 1847^{3}–1850^{3}; ent. R.N.; Lieut. H.M.S. 'Vengeance'; served in the Crimea; was present at the Bombardment of Sebastopol; med. and clasp, Turkish med.; served in H.M.S. 'Nile' in the Baltic 1855 (med.); joined 1st Life Gds. 1861; served as a Vol. with Gen. McClellan's Staff in the American Civil War 1862; ret. from 1st Life Gds. 1863; *m.* Mary Agnes, *d.* of James Block of Charlton, Salisbury; died Feb. 14, 1866.

Cookesley *mi.* (W.G.C.) — CAPT. EDWARD MURRAY. Son of Rev. H. P. C. of Wimborne; 1850^{2}–1856^{3}; Capt. 22nd Regt.; served with the 97th Regt. in the Indian Mutiny (ret. 1870); *m.* Margaret Deborah, *d.* of John Bingley Garland of Stone, Wimborne. 7 *Cromwell Place, S.W.*

UNPLACED.

Fane (Mrs. de R., F.E.D.) — EDWARD BOYD. Eld. son of Rev. F. A. S. F of Priors, Brentwood, and Vicar of Norton Mandeville, Essex; 1850^{2}–1856^{3}; Eton XI. 1854–6, Capt. 1855–6; Keeper of Upper Club 1854–5; Field XI. 1854–5, Keeper 1855; died June 22, 1868.

George (W.J.) — JOHN D'OLIER. Eld. son of R. D. G. of Cahore House, Gorey; 1850^{2}–1853^{3}; formerly 60th Rifles; dead.

LOWER SCHOOL.

THIRD FORM.—UPPER GREEK.

Gledstanes *mi.* (W.L.E.) — HUGH BARTON. Son of J. H. G. of Cheshunt, Waltham Cross; 1847^{3}–1853^{3}; formerly Capt. 75th Regt.; aft. in the Cape Mounted Rifles; died March 3, 1872.

Pryor *mi.* — HENRY MACLEAN. 2nd son of J. P. of Baldock, Herts; 1849^{1}–1853^{3}; formerly Capt. 60th Rifles, aft. Major 1st Bols Rifle Vol.; *m.* Margaret de Vins, *d.* of Rev. Charles James Wade, Rector of Gravenhurst, Ampthill. *Clifton Lodge, Biggleswade.*

Knatchbull-Hugessen *mi.* (E.B.) — WILLIAM WESTERN. 10th son of Rt. Hon. Sir Edward Knatchbull, 9th Bt., of Mersham Hatch, Ashford, Kent, and brother of 1st Lord Brabourne; 1849^{1}–1855^{1}; Magd. Coll. Oxf.; died at Hastings, Sept. 6, 1864.

Vidal *mi.* (F.V., W.B.M.) — CAPT. JOHN HENRY, R.N. Son of Rev. F. V. of Sutton Vicarage, Woodbridge; 1848^{3}–1853^{3}; Capt. R.N. (ret.); med. for Fenian Raid, 'Canada' 1865; *m.* Julia Ursula Bancroft, *d.* of Hon. Peter Alexander Espeut of Jamaica. 1 *Park Road, Sunderland.*

Campbell — HENRY FRANCIS. 1850[2]–1852[1]; formerly Lieut. 72nd Highl.

Desborough — LAURENCE WILLIAM. 1848[3]–1852[1]; formerly Lieut. 27th Regt.

Stevens (T.H.S., F.E.D.) — THOMAS COMINS. Eld. son of T. H. S. of Eton; 1847[3]–1850[2]; died 1851.

Tarver *ma.* (Home, W.G.C.) — ARTHUR GORE. Son of J. C. T. of Eton; 1850[2]–1851[3]; died Dec. 25, 1857.

Thomas (J.W.H. & R.D., R.D.) — COL. MORGAN DALRYMPLE (aft. Treherne). Eld. son of M. T. of Gate House, Mayfield, Sussex; 1848[3]–1856[2]; Field, Opp. and Mixed Wall XI.'s 1855; formerly Col. Royal W. Kent Regt.; *m.* Agnes, Countess Waldstein, *d.* of Baron F. Fiath and widow of Connt Waldstein. *Villa Agnese, San Remo, Italy.*

Jackson (W.E.) — WILLIAM GODDARD. Son of W. G. J. of Duddington; 1848[3]–1853[1]; formerly a Solicitor at Wisbech; J.P. co. Northants, High Sheriff 1878; *m.* Selina Barbara Maria, *d.* of Lieut.-Gen. William A. Johnson of Wytham, Oxf. *Duddington Hall, Stamford.*

LOWER GREEK.

Vesey *mi.* (J.E.Y.) — GEORGE FRANCIS. 1849[1]–1851[1]; formerly Lieut. 19th Regt.; was a Midshipman in the Baltic Fleet 1854.

Dent (J.W.H., H.D. & J.E.Y.) — HENRY FRANCIS. Son of J. D. of Ribston Hall, Wetherby; 1849[1]–1855[1]; Trin. Coll. Camb.; formerly Major 7th Dragoon Gds.; J.P. for N. and E. Ridings of Yorks; *m.* Isabella, *d.* of Rev. John Tomkyns. *Menethorpe, Malton.*

Lubbock *min.* (J.L.J.) — BEAUMONT WILLIAM. 4th son of Sir J. W. L., 3rd Bart., of High Elms, Down, Farnborough, Kent; 1849[1]–1857[3]; Eton VIII. 1856–7; Partner in Robarts, Lubbock & Co., Bankers, 15 Lombard St., E.C. 7 *Clarges Street, W.*

Pryse — SIR PRYSE, 1st Bt. Son of Pryse Loveden (formerly Pryse) of Gogerddan; 1849[1]–1851[1]; Cornet, Royal Horse Gds., ret. 1885; J.P. and D.L. co. Cardigan, High Sheriff 1861; *m.* Louisa Joan, *d.* of Capt. John Lewes of Lianlear, co. Cardigan. *Gogerddan, Bow St., R.S.O., co. Cardigan.*

Pennant *mi.* (J.L.J.) — LIEUT.-COL. HON. ARCHIBALD CHARLES HENRY DOUGLAS-. 2nd son of Edward Gordon, 1st Lord Penrhyn; 1850[2]–1853[1]; Lieut.-Col. Gren. Gds.; *m.* Hon. Harriet Ella, *d.* of Robert Francis, 2nd Lord Gifford; died Sept. 7, 1884.

Hancock (E.C.) — SIR HENRY JAMES BURFORD BURFORD-, C.M.G. Son of H. H., Professor, Royal Coll. of Surgeons (Eng.); 1850[3]–1856[3]; ent. 45th Foot; called to the Bar, Inner Temple, 1864; Chief Justice successively of Leeward Islands, Gibraltar, and Jamaica; *m.* 1st, Hannah, *d.* of Capt. Settle, R.N.; 2nd, Alice Maud, *d.* of Rev. John Nankivell, Chaplain of Crediton; died at Jamaica 1895.

Pilcher *mi.* (W.J.) — ARTHUR. Son of J. P. of Worthing; 1849[3]–1851[3]; Lawyer; *m.* Miss Holyoake; dead.

Colebrooke — JAMES ROBERT ALFRED. 1849[3]–1855[1] formerly 83rd Regt.

SENSE.

Tarver *mi.* (Home, W.G.C.) — EDWARD JOHN. Son of J. C. T. of Eton; 1848[3]–1855[2]; Architect; *m.* Edith Harriet, *d.* of R. N. Wornum; died June 7, 1891.

Pakenham — EDMUND POWERSCOURT. 5th son of Lieut.-Gen. Hon. Sir H. R. P., K.C.B., of Langford Lodge, co. Antrim; 1849[1]–1852[2]; Capt. 52nd Lt. Infantry; died at Gwalior Fort, India, Sept. 28, 1861.

Hawtrey (R.D.) — RALPH DE BEAUVOIR. Eld. son of Rev. M. H.; 1850[2]–1854[2]; Comm. R.N. (Baltic Med.); *m.* Mary Whitney, *d.* of William Richards; drowned near New Zealand, 1873.

Lord Earlsfort — JOHN HENRY REGINALD (4th Earl of Clonmell). Eld. son of John Henry, 3rd Earl of C.; 1851[3]–1854[2]; formerly Lieut. 1st Life Gds.; D.L. co. Kildare; died unm. June 22, 1891.

Mr. Scott — HON. THOMAS CHARLES (5th Earl of Clonmell). 2nd son of John Henry, 3rd Earl of C.; 1850[2]–1854[2]; Lieut.-Col. Rifle Bgde.; A.D.C. to Lord-Lieut. of Ireland; D.L. co. Kildare; *m.* Agnes, *d.* of Robert Godfrey Day; died June 18, 1896.

Price — WILLIAM EDWIN. Of Hillfield, Gloucester; son of W. P. P. of Tibberton Court, Gloucester; 1850[2]–1857[1]; London Univ. B.A.; F.G.S.; R.M. Academy, Woolwich; formerly in 36th Regt., aft. Major Glones. Militia; M.P. for Tewkesbury; *m.* Margaret, *d.* of Robert Needham Philips of The Park, Prestwich, Manchester; died 1886.

NONSENSE.

Lane-Fox *mi.* (F.E.D.) — JAMES THOMAS RICHARD. 2nd son of G. L.-F. of Bramham Park; 1849[1]–1857[1]; Capt. Gren. Gds. 1858–68; J.P. and D.L. for W. Riding of Yorks; *m.* Lucy Frances Jane, *d.* of Humphrey St. John-Mildmay. 26 *Upper Grosvenor Street, W., and Bramham Park, Boston Spa, R.S.O., Yorks.*

Oliveira — BENJAMIN. Eld. son of — O., M.P. for Pontefract; 1849[3]–1852[2]; R.M. Coll., Sandhurst; aft. Civil Service.

Cleland *mi.* — JAMES VANCE. Of Ennismore, co. Armagh; 2nd son of S. J. C.; 1849[3]–1851[3]; formerly Capt. 3rd Hussars; *m.* Emily Catherine, *d.* of Sir George King Adlercron Molyneux, 6th Bt.; died 1886.

Pakenham — CAPT. HAMILTON SANDFORD. 5th son of Very Rev. Hon. H. P., Dean of St. Patrick's, Dublin; 1850[2]–1854[3]; Capt. 2nd Life Gds.; *m.* Gwenwyld Frances, *d.* of Col. Hon. Richard Thomas Rowley; died Oct. 20, 1864.

P

INTERMEDIATE LIST.

Names of Boys entered between Election 1847 and 1850, who left Eton before Election 1850, and are therefore not included in the foregoing list.

Mr. Liddell (J.E.Y.) — HON. ATHOLL CHARLES JOHN (3rd Earl of Ravensworth). 5th son of Henry Thomas, 1st Earl of Ravensworth; 1847^{2}–1847^{4}, formerly Capt. 60th Rifles; D.L. co. Durham; J.P. for Northumberland; *m.* Caroline, *d.* of Hon. George Edgcumbe. *Winter Villa, Stonehouse, Plymouth, and Ravensworth Castle, Gateshead.*

Battiscombe (Mrs. Ro., W.L.E.) — HENRY LUMSDEN. Son of Rev. — B., Vicar of Barkway, Royston, Herts; 1847^{2}–1848^{3}; formerly Capt. 38th Regt.; wounded at Inkerman. *Tregew, Jervis Road East, Bournemouth.*

Llewelyn (J.W.H.) — WILLIAM MANSEL DILLWYN-. Son of J. D.-L., F.R.S., of Penllergare, Swansea; 1847^{3}–1850^{1}; Lieut. 4th Hussars; died March 29, 1866.

Beadon *ma.* — AUGUSTUS FREDERICK. Son of Rev. — B., Vicar of Burnham, Somerset; 1847^{3}–1848^{1}; died at Eton, 1848.

Beadon *mi.* — REGINALD HENRY. Son of Rev. — B., Vicar of Burnham, Somerset; 1847^{3}–1848^{4}; ent. again 1851^{3}–1852^{3}; formerly Capt. 60th Rifles.

Gregory (W.L.E.) — CAPT. ARTHUR MORGAN GROSVENOR HOOD. Of Styvechale, Coventry; eld. son of A. F. G. of Styvechale; 1847^{3}–1849^{3}; formerly Capt. Scots Fusilier Gds.; served in the Crimea; died num. May 17, 1883.

Prendergast (C.O.G.) — MAJ.-GEN. GUY ANNESLEY. Son of G. L. P.; 1847^{3}–1849^{2}; Maj.-Gen. Bengal Cav.; *m.* Catherine Cortlandt, *d.* of Major Philip Cortlandt Anderson. 8 *Bramham Gardens, S.W.*

Baring (W.A.C.) — RICHARD. 1847^{3}–1849^{1}.

McCrea (W.G.C.) — JOHN BENJAMIN. Son of Rev. J. B. M. of Windsor; 1847^{3}–1849^{2}.

Goren (C.L.) — AMES. 1847^{3}–1850^{1}; formerly Capt. 19th Regt.; dangerously wounded in the Crimea.

Hartopp (E.H.P.) — WILLIAM WREY. Son of E. B. H. of Dalby Hall, Melton Mowbray; 1847^{3}–1849^{2}; formerly Capt. Royal Horse Gds.; *m.* Lina, *d.* of Thomas Howe; died 1874.

Graham (Mrs. Vav., W.J.) — JAMES STANLEY. 3rd son of Rt. Hon. Sir J. R. G. G., 2nd Bt., of Netherby, Carlisle; 1847^{3}–1849^{1}; Capt. R.N.; died Feb. 3, 1873.

Wickham (Mrs. Ro., W.J.) — VERY REV. EDWARD CHARLES, D.D. Son of Rev. E. W., Vicar of Preston Candover, Basingstoke; 1847^{3}–1847^{3}; New Coll. Oxf.; 1st Cl. Mods. 1854; 2nd Cl. Lit. Hum. 1856; Chanc. Prize for Latin Verse 1856; Latin Essay 1857; Fellow of New Coll. and Tutor 1850–73; Headmaster of Wellington 1873–93; Dean of Lincoln since 1894; Hon. Fellow of New Coll.; *m.* Agnes, *d.* of Rt. Hon. W. E. Gladstone. *The Deanery, Lincoln.*

Chatfield (Mrs. Ro., W.J.) — GEORGE KEMP. Son of Rev. A. W. C., Vicar of Much Marcle, Gloucester; 1847^{3}–1848^{3}; Capt. 91st Regt.; *m.* Caroline, *d.* of D. Blair, M.D.; died at sea April 20, 1862.

O'Dowda (R.O.) — ROBERT CHARLES. 1847^{3}–1848^{1}.

Grove-Price (C.J.A.) — STANHOPE. Son of — G.-P., M.P. for Sandwich; 1847 [illegible]–18[illegible]; formerly Lieut. R.N.

Malloek (Mrs. Ro. and Mrs. de R., C.O.G.) — COL. HENRY ARCHIBALD. Son of J. M. of Axminster; 1848^{1}–1850^{4}; served in the Indian Mutiny 1857 (Med.); Afghanistan 1879–80 (Med.); *m.* 1st, Mary Jane, *d.* of Sir William O'Shaughnessy; 2nd, Emma Louise Arundell, *d.* of Capt. Morton Grove Mansel of Puncknoll, Dorchester, Dorset. *Friarmayne House, Broadmayne, Dorchester.*

Bradford (Mrs. P., H.M.B.) — HAMILTON WILLIAM KINDERSLEY. 1848^{1}–1849^{1}; formerly Madras Infantry, aft. Capt. 108th Regt.

Heaton (T.H.S., C.O.G.) — WILLIAM HENNIKER. Of Bryn-Issa, co. Worcester; 4th son of J. H. of Plas Heaton, Trefnant, co. Denbigh; 1848^{1}–1848^{1}; formerly Lieut. R.N.; *m.* 1st, Henriette Mary, *d.* of Thomas Paterson Anderson; 2nd, Dorothy Kenrick, of Reigate; died 1898.

Parks — EDWARD ALEXANDER HAWTREY. Son of — P. of Woodside, Old Windsor; 1848^{1}–1849^{1}; formerly in the 20th Regt.

Jervis (E.B.) — EDWARD LENNOX. Formerly of Fairhill, Tonbridge; 2nd son of Chief Justice Sir J. J. of the Court of Common Pleas; 1848^{1}–1849^{2}; formerly Major 6th Dragoon Gds.; served in the Crimea; horse shot under him at Balaclava; med. with four clasps and Turkish med.; J.P. for Kent; died May 6, 1900.

Chambers (J.W.H.) — WILLIAM HENRY. 1848^{1}–1849^{2}; 2nd entry 1853^{3}–1855^{1}.

Pearson (W.E., E.H.P.) — CHARLES BURGESS NICHOLAS. Son of — P. of Tempsford Hall, St. Neots; 1848^{1}–1849^{2}.

Warren (Mrs. Vav., H.D.) — REV. SAMUEL LUCKENDRY. Son of S. W., Q.C.; 1848^{2}–1850^{1}; Wadham Coll. Oxf.

Mr. Monson (H.D.) — H.E. RT. HON. SIR EDMUND JOHN, P.C., G.C.B., G.C.M.G., D.C.L. 4th son of William John, 6th Lord Monson; 1848^{2}–1849^{2}; Ball. Coll. Oxf.; 1st Cl. Mod. Hist., and Fellow of All Souls 1855; M.A.; Hon. D.C.L.; 1st Cl. Law and Hist. 1855; Examiner for Taylorian Scholarships 1868; Attaché to Paris 1856, Florence 1858, Paris 1858, Washington 1858; Priv. Sec. to Lord Lyons 1858–63, Attaché to Hanover 1863; promoted 3rd Sec. 1863; transferred to Brussels 1863, resigned 1865; Consul in the Azores 1869–71; Consul-Gen. Hungary 1871–9; 2nd Sec. H.M.'s Embassy at Vienna 1874; Special Service in Dalmatia and Montenegro 1876–7; C.B. 1878; Min. Res. and Consul-Gen. to Republic of Uruguay 1879–84; Envoy Extra. and Min. Plen. to Argentine Republic, and Min. Plen. to Paraguay 1885, to King of Denmark 1885–8, to King of the Hellenes 1888–92; K.C.M.G. 1886; Arbitrator between Denmark and United States, 'Butterfield' Claim, 1888; Envoy Extra. and Min. Plen. to King of the Belgians 1892–3; G.C.M.G. 1892; Ambass. Extra. and Plen. to Emperor of Austria 1893–6; P.C. 1893; Ambass. Extra. and Plen. to French Republic; *m.* Eleanor Catherine Mary, *d.* of Maj. James St. John Munro, H.B.M. Consul at Monte Video. *British Embassy, Paris.*

Waddington (Mrs. Vav., C.O.G.)

HORACE. Son of Maj.-Gen. C. W., C.B., of H.E.I.C. Bombay Engineers: 1848^3–1848^3; Univ. Coll. Oxf. M.A.: 1st Cl. Mods. and 1st Cl. Final Class.; H.M.'s Inspector of Schools 1863–95; *m.* 1st, *d.* of David Thomas; 2nd, Emily, *d.* of Fred. North. *Roseneath, Godalming.*

Robertson (R.O.)

JOHN MARJORIBANKS. 1848^3–1849^3; died 1861.

Judd (W.L.E.)

JOHN MORLEY. Son of J. P. J. of Maces Place, Rickling, Essex; 1848^3–1849^3; killed while serving as a Midshipman on H.M.S. 'Arethusa,' July 28, 1854.

Boilean (W.G.C.)

CHARLES AUGUSTUS PENRHYN. 4th son of Sir J. P. B., 1st Bt.: 1848^3–1849^2; Lieut. Rifle Bgde.; died at Malta of wounds received before Sebastopol, Aug. 1, 1855.

Kekewich (Mrs. P., H.M.B.)

LEWIS. 3rd son of S. T. K. of Peamore House, Exeter: 1848^3–1848^3; Lieut. 20th Regt., served in Crimea (at Alma, Balaclava and Inkerman), wounded at Inkerman; died at Corfu Feb. 16, 1855.

Suttie (W.L.E.)

GEORGE GRANT-. 3rd son of Sir G. G.-S., 5th Bt.; 1848^3–1849^2: formerly Major 75th Regt.: served with the 3rd Buffs in the Crimea; died Jan. 1875.

Mr. Pennington (W.A.C.)

HON. JOSSLYN FRANCIS (5th Lord Muncaster). 3rd son of Lowther Augustus John, 3rd Lord M.; 1848^3–1850^1; formerly Capt. 90th Lt. Infantry; served in Crimea 1854–6 (med.): in trenches and two attacks on Redan and storming party (med. and clasp, Turkish med.): aft. Capt. Rifle Bgde.: M.P. W. Cumberland 1872–80, Egremont Div. of Cumb. 1885–92; Col. E. York Militia; formerly Lieut. Yorks Hussars; Lord-Lieut. of Cumberland since 1876; J.P. and D.L. co. York; Director of the Furness Rly.; *m.* Constance Ann, *d.* of Edmund L'Estrange of Tynte Lodge, co. Leitrim. 5 *Carlton Gdns., S.W., and Muncaster Castle, Ravenglass, R.S.O., Cumberland.*

Basset (H.D.)

GUSTAVUS LAMBART. Of Tehidy Park, Camborne: 3rd son of F. B. of Tehidy; 1848^1–1848^3; J.P. and D.L. for Cornwall; *m.* Charlotte Mary, *d.* of William Elmhirst of West Ashby, Horncastle; died July 25, 1888.

Lord Belmore (W.G.C.)

SOMERSET RICHARD LOWRY-CORRY (4th Earl of Belmore), P.C., G.C.M.G.; eld. son of Armar, 3rd Earl of B.; 1848^3–1849^2: Trin. Coll. Camb. M.A.: Under-Sec. Home Dept. 1866–7; P.C. 1867; Gov. New South Wales 1868–72; K.C.M.G. 1872; G.C.M.G. 1890; Pres. of Commn. on Trin. Coll. Dublin 1877, and the Manual and Practical Instruction Commission 1897; served as one of the Lords Just'ces Gen. and Gen. Governors of Ireland, and on Judicial Committee of the Irish Privy Council; formerly Major London Irish R.V.; Lord-Lieut. of co. Tyrone; J.P. cos. Fermanagh, Tyrone, and Kent: *m.* Anne Elizabeth Honoria, *d.* of Capt. John Neilson Gladstone, R.N., of Bowden Park, Wilts. *Castle Coole, Enniskillen.*

Mostyn (Mrs. Vav., W.A.C.)

MAJOR GEN. HON. SAVAGE LLOYD-, C.B. 3rd son of Edward, 2nd Lord Mostyn, of Mostyn Hall, Holywell, Flints; 1848^3–1849^2; ent. Army, 23rd Fusiliers 1853; served in the Crimea, inc. Sebastopol, and attack on Redan (med. with clasp, Turkish med.) 1855; Indian Mutiny, inc. Lucknow (med. with two clasps) 1857–8; Comm. Headquarters Gold Coast throughout 2nd phase Ashanti war (several times mentioned in despatches, C.B., med. with clasp) 1874; Comm. a Regimental District 1880–5; Major-Gen. 1885 (ret.): *m.* E[illegible], *d.* of Rev. George Earle Welby, Rector of Barrowby, Grantham. *Ma[illegible]-y-Nant, Wrexham.*

Wheler (H.D.)

CHARLES WHELER. Of Otterden Place, Faversham; son of Rev. C. W. of Otterden: 1848^3–1849^3; Ch. Ch. Oxf. M.A.; formerly Lieut. E. Kent Rifles; J.P. and D.L. for Kent, High Sheriff 1891; J.P. W. Riding of Yorks; *m.* Elizabeth Townsend, *d.* of William Hall of Syndale, Kent; died Aug. 6, 1899.

Beaumont (R.O.)

GODFREY WENTWORTH. Son of Capt. R. B., R.N., of Bossall House, co. Yorks; 1848^3–1850^1: Lieut.-Col. Scots Fusilier Gds.; *m.* Anna Maria, *d.* of Sir Edward Blackett, 6th Bt., of Matfen Hall, Corbridge, Northumberland; died 1876.

SAMUEL MASTERS. 1848^3–1849^3.

Davies (Mrs. P., W.J.)

Barrett-Lennard (Mrs. P., C.O.G.)

WALTER JAMES. 8th son of Sir T. B.-L., 1st Bt., of Belhus, Aveley, Purfleet, S.O., Essex; 1848^3–1849^2; *m.* Caroline, *d.* of Samuel Dormer; died June 6, 1899.

Wiggett (F.E.D.)

JAMES ALLAN. Son of Rev. J. S. W. of Allanbay; 1848^3–1849^1; Trin. Coll. Oxf. B.A.; J.P. for Berks; *m.* Caroline Frederica, *d.* of Gen. D'Oyly. *Allanbay, Binfield, Bracknell.*

Edgeworth (F.V., W.A.O.)

CAPT. WILLIAM. Eld. son of F. B. E. of Edgeworthstown, Ireland: 1848^3–1849^1: Capt. 5th Lancers, aft. 3rd Dragoon Gds.; died unm. June 26, 1863.

Burnett (W.L.E.)

FRANK REDFEARN. Eld. son of Col. — B. of Gadgirth, Ayrshire; 1848^3–1849^1; formerly Bombay Lt. Infantry, aft. Lieut. 106th Regt.

Ridehalgh

GEORGE JOHN MILLER. Of Fell Foot, Newby Bridge, Ulverston; son of G. L. R. of Winkfield House, Berks; 1849–1849^1; Hon. Col. and Lieut.-Col. Westmorland R.V.; *m.* 1st, Fanny, *d.* of Henry Reade; 2nd, Elizabeth, *d.* of Robert Ridehalgh of Foulridge, Colne; died 1892.

Heigham. (Mrs. Dr., R.O.)

HENRY. 2nd son of J. H. H. of Hunstan Hall, Bury St. Edmunds; 1849^2–1850^2; *m.* Winifred, *d.* of H. Griffin of Ottawa; dead.

Pennefather (W.E., E.B.)

RICHARD. Son of R. P. of Darling Hill, co. Tipperary; 1849^2–1850^1; Trin. Coll. Camb.; in the Diplomatic Service; died Mar. 5, 1863.

Fitzgerald (H.D.)

RICHARD PUREFOY. Of North Hall, Preston Candover, Basingstoke; son of T. F. of Shalstone, Buckingham; 1849^2–1849^2; formerly Lieut. R.N., aft. Hon. Col. Bucks Yeo.; J.P. for Hants; *m.* Henrietta Mary, *d.* of Rev. Anthony Chester of Chicheley Hall, Bucks; died Feb. 28, 1895.

ARTHUR FERDINAND. 1849^2–1849^2; Major 49th Regt.; died of illness at Scutari, Aug. 11, 1855.

Platt (Mrs. Hor., E.H.P.)

Caulfeild (W.A.C.)

WILLIAM HARRIS. 2nd son of Lieut.-Gen. J. C., C.B., M.P.; 1849^2–1849^3; Bengal Civil Service; died of cholera at Benares, Sept. 17, 1857.

Wade (W.J.)

LOWRY WILLIAM HARRIS. 1849^2–1849^3; died Dec. 1849.

Strachey (C.O.G.)

RICHARD CHARLES. Of Ashwick Grove, Oakhill, Bath; eld. son of R. S. of Ashwick Grove; 1849^3–1850^1; C.C.C. Camb.; formerly N. Somerset Yeo.; Master of Blackmoor Vale Foxhounds; J.P. for Somerset; *m.* Charlotte Lindsay, *d.* of Ralph Barchard Hankin of Bedford; died July 30, 1901.

CHARLES THOMAS. 1850^1–1850^1; Camb. M.A.; Barrister.

Luck (W.G.C.)

Vonles *min.* (W.[illegible])

HERBERT AUGUSTUS. Son of C. S. V., [illegible], of W[illegible]sor; 1850^2–1852^1; formerly [illegible] Army; dead.

INDEX TO THE ETON SCHOOL LISTS

FOR THE YEARS 1841-50.

*** *The year in the first column is the last in which a Boy's name occurs, and where particulars will be found. The last column indicates the page.*

AB—AR

AR—BA

BA—DE

DE—ED

ED—FE

FE—FR

LE—LU

LU—MA

MA—MO

SH—SP

ETON
PRINTED BY SPOTTISWOODE AND CO. LTD

CPSIA information can be obtained
at www.ICGtesting.com
Printed in the USA
BVHW010035060821
613731BV00023B/115